The Prague Spring and the Warsaw Pact Invasion of Czechoslovakia in 1968

The Prague Spring and the Warsaw Pact Invasion of Czechoslovakia in 1968

Edited by
Günter Bischof,
Stefan Karner, and
Peter Ruggenthaler

LEXINGTON BOOKS
A division of
ROWMAN & LITTLEFIELD PUBLISHERS, INC.
Lanham • Boulder • New York • Toronto • Plymouth, UK

Published by Lexington Books
A division of Rowman & Littlefield Publishers, Inc.
A wholly owned subsidiary of The Rowman & Littlefield Publishing Group, Inc.
4501 Forbes Boulevard, Suite 200, Lanham, Maryland 20706
http://www.lexingtonbooks.com

Estover Road, Plymouth PL6 7PY, United Kingdom

British Library Cataloguing in Publication Information Available

Library of Congress Cataloging-in-Publication Data

The hardback edition of this book was previously cataloged by the Library of
Congress as follows:

The Prague spring and the Warsaw Pact invasion of Czechoslovakia in 1968 /
    edited by Günter Bischof, Stefan Karner, and Peter Ruggenthaler.
      p. cm. — (Harvard Cold War studies book series)
    Includes bibliographical references and index.
    1. Czechoslovakia—History—Intervention, 1968. 2. Czechoslovakia—
    Politics and government—1968–1989. 3. Czechoslovakia—Foreign
    relations—1945–1992. 4. World politics—1965–1975. I. Bischof, Günter,
    1953– II. Karner, Stefan, 1952– III. Ruggenthaler, Peter, 1976–
    DB2232.P743 2010
    943.704'2—dc22   2009036547

ISBN: 978-0-7391-4304-9 (cloth : alk. paper)
ISBN: 978-0-7391-4305-6 (pbk. : alk. paper)
ISBN: 978-0-7391-4306-3 (electronic)

Printed in the United States of America

Dedicated to the memory of Saki Ruth Dockrill
(14 December 1952–8 August 2009),
Cold War scholar extraordinaire

Contents

Foreword

The year 2008 serves as an important anniversary of the many crucial events that have shaped Czech history—the ninetieth birthday of the founding of the first Czechoslovak Republic in 1918; the seventieth commemoration of the 1938 Munich Agreement which gave the Sudetenland to Germany and de facto control of Czechoslovakia to Hitler, thereby dismembering the country and putting an end to democracy in Czechoslovakia; and the pivotal Communist coup in 1948 and the Warsaw Pact invasion of Czechoslovakia in 1968.

Now, as the Czech Republic is poised to assume the presidency of the European Union during the first half of 2009, we find ourselves in a position to contemplate these historical anniversaries marked in the year 2008 and the changes that have led us to where we are today. The events that took place in Czechoslovakia in 1968 were a milestone in Czech, Slovak, European, and transatlantic history. As they had in 1938, the Czechoslovak people felt again in 1968 that the West was not prepared to fight for a strange country, and instead it let us down. I was six years old in 1968 when the tanks rolled into the country. As a young boy, I was excited to see the tanks in the streets and didn't understand why my mom was crying and why my dad was angry. After that, I began to understand the true meaning of those tanks.

Two lessons arose from the Warsaw Pact intervention of 1968. First, intellectuals in the East and West came to realize that building socialism with a human face is not feasible. The second lesson of 1968 for the United States and the West is that the Czech Republic must not be abandoned again. This second lesson helped us gain entry into NATO in 1999 and has led to an alliance between the United States, the Czech Republic, and Central Europe that is stronger than ever before.

I thank the University of New Orleans, CenterAustria, and all those involved for organizing the "Prague Spring and the Warsaw Pact Invasion of Czechoslovakia in 1968" conference. I am grateful to have the opportunity to mark these defining milestones in Czech history with you.

Petr Kolář
Ambassador of the Czech Republic to the United States
University of New Orleans
New Orleans, Louisiana
3 April 2008

I

INTRODUCTION AND HISTORICAL CONTEXT

1

Introduction

Günter Bischof, Stefan Karner, and Peter Ruggenthaler

The day of 20 August 2008 marked the fortieth anniversary of the invasion of the Czechoslovak Socialist Republic (ČSSR). The Ludwig Boltzmann Institute for Research on War Consequences in Graz, Austria, organized an international network of Cold War scholars to produce a collective new scholarly analysis on the Prague Spring within the context of the international crisis year 1968. Some eighty scholars and eyewitnesses of these signal events in 1968 produced essays for the massive scholarly volume *Prager Frühling: Das Internationale Krisenjahr 1968*.[1] A selection of these papers are reproduced in this volume in English as an offspring of the conference "The Prague Spring and the Warsaw Pact Invasion of Czechoslovakia in 1968" organized by CenterAustria of the University of New Orleans in April 2008. The essays by Mark Kramer, Mark Carson, and Alessandro Brogi were delivered in New Orleans for the first time and are new and original contributions to this collection. Together this multinational collective research collaborative produced a vigorous scholarly reassessment of this turning point in the Cold War. This reassessment is particularly timely and up-to-date since the essays are based on numerous new and unknown documents from Moscow archives and an additional three dozen archives from around the world. The key documents collected for this project have been published in both the original Russian language (and in some cases English) and a parallel German translation in a second documentary volume, complementing the essays.[2] Taken together, this collective history amounting to almost three thousand pages in these two volumes constitutes a major contribution to Cold War history and is made available here in an abbreviated English version.

The "global disruption" of 1968 challenged the authority of many governments in both the East and West and sparked the quickening of the nascent policy of détente to reconstruct international order from the top down.[3] The bloody war in Vietnam fueled much of the energy of the global protest movement.[4] The heady reforms of the Czechoslovak Communist Party during the "Prague Spring" of 1968 and the invasion by the Warsaw Pact stopping the liberalization and democratization of this Soviet puppet state were key moments during this momentous year of crises in 1968.[5] The Warsaw Pact invasion ended President Lyndon B. Johnson's policy of "bridge-building" with Eastern Europe.[6] It arrested Johnson's policy of détente with the Soviet Union for the time being, but did not end this process of easing tensions with Moscow.[7] The invasion of Czechoslovakia "doomed the summit and arms control negotiations," concludes a major new history of U.S. foreign relations.[8] During the hot summer of 1968, Johnson was hoping to arrange a summit meeting with the Soviets to produce results on strategic arms control as a principal foreign policy legacy of his presidency. The invasion of Czechoslovakia stopped all those efforts in their tracks. Had Johnson been able to negotiate the freeze on nuclear weapons he was looking for in 1968, it might have saved both superpowers billions of dollars in arms expenditures and avoided many of the averse political consequences of the 1970s and 1980s.[9] Ironically, the Warsaw Pact invasion of Czechoslovakia stabilized the region where the Cold War had begun and provided a solid basis for détente. After 1968, neither side seriously contemplated going to war in Europe, let alone nuclear war. During the Czechoslovak crisis, both sides "showed a prudent disposition to underestimate their own strength and overestimate the strength of the adversary," concludes one scholar.[10] Johnson's inaction and marked aloofness during the Prague Spring and in response to the Warsaw Pact invasion also spelled the beginning of the end of U.S. hegemony in the global arena.[11] Literature on Johnson's foreign policies, the international crises of 1968, and the Czechoslovak crisis of 1968 has grown by leaps and bounds,[12] including solid documentary collections from Soviet and former Warsaw Pact countries' archives.[13]

The Prague Spring and the Warsaw Pact invasion of Czechoslovakia were a turning point in the Cold War.[14] These events spawned the "Brezhnev Doctrine" and Soviet claims for the right of intervention in its own sphere of influence if its "sovereignty" was threatened. The Soviet Union and its allies would guarantee the survival of socialism in their own sphere of influence.[15] It alienated the Communist parties of Italy, France, and Spain.[16] It launched negotiations for the Conference of Security and Cooperation in Europe (CSCE), including the Canadians and reluctant Americans, culminating in the Helsinki meeting of 1975, generally regarded as the high point of détente. It unleashed West German chancellor Willy Brandt's *Ostpolitik,* improving relations with the Soviet Union and the Soviet satellites, including the German Democratic Republic (GDR). It spawned the development of the Soviet SS-20 medium range rockets to improve Soviet nuclear defenses by uncoupling militarily inferior Western Europe from U.S. nuclear deterrence. This produced NATO's "double track" decision and unleashed a new arms race in the 1980s (including Ronald Reagan's "Strategic Defense Initiative") that was economically more harmful to Moscow than Washington. The Soviet Bloc's increasing technological and economic backwardness and lagging behind the West were crucial factors in bringing down the Soviet Empire and the Soviet Union and ending the Cold War. Moreover, Prague's 1968 "socialism with a human face" model of reforming communism may also have influenced Mikhail Gorbachev's reforms in the later 1980s that ultimately brought down communism by way of their spillover effects into the Soviet sphere, exactly as Moscow and its satellites feared in 1968. Neither should the factor of the Czechoslovak dissident movement of "Charta 77" on other dissidents movements in the Communist world and their impact on the end of the Cold War be underestimated.[17]

The invasion of Czechoslovakia surprised official Washington. The reforms of the Prague Spring had been going on for months without direct Soviet interference. Many keen observers expected a Soviet intervention. When it did not come, they thought the Czechoslovaks might get away with their reforms. Yet during the night of 20/21 August 1968, troops of the Warsaw Pact from the Soviet Union, Poland, Hungary, and Bulgaria marched into Czechoslovakia, which was also a member of the pact. In doing so, they aborted the Prague Spring, the attempted democratization of the Communist system of the ČSSR under its leader, Alexander Dubček.[18] The political goals of the military intervention had been defined by the Communist Party leaders of the Eastern Bloc countries at several meetings in the months that preceded the intervention: putting an end to the reform process ("socialism with a human face"), defeating the "counterrevolution," putting the ČSSR back on a course loyal to Moscow, preventing the democratization of Czechoslovakia and the country's leaving the Warsaw Pact, and staging a "bureaucratic" coup of the "healthy forces" loyal to Moscow against the reformers within the Communist Party of Czechoslovakia (*Komunistická strana Československa* or KSČ).[19] The result is well known.

The reforms initiated by the KSČ, of course, were suspiciously viewed from the very beginning by the "fraternal states," notably the hard-line Communist regimes in East Berlin, but also in Warsaw and Sofia. In the Soviet Union's satellite states, political decision making resembled that of the Communist Party of the Soviet Union (*Kommunisticheskaya Partiya Sovetskogo Soyuza or CPSU*) in that it took place above all as a series of reactions to reformist developments in Czechoslovakia. The German Democratic Republic's Socialist Unity Party (*Sozialistische Einheitspartei*

Deutschlands or SED) under Walter Ulbricht was the first fraternal party to declare the reforms of the Prague Spring counterrevolutionary in character as early as March 1968.[20] Support for and validation of the SED's diagnosis was forthcoming above all from Leonid Brezhnev himself and from the Communist Party heads of Poland and Bulgaria, Władysław Gomułka and Todor Zhivkov. From March 1968 onward, stopping the "counterrevolutionary" reform process in Prague was the line to which the fraternal countries adhered. The weaker Warsaw Pact allies exerted considerable leverage on the imperial center in Moscow.

FROM THE JANUARY CENTRAL COMMITTEE PLENUM OF THE KSČ TO DRESDEN

The Kremlin's "politics of intervention" during the Czechoslovak crisis in 1968 can be subdivided into five phases. Phase I spans the time from January to March 1968, when Moscow "still kept relatively quiet regarding the events in the ČSSR."[21] Moscow confined itself to calling the situation in the country difficult and contradictory. The Kremlin was offering "maximum help to the Czechoslovak leadership." The abolition of censorship in Czechoslovakia and the mass dismissal of party functionaries of the middle and lower levels caused alarm bells to start ringing in Moscow.[22] In the run-up to the March conference in Dresden, which was officially convened to debate economic questions only, Moscow was beginning to worry seriously about Czechoslovakia's future. On 15 March, the Politburo of the Communist Party of the Soviet Union (CC CPSU) debated a report by Foreign Minister Andrei Gromyko and Committee for State Security (KGB) chief Yuri Andropov. It outlined a worst-case scenario that was all but imminent in the Kremlin's eyes: introduction of capitalism in Czechoslovakia and the splitting up of the Warsaw Pact.[23]

Moderate Moscow, on the one hand, at least initially conveyed again and again to the KSČ leadership its approval of the resolutions of the January plenum and the reform course on which Czechoslovakia had embarked. On the other hand, the hard-line East German, Polish, and Bulgarian leaders took a much more critical view of events and condemned them categorically. East German leader Walter Ulbricht always acted with his eyes anticipating or following the Soviet course. The political changes in Czechoslovakia, in evidence at least since 1967, were also painstakingly charted by Bulgarian diplomats. Bulgaria's ambassador to Prague warned of growing discontent in Czechoslovakia. From the end of 1967, Todor Zhivkov, the bullish head of the Bulgarian Communist Party, insisted on personally reading the diplomatic dispatches from Prague. After the dismissal of the KSČ's first secretary, Antonín Novotný, who enjoyed Bulgarian sympathies, Dubček assured the Bulgarians that the unity of the party was not in danger. Sofia's worries were assuaged only mildly. While Zhivkov noted the exchange of the entire Czechoslovak state leadership, he was not the only one gravely concerned with it.[24] Having been given the green light by Moscow, Władysław Gomułka, the head of the Polish Communist Party, had already had a meeting with Dubček as early as the beginning of February. Dubček tried to paint the situation in his country in the best possible light, but failed to convince Gomułka. The Polish party chief feared that the reforms would lead to a significant weakening of the party.[25]

In this first phase, the East German SED leadership was trying to gauge the consequences of Novotný's ousting by Dubček; it prepared a first assessment of the new situation in the run-up to the meeting in Dresden on 23 March. The GDR Embassy in Prague sent regular reports to East Berlin, expressing their view of an impending threat: "The activities of the oppositional forces have been . . . stepped up and are displaying increasingly openly counterrevolutionary characteristics." The Prague reformers' key word—"democratization"—was synonymous for the SED with the desire for a counterrevolutionary regime change. This had to be prevented at all costs. Yet it accurately described the goal of the SED's interventionist policy. The direction of East German goals paralleled Moscow's: the Czechoslovak reforms had to be stopped! The power monopoly of the KSČ had to be restored! For the SED, the gist of the reforms in the ČSSR was perfectly clear: a counterrevolution was underway in Prague![26]

The Dresden Warsaw Pact meeting ended the opening phase of the policy of intervention. It was the first of five meetings of the fraternal parties prior to 21 August. The party and state leaderships of Bulgaria, Hungary, the GDR, Poland, and the USSR were in attendance at these meetings. On 6/7 March, Zhivkov had already issued assurances in a Sofia meeting with Brezhnev and Aleksei Kosygin that Bulgaria stood ready to use its armed forces if necessary. However, Zhivkov's willingness to use force can hardly be seen as the first proposal to use military force to end the reform process in Czechoslovakia. Rather, Zhivkov was aiming "to provide further proof of Bulgaria's traditional role as a loyal and unflinching ally of the USSR." Solving problems within the Warsaw Pact with armed force was a staple of his policy, even though he considered the "Stalinist methods of the past" no longer necessary.[27] Yet despite such caveats, Zhivkov's proposal is the earliest documented statement of the *military* option for the "solution" of the Czechoslovak question contemplated by the "Warsaw Five" (USSR, Hungary, Poland, Bulgaria, and East Germany). This is corroborated by Marat Kuznetsov, the former counselor in the Soviet embassy, who had accompanied the Soviet delegation to Sofia. The issue of an invasion of Czechoslovakia was raised: "Suddenly I noted to my surprise that the conversation had turned to an invasion of Czechoslovakia by Soviet troops.

I was amazed. . . . Brezhnev himself seemed to be of two minds. It was a tug of war. . . . In Sofia the issue of the invasion was not on the agenda as such but it was discussed in private between members of the Warsaw Pact delegations."[28]

In the final meetings of the Soviet Central Committee's Politburo before Dresden, Moscow's political decision makers advanced the idea for the first time that it might be necessary to enter into deliberations *"along military lines."* Kirill Mazurov was a Politburo member and the first vice president of the Council of Ministers of the USSR. Before and after the August 1968 invasion of Czechoslovakia, he also operated as "Brezhnev's man" in Prague. Mazurov openly addressed the already prevalent anxiety when he averred in no uncertain terms: *"We have to prepare for the worst"* (emphasis added).[29]

FROM DRESDEN TO WARSAW

The invitation to the March meeting in Dresden also included the KSČ leadership. The official purpose given for this Warsaw Pact gathering was a discussion of economic issues. Dubček himself is supposed to have suggested to Brezhnev to paint the conference as an economic meeting.[30] Dubček, however, left his Czechoslovak comrades in the dark. He was at pains after the meeting to create the impression that the Czechoslovak side had been confronted out of the blue with the "counterrevolution" charges leveled against them in Dresden. Instead of discussions on economic issues, the Czechoslovak delegation found itself arraigned as if the meeting were a tribunal. In his initial statement, Brezhnev solemnly declared that the issues on the agenda were much too grave to tolerate any keeping of minutes. Yet contrary to the directive of the general secretary of the CPSU, the SED arranged for the proceedings to be recorded anyway.

These minutes are a blessing to historians of the crisis, for the East German minutes clearly document how severely their Communist brethren took the Prague reformers to task. Dubček first had to explain his party's political course. Brezhnev then asked him what meaning he attached to the concept of "liberalization of society." The Soviet party chief also bluntly asserted that a "counterrevolution" was imminent in Czechoslovakia. Gomułka told Dubček in plain words: "We are well aware of the dangers, the real dangers confronting the Czechoslovak party and the Czechoslovak people and we are convinced that it is still possible today to overcome these dangers, I mean to overcome them in a peaceful manner." The aggressive Polish party chief added: "This calls for a forceful counteroffensive that would in our view have to be carried out by the leadership of the Communist Party of the ČSSR against the counter-revolutionary forces, against the reactionary forces that have surfaced and are active on a grand scale in the ČSSR."[31]

In no uncertain terms, Brezhnev demanded Dubček restore the KSČ's monopoly of power. The CPSU did not see the events in the ČSSR in the light of an "experiment," but as a "calculated project," in other words, as a deliberate attempt to change the system: "We have been empowered by our Politburo to . . . express the hope that you as the leaders will be in position to bring about a reversal of these events and to put an end to this very dangerous development. We are prepared to help . . . you." In a more ominous tone he added: "If this should prove impossible . . . we cannot remain passive onlookers of the development in the ČSSR. We are inseparably linked to each other through ties of friendship, through obligations of an internationalist kind, through considerations for the security of the socialist countries." This was a clear indication of the limits of Moscow's patience. The forcible removal of "a link in the chain" that tied together the Socialist community could not be tolerated.

Yet the demands that were put to the Czechoslovak Communist Party were unequivocal. The Communist Party must reestablish its monopoly of power in Czechoslovakia and suppress the "counterrevolution" by every means at its disposal. The Warsaw Pact allies expected the KSČ to deal with the "problem" itself; after all, it was of its own creation. This, then, was the only alternative offered to the Czechoslovaks by the CPSU and its vassals: to reestablish order as understood by the Warsaw Pact through the use of all political means available in order to avoid a military "solution" that had been in the cards even before the Dresden meeting.

Everybody present at the Dresden meeting agreed to cloak it in absolute silence. Such a conspiratorial stipulation was observed above all by Dubček himself, who left his own party leadership in the dark about the Warsaw Pact allies' demands. Dresden marks the end of the "reconnaissance phase," which assessed the nature of goings-on in Czechoslovakia. The Warsaw Pact allies' stark conclusion, stated openly and shared also with the Czechoslovaks present at the meeting, was that Prague had indeed embarked on a "counterrevolution." In the ensuing phases moving toward intervention, the fraternal states increasingly subjected the Czechoslovak leadership to growing "political pressure."[32]

Phase II lasted from the end of March to the publication of the "2,000 Words" and/or the Warsaw meeting in mid-July. Shortly before dissolving, the Central Committee of the Czechoslovak Communist Party passed an "Action Program" on 1 April calling for domestic pluralism and changing the composition of the party leadership in favor of the reformers by way of elections. This bold Action Program was the first step in a transition from Stalinist Soviet-style socialism to democratic socialism "with a human face." Ulbricht's SED fretted that the Action Program was no longer recognizable as the program of a Marxist-Leninist Party and that the Czechoslovak Communist Party could no longer be considered belonging to that select league.

It should not come as a surprise, then, that the Action Program was neither published in the GDR, nor did the press comment on it.[33] Clearly, anxiety about the spillover of Czechoslovak reforms to the neighboring fraternal countries was growing ominously.

Moscow's reactions were more muted. The Kremlin felt that while the Action Program had a number of deficiencies it was hardly reasonable to expect the Czechoslovaks "to come up with anything better."[34] The Kremlin leaders had had an opportunity to familiarize themselves with the Action Program since mid-March, when KGB circles close to Novotný had passed it on to them.[35] It had already provoked a storm of criticism in Dresden. Yet the KSČ nevertheless stood by it and emerged from Dresden unscathed. Until early April, it had only been a topic in internal discussions in the Soviet leadership. In his speech opening the plenum of the Communist Party's Central Committee meeting, taking place from 6 to 10 April, Brezhnev attacked the Action Program openly for the first time and called it "revisionist," a term pregnant with sinister meaning in the Communist dictionary.[36] This April Party Plenum marked the end of Soviet tactical forbearance, notably displayed by Brezhnev since the beginning of the Czechoslovak crisis.

The hard-line fraternal parties, led by the GDR, immediately responded to this signal from Moscow—a clear case of the tail wagging the dog.[37] Poland's Gomułka urged the Soviet military "to consider, within the framework of the Warsaw Pact Treaty, the occupation of Czechoslovakia by Soviet forces."[38] Such assessment of the Action Program by Eastern European hardliners encouraged Kremlin dogmatists in Moscow, such as the Communist Party chief ideologist Mikhail A. Suslov and Ukrainian party chief Petro Shelest, to go on the offensive. Shelest, who was also a full member of the Politburo, was highly anxious that the Czechoslovak reforms might soon spill across the border into Ukraine and the rest of the Soviet empire. At the same time, he was aware that military intervention might not solve all the problems and could raise additional ones.

In April, Soviet hawks were pushing for military intervention. For Soviet minister of defense Andrei Grechko, however, the matter had reached a point of clarity: "We are ready at a moment's notice, provided the Party passes such a resolution, *to assist the Czechoslovak people with the armies of the Warsaw Pact countries*, in case imperialists and counterrevolutionaries attempt to tear away the socialist ČSSR from the other socialist countries" (emphasis added).[39] Two days earlier, the Soviet leadership had already decided to start military preparations. On 8 April, the commander in chief of the Soviet airborne troops, General Margelov, received a directive to start planning the deployment of airborne troops in Czechoslovakia. Margelov's paratroopers were directed to be ready for deployment at a moment's notice. In case the troops of the Czechoslovak armed forces took a friendly view of the Soviet paratroopers landing on their territory, suitable forms of cooperation were to be organized. If they resisted, they would be disarmed.

Moscow regarded military measures throughout the crisis as *the option of last resort*. Yet throughout the Prague Spring, military measures were never off the table.[40] The loss of Czechoslovakia, a Central European country of key strategic importance within the framework of the Warsaw Pact, was considered unacceptable. It would have created a grave security problem for the Soviet military, irrespective of the larger political repercussions in the Cold War. The key importance of the military-industrial complex (MIC) receiving enormous attention under Brezhnev must also be kept in mind. In the 1960s and 1970s, the USSR sped up the development of a number of new defense programs. The KGB in particular did a great deal to further its own interests in the vast Soviet arms industry.[41] Special favors for the military-industrial complex originated with both KGB chief Andropov and defense minister Dmitrii Ustinov having their roots in the MIC. Not surprisingly then, both Andropov and Ustinov "were the most categorical advocates of a military solution" during the Czechoslovak crisis.[42]

In the larger scheme of things, the Prague Spring and its long-range repercussions created a "hunger for innovation" and also an increasing bureaucratization of the structures of the military-industrial complex. From the spring of 1968 onward, all KGB activities in Czechoslovakia were made to serve the preparations for the invasion of the Red Army. With this objective in mind, the KGB produced fake evidence of the "inevitable intervention of the West" and put it into circulation. This was a precautionary measure in case the leadership of the USSR, losing its nerve, conceded freedom of action to Dubček, and was thus designed to drive home to the Soviet party leadership the necessity of a military solution.[43]

Yet the key hawks and most important catalysts outside the Kremlin for a "military solution" of the Czechoslovak "issue" were Ulbricht and Gomułka.[44] In their eyes, all the key ingredients calling for intervention—ideological, political, and military—were in play. Particularly for Ulbricht, who was never tired of warning of the potential consequences and spillover effects into the Bloc and the Soviet Union itself, his own survival in power was at stake. Viewed from the perspective of 1989, when the countries of the Soviet Bloc fell like dominoes, his anxieties seem quite prescient.

A couple of weeks after the April plenum of the CC CPSU, the "reactions" of the fraternal states and their recommendations had been brought to the Kremlin's notice. Konstantin Rusakov acted as the head of the Department of Liaison with the Communist and Workers' Parties of the Socialist Countries. On 26 April, he presented a secret report to the CC CPSU underlining the SED's contention that it was imperative for the fraternal parties to offer "collective help, including measures of last resort . . . in order to defend

Socialist achievements in the ČSSR if circumstances require it."[45] Gomułka also supported the idea of an "armed intervention." He even let it be known that for the time being he saw no alternative to "marching the troops of the Warsaw Pact, including the Polish army, into the territory of the ČSSR." The Bulgarians had likewise opted immediately after Dresden "for taking the required measures forthwith, including military ones, if need be." The only ones to drag their feet were the Hungarian party leaders. Raising the old bogey of Western subversion in the Bloc, Zhivkov declared in Sofia: "Western points of contact have been established and are active there. In the ČSSR as well as in Poland Zionism is playing a major role." He added: "It is not necessary to revert to the Stalinist methods of the past yet we have to choose methods that will enable us to reestablish order in Czechoslovakia, Romania and subsequently also in Yugoslavia."[46]

At the end of April, Zhivkov came to Prague on a state visit and met Dubček in person for the first time. Dubček tried to defend his reforms. Yet for Zhivkov, it was a foregone conclusion that Dubček was a revisionist. After having seen the situation in the country with his own eyes, Zhivkov concluded that a counterrevolution was unfolding in Czechoslovakia and that capitalism was being restored. Nowhere else but in Slovakia had he found sympathetic ears to his concerns, evident in talks with Bil'ak, not least because he had told the Slovak "healthy" forces loyal to Moscow that he himself sympathized with the project of a "federalization" of the ČSSR, namely giving the Slovaks more rights.[47]

Upon their return to Sofia, the Bulgarian party leadership informed the fraternal parties of the upshot of their state visit to the ČSSR. Like the East Germans, the Bulgarians had identified two revisionist hot spots within the leadership of the KSČ. They were emphatic that the devious counterrevolutionary process was still unfolding. Ulbricht had come to the same conclusion and suggested yet another meeting.[48] It unfolded in Moscow on 8 May,[49] just a few days after yet another round of bilateral talks in Moscow between the Soviets and Czech Communist leaders. The most important result of that meeting was that the Prague leadership reluctantly consented to the Warsaw Pact's proposal to conduct military maneuvers on Czechoslovak territory.[50] The fact that the Soviet leadership once again had received only unsatisfactory answers from the Czechoslovaks during this bilateral meeting was presumably the reason why the Czech Communist leadership was not invited to attend the meeting with the leaders of the fraternal parties scheduled a few days later.

The gathering of fraternal parties, entirely devoted to a discussion of Czechoslovakia, was marked by a high level of tension. The leaders of the CPSU found themselves wedged between a rock and a hard place in a situation without precedent in the history of the Soviet Union. On the one hand, the fraternal parties were clamoring for extreme measures. On the other hand, the Kremlin was well aware that these extreme measures would only be justified as a last resort if all political options had been exhausted. Brezhnev was not prepared to abandon his burning desire for détente.[51] Leaders of the fraternal parties deemed it inadvisable to attack the Czech Communist leadership in its entirety. There was still a residue of hope that the "healthy forces" in Czechoslovakia were on the verge of gaining political clout. Brezhnev, however, knew that the odds for such a development occurring were rather long and stated that "we may have to meet again in this matter, and presumably more than once."[52]

During this Moscow meeting, Ulbricht explicitly welcomed Warsaw Pact military maneuvers as an opportunity to demonstrate military strength. He desired them to take place in close proximity to the West German border. He also suggested providing additional outside support for the "healthy forces" in the KSČ to strengthen them in their intra-party struggle. Dubček was a hopeless case, Ulbricht decreed in Moscow. Gomułka polemicized vehemently against Hungarian party chief Janoš Kádár, who adamantly refused to recognize the "counterrevolution" unfolding in neighboring Czechoslovakia. Conversely, Ulbricht's clear-cut diagnosis was grist to the Polish party chief's mill.[53] Gomułka was as fond of using the term "counterrevolution" as Ulbricht and Brezhnev.

In Moscow, the time had arrived to put the military option on the table openly. Brezhnev presented a written draft to the four leaders of the fraternal parties.[54] He suggested installing a "red telephone" to facilitate communication between the five allies. The CPSU and the SED created a working group to monitor and analyze developments in Czechoslovakia. From May onward, the "Czechoslovak question" was on the agenda of the Politburo of the CC CPSU at least once a week. His analysis of the Politburo materials has led Mikhail Prozumenshchikov to conclude that in spite of the deterioration of the situation in Czechoslovakia the Kremlin was now inclining toward a more moderate assessment of the situation than in the spring. In his view, there are two reasons for this: on the one hand, Moscow did not want to lay itself open to the charge it was exerting "undue pressure" on Prague; on the other hand, hope was still alive that "Dubček might be induced . . . to impose order in the country of his own accord."[55]

Significantly, in internal discussions parallels were drawn with increasing frequency to the scenario of Hungary in 1956. KGB chief Yuri Andropov, who had been Soviet ambassador and stage manager of the Soviet intervention in Budapest in 1956, had pointed out as early as March that "methods and appearances . . . were strongly reminiscent of the ones in Hungary. This was what the beginnings looked like in Hungary." The results of the abolition of media censorship in Czechoslovakia supplied Kremlin hawks such as Andropov and Ustinov with arguments and "proofs" galore that the "counterrevolution" was rapidly advancing toward its goal and that forceful measures would be required to crush it.[56]

The role of the uncensored Czechoslovak mass media proved to be the greatest irritant for the Kremlin and was ultimately one of the most important factors in triggering the decision for military intervention. The proverbial last straw was the publication of Ludvík Vaculík's "2,000 Words." This manifesto vehemently advocated a continuation of the reforms and indeed voiced public doubts as to their viability. For the Kremlin, this marked a climax of the "counterrevolution" in Prague and signaled the beginning of the phase characterized by increasing military pressure on Prague. At the same time, options for a political solution to the crisis in the Soviet Bloc were waning, looking increasingly unrealistic. The Kremlin hawks were visibly gaining in strength. They now favored a military solution without thinking about the political consequences of an invasion. The hardliners in the fraternal parties aided and abetted their line. Seen in this light, Vaculík's "2,000 Words" was "a proclamation of the counterrevolution."[57]

FROM WARSAW TO BRATISLAVA

Phase III began with the "2,000 Words" and was characterized by the actual military-political and operative preparations for the intervention and occupation of Czechoslovakia being put into practice. On 15 July, the die was cast for the intervention. The CPSU convened yet another meeting with the four fraternal parties in Warsaw, so there would be no lack of consultation.[58] Moscow reserved the final decision as to the deployment of the troops for itself. Sensing what was in store in Poland, the Czechoslovak Communist Party leadership had declined to attend.[59] The five parties sent a joint letter, the "Warsaw Letter," to the KSČ. It contained a demand for a swift change of the reformist political course couched in the terms of an ultimatum.[60] The Warsaw Five were no longer willing to credit the KSČ with having the energy needed to turn things around according to their wishes. For Zhivkov, the occupation of the ČSSR by Warsaw Pact troops was the precondition for victory over the forces of the "counterrevolution." None of the other party leaders contradicted him; rather, Gomułka and Ulbricht joined him in clamoring for a military intervention. Ulbricht attacked Kádár in the strongest terms and declared that as far as the KSČ was concerned the Czechoslovaks were not merely guilty of "revisionism" (as Kádár maintained), but of staging a counterrevolution. "The next strike," Ulbricht said, casting himself in the role of the prophet, "will be directed against you, against Hungary." Brezhnev still harbored vestigial feelings of responsibility toward Dubček, "his man in Prague." The hesitant Soviet party chief was the last one among the Communist leaders in Warsaw to advocate a more moderate course. Yet during the Warsaw meeting, the thunder of imminent military action could be heard clearly.[61]

On their leaders' return from Warsaw, the mighty Communist Party of the Soviet Union convened a plenum at very short notice. Many Central Committee members were on holiday and did not make it back to Moscow in time to attend. At the plenum, Brezhnev all but prepared the party for a military invasion, a decision that was applauded in principle by those present. However, Brezhnev, ever the *cunctator* on this issue, was still insisting that "before measures of last resort are taken we will exhaust all political means, together with the fraternal parties, to help the KSČ . . . retain and defend its socialist achievements."[62]

In view of the rapidly fading hope of the Czechoslovak Communist Party bringing about a change of course, the Kremlin intensified its preparations for military operations. On 19 July, four days after the meeting in Warsaw, the Politburo put the elaboration of the "extreme measures" at the top of its agenda.[63] This was made easier for the Kremlin by the reassuring signals from Washington that were starting to arrive precisely in those days, intimating that the United States had no intention of interfering in Czechoslovak affairs.[64] The following week was devoted to ongoing military preparations. On 20 July, the Soviet government dispatched a note to the Czechoslovak government protesting the criticism of the Warsaw Letter unleashed in the Czechoslovak media. The Kremlin also upbraided Prague for the inadequate security arrangements in place at the Czechoslovak-Austrian border, which it considered a threat to the security of the entire Socialist camp. On 22 July, the Politburo mandated Minister of Defense Marshall Grechko to take "measures . . . in accordance with the exchange of opinions at the meeting of the Politburo."[65] These measures also included political arrangements for the installation of a revolutionary government of the ČSSR after the invasion. A number of declarations and proclamations were drafted that were ultimately supposed to help legitimate the intervention after the fact.

Even at this late point in the game, Brezhnev and some in the Kremlin hesitated.[66] Before the Politburo passed the final resolution to authorize the intervention, a final attempt was to be made to browbeat Dubček and the KSČ leadership into accepting a "political solution" on the basis of the Dresden demands. At the end of July, Soviet-Czechoslovak bilateral negotiations took place in the Slovak town of Čierná nad Tisou at the Czechoslovak-Soviet border. Contrary to the Kremlin's expectations, these talks seemed to hold out some promise after all.[67] In the run-up to the meeting in Čierná nad Tisou, yet another meeting of the Warsaw Five in Moscow had been in the pipeline. This was canceled at short notice by the Politburo of the CC CPSU. For the first and only time in the history of the USSR, the entire Soviet Politburo ventured to go abroad across the border to the Čierná meeting. Dubček was given a very last chance to stop the "counterrevolution" himself. After the bilateral Čierná meeting in eastern Slovakia, the

Warsaw Five met with the Czechoslovak Communist Party leaders in the Slovak capital of Bratislava on 3 August. The Soviet leadership felt it was important "to record the results of our negotiations with the KSČ leadership in a joint document." This was tantamount to putting the agreements on an international basis, which was done during the Bratislava meeting: "In principle . . . the results of the negotiations were laid down in the declaration of Bratislava."[68]

Today, it seems safe to assume that the Czechoslovak side agreed to implement the Soviet demands for cadre changes and dismissals as a result of the Čierná meeting. The signing of the declaration of Bratislava provided the Soviet side with a frame of reference that, as they saw it, made their own further actions and the actions of the Warsaw Five appear legitimate. The result of Bratislava was a last attempt before a military intervention in Czechoslovakia to achieve a compromise on the basis of the Soviet draft agreement between the parties involved. This legitimated the "bureaucratic coup" already being prepared by the "healthy forces" in the presidium of the KSČ. In the course of the meeting, Bil'ak handed the Soviet delegation the notorious "letter of invitation by the healthy forces" in the KSČ, asking the five interventionist states to provide "collective assistance." The letter reputedly changed hands in a men's bathroom.

Signing the declaration of Bratislava also provided a point of reference for the programmatic preparation of the "bureaucratic coup" that was being planned by Bil'ak and his comrades in the presidium. Dubček's nonadherence to the declaration of Bratislava was ultimately used by the Soviet side to justify the invasion. Moscow needed time to organize the "bureaucratic coup," which was planned to unfold in the presidium of the KSČ at the same time as the military invasion was occurring. If Dubček failed to adhere to the agreement—which was quite inevitable—the "healthy forces" had a lever with which to oust him from his position.[69]

Dubček would not be bullied, and Brezhnev did what he had threatened to do: "I may look soft, but I can strike so hard that afterwards I feel sick for three days."[70] The military intervention of the Warsaw Five put an end to all attempts on the part of the Five to solve the "crisis" in the ČSSR by political means. It marked the transition to Phase IV, the military phase, which had begun with the Warsaw Pact maneuvers in Czechoslovakia in May. The military preparations had been completed by 30 July. The Politburo of the CPSU took the final decision as to the date of the intervention as late August. A day later, Zhivkov, Kádár, Ulbricht, and Gomułka arrived in Moscow. Brezhnev informed them of the decision to reestablish the "old order" in Czechoslovakia by military means, and they all signaled full agreement. Newly accessible Soviet sources document that Moscow concurred with the request of the "healthy forces" in Czechoslovakia urging the exclusion of the GDR's National People's Army from the military action as such. Ulbricht and the SED leadership, which had been among the most vociferous advocates of an intervention, found it difficult to stomach that they should not be part of the forces that would snatch the country from the jaws of the "counterrevolution." In 1968, as in 1953 and 1956, the Soviet empire was still kept in place by coercion.[71]

THE FLOW OF INFORMATION

Gathering information on the situation in the ČSSR was above all the task of the Soviet embassy in Prague, the consulate in Bratislava, and the KGB on the ground. After Moscow had acceded to the suggestions of the Czechoslovak secret service in May 1968, the KGB advisers of the state security services of the ČSSR were withdrawn from the country and replaced by new personnel, who were active in the country "protected by the embassy and their diplomatic status."[72]

Writing up detailed reports on the situation in the ČSSR was part of the routine work of the Soviet embassy in Prague. Stepan Chervonenko, the Soviet ambassador in Prague, was "familiar with working against the background of diplomatic crises," having served as Soviet ambassador to Peking (during a period crucial for Soviet-Chinese relations) before his stint in Prague. Chervonenko reported directly to Brezhnev's secretariat, the Foreign Ministry, and the CC CPSU. He and the majority of his staff were in close contact above all with politicians from Novotný's entourage. This was the most important reason for the lack of trust in the new leadership of the KPČ, which became more and more pronounced over the course of time. The man below Chervonenko in rank was Ivan Udal'tsov, who was in charge of the basic operations of secret service activities of the embassy. As opposed to Chervonenko, who resembled Brezhnev in that he was bent on exhausting all political possibilities in a crisis, Udal'tsov was much stricter and more rigorous ideologically. Any deviation from the Soviet model of Marxism-Leninism was anathema to him. He viewed Dubček very critically from the start. This often led to differences of opinion between him and Ambassador Chervonenko in the assessment of the situation in the ČSSR. The embassy's "troika" was completed by Vasilii Grishanov, the secretary of the party organization.

While the official diplomatic channel was reserved for reports filed by the ambassador and the embassy counselor to Brezhnev's secretariat, all the other staff members' reports, following routine practice, were filed to the Foreign Ministry. All incoming reports were scheduled to cross the desk of Evgenii Gromov, the head of the 4th European Department (responsible for a number of European countries including Czechoslovakia). Analyses were made under his supervision and submitted to the CC CPSU. The reports of the most senior diplomats were also filed directly to Foreign Minister Gromyko and Konstantin Rusakov, the head of the Department of Liaison with the Communist and Workers' Parties of the Socialist Countries in the CC CPSU, and to Brezhnev's secretariat. Foreign Minister Gromyko and the party's chief ideologue Mikhail Suslov, along with Brezhnev, were the only members of the Politburo, the Soviet Union's top decision making body in 1968, to have direct access to all secret diplomatic reports.

Mention of "the first symptoms of a worsening of the antisocialist mood and of the criticism leveled against the USSR" in Czechoslovakia can be found, according to the Russian historian Ol'ga Pavlenko, in a report of 22 November 1966, filed by the Department of Liaison with the Communist and Workers' Parties. The report was signed by Yuri Andropov, secretary of the CC CPSU from 1962 and formerly the head of that department. Shortly afterwards, Andropov was made head of the KGB. Moscow's focus on the crisis in Prague had reached a critical stage after Novotný's dismissal, and the Kremlin started monitoring Czechoslovakia closely, with Andropov serving as a member of all commissions dealing with the situation in the ČSSR. "KGB chief Andropov," asserts Russian historian Nikita Petrov, "played an important role in all discussions on Czechoslovakia."

After the withdrawal of the Soviet advisers of the Czechoslovak state security services from the country, Moscow was forced to switch to a new ball game. Nikolai Semyonov, a counterespionage cadre officer, was recalled from Estonia to Moscow for a half-year briefing in the First Chief Directorate to equip him for his mission in Prague. The KGB continued to be the hub for gathering the most diverse kinds of information on the ČSSR. An analysis in May 1967, which was based primarily on information from the Czechoslovak Ministry of the Interior, concluded that widespread discontent was due above all to mistakes in the economic reforms. This first set off alarm bells in the KGB.[73]

In the following months, the debate centering on freedom of expression in the media became more and more prominent in the KGB's analyses, focusing on one of the root causes of all ills. Since 1964, Jiří Pelikan, the head of Czechoslovak National Television, had been producing in cooperation with ORF, the Austrian National Television corporation, a program called *Stadtgespräche Wien-Prag*. These lively "city communications" between Vienna and Prague were a historic first, featuring uncensored, live TV conversations across the Iron Curtain on a wide variety of topics.

In a timely show of its decisiveness, the KGB diagnosed a rapidly spreading crisis in Czechoslovakia. Andropov immediately stepped up the pressure on the Czechoslovak reformers. Leaving aside the differences of opinion on the "solution of the Czechoslovak problems" within the Soviet leadership, they had one thing in common: unanimity that the reforms must be stopped, ideally by the KSČ leaders themselves. This soon appeared to be wishful thinking in Moscow. So Andropov started to devise a worst-case scenario that outlined what might happen if the reformers were not stopped. Since Andropov had witnessed the victory of the "counterrevolution" in Budapest in 1956, parallels with and historical lessons from the Hungarian Revolution were becoming more prominent by the day. By mid-March, the KGB had definitive proof that its worst fears were justified. The Action Program of the KSČ had been passed on to them by friendly party members. On 13 March, the Action Program and the reforms planned by the KSČ were on the agenda of the Politburo's meeting in Moscow. The Soviet leadership's patience and forbearance were being exhausted. Two days later, the Politburo dispatched a letter to the KSČ bristling with the tough rhetoric of class struggle. Dubček was still able to dissuade the Soviets from taking action right away. The meeting in Dresden marked a compromise of a kind between Dubček, the Kremlin, and the leaders of the fraternal parties. Among them, Ulbricht had also done his homework, in a manner comparable to Andropov and Suslov. Dresden was the first of several meetings of the scheming fraternal parties from which the KSČ was subsequently excluded. The hardliners in these fraternal parties exerted their influence on the Kremlin's course of planning for an intervention by underwriting, boosting, and endorsing it. The tail was wagging the dog, and the *leverage of the weak* was felt once again in the Cold War alliance structures.

LBJ'S ALOOFNESS: THE "NO ACTION" AMERICAN RESPONSE

The response of the administration of Lyndon B. Johnson not to intervene after the Warsaw Pact Invasion of Czechoslovakia was quite predictable given previous U.S. behavior vis-à-vis crises in the Soviet Bloc. During the Soviet intervention in the German Democratic Republic in 1953 and in Hungary in 1956, the U.S. response had been minimal, too. Even when it was in an overall much more favorable strategic position during the Cold War than the Johnson administration was in the late 1960s, the Eisenhower administration had engaged in some tough "liberation of captive peoples" rhetoric, but refrained from considering any direct military response, nor did it unleash Central Intelligence Agency (CIA) covert operations.

The international environment and the U.S. position in the Cold War had changed considerably since the mid-1950s. The global U.S. position and the country's relationship with its allies were under stress. The deepening quagmire of the Vietnam War, demands for NATO reforms and sharing of defense burdens, and hopes for launching arms control with the Soviets as well as a vigorous détente regime, kept the Johnson administration off balance. Moreover, the Johnson administration faced a deepening domestic crisis in 1968 during a highly contentious and divisive national election. The American youth were rebellious over the deepening and interminable Vietnam War. Johnson also faced a growing resistance in his own party to his policies in the Vietnam War after the Tet Offensive by the North Vietnamese and the Vietcong. During this deepening vortex of domestic unrest in late March 1968, Johnson made the momentous and surprising decision not to run again for reelection.[74] The assassinations of Martin Luther King Jr. in April and Robert Kennedy in June added to the national trauma. In this deepening domestic crisis, President Johnson was incapable of responding to—let alone resisting—the burgeoning Soviet pressure on Dubček.

Johnson's nonresponse to the Warsaw Pact invasion was clearly foreshadowed in an early May exchange between Undersecretary of State Eugene V. Rostow and Secretary of State Dean Rusk. Rostow wanted Rusk to send a strong deterrent signal to Moscow not to intervene in Czechoslovakia. Rostow reasoned: "In retrospect, our failure to deter the Communist takeover of Czechoslovakia in 1948 was one of the most serious mistakes of our foreign policy since the war." He reminded Rusk: "Similarly, stating in public that the U.S. would not intervene during the Hungarian crisis in 1956 . . . gave the Soviets full license." Rostow sternly admonished the Secretary of State that the Russians were hesitating and that "the moment to give them a deterrent signal is therefore now." Rusk wrote two words on top of the one-page memorandum and initialed them with "DR": "No action."[75] While State Department diplomats had been expecting some form of Soviet intervention ever since the more radical reforms of the Prague Spring were unfolding, the CIA was circumspect and full of wishful thinking that somehow the Czechoslovaks might get away with their reform agenda.

On 22 July, Rusk issued a cautious warning to Soviet ambassador to the United States Anatolii Dobrynin for the first time. Rusk noted that "the USA has been against interference in the affairs of Czechoslovakia from the very start." In the message summarizing this conversation Dobrynin sent to the Politburo, Rusk apparently added: *"This is a matter for the Czechs first and foremost. Apart from that, it is matter for Czechs and other nations of the Warsaw Pact"* (emphasis added).[76] As noted above, Russian historian Prozumenshchikov has interpreted this message as a "green light" from Washington to Moscow that they would not intervene if the Kremlin cleaned up the Czechoslovak mess. This may well have been Moscow's perception, but it was hardly the precise meaning of Washington's message. These vital signals from Washington undoubtedly provided grist to the mills of the Kremlin hawks who had been demanding a military intervention for weeks. Given that Dubček's promises had all been empty ones, those Kremlin decision makers who had warned about the international consequences of an intervention were muted.

When the Warsaw Pact invasion came on 20 August, the Johnson administration was surprised and reacted with the same passivity with which Eisenhower had reacted to the 1953 and 1956 crises. The president himself was deeply disappointed that the invasion shattered his dreams for détente to salvage at least one signal foreign policy success as a legacy of his troubled presidency. Clearly he was not prepared to test Soviet resolve with a military response as the late night discussions of the National Security Council on the day of the invasion on 20 August suggest. Secretary of Defense Clark Clifford noted that Johnson felt doubled-crossed by the Kremlin leaders and only reluctantly agreed to cancel the summit meeting that was already scheduled for early October in Leningrad. Secretary of State Dean Rusk averred that the United States could do little to help Prague; the Czechs had to help themselves. General Earle G. Wheeler, the chairman of the Joint Chiefs of Staff, made it abundantly clear that a military U.S. response was out of the question: *"We do not have the forces to do it"* (emphasis added). The United States found it impossible to respond to two major international crises at the same time. All that could be done was "giving the Russians hell" by castigating their intervention in the United Nations and registering a formal protest via the Soviet ambassador with the Kremlin.[77] During the 1968 Czechoslovakia events, CIA director Richard Helms did not play the role of *primus inter pares* that Allen Dulles had enjoyed as key adviser to Eisenhower during crises in the Soviet Bloc.[78]

"No action" characterizes Johnson's response to the invasion of Czechoslovakia in 1968. Over the next weeks, Rusk and the State Department were busy rejecting charges about prior U.S.-Soviet "collusion" tolerating a Soviet intervention. Charges from French president Charles de Gaulle's government that the Yalta spheres of influence agreement explained the meek U.S. response were particularly galling. The Americans were worried about a possible spillover of the crisis into Romania or Yugoslavia and cautioned the Soviets about further invasions in the Bloc. Washington used the invasion crisis without hesitation to stop all Congressional talk of withdrawing American forces from Europe. The Johnson administration ironically seized the opportunity of the advance of Warsaw Pact forces along Czechoslovakia's West German border to strengthen NATO and demand higher Western European contributions to their own defense. Efforts at East-West détente were put on ice, but not for very long.[79] The Warsaw Pact invasion of Czechoslovakia and the pronouncement of the Brezhnev Doctrine caused only minor ripples in the fall of 1968 during the divisive presidential campaign. Unlike during the Hungarian crisis, the cold warriors of Radio Free Europe in Munich stuck by their scripts during the crisis in Czechoslovakia and did not escalate propaganda warfare. As far as we know, no CIA covert operations were launched behind the Iron Curtain (despite unsubstantiated Soviet propaganda that U.S. "green berets" had infiltrated Czechoslovakia through neutral Austria). The debate in the United Nations quickly fizzled out, too. Soviet control of the Western frontiers of its Eastern European sphere of influence was firmly respected in Washington, particularly at a time when the U.S. military was overburdened by the war in Vietnam. It was also obvious that President Johnson did not want to risk nuclear war with either a U.S. or a NATO military intervention in Czechoslovakia.[80]

SUMMARY

The "reconnaissance phase," in which the nature of the events in Prague was assessed, ended in Dresden in March 1968. From then on, the Czechoslovaks saw themselves confronted with demands for an end of their reforms and the restoration of the status quo ante. The ensuing phases were marked by the search for ways and means to realize these demands. The next phase of "political pressure" gave way in May 1968 to a combination of "political and military pressure." The publication of the "2,000 Words" was grist to the Kremlin's mill and enabled it to turn up the heat on the KSČ leadership. The die was cast finally in Warsaw in mid-July. After the meeting of the Warsaw Five in Poland, the Politburo of the CC CPSU passed a resolution in favor of a military intervention and the political preparation of a "bureaucratic coup," counting on the support of "healthy forces" in Prague loyal to Moscow around Vasil Biľak and Alois Indra. The military intervention went according to plan, but the machinations to topple Dubček failed miserably. After the invasion, the Kremlin quickly reached a political dead end. The Kremlin then played the "national card" and courted the Slovak Gustav Husák. Moscow could always count on the support of the fraternal parties throughout the crisis and got Czechoslovakia back on the road of "normalization." Communist rule in Czechoslovakia was consolidated once again without rescinding all the reforms right away, but by slowly reestablishing a Communist government along neo-Stalinist lines. This postinvasion reestablishment of Communist control in Czechoslovakia was Phase V.

On the basis of hitherto inaccessible resolutions of the Politburo of the CC CPSU, historians now can fill in the details about Soviet preinvasion decision making.[81] By mid-July, the invasion was a foregone conclusion. The meeting in Čierná nad Tisou at the end of July was the very last attempt to substitute a "political" solution for the military one. It was Dubček's last chance to deal with the "counterrevolution" on his own terms, without having his arm twisted by "fraternal assistance." Despite the prevalence of the opinion that Dubček would never be able to deliver on his promises, in an unprecedented step the entire Politburo of the Soviet Communist Party traveled to eastern Czechoslovakia to meet their counterparts. The heads of the Communist parties of the fraternal countries were scheduled to meet on the very next day in Moscow. This meeting was canceled at short notice after Dubček had managed to convince Brezhnev that he was still in charge.

Early first hints that Moscow was considering a military "solution" to the "Czechoslovak crisis" exist. During the April plenum of the CC CPSU, Soviet minister of defense Grechko intoned that the Red Army was ready to play its role and launch an invasion if the party ordered it. We must also keep in mind that positions of individual actors in the Kremlin were by no means immune to change or clear cut. One might speak of two distinct camps inside the Kremlin, hawks and moderates. Kremlin insiders considered Kosygin, for instance, a hawk, yet after his trip to the ČSSR, he switched to a more "moderate" role.[82] Given his background during the Hungarian crisis, Andropov saw events in the ČSSR entirely in light of the situation in Hungary in 1956. The hawkish KGB chief contributed to making the situation appear more ominous than it was. The duplicitous Andropov went so far as to misinform the Politburo members in order to buttress arguments for a drastic "solution."

Brezhnev's astounding hesitancy throughout the crisis comes as the biggest surprise. Brezhnev would have preferred a "political" solution to the Czechoslovak crisis. Even as late as early August, he engaged in wishful thinking, hoping that his friend Dubček and the KSČ might recognize the danger of a "counterrevolution" on their own and stop the reforms. But Brezhnev was not averse to the last resort of a military solution and did not need to be persuaded by others to accept it (and certainly did not need to be outvoted in the Politburo).

The *leverage of the weak*—the influence of the fraternal parties on the decision-making process in the Kremlin and their reckless abandon in calling for the military solution—emerges powerfully in these new documents. Ulbricht was the first to use the term "counterrevolution" in Prague. He received substantial support from Zhivkov and Gomułka in this matter. Zhivkov and Gomułka identified a "second center" within the KSČ leadership, and later even a "Zionist" conspiracy, as the old Stalinist diction put it. The leaders of these three fraternal parties became crucial *outside catalysts* to drive the decision-making process in the Kremlin. Janoš Kádár, the head of the Hungarian Communist Party, played his own special role. After the crushing of the Hungarian uprising twelve years earlier, Kádár had been responsible for steamrolling his countrymen back on a course loyal to Moscow. In this particular "band of brothers," he was the least inclined to advocate a repetition of this scenario. Yet in the end he supported Moscow's decision without reservations. All his attempts at mediation failed.[83]

Ulbricht may have been the most adamant from the get go to enforce the end of the reform process in Prague. He is credited even today with having shown restraint in his attitude toward the Czechoslovaks. Some also give him credit for having wisely decided to refrain from dispatching German troops into Czechoslovakia and thus refraining from stirring painful memories of Hitlerite aggression.[84] Newly opened archival sources from Moscow tell a different story. The last-minute decision not to include the East German National People's Army in the Warsaw Pact invasion force was requested by Czechoslovak Communists loyal to Moscow. The German comrades, according to Brezhnev, were bitter about their exclusion from the invasion force.[85]

Alliance politics drove the Warsaw Pact. Keeping the Eastern European Communist parties together in a close alliance was of paramount concern. The Kremlin needed to shore up the Communist Bloc and contain China's hegemonic demands that were increasingly in evidence ever since the Sino-Soviet split. Brezhnev himself summed up the matter at the Communist Party Plenum in October 1968 when he noted that the Soviet leadership had been so engrossed with China politics that it failed to devote sufficient attention to Soviet Bloc matters.[86] For this reason, it was crucially important for the Kremlin in 1968 to paint the military intervention as an action of Warsaw Pact solidarity. To the Kremlin, it mattered that the intervention was an "internationalist socialist measure" originating with the joint deliberations among the fraternal parties. The Soviet Union was deeply concerned with preserving the status quo in Europe as laid down by the Yalta agreements. Moscow was just as concerned with consolidating its own hegemonic position within the Communist world against the challenge of China's ascendancy in acting as a competing power in Asia and the Third World. The invasion of Czechoslovakia also mattered in terms of solidifying Moscow's premier hegemonic position in the Communist world.

Alliance politics drove the U.S. response to the Warsaw Pact invasion as well. The Johnson administration was deeply concerned over escalating the crisis toward the nuclear threshold with a military response. The United States was stuck in its Vietnam morass and was running out of military manpower to fight the war. Since the United States had failed to convince its NATO allies to support it in Vietnam, it put pressure on its NATO allies in Europe to carry more of their own defense burden. In this sense, the invasion of Czechoslovakia was a "blessing in disguise" for NATO, concludes Saki Dockrill. Indeed, London and Paris were equally disinclined to confront the Warsaw Pact over Czechoslovakia.[87] In a veritable "war of nerves," Washington and NATO perceived the greatest threat after the invasion of Czechoslovakia as being a possible spillover of the crisis to reluctant pact-ally Romania, or nonaligned Yugoslavia, or neutral Austria, or even exposed West Berlin. In spite of considerable paranoia, both sides kept their cool through the aftereffects of the Czechoslovak crisis.[88] Those were the fearful crisis scenarios in 1968 that did not come to pass.

While the old Warsaw Pact is now on the ash heap of history, the politics of history remind us of the legacies of the 1968 invasion of Czechoslovakia today. On 1 December 1989, a mere three weeks after the fall of the Berlin Wall, the People's Parliament of the GDR declared that "in response to the manifest will of the citizens of our country . . . it sincerely regrets the GDR's involvement in military actions in the states of the Warsaw Pact in connection with internal struggles within the ČSSR in August 1968 and apologizes for it on behalf of the people of the GDR to the peoples of the ČSSR."[89] On 1 March 2006, Vladimir Putin, the president of the Russian Federation, conceded in a meeting with Václav Klaus, president of the Czech Republic, that Russia as legal successor to the Soviet Union, accepted "moral" but not legal responsibility for the 1968 invasion of Czechoslovakia. He added that excessively dwelling on the past would lead nowhere.[90] Yet apologies do matter as a form of restitution for past injustice for those who have been victimized, particularly to a people who had suffered two brutal invasions within a period of thirty years from totalitarian regimes in the twentieth century.

ACKNOWLEDGMENTS

To launch their research project for completion before the 2008 fortieth anniversary of the 1968 Czechoslovak crisis, the Boltzmann Institute for Research on War Consequences and the Russian State Archive for Contemporary History and the Russian Academy of Sciences signed a declaration of intent regarding a joint publication on the Prague Spring as early as 2003. They immediately initiated the planning and realization of the project. In a historic first step, the former Central Committee Archive made the relevant Politburo resolutions from the period of 1967 to 1969 systematically accessible for the first time ever. In July 2006, the actual analysis of these thousands of newly accessible files began. The result of this collaborative effort is the two volumes mentioned at the beginning of this introduction.

Altogether more than one hundred researchers from Europe, Russia, and the United States, including prominent eyewitnesses to those events, cooperated in an extensive international research network established under the aegis of the Ludwig Boltzmann Institute for Research on War Consequences in Graz. The key partners in this research collaborative were the Russian State Archive for Contemporary History (formerly the Archive of the CC CPSU under the directorship of Natalya Tomilina), the Russian Academy of Sciences in Moscow (Institute of World History of the Russian Academy of Sciences, directed by Alexander Chubaryan), Center Austria of the University of New Orleans (Günter Bischof), the Institute for Contemporary History of the Czech Academy of Sciences in Prague (Oldřich Tůma), the Institute for Contemporary History, both in Munich and Berlin (Horst Möller) and Manfred Wilke, Berlin. Stefan Karner headed the entire project.

The coordination of the project lay in the hands of Peter Ruggenthaler (Graz), Mikhail Prozumenshchikov, and Viktor Ishchenko (Moscow). An additional three dozen research institutions were involved in Austria, Russia, Czechoslovakia, the United States, Germany, Azerbaijan, Belarus, Bulgaria, Croatia, Denmark, Estonia, Finland, France, Hungary, Italy, Latvia, Lithuania, Poland, Romania, Slovakia, Ukraine, and the United Kingdom during the course of the two-year collection effort from 2006 to 2008.

Needless to say, such a vast collective research endeavor would have been impossible to launch without many generous sponsors and supporters. Funding from the Austrian Federal Ministry for Education, Science, and Culture (since 2007 the Federal Ministry for Science and Research) was essential in launching the project. We owe the respective Ministers of Science Elisabeth Gehrer and Johannes Hahn our deepest gratitude, along with their dedicated ministry staff Anneliese Stoklaska, Gisela Zieger, Alois Söhn, Peter Kowalski, and Elmar Pichl. Other significant sponsors were the provincial government of Styria, where Governor Franz Voves showed great interest in the progress of the research effort. Also Mayor Siegfried Nagl and the City of Graz enthusiastically supported the project. Additional generous sponsors were the *Dokumentationsstelle Zeitgeschichte/Volksgruppenbüro* of the provincial government of Carinthia and its head, Peter Karpf; the Federal Foundation for the Reappraisal of the SED Dictatorship in Berlin with the help of Anna Kaminsky, Markus Meckel, and Ulrich Mählert; the Gerda Henkel Foundation, Düsseldorf; the Diplomatic Academy in Vienna and its director, Ambassador Jiři Gruša; and the Austrian Cultural Forums of the Austrian Federal Ministry for European and International Affairs, which made significant contributions to the conferences in Moscow (May/June 2007), New Orleans (April 2008), and Vienna-Graz (20–22 August 2008), with the enthusiastic support of Ambassador Emil Brix. Ewald Stadler has been extremely helpful both as director of the Austrian Cultural Forum in Budapest and then in New York, where Martin Rauchbauer also lent us his helping hand. Aleksandr Bezborodov, Ol'ga Pavlenko, and Viktor Ishchenko organized an interim conference in early summer 2007 at the Russian State University for the Humanities, Moscow. This allowed project scholars an opportunity to discuss emerging theses and arguments intensively and shape the future conception and direction of the two volumes.

The research demands of this Boltzmann Institute project also found wonderful supporters at the Austrian embassy in Moscow. Special thanks must go to Ambassadors Franz Cede and Martin Vukovich who both offered their contact networks unstintingly to direct us toward valuable resources. They kindly offered embassy facilities on more than one occasion to project coordinators for meetings with Russian counterparts. While we are indebted to many kind staffers at the embassy, this applies especially to attaché Sieglinde Presslinger for the help she has unfailingly given us over several years. In Vienna, we have always been able to count on the help from the Russian embassy, especially from Ambassador Stanislav Ossadtchii.

The Ludwig Boltzmann Gesellschaft in Vienna, above all President Christian Konrad and Managing Director Claudia Lingner, have been extremely helpful with this project throughout its duration. We owe them a great debt of gratitude.

At CenterAustria in New Orleans, where the English version of this book was completed, we would like to thank Gertraud Griessner, Marion Wieser, Sandra Scherl, Michael Maier, and Christina Sturn. Susan Krantz, Dean of the College of Liberal Arts, quietly gave CenterAustria her support when needed. Scott Manguno assisted Günter Bischof in his research. Jennifer Shimek of Loyola University performed her usual wonders as copy editor of this volume. In Graz, Harald Knoll and Silke Stern came through whenever their help was needed. We would like to thank Otmar Binder, Vienna, for his smooth translations of nine of the articles in this volume from German into english. We are extremely grateful to Mark Kramer for including this volume in his Cold War History Series with Lexington Books without any hesitation and with much good cheer to help us pull through the final production effort.

NOTES

1. Stefan Karner, Natalja Tomilina, Alexander Tschubarjan, Günter Bischof, Viktor Iščenko, Michail Prozumenščikov, Peter Ruggenthaler, Oldřich Tůma, Manfred Wilke, eds., *Prager Frühling. Das internationale Krisenjahr 1968: Beiträge*, Veröffentlichungen des Ludwig Boltzmann-Instituts für Kriegsfolgen-Forschung, Sonderband 9/1 (Vienna: Böhlau, 2008) (hereinafter abbreviated throughout this book as Karner et al., *Beiträge*, with corresponding page numbers).

2. Stefan Karner, Natalja Tomilina, Alexander Tschubarjan, Viktor Iščenko, Michail Prozumenščikov, Peter Ruggenthaler, Oldřich Tůma, Manfred Wilke, with the support of Irina Kazarina, Silke Stern, Günter Bischof, Aleksei Filitov, and Harald Knoll, eds., *Prager Frühling. Das internationale Krisenjahr 1968. Dokumente. Prazhskaya vesna. Mezhdunarodnyi krizis 1968 goda. 2. Dokumenty*, Veröffentlichungen des Ludwig Boltzmann-Instituts für Kriegsfolgen-Forschung. Sonderband 9/2 (Vienna: Böhlau, 2008) (hereinafter abbreviated throughout this book as Karner et al., *Dokumente*, with corresponding document number in the collection).

3. Jeremi Suri, *Power and Protest: Global Revolution and the Rise of Détente* (Cambridge, MA: Harvard University Press, 2003), 211–13; Jeremi Suri, "Lyndon Johnson and the Global Disruption of 1968," in *Looking Back at LBJ: White House Politics in a New Light*, ed. Mitchell B. Lerner (Lawrence: University of Kansas Press, 2005), 53–57.

4. Norbert Frei, *Jugendrevolte und globaler Protest* (Munich: DTV, 2008), 50; see also Ingrid Gilcher-Holtey, *1968: Eine Zeitreise* (Frankfurt am Main: Suhrkamp, 2008); Wolfgang Kraushaar, *Achtundsechzig: Eine Bilanz* (Berlin: Propyläen, 2008).

5. On the crisis year 1968, see Mark Kurlanski, *1968: The Year That Rocked the World* (New York: Ballantine, 2004); Ronald Fraser, ed., *1968: A Student Generation in Revolt* (New York: Pantheon, 1988). For the larger context of the 1960s, see Terry H. Anderson, *The Movement and the Sixties: Protest in America from Greensboro to Wounded Knee* (New York: Oxford University Press, 1995); David Bruner, *Making Peace with the 60s* (Princeton, NJ: Princeton University Press, 1996); Arthur Marwick, *The Sixties: Cultural Revolution in Britain, France, Italy, and the United States, c. 1958–c. 1974* (Oxford: Oxford University Press, 1998); Udo Wengst, "'1968'—40 Jahre danach. Ein Literaturbericht," *Sehepunkte* 9, no. 1 (2009), http://www.seh epunkte.de/2009/01/14414.html (accessed 26 January 2009).

6. Mitchell Lerner, "Trying to Find the Guy Who Invited Them: Lyndon B. Johnson, Bridge Building and the End of the Prague Spring," *Diplomatic History* 21, no. 3 (2008): 77–103.

7. Alan Schwartz, *Lyndon Johnson and Europe: In the Shadow of Vietnam* (Cambridge, MA: Harvard University Press, 2003), 210–22; H. W. Brands, ed., *The Foreign Policies of Lyndon Johnson beyond Vietnam* (College Station: Texas A&M University Press, 1999), 118–21.

8. George C. Herring, *From Colony to Superpower: U.S. Foreign Relations since 1776*, The Oxford History of the United States, ed. David M. Kennedy (Oxford: Oxford University Press, 2008), 756.

9. John Prados, "Prague Spring and SALT II," in Brands, *The Foreign Policies of Lyndon Johnson beyond Vietnam*, 32–35.

10. Vojtech Mastny, "Was 1968 a Strategic Watershed of the Cold War," *Diplomatic History* 29, no. 1 (2005): 149–77, here 176.

11. H. W. Brands, *The Wages of Globalism: Lyndon Johnson and the Limits of American Power* (New York: Oxford University Press, 1995), 254–64; George C. Herring, "Tet and the Crisis of Hegemony," in *1968: The World Transformed*, ed. Carole Fink et al., Publications of the German Historical Institute, Washington, DC (Cambridge: Cambridge University Press, 1998), 31–53.

12. Vladislav M. Zubok, *A Failed Empire: The Soviet Union in the Cold War from Stalin to Gorbachev* (Chapel Hill: University of North Carolina Press, 2007); Mark Kramer, "The Czechoslovak Crisis and the Brezhnev Doctrine," in Fink et al., *1968: The World Transformed*, 111–72; Robert A. Divine, *The Johnson Years*, vol. 3, *LBJ at Home and Abroad*, ed. Robert Divine (Lawrence: University of Kansas Press, 1994), 239–79; Mitchell B. Lerner, ed., *Looking Back at LBJ: White House Politics in a New Light* (Lawrence: University of Kansas Press, 2005); Warren I. Cohen and Nancy Bernkopf Tucker, eds., *Lyndon Johnson Confronts the World: American Foreign Policy, 1963–1968* (Cambridge: Cambridge University Press, 1994); Lawrence Kaplan et al., eds., *NATO after Forty Years* (Wilmington, DE: Scholarly Resources, 1990); Hal Brands, "Progress Unseen: U.S. Arms Control Policy and the Origins of Détente, 1963–1968," *Diplomatic History* 30, no. 2 (2006): 253–85; John C. McGinn, "The Politics of Collective Inaction: NATO's Response to the Prague Spring," *Journal of Cold War Studies* 1, no. 3 (1999): 111–38; A. Paul Kubricht, "Confronting Liberalization and Military Invasion: America and the Johnson Administration

Respond to the 1968 Prague Summer," *Jahrbücher fur Geschichte Osteuropas* 40, no. 2 (1992): 197–212; Andreas Daum et al., eds., *America, the Vietnam War, and the World: Comparative and International Perspectives*, Publications of the German Historical Institute, Washington, DC (Cambridge: Cambridge University Press, 2003); Alexandra Friedrich, "Awakenings: The Impact of the Vietnam War on West German-American Relations in the 1960s" (Ph.D. diss., Temple University, 2000).

13. Jaromír Navrátil et al., eds., *The Prague Spring 1968*, National Security Archive Cold War Readers (Budapest: Central European University Press, 1998); Vojtech Mastny and Malcolm Byrne, eds., *A Cardboard Castle? An Inside History of the Warsaw Pact, 1955–1991*, National Security Archives Cold War Readers (Budapest: Central European University Press, 2005); on new sources, see also the chapter by Mark Kramer in this volume.

14. The idea of turning points in the Cold War is explicated in the volume by Kiron K. Skinner, ed., *Turning Points in Ending the Cold War* (Stanford, CA: Hoover Institution Press, 2008).

15. Matthew J. Ouimet, *The Rise and Fall of the Brezhnev Doctrine in Soviet Foreign Policy* (Chapel Hill: University of North Carolina Press, 2003).

16. See the chapter by Alessandro Brogi in this volume.

17. A good summary of some of these factors is Gerhard Wettig, "Längerfristige Folgewirkungen des Reformkommunismus und der Militärintervention in der ČSSR im Jahr 1968," *HISTORICUM* (Winter 2007/2008–Spring 2008): 69–76; see also the chapter by Mark Kramer in this volume.

18. For details see above all Jan Pauer, *Prag 1968: Der Einmarsch des Warschauer Paktes: Hintergründe—Planung—Durchführung* (Bremen: Edition Temmen, 1995), which was for a long time the only work of reference in German to be based on Soviet files.

19. Parts of this introduction are based on the extensive introduction by the same authors to Karner et al., *Beiträge*, 17–67.

20. See the chapter by Manfried Wilke in this volume. See also appendix 1.

21. For details here and subsequently, if no other references are specifically cited, see Karner, Bischof, Wilke, and Ruggenthaler's introduction, in Karner et al., *Beiträge*, 17–67.

22. See Mikhail Prozumenshchikov's chapter in this volume.

23. See Prozumenshchikov's chapter in this volume.

24. Iskra Baeva, "Bulgarien—der treue Vasall des Kreml," in Karner et al., *Beiträge*, 461–80.

25. Paweł Piotrowski, "Polen und die Intervention," in Karner et al., *Beiträge*, 447–60.

26. See the Wilke chapter in this volume.

27. Baeva, "Bulgarien—der treue Vasall des Kreml," 468.

28. AdBIK, transcript of the conference "Sovetskii Soyuz, Avstriya i mezhdunarodnyi krizis 1968 goda," Russian State University of the Humanitites, Moscow, 31 May–1 June 2007.

29. Ol'ga Pavlenko, "Der Informationsfluss an die Moskauer Machtzentrale," in Karner et al., *Beiträge*, 243–78.

30. See the chapter by Csaba Békés in this volume.

31. SAPMO-BA, DY 30/11834, pp. 1–271, stenographic transcript of the consultations between the five fraternal parties and the KSČ in Dresden, 23 March 1968, in Karner et al., *Dokumente*, #75.

32. On the fear of counterrevolution and its contagiousness on the regime of fraternal states, see the chapter by Mark Kramer in this volume.

33. See the Wilke chapter in this volume.

34. See the Prozumenshchikov chapter in this volume.

35. Pavlenko, "Der Informationsfluss an die Moskauer Machtzentrale," 267.

36. RGANI, F. 2, op. 3, d. 95, pp. 3f., 73–87, speech of the general secretary of the CC CPSU, L. I. Brezhnev, "On current problems of the international situation and on the CPSU's struggle for the unity of the worldwide communist movement," at the plenum of the CC CPSU, 6 April 1968, reprinted in Karner et al., *Dokumente*, #31.

37. Pavlenko, "Der Informationsfluss an die Moskauer Machtzentrale," 273.

38. Gomułka's meeting with Marshall Yakubovskii on 19 April is cited in Piotrowski, "Polen und die Intervention," 449; see also Mastny, "Was 1968 a Strategic Watershed in the Cold War?" 156. The Germanophobe Gomułka also urged the Soviets not to deploy any East German troops in such an operation. The maneuvers launched in Czechoslovakia soon thereafter also were supposed not to include forces of the East German *Nationale Volksarmee* (NVA). Only after Ulbricht's massive lobbying in Moscow were NVA troops included. Ulbricht also insisted on being part of the military preparations for the invasion and the inclusion of the NVA. Only upon sincere pleading by faithful Czechoslovak Communists in Moscow were East German forces asked not to join the operational forces in the final hours before the invasion. Gomułka tried to trivialize the marginalization of the East Germans before a group of the Polish Central Committee in Warsaw. He argued that the NVA troops were scheduled from the very beginning only to occupy adjoining border areas to the GDR. Gomułka wanted to convince his party colleagues that he had considerable pull in Moscow. The NVA's exclusion from the invasion operations is covered in Rüdiger Wenzke, "Die National Volksarmee der DDR: Kein Einsatz in Prag," in Karner et al., *Beiträge*, 673–86, as well as the Wilke chapter in this volume; Gomulka's intrigues vis-à-vis the NVA are also covered in Pauer, *Prag 68*, 229.

39. RGANI, F. 2, op. 3, d. 94, pp. 1–15, speech of the minister of defense of the USSR, A. A. Grečko, at the plenum of the CC CPSU, 10 April 1968, reprinted in Karner et al., *Dokumente*, #33. Partly reprinted in this volume as appendix 2.

40. Valerij Vartanov, "Die militärische Niederschlagung des 'Prager Frühlings,'" in Karner et al., *Beiträge*, 660–73.

41. Aleksandr Bezborodov, "Sowjetische Hochrüstung als Folge des Einmarsches," in Karner et al., *Beiträge*, 701–16.

42. Bezborodov, "Sowjetische Hochrüstung als Folge des Einmarsches," 716.

43. See the Nikita Petrov chapter in this volume.

44. Pavlenko, "Der Informationsfluss an die Moskauer Machtzentrale," 271.

45. Pavlenko, "Der Informationsfluss an die Moskauer Machtzentrale," 271; RGANI, F. 5, op. 60, d. 313, pp. 5–23, report of the CC CPSU head of the Department of Liaison with the Communist and Workers' Parties of the Socialist Countries, K. Rusakov, on the Socialist countries' reactions to the events in the ČSSR, 26 April 1968, reprinted in Karner et al., *Dokumente*, #163.

46. Baeva, "Bulgarien—der treue Vasall des Kreml," 468.

47. Baeva, "Bulgarien—der treue Vasall des Kreml," 470.

48. Pauer, *Prag 68*, 73; see also the Wilke chapter in this volume.

49. RGANI, F. 10, op. 1, d. 235, p. 27, minutes of the meeting of the leadership of the CC CPSU with the leaders of the Communist parties of Bulgaria, Hungary, the GDR, and Poland, 8 May 1968. The stenographic transcript of the meeting is reprinted in Karner et al., *Dokumente*, #77.

50. The maneuvers codenamed "Šumava" (*Böhmerwald*) "were staged to demonstrate that the Czechoslovak army was not up to its task," argues Vojtech Mastny who adds, "perhaps the only military exercise in history meant to show that forces taking part in it, were *not* ready to fight." See his "Was 1968 a Strategic Watershed in the Cold War?" 158. The pitiful state of the Czechoslovak Army is also part of an early July conversation between Yakubovskii and Dzúr, see SAPMO-BA, DY 30/3618, pp. 80–87, reprinted in Karner et al., *Dokumente*, #89.

51. Melyn P. Leffler, *For the Soul of Mankind: The United States, the Soviet Union and the Cold War* (New York: Hill and Wang, 2007), 234–58; for Brezhnev's intense interest in the success of détente, see also Zubok, *Failed Empire*, 207–9, 218–22.

52. Karner et al., *Dokumente*, #89.

53. Karner et al., *Dokumente*, #89.

54. Baeva, "Bulgarien—der treue Vasall des Kreml," 471–72.

55. See the Prozumenshchikov chapter in this volume.

56. See Prozumenshchikov's chapter in this volume; Kramer also stresses the importance of the Hungary 1956 historical analogy for Kremlin decision makers.

57. See the Wilke chapter in this volume.

58. The stenographic transcript of the meeting's proceedings is reprinted in a German translation in Karner et al., *Dokumente*, #82. Excerpts in English are reprinted in Navrátil et al., *Prague Spring 1968*, 212–33.

59. Pauer, *Prag 68*, 108–9.

60. Pauer, *Prag 68*, 123–26.

61. Pauer, *Prag 68*, 116–23; SAPMO-BA, DY 30/11836, pp. 1–116, stenographic transcript of the meeting of the interventionist coalition Warsaw, 14/15 July 1968, reprinted in Karner et al., *Dokumente*, #82.

62. RGANI, F. 2, op. 3, d. 114, p. 118, stenographic transcript of the meeting of the plenum of the CC CPSU, closing speech of the general secretary of the CC CPSU, L. I. Brezhnev, 17 July 1968, reprinted in Karner et al., *Dokumente*, #38; see also Pauer, *Prag 68*, 127, partly reprinted in this volume as appendix 4.

63. See the Prozumenshchikov chapter in this volume.

64. It is not possible to go into further detail here; see the chapter by Günter Bischof in this volume.

65. RGANI, F. 3, op. 72, d. 189, pp. 2, 4, Politburo resolution of the CC CPSU p. 92 (II), "On the question of the situation in Czechoslovakia," 20 July 1968. See also the chapter by Mark Kramer in this volume.

66. Brezhnev's health began to suffer from the stress of the ongoing crisis; he feared that "losing Czechoslovakia" would leave him politically vulnerable to potential rivals; on this strain and Brezhnev's continued hesitation, see the chapter by Mark Kramer in this volume and Zubok, *Failed Empire*, 208.

67. For details, see the chapter by Peter Ruggenthaler and Harald Knoll in this volume.

68. See the chapter by Peter Ruggenthaler and Harald Knoll in this volume.

69. See the chapter by Peter Ruggenthaler and Harald Knoll in this volume.

70. Brezhnev quoted in Zubok, *Failed Empire*, 208.

71. John Lewis Gaddis, *We Now Know: Rethinking Cold War History* (Oxford: Clarendon, 1997), 17.

72. Pavlenko, "Der Informationsfluss an die Moskauer Machtzentrale," and the chapter by Petrov in this volume.

73. Pavlenko, "Der Informationsfluss an die Moskauer Machtzentrale," and the chapter by Petrov in this volume.

74. The background was the worsening situation in Vietnam after the Tet Offensive and the monumental struggle between his principal foreign policy advisers over launching a peace initiative vis-à-vis North Vietnam; see Thomas J. Schoenbaum, *Waging Peace & War: Dean Rusk in the Truman, Kennedy & Johnson Years* (New York: Simon and Schuster, 1988), 465–91.

75. "Soviet threat to Czechoslovakia," Rostow to Rusk, 10 May 1968, Folder "6/1/68," Box 1558, POL-Czech, RG 59, NARA, reprinted as appendix 3 in this volume. See also the chapters by Günter Bischof and Donald P. Steury in this volume.

76. See Ouimet, *Rise and Fall of the Brezhnev Doctrine*, 34, and the Bischof chapter in this volume. In the State Department minutes of the 22 July conversation with Dobrynin, Rusk's message is less direct than Dobrynin's dispatch sent to Moscow— the Warsaw Pact is not mentioned: "*He said we had not wished to involve ourselves directly in this matter, that the U.S. had been attempting to develop better relationships with Eastern European countries as well as with the Soviet Union*" (emphasis added), see *Foreign Relations of the United States, 1964–1968*, vol. 8, *Eastern Europe* (Washington, DC: U.S. Government Printing Office, 1996), 212–14. In a 26 July resolution by the Politburo, reference is made to the 22 July Rusk-Dobrynin conversation, in which the secretary of state noted "that events in Czechoslovakia were a matter that concerned solely the Czechs and the other countries of the Warsaw Pact," see RGANI, F. 3, op. 72, d. 191, pp. 84–85. Politburo resolution of the CC CPSU P 92 (82), 26 July 1968, partly reprinted in this volume as appendix 5.

77. "Notes of Emergency Meeting of the National Security Council," 20 August 1968, 10:15 p.m., in *FRUS, 1964–1968*, vol. 8, *Eastern Europe*, 236–41; also reprinted in Navrátil et al., *Prague Spring '68*, 445–48; see also the Bischof chapter in this volume. Mastny also noted this discrepancy in the U.S. and Soviet records and observes tongue in cheek that each side included the details they felt suitable "to embellish its own record," surely a cautionary tale for diplomatic historians, see "Was 1968 a Strategic Watershed in the Cold War?" 162.

78. It may be good thing that Allen Dulles was no longer advising presidents in 1968, for during both the 1953 and 1956 crises, he had made disparaging remarks about the Czechs. During the National Security Council discussion following the East German uprising, he had observed that among the peoples of the satellites "the Czechs were certainly the most phlegmatic and the least likely to rise in revolt," see Christian F. Ostermann, ed., *Uprising in East Germany, 1953*, National Security Archives Cold War Readers (Budapest: Central European University Press, 2001), 227. When President Eisenhower asked Allen Dulles about the Czech reaction to

the invasion of Hungary, Dulles answered that he did not know, but it did not matter much since "all the potential Gomułkas in Czechoslovakia had been pretty well slaughtered," in Csaba Békés et al., eds., *The 1956 Hungarian Revolution: A History in Documents*, National Security Archive Cold War Readers (Budapest: Central European University Press, 2002), 241. Incidentally, Dubček had survived the purges.

79. The Soviet ambassador to the United States, Dobrynin, also came to the same conclusion after the invasion of Czechoslovakia; see Dobrynin's report, RGANI, F. 5, op. 60, d. 469, pp. 57–69, partly reprinted in this volume as appendix 10.

80. See also Bennett Kovrig, *Of Walls and Bridges: The United Sates and Eastern Europe* (New York: New York University Press, 1991) and Brands, *Wages of Globalism*. On the role of the Vietnam War, see the chapter by Mark Carson in this volume; see also George C. Herring, "Tet and the Crisis of Hegemony," in Fink et al., *1968: The World Transformed*, 31–53; Schwartz, *Lyndon Johnson and Europe*; Hubert Zimmermann, "Who Paid for America's War? Vietnam and the International Monetary System, 1960–1975," in Daum et al., *America, the Vietnam War, and the World*, 151–73; Frank Costigliola, "Lyndon B. Johnson, Germany, and 'the End of the Cold War,'" in Cohen and Tucker, *Lyndon Johnson Confronts the World*, 173–210; see also the chapter by Günter Bischof in this volume.

81. For details, see Pavlenko, "Der Informationsfluss an die Moskauer Machtzentrale," and the chapter by Prozumenshchikov in this volume.

82. For details, see Pavlenko, "Der Informationsfluss an die Moskauer Machtzentrale," and the chapter by Prozumenshchikov in this volume.

83. For further details on Kádár's role, see the Békés chapter in this volume.

84. Hans Modrow, *In historischer Mission: Als deutscher Politiker unterwegs* (Berlin: Edition Ost, 2007), 173, writes: "On 4 December 1989 representatives of the states of the Warsaw Pact, who had assembled in Moscow for consultations, issued an apology to the Czechs and Slovaks for the military intervention in August 1968. The NVA did not take part in the operation. Walter Ulbricht was wise enough not to let a single German soldier cross the border. In view of the experiences of 1938/1939 the decision was perfectly justified. The GDR provided logistical support, that is correct. But this is where the matter ended."

85. For details, see Wenzke, "Die Nationale Volksarmee der DDR: Kein Einsatz in Prag," in Karner et al., *Beiträge*, 673–86. RGANI, F. 89, op. 38, d. 57, pp. 1–19, stenographic transcript of the meeting between the Soviet leadership and the state president of the ČSSR, L. Svoboda, and M. Klusák, 23 August 1968, reprinted in Karner et al., *Dokumente*, #107. According to Gomułka, the NVA was kept back at the express request of the group around Bil'ak and Indra. On this, see Pauer, *Prag 1968*, 229, partly reprinted in this volume as appendix 8.

86. RGANI, F. 2, op. 3, d. 130, pp. 1–26, speech by L. I. Brezhnev at the session of the plenum of the CC CPSU, 31 October 1968, reprinted in Karner et al., *Dokumente*, #122.

87. See the chapters by Saki Ruth Dockrill and Georges-Henri Soutou in this volume.

88. In considerable detail (including Romanian sources), see also Mastny, "Was 1968 a Strategic Watershed of the Cold War?" 169–72; on Yugoslavia, see the Tvrtko Jakovina chapter in this volume.

89. *Neues Deutschland*, 2 December 1989, in *Deutschland Archiv* 1 (1990): 137; Lutz Prieß et al., *Die SED und der "Prager Frühling" 1968: Politik gegen einen "Sozialismus mit menschlichem Antlitz"* (Berlin: Akademie Verlag, 1968), 17.

90. On Vladimir Putin's visit to Prague, see *Die Welt*, 1 March 2006.

2

The Prague Spring and the Soviet Invasion in Historical Perspective

Mark Kramer

When turmoil engulfed many parts of the world in 1968, the Soviet Bloc was not wholly immune. A series of momentous events in Eastern Europe in 1968 marked a turning point in the Cold War. Until then, the Iron Curtain separating Communist states in the East from democratic countries in the West had seemed impermeable. The division of Europe had, ironically, been reinforced when violent rebellions erupted in several of the East Bloc countries in the first few years after Josef Stalin's death—in Czechoslovakia and the German Democratic Republic (GDR) in June 1953, in Poznań, Poland in June 1956, and in Hungary in October 1956. Faced with violent instability and the imminent collapse of the East German regime in 1953 and the Hungarian government in 1956, Soviet leaders deployed vast numbers of combat troops to crush those challenges and restore orthodox Communist rule. The Soviet Army's success in quelling the two uprisings consolidated the USSR's sphere of influence in Eastern Europe and exposed the hollowness of U.S. rhetoric promising the "rollback" of communism from the region.

A very different problem arose for the Soviet Union in 1968, when Czechoslovakia embarked on a dramatic but entirely peaceful attempt to change both the internal complexion of communism and many of the basic structures of Soviet–East European relations. This eight-month-long experiment, widely known as the "Prague Spring," came to a decisive end in the early morning hours of 21 August 1968, when hundreds of thousands of Soviet and Warsaw Pact troops invaded and occupied Czechoslovakia on behalf of "healthy forces" in the local Communist Party who set about reinstating a hard-line Soviet-style regime.

Neither the Soviet Union nor Czechoslovakia exists any longer, but the legacy of the Prague Spring and the Soviet invasion is still being felt. The reforms that took place in Czechoslovakia in 1968 under the leadership of Alexander Dubček offered the first opportunity for an East European Communist regime to earn genuine popular support. Moscow's unwillingness to tolerate those liberalizing reforms ensured that, from then on, stability in the Eastern Bloc could be preserved only by the threat of another Soviet invasion.

That threat sufficed to hold the Bloc together for more than twenty years, even when tested by severe crises like the one in Poland in 1980–1981. But soon after Mikhail Gorbachev came along and was no longer willing to use military force in Eastern Europe, the whole Soviet Bloc collapsed. Because of the legacy of 1968, all the East European regimes still lacked the legitimacy they would have needed to sustain themselves without Soviet military backing. The invasion of Czechoslovakia saved Soviet-style communism in Eastern Europe for more than two decades, but it could not forestall the eventual demise of the Bloc.

EARLIER RESEARCH AND SOURCES

During the Cold War, historians and political scientists devoted a great deal of scrutiny to the Prague Spring and the invasion of Czechoslovakia. Countless books, monographs, and articles about the invasion and the events preceding and following it appeared in the West. For many years, all such studies had to rely exclusively or almost exclusively on open sources. Although new firsthand information about the Soviet-Czechoslovak crisis became available in the late 1970s and 1980s when some valuable memoirs and interviews appeared, these retrospective accounts were not enough to make up for the total unavailability of secret documentation in the Warsaw Pact countries. Declassified cables, memoranda, and reports from the U.S. government and from some of the West European countries helped to fill in certain gaps, but the lack of archival evidence and solid memoirs from the Soviet Bloc posed formidable problems.

By the mid-1980s the existing, open-source materials had been thoroughly mined. Without access to the Soviet and East European archives, researchers had little prospect of coming up with many additional insights. But until the late 1980s there seemed almost no chance that the East Bloc archives would ever be accessible. Given the continued sensitivity of the topic, the closed nature of the Soviet and East European societies, and the lack of any procedures in the Communist Bloc for requesting the declassification of documents (even for purely scholarly purposes), secret archival materials about the Prague Spring seemed destined to remain unavailable to scholars. Not until 1988 and 1989, when Gorbachev's policy of glasnost (official openness) sparked bolder public discussions of Soviet foreign policy, did the opportunities for research begin to expand. Former officials—and even some active officials—in both the USSR and Eastern Europe began reassessing the whole question of the Prague Spring and the Soviet invasion. This auspicious trend gained vastly greater momentum after the collapse of East European communism in 1989 led to free elections that brought noncommunist governments to power in the former Soviet Bloc countries. The trend accelerated still further when the Communist Party of the Soviet Union (CPSU) and the Soviet state disintegrated in late 1991. Sensitive documents and firsthand accounts of the events leading up to and following the 1968 invasion, which once would have been wholly off-limits to Western (and Eastern) scholars, suddenly were available in abundance. Although many difficulties have persisted in gaining access to archival collections in Moscow and elsewhere, researchers are at last able to pore over key materials that only recently were kept under tight guard.

NEW SOURCES

The recently declassified documents include stenographic accounts of all the multilateral Soviet–East European conferences in 1968; transcripts of all bilateral Soviet-Czechoslovak negotiations; transcripts of meetings of the Presidium and Central Committee of the Communist Party of Czechoslovakia (*Komunistická strana Československa*, or KSČ); transcripts and supporting documents from CPSU Politburo sessions and CPSU Central Committee plenums; transcripts of meetings of the ruling organs of the Communist parties in other East European countries; the texts of secret high-level letters and messages; the detailed contemporaneous diaries of a CPSU Politburo member, Petro Shelest, who played an important role in the crisis; transcripts of high-level phone conversations; secret military directives and planning materials; reports on military exercises; memoranda and cables from the Soviet embassy in Czechoslovakia; records amassed by CPSU Central Committee departments; records from the Czechoslovak embassies in Moscow and other East Bloc capitals; reports by senior officials from other East European countries; the text of the Moscow Protocol and associated documents; and many other items. Many illuminating retrospective accounts by top-ranking participants in the crisis are also now available.

In addition to all these materials from former East Bloc countries, many additional documents from the United States, West European countries, and the headquarters of the North Atlantic Treaty Organization (NATO) are also now available. Although some important Western (especially U.S.)

records were available well before the Cold War ended, access to U.S.,
West European, and NATO documents has increased immensely since
1991. Huge collections from the U.S. State Department, National Security
Council, Defense Department, and Central Intelligence Agency, including
many items originally released through the Freedom of Information Act or
Mandatory Review Requests, are available at the U.S. National Archives in
College Park, Maryland, and the Lyndon Baines Johnson Library in Austin,
Texas. Similar types of documents, albeit less numerous and with larger
gaps, can be found in the national archives of most of the West European
countries as well as at NATO's main archive in Brussels. Although Western
diplomatic and intelligence analyses of Soviet decision making during the
1968 crisis were imperfect at best (in this respect, the documents indirectly
confirm that Western governments were unable to recruit sources anywhere
near the highest levels of the Soviet regime), the Western documents provide vital information about the policies of the U.S. and West European
governments and also contain some information about the Soviet and East
European armed forces that is currently, and will for many years likely remain, unavailable from the Russian and other former East Bloc archives. A
case in point is a September 1968 U.S. Army intelligence report offering a
remarkably detailed overview of the Soviet Army's use of electronic warfare
(EW) and jamming during the invasion.[1] No documents pertaining to EW
or other sensitive operational matters have been released from the Russian
Defense Ministry's Main Archive.

This huge outpouring of new sources has greatly enriched earlier accounts of the Prague Spring and of the crisis that emerged between the
hard-line Warsaw Pact countries (including the USSR) and Czechoslovakia.
Previously unknown aspects of these events have now come to light, and
countless important details have been filled in, as is evident in the many
fine chapters of this book. Although the new sources do not drastically
change our basic understanding of the Prague Spring (which was superbly
analyzed in H. Gordon Skilling's landmark book published in 1976, as well
as in dozens of other books and many hundreds of articles), they do allow
us to gain a much more nuanced and comprehensive sense of what went on
in Czechoslovakia.[2] More importantly, the new archival evidence permits a
far more complete and accurate picture of Soviet decision making, interactions within the Warsaw Pact, and the events that led up to the August 1968
invasion. Although Karen Dawisha, in her 1984 book analyzing Soviet decision making vis-à-vis Czechoslovakia, did an admirable job on the basis of
the exiguous information that was available as of the early 1980s, her book
(not to mention other analyses that were less perceptive) has now been
overtaken by the deluge of new archival evidence and firsthand testimony.[3]
No scholar writing about this subject can any longer hope to do a satisfac-

tory job without taking account of the vast quantity of recently declassified documents, memoirs, and interviews from both East and West.

THE PRAGUE SPRING AND ITS RECEPTION IN MOSCOW

The new evidence underscores just how bold the changes in Czechoslovakia were, even in the face of relentless pressure from the Soviet Union and its hard-line Warsaw Pact allies (especially the GDR and Poland). Far-reaching reforms early in the Prague Spring, including the elimination of censorship, the emergence of unofficial political "clubs," the removal of orthodox Communist officials, and the general effort to forge "socialism with a human face," brought a sweeping revival of political and cultural life in a country that had long been one of the most repressive in the Soviet Bloc. As the reform program gained pace and public support grew, the Prague Spring took on a life of its own and gradually eluded the control of the KSČ. Traditional Marxist-Leninist institutions in Czechoslovakia were on the verge of being swept away.

Officials like Dubček remained loyal Communists, but their willingness to press ahead with wide-ranging political liberalization facilitated the emergence of more radical reformers within the party and the growing visibility of proponents of liberal democracy outside the KSČ. The new evidence confirms that senior Czechoslovak officials who were especially bold in supporting reforms, such as Ota Šik (a deputy prime minister), Jiří Pelikán (the head of state television), and even František Kriegel (a member of the KSČ Presidium), envisaged a greatly liberalized version of communism that would fundamentally depart from the standard Soviet model. Šik enunciated this new approach at a student rally in Prague in May 1968:

> I believe that our peoples [Czechs and Slovaks], with their strong democratic traditions and their deep revulsion toward any political restrictions and oppression, can put into practice the kind of socialist democracy we have not seen anywhere else. We can create a model of socialist society that will become genuinely attractive for the working people of all capitalist countries and that will have a tremendous impact on the development of left-wing movements in Western countries.[4]

In pledging to foster a liberal form of socialism that "we have not seen anywhere else," Šik made clear that he did not regard the Soviet Union as an example worth following. His aim of creating a "socialist democracy" that would "become genuinely attractive for the working people of all capitalist countries" was an obvious acknowledgment that Soviet-style socialism was *not* "genuinely attractive for working people."

Soviet leaders, as the new evidence shows, were unnerved by this sort of rhetoric and by the rise of influential political groups outside the KSČ. Officials in Moscow worried that even if Dubček did not intend to push in a radical direction, the outspoken proponents of liberal democratic reform in Czechoslovakia would increasingly eclipse him and steer the country along an "antisocialist" path. Such a development, they feared, would, if left unchecked, create an ominous precedent for the rest of the Soviet Bloc. Although the process of political, economic, and cultural revitalization in Czechoslovakia in 1968 was peaceful throughout, the lack of any violent turmoil did not prevent Soviet leaders from repeatedly drawing analogies to an event they had collectively experienced twelve years earlier—the violent rebellion in Hungary in October–November 1956, which was eventually subdued by the Soviet Army. As early as 15 March 1968, at a meeting of the CPSU Politburo, the head of the Soviet state security committee (KGB), Yuri Andropov, who had served as Soviet ambassador in Budapest during the 1956 revolution, claimed that events in Czechoslovakia "are very reminiscent of what happened in Hungary."[5] The CPSU general secretary, Leonid Brezhnev, who in 1956 had taken part in all the high-level discussions that led to the Soviet invasion of Hungary, concurred with Andropov's assessment, adding that "our earlier hopes for Dubček have not been borne out." Brezhnev phoned Dubček during a break in the CPSU Politburo's deliberations and emphasized his "grave concern" about the situation in Czechoslovakia, especially the "growth of patently antisocialist forces." The Soviet leader warned Dubček that "the Hungarian events of 1956 might soon be repeated in [Czechoslovakia]," but, to Brezhnev's disappointment in subsequent weeks, the phone call did not spur Dubček to rein in the Prague Spring.[6]

When the Soviet Politburo reconvened on 21 March, the assembled leaders expressed dismay that political liberalization in Czechoslovakia was continuing and that orthodox members of the Communist Party of Czechoslovakia (KSČ) were in danger of being removed from the scene altogether.[7] Likening the situation to the changes that occurred in Hungary just before the 1956 revolution, Brezhnev claimed that events in Czechoslovakia were "moving in an anti-Communist direction" and that many "good and sincere friends of the Soviet Union" had been dismissed. He also noted that the Prague Spring was beginning to spark ferment among Soviet "intellectuals and students as well as in certain regions" of the USSR, notably Ukraine. Brezhnev's misgivings were echoed by other Politburo members, including Soviet prime minister Aleksei Kosygin, who insisted that the Czechoslovak authorities were "preparing to do what was done in Hungary" in 1956. The Ukrainian party leader, Petro Shelest, also stressed the potential for violence to erupt in Czechoslovakia and to spill over into Ukraine—a development that in his view would determine "not only the fate of socialism in one of the socialist countries, but the fate of the whole socialist camp." Aleksandr Shelepin and Mikhail Solomentsev spoke in similarly ominous tones about the effect of the Prague Spring on Soviet students and intellectuals. They joined Shelest in urging the Soviet Union to prepare to take "extreme measures," including "military action." This proposal was strongly endorsed by Andropov, who argued that "we must adopt concrete military measures" as soon as possible.[8]

The growing unease in Moscow was reinforced by the much harsher complaints expressed in other East Bloc capitals, especially Warsaw and East Berlin. From the outset, the Polish leader Władysław Gomułka and the East German leader Walter Ulbricht were determined to counter the "growth of inimical, anti-socialist influences" along their borders. The two men feared that events in Czechoslovakia would prove "contagious" and would create political instability in their own countries. As early as mid-January, when a high-level Soviet delegation led by Brezhnev paid an unofficial visit to Poland and East Germany, both Gomułka and Ulbricht expressed disquiet to their Soviet counterparts about recent developments in Czechoslovakia.[9] Gomułka reiterated his concerns in a private conversation with Dubček a few weeks later in the Moravian city of Ostrava, warning that "if things go badly with you [in Czechoslovakia], we in Poland, too, will find hostile elements rising against us."[10] In subsequent weeks, Gomułka's and Ulbricht's views of the Czechoslovak reform program took on an increasingly alarmist edge; and before long, both of the East European leaders were calling, with ever greater urgency, for intervention by Warsaw Pact troops to halt the Prague Spring.

THE ROAD TOWARD CONFRONTATION

The concerns expressed by Polish and East German leaders, combined with the disquiet that senior officials in Moscow were beginning to feel, induced the CPSU Politburo to give high priority to the "Czechoslovak question."[11] From mid-March 1968 on, the issue was constantly at the top of the Politburo's agenda. The transcripts of the Politburo sessions and the records of other high-level CPSU bodies, as well as materials from Brezhnev's personal papers (*lichnyi fond*), reveal that the CPSU general secretary consulted and worked closely with his colleagues on all aspects of the crisis, thereby ensuring that responsibility for the outcome would be borne collectively. Unlike in December 1967, when Brezhnev resorted to "personal diplomacy" during a sudden visit to Prague as the pressure for political change in Czechoslovakia was coming to a head, the growing "threat" in Czechoslovakia by the spring of 1968 gave him an incentive to share as much of the burden as possible with the rest of the Politburo and Secretariat. In particular, he ensured that his two top colleagues (and potential rivals), Aleksei Kosygin and Nikolai Podgornyi, were prominently involved in all key decisions and negotiations, linking them in an informal troika (with Brezhnev) that represented—and often acted on behalf of—the full Politburo. Much the same was true of Brezhnev's reliance on two other senior Politburo members: Mikhail Suslov, who oversaw ideological matters; and Petro Shelest, whose responsibilities in Ukraine did not prevent him from playing a key role during the crisis.

At the same time, Brezhnev was careful not to get bogged down by lower-level bureaucratic maneuvering. Throughout the crisis the CPSU Politburo, led by Brezhnev, exercised tight control over Soviet policy. The Politburo eventually set up a high-level "commission on the Czechoslovak question," consisting of Podgornyi, Suslov, Arvīds Pel'she, Aleksandr Shelepin, Kirill Mazurov, Konstantin Rusakov, Yuri Andropov, Andrei Gromyko, and Aleksei Epishev. The commission kept a daily watch on events in Czechoslovakia, functioning as an organ of the Politburo that was directly accountable to Brezhnev. (Six of the nine members of the commission, including Podgornyi and Suslov, were full or candidate members of the Politburo, and the three other commission members had been taking an active part in the Politburo's deliberations on Czechoslovakia.)[12] The commission's updated findings and recommendations were regularly brought before the full Politburo for consideration. Brezhnev himself carefully guided the Politburo's proceedings and took direct responsibility for bilateral contacts with Dubček.

Throughout the spring and summer of 1968, analogies with the violence in Hungary in 1956 remained salient in the Soviet Politburo's deliberations about the Prague Spring, despite the lack of any violent unrest in Czechoslovakia. When Dubček and other reform-minded Czechoslovak officials spoke with Soviet leaders, they tried to convince them that the situation was not at all like Hungary twelve years earlier:

> [T]he current events [in Czechoslovakia] are not a repetition of the events of 1956 in Hungary. In Hungary the popular masses rose up against the party and Central Committee, whereas in Czechoslovakia the masses are speaking out only against the conservatives and the group around [the hard-liner Antonín] Novotný and are supporting the [KSČ], the Central Committee, and friendship with the Soviet Union.[13]

These assurances, in the absence of concrete steps demanded by the Soviet authorities, failed to mollify leaders in Moscow. Although Soviet officials acknowledged that no violent upheavals were occurring in Czechoslovakia ("at least not yet"), they argued that this was purely because "the American and West German imperialists" had "shifted tactics" and were "resorting to a new, step-by-step approach." The extensive evidence now available in

Western and former East Bloc archives makes clear that, contrary to these allegations of "imperialist" involvement, Western governments were in fact not masterminding or even doing much to help out the Prague Spring. The reform program in Czechoslovakia was devised from within.

For Soviet leaders, however, the allegations served a clear purpose. By repeatedly accusing the U.S. and West German governments of conspiring with "reactionary" forces in Czechoslovakia, they sought to discredit the Prague Spring. They argued that Western governments had been chastened by the experience in 1956 (when Soviet troops forcefully quelled the Hungarian Revolution) and were therefore now adopting a subtler approach. At a closed party gathering in April 1968 the Soviet Politburo member Petro Shelest explained this alleged shift in Western tactics:

> In Hungary in 1956 the imperialists urged the local reactionaries to embark on an armed attack to seize power, whereas in Czechoslovakia they are trying to establish a bourgeois order by "peaceful means." That is, they are trying gradually to change the situation so that the reactionaries can gradually seize one position after another. . . . [The anti-Soviet elements in Czechoslovakia] do not dare to speak out openly in support of anti-Communist and anti-Soviet demands. They understand [from the decisive Soviet response in 1956] that this game is over once and for all. The enemies provide cover for themselves with demagogic statements about "friendship" with the Soviet Union, while at the same time sowing doubts about some sort of "inequality" and about the pursuit of a special, "independent" foreign policy. They are also trying to undercut the leading role of the [Communist] Party.[14]

Shelest claimed that he was still hoping that "the healthy forces in the KSČ will be able to regain control of the situation and guide the country back onto the socialist path." But he added that "in the event of danger," the CPSU Politburo "will use all of our capabilities," including military forces, "to thwart the intrigues of our enemies who want to rip fraternal Czechoslovakia out of the commonwealth of socialist countries."[15]

Shelest's argument signaled a far-reaching change of policy that was later reflected in the Brezhnev Doctrine. The implication of his comments was that even if violence did not ever break out in Czechoslovakia, the peaceful "seizure of power" by "hostile forces" (supposedly "in collusion with Western imperialists") could eventually pose the same sort of "mortal danger" that arose in Hungary in 1956, necessitating the same type of Soviet response. This line of reasoning was publicly codified in an article in the main CPSU newspaper, *Pravda*, in July 1968, a few days before Soviet leaders met in Warsaw with the leaders of East Germany, Poland, Bulgaria, and Hungary to decide what to do about Czechoslovakia. The article, titled "Attack against the Foundations of Socialism in Czechoslovakia," asserted that "the tactics of those who would like to undermine the foundations of socialism in Czechoslovakia are even more cunning and insidious" than the "frenzied attacks launched by counterrevolutionary elements in Hungary in 1956."[16] Because the "champions of counterrevolution" in Czechoslovakia and their Western backers were aware that open revolt would provoke a Soviet military response, they were "carrying out a stealthy counterrevolution" that would peacefully "subvert the gains of socialism."

The significance of this new Soviet rhetoric was not fully understood in Prague until it was too late. Although Dubček was well aware that internal reforms in Czechoslovakia had sparked consternation in Moscow, he assumed that he could offset this hostility by constantly reassuring Soviet leaders about the firmness of Czechoslovakia's commitment to the Warsaw Pact and the "socialist commonwealth."[17] Looking back to the events of 1956 in Hungary, Dubček and other senior KSČ officials concluded that by upholding Czechoslovakia's membership in the Warsaw Pact and maintaining broad control over the reform process, they could carry out sweeping domestic changes without provoking Soviet military intervention.[18] This conclusion, as we now know, was erroneous even about the earlier case of Hungary. The CPSU Presidium's decision at the end of October 1956 to quell the revolution in Hungary through a full-scale invasion predated Hungary's announced intention to withdraw from the Warsaw Pact.[19] Whether valid or not, however, the "lesson" that Czechoslovak officials drew from the 1956 crisis—that internal reform would be tolerated so long as membership in the Warsaw Pact was not questioned—induced them to make frequent references to Czechoslovakia's "unbreakable friendship and alliance" with the USSR.[20] As domestic liberalization gathered pace, Dubček was particularly careful to issue repeated expressions of solidarity with Moscow and to pledge that Soviet interests would be safeguarded under all circumstances.

Although Dubček was undoubtedly sincere in his professions of loyalty to the Soviet Union, his statements failed to defuse the crisis. Not only did Soviet leaders worry that the Prague Spring would eventually undermine Czechoslovakia's commitment to the Warsaw Pact, but they also believed that the internal changes in Czechoslovakia were themselves a threat to the "unity and cohesion of the Communist movement." In the spring and summer of 1968, the Soviet Politburo consistently emphasized three main demands—that the KSČ reintroduce strict censorship over the Czechoslovak mass media; that Dubček remove the most outspoken officials, including Jiří Pelikán and General Václav Prchlík; and that the Czechoslovak authorities promptly disband and outlaw the unofficial political "clubs." Soviet leaders brought up these points whenever they met or spoke by phone with their Czechoslovak counterparts, and they voiced similar demands in multilateral forums. Dubček could have been under no illusions about what the Soviet Union wanted, but he consistently tried to defer or avoid any concrete steps to fulfill the demands.

In the absence of a major turnaround in Czechoslovakia, analogies with the Hungarian Revolution, no matter how dubious, persisted in the Soviet Politburo's deliberations. Even so, the lack of any violence in Czechoslovakia in 1968 meant that Brezhnev and his colleagues had more time to resolve the situation than was available to Soviet leaders in either 1953 (when an uprising broke out in East Germany) or 1956 (when violent protests erupted in Hungary). The violence that accompanied those earlier crises necessitated prompter action. In 1968, by contrast, the Soviet Politburo deliberated for several months before reaching a consensus about the best way to end the crisis. Shelest noted in his diary that as late as the summer of 1968, the differing approaches of Brezhnev, Kosygin, Podgornyi, Suslov, and other senior officials "kept the Politburo from being firmly united about how to deal with the question of Czechoslovakia."[21] The declassified transcripts of the Soviet Politburo's discussions and of other high-level meetings amply corroborate Shelest's point. The transcripts show that some Politburo members, such as Andropov, Podgornyi, and Shelest, were consistent proponents of military intervention, whereas other members, particularly Suslov, were far more circumspect. The transcripts also indicate that several figures, including Kosygin, Aleksandr Shelepin, and Pyotr Demichev, fluctuated during the crisis, at times favoring "extreme measures" (that is, military action) and at other times leaning toward a political solution.

Nevertheless, even when the members of the Soviet Politburo disagreed with one another, their disagreements were mainly over tactics rather than strategic considerations or fundamental goals. All of the Politburo members agreed that the reform process in Czechoslovakia was endangering the "gains of socialism" and the "common interests of world socialism," just as the Hungarian Revolution had in 1956. By the late spring of 1968, most of the Politburo members sensed that drastic Soviet action would be necessary to curtail the Prague Spring. Although some still hoped that Dubček himself would be willing to crack down, many had begun to suspect that it was no longer possible to count on a purely "internal" solution.

One of those who did still hold out at least some hope of achieving an internal solution was Brezhnev. In July and early August 1968, he and other Soviet officials repeatedly urged Dubček to clamp down on "antisocialist" groups, restore censorship of the mass media, and remove the KSČ officials who ardently supported "socialism with a human face." The Soviet Union's relentless pressure on the Czechoslovak authorities was reinforced by Poland, East Germany, Bulgaria, and antireformist members of the KSČ Presidium. Brezhnev used a variety of bilateral channels to exhort Czechoslovak officials to combat "antisocialist" and "counterrevolutionary" elements, and he even approached a few of Dubček's reformist colleagues surreptitiously in the hope of finding a suitable replacement who would be willing to crack down.[22] The Soviet government also convened multilateral Warsaw Pact conclaves to generate further pressure on Dubček. Highly publicized meetings in Warsaw in mid-July and in Bratislava at the beginning of August featured harsh criticism and threats of joint action to "defend the gains of socialism" in Czechoslovakia.[23]

None of these efforts, however, proved successful in derailing the Prague Spring. As Brezhnev and other leaders increasingly realized that an internal crackdown was not going to materialize, the high-level debate in Moscow moved toward consensus. The Soviet Politburo tentatively decided at its meetings on 22 and 26/27 July to proceed with a full-scale invasion sometime in mid- to late August if the situation in Czechoslovakia did not fundamentally change. When the Soviet Politburo reconvened in an expanded session on 6 August to review the latest developments, no one any longer really expected that military action could be averted. Although a few participants voiced reservations about the potential costs of an invasion—especially if, as Defense Minister Andrei Grechko warned, the incoming troops encountered armed resistance—the Politburo reached a consensus on 6 August to proceed with military intervention in Czechoslovakia unless Dubček took immediate, drastic steps to comply with Soviet demands.[24] This consensus did not yet signify an irrevocable decision to invade, but it did mean that Brezhnev and other Soviet leaders had essentially abandoned hope that "anything more can be expected" of Dubček.

A CONSENSUS IN FAVOR OF MILITARY INTERVENTION

As the time for military action approached, Brezhnev made one final attempt to pressure Dubček to reverse course. The strain of the crisis was beginning to take a serious toll on Brezhnev's health, but he was still determined to exhaust all other options before resorting to military action.[25] Although he confided to his aides that he was deeply worried about "losing Czechoslovakia" and "being removed from [his] post as General Secretary," he also was concerned that an invasion would exact high political costs of its own.[26] He and other Soviet leaders were in the Crimea during the second week of August, but he kept in close touch with Dubček by phone throughout that time. Brezhnev also maintained contact with Dubček via the Soviet ambassador, Stepan Chervonenko. In a phone conversation with Dubček on 9 August, Brezhnev tried to compel the KSČ leader to act. Brezhnev emphasized how "dire" the situation had become, and he urged Dubček to live up to "the conditions we jointly approved and agreed on [at the beginning of August after holding bilateral negotiations] in Čierna nad Tisou."[27] In a follow-up telephone conversation four days later, Brezhnev was far more aggressive and belligerent, accusing Dubček of "outright deceit" and of "blatantly sabotaging the agreements reached at Čierna and Bratislava."[28] The Soviet leader warned that in the "entirely new situation that has emerged" the USSR "would be obliged to consider adopting new, independent measures that will defend both the KSČ and the cause of socialism in Czechoslovakia."

Soon after the phone conversation on the 13th, Brezhnev sent an urgent cable to Chervonenko ordering him to meet with Dubček as soon as possible to reemphasize the "extraordinary gravity" of the situation and the need for immediate action.[29] Chervonenko did so that same evening, but his efforts, too, were of no avail. The failure of these different contacts seems to have been what finally spurred Brezhnev to conclude that "nothing more can be expected from the current KSČ CC Presidium" and that a military solution could no longer be deferred.[30] From then on, the dynamic of the whole situation changed. Brezhnev, during his break in the Crimea, had been conferring with other senior members of the CPSU Politburo and Secretariat, most of whom were vacationing nearby.[31] Ad-hoc sessions of the Politburo were convened on 13, 14, and 15 August to discuss appropriate responses. Brezhnev and his colleagues acknowledged that a military solution "would be fraught with complications," but they all agreed that any delay in acting "would lead to civil war in Czechoslovakia and the loss of it as a socialist country."[32]

On 17 August, with all the top leaders back in Moscow, the Soviet Politburo convened and voted unanimously to "provide assistance and support to the Communist Party and people of Czechoslovakia through the use of [the Soviet] armed forces."[33] No one on the Politburo expressed doubt about the decision. The following day, at a hastily convened meeting in Moscow, Brezhnev informed the leaders of East Germany, Poland, Bulgaria, and Hungary about the decision.[34] Similar briefings were held in Moscow on 19 August for the members of the CPSU Central Committee, for the heads of union-republic, regional, and municipal party organizations, and for senior government officials. After the briefings on the 19th, the CPSU Politburo convened for several hours to review the military and political aspects of the upcoming operation.[35] Detailed presentations by Defense Minister Grechko and the chief of the Soviet General Staff, Marshal Matvei Zakharov, provided grounds for optimism about the military side of the invasion, but the political preparations received less scrutiny. Although most of the Politburo members expressed confidence that the "healthy forces" in Czechoslovakia (a group of KSČ hardliners who secretly conspired with the Soviet Union before the invasion) would carry out their plan to seize power, a few Politburo members seemed more skeptical about "what will happen after our troops enter Czechoslovakia."[36]

Over the next day, Soviet officials and military commanders kept in close touch with their East European counterparts. Unlike in 1956, when Soviet troops intervened in Hungary unilaterally (after turning down offers of help from Romania, Czechoslovakia, and Bulgaria), Brezhnev was determined to give the invasion in 1968 a multilateral appearance. Combat soldiers from Poland, Bulgaria, and Hungary and a liaison unit from East Germany took part in the invasion, which began at 11:00 p.m. (Moscow time) on 20 August.

THE INVASION AND ITS AFTERMATH

The Soviet High Command went to great lengths to make sure that the incoming forces would not encounter any armed resistance. When the first Soviet troops crossed the border, Marshal Grechko phoned the Czechoslovak national defense minister, General Martin Dzúr, and warned him that if Czechoslovak soldiers fired "even a single shot" in resistance, the Soviet Army would "crush the resistance mercilessly" and Dzúr himself would "be strung up from a telephone pole and shot."[37] Dzúr heeded the warning by ordering all Czechoslovak troops to remain in their barracks indefinitely, to avoid the use of weapons for any purpose, and to offer "all necessary assistance to the Soviet forces."[38] A similar directive was issued by the Czechoslovak president and commander in chief Ludvík Svoboda after he was informed of the invasion—in more cordial terms—by Ambassador Chervonenko shortly before midnight.[39] Neither Dzúr nor Svoboda welcomed the invasion, but both of them believed that armed resistance would merely result in widespread, futile bloodshed. The KSČ Presidium and the Czechoslovak government also promptly instructed the army and security forces not to put up active opposition; and the Soviet commander of the invasion, General Ivan Pavlovskii, issued a prepared statement in the name of the Soviet High Command urging Czechoslovak soldiers to remain in their barracks.[40] As a result of all these appeals, the Soviet and Warsaw Pact troops faced no armed resistance at all.

Soviet airborne forces and KGB special operations personnel spearheaded the invasion, and they were followed within a few hours by nearly 170,000 regular Soviet troops. (In subsequent days, nearly 300,000 more Soviet soldiers moved into Czechoslovakia, bringing the total to around 450,000-500,000.) Within hours, the Soviet-led units seized control of Czechoslovakia's transportation and communications networks and surrounded all the main Communist Party and government buildings in Prague and other cities. Soviet troops then began methodically occupying key sites (including military bases and airfields) and setting up new communications and broadcasting facilities. In the early morning hours of 21

August, Soviet commandos from the elite Taman division, accompanied by KGB officers and Czechoslovak State Security forces, entered the KSČ Central Committee headquarters and arrested Dubček and the other KSČ Presidium members who had supported the Prague Spring (except for Prime Minister Oldřich Černík, who had been arrested earlier at his office in the Government Ministers' building).[41] Soon after Dubček and the other KSČ officials were spirited away, the whole of Czechoslovakia fell under Soviet military control.

Decisive as the military results may have been, they seemed rather hollow when the invasion failed to achieve its immediate political aims.[42] The Soviet Union's chief political objective on 20/21 August was to facilitate a rapid transition to a pro-Moscow "revolutionary government," as had been done in Hungary in November 1956 when Soviet troops installed a "workers' and peasants' government" under Janoš Kádár. In Czechoslovakia, however, a pro-Moscow government failed to materialize immediately after the invasion. The "healthy forces" in Czechoslovakia were unable to gain majority support on the KSČ Presidium. The resulting confusion was well described in an emergency cable to Moscow from Kirill Mazurov, a Soviet Politburo member who had been sent to Czechoslovakia to oversee the political side of the invasion. Mazurov reported that the KSČ hardliners had "gone a bit haywire" and had "lost their nerve when Soviet military units were slightly late in arriving" at the KSČ Central Committee headquarters.[43] Upon learning that troops had crossed into Czechoslovakia, the KSČ Presidium had voted seven to four to adopt a statement condemning the invasion, and this statement was broadcast repeatedly on radio and television over the next several hours and was published in full on the front page of a special edition of the main KSČ newspaper, *Rudé právo*, on 21 August.[44] These developments, according to Mazurov, caused even greater disarray and panic among the "healthy forces," who were "unable to recover from the shock."[45]

Despite this setback, Soviet leaders were reluctant to abandon their initial plan, apparently because they had neglected to devise any fallback options. It is surprising, even in retrospect, that they would have committed themselves so heavily to such a dubious strategy without having devised a viable alternative. No doubt, this was partly the fault of Soviet embassy officials in Prague and Soviet KGB sources who had assured the CPSU Politburo that the "healthy forces on the KSČ Presidium have finally consolidated themselves and closed their ranks so that they are now a majority."[46] The members of the CPSU Politburo genuinely expected that the invasion would earn widespread official and popular support (or at least acquiescence) once the "right-wing opportunists" in the KSČ were removed and the initial shock of the invasion wore off. Although martial law was to be imposed in certain parts of Czechoslovakia on 21 August, it was intended as a temporary and selective measure that could be lifted as soon as a "revolutionary government" was in place and the "antisocialist" and "counterrevolutionary" forces had been neutralized.[47] The lack of any attempt by the invading troops to take over the functions of the Czechoslovak government or parliament, the very limited scale of the initial Soviet propaganda effort inside Czechoslovakia, and the meager quantity of provisions brought in by the Soviet and East European forces (because they assumed that they would be promptly resupplied by a friendly Czechoslovak government) all confirm that Soviet leaders were expecting a swift transition to a pro-Moscow regime.[48]

Only after repeated efforts to set up a post-invasion government had collapsed and the invasion had met with overwhelming opposition in Czechoslovakia—both publicly and officially—did Soviet leaders get an inkling of how unfavorable the conditions in Czechoslovakia were.[49] An internal Soviet Politburo report shortly after the invasion conceded that "75 to 90 percent of the [Czechoslovak] population . . . regard the entry of Soviet troops as an act of occupation."[50] Reports from Soviet diplomats indicated that even most KSČ members viewed the invasion in "highly negative" terms.[51] Brezhnev and his colleagues acknowledged this point but were loath to admit that they had fundamentally misjudged the situation and had failed to take adequate precautions. Instead, they ascribed the fiasco solely to the "cowardly behavior" of the "healthy forces" in Czechoslovakia and the "lack of active propaganda work" by Soviet units.[52]

Faced with massive popular and official resistance in Czechoslovakia, the Soviet Politburo decided to open negotiations on 23 August with Dubček and other KSČ officials who had been arrested on the morning of the 21st. After four days of talks, the two sides agreed to sign the Moscow Protocol, which forced the reversal of several elements of the Prague Spring but also ensured the reinstatement of most of the leading reformers, including Dubček. The decision to bring back key Czechoslovak officials did not go over well with some Soviet Politburo members and with hard-line leaders in Eastern Europe. At a Warsaw Pact conclave on 24 August, Gomułka insisted that Soviet and East European troops should be "ordered to combat the counterrevolution" and take "whatever steps are necessary" to "prevent rightists and counterrevolutionaries from regaining power."[53] In his view, "the situation in Hungary [in 1956] was better than in Czechoslovakia today." Gomułka's complaints were echoed by Ulbricht, who declared that "if Dubček and Černík are going to be back in the leadership, what was the point of sending our troops there in the first place?"[54] Ulbricht warned that the KSČ reformers had "deceived us at Čierna and Bratislava" and "will deceive us again." Both he and Gomułka joined the Bulgarian leader, Todor Zhivkov, in calling for the imposition of a "military dictatorship" in Czechoslovakia. Their views were endorsed by Andropov, Shelest,

Podgornyi, and a few other Soviet officials during a meeting of the CPSU Politburo the following day.[55] Alluding to what was done in Hungary after Soviet troops invaded in 1956, Andropov proposed that a "revolutionary workers' and peasants' government" be installed in Czechoslovakia to carry out mass arrests and repression. His suggestion was backed by another candidate Politburo member and CPSU secretary, Dmitrii Ustinov, who emphasized that "we must give a free hand to our troops."

These calls for a much more vigorous (and presumably bloodier) military crackdown were rejected by Brezhnev, Kosygin, and other officials. Although Brezhnev was prepared, in extremis, to impose direct military rule in Czechoslovakia for as long as necessary, he and most of his colleagues clearly were hoping to come up with a more palatable solution first. The task of finding such a solution was seriously complicated by the collapse of Moscow's initial political aims, but a sustained period of repression and "normalization" gradually negated the defiant mood of the Czechoslovak population and consolidated the military and political gains of the invasion.[56] In April 1969, Dubček was removed from office for good.

THE BREZHNEV DOCTRINE

The implications of the 1968 crisis for Soviet responses to nonviolent political change in East-Central Europe were codified in the so-called Brezhnev Doctrine (a term coined in the West in September 1968 after the Soviet Union published a number of authoritative statements justifying the invasion of Czechoslovakia). The Brezhnev Doctrine laid out strict "rules of the game" for the Communist Bloc by linking the fate of each socialist country with the fate of all others, by stipulating that every socialist country must abide by the norms of Marxism-Leninism as interpreted in Moscow, and by rejecting "abstract sovereignty" in favor of the "laws of class struggle." Under the Brezhnev Doctrine, the Soviet Union had both a right and a "sacred duty" to preserve the "socialist gains" of all Warsaw Pact countries.[57] The Soviet Politburo therefore would be obliged to use military force not only to respond to violent outbursts—as in the case of Hungary in 1956—but also to preempt "impermissible deviations from socialism," even if these were carried out through entirely peaceful means. Although a preemptive military option had always existed for the Soviet Union, the Brezhnev Doctrine made it explicit by proclaiming that the Warsaw Pact states would never again risk "waiting until Communists are being shot and hanged," as in the autumn of 1956, before sending Soviet and allied troops to "help the champions of socialism."[58]

The Brezhnev Doctrine thus reflected the Soviet Union's profound hostility to any meaningful change in the political complexion of East-Central Europe, regardless of whether such change was achieved through nonviolent civil resistance or violent rebellion. But this engrained attitude did not necessarily mean that Soviet troops would intervene promptly or indiscriminately during future crises in the Soviet Bloc, any more than they had in 1968. Brezhnev went to great lengths in 1968 to pursue an internal solution in Czechoslovakia that would preclude the need for a full-scale invasion. He and other Soviet officials tried for months to pressure Dubček to crack down, and it was only when their repeated efforts failed and when the dates of party congresses in Czechoslovakia were looming (congresses that would have resulted in sweeping replacements of KSČ hardliners) that the Soviet Politburo finally approved the dispatch of Soviet troops. This pattern of trying every option to find an internal solution before resorting to military force was repeated during all subsequent crises in East-Central Europe under Brezhnev.

NET ASSESSMENT

In retrospect, given what the latest evidence reveals about the Soviet Union's objectives at the time, we can safely conclude that no real opportunity existed in 1968 for truly radical change in Czechoslovakia. Significant reforms would of course have been possible, as had been occurring in Hungary since 1962. But the much more far-reaching transformation envisaged by the boldest reformers in Czechoslovakia was unacceptable to the leaders in Moscow. Because Brezhnev and his Soviet colleagues had sufficient power to determine the political fate of Czechoslovakia, their preferences ultimately prevailed in 1968. Fundamental change in Czechoslovakia and in other Central and East European countries required a fundamental change in Soviet policy, and this did not occur until the end of the 1980s. Only then were the ideals and central elements of the Prague Spring, especially its democratic thrust, allowed to bear full fruit.

Nonetheless, even if radical change could not have taken lasting hold in Central and Eastern Europe under the circumstances that existed in Moscow in 1968, this does not diminish the drama and audacity of the Prague Spring. Soviet leaders rightly sensed that the far-reaching reforms in Czechoslovakia would have a fissiparous effect within the Communist Bloc. To be sure, it is impossible to know whether the reform program in Czechoslovakia would eventually have produced a genuinely democratic polity. Even if the external environment had been more benign, the internal obstacles to radical change were formidable. The well-known Czech writer Antonín Liehm, who was a leading reformer in 1968, recently acknowledged that "skepticism and disillusion" might eventually have ensued in Czechoslovakia, even without the external pressure.[59] But Liehm also aptly noted that the boldest of the reformers were "sincere" in wanting to "abandon militarized socialism" and to "push for real political freedom."

In that respect, it is unfair and misleading for Czech officials nowadays to dismiss the Prague Spring as merely an insignificant exercise in "warmed-over communism"—the sort of dismissal voiced often by Václav Klaus and some other Czech politicians who themselves kept their heads down in 1968. (Klaus was a twenty-seven-year-old economist in 1968 and took no part in the reform efforts.) Klaus has been wont to condemn the leaders of the Prague Spring for having "believed in socialism with a human face" rather than genuine democracy, but this sort of criticism is largely ahistorical.[60] Given the constraints posed by the Soviet Union's hegemonic position in the Warsaw Pact, "socialism with a human face" (*socialismus s lidskou tváří*) was a remarkably bold goal for an East European country to seek. The slogan itself—"socialism with a human face"—not only heralded the sweeping changes that Czechs and Slovaks were hoping to achieve, but also implied that socialism elsewhere in the Soviet Bloc lacked a "human face." Oldřich Černík, the Czechoslovak prime minister in 1968, later recalled that Brezhnev angrily confronted Dubček over precisely this issue in May 1968: "In one of the Kremlin corridors [Brezhnev] kept asking Alexander Dubček: 'What's with this human face? What kind of faces do you think we have in Moscow?' Dubček sought to mollify him by answering that this, you know, is just some catchy phrase that the people like."[61]

Even though the slogan meant different things to different people in Czechoslovakia, opinion polls taken in 1968 revealed that a large majority of Czechs and Slovaks were supportive of Western-style democracy.[62] Soviet troops put a forceful end to those aspirations, but the goal never really disappeared. Thus, looking back, we can view the spirited attempts at reform in Czechoslovakia in 1968, and the tragic way in which they ended, as adumbrating the eventual downfall of the Communist Bloc and of the USSR itself.

NOTES

1. U.S. Defense Intelligence Agency, *DIA Intelligence Supplement: Soviet Electronic Countermeasures during Invasion of Czechoslovakia*, DIAIS UP-275-68 (Secret—No Foreign Dissemination), 1 October 1968, declassified October 2002, in Lyndon Baines Johnson Library, National Security File, Europe and USSR, Czechoslovkia, Czechoslovakia Memos, Vol. IV: 9/68–1/69.

2. H. Gordon Skilling, *Czechoslovakia's Interrupted Revolution* (Princeton, NJ: Princeton University Press, 1976).

3. Karen Dawisha, *The Kremlin and the Prague Spring* (Berkeley: University of California Press, 1984).

4. "Cesty ke svobodě," *Rudé právo* (Prague), 13 May 1968, p. 1.

5. "Rabochaya zapis' zasedaniya Politbyuro TsK KPSS ot 15 marta 1968 g.," verbatim transcript (top secret), 15 March 1968, in Arkhiv Prezidenta Rossiiskoi Federatsii (APRF), Fond (F.) 3, Opis' (Op.) 45, Delo (D.) 99, Listy (Ll.) 123–24.

6. "Rabochaya zapis' zasedaniya Politbyuro TsK KPSS ot 15 marta 1968 g.," L. 127.

7. "Rabochaya zapis' zasedaniya Politbyuro TsK KPSS ot 21 marta 1968 g.," verbatim transcript (top secret), 21 March 1968, in APRF, F. 3, Op. 45, D. 99, Ll. 147–58.

8. "Rabochaya zapis' zasedaniya Politbyuro TsK KPSS ot 21 marta 1968 g.," Ll. 148, 151–53, 156.

9. See the materials pertaining to these discussions in Archiwum Akt Nowych (AAN), Warsaw, Archiwum Komitetu Centralnego Polskiej Zjednoczonej Partii Rabotniczej (Arch. KC PZPR), Paczka (P.) 32, Tom (T.) 114.

10. "Protokół z rozmowy Pierwszego Sekretarza KC PZPR tow. Władysława Gomułki z Pierwszym Sekretarzem KC KPCz tow. Aleksandrem Dubczekem," 7 February 1968 (Secret), in AAN, Arch. KC PZPR, P. 193, T. 24, Dok. 3.

11. A. M. Aleksandrov-Agentov, *Ot Kollontai do Gorbacheva: Vospominaniya diplomata, sovetnika A. A. Gromyko, pomoshchnika L. I. Brezhneva, Yu. V. Andropova, K. U. Chernenko i M. S. Gorbacheva* (Moscow: Mezhdunarodnye otnosheniya, 1994), 147–49.

12. "Rabochaya zapis' zasedaniya Politbyuro TsK KPSS ot 23 maya 1968," verbatim transcript (top secret), 23 May 1968, in APRF, F. 3, Op. 45, L. 262.

13. Cited in "TsK KPSS," memorandum no. 1/22 (top secret) from P. Shelest to the CPSU Politbyuro, 21 March 1968, in Tsentral'nyi Derzhavnyi Arkhiv Hromads'kykh Ob'ednan' Ukrainy (TsDAHOU), Kyiv, F. 1, Op. 25, Sprava (Spr.) 27, Ll. 18–23. See also Emil Šip, "Prvomájové referendum," *Rudé právo* (Prague), 3 May 1968, p. 2.

14. "Doklad P. E. Shelesta 'Ob itogakh aprel'skogo plenuma TsK KPSS,'" speech text (top secret), 25 April 1968, in TsDAHOU, F. 1, Op. 25, Spr. 97, Ll. 8–9.

15. "Doklad P. E. Shelesta 'Ob itogakh aprel'skogo plenuma TsK KPSS,'" L. 11.

16. I. Aleksandrov, "Ataka protiv sotsialisticheskikh ustoev Chekhoslovakii," *Pravda* (Moscow), 11 July 1968, p. 4.

17. See the retrospective comments of Jiří Hájek, who served as Czechoslovak foreign minister in 1968, in *Dix ans après: Prague 1968–1978* (Paris: Éditions du Seuil, 1978), 110–15, 163–64, 172–79.

18. See Dubček's comments on this matter in *Hope Dies Last: The Autobiography of Alexander Dubček*, trans. by Jiří Hochman (New York: HarperCollins, 1993), 178–79.

19. Mark Kramer, "The Soviet Union and the 1956 Crises in Hungary and Poland: Reassessments and New Findings," *Journal of Contemporary History* 33, no. 2 (April 1998): 163–214.

20. See, for example, "Projev soudruha Alexandra Dubčeka," *Rudé právo* (Prague), 25 April 1968, pp. 1–2.

21. "Dnevniki P. E. Shelesta," in Rossiiskii Gosudarstvennyi Arkhiv Sotsial'no-Politicheskoi Istorii (RGASPI), F. 666, Tetrad' (Te.) 6, L. 27.

22. See the interview with Josef Smrkovský in "Nedokončený rozhovor: Mluví Josef Smrkovský," *Listy: Časopis československé socialistické opozice* (Rome) 4, no. 2 (March 1975): 17; and the interview with Oldřich Černík in "Bumerang 'Prazhskoi vesnoi,'" *Izvestiya* (Moscow), 21 August 1990, p. 5. Both Smrkovský and Černík were members of the KSČ Presidium in 1968. Smrkovský was also president of the National Assembly and a leading architect of the Prague Spring; Černík was the Czechoslovak prime minister. Shelest describes an incident in his diary ("Dnevniki P. E. Shelesta," in RGASPI, F. 666, Te. 4, L. 80) that suggests the overtures may have found a receptive audience in Smrkovský, but no further corroboration of this incident has emerged.

23. For a verbatim transcript of the meeting in Warsaw, see "Protokół ze spotkania przywódców partii i rządów krajów socjalistycznych—Bulgarii, NRD, Polski, Węgier i ZSRR—w Warszawie, 14–15 lipca 1968 r.," Copy No. 5 (Top Secret), 14–15 July 1968, in AAN, Arch. KC PZPR, P. 193, T. 24, Dok. 4. See also the lengthy interview with the Hungarian leader János Kádár, who took part in these meetings, in "Yanosh Kádár o 'prazhskoi vesne,'" *Kommunist* (Moscow), no. 7 (May 1990): 96–103.

24. "Rabochaya zapis' zasedaniya Politbyuro TsK KPSS ot 6 avgusta 1968 g.," verbatim transcript (top secret), 6 August 1968, in APRF, F. 3, Op. 45, D. 99, L. 462.

25. A firsthand account of Brezhnev's medical problems during the crisis can be found in the memoir by Brezhnev's physician, Evgenii Chazov, *Zdorov'e i vlast': Vospominaniya "kremlevskogo vracha"* (Moscow: Novosti, 1992), 74–79.

26. Quoted in an interview with Brezhnev's closest aides in Leonid Shinkarev, "Avgustovskoe bezumie: K 25-letiyu vvoda voisk v Chekhoslovakiyu," *Izvestiya* (Moscow), 21 August 1993, p. 10.

27. "Telefonický rozhovor L. Brežněva s A. Dubčekem, 9.8.1968," verbatim transcript (top secret), 9 August 1968, in Ústav pro soudobé dějiny, Sbírka Komise vlády ČSFR pro analyzu udalostí let 1967–1970 (ÚSD-SK), Z/S 8.

28. "Rozgovor tovarishcha L. I. Brezhneva s tovarishchom A. S. Dubchekom," verbatim transcript (top secret), 13 August 1968, in APRF, F. 3, Op. 91, D. 120, Ll. 1–18.

29. "Vypiska iz protokola No. 94 zasedaniya Politbyuro TsK KPSS 13 avgusta 1968 g.," No. P94/101 (Top Secret), 13 August 1968, in APRF, Prot. No. 38.

30. Cited in Tibor Huszár, *1968: Prága, Budapest, Moszkva. Kádár János és a csehszlovákiai intervenció* (Budapest: Szabad Tér, 1998), 180. For a translation into Czech, see "Vystoupení J. Kádára na zasedání ÚV MSDS a rady ministrů 23.8.1968 k maďarsko-sovětskému jednání v Jaltě, 12.–15.8.1968," in ÚSD-SK, Z/M 19.

31. Declassified documents reveal that Brezhnev met several times in the Crimea with Aleksei Kosygin, Nikolai Podgornyi, Petro Shelest, Mikhail Suslov, Aleksandr Shelepin, Arvīds Pel'she, Kirill Mazurov, Gennadii Voronov, Viktor Grishin, Dinmukhamed Kunaev, Pyotr Masherov, Sharaf Radishov, Vladimir Shcherbitskii, and Konstantin Katushev.

32. For a valuable, firsthand account, see "Dnevniki P. E. Shelesta," in RGASPI, F. 666, Te. 6, Ll. 190–91, 193. Evidently, no full transcript of the ad-hoc sessions was compiled.

33. "K voprosu o polozhenii v Chekhoslovakii: Vypiska iz protokola No. 95 zasedaniya Politbyuro TsK ot 17 avgusta 1968 g.," Resolution No. P95/1 (top secret), 17 August 1968, in APRF, Prot. No. 38.

34. "Stenogramma Soveshchaniya predstavitelei kommunisticheskikh i rabochikh partii i pravitel'stv NRB, VNR, GDR, PNR i SSSR po voprosu o polozhenii v Chekhoslovakii," verbatim transcript (top secret), 18 August 1968, in Rossiiskii Gosudarstvennyi Arkhiv Noveishei Istorii (RGANI), F. 89, Op. 38, D. 57, Ll. 1–22.

35. "Rabochaya zapis' zasedaniya Politbyuro TsK KPSS ot 19 avgusta 1968 g.," 19 August 1968 (top secret), in APRF, F. 3, Op. 45, D. 99, Ll. 474–82.

36. Comments recorded in "Dnevniki P. E. Shelesta," in RGASPI, F. 666, Te., 7, L. 213.

37. Cited in "Dnevniki P. E. Shelesta," Ll. 213–14. See also the interview with Shelest in Leonid Shinkarev, "Avgustovskoe bezumie: K 25-letiyu vvoda voisk v Chekhoslovakiyu," *Izvestiya* (Moscow), 21 August 1993, p. 10, and the recollections of Pavlovskii, "Eto bylo v Prage," 5.

38. "Obdobie od 21.srpna do konca roku 1968," from a report by Czechoslovak national defense minister General Martin Dzúr, 9 June 1970, in Národní Archiv České Republiky (NAČR), Archiv Ústředního výboru Komunistické strany Československa (Arch. ÚV KSČ), 4. oddělení (Spr. G. Husák).

39. See the "extremely urgent" (*vne ocheredi*) cable from Chervonenko to the CPSU Politburo, 21 August 1968, in ÚSD-SK, Z/S-MID, Nos. 37 and 39.

40. "Prohlášení předsednictva ÚV KSČ z 21.8.1968," *Rudé právo* (Prague), 21 August 1968 (2nd ed.), p. 1. For Pavlovskii's statement, see "Obrashchenie Chekhoslovatskoi narodnoi armii," in Arkhiv Vneshnei Politiki Rossiiskoi Federatsii (AVPRF), F. 059, Op. 58, Papka (P.) 127, D. 586, Ll. 33–35.

41. For firsthand accounts, see "Nedokončený rozhovor," 16–18; Zdeněk Mlynář, *Nachtfrost: Erfahrungen auf dem Weg vom realen zum menschlichen Sozialismus* (Köln: Europäische Verlagsanstalt, 1978), 181–87; František August and David Rees, *Red Star over Prague* (London: Sherwood, 1984), 134–42; Dubček, *Hope Dies Last*, 182–84; and Historický ústav ČSAV, *Sedm pražských dnů, 21.–27. srpen 1968: Dokumentace* (Prague: ČSAV, 1968), 53–58. On Černík's arrest, see the firsthand account by Otomar Boček, chairman of the Supreme Court, delivered to the 14th Congress in Vysočaný, in Jiří Pelikán, ed., *Tanky proti sjezdu: Protokol a dokumenty XIV. sjezdu KSČ* (Vienna: Europa-Verlag, 1970), 66–68.

42. The military operation itself, it should be noted, was not wholly flawless. See Leo Heiman, "Soviet Invasion Weaknesses," *Military Review* 49, no. 8 (August 1969): 38–45. However, the same is true of almost any large-scale use of military force against a foreign country. Unexpected glitches are bound to arise.

43. "Shifrtelegramma," 21 August 1968 (top secret), in AVPRF, F. 059, Op. 58, P. 124, D. 574, Ll. 184–86. For Mazurov's retrospective account of his role in the invasion, see Pavlovskii, "Eto bylo v Prage," 5.

44. "Prohlášení předsednictva ÚV KSČ z 21.8.1968," 1.

45. "Shifrtelegramma," 21 August 1968 (top secret), in AVPRF, F. 059, Op. 58, P. 124, D. 574, Ll. 184–86.

46. "Shifrtelegramma," 7 August 1968 (top secret), from S. V. Chervonenko, Soviet ambassador in Czechoslovakia, to the CPSU Politburo, in AVPRF, F. 059, Op. 58, P. 124, D. 573, Ll. 183–85. For further relevant citations from the ex-Soviet archives, see Kramer, "The Prague Spring and the Soviet Invasion of Czechoslovakia," 6–8, 13, 54. See also Zdeněk Mlýnář, *Československý pokus o reformu, 1968: Analyza jeho teorie a praxe* (Köln: Index, 1975), 232–33.

47. "Rozkaz správcu posádky čislo 1, Trenčín, 21. avgusta 1968: Správca posádky Soivetskej armády podplukovník ŠMATKO," in ÚSD-SK, A, from I. Šimovček. See also Historický ústav ČSAV, *Sedm pražských dnů: Dokumentace* (Prague: Historický ústav ČSAV, 1968), 123, 278–81, and 324–25.

48. See "TsK KPSS," Memorandum No. 24996 (top secret), 6 September 1968, from Aleksandr Yakovlev, deputy head of the CPSU Propaganda Department, and Enver Mamedov, deputy head of Soviet television and radio, to the CPSU Politburo, in RGANI, F. 5, Op. 60, D. 19, Ll. 200–206; and "Nekotorye zamechaniya po voprosu podgotovki voenno-politicheskoi aktsii 21 avgusta 1968 g.," Politburo Commission report (special dossier/strictly secret), 16 November 1968, in RGANI, F. 5 "OP," Op. 6, D. 776, Ll. 128–44.

49. "Shifrtelegramma," 21 August 1968 (top secret), from Kirill Mazurov to the CPSU Politburo, in AVPRF, F. 059, Op. 58, P. 124, D. 574, Ll. 184–86.

50. "Nekotorye zamechaniya po voprosu podgotovki voenno-politicheskoi aktsii 21 avgusta 1968 g.," L. 137.

51. "Informatsiya o druzheskikh svyazyakh oblastei i gorodov Ukrainskoi SSR s oblastyami, voevodstvami, okrugami, uezdami i gorodami sotsialisticheskikh stran v 1968 godu," 20 December 1968 (secret), in RGANI, F. 5, Op. 60, D. 2, Ll. 46, 64–65.

52. The first quotation is from the Soviet participants in a high-level "Warsaw Five" meeting shortly after the invasion, "Záznam ze schůzek Varšavské pětky v Moskvě ve dnech 24.–27.8.1968," verbatim transcript (top secret), 24–27 August 1968, in ÚSD-SK, Z/M 21; and the second quotation is from "Nekotorye zamechaniya po voprosu podgotovki voenno-politicheskoi aktsii 21 avgusta 1968 g.," L. 129. This was also the view put forth by the four East European leaders of the "Warsaw Five." See, for example, Gomulka's secret speech on 29 August 1968 to the PZPR Central Committee, reproduced in "Gomułka o inwazji na Czechosłowacje w sierpniu '68: Mysmy ich zaskoczyli akcja wojskowa," *Polityka* (Warsaw), No. 35 (29 August 1992): 13.

53. "Záznam ze schůzek Varšavské pětky v Moskvě ve dnech 24.–27.8.1968," L. 3.

54. "Záznam ze schůzek Varšavské pětky v Moskvě ve dnech 24.–27.8.1968," L. 5.

55. "Rabochaya zapis' zasedaniya Politbyuro TsK KPSS ot 25 avgusta 1968 g.," verbatim transcript (top secret), 25 August 1968, in APRF, F. 3, Op. 45, D. 99, Ll. 484–91.

56. For an assessment of the postinvasion period based on declassified archival materials from former Czechoslovak archives, see Kieran Williams, *The Prague Spring and Its Aftermath: Czechoslovak Politics, 1968–1970* (New York: Cambridge Univeristy Press, 1997), 39–59, 144–253.

57. "Rech' tovarishcha L. I. Brezhneva," *Pravda* (Moscow), 13 November 1968, p. 2.

58. S. Kovalev, "O 'mirnoi' i nemirnoi kontrrevolyutsii," *Pravda* (Moscow), 11 September 1968, p. 4.

59. "Proti zapomnění a manipulaci: O co šlo v roce 1968," *Lidové noviny* (Prague), 12 March 2008, p. 3.

60. "'Fast alle glaubten an diesen Traum': Der tschechische Staatspräsident Václav Klaus im *Standard*-Interview über die Niederschlagang des Prager Frühlings," *Der Standard* (Vienna), 27 March 1968, pp. 1, 5.

61. Interview with Černík, transcribed in "Bumerang 'prazhskoi vesny,'" *Izvestiya* (Moscow), 21 August 1990, p. 7.

62. Lubomír Brokl et al., *Postoje československých občanů k demokracii v roce 1968*, Working Paper No. 99:8 (Prague: Sociologický ústav Akademie věd České republiky, 1999).

II

CZECHOSLOVAKIA, THE SOVIET UNION, AND THE "PRAGUE SPRING"

3

Reforms in the Communist Party: The Prague Spring and Apprehension about a Soviet Invasion

Oldřich Tůma

For many contemporary observers, the events in Czechoslovakia in 1968 were already directly linked at the time to one symbolic figure: Alexander Dubček. This was undoubtedly even more the case for observers from abroad (and to a certain extent also for Slovak observers). Factors that contributed to this impression were photos, sound recordings, and even mere ideas: Dubček smiling, with an enthusiastic crowd milling around him in spring 1968; Dubček anxious, talking to Leonid Brezhnev at the end of July in Čierná nad Tisou;[1] Dubček on his way to an uncertain future on 21 August, as he is being deported from the country (perhaps handcuffed) by Soviet military personnel;[2] Dubček on 27 August, addressing Czechs and Slovaks on the radio and explaining with a faltering voice the necessity of reaching a compromise with the Kremlin and appealing to the population to end their resistance to the intervention.[3] In the memories of 1968, Dubček does indeed play the role of an icon of the "Prague Spring," and these events also signaled, in a certain sense, his own breakthrough: Dubček the reformer of socialism, Dubček the defender of Czechoslovak sovereignty and independence, Dubček the precursor of Mikhail Gorbachev.[4]

A certain simplification in the interpretation of past events and their identification with the most significant actors are not unusual in connection with historical memory, all the more so in the case of a memory that relies above all on the media reportage of the period: headlines, photos, and TV material. In all of them it is, unsurprisingly enough, people and their names that play a key role and that eclipse to some extent the continuum or the changes and developments in the attitudes and the reactions of the public, the hidden interdependencies, the decision making, and all the rest that tends to get lost in day-to-day reporting. These were the decisive factors shaping the

information about the events of 1968 in Czechoslovakia that was brought to
the attention of a non-Czechoslovak public, which—according to the rules
applicable at the time—was a Western one. The "Dubček myth"—the idea
that, first, the Prague Spring amounted to a single-handed attempt by the
Communist Party of Czechoslovakia (*Komunistická strana Československa* or
KSČ) to reform the Communist regime and that, second, the initiator and at
the same time the political leader responsible for that attempt was Alexander
Dubček—is erroneous twice over. This myth is, moreover, decidedly unhelp-
ful if we want to understand what actually happened in Czechoslovakia in
1968 and complicates the interpretation of the Soviet decision and of the
reasons for the military intervention even further. By the same logic, this
myth will prevent us from fully appreciating the lessons to be learned from
the Prague Spring and its consequences for the following decades.

It must be borne in mind that the Prague Spring was not only an attempt
to reform the Communist regime in Czechoslovakia, it was a major crisis of
the regime as such. For an understanding of what was at stake in Czechoslovakia in 1968, we must not content ourselves with an analysis of the
reforms that the KSČ leadership sought to implement. It is not enough to
focus on "socialism with a human face," and it would be a great mistake to
analyze the motives behind the Soviet decision to intervene purely in terms
of the Soviet determination to put a stop to the Czechoslovak reforms.

If we are to understand the dynamics and the meaning of the events of
1968, we must proceed from the fact that the developments of the spring
and summer were not exclusively (and not even primarily) masterminded
by the reformers within the leadership of the KSČ. We must assume that
the reforms were not the outcome of some political strategy that had been
devised in detail in advance and that was backed by a unified and clearly
defined group of reformers. Even less were they the work of one key player,
that is, Alexander Dubček. In Czechoslovak society, other forces were at
work as well, forces whose strivings for reform influenced each other, which
took turns in the role of pioneers, which took inspiration from each other,
but which were at the same time far from identical in terms of their objectives, their political platforms, and their orientation.

The majority of Czech and Slovak society hoped for much more in terms
of freedom and democracy than the reform agenda of the KSČ attempted;
their desires, if played out to their logical conclusion, were incompatible
in principle with any Communist program, including that of the reform
Communists. Saying that here was a movement that was incompatible
with communism by its very nature does not necessarily imply that it was
not also supported by people who chose to remain members of the KSČ.
These people even had considerable clout in some of the party organizations, most notably in the city committees in Prague and Brno as well as
among Communist artists and intellectuals. Yet the far greater part of the

movement had no truck with the Communist Party, and it is important to remember that this movement or societal force had neither one leader nor a clearly formulated program. These handicaps were compensated for by the existence of specific groups, such as journalists, artists, and, increasingly, students, who were the group with the clearest political profile.[5] On the whole, one opted for noncommittal discussions of a whole range of political programs and visions rather than for serious and conscientious political preparations. Prototypical in a way were Václav Havel's musings in the first issue of the Writers' Association's revived weekly *Literární listy* at the beginning of April on the possibility of the implementation of a political system that had as its basis the competition between two parties, the Communists and the Democratic Party.[6] Yet deliberations on democracy, pluralism, civil society, basic civic rights, and the sovereignty of state and nation were definitely part of the societal discourse as well. Deliberations proved by no means the end of it; very soon a clamoring for their gradual realization arose. An almost unrestricted freedom of speech existed, and several organizations (including youth organizations, cultural organizations, some trade unions, and the like) emancipated themselves from the tutelage of the KSČ. Openly political groupings took shape and became active, such as the Association of Former Political Prisoners K231 or the Club of Committed Non-Partisans (KAN), the attempt to relaunch social democracy,[7] the establishment of an independent student organization (Association of University Assistants), and the existence of critical public opinion.[8] All this amounted already to a de facto pluralistic environment: a state of affairs, in other words, that the KSČ reformists' program did not take into account but that was nevertheless an indisputable fact. These "protodemocratic" forces did not succeed in gaining a sufficiently strong foothold in public before August. Their activities were confined to discussions of a theoretical nature in the press or in various debating shops. They preferred this to voicing their demands in the streets. Nevertheless, it was clear that the movement had potential, and it was, therefore, eyed with apprehension by Moscow. In the eyes of the Kremlin, it was clearly an antisocialist and counterrevolutionary movement. The reform Communists, too, felt displeasure at the existence of such societal forces. Under certain conditions, if it had not been thrown off course by external pressure and, subsequently, by the intervention, such a "protodemocratic" movement could have flourished and would—if we follow this line of thought through for a moment—necessarily had to engage in conflict with the reform Communists. This is, of course, a matter of pure speculation and cannot be decided one way or another.

Reforms of the different spheres of societal life were prepared in Czechoslovakia with considerable thoroughness. This is by no means only true of 1968, but of the first half of the 1960s as well, even though this is not always fully appreciated.[9] Sizable groups of cadres advocated reform at different levels of the party apparatus, in the state administration, and in the economic and scientific communities. With a bit of simplification, one might say that it was these people who had, after 1945 and when they were still young, supported the Communist seizure of power and the construction of the Communist system out of conviction, sometimes even in a spirit of fanaticism. In the 1950s, a number of different circumstances subsequently led many of these people to view critically the reality that had developed after 1948; they noticed that it had little in common with the idealistic notions they had initially harbored. Any criticism within the party was suppressed until 1956 and did not resurface until the beginning of the 1960s. In the meantime, many of these critical thinkers had reached relatively important positions. The reasons for their disenchantment were to be found in a number of different areas: the weak economy, cases of blatant disregard for the law, the suppression of artistic freedom, and so forth. In addition to these, the nagging sense that Czechoslovakia was hopelessly trailing the countries to the west of its borders, countries with which Czechoslovakia had shared the same or a similar standard of living immediately after 1945, existed. The sense that the country was falling behind concerned not only the economy, but also technology, culture, and civilization in general. When the strict isolation in which the country had found itself in the 1950s was beginning to yield, the gap became very apparent. A solution, perhaps the proverbial five-to-twelve doomsday scenario, to give the country a break appeared to lie in the preparation and implementation of fundamental reforms. These reforms were meticulously planned. On the basis of close cooperation between institutions of the party, the state and academic teams were put together to orchestrate reforms in different spheres: one team, with Ota Šik at its head, was to deal with the economy, Zdeněk Mlynář headed another that was supposed to fix the political system, and Radovan Richta and his team were to devote themselves to the environment. The teams received relatively generous support in terms of money and the possibility of traveling abroad for study purposes. This proved somewhat counterproductive: the insights these people gained abroad served mainly to strengthen their conviction that far-reaching changes were necessary.

The reform program was underpinned not only by a general awareness that Czechoslovakia had significantly fallen behind the West and that the system as such was dysfunctional, but also by an ideological basis. The ratification of the new constitution in 1960 entailed the assessment that the process of the construction of socialism had been successfully concluded in Czechoslovakia and that the time had now come—in accordance with the classics of Marxism-Leninism—to discuss the transition from the dictatorship of the proletariat to a state for the entire population and the need and/or the possibility of a reduction of state control in view of the new situation. The reform program was hammered out and ratified under the aegis of Antonín Novotný. Economic reform, which was formulated down to the last detail and which was to combine state ownership and central planning with a dose of market economy principles, was begun as early as 1965. The program aiming at a reform of the political system was much more cautious in its scope and did not allow for the emergence of a certain limited political pluralism for at least another decade.

The general acceptance of the inevitability of reforms was one thing; quite another was their consistent implementation, which was viewed by the KSČ leadership and by important segments of the party and state apparatus with apprehension and distaste. Evidence for this can be found in such examples as the attempted economic reform and the reform of the domestic secret service. As regards the reform of the economy it was, paradoxically enough, its initial successes—an increase in the profits of several businesses and the ensuing wage rises—that evoked in Novotný a nightmare that Communist functionaries knew only too well: the fear that demand and supply might be thrown out of sync in that the supply of goods available in the market might prove inadequate in relation to the workers' increasing spending power. Novotný therefore began to backpedal, to slow the pace of the reform, delay its implementation, and generally make sure it was no more than a half-hearted attempt. In the case of the transformation of the domestic secret service from an organ that was supposed to form the vanguard in the exacerbating class struggle into one that was to protect the state against external enemies—which was the totality of Minister of the Interior Lubomír Štrougal's blueprint for reform—the decisive opposition came from below. The majority of the service's staff never accepted this transformation, sabotaged it as best they could, and did everything to reverse it.

In 1967, the demarcation line that separated the inimical camps within the KSČ leadership became apparent: those who supported a continuation and intensification of the reforms and those under Novotný's aegis who, motivated by fear of further progress, opted for indecisive and incomplete solutions. However, at the crucial moment toward the end of the year there were a number of additional fault lines which caused these forces within the Central Committee to split into opposing factions. There were those who joined the anti-Novotný camp for various personal reasons, and the Slovak question was another key factor. Novotný's lack of sensitivity in handling Slovak matters and Slovakia's declared wish to be granted a certain maneuvering space at the expense of strict central control resulted in a Slovak front practically unified against Novotný. By another paradoxical twist, one of the protagonists in the activities that led to Novotný's dismissal, Vasil Bil'ak, was to assume a leading role a few months later in a plot that staged a coup in the KSČ with Moscow's help and engaged in preparations for the military invasion of Czechoslovakia.

Some of the measures adopted by the new party leadership after January 1968 were merely designed to reduce further the standing of Novotný and his supporters and, therefore, lacked the logic of a consistent reform program. The key decision at the end of February 1968 to abolish censorship must be seen in that context. This decision was taken in the illusory conviction that the party's control of the media was guaranteed by the KSČ members being among the editors and that society could be counted on in its entirety to support the reform program and nothing else. This quickly proved a misjudgment. The media totally emancipated themselves from any control within weeks and assumed the role of one of the most important political actors. The nascent civil society and the critical public opinion generated demands that went much further than the planned reforms, which, moreover, had at least in part been conceived in an academic environment and were still far from having assumed the form of a concise political program.

Incidentally, the reformist movement within the KSČ did not achieve by any means a stable or fixed identity during the eight months of the Prague Spring, the time between Alexander Dubček's acceptance of the party leadership and the intervention in August. It was itself in a state of flux; it accommodated a variety of different viewpoints, nuances, priorities, and a whole range of different assessments as to the envisaged scope of the reforms. It was, therefore, not highly developed in terms of its program nor even, for a long time, in terms of its membership. The line of demarcation between reformers and orthodox Communists that eventually split the KSČ leadership emerged slowly and by degrees. It did not imply radically different programmatic viewpoints; what set the camps apart was, rather, a difference in the way they represented their viewpoints in public and the attitudes they displayed toward the Warsaw Pact "allies." For the reader of the minutes of the speeches delivered at the sessions of the KSČ's governing bodies in April or May 1968, it is virtually impossible to tell which of the speakers would end up after the suppression of the Prague Spring with the tag "revisionist" and "opportunist" and which would be counted among the "healthy forces." Utterances that are characteristic for us of the way the Kremlin viewed the situation in Czechoslovakia were voiced in the spring of 1968 not only by those members of the KSČ leadership who in the end threw in their lot with the "allies" of the Warsaw Pact and took part in preparing the intervention, but also (and on a fairly regular basis, too) by the protagonists of the reform movement. Dubček himself as well as the head of the government Oldřich Černík, the president of the National Assembly Josef Smrkovský, Central Committee Secretary Zdeněk Mlynář, and others routinely referred to the imminence of the counterrevolution, to the need to leave the people's militias (the KSČ's armed units) intact because it might become necessary to deploy them, to tanks and the use of force as extreme but, perhaps, inevitable possibilities. They, too, voiced regular complaints about the party's increasing loss of control of the media and peremptorily demanded a change of this intolerable situation. They did mention, it is true, other things as well, such as the positive transformation program for which the party had to muster and retain public support. (The reasons given for this included the need not to concede terrain to "right-wing anti-socialist forces.")[10] Above all, they used a somewhat different diction when their words were designed for public consumption. Yet it reflects to their credit that they were capable of heeding the mood and the expectations of the public, of respecting them and taking them into account. This was not necessarily due to their unprincipled, opportunist "Janus-headed politics" (epithets used later by the "normalized" KSČ leadership and the "normalized" media to characterize their approach), but is regarded as evidence of the increasing regeneration of society's potential in the direction of an open society and a normal interaction between the public and the political elites. A situation characterized by almost complete freedom of speech and the restoration of public opinion was simply too propitious to be ignored. Dubček's own position was somewhere in the middle. He tried to defuse extremist positions, he tacked and veered, and his increasing popularity was due primarily to his likable appearance, which did indeed set him apart from leading Communist functionaries both before and after him.

The mainstream of this reformist movement did not by any means advocate the abolition of the existing political and economic system. The goals were innovation, rationalization, increased productivity, and undoubtedly also a certain upgrading of the regime in humane terms. It is possible to document with some precision that this applied both to those who chiefly represented the reform movement—in a word, Dubček and his entourage—and to the majority within the KSČ at the time. Mlynář later estimated in his memoirs, which were first published in the West,[11] that this group represented roughly 80 percent of the party. It was this reformist majority that emerged victorious in spring 1968 from the KSČ's district and regional conferences and that would have triumphed at the extraordinary party conference scheduled for September, which never took place. The programmatic key document of the reformist movement, the so-called Action Program, which the KSČ leadership passed on 5 April 1968, displays a disconcerting lack of focus and considerable internal contradictions.[12] There is, of course, no disputing that parts of the reformist program aimed for a far-reaching enfranchisement in the areas of culture and the sciences, for the removal of obstacles that hampered the professional careers of nonparty members, for a program of rehabilitation and compensation for the victims of injustice, and so forth. The same applies to the emphasis on the autonomy of the organs of the state (government, parliament, and regional and local authorities). The Communist Party's task was perceived not to lie in day-to-day administration, but in the definition in political terms of the direction in which society was to move. This was, indeed, a striking innovation: the party was to resign its role of an omnipresent force that dominated everything, reducing all other social organizations and institutions to cogs and levers for the transmission of Communist power. Questions concerning political power and the admissibility of political pluralism were off limits. Should it ever become possible to address them, this would be in a distant future and in a manner that was far from clear in 1968.[13] In simple terms, one could say that the reformers within the party leadership were not aiming for the democratization but for the liberalization of the system. It goes without saying that even this political course differed substantially from anything for which the KSČ had stood prior to 1968 and would stand for from 1969 onward. It was also a course that propelled Czechoslovakia, through the unplanned but nevertheless real synergy with the dynamics of an agitated social movement, beyond the confines of "really existing socialism."

An issue that this program avoided altogether was the restoration of the sovereignty of state and nation; it did not touch on Czechoslovakia's membership or position within the Soviet Bloc. All questions relating to the country's foreign policy were deliberately sidelined or excluded altogether. This was done presumably under the naive perspective that unquestioning loyalty on the level of global politics was going to ensure a safe climate for domestic reforms. This was, of course, a cardinal mistake. The intervention was to become reality.

It is obvious that the intervention was not triggered by worries occasioned by the reform agenda of the KSČ. The reason was that the Soviet leadership had lost confidence in Dubček's ability (and indeed in his willingness) to get a situation under control in which the system was gradually being eroded.[14] There were other sponsors of the intervention in addition to the Communist Party of the Soviet Union (*Kommunisticheskaya Partiya Sovetskogo Soyuza* or CPSU) leadership, notably the orthodox faction in the KSČ leadership and the party leaders in the satellite countries. Among them, the attitude of the Polish and the East German Communists, who explicitly endorsed the invasion, was particularly important.[15] It is understandable that the final assessment, arrived at in Moscow not without hesitation or controversy, carried considerable weight. In view of what we know today, one of the interpretations that were once common in Czechoslovakia and in leftist Western circles can hardly be upheld any longer, namely that the Soviet leadership misjudged the situation entirely, meddled when the Communist regime was under no threat, and discredited itself through its aggressive communism with lasting consequences. Let us, for instance, recall the poster that was on display everywhere in the streets of Prague depicting Brezhnev as the grave digger of world communism or the slogan that was making the rounds at the same time: "Wake up, Lenin, Brezhnev has gone nuts." In fact, the reverse was true. The Soviets remained true to the logic of the system that they represented. Consequently, the intervention stifled the movement that had the potential to bring about the collapse of the Communist regime in Czechoslovakia and, for all the Soviets knew, was already in the process of doing so. This would have amounted to a serious destabilization of the regimes of the neighboring countries in a manner that was ultimately to materialize in the domino effect of 1989. It may very well have been the case that the intervention extended the lease on life for these regimes by another twenty years.

That such an assessment ultimately gained credence in the Soviet leadership is due to a number of factors, not least of which is the tactics that the KSČ leadership used in their negotiations with the Soviets or, to assign names to the dramatis personae, that Dubček used in his negotiations with Brezhnev. It is difficult to judge whether a different strategy than the one chosen by Dubček, which consisted basically in playing for time, would have had more of a chance of success. Its rationale was the realization on the part of the Dubček faction that it was of paramount importance for them to hold out until the beginning of the extraordinary party conference of the KSČ, which was scheduled for 9 September; the conference would boost the reformers and quite likely blow the position of the leadership's orthodox, Moscow-beholden faction to smithereens. But, of course, the Soviets were equally capable of a rational assessment of the situation. Dubček's ceaseless attempts to paint the situation in rosier colors than was actually justified (and also rosier than it had repeatedly been depicted in speeches by the leading reformers, speeches with which the Soviets were, of course, familiar), to pacify the Soviets with promises holding out the prospect of various measures and changes, to embark subsequently on a course of procrastination and then to serve up excuses of one kind or another for the delays—all these maneuvers were effective for a time, but the moment when enough was enough finally arrived. The transcripts of the telephone conversations that took place between Dubček and Brezhnev only days before the intervention, on 9 and 13 August 1968, when Dubček attempted to justify himself by citing all kinds of reasons why he had not yet followed up on the pledges he had made two weeks earlier in Čierná nad Tisou, demonstrate quite clearly the limits and also the counterproductivity of such tactics.[16] The majority of the CPSU leadership could not but arrive at the conclusion that the KSČ had not only lost all control over the media and was in the process of losing control over the organs of power, but that it had entirely lost its ability to act and to hold the party together.

To return to this point once more: it is, of course, impossible to tell in retrospect whether a different approach might have prevented the intervention. Yet it is undoubtedly true that the leaders of Poland's Communist Party, Władysław Gomułka in 1956 and Stanisław Kania and Wojciech Jaruzelski in 1980 and 1981, confronted the Soviets when the country was in a comparable situation far more resolutely than Dubček with his words,

"Comrade Brezhnev, you should resort to all the measures that your CC Politburo believes are appropriate." One must add, however, that in their negotiations with Moscow the Poles not only displayed much more determination to stave off an intervention, they were also as good as their word in actually carrying out the measures they had pledged. The fact that they did not implement measures that would no doubt have been construed as endorsement of the Soviet interference and that would, moreover, have meant reneging significantly on liberalization and reform (reintroduction of censorship, changes in the Ministry of the Interior, a number of new appointments) would have reflected well on the KSČ leadership under Dubček in 1968, if they had also had the gumption in the first place to reject such demands out of hand in the talks with the Soviet leaders, instead of half-heartedly acceding to them and following this up with equally halfhearted delays. What made matters even worse was that these same reformist party leaders then played a role in the downward spiral that followed the intervention, in autumn 1968 and in 1969, in a situation in which they were no longer constrained by tactical considerations to defend themselves, in which the last traces of their reform program had been swept away as well as the last shreds of their own political careers. A case in point is the Legal Measure of the Presidium of the Federal Assembly of 22 August 1969. It was passed after several days of rioting in connection with the first anniversary of the intervention. It amounted to the proclamation of a temporary state of siege and became an important tool for quelling resistance at the beginning of the process of "normalization," that is, the consolidation of Communist rule in Czechoslovakia. It bore the signatures of President Ludvík Svoboda, of the head of the government, Černík, and Dubček, who had already been reduced to the role of president of the Federal Assembly.[17]

Raising the question to what extent this or that negotiation tactic of the KSČ leadership contributed to Soviet decision making does not mean attempting a reallocation of the roles of victim and aggressor (which is part of the agenda of some Russian historians).[18] The aggressor, irrespective of what reasons led to its decision, was the Soviet Union; the role of accomplice and initiator of the intervention was the domestic "fifth column": the orthodox Communists within the party leadership of the KSČ and other plotters in the party and the state apparatus.

The intervention and the resistance it evoked led to a tremendous mobilization of the Czechoslovak society and gave it ethical and emotional foundations that were to serve as a basis for the unparalleled awakening of civic self-confidence and responsibility. On 21 August, the threat of an attack from outside ceased to be relevant any longer; while it had been imminent, it had slowed down political activity during the preceding months by forcing people to respect self-imposed limits. In a strange way, that first week after the invasion gave the Czechoslovak public an intense foretaste of unlimited freedom. It was only then that the forces pent up in society, which had been something of an object for speculation before August, revealed themselves in full. Brezhnev and others in Moscow were right in the way they assessed the activities of the "Right" immediately after the invasion. Gomułka even said: "We are the wiser for the experience: it's in fact possible to stage a counterrevolution before the very eyes of the Soviet military. The situation is worse than we thought."[19]

The two different movements that had powered the Czechoslovak Spring of 1968, the reformist and the socially more Catholic "protodemocratic" one that embraced society in its entirety, were briefly united in the struggle against the military intervention. This struggle was admirable in a way, and it succeeded temporarily in upsetting the political mise-en-scène of the intervention and forced the Kremlin to improvise. This improvisation made a calculating use of the leading reformers and the practically unlimited trust that was placed on them by the Czech and Slovak societies. After 21 August the KSČ, with a few insignificant exceptions, massively supported the countrywide resistance. However, this situation did not last long, and after the signing of the Moscow Protocols and the accession to power in Czechoslovakia of the pragmatists, opportunists, and the orthodox Communists, the party found itself once again in opposition to mainstream society.

Relying on the presence of foreign troops, it managed to consolidate the regime for another two decades. The protagonists of the reforms came to realize at different times (if they did not opt for the shortcut of switching sides, which some of them managed to do with remarkable bravura) that a reform of the Communist system was doomed to failure and that their attempts at reform and the tactics with which they had tried to establish contact with a society whose control eluded them had actually paved the way for a much more radical change. Some of them understood this immediately after 21 August, others later, when they found themselves in the ranks of the dissenters, in exile, or even in prison, where Gustáv Husák's normalization regime had put them. Some did not arrive at what was for them a bitter insight until November 1989—and this presumably applied to Dubček.[20]

The defeat that was inflicted on the Czechoslovak society between August 1968 and 1969 took a long time to be reversed. Yet there is no doubt that in the history of the long, drawn out failure and eventual collapse of the Communist regime, the events of 1968 played a key role. The years 1968 and 1969 made a significant contribution to the emancipation of the Czech and Slovak societies from communism, particularly as regards the younger generation. In the terms of power politics, the regime had been consolidated again, but it had lost those roots in society that would have been necessary for a genuine revitalization.

NOTES

Translated from German into English by Otmar Binder, Vienna.

1. Photos depicting Dubček can be found online at http://www.68.usd.cap.cz (accessed 8 May 2008).

2. Throughout 1981, General Jaruzelski kept on recalling Dubček's fate, which, according to the testimony of his memoirs, had great influence on his own decisions. See Wojciech Jaruzelski, *Mein Leben für Polen* (Munich: Piper, 1993); Wojciech Jaruzelski, *Hinter den Türen der Macht: Der Anfang vom Ende einer Herrschaft* (Leipzig: Militzke Verlag, 1996).

3. The recording is available for download at http://www.68.usd.cap.cz/content65/93/lang,cz/ (accessed 8 May 2008). The text of the address has been published in Jitka Vondrová and Jaromír Navrátil, eds., *Komunistická strana Československa. Kapitulace. srpen—listopad 1968*, vol. 9, no. 3, *Prameny k dějinám československé krize* (Prague: Ústav pro Soudobé Dějiny, 2001), 120–24.

4. See Antonín Benčík, *Utajovaná pravda o Alexandru Dubčekovi: Drama muže, který předběhl svou dobu* (Prague: Ostrov, 2001).

5. On the role played by the students, see Milan Otáhal, *Studenti a komunistická moc v českých zemích, 1968–1989* (Prague: Dokořán 2003).

6. See Jiří Hoppe, ed., *Pražské jaro v médiích: Výběr z dobové publicistiky*, vol. 11, *Prameny k dějinám československé krize* (Prague: Ústav pro Soudobé Dějiny AV ČR, 2004), 114–19.

7. On the attempted revival of the Social Democratic Party, see Přemysl Janýr, *Neznámá kapitola roku 1968: Zápas o obnovení činnosti Československé sociální demokracie* (Prague: Ústav pro Soudobé Dějiny AV ČR, 1998); Jiří Hoppe, "Die Wiedererlebung von Politik und bürgerlicher Gesellschaft: die tschechischen Sozialdemokraten im Jahre 1968," *ZfG* 46 (1998): 710–19.

8. On the emancipation of the society, see inter alia Vilém Prečan, "Lid, veřejnost, občanská společnost jako aktér Pražského jara 1968," in *Proměny Pražského jara 1968–1969*, ed. Jindřich Pecka and Vilém Prečan (Prague: Ústav pro Soudobé Dějiny AV ČR, 1993), 13–36; Vilém Prečan, "Seven Great Days: The People and Civil Society during the 'Prague Spring' of 1968–1969," in *La Primavera di Praga*, ed. Francesco M. Cataluccio and Francesca Gori (Milan: F. Angeli, 1990), 165–75; Petr Pithart, "La dualité du Printemps tchécoslovaque: Société civile et communistes réformateurs," in *Le Printemps tchécoslovaque 1968*, ed. Francois Fejto (Brussels: Éd. Complexe, 1999), 77–86; Petr Pithart, *Osmašedesátý* (Prague: Rozmluvy, 1990); H. Gordon Skilling, *Czechoslovakia's Interrupted Revolution* (Princeton, NJ: Princeton University Press, 1976).

9. For details on the preparations of the reforms and the roots of the "Prague Spring" in the Communist Party and society, see above all Karel Kaplan, *Kořeny československé reformy 1968*, I. *Československo a rozpory v sovětském bloku*, II. *Reforma trvale nemocné ekonomiky* (Brno: Doplněk, 2000); Karel Kaplan, *Kořeny československé reformy 1968*, III. *Změny ve společnosti*, IV. *Struktura moci* (Brno: Doplněk, 2002); see also Karel Kaplan, "Die Wurzeln der 1968er Reform," in Karner et al., *Beiträge*.

10. See also the minutes of the most important KSČ bodies in spring 1968 in Jitka Vondrová et al., eds., *Komunistická strana Československa. Pokus o reformu (říjen 1967–květen 1968)*, vol. 9, no. 1 (Prague: Doplněk, 1999).

11. Zdeněk Mlynář, *Mráz přichází z Kremlinu* (Prague: Mladá fronta, 1990); in German translation, Zdeněk Mlynář, *Nachtfrost: Das Ende des Prager Frühlings* (Frankfurt am Main: Athenäum, 1988).

12. See Vondrová et al., *Komunistická strana Československa*, 320–59; for excerpts in English, see Jaromír Navratíl et al., eds., *The Prague Spring 1968: A National Security Archive Documents Reader* (Budapest: Central European University Press, 1998), 92–95.

13. Zdeněk Mlynář, *Československý pokus o reformu 1968: Analýza jeho teorie a praxe* (Cologne: Index, 1975).

14. On the process of Soviet decision making with regard to the intervention, see Mikhail Prozumenshchikov, "Inside the Politburo of the CPSU: Political and Military Decision Making to Solve the Czechoslovak Crisis," in this volume; Václav Kural et al., eds., *Československo roku 1968* (Prague: Parta, 1993); Jan Pauer, *Prag 1968, Der Einmarsch des Warschauer Paktes: Hintergründe, Planung, Durchführung* (Bremen: Ed. Temmen, 1995), 34–228; Kieran Williams, *The Prague Spring and Its Aftermath: Czechoslovak Politics, 1968–1970* (Cambridge: Cambridge University Press, 1997); Jiři Valenta, *Soviet Intervention in Czechoslovakia, 1968: Anatomy of a Decision* (Baltimore: Johns Hopkins University Press, 1991).

15. For more details, see Manfred Wilke, "Die DDR in der Interventionskoalition," and Pawel Piotrowski, "Polen und die Intervention," in Karner et al., *Beiträge*.

16. See Jitka Vondrová and Jaromír Navrátil, eds., *Mezinárodní souvislosti československé krize 1967–1970, Červenec—srpen 1968*, vol. 4, no. 2 (Brno: Doplněk, 1996), 164–66, 172–81; RGANI, F. 89, op. 76, d. 75, pp. 1–18, telephone conversations of L. I. Brezhnev with A. Dubček, 13 August 1968, reprinted in Navrátil et al., *The Prague Spring 1968*, 343–56; and in German and Russian in Karner et al., *Dokumente*, #57.

17. See Oldřich Tůma et al., eds., *Srpen '69. Edice dokumentů* (Prague: Maxdorf, 1996); Oldřich Tůma, "Ein Jahr danach. Das Ende des Prager Frühlings im August 1969," *ZfG* 46 (1998): 720–32.

18. See also R. G. Pikhoya, "Chekoslovakiya, 1968 god. Vzglyad iz Moskvy. Po dokumentam TsK KPSS," *Novaya i noveyshaya istoriya* 6 (1994): 3–20, and in *Novaya i noveyshaya istoriya* 1 (1995): 34–48.

19. Vondrová and Navrátil, *Mezinárodní souvislosti československé krize 1967–1970*, 277.

20. For Dubček's views as voiced in conversations, letters, and other texts dating from the spring and summer of 1989, see Alexander Dubček, *Od totality k demokracii. Prejavy, články a rozhovory, výber 1963–1992* (Bratislava: Veda, 2002), 293–313.

4

Soviet Society in the 1960s

Vladislav Zubok

On 18 August 1968, Aleksandr Tvardovsky, the Russian poet and editor of the literary journal *Novy Mir*, spent hours at his dacha near Moscow with his short-wave radio. He listened to the news broadcast about Czechoslovakia by Western stations, among them Radio Liberty, Voice of America, and Deutsche Welle. He also listened to the open letter "2,000 Words to Workers, Farmers, Scientists, Artists, and Everyone," composed by the Czech writer Ludvík Vaculík, which concluded: "This spring, as after the war, we have been given a great chance. Again we have the chance to take into our own hands our common cause, which for working purposes we call socialism, and give it a form more appropriate to our once-good reputation and to the fairly good opinion we used to have of ourselves."[1]

These words resonated powerfully in Tvardovsky's soul. He wrote in his diary on the next day: "I would have signed [a similar letter], regarding our situation. And I would have written an even better one." During the tense Soviet-Czechoslovak talks at Čierná nad Tisou in early August, Tvardovsky, for the first time in his life, spent hours glued to his short-wave radio. He felt euphoric when he learned that the Czechoslovak reformists enjoyed national support and would not bend to Soviet pressure: "I never imagined I could feel such joy at this discomfiture, political and moral, of my country in the eyes of the whole world." At the same time, as Tvardovsky admitted, there was a great polarization of opinions in the Soviet Union regarding the Prague Spring. "What a multitude of people in our land has been listening to all this: some feel great compassion and sympathy, yet others feel tense, apprehensive, and are full of hatred. They think: 'These Czechs allow themselves too much!'"[2]

Understanding Soviet responses to the Prague Spring sheds light on inner divisions, feelings, ambiguities, hopes, and fears that existed in Soviet society at the time. Recent studies reveal the "spillover effect" of the events in Czechoslovakia on the USSR. Yet the resonance of the Prague Spring with Soviet society cannot be fully understood in the synchronic perspective. Nor can it be correctly explained as a one-sided impact or emanation of the Czech events on the Soviet body politic and the social-intellectual scenery. A much more adequate perspective, as this essay will argue, is a diachronic one that explains various Soviet attitudes to the Prague Spring as the products of *previous* Soviet internal arguments and struggles over the issues of de-Stalinization, liberalization, and the possibility of a reformed communism "with a human face."

The main argument of this chapter is that the Soviet experience of de-Stalinization (which preceded the Czech developments) had produced passions, hopes, and fears as well as lessons and memories that would produce fundamental divisions in Soviet society's reaction to the Prague Spring and the Soviet intervention of 1968. This chapter focuses on the Russian part of Soviet society and the central Soviet elites located in Moscow and other Russian cities. The responses, lessons, and memories in the non-Russian parts of the USSR, especially in the western borderlands, were markedly different and have been studied elsewhere.[3] This chapter draws on the growing body of archival research as well as the numerous sources this author was able to study for his large-scale project on the role of intellectuals in Soviet society.[4] First, Soviet de-Stalinization as it developed is explored. Then the focus shifts to the divisions and options Soviet de-Stalinization created, and the reasons why de-Stalinization and the movement for liberalization and reformed communism had such a limited and abortive nature in Soviet society and elites are discussed. Next, the ambiguous social developments and ideological trends in Moscow in the years preceding the Prague Spring are examined. A brief address of the lack of protest in the Soviet Union after the invasion follows. Finally, the short-term and long-term fallout of the aborted Czech experiment for Soviet polity and society is considered.

DE-STALINIZATION IN SOVIET SOCIETY, 1953–1963

It is important to recognize two facets of Soviet de-Stalinization: first, institutional and ideological de-Stalinization (from above), carried out by the Kremlin leadership, and second, the social, intellectual, and even spiritual de-Stalinization (from below) that took place in the minds, hearts, and souls of individual Soviet citizens. Both processes interacted and affected Soviet society. Both began at the moment of Stalin's death, yet they did not develop in unison. The first attempts of the post-Stalin leadership (by the likes of Lavrenty Beria and Georgi Malenkov) in 1953 to raise the issue of the "cult of personality" of Stalin did not resonate much with the party elites or with society at large (with the notable exception of the gulag). Some departures from Stalinism in 1953–1955, such as amnesties and rehabilitations, reconciliation with Josip Tito, and withdrawal from Finland and Austria, evoked more confusion than approval among Soviet citizens. A very narrow stratum of cultural elites, educated public, and students participated in the cultural Thaw, yet even among these many remained genuine admirers of Stalin and his international and domestic legacy.

Therefore, Nikita Khrushchev's Secret Speech of February 1956 produced a profound, unprecedented shock among the elites and the general public. That speech made irreversible the end of such key features of Stalinism as mass terror and permanent war mobilization. The speech unleashed de-Stalinization from below, yet it also produced powerful resistance in society. The Kremlin authorities, especially Khrushchev himself, were largely unaware of the Pandora's box they opened. They did not prepare the propaganda apparatus for enormous tasks facing them in the new situation after the speech was read to millions of party and nonparty members. In fact, only in July the Politburo issued clarification to the party propagandists that interpreted Stalinist crimes as deviations dictated by the prewar circumstances. As a result, for months after the Secret Speech, people were left with their own perceptions and interpretations. Khrushchev's attempts to avoid the public discussion of his speech and to divert public attention to other topics were counterproductive.[5]

From March to November 1956, spontaneous de-Stalinization occurred among students and young scientists, above all among those in the educational, cultural, and scientific institutions of Moscow and scientific-technical labs outside the capital, all of them linked to the military-industrial complex. There were attempts to reform the Komsomol, to search for "truth" and "sincerity" in literature, to forge new cultural and intellectual identities, and even sporadic collective actions to defend basic rights. Many students in Moscow, Leningrad, Sverdlovsk, Gorky, and other university centers of Russia tried to find out more about the Polish and Hungarian Revolutions. Some even sympathized with the Hungarian rebels and criticized the Soviet invasion of Hungary. In Leningrad in late November and early December, some students plotted to hold a rally in support of Hungary. Mikhail Molostvov, student of philosophy at Leningrad State University, wrote an essay entitled "Status Quo," demanding glasnost and an end to the tyranny of the bureaucracy. Victor Trofimov and Boris Pustyntsev, both students of the Herzen Institute, were motivated by the same ideas and organized a secret group of "Decembrists." A young party official and professor at Moscow State University, Lev Krasnopevtsev modeled his idea of organizing a revolutionary underground organization among junior faculty and graduate students on the Hungarian events. Hungary, he recalled later, "turned us upside down."[6]

The confusion, inaction, and blunders by the Soviet authorities were, in part, the result of inexperience, but they also stemmed from Khrushchev's convictions and overconfidence. The Soviet leader firmly believed that the selective dismantling of the Stalinist regime would only remove the roadblocks in the way of the ultimately inevitable triumphal march of communism. Khrushchev's "communism" was not only a not-so-distant goal (as he famously proclaimed in 1959), but also the sum of past experiences, including the "war communism" of 1918–1921 and the "socialist construction" of 1928–1934, when Stalin had not yet stifled "party democracy." This revolutionary epistemology blinded Khrushchev to the long-term dangers of radical de-Stalinization. At the same time, it made him alert to the short-term dangers of the loss of political control as a result of "bourgeois" or "revisionist" influences. Alarmed by the tragic Hungarian events, Khrushchev unleashed the Committee for State Security (KGB) on suspected agents of domestic "revisionism." He believed that the arrest of a few "loudmouths" among intellectuals, scientists, and students would end the social confusion.

Still, de-Stalinization from above continued. It involved large-scale events and campaigns: the World Youth Festival in Moscow (1957), the mass mobilizations to the Virgin Lands (reviving the revolutionary traditions of "socialist labor" as opposed to the camps' labor), Western exhibitions, development of foreign tourism, the emergence of "new" investigative journalism (in newspapers such as *Komsomolskaia Pravda* and *Izvestiya*, led by Khrushchev's son-in-law A. Adzhubei), and the second attack on Stalin and his accomplices at the 22nd Party Congress (October 1961). Khrushchev promoted the "rejuvenation" of the party cadres. A group of reform-minded idealists worked in the Komsomol, among them sociologists, literary critics, and philosophers who sought to rebuild the damaged bridges to the university students in order to regain their trust and participation in public life.

Khrushchev's massive housing construction and other life-improving social policies became a powerful factor in de-Stalinization. The movement of millions of urbanites from "communal" apartments to private apartments sharply reduced the social space that had helped generate "ordinary" Stalinists, secret police informers, and vigilantes.[7] The rapid growth of private social space boosted the proliferation of informal groups of young educated people (*kompaniyi*), a vital ingredient of the growing free-thinking milieu of middle-class professionals. Among the students during the 1950s, the private space of informal groups was far more important than the public activities in the Komsomol, which were increasingly viewed as bureaucratized and sterile. Groups of educated youth became the most important engine of intellectual, cultural, and spiritual de-Stalinization.[8]

Another significant factor was Khrushchev's promotion of the scientific-technical revolution after the successful Soviet launch of the first Sputnik. Ideologically cautious and inconsistent as this course was (such as when Khrushchev restored the infamous Trofim Lysenko, the enemy of genetics, to power), it produced the increasingly well-funded, confident, and socially prestigious academic and scientific-technical elites. In contrast to the universities that remained under stringent control, these elites existed in the "oases" of relatively free thinking and discussion, with access to information and enormous resources. The media reporting on the formerly secret scientific lab in Dubna near Moscow and the construction of a privileged "Academic City" near Novosibirsk epitomized the greater autonomy of the intellectual elites from the party-state as well as the recognition of the growing dependence of the latter on the former. Scientists became a privileged class and took advantage of this to help and promote their colleagues from the social sciences, biology, and creative arts—the other fields where the party-state's ideological controls remained strong.[9]

In the late 1950s and early 1960s, de-Stalinization from below began to develop a momentum of its own in Moscow and a few other cultural centers of Russia. These informal educated groups and networks in Moscow generated a new phenomenon unthinkable under Stalinism: *samizdat,* the unofficial alternative system of information exchange and cultural-intellectual interaction, free from state censorship. The Moscow branches of the "creative unions" of writers and artists—those Stalinist guilds created to corrupt and control the creative elites—became engines of cultural liberalization during the Thaw. There was a process of "rejuvenation" of these associations with the advent of younger cohorts of writers, poets, painters, and sculptors who sought to express "the truth" about the war, Stalinism, and everyday Soviet life and its meaning. The dominant direction of cultural and literary self-expression was modernist: young creative people took revolutionary experimental art as well as contemporary Western art as their models.[10]

The time between the spring of 1960 and December 1962 produced the "second Thaw" with its soaring hopes for liberalization among the Moscow cultural, intellectual, and scientific elites. A number of events created a synergistic effect: the spontaneous demonstrations after the space flight of Yuri Gagarin; the Cuban revolution and the surge of "revolutionary romanticism" with regard to the Third World, the adoption of the party's new program of "construction of communism" by 1960, and Khrushchev's second attack on Stalin at the 22nd Party Congress. All this took place against the background of an unprecedented expansion of the institutions of higher education, culture, and science; the peak of public faith in the scientific-technical revolution; and the rapid expansion of middle-class professional groups. The values of those groups, in contrast to the middle-class values of late Stalinism, focused not only on material well-being, but also on intellectual and cultural emancipation from the authoritarian controls. Publications in literary journals, popular scientific journals, and "investigative" newspapers, such as *Novy Mir, Nauka i Zhizn'* (*Science and Life*), and *Izvestiya*, created the new phenomenon of a nation-wide, educated readership whose minds, souls, hearts, and ultimately civic loyalty belonged not to the party-state leadership, but to the intelligentsia. The notion of intelligentsia was a contested one, with different people imparting different meanings to it. Traditionally in Russia, however, this notion meant individual social responsibility, autonomy from the repressive authoritarian regime, and searching for the moral meaning of life.[11] The phenomenal popularity of poet Yevgeny Yevtushenko, writer Vassily Aksyonov, and bard Bulat Okudzhava, among many others, signified the reemergence of a collective identity familiar from history (the Russian intelligentsia) with a new mass following among the Soviet-era professional educated middle classes.

In November 1962, Tvardovsky, the editor of *Novy Mir*, obtained Khrushchev's permission to publish the novel *One Day in the Life of Ivan Denisovich* by Aleksandr Solzhenitsyn, a completely unknown teacher of mathematics in Ryazan and an ex-convict of the gulag. Finally, de-Stalinization from above (Khrushchev) and from below (intelligentsia) appeared to act in synchrony against the forces of Stalinism in the bureaucracy and society. Tvardovsky told Khrushchev: "*Novy Mir* and the Soviet government belong to the same camp." He suggested abolishing the censorship of literary journals, and Khrushchev nodded sympathetically and, according to Tvardovsky, even expressed his "complete agreement" with the writer.[12] When Solzhenitsyn's piece was published, the Thaw seemed to be turning into the Moscow Spring. As one Moscow school teacher wrote in her diary, "[F]rom that moment, people would begin to speak and think freely, and not a single scoundrel would be able to indict them for anti-Soviet speeches."[13] Anna Akhmatova believed at that moment that everything she wrote about the Great Terror would soon be published.[14]

Instead, in December 1962 came frost, not spring. Khrushchev personally led the attack against the liberalizing trends and their "agents" in Soviet arts and culture: closing the young artists' exhibition in the Manege Exhibition Hall near the Kremlin and lashing out at poets and artists at two meetings with the "creative intelligentsia" (December 1962 and March 1963). The accounts, all written from the liberal perspective, blame the crackdown on the "Stalinist conspiracy." The latest Khrushchev biography cites the leader's neurotic instability, anti-intellectualism, and flawed vision of reforms and de-Stalinization. This turnabout, however, was totally abrupt and inexplicable for Moscow-based intellectuals and artists, the supporters of cultural liberalization. For a while, they continued to believe that "Stalin stalwarts seemed to be routed completely. One no longer had to fight with them. It was sufficient to laugh them off."[15] Abetted from the top, the crackdown, however, grew into a cultural-ideological backlash, reminiscent both of the Stalinist campaigns of 1946–1949 against "cosmopolitans" and of McCarthyist witch hunts. To many, this campaign also reminded them of a recent public attack on poet Boris Pasternak. Most shockingly, the established Soviet cultural elites, driven by fear and self-protection, became actively engaged in the campaign, denouncing each other, as if there had been no de-Stalinization or revelations by Solzhenitsyn. The momentum of the Moscow Spring was dead.[16]

The fragmentation and weakness of public support for cultural liberalization requires us to turn to the divisions, fears, and illusions produced by de-Stalinization in Soviet society, and ultimately to the abortive nature of this de-Stalinization.

LIMITATIONS OF RUSSIA'S DE-STALINIZATION

De-Stalinization was an international phenomenon. In Eastern and Western Europe, Khrushchev's Secret Speech split the Communist world into "Stalinists" and "reformed Communists." Numerous people abandoned their Communist beliefs altogether. The Hungarian Revolution was launched by the students and intellectuals who believed in liberalization, but also in "socialism"; their movement was supported by "reformed Communists" in the ruling party. Yet this revolution very quickly developed into an anticommunist, nationalist, anti-Russian movement that "reformed Communists" were unable to control any longer. In Poland, another option prevailed in 1956: ex-Stalinist Władysław Gomułka hoisted himself into the saddle of a popular movement, which blended "reformed communism" with liberalism and heavily anti-Russian Polish nationalism, which was the predominant driving force.

At the risk of crude generalization, the events in Poland and Hungary, as well as in less dramatic ways in Romania, revealed three discourses that emerged in the wake of Stalinism's "decapitation" by Khrushchev. The Stalinist discourse survived in part as a language of "realism" and cold war, and it remained the language of Communist regimes which stayed in power. These regimes, however, tapped into two other discourses to boost their legitimacy. One was the powerful language of nationalism, both in its liberal and illiberal versions, harking back to earlier collective memories, especially war traumas. Another was an idealistic discourse of reform communism that rejected liberal democracy and economic liberalization as "the return to capitalism" and sought to refurbish and revive the egalitarian promises of the Communist faith, combining them with the dreams of democratization and respect for civil rights.

It is obvious in retrospect that reform communism was a transitional phenomenon on the road from the authoritarian regime toward democratization and full national sovereignty from the Soviet Union. Even before the Prague Spring, the proponents of reformed communism were losing ground everywhere in Eastern Europe either to Stalinists (Poland and Romania of the 1960s) or to radical liberal nationalism (briefly in Budapest in 1956). Yet the mirages associated with reformed communism continued to attract intellectuals and artistic elites everywhere from Moscow to Warsaw and Prague, and from there to Berlin and Paris. The rebellious *Zeitgeist* of the 1960s in the West, especially the continued ideological fascination with Karl Marx, Vladimir Lenin, and Mao Zedong among Western intellectuals and students, supported and nourished these illusions and spread them among millions of believers in the rapidly growing ranks of university students and the professional middle classes.[17]

De-Stalinization proceeded very differently in various regions of the Soviet Union. In the Baltic republics, Ukraine, and in South Caucasus, especially in Georgia, the nationalist discourse was predominant. In Soviet Russia, it was a more complicated and contradictory process. The crisis of 1956 had already revealed important things about Russian Soviet society. The shock of revelations of Stalin's crimes created the possibility for spiritual catharsis, for self-questioning. Some Moscow intellectuals, scientists, and students perceived themselves as a vanguard of de-Stalinization from below. Very few of them were ready, however, to question the entire revolutionary legacy. It was customary among intellectual hot-heads to rediscover the traditions of the Russian struggle against the Tsarist autocracy. Reformed communism contrasted "moral" Bolshevism with Stalinism, thereby preserving the basic myth of the leftist intelligentsia about its special mission in remaking and saving Russia. Poet David Samoilov wrote in his diary in 1957 that Stalin brought to power *meschanstvo*, the anti-intellectual lower-middle class, the embodiment of provincial darkness and crass materialism; the task of the intellectuals was to fight against this group.[18] This line of thinking is typical of the time.

Just like many liberal-minded and reform-Communist intellectuals in Central Europe then and later, many of the anti-Stalinist intellectuals in Moscow came from the families of Old Bolsheviks and passionate believers in the revolution. Most of them still thought that a "return to Lenin" and "purification" of the revolutionary cause from Stalinism was the correct path to the future. For a decade after 1956, some of them would search for "a flaw in the original design" of Marxism in history, philosophy, sociology, and political economy. Others would propagate the idea of genuine revolution and honest and moral revolutionaries including Lenin (as opposed to Stalin and Stalinists) in theater, cinema, art, and literature.[19]

At the same time, in contrast to Central Eastern Europe, the Russian Soviet society failed to develop a potent nationalist alternative to discredited Stalinism. In part, this incapacity was the reflection of Russian history, traditions, and the composition of society. Unlike the Hungarians in 1956 and the Czechs in 1968 who remembered life before "communization," the vast majority of Russians in 1956 and later remembered only the Soviet past. In Budapest and Prague, there were deep-seated liberal traditions and culture rooted in historical memories and the recently destroyed bourgeois, middle-class milieu. Virtually none of these existed in Moscow or elsewhere in Russia by 1953. Stalinism had reshaped and debased Russian society more than the societies of Central Europe. In Leningrad, the only truly European city of Russia, the bourgeois-liberal milieu had been destroyed by waves of terror and resettlements. In Moscow, numerous members of the cultural elites enjoyed in some ways bourgeois and middle-class standards of life, yet they developed the ingrained "court" mentality of time-serving cynics. Many of them fully accepted their role as the servants of the regime and abdicated their spiritual and moral responsibilities to society. They were prepared to stamp out any heretics and revisionists that dared to break the rules and cross the boundaries of the permissible. In 1958–1959, these "court" cultural elites, unleashed by the Kremlin, hunted down poet Boris Pasternak after he published his novel *Doctor Zhivago* (treating the Russian revolution as a deeply tragic, rather than historically progressive development) abroad and received the Nobel Prize for literature. Later, in 1963–1965, they supported repression against their fellow poets, writers, and filmmakers.

The Cold War fortified Stalinist discourse and undercut any attempts to form a Russian national alternative to Stalin's empire. Cold War propaganda strengthened the illiberal reactions and predilections of Russian society and elites. After all, the Soviet Union opposed the most radical liberal democracy of all, the United States. The Kremlin leadership successfully argued that cultural liberalization and ideological deviations could only hand powerful weapons to the enemy, and the loss of stability in the USSR and the loss of the Soviet empire in Eastern Europe would then be inevitable. The vast majority of the Russian ethnic "core" of the Soviet Union supported the center against the anti-Russian periphery (the Balts, West Ukrainians, and Georgians). An even greater majority of Russians, including the cultural-intellectual elites and students, strongly associated themselves with the Soviet victory in the Great Patriotic War. Faced with a choice between liberalization and the Soviet postwar empire, most of them chose the latter. "The hegemony over East Central Europe," as one historian aptly remarked, "became the most visible and palpable prize of the great Soviet victory and therefore functioned as a powerful moral bond between the regime and its peoples and among the various sectors of the Soviet elite."[20]

Even worse, Russians were deeply divided among themselves on the meaning of de-Stalinization. In Western and dissident literature, the division between "Stalinists" and "anti-Stalinists" became the standard binary formula to analyze and discuss politics and cultural divisions during the Khrushchev period and in the post-Khrushchev years. Useful as it was, this formula nevertheless simplified motivations and feelings behind "Stalinist" and "anti-Stalinist" façades. Above all, it failed to explain the remarkable resilience and strength of "Stalinist" attitudes in the Soviet society, as well as the chronic weakness of the "anti-Stalinist" camp.

In Soviet Russia, Stalinism had cultivated powerful identities that outlived Stalin because they appealed to Russian historical memories, pride, and fears. For millions, the Stalinist past embodied three decades of incredible suffering, destruction and executions, torture and slave camps. Yet for other millions of Russians, Stalinism symbolized an era of unparalleled achievements, great upward social mobility, enthusiasm, and triumphs, including victory in World War II. Vladimir Kozlov discovered the widespread phenomenon of anti-Khrushchevian "popular Stalinism" that was illiberal and immune to the values of individualism and human rights. Many felt repulsed seeing how Khrushchev and other Soviet "bosses" distanced themselves from Stalin, while retaining their power and privileges and pretending they still had the right to lead and rule. In many regions of Russia, people believed that Stalin's terror in 1934–1938 was retribution to Communist bosses who had oppressed the "common people" and brutally enforced collectivization. Finally, many people remembered Stalin as the indispensable wartime leader who had led the country to victory.[21]

Even among intellectuals there was a curious attitude: *anti*-anti-Stalinism. They felt that Khrushchev's denunciation of Stalin and the way he stifled any discussion in society was wrong and profoundly immoral.[22] Writer Konstantin Simonov once told Khrushchev that his denunciation of Stalin was like reversing a car that was moving forward at full speed. "You have to stop first and switch gears. I believe we should take a timeout and think."[23] This kind of reaction reflected the traditional alienation between the regime and those who viewed themselves as the heirs to the left-liberal Russian intelligentsia of the nineteenth century and who experienced a profound feeling of social duty and moral responsibility.

Instead of presenting a credible alternative to Stalinist discourse, nationalism in Soviet Russia played a highly divisive role, putting sharp limits on de-Stalinization in Soviet Russian society. Stalin had successfully used the pre-revolutionary arsenal of the Great Russian imperial ideology to build up his cult. He also directed people's discontent against the Jews. Late Stalinism revived and exploited Russian traditional identities, which had more in common with the prerevolutionary Black Hundred anti-Semitic nationalist movement than with Marxist-Leninist ideology. Many young intellectuals, ethnic Russians, imbibed anti-Semitism along with Great Russian chauvinism, and 1956 did not change their views. They became "Russian patriots" who hated liberals and cosmopolitan intellectuals, viewing their activities as treasonous.

Russian-Jewish intellectuals and cultural figures, victims of the anti-Semitic campaign, children of Old Bolsheviks and true believers in communism, were among the first who embarked on the process of de-Stalinization from below. They played a uniquely active role in the formation of the vanguard of cultural, intellectual, and spiritual liberalization.[24] Most of them continued to perceive Stalinism as a deviation from the correct historical path, and from the legacy of the Russian revolution. The uniting discourse of this group was reform communism or "democratic socialism." Educated as Soviet patriots, these people were shocked by the Soviet invasion of Hungary in 1956 and believed that principles were more important than the preservation of Stalin's empire. The priority of these artists and intellectuals was cultural and intellectual emancipation, not traditional organized politics, and they rejected violence in the name of social change. A few them began to break with the faith of their Old Bolshevik parents, and some even became radical liberals, if not libertarians. They rejected the Soviet regime as a hostile force, and resented the official doctrine of socialist realism as a form of cultural oppression. Alexander Ginzburg, the father of *samizdat*, remarked to the writer V. Aksyonov in 1960: "It is a new environment where [the KGB] can no longer shadow all of us. There are just too many of us. This generation turned out to be like that, too many are marching out of lockstep."[25]

During the late 1950s and early 1960s, the rift deepened between "Russian patriots" and "liberals" (they gave different definitions to each other) inside the cultural elites, especially in the Writers' Union. While similar tensions existed in Communist Poland, Hungary, and even in Czechoslovakia, there were also, at various historical moments, broad national democratic coalitions that included "Jews" and even had them play the key role as the adepts of liberal or reform Communist ideas. It did not happen in Soviet Russia. Before the Thaw, "Russian patriots" victimized "cosmopolitans"; during the Thaw, the latter tried to settle their score with the former in kind. The constant rivalry precluded the formation of any new brand of liberal democratic movement that could simultaneously appeal to Russian national feelings. The "Russian patriots" rejected the ideas of reform communism and liberal socialism as the manifestations of the cosmopolitan "Jewish" spirit, which they regarded as destructive for Russians.[26] Members of the cultural vanguard of the early 1960s regarded Russian nationalism as a reactionary, anti-Semitic, and potentially "fascist" phenomenon. Both sides periodically looked to powerful allies in the Soviet party apparatus for support.[27]

Against the background of these divisions, it is surprising that the ideas and values of the "third way," "democratic socialism," cultural liberalization, and economic reforms still played a prominent role in the Soviet Union in the years preceding the Prague Spring.

BIRDS OF SPRING: "PEOPLE OF THE SIXTIES"

Khrushchev's de-Stalinization actions and the Thaw created an unusual phenomenon in Soviet society: a growing number of men and women, including many from the postwar cohorts of the "Soviet intelligentsia" and educated professionals as well as survivors belonging to the pre-Stalinist intelligentsia, began to think of themselves as an informal and nonpolitical community. In public life, many of these people were party members and Komsomol activists. Privately, however, they stood in aesthetical and ethical opposition to the bulk of the party-state *nomenklatura* and the country's leadership, considering them uneducated, crude, and repulsive. At the core of this phenomenon was the rejection of Stalinism in favor of liberal humanist values and ideas of individual dignity, the rejection of the turgid canon of socialist realism, the faith in historical progress, and a youthful sense of opening horizons. The most common, if very loose, name for this community was "people of the Sixties" (*shestidesyatniki*). It implied not so much the generational change (although it was visible) as a cultural, ethical, and aesthetical distancing from the Stalinist past.

The social base of this informal community grew rapidly in the postwar years. The logic of competition with the United States forced the Soviet leadership to expand higher education and to foster the growth of scientific and engineering elites. From 1928 to 1960, the number of college students in the USSR grew twelve-fold and reached 2.4 million. The number of college-educated professionals increased from 233,000 to 3.5 million.[28] The number of scientists reached 665,000 by 1965, a six-fold growth in fifteen years.[29] The students who graduated during the 1950s formed the *majority* of Soviet educated classes, and they joined the workforce during a period of unprecedented, Cold War–fueled job growth, the scientific-technical revolution, and Soviet social and educational programs. A huge gap separated these young cohorts, numerous, optimistic, and idealistic, from their predecessors who had been decimated by war and Stalin's terror and whose authority was tarnished by their Faustian bargains with the regime. Gradually, some members of the young intelligentsia in Moscow and Leningrad began to look for inspiration and guidance from the remnants of the Russian intelligentsia.

The community had neither the desire nor the opportunity for political organization. The *shestidesyatniki* possessed only the "soft power" of cultural innovation, moral reflection, and thought-provoking intellectualism. Yet there were several trends that enhanced this "soft power." First, there was the continuing discovery and production of the treasures of high culture. There was a long row of banned and suppressed Russian writers, poets, and artists to be discovered and "rehabilitated." Also, there was the rising cultural tide that found its way into the Soviet Union through the breaches in the Iron Curtain made under Khrushchev: Italian neorealist films, British theater, French impressionists, Picasso, and many others. The translation and emulation of literature and art from Central Europe (Bertold Brecht, Polish films and novels, Czech essays, Hungarian poetry, and so forth) supplied the Soviet Russian intellectuals with Western elements that were conspicuously absent from their cultural and spiritual diet.

Despite Khrushchev's crackdown on formalist poetry and art, the ferment of creativity continued to make itself felt in filmmaking through the work of Andrei Tarkovsky, Andrei Konchalovsky, and many other young directors; in the theater by companies such as Oleg Yefremov's Contemporary Theater and Yuri Liubimov's Taganka Theater; and in literature. *Novy Mir* under Tvardovsky's leadership developed into the best literary journal of the Soviet era. The journal's publications broke the taboos of officially sanctioned socialist realism one by one, presenting the prose of "lieutenants" about war, the "village prose" about the tragic end of Russian peasantry, and critical essays discussing democratic and revolutionary traditions before Stalinism. Tvardovsky, together with a group of dedicated publishers, literary critics, writers, and poets, attempted to use the great traditions of Russian literature to refurbish—not discard—the Soviet identity.[30] One of the key elements in this attempt was the profound conviction that only a "sincere" and "truthful" exploration of the Stalinist era could provide a basis for the future existence of a *Soviet* internationalist and humanist society. Tvardovsky gradually came to the firmly held belief that the ill-educated bureaucracy needed the intelligentsia as a mediator between the state and the people. Only talented and sincere artists and writers would be able to help prepare the moral and spiritual ground for a future egalitarian society.

The 1960s also produced an ever-growing informal culture on the crossroads between the classical Russian high culture canon, new democratic liberal values, and unflagging beliefs in the revolutionary mythology and historical determinism. This informal culture was born below and found its most visible expression in the cult of informal songs written by bards not recognized by the cultural elite, but loved by the new educated cohorts. Songs by Bulat Okudzhava, Vladimir Vysotsky, Yuri Vizbor, Aleksandr Galich, Aleksandr Gorodnitsky, Evgenii Kliachkin, and others spread among millions with the help of private tape-recorders (*magnetizdat*). Tens of thousands of people gathered every summer in the countryside to perform, sing, and exchange cultural information.

The most influential segment of the *shestidesyatniki* was in the military-industrial complex, which employed over three million in the 1960s. Scientists, designers, and engineers were avid readers of thick literary journals and consumers of "honest" cultural products. These groups extended assistance to the "lyricists"—poets, writers, artists—when the latter got into trouble in 1963–1964. Academic and scientific institutes acted not only as "oases of free thinking," but as cultural stages. At the same time, scientists and professionals of the military-industrial complex harbored strong technocratic illusions in that they were confident that in the future the national leadership would have to turn to them, not to the poets and writers, for guidance. The Cold War arms race boosted their prestige and confidence and so did the decline in the growth of the Soviet economy in 1959–1964. It forced the Communist Party to turn for help to the professionals. It was the high noon for the technocrats and their supporters in the state bureaucracy.

In return for their vital services, the scientists gained more intellectual autonomy than they had ever had before. Scientists in the "closed" cities and labs of the military-industrial complex had virtually uncensored access to global information. Even outside this complex, a slew of privileged scientific conglomerates also enjoyed relative academic freedom. In 1965, Akademgorodok near Novosibirsk was, as one veteran recalled, "the most liberal locale in the country," with forty-seven academicians, eighty-five doctors of science, and over one thousand younger scientists. There was virtually no party or secret police supervision there. The intensity of intellectual discussions in the Akademgorodok, one witness recalled, resembled that at Berkeley.[31]

The first post-Khrushchev years, 1965–1967, saw the peak of influence of the intellectual-professional elites on the Soviet regime. Sociologist Vladimir Shlapentokh recalled that "never in Soviet history had the officially recognized role of the intellectuals been so great."[32] In the race for strategic parity with the West, the Soviet regime could only count on scientists. Even the KGB needed the scholarly elite and their brains to deal with the challenges from the West.[33] In 1962–1965, the Kremlin authorized economic discussions; central and regional authorities employed sociologists and paid for public opinion polls to learn more about social processes. Economists, mathematicians, and sociologists used the "rehabilitated" and now fashionable discipline of cybernetics to offer solutions to reverse the slowing of the Soviet economy. *Pravda, Izvestiya*, and other newspapers and journals published "discussion articles" on possible economic reforms. These reforms were launched with pomp and circumstance at the Party Plenum in September 1965.[34]

Another trend in 1965–1967 was a growing public standoff between the post-Khrushchev leadership in the Politburo and the small group of the pro-liberalization and reform-Communist intellectuals and artists in

Moscow. This standoff was triggered by the Kremlin's decision to cancel de-Stalinization from above. Instead, the regime attempted to boost its national legitimacy by creating the cult of the Great Patriotic War. Against this ominous background, the arrest and trial of two writers, Andrei Sinyavsky and Yuli Daniel, took place. The trial was part of a campaign promoted by "hardliners" in the KGB and the Politburo in order to fight "Western influences" and "liberal rot" that had accumulated in the Moscow educated circles, as the hardliners believed, during Khrushchev's rule. Protest against this campaign brought to life a "movement" primarily located in Moscow. Solzhenitsyn recalled that "*Samizdat* gushed like a spring flood, new names joined the protests. It seemed that we would start breathing freely with one more push."[35] Historian Roy Medvedev recalled that in 1966–1967 this movement enjoyed emotional and material support among large groups of the intelligentsia, Old Bolsheviks, and even some people of the central party apparatus. Among the latter were experts in international affairs, culture, and science, recruited into the apparatus during Khrushchev's Thaw (A. Rumyantsev, F. Burlatsky, N. Inozemtsev, O. Bogomolov, A. Bovin, G. Shakhnazarov, and A. Chernyaev, among others). Some of them became directors of think-tanks preparing international "détente" and writing speeches for Leonid Brezhnev. At the same time, they helped artists and historians who became the targets of neo-Stalinist attacks.[36] There was an informal alliance between reform Communists in the apparatus and the anti-Stalinist cultural elites, including some "liberals" among them.

It is obvious that both trends failed to produce the forces of historic change. Moreover, the chances, in retrospect, look even bleaker than they had looked at the time. In general, reform communism never gained many converts in the party apparatus; it remained limited to a few smatterings of educated ("enlightened") apparatchiks, specializing in international relations, culture, science, and technology. Soviet Russian reform Communists still believed in the Leninist revolution and "purification" of the Leninist legacy from Stalinism, and they hesitated to see that Stalin's empire was doomed. Yet, at the same time, Khrushchev's revelations of the blood-soaked past created a strong aversion to violence among these intellectuals. They no longer viewed mass politics as the major force of history. On the contrary, they gave priority to cultural enlightenment or scientific/technical progress. They regarded Soviet bureaucracy as the primary enemy of "genuine socialism" and ascribed to themselves and the growing groups of intellectuals and artists the same role that Karl Marx and Friedrich Engels had ascribed to the proletariat.

As for liberals in the broader sense, they limited their aspirations to the sphere of culture and abhorred public politics. They were especially prominent among the cultural and artistic elites, ensconced in the official unions, and firmly embedded in the system of material privileges of the regime, which they were afraid to lose. Overall, fear remained a dominant motive in their actions. It had stayed in their marrow since Stalin's times. Only a tiny minority of the reform Communists and liberals had the courage for making public protests. The vast majority had long learned to live a double life, even more so than their Central European colleagues. Their favorite way to compensate themselves for their public life as conformists and obsequious time-servers was the cultivation of refined cultural tastes. Many of them looked at the aesthetic and ethical spheres as a purely private affair, which helped them to "save their souls" and withstand the repulsive realities of Soviet Russian life.

For all its social and intellectual capital, the Soviet technocratic intelligentsia was as split and divided as the writers and the rest of the educated classes; they all spoke different discourses typical of the era, including Stalinist, reform Communist, and nationalist ones. Consistent "liberals" were a minority even in the Akademgorodok. Even those technocrats who were highly critical of the existing economic system continued to believe that alternatives and new solutions could only be found in "improving the socialist model," not in returning to capitalism.[37] The main reformist ideas included de-centralization without the dismantling of the centrally planned economy, introduction of new labor incentives without creation of a free labor market, and introduction of the notions of "price," "value," and "competition" without abolition of total price control or the restitution of private property. The rejection of liberal economic thinking was the result of ideological blindness and ignorance about Western concepts, but it also reflected the "natural" social habitat of the reformers and their intellectual milieu. In the Academy of Science, including Akademgorodok, as well as in the two dozen "secret cities" of the military-industrial complex, tens of thousands of scientists, engineers, and their families lived a privileged life in which all their needs were taken care of within the framework of a property-less, centralized economy. Why wish for its destruction?

The birth of the "movement" in 1966–1967 and the flurry of activities (collective petitions, promotion of "honest" works of history and literature, providing assistance to the families of political prisoners) seemed to break the paralyzing fear. It created the men and women of a new political-ideological quality, the dissident counter-elite. It is worth reminding the contemporary reader that many dissidents had grown up as Soviet patriots and true believers in communism. Many had joined the party during the war or after Khrushchev's Secret Speech. Practically all of them lived in Moscow and worked in the state-funded (there were no others) institutions of culture, education, and science. The group also included a very high percentage of children and relatives of the victims of Stalinist terror, children of Russified Jews, and innovative artists in aesthetic "rebellion" against the canon of socialist realism. In 1966–1967 they were united by the visceral hatred of Stalinism, "Stalinists," and the KGB, and by the values of the left-leaning Russian intelligentsia of the nineteenth century as well as by the newly developed concept of human rights from postwar legal terminology.

The most active dissidents felt contemptuous of both their conformist colleagues and the reform Communists in positions of authority. Yet as far as a political platform, specific programs, and ideology were concerned, the dissidents were also in disarray. The same deep split existed between the movement's liberals, socialists, and nationalists as everywhere else. Characteristically, the informal leader of the movement at the time, the writer Aleksandr Solzhenitsyn, was a profoundly illiberal thinker and Russian nationalist. He despised Moscow intellectual "smatterers" and nursed a grudge against Jews for their support of communism and the Soviet regime in the past.

Above all, reform Communists, liberal dissidents, and technocratic scientists were just the icing on the cake, the rarified urban intellectuals estranged from the masses of the Russian people.[38] These masses, especially the workers and peasants, saw the party apparatchiks and the intelligentsia as different segments of the same ruling elite.[39] Soviet Russian reform Communists mistrusted mass politics; they were afraid of the mass support for "Russian fascism" in the near future. As far as the liberals among the dissidents were concerned, the logic of their opposition to the Brezhnevite neo-Stalinism increased their mistrust in the Russian people, alternatively imagined as passive and slovenly and as aggressive, neo-fascist, and nationalistic. Some dissidents tilted toward an alliance with non-Russian nationalities in the Soviet Union and, most importantly, with Western scientists, scholars, journalists, and, possibly, even people connected to Western secret services. Finally, the technocratic-minded dissidents felt that the masses lacked, by definition, education and an understanding of the meaning of progress. In other words, the masses and the bulk of Communist apparatchiks belonged to the kingdom of darkness.

Sociologists haltingly began to plumb the depths of Soviet Russian society. Focusing on their own problems with the post-Khrushchev regime, they were slow to admit that society was evolving away from, not toward, their elevated ideas and schemes.[40] Most remarkably, there was no student movement in Moscow in the 1960s. The new cohorts of Soviet students were much more conformist and less ideologically active than the cohorts of 1956–1958. John Scott, a contemporary American observer, remarked that education did not stimulate social activism anymore, but rather stimulated "desire for more privacy and mobility—one's own room or apartment; the right to turn off the cliché-ridden political program on television, the desire for one's own car; the chance to visit Paris."[41] Soviet opinion polls as well as KGB reports recorded a continuing decline of romanticism and idealism and the spread of cynical conformism. In comparison with the data of 1960–1961, many more young men and women seemed to become materialistic, indifferent to ideas, principles, and big social issues.[42]

In Soviet Russian society, the credibility of the Brezhnev regime grew between 1965 and 1967; it did not decrease. Among the contributing factors was the second round of the extension of visible social benefits to millions of people (the first round took place under Khrushchev in 1955–1958), which included free housing, education, medicine, childcare, and pensions. According to Western estimates, public consumption in the USSR grew annually by 4.6 percent after 1964 (before it was 3.2 percent). The Kremlin combined increases in the purchase of wheat and consumer goods abroad with subsidized low prices for basic food and consumer items.[43] Sociologists began to notice that not only the Communist *nomenklatura*, a predictable suspect, resisted economic reforms; even bigger resistance came from the majority of the workers and employees who preferred equality in payment to hard work and social protection to efficiency. Even before 1968, economic reforms began to grind to a halt simply because the profits of the few efficient enterprises and economic sectors were spread around the entire economy via the central budget. Even before the Prague Spring, the USSR began to drift from dynamic reformism into stagnation.[44]

The political culture of the majority of people in Soviet Russian society continued to be defined by the search for stability and peace, not by the quest for civil freedoms. The traditional Cold War enemy images, blurred among the educated strata and reversed among the liberal dissidents, remained very strong in the society's depth. The regime's propaganda successfully used the Vietnam War and the brutal U.S. bombing of the North Vietnamese to discredit the "American enemy" in the eyes of the majority. Against this backdrop, the Soviet "right" to control Central Eastern Europe remained nondiscussible and sacrosanct.

SURVIVING THE INVASION

The truth about the Prague Spring was in the beholder's eye. The reform Communists, including the "enlightened" apparatchiks, viewed the Czech developments as an unexpected second chance for a profound de-Stalinization of the Soviet society and for the ousting of the neo-Stalinist old guard. Some of them had lived in Prague for years, working for the journal *The Problems of the Peace and Socialism*.[45] They warned the party leadership that military intervention in Czechoslovakia would lead to a split with the Western Communist parties and jeopardize the Soviet position in the world.[46] One observer who worked in the party Central Committee's building in the summer of 1968 recalled: "Never before or since have I seen so much room for liberalism in the highest Soviet quarters. One could walk along the corridor inside the party Central Committee and shout at the top of one's lungs: 'It is impossible to send tanks into Czechoslovakia!'"[47] Aleksandr Bovin wrote in his diary on 19 August, "In our Department [of the Central Committee], in the Foreign Ministry [intervention] is considered an unjustified step, at least a premature one."[48]

The brio of the Prague Spring seemed to have brought reform Communists and Liberals together again, at least in Muscovite intellectual circles. Active Russian Jewish dissident Mikhail Agursky recalled: "The Prague Spring of 1968 briefly brought me back to the eschatological expectations of Good Communism. I still shared hopes that salvation would come from the outside: Poland, Hungary, the Italian Communist Party and now from Czechoslovakia."[49] Journalist Vladimir Lukin, a man with strong identity of *shestidesyatnik* and with extensive contacts to innovative artists and formalist poets, returned early in 1968 from Prague to Moscow for a leave and found that "the entire Moscow" of dissidents and semi-dissidents flocked to his apartment, eager for news about Czechoslovakia.[50]

The Prague Spring was closer to the hearts and minds of the Moscow-based intellectuals and artists than the Western New Left radicalism that erupted at the same time. The anti-Vietnam protest among radical youth in the West did not find the slightest response in the quarters of the dissident movement. Moscow intellectuals also refused to share the Western radical infatuation with Maoist Cultural revolution in China. In the opinion of one Moscow witness of the May events in Paris, French neo-Marxist intellectuals and students were "possessed by Satanic powers." They worshipped revolutionary violence, while Soviet liberals and reform Communists abhorred it.[51] Russian film critic Maya Turovskaya recalled: "In 1968 the West experienced 'its' Sixties. And we did not understand why Western Leftists could be so blind to what was happening in the Soviet Union. We felt like being on a train going in the opposite direction."[52]

In April–June 1968, Andrei Sakharov formulated a paradigm of technocratic-minded Soviet intellectuals in a pamphlet: "Reflections on Progress, Peaceful Coexistence, and Intellectual Freedom." He appealed to the Western political and intellectual classes with a call for the convergence of the two opposed systems. Sakharov emphasized the need of intellectual freedom and of the "scientific-democratic approach to politics, economics, and culture." He stressed that he held "socialist" views. Yet his emphasis was not on revolution or mass politics, but on peaceful evolution and scientific/technical progress. Sakharov rejected violence and revolutionary changes. He feared that any political coup or revolution in Soviet society would cause a regression to violent chaos. The only alternative could be "scientific-democratic" reforms brought about by a gradual evolution in politics, economics, and culture. Sakharov believed that the intelligentsia, scientists and artists, should play a crucial role in such a transformation, provided they were given freedom of information, travel, and speech.[53]

The invasion of Czechoslovakia by the Warsaw Pact troops on 21 August 1968 took everybody in Russia by surprise. Earlier news broadcasts had not prepared people for the use of military force. Many were on summer vacations, in a mood that was far from political or concerned with international events. KGB and party reports invariably spoke of "absolute calm" in all the Soviet regions and cities. Even in comparison with 1956, protest in Moscow and Leningrad was remarkably insignificant. In Prague, Lukin and other Russians in sympathy with the Prague Spring refused to propagate lies about the invasion and quickly lost their jobs. In Russia, there was one perhaps rather spectacular protest that took place in Red Square on 25 August. There were only seven protesters, all of them from the ranks of the post-1965 movement of human rights defenders: Konstantin Babitsky, Larisa Bogoraz, Vadim Delone, Vladimir Dremliuga, Pavel Litvinov, Natalia Gorbanevskaya, and Vladimir Fainberg. They tried to unfurl small Czech flags and posters. One poster read: "Long live a free and independent Czechoslovakia!" On another poster was the famous slogan of the Polish nationalist revolutionaries of the nineteenth century: "For your freedom and for ours!" The KGB quickly arrested the protesters.[54]

Ill-informed and deceived by the Kremlin propaganda, the vast majority of Russian people took the invasion as a necessity. Some in the KGB and among the officials were all too eager to depict the Czech reforms as a "Jewish-led affair," drawing parallels to the dissidents in the USSR. This had the potential of unleashing anti-Semitic reactions.[55] Yet this did not happen. Security interests and Cold War bipolarity remained the trump card of official propaganda. For many, the fact that Czechoslovakia bordered on West Germany was enough to justify the invasion. "What occupation?" asked some people regarding the seven dissident protesters in Red Square. "Of Czechoslovakia? But we liberated them in 1945. Two hundred thousand Russian soldiers died there. And now they've staged this counterrevolution. We cannot give up Czechoslovakia and leave it to the Americans."[56] This echoed typical views, shared by many Russians who had lost relatives in the Second World War.[57]

The invasion fatally tipped the domestic balance: the potential democratic-socialist coalition, uniting idealistic Communists and liberal intellectuals, was no longer in the cards. The regime proved it was not afraid of resorting to brutal force and got away with insignificant reactions from the Western powers and total quiescence inside the USSR and the Communist Bloc. Among advocates of cultural liberalization and reform Communists alike, a feeling of intense shame was compounded with a sense of impotence. They felt dishonored, for their ideals had been trampled on and defiled. More and more of them became, as Elena Bonner put it, "foreigners at home."[58] Writer Aksyonov railed against the criminal regime. Poet Yevtushenko shed "the tears of a deceived idealist." Yevtushenko sent two cables: one to Brezhnev, protesting the invasion, another to the Czech embassy in Moscow, expressing moral solidarity. Then he hurried to his dacha near Moscow to burn his manuscripts and letters, expecting the KGB to come and search or even arrest him. In the "oases of free thinking," the think-tanks and labs in Moscow, Akademgorodok and elsewhere, the arrogant and confident technocrats of the scientific elite promptly "changed tapes": now they marched to hard-line music. The editor of *Literary Gazette*, Aleksandr Chakovsky, launched a campaign to collect signatures of writers to support the invasion.[59] There was no widespread campaign among established pro-liberalization intellectuals and artists to defend the rights of the arrested dissidents. Fear of being branded anti-Soviet and the inability to speak against Stalin's empire at the time of the Cold War were as paralyzing in 1968 as in 1956.

The self-immolation of Jan Palach, the Czech student, underlined the pain of isolation felt by the liberal-reformist minority of Soviet intelligentsia. On 20 January 1969, Igor Dedkov, another veteran of the student activism of 1956, wrote in his diary: "A Czech student died yesterday. Our radio stations and newspapers are silent. They report on anything but Czechoslovakia. Nothing we have been writing makes any sense: cheap, cowardly acting, boot-licking, and prostitution." Some students of the Moscow State Institute for International Relations (MGIMO), the elite factory of Soviet diplomats, stood silently with glasses of vodka raised—the old Russian tradition of mourning the dead. Still, in Russia, in contrast to the Baltics and the Ukraine, Palach found no followers.[60]

While the invasion demoralized the reformist intellectuals, it energized their enemies. Mikhail Gorbachev, then the regional party boss in the Stavropol region, recalled: "From 21 August on, an ideological 'toughening' began, the repression of any free thinking." Instructions from the party Central Committee ordered regional committees to "take decisive actions in the ideological sphere. The struggle against dissident movements took on a massive and ubiquitous character."[61] Numerous reform Communists and those involved in the movement of 1966–1967 were expelled from the party. The very word "reform" became a taboo in the public lexicon for almost two decades. In January 1970, after many months of strangulation of *Novy Mir* by censors and party hard-liners, Tvardovsky resigned from the journal and died soon afterwards.

In November 1969, Mikhail Gorbachev and another regional party leader, Yegor Ligachev, visited Prague with an official Soviet delegation. Gorbachev knew that his university classmate Zdeněk Mlynář was an active participant in the Prague Spring. At first, Gorbachev tended to agree with the majority in Russia that the invasion was necessary, for his father had been badly wounded liberating Slovakia in 1944. Yet he could not help feeling dismayed by the paralysis and the unmitigated hostility displayed toward the Russians in Prague and Bratislava. After the trip to Czechoslovakia, he recalled, he "returned home overpowered by grave thoughts, realizing the direct connection of what was happening over there with the events of August 1968." In his memoirs, published in 1995, he called this trip "the most difficult" of all foreign trips he made.[62] It would take Gorbachev years to come round to the views on the Czech reforms espoused in 1968 by Alexander Dubček and other reform Communists.

POSTMORTEM

The short-term effect of the 1968 invasion on Russian society was extremely limited. Except for a few dissidents, no elements in Soviet society were prepared to take their discontent and protest into the public realm. On the other hand, the longer-term effect of the abortion of the Prague Spring was very significant. The disillusionment with the prospects of "democratic socialism" similar to the Czechoslovaks' "communism with a human face," terminated any possibility of a unity between the liberals in the Muscovite cultural milieu and reform-Communist apparatchiks. The hopes for an evolutionary improvement of the Soviet regime were gone among the cultural Muscovite elites. Meeting in their kitchens, they raised bitter toasts to the "success of our hopeless cause." From now on, their priority was the preservation of their individual moral and intellectual integrity, not the transformation of society. Among the intellectuals who had toyed with neo-Marxist ideas in the 1960s, there was a widespread sense that history "betrayed" them.[63] Social philosopher Dmitry Furman recalled about that time that the fad of Marxism-Leninism among his friends and colleagues in Moscow "died a quiet death sometime during the reign of Brezhnev."[64]

Some intellectuals now turned to the West and the "free world" as a last resort. "The West will help us," became a favorite toast among those "defectors-in-place." For dissidents, friendship with Western journalists became essential. Foreigners who resided in Moscow with their families, the hordes of the "messengers of détente" who descended on Moscow and Leningrad, exchange scholars, and participants in scientific conferences carried information in and out of the Soviet Union, helping to spread the news about the arrests and persecutions and to erode the xenophobic encirclement. Numerous sympathizers of the "movement" of 1966–1967 who had begun to "feel foreign" in Soviet society began to seek an exit not only from the ideological utopia, but also from the Soviet Union itself. From 1970 onward, the possibility of such an exit existed in the form of the so-called Jewish immigration.

Reform communism was dead in Russian Soviet society, yet miraculously it survived in the party apparatus. It continued to exist among intellectuals and "enlightened" party members in the Russian provinces and among the tiny group of "enlightened" party apparatchiks in Moscow. The very fact that the Prague Spring (as well as the earlier Moscow Spring) was aborted helped those people to live with their illusions. This meant that, if the democratic reforms had been allowed to proceed instead of being brutally crushed, they would have attracted mass support and created preconditions for the peaceful transformation of the Soviet system.

Inspired by this scenario, two decades later in 1988–1989, Mikhail Gorbachev decided to repeat the Prague Spring in the Soviet Union. The dismal failure of this attempt was overdetermined by a host of economic, financial, and social-political factors. It proved, once and for all, that there was no possibility for a "third way" in the Soviet or Central European countries for societies to develop without the authoritarian state. The abolition of censorship, cultural liberalization, and political democratization produced an avalanche that swept aside the artificial elitist constructions of reform communism. Then as before in Russian society, reform Communists lacked any genuine base even among the elites, not to mention Russian society at large. Very quickly, the discourse of "democratic socialism" practiced by Gorbachev lost its mass support among educated Russians and even in the Russian segment of the Communist Party. Shattered by the revelations of Gorbachev's glasnost in 1986–1989, Russian nationalism underwent a remarkable transformation: it rejected the vision of Stalin's empire and embraced the prospect of Russia's independence from this empire. This transformation is not the subject of this article. Still, it demonstrated the transitional and illusory nature of the ideas and values that had inspired the Moscow Thaw and the *shestidesyatniki* in the years preceding 1968.

NOTES

1. "Dva tisíce slov," *Literarni listy*, 27 June 1968, reproduced in Jaromír Navrátil, ed., *The Prague Spring 1968* (Budapest: CEU, 1998), 177–81.

2. Aleksandr Tvardovsky, "Rabochie tetradi," *Znamia* 9 (2003): 142–43, 149.

3. Amir Weiner, "Déjà vu All Over Again: Prague Spring, Romanian Summer, and Soviet Autumn on the Soviet Western Frontier," *Contemporary European History* 15, no. 2 (2006): 159–94; Mark Kramer, "Ukraine and the Soviet-Czechoslovak Crisis of 1968," *Cold War International History Project Bulletin* 10 (March 1998).

4. Vladislav Zubok, *Zhivago's Children: The Last Russian Intelligentsia* (Cambridge, MA: Belknap Press of Harvard University Press, 2009).

5. Susanne Schattenberg, "'Democracy' or 'Despotism'? How the Secret Speech Was Translated into Everyday Life," in *The Dilemmas of De-Stalinization: Negotiating*

Cultural and Social Change in the Khrushchev Era, ed. Polly Jones (London: Routledge, 2006), 64–79.

6. S. D. Rozhdestvensky, "Materiali k istorii samodeiatel'nikh politicheskikh ob'edinenii v SSSR posle 1945 goda," *Pamyat': Istoricheskii sbornik*, Vypusk 5 (Moscow: IMCA, 1981–1982), 231–33; interview of Tatiana Kosinova with Lev Krasnopevtsev, 10 August 1992, the Archive of Memorial Society, Moscow.

7. Katerina Gerasimova, "Public Privacy in the Soviet Communal Apartment," in *Public Spheres in Soviet-Type Societies*, ed. Gabor Rittersporn et al. (Frankfurt am Main: P. Lang, 2003); Orlando Figes, *The Whisperers: Private Life in Stalin's Russia* (New York: Metropolitan Books, 2007), 174–86.

8. Ludmilla Alexeyeva and Paul Goldberg, *The Thaw Generation: Coming of Age in the Post-Stalin Era* (Pittsburgh: University of Pittsburgh Press, 1990).

9. Paul R. Josephson, *New Atlantis Revisited: Akademgorodok, the Siberian City of Science* (Princeton, NJ: Princeton University Press, 1997); Anna Eremeeva, *Rossiyskie uchyonye v usloviyakh sotsial'no-politicheskikh transformatsiii XX veka* (St. Petersburg: Nestor, 2006), 137–49.

10. Emily Lygo, "The Need for New Voices: Writers' Union Policy towards Young Writers, 1953–1964," and Susan E. Reid, "Modernizing Socialist Realism in the Khrushchev Thaw: the Struggle for a 'Contemporary Style' in Soviet Art," in Jones, *The Dilemmas of De-Stalinization*, 193–230.

11. On the transformations and contested meanings of the intelligentsia in Soviet Russia see Lynn Mally, *Culture of the Future: The Proletkult Movement in Revolutionary Russia* (Berkeley: University of California Press, 1990); Mark D. Steinberg, *Proletarian Imagination: Self, Modernity, and the Sacred in Russia, 1920–1925* (Ithaca, NY: Cornell University Press, 2002); Katerina Clark, *Petersburg, Crucible of Cultural Revolution* (Cambridge, MA: Harvard University Press, 1995); Boris Uspensky, "Russkaya intelligentsia kak spetsificheskii fenomen russkoy kul'turi," in *Etyudi o russkoy istorii* (St. Petersburg: Azbuka, 2002); D. S. Likhachev, ed., *Russkaya intelligentsia: Istoriya i sud'ba* (Moscow: Nauka, 1999).

12. *Znamya* 7 (2000): 136.

13. Aleksander Solzhenitsyn, *Bodalsya Telenok s Dubom: Ocherki literaturnoy zhizni* (Paris: IMKA, 1975), 63; the diary of Communa-33, TsADKM, f. 193, op. 1, d. 3, ll. 91–92.

14. Kornei Chukovsky on 19 November 1962 in his *Dnevnik 1930–1969* (Moscow: Sovetskii pisatel, 1994), 328; Lidia Chukovskaya, *Zapiski ob Anne Akhmatovoy*, vol. 2 (Paris: YMCA, 1976), 536–57, 552, 556, 560–62.

15. Raisa Orlova and Lev Kopelev, *My zhili v Moskve* (Moscow: Kniga, 1990), 83–84.

16. William Taubman, *Khrushchev: The Man and His Era* (New York: Norton, 2003), 582, 590–95; Rabichev, "Manezh 1962," 132; Andreï Voznesensky, *Proza* (Moscow: Vagrius, 2000), 190–91; Yevgeny Yevtushenko, "Fekhtovanie s navoznoy kuchey," *Volchii pasport* (Moscow: Vagrius, 1998), 196.

17. On the spirit of the 1960s as the ephemeral search for the Third Way, see Tony Judt, *Postwar: A History of Europe Since 1945* (New York: Penguin, 2005), chaps. 11–12.

18. David Samoilov, *Podennye zapisi* (Moscow: Vremia, 2002), 1, 268.

19. Anatoly Smeliansky, *The Russian Theater after Stalin* (Cambridge: Cambridge University Press, 1999), 24–29.

20. Joseph Rothschild and Nancy M. Wingfield, *Return to Diversity: A Political History of East Central Europe since World War II*, 3rd ed. (New York: Oxford University Press, 2000), 73.

21. Vladimir Kozlov and Sergei Mironenko, eds., *Kramola: Inakomyslie v SSSR pri Khrushcheve i Brezhneve 1953–1982 gg.* (Moscow: Materik, 2005), 125; Mikhail Gorbachev, *Zhizn' i reformy*, kniga 1 (Moscow: Novosti, 1995), 84.

22. Vera Sandomirsky-Dunham's recollections during her meeting with the author, Washington, DC, 3 October 1999.

23. Recollection of Rada Adzhubei, in *Pressa v obshchestve*, 18; Aleksei Adzhubey, *Krushenie illyuzii* (Moscow: Izd-vo SP "Interbuk," 1991), 205.

24. For an explanation of this phenomenon, see Yuri Slezkine, *The Jewish Century* (Princeton, NJ: Princeton University Press, 2004).

25. Vassily Aksyonov, "TsPKO im. Ginzburga," *Moskovskie Novosti*, 8 August 2002.

26. Vladimir Shlapentokh, *Strakh i druzhba v nashem totalitarnom proshlom* (St. Petersburg: Zvezda, 2003), 132.

27. On the role of the intelligentsia as a generator of nationalism and the special inhibitions operative in the Russian case, see Nathaniel Knight, "Was the Intelligentsia Part of the Nation? Visions of Society in Post-Emancipation Russia," *Kritika* 7, no. 4 (Fall 2006): 733–58. On the nationalist trends among Russian intellectuals, see Yitzhak M. Brudny, *Reinventing Russia: Russian Nationalism and the Soviet State, 1953–1991* (Cambridge, MA: Harvard University Press, 1998); Nikolai Mitrokhin, *Russkaya partiya: Dvizhenie russkikh natsionalistov v SSSR 1953–1985* (Moscow: Novoe literaturnoe obozrenie, 2003); Geoffrey Hosking, *Rulers and Victims: The Russians in the Soviet Union* (Cambridge, MA: Harvard University Press, 2006), 345–52.

28. S. V. Volkov, *Intellektualnyi sloi v sovetskom obshchestve* (Moscow: Fond Razvitie, 1999), 30–31, 126–27.

29. Paul R. Josephson, *New Atlantis Revisited*, 23; L. G. Churchward, *The Soviet Intelligentsia* (London, Routledge, 1973), 9.

30. The role of Tvardovsky and *Novy Mir* in the 1960s remains contested in Russian publications to this day. See, for example, Yuri Burtin, "O Staliniste Tvardovskom, kotoryi terpel i molchal," *Nezavisimaya gazeta*, 8 April 2000; Regina Romanova, *Alexandr Tvardovsky: Trudy i dni* (Moscow: Vodolei, 2006); E. Vysochina, ed., *A. Tvardovsky, M. Gefter: XX vek, Gologrammy poeta i istorika* (Moscow: Novii khronograf, 2005).

31. Vladimir Shlapentokh, *Strakh i druzhba v nashem totalitarnom proshlom* (St. Petersburg: Zvezda, 2003), 169–74; physicist Arseny Berezin to the author, interview in Washington, DC, 15 November 2000.

32. Shlapentokh, *Soviet Intellectuals and Political Power: The Post-Stalin Era* (Princeton, NJ: Princeton University Press, 1990), 172; also see Malin notes in A. A. Fursenko, ed., *Prezidium TsK. 1954–1964. Chernovyie protokol'nyie zapisi zasedanyi. Stenogrammi. Postanovleniya*, vol. 1 (Moscow: ROSSPEN, 2003), 865; and Rudolf Pikhoia, *Sovetskii Soiuz: Istoriya Vlasti, 1945–1991* (Moscow: RAGS, 1998), 283.

33. KGB to the CC CPSU, 3 March 1965, RGANI f. 5, op. 30. 462. ll. 19–22.

34. On Soviet economic debates, see Moshe Lewin, *Stalinism and the Seeds of Soviet Reform: The Debates of the 1960s* (Armonk, NY: M. E. Sharpe, 1991), 134–35; Pekka Sutela, *Socialism, Planning, and Optimality: A Study in Soviet Economic Thought* (Helsinki: Societas Scientiarum Fennica, 1984). On the role of cybernetics, see Slava Gerovitch, *From Newspeak to Cyberspeak: A History of Soviet Cybernetics* (Boston: MIT Press, 2002); Nikolai Krementsov, *Stalinist Science* (Princeton, NJ: Princeton University Press, 1997).

35. Roy Medvedev, "Dissidenty o dissidentstve," *Znamya-plus* (1997/1998): 171; Aleksandr Solzhenitsyn, "Obrazovantshina," in *Iz-pod glyb* (Paris: YMCA, 1974) and reprinted in Likhachev, *Russkaya Intelligentsia*, 136.

36. Robert English, *Russia and the Idea of the West: Gorbachev, Intellectuals, and the End of the Cold War* (New York: Columbia University Press, 2000).

37. Report of Martin Schtigler, "The Youth of the Soviet Union," 14th Conference of the Institute for the Study of the USSR, Munich, 1962, 70, the Open Society Archive, Budapest, The Collection of "The Red Archive," Box 497; Philip Hanson, *The Rise and Fall of the Soviet Economy* (London: Longman, 2003), 97.

38. An American journalist wrote in October 1968 that most signers of collective letters (*podpisanty*) were from Moscow. In terms of professions, the group's composition was as follows: thirty-four civil engineers, twenty-four physicist-mathematicians, twenty-two philologists, twenty writers, seventeen mathematicians, seventeen teachers, fifteen scientific researchers, thirteen undergraduate students, ten literary critics, ten historians, nine editors, nine graduate students, eight physicists, eight philosophers, seven economists, seven translators, seven linguists, and six art critics, among others. The only sizable group outside the capital included the scientists from the Novosibirsk Akademgorodok. Paul A. Smith Jr., "Protest in Moscow," *Foreign Affairs* (October 1968).

39. Vladimir Shlapentokh, *Soviet Intellectuals*, 174.

40. B. A. Grushin, *Chetyre Zhizni Rossii v zerkale oprosov obshchestvennogo mneniya. Epokha Brezhneva (1)* (Moscow: Progress-Traditsiia, 2003), 29–30.

41. John Scott's speech for the NYU Radio Liberty Conference, "On Communication with Soviet Youth, 10 March 1967," The Open Society Archive, Budapest, 300/80, Box 496.

42. Grushin, *Chetyre zhizni Rossii v zerkale oprosov obshchestvennogo mneniya*, 101–15; KGB to the CC CPSU, 5 November 1968, *Istoricheskii arkhiv* 1 (1994): 175–207.

43. Jeremi Suri, "The Promise and Failure of 'Developed Socialism,'" *Contemporary European History* 15, no. 2 (2006).

44. Victor Zaslavsky, *The Neo-Stalinist State* (Armonk, NY: M. E. Sharpe, 1982), 48–51.

45. More details in English, *Russia and the Idea of the West*, 70–72.

46. Aleksandr Bovin, *XX vek kak zhizn'. Vospominaniya* (Moscow: Zakharov, 2003), 180–84; Nikolai Shmelev, "Curriculum vitae," *Znamya-plus* (1997–1998): 112.

47. Shmelev, "Curriculum vitae," 112.

48. Bovin, *XX vek kak zhizn'*, 189.

49. Mikhail Agursky, *Pepel Klaasa* (Jerusalem: URA, 1988), 328.

50. Vladimir Lukin, "Tanki na zakate leta," *Literaturnaya Gazeta*, 18 August 1993; English, *Russia and the Idea of the West*, 110–11.

51. Arkady Vaksberg, *Moya zhizn' v zhizni*, vol. 1 (Moscow: Terra Sport, 2000), 342, 391, 397.

52. Maya Turovskaya to the author, 25 June 2000, Moscow; also Tony Judt, *Postwar*, 421.

53. Andrei Sakharov, *Progress, Peaceful Coexistence, and Intellectual Freedom* (New York: Norton, 1968).

54. Yevtushenko, *Volchii passport*, 299–301.

55. Weiner, "Déjà Vue All Over Again," 181; Augursky, *Pepel Klaasa*, 329; A. Alexandrov to the CC CPSU, 3 July 1969, in V. I. Fomin, *Kino i Vlast'. Sovetskoe kino—1965–1985 godi. Dokumenti. Svidetel'stva. Razmyshleniya* (Moscow: Materik, 1996), 337–42.

56. Recollections of Natalia Gorbanevskaya, "Chto pomniu ia o demonstratsii," *Prava Cheloveka v Rossii*, http://www.hro.org/editions/karta/nr21/demonstr.htm (accessed 13 July 2008).

57. Mikhail Gorbachev, *Zhizn' i reformy*, vol. 1 (Moscow: Novosti, 1995), 117–19, 157–59.

58. See English, *Russia and the Idea of the West*, 111.

59. Yevtushenko, *Volchii passport*, 299–301.

60. Igor Dedkov, "Kak trudno dayutsia inye dni!—Iz dnevnikovikh zapisey1953–1974 godov," *Novyi Mir* 5 (1996): 144; Information from Vladimir Pechatnov, MGIMO student in 1968, 11 November 2006; Weiner, "Déjà Vu All Over Again," 190.

61. Gorbachev, *Zhizn' i reformy*, 1:119.

62. Gorbachev, *Zhizn' i reformy*, 1:157–59.

63. G. S. Batygin, ed., *Rossiiskaya sotsiologiya shestidesiatykh godov v vospominaniyakh i dokumentakh* (St. Petersburg: Russkii khristianskii gumanitarnii institut, 1999), 398; Smeliansky, *The Russian Theater after Stalin*, 29–30.

64. Dmitry Furman, "Perestroika glazami moskovskogo gumanitariya," in *Proriv k svobode. O perestroyke dvadtsat' let spustia (kriticheskiy analiz)*, ed. Boris Kuvaldin (Moscow: Alpina Biznes Buks, 2005), 316–19.

5

Politburo Decision-Making on the Czechoslovak Crisis in 1968

Mikhail Prozumenshchikov

You will understand that we had no choice.

The forty years that separate us from the Czechoslovak crisis in 1968 is, historically speaking, a relatively short time span for historians to arrive at a balanced analysis of those events and to publish both the key facts and the relevant details that are needed for a comprehensive historical reconstruction of the "Prague Spring." This kind of reconstruction has, in part, been made possible by archives in the countries of the former Socialist system becoming accessible and above all by the possibility of doing research on documents of the supreme organ, the Communist Party of the Soviet Union (CPSU), which ceased to exist in 1991.[1] Archival material that has become available for the first time only during the last few years has been the basis for studying the most diverse aspects of the Prague Spring, notably the political processes that were played out among the top ranks of the Soviet leadership and that ultimately resulted in the military invasion of the independent "fraternal state."

What is of supreme interest in the present context, in addition to drafts of resolutions and other documents that served as the basis for forthcoming announcements, are resolutions of the Politburo of the Central Committee (CC) of the CPSU, the de facto, though not the de jure, highest organ in the system of the Soviet party and the Soviet state. An analysis of these documents enhances our understanding of how the mixing of political ingredients was actually performed and of what mechanisms were at work in decision making with regard to the Czechoslovak crisis. Obviously, quite a few of the decisions that were to prove final were made on the spur of the moment during actual Politburo meetings. However, as a rule these meetings served for the rubberstamping of documents that had been elaborated in advance and had already met with all-round approval. It was an exception for these documents to be returned to the sender for further elaboration, and it was even more unusual for them to be rejected altogether. In cases where discussions flared up in the Politburo and issues were hotly contested—the atmosphere in the meetings encouraged speeches which were often emotional rather than coolly rational in character—participants' role in the meeting was to demonstrate agreement with the leading figures of the party hierarchy. The final editing of the documents then took place in calmer waters, and the politician in charge of putting the final touches to the draft had the opportunity and, above all, the leisure to weigh carefully all the pros and cons and to come up with a result that was as finely honed for the purpose as possible. The many instances in which Soviet leaders returned to drafts of documents again and again to introduce major changes to texts that had already been edited by their own hand before are all cases in point.

The materials of the Politburo of the CC CPSU from the months before the invasion can be grouped as belonging to four different stages, by means of which it is possible to trace the change of heart on the part of the Soviet leadership with regard to the "Czechoslovak problem."

THE PERCEPTION OF THE PRAGUE SPRING
BY THE POLITBURO OF THE CC CPSU

In what may be considered the first stage, January and February 1968, relative calm was observed in Moscow vis-à-vis developments in the Czechoslovak Socialist Republic (ČSSR). Activities were limited to noting that the situation in the country was difficult and contradictory and to attempting to "give support" to the Czechoslovak leadership, be it in political, economic, or military/technical terms.[2]

The beginning of the second stage can be dated to March 1968 when a far-reaching review of the Soviet position took place with regard to Soviet-Czechoslovak relations. Prior to this date, it had been the resolution of the Central Committee of the Communist Party of Czechoslovakia's (CC KSČ) presidium to abolish censorship in Czechoslovakia that had been the greatest cause for worry for the USSR; now, at the beginning of spring, the incipient mass dismissal of "preselected" functionaries at the medium and lower levels, for which the free press was largely responsible, rattled Moscow.[3] It did so all the more since all attempts by the USSR to obtain from the Czechoslovak leadership an assessment of the situation had produced no solid result so far. What Prague transmitted to Moscow was reassuring announcements that everything was under control. At the same time, members of the presidium of the CC of the Communist Party of Czechoslovakia

(KSČ) were making statements in their speeches to huge audiences that diametrically contradicted this.

The first signal that might have alerted observers to the fact that Moscow had moved beyond the stage of carefully monitoring developments in the ČSSR and was now beginning to nurse grave misgivings was a letter of the ČSSR CPSU to the KSČ leadership, which was discussed in the Politburo meeting of the CC CPSU on 15 March. The draft of the letter, prepared by Foreign Minister Andrei Gromyko and the then head of the CC Department for Relations with Communist Parties in Socialist Countries and the head of the KGB, Yuri Andropov, was drastically revised.[4] The revision resulted in underscoring the two key theses: anticommunist forces were trying to establish a capitalist system in Czechoslovakia, and the Western countries were trying to drive a wedge between the members of the Warsaw Pact by dragging "free" Czechoslovakia off to join NATO. Formulations that appeared to take matters to extremes (such as statements like "While you are coasting along in the wake of the reactionaries, Fascism is rearing its head in Germany"[5]) were ultimately left out, yet the overhauled document was still quite harsh in comparison to the first version.

On the same day, three letters of the Ministry of Defense to the Czechoslovak leadership were discussed in the Presidium session. The topics of these missives were the visit of a delegation of the Political Administration of the Red Army and the Navy, command-staff exercises to be conducted by the armies of Warsaw Pact countries on the territory of Czechoslovakia, and an invitation to the USSR of a Czechoslovak military delegation.[6] Three days later, it was decided that only the last letter was actually going to be forwarded to Prague; a brief note attached to this resolution states that "the missives regarding the command-staff exercises and the Soviet military delegation's visit to the ČSSR . . . have not been dispatched on account of the ongoing changes in the leadership of the ČSSR."[7] The changes mentioned here apparently referred to the enforced resignation of Antonín Novotný from the post of president of the ČSSR. This development caused great ill feeling among Soviet leaders, for only two months earlier, when Novotný had had to vacate the post of general secretary of the CC KSČ to accommodate Alexander Dubček, both Novotný himself and Moscow had been given assurances that Novotný would be safe in his post as president of the state under any circumstances. It does not come as a surprise therefore that, given the latest twist, the Soviet leadership felt downright betrayed by the new KSČ leaders.[8]

It has to be borne in mind that the general secretary of the CC CPSU, Leonid Brezhnev, was caught in a most precarious dilemma at that stage. Through his trip to Prague in December 1967, when the "endless plenum" of the CC KSČ was in session there, he de facto gave a hand up to the leader of the "new wave," Dubček; afterwards, feeling responsible for his protégé, he constantly tried to defend and protect him. Even within the Socialist camp, he singled out Dubček for special support. On the occasion of the twentieth anniversary of the Communist takeover of power (the "Victory of the Czechoslovak Working Class" in February 1948),[9] for instance, it was none other than Brezhnev who insisted that the Eastern European countries dispatch their highest ranking party delegations to Prague.[10] At the same time, the majority of members of the CC CPSU felt intensely uncomfortable about the new KSČ leader right from the start. He was criticized for his indecisiveness, for the constant concessions he made to rightist forces, for his weak interpretation of Marxism, and so forth. This criticism hurt Brezhnev as well, if indirectly, and he was compelled at a later stage, when the misgivings of the Soviet leaders concerning Dubček increasingly turned out to be justified, to prove to all and sundry that he had supported "Sasha"[11] only until the latter began, through his activities (or the lack thereof), to jeopardize the "achievements of socialism" in Czechoslovakia.[12]

If there were differences of opinion in the Politburo of the CC CPSU regarding developments in Czechoslovakia, these did not go beyond what was usual in discussions. They most certainly did not amount to a split of the Soviet leadership into a "liberal Western" and an "internationalist Leninist" camp, as is sometimes asserted in the literature, notably in Western literature. A comparable split of the CPSU leadership (into "conservatives" and "revisionists") occurred much later. At the time being discussed in this chapter, the positions held by the Soviet leaders were determined in many ways by their personal perception of the Czechoslovak crisis; their perception was, in turn, shaped by the amount of information to which they had access, by their own political experience, and by the position they occupied in the hierarchies of party and state. The imperative calls to "reestablish order" in Czechoslovakia articulated by the defense minister of the USSR, Andrei Grechko, and by Petro Shelest, a Politburo member, are easy enough to understand as justified, given their point of view. The former worried about weakening the defensive potential of the Warsaw Pact on the one hand and, on the other, about a possible "depropagandization" of the soldiers of the Czechoslovak People's Army which might result, should the "Day X" dawn, in former "brothers in arms" turning into a military power bent on active resistance.[13] Shelest, who was also the general secretary of the Communist Party of Ukraine, feared that the "Czechoslovak contagion" might spread to his republic, particularly to its western regions. The positions of other Soviet leaders were not quite as clear cut and were occasionally modified in one direction or another, dependent on circumstances.

Mikhail Latysh in particular comes to the conclusion, in the light of the interviews he conducted and recorded at the end of the 1980s and the beginning of the 1990s with people who had inside knowledge of the apparatus of the CC CPSU—namely Vadim Zagladin, Ivan Udal'tsov, and

Aleksandr Bovin—that the Soviet prime minister, Aleksei Kosygin, always considered rather "weak" in the West, maintained, in fact, a "consistently rigorous" attitude toward both the ideas of the Prague Spring and the majority of the Czechoslovak political leaders associated with it.[14]

On the one hand, this view might well be true. What commends it, for example, is the CC CPSU missive of 15 March mentioned above. Kosygin's comments on the draft of this resolution were by far the most rigorous and the least inclined to compromise.[15] On the other hand, it must be remembered that on his return from Karlovy Vary, where he was said "to be taking the waters,"[16] the same Kosygin gave a very moderate assessment of the situation in the ČSSR;[17] later, he tried repeatedly—and urged his colleagues in the part leadership to do the same—to come up with an answer to the most difficult of questions, namely: "So, having marched our troops into Czechoslovakia, what do we do next?"[18] He was raising the issue of an exit strategy.

Differences in the assessment of the situation in the ČSSR and of the extent of a potential interference in its internal affairs were to be observed not only in the higher reaches of the political hierarchy. The *Pravda* correspondent Aleksei Lukovets, who had spent the month of May in Prague, reported on serious differences of opinion within the Soviet embassy in Prague on the "crisis in the country." Even though Ambassador Stepan Chervonenko favored, according to the journalist's reports, an objective assessment and warned against mistakenly equating the KSČ's line with the opinions of isolated individuals, the embassy's minister, Udal'tsov, insisted that the only proper course to take was rigorously to criticize all developments in the country, including the line taken by the leadership of the CC KSČ and continued to dispatch notably negative reports to Moscow.[19] It was obvious that Udal'tsov's course was in alignment with that of the Kremlin hardliners. It must, however, be borne in mind that the information issuing from the embassy nevertheless contributed, whether by design or otherwise, to the assessment the Soviet leadership formed of the Czechoslovak crisis.

The Kremlin's frantic search for solutions to the "Czechoslovak problem" and the ambivalent positions of the Soviet leaders with regard to this issue become apparent from the genesis of another Politburo resolution. This resolution concerns the preparation of an information communiqué for Communist Party leaders in a number of Eastern European countries on the results of Kosygin's visit to Karlovy Vary. The original draft was again subjected to several rather drastic revisions (not all of which were subsequently incorporated into the final text). The contradictory nature of those that were incorporated imparts an air of incompleteness and ambivalence to the final result.

Among the proposals was the inclusion of several lengthy passages (the so-called expanded version of the missive), which contained a more detailed description of the situation in the ČSSR and in the KSČ leadership and was designed to illustrate the salient points of the developments by means of concrete examples.[20] One of the sponsors of this variant was the Chairman of the Supreme Soviet of the USSR, Nikolai Podgornyi, who had been Shelest's predecessor as party leader of Ukraine. The following points of his variants are particularly noteworthy, even though they were not included in the final document. First, more emphasis was put on the understanding Dubček and the other Czechoslovak leaders showed for the situation that had developed in the ČSSR. Secondly, it repeated the urgent request voiced by leading figures in the KSČ and addressed to the CPSU and the other fraternal parties "not to take any steps that might speculatively be exploited by the enemies of socialism to undermine the authority of the present KSČ leadership and of the ČSSR and that might give comfort within Czechoslovakia to tendencies hostile to fraternal countries and parties."[21] All this was left out in the final version of the document.

In what was arguably a first, doubts were expressed openly in the resolution as to the capability of the KSČ leadership and of the ČSSR "to rally the healthy forces around them, take the initiative into their own hands and strike back at the intrigues of the counterrevolution."[22] The final version of the document, which was ultimately dispatched to the leaders of those countries that were soon to participate in the invasion, referred to the fact that it was impossible to say with certainty whether the ČSSR leadership was capable, if the need arose, to take "decisive action, including the use of force, for instance, by workers' militias."[23] Yet in the preparatory stage of the document, part of the Politburo successfully advocated the inclusion of an additional formulation of proposals to assist the KSČ and the ČSSR that would readily be understood by everyone, including "an alternative type of help that might become necessary if events take a negative turn."[24]

Evident from the documents are the shifts in the Soviet leaders' position regarding the possibilities and capabilities of the so-called healthy forces in the Czechoslovak leadership to keep the situation under control. At the beginning of 1968, the KSČ leadership is perceived in the Soviet documents as a monolithic force engaged in the struggle against the class enemy's "hostile" and "antisocialist" intrigues. In a next stage, particularly after the mass dismissal of party leaders of the old guard, which was implemented under the motto of "new politics with new people," a terminology is promptly at hand in the Kremlin for the groups to which the Czechoslovak leaders are supposed to belong: "the rightists," "the indecisive," and "the healthy forces." Even Dubček was counted among the "indecisive" more and more often, even if it was impossible for the USSR to discount his enormous popularity in the party and in the country. This was also the reason why there was little else that could be done in the existing situation than regularly and insistently to tell Dubček to be guided by the judgment of the "healthy forces" within the KSČ leadership, to rely on them, and so forth. It was noted in Moscow with growing unease that these "healthy forces" were getting steadily fewer and weaker. One of the alterations that Brezhnev undertook in the above-mentioned resolution "On the Results of Kosygin's Visit to the ČSSR" may look insignificant at first sight, yet it is, in fact, extremely telling in this context. In the sentence "The majority of the KSČ and the ČSSR leaders make noticeable efforts to consolidate the healthy forces around them," the general secretary substituted the phrase "part of" for "the majority."[25] The resolution was passed with this alteration. It is obvious that the Soviet head of state was motivated in this by the information he had received from Czechoslovakia (and above all by what Kosygin's visit had netted). This amounted to a virtual acceptance of the fact that the "healthy forces" in the Czechoslovak leadership were no longer in the majority and had, in fact, lost control of the situation.

That the situation in the ČSSR dominated Soviet foreign policy in the summer of 1968 can be inferred from the steadily growing number of CC decisions and resolutions revolving around the Czechoslovak problem. From May onward, issues related to Czechoslovakia were on the agenda of Politburo sessions at least once a week and sometimes more often. During the same period, a special commission was called into being by a Politburo decision and charged with the task "of dealing with questions concerning Czechoslovakia in an operative manner and to submit, when called upon to do so, their proposals in the CC CPSU."[26] The amount of information reaching the CC from a number of different organizations and from Soviet individuals who were either permanently residing in the ČSSR or visited the country in an official capacity (delegations of party officials, representatives of twin towns, scientists, artists, and so forth) rose steadily.

As regards the analysis of decisions and resolutions on Czechoslovakia that were hammered out and adopted in Politburo sessions, it is necessary to underscore several characteristic peculiarities. There was above all the tendency to adopt a more cautious and moderate attitude in assessing the situation. CC documents dating from spring 1968 mostly tended to assume a more demanding, threatening tone in the final version compared to their original draft. At times, one gets the impression that Moscow was ready every day to use military force. The beginning of summer saw a complete reversal of this situation. Much confrontational language was either deleted from the drafts altogether or at least toned down. This was all the more remarkable because the situation in the ČSSR deteriorated steadily in the eyes of the leading Soviet figures themselves! This can be explained, in part, by Moscow worrying it was exposing itself to charges of exerting "excessive pressure" on Prague. In addition to this, the Soviet leadership, which was well aware of the complexity of the situation, was still trying to get Dubček to "re-establish order in the country of his own free will," as he had already repeatedly promised.

In Politburo documents dating from this phase, other, more general common characteristics are to be found. First, all the numerous references were deleted from almost all final versions of resolutions pertaining to "rightists" in Czechoslovakia rallying under the banners of the struggle against the "legacy of the personality cult," the "dominance of the conservative party nomenclature," and so forth. Secondly, care was taken not to conjure up facile associations by avoiding in the documents all kinds of comparison of the situation in the ČSSR with the events in Hungary twelve years earlier. On the other hand, in drafts of Politburo resolutions as well as in analyses of the Czechoslovak crisis within the framework of the Warsaw Pact and even in speeches before Soviet audiences (for instance in Brezhnev's speech in the plenum of the CC CPSU on 17 July), such comparisons were openly made.[27]

At the same time, the unmistakable parallels inevitably influenced the Soviet leaders in elaborating and adopting resolutions on Czechoslovakia. Andropov, who had been the Soviet ambassador to Budapest in 1956 and had witnessed the Hungarian Revolution on the spot, said as late as March 1968 that "the methods and forms that were being applied in Czechoslovakia, were strongly reminiscent of the Hungarian ones. . . . In Hungary things also started to get moving in this way."[28] In addition to broad similarities in terms of the general situation (economic problems, a precipitous decline in the authority of the Communist Party, demands for changes in the political system, the revitalization of diverse political clubs and civic associations, strongly marked anti-Soviet and anticommunist tendencies in the mass media), there were less obvious correspondences, which might have escaped an outside observer, but did not go unnoticed in the Kremlin. Just as in the summer of 1956, when Moscow was driven by the fear "to betray its principles and show weakness" and did everything in its power to keep the Stalinist Mátyás Rákosi in power, so now the USSR was just as desperate (and equally unsuccessful!) in keeping Novotný at least in the post of the Czechoslovak president. In 1956, the future Hungarian Communist Party leader János Kádár rose in the eyes of the Kremlin within a few months from a "right-wing opportunist" to a "dedicated Marxist-Leninist"; in Czechoslovakia twelve years later, Gustáv Husák, who had been classified as "politically suspect" only a short while, before quickly accumulated bonus points in the assessment of the Soviet leaders, who were casting around for an acceptable candidate to replace Dubček. Another similarity, if a coincidental one, is the fact that in both cases Poland played a role in the initial stages.[29] There was one more detail which was deeply embarrassing for the USSR under the existing circumstances, namely the tenth anniversary of the execution in the summer of 1958 of Imre Nagy—his face one of the emblems of the Hungarian Revolution. The Czechoslovak "free press" commemorated this event with an openly anticommunist article, which caused great indignation in Moscow. An explanation was immediately supplied by Dubček.[30]

There were, however, also basic differences between events in Hungary and in Czechoslovakia. This is particularly noticeable in the attitudes of the leading Soviet figures, most of whom were working hard to avoid a solution that involved the use of force. Moscow realized that however much cause the USSR might have to complain to the world about the intrigues of imperialism and Western plots against Socialist Czechoslovakia, "reestablishing order" in the Eastern Bloc through the use of military means was only going to give the world at large one more reason to doubt the viability and the progressive character of socialism. This is presumably why the military maneuver of the Warsaw Pact countries, which were conducted on Czechoslovak territory in June 1968, did not escalate into a military intervention, despite the fears (or conversely, the expectations) harbored by many. Not even the delay in the evacuation from Czechoslovakia of the Soviet troops after the maneuver, which was immediately branded as "massive meddling in the internal affairs of the ČSSR" by the country's press, was directly related to the invasion, the preparations for which had already been completed.[31]

By the standards of the Hungarian revolutionaries, the Czechoslovak reformers proceeded with extreme caution and circumspection, for the simple reason that they, too, feared a replay of the events in Hungary. They also had many more possibilities for maneuvering and for accomplishing the tasks they had set themselves one by one. In Hungary, Rákosi was succeeded by András Hegedűs (who actually pursued the same course as his predecessor), and the reformer Nagy did not take over as head of state until the revolution was already underway. By contrast, Dubček assumed power in Czechoslovakia straightaway; there were no intermediaries, even though candidates for the part might have been found among Novotný's supporters, such as Josef Lenárt, Bohumír Lomski, or other top functionaries.

Yet it was precisely this evolutionary development of events which seemed most ominous to the Soviet nomenclature and almost automatically spurred them into decisive action. Fear was rife in the USSR that one might fail to notice—and preempt—that moment when Czechoslovakia would metamorphose into a bourgeois, democratic country with all the baleful consequences for the Socialist camp. There was, of course, the additional prospect that a restoration of the capitalist system was not going to be accomplished without bloodshed; in Moscow, there was even talk of the danger of a civil war in Czechoslovakia. Whatever the scenario, it was reasonable to assume that military intervention under the rapidly changing circumstances would take a great toll, both in human lives and in political and economic terms. The fear of "delaying the re-establishment of order" until it was too late, on the one hand, and the blatant difference between the bloody uprising of the people in Budapest in October 1956 and peaceful Prague in July 1968, on the other, created a situation that made it extremely difficult for Moscow to explain even to its most stalwart supporters its reasons for what looked from outside like a totally inadequate reaction to the developments in the ČSSR.

To an extent, Dubček himself also contributed to the invasion in that his constant promises of an imminent improvement in the situation (which never materialized) caused the number of Soviet leaders who advocated the use of force to solve the problem to grow. Dubček even gave specific dates. First the promise was made that sweeping changes for the better would occur after the "April plenum" of the CC KSČ, which was going to give the green light to the Czechoslovak Communist Party's "Action Program." In Moscow, some felt the "program" had several flaws, yet given the circumstances, it was not reasonable to expect that anything better could be cobbled together. This "program" was never realized. At the end of May, Dubček gave a new pledge to Kosygin that the forthcoming plenum was going to make all the difference. The resolutions that were going to be adopted by it would bring about a drastically altered situation and enable the KSČ leader at long last to take an "offensive line."[32] The plenum came, the plenum went, and things continued the same as before. The same scenario was played out again at the next plenum, on which Dubček had also pinned the hope that it was going to make a change. It was, therefore, no coincidence that there was no one left in Moscow who still gave credence to the assurances of the Czechoslovak party leader that the forthcoming 14th Party Conference of the KSČ was going to bring the "breakthrough." To be precise, it was the other way round. A commonly held belief in the USSR was that this party conference would prove "decisive," but not in the sense Dubček meant. The belief had taken hold that this party forum was going to yield the result that the Czechoslovak party leader and his supporters were ousted from power, that the KSČ would end up demoralized and in a shambles for good, and that power would be seized by "reactionary" forces. It was a deeply apprehensive Brezhnev who voiced these concerns and who remarked that "a way out of the present impasse could also be the elimination of all the present members of the Presidium of the CC KSČ from the party leadership."[33]

Any discussion of the demands and claims that Moscow addressed to Prague must underscore the fact that issues connected to reforms of the ČSSR's economy always took second place, even though Ota Šik's reforms were clearly angled at a market economy. In part, this may have been due to the Soviet leadership's deeply held conviction that these reforms were doomed to early failure—price rises, soaring rates of unemployment, and other side effects of such reforms would necessarily, in the Kremlin's rationale, trigger vociferous protest among the majority of Czechoslovakia's population, particularly among the working class. This assessment was compounded by an assumption that was widely shared in the Soviet Union and in the other East European countries—namely that the actual economic situation in the ČSSR was not as bleak as the Czechoslovak leadership as well as the "rightist forces" chose to paint it. The leader of the Socialist Unity Party of Germany (*Sozialistische Einheitspartei Deutschlands*, or SED), Walter Ulbricht, went so far as to assume that the ČSSR's regular pleas directed at the USSR for economic and financial aid were no more than moves in the great political game the Czechoslovak leadership was playing and had one sole objective: in case the request was turned down by the USSR, the ČSSR would "have no choice" but to turn to the West for help.[34]

On the other hand, such problems as free mass media and a possible shift in the political system of ČSSR which would include the creation of a multiparty system, featured prominently in Soviet party documents. It may be said that the Kremlin was panic-stricken at the idea of the Czechoslovak society losing its ideological focus, a process signaled, in the eyes of the Politburo members, by the stirrings of the Czechoslovak Social Democrats. It was feared in Moscow at first that once the Social Democrats returned to the political stage, they would develop into a major player capable of toppling the Communists, seizing power, and guiding the country to the "bourgeois fold." However, as events unfolded the danger increased that the KSČ itself was doomed for a de facto disintegration and that part of it was going to become the basis for the newly emergent social democracy. This was a development that had to be prevented by the USSR at all costs. Since a comparable scenario was within the bounds of probability at the 24th Party Conference of the KSČ, which was scheduled for autumn, the very fact that this party forum was drawing near, particularly when seen in conjunction with the ambivalence of the policies of the KSČ leadership, was one of the reasons for the ultimate fatal twist in this saga.

One of the virtually insoluble problems was that Czechoslovakia's mass media had been freed from the constraints of censorship in January 1968. Originally, the USSR had even been prepared to accept a measure of Czechoslovak glasnost until the consistent one-sidedness of what was happening became evident.[35] The pendulum abruptly changed direction. In the past, it had been impossible to circumvent the control of the party and get into print negative reports on the CPSU, the KSČ, Soviet-Czechoslovak relations, and so forth. Now it was almost equally impossible to find any positive reports in the Czechoslovak mass media on any of these topics. In the USSR, statesmen noted with rising indignation that in the Czechoslovak mass media "all Communists" were automatically tagged as conservative; that "Communists who had become the target of public criticism and vilification had no possibility of defending their point of view," simply because papers would not accept their statements for publication; and that "there was no freedom of information" any longer in Czechoslovakia, only "freedom for political thuggery and the complete and utter defenselessness of those who were methodically victimized by the press."[36]

Such grievances may sound strange, particularly when uttered by political leaders who had been using similar and even more drastic methods in the struggle with their political opponents for decades. Nevertheless, it was the activities of the Czechoslovak mass media that irked the Soviet leadership the most, and in the last resort, they provided one of the most important impulses for the USSR's decision in favor of armed intervention. Both in Moscow and in Prague, people knew only too well what a crucial role the Czechoslovak mass media and the propaganda spread by them was playing in the situation as it actually existed. This was also why a compromise in this area was improbable from the start. Even in the earliest stages of the military operation Soviet leaders claimed repeatedly that Prague was rife with underground radio stations ("One radio station has its neck twisted; another one takes its place"), and Soviet troops encountered the first major resistance precisely when they were about to take the radio and TV center in Prague.[37]

Ultimately the main charge that was leveled at the KSČ's leadership was one of utter helplessness and ineptitude (or a lack of inclination) when confronted with the task of reestablishing control of the country. Moscow did what it could to alert Dubček to the fact that many local party organizations either ignored or contravened the resolutions of the presidium of the CC; that members of the presidium kept on announcing in public the most contradictory political principles; and that the KSČ leadership did not muster the resistance that was required—not even when socialism and the party itself were targeted. One of these attacks—the opposition manifesto of the "2,000 Words," which the Czechoslovak leadership again failed to rebuff adequately in the Kremlin's opinion—became in many ways the point of no return in Soviet-Czechoslovak relations and marks the beginning of the third stage.

This stage is marked by the fact that the majority of Soviet leaders had come to the conclusion that a military intervention was inevitable. Moscow's final running out of patience can be reconstructed in detail from the discussion and elaboration of the following memorandum of the CC CPSU to the CC KSČ (particularly on the occasion of the manifesto of the "2,000 Words") as well as from the steps that Soviet leadership took immediately afterwards.

The first draft of the memorandum as well as the outlines for the meeting between the Soviet ambassador and Dubček at Brezhnev's behest were prepared by Mikhail Suslov, Boris Ponomaryov, and Konstantin Rusakov and presented to the members and candidate members of the Politburo of the CC CPSU on 29 June 1968.[38] The prepared document did not satisfy the majority of the Soviet leadership despite the harshness of a number of formulations. Comments and suggestions poured in from all sides whose common denominator was a hardening of the Soviet position and demanding from the Czechoslovak leaders decisive and, above all, immediate, action.[39] Even from faraway Uzbekistan, a cable arrived from first secretary of the Communist Party of that republic containing similar demands.[40] The arguably weightiest proposals came from Aleksandr Shelepin, who not only demanded finalizing an agreement with the CC KSČ that would cover all the details but a redraft of the entire text of the document,[41] for he considered it "pointless" to dispatch the original version, given the fact "that we have already spoken on more than one occasion with [the KSČ leaders] along the selfsame lines contained in the memorandum that has now been forwarded to the comrades in the Politburo."[42]

After a number of alterations the document wound up being discussed in a session of the Poliburo for two days, on 2 and 3 July, and it took several rounds of voting for it to be passed by the leaders of the CPSU.[43] The resolution was fairly nonpartisan in tone, despite the fact that not nearly all proposals put forward by some in the Soviet leadership were incorporated into the final text. For instance, a passage claiming that the CPSU "was sympathetic to the resolutions of the latest plenum of the CC KSČ, which were aimed at streamlining administrative procedures and methods and at speeding up progress along the road of Socialism," was deleted from the original version. After the statement that "rightist forces had no support among the broad mass of the workers" the warning was inserted that, the situation being what it was, this "did not mean they might not be successful after all"; this warning had been missing in the first draft.[44] In some cases, compromise variants carried the day. The draft of the missive spoke of "many" Czechoslovak mass media outlets that were controlled by elements hostile to the party. The hardliners wanted to substitute "nearly all" for "many"; the final version has the more moderate phrase "the most important mass media."[45]

At the same time, open attacks on the KSČ group of leaders gained no traction, and grave accusations, which charged them, among other things, with cowardice and apathy, were dropped. In an attempt not to cause emotions to flare, passages such as "We are firmly convinced that openly anti-Communist assaults of reactionary elements are literally possible any day" were left out of the text. At the end of the session, Shelepin's proposal to dispatch Brezhnev, Kosygin, and Podgornyi to the ČSSR as soon as possible so that they could form their own impression of the situation fell through.[46] In its place, a resolution was adopted in the Politburo to forward the memorandum to the party Action Committee, to dispatch copies to the party leaders of Hungary, Bulgaria, Poland, and the German Democratic

Republic (GDR), and to organize a meeting of the party leaders of these countries, to which representatives of the ČSSR would also be invited.[47]

Of the greatest importance was editing the key paragraph of the memorandum where the final version has a passage saying that the KSČ's leaders could always count on "help as required" from the CPSU and the Soviet government.[48] In the original version, this phrase had a much blander ring:

> If the situation continues to develop in a dangerous direction and if the threat for Socialist achievements in Czechoslovakia keeps on growing, we, mindful of the principles of proletarian internationalism and of the obligations imposed on us by the Warsaw Pact, want to assure you in a fraternal manner that we will be prepared to come to the assistance of the Czechoslovak people with all means at our disposition.[49]

These editorial changes and corrections may not look spectacular at first sight if it were not for a huge "but": they may be unspectacular, but every word that was added or deleted affected the fates of thousands of people and of entire nations. Therefore, a whole week passed from the first appearance of the missive to its final dispatch.

The CPSU informed its own party Action Committee and the Soviet public of developments in Czechoslovakia in "open" and "secret" letters and in the plenum of the CC CPSU; the same purpose was served as regards the USSR's close allies in the Warsaw Pact—the GDR, Poland, Hungary, and Bulgaria—through regular meetings devoted to this topic.[50] The results of these discussions usually had a profound effect on the activities of the Soviet Union. At first these meetings of the allies included the ČSSR, as in Dresden in March 1968, where the KSČ leaders were confronted for the first time with critical questions on developments in their country and on the future course the party proposed to adopt. Their efforts notwithstanding, the participants of the meeting did not manage to extract conclusive answers from either Dubček or his colleagues, nor were the Soviet leaders any more successful at a bilateral meeting with a KSČ delegation, which had come to Moscow at the beginning of May. This was obviously the reason why no Czechoslovak representatives were invited to the Moscow conference of the party leaders of the five East European Communist parties which was scheduled for 8 May. The conference itself was entirely given over to a discussion of the situation in the ČSSR. The prevailing tone was a relatively agitated one: all speakers mentioned the activation of antisocialist forces in the ČSSR, the feebleness and haplessness of the KSČ leadership, the targeted discrediting of Socialist ideas, and so forth.[51] Nevertheless, the Soviet leaders succeeded in persuading the participants of the conference to refrain "for the time being from launching wholesale attacks on the KSČ leadership," in the hope that the "healthy forces" in the ČSSR might ride to the rescue (with, perhaps, the planned military maneuvers of the Warsaw

Pact countries on Czechoslovak territory to encourage them). Brezhnev, who presumably did not consider this scenario realistic, expressed his opinion that "we will have to meet again, perhaps several times, to sort these matters out." He underscored the "readiness on our part to fly wherever is necessary, be it day or night, we can be on the spot in a matter of two to three hours, however busy we are."[52]

The fact that no representatives of the ČSSR had been invited to attend the conference caused considerable irritation in Prague; Moscow had to justify its decision and set out to prove that the participants "had no secrets they did not want to share with the KSČ" and that the agenda had consisted exclusively of issues that had already featured at the meeting of the heads of state of the two countries in the USSR not long before. The Soviets also pointed out that "another visit of the Czechoslovak leaders in Moscow within such a short time" might have given rise "to any number of interpretations and speculations about presumptive 'difficulties' in the relations between the CPSU and the other fraternal countries, on the one hand, and the KSČ, on the other."[53] When the Soviet Union proposed a meeting in July in Warsaw, the KSČ leaders declined the invitation, knowing only too well what would be in store for them there. They proposed to hold a number of bilateral meetings instead, involving the leaders of the "fraternal parties" (notably those of the CPSU). The reason they gave for not accepting the invitation to Warsaw was that "at that time, attending a meeting would overly exacerbate the work load on our party."[54] The KSČ letter containing the negative reply was not dispatched until 13 July. At that time, the delegation of all parties had already arrived in Warsaw. For this reason, the draft of a reply was written on the spot in Poland by Brezhnev, Kosygin, Podgornyi, and Shelest. The party apparatus back in Moscow was given the order "to vote on the resolution, to adopt it, and to dispatch it to the indicated address."[55]

The way the leadership of the ČSSR acted played directly into the hands of the hawks in the Kremlin. This state of affairs was further compounded by the fact that Brezhnev was presumably the only one among the Soviet participants of the meeting in Warsaw to still pursue a moderate course. The party leaders of Poland and Bulgaria, Władysław Gomułka and Todor Zhivkov—and even more the GDR's Walter Ulbricht—only poured oil onto the fire. They all emphatically advocated a military intervention. The latter had already classified Dubček as "a basket case" during the Moscow meeting in May;[56] in Warsaw, he declared with a sideswipe at Kádár that the KSČ and the ČSSR was no longer about a struggle with the revisionists (as the Hungarian leader had claimed), but about fighting the counterrevolution and asserted that "the next blow will be directed against you, against the Hungarian People's Republic."[57] Even though no groundbreaking resolutions were officially adopted at the conference[58] and the leaders of the

CPSU declared they were prepared to hold another bilateral meeting with the ČSSR leadership, the distant thunder of the imminent military operation was sounding for everyone to hear. When Kádár told the story of how Dubček and Černik had burst into tears in the middle of a discussion with him about the party and the country's situation, not even Brezhnev could help remarking mordantly, "They are always bursting into tears!"[59]

At the beginning of July, with the CC CPSU still busy putting the final touches on the abovementioned letter to the CC KSČ, another missive was dispatched from Berlin to Prague, where, as opposed to the Soviet variant, the readiness of the GDR was openly offered "to support all your resolutions and measures according to the obligations that member states of the Warsaw Pact are bound by in the spirit of Socialist internationalism."[60]

In this context, the Warsaw Conference became for Moscow the next indispensable step in the preparations for the military operation, which were visibly gaining in momentum. Only a day after the end of the conference, on 17 July, the plenum of the CC CPSU was convened in order to rubber-stamp the imminent intervention. The extremely short notice at which this important party forum was convened is also in evidence in the composition of the participants: it was hardly due to the holiday season that twenty CC members, thirty-one candidate members, and ten members of the Central Revision Committee failed to turn up—they simply could not make it to Moscow in time.[61] Most of those who were present wanted to move from words to deeds and signaled agreement with launching a military operation against Czechoslovakia.[62] At the same time, remembering his promise to conduct one more bilateral meeting with the KSČ leadership, Brezhnev underscored both in his speech and in his closing remarks that "before extreme measures are taken, we will exhaust, together with the fraternal parties, all political means at our disposal to assist the Communist Party of Czechoslovakia and the Czechoslovak people in keeping and defending the achievements of Socialism."[63]

This promise, however, did not impede the buildup of preparations for the military operation. On 19 July, the Politburo began the planning of the "extreme measures," which took a week to complete. On 20 July, the government of the USSR sent a note to the government of the ČSSR to protest against the criticism that had been voiced in Czechoslovakia with reference to the "Warsaw Letter" as well as against negligent security at Czechoslovakia's border with Austria. This was a threat to the security of the entire Socialist camp.[64] On 22 July, Defense Minister Andrei Grechko was given the permission, apropos developments in Czechoslovakia, "to take measures in accordance with planning dates and the exchange of opinions in the session of the Politburo." It goes without saying what "measures" were meant; after all, at the same time documents were being prepared in Moscow that were later claimed to have been authored by the future ČSSR leadership, which was to replace the one presently in power according to Soviet planning. On 20 July, a first version of a Declaration of the Presidium of the CC KSČ and the Revolutionary Government of the ČSSR on the country's domestic and foreign politics was prepared, which was followed by the second version and a speech to the Czechoslovak people on 26 July.[65] On the following day, 27 July, the Politburo rubberstamped the speeches to the Soviet people and to the Czechoslovak People's Army.[66] All these documents had to be published once the invasion of Czechoslovakia began.

At this stage, the world at large, both foes and friends, had to be prepared for what lay ahead. Dealing with the foes was the easier task, as is frequently the case. The United States was tied down in Vietnam and was hoping the USSR would act as an intermediary between the parties. On 22 July, Secretary of State Dean Rusk expressed to the Soviet ambassador to Washington, Anatolii Dobrynin, the U.S. government's concern with "the increasingly serious Soviet accusations that the U.S. was meddling in Czechoslovak affairs." On the very next day, the CC CPSU confirmed it was drafting a resolution to acknowledge Rusk's statement "that developments in Czechoslovakia concerned solely the Czechs and the other Warsaw Pact countries";[67] this statement was of the greatest importance for the Soviets, as it virtually gave them the green light for their planned moves in Czechoslovakia.

Moscow found dealing with its own allies much more difficult. The publication in Pravda of the letter the five parties had addressed from Warsaw to the CC KSČ on 18 July was the CPSU party leaders' attempt to mobilize "the Communist community in all countries to support this important document."[68] Not only did Romania and Yugoslavia express open sympathies, but there were also Communist parties in capitalist countries that warned of a potential interference in the affairs of the ČSSR and/or that exhibited "no awareness of how critical the situation was and what consequences might arise from it,"[69] as the Soviet leadership put it. The Communist parties of Italy and France proved particularly recalcitrant. Italian Communist Party (PCI) leader Luigi Longo opined that the KSČ must be left to follow "the road of the purges" to the end and then had to start "from scratch." Without consulting the CPSU, the French wanted to convene a conference of the European Communist and workers' parties on developments in Czechoslovakia.[70] Such a conference was, of course, impossible to reconcile with USSR planning, which was already in the middle of the preparations for the military operation. The Soviet leadership had to expend a great deal of time and energy in order to get the leaders of the CPI[71] and the representatives of the other "procrastinating" Communist parties to "understand" their view of the developments in Czechoslovakia.[72]

There is one more important detail in this phase that must not go unmentioned. In the second half of July, the resolutions that were passed by the CC CPSU in connection with Czechoslovakia came to acquire an increasingly laconic tone. It was not just words or phrases that were deleted in the original drafts, but whole sentences, entire paragraphs. Such strict editing can certainly not be accounted for merely on the grounds that these documents were written under great pressure. Because it was a foregone conclusion that the situation would lead to military intervention, Moscow began to doctor the documents and to remove passages that could either be interpreted as proof of the USSR's readiness to use military force or, conversely, as proof of the USSR committing itself to exclusively using peaceful means for the solution of the crisis.[73]

On 19 July, when the Politburo briefed the ambassadors of the USSR to inform the leaderships of thirty-three Communist parties on events in Czechoslovakia and the results of the conference in Warsaw, the following phrase was removed from the document at the very last moment: "Make sure you leave no doubt that if the situation exacerbates any further, the CC CPSU will be prepared alongside the other fraternal parties, who took part in the meeting in Warsaw, to take the most drastic measures to defend the position of Socialism in the ČSSR."[74] Despite the fact that the USSR had lost all belief in Dubček and the entire KSČ leadership's capacity to take any constructive course of action, preparations were underway in Moscow for another meeting. Almost the entire leadership of the CPSU traveled to Čierná nad Tisou at the Czechoslovak side's request, but not without laying down a number of conditions for the Czechoslovaks: communiqués for the press would be given after the meeting, not before; the stenographic minutes of the negotiations would be recorded separately by each of the two sides; no audio taping of the negotiations would occur; and no gatherings, demonstrations, or journalists near the conference facilities would be permitted.[75] No sooner were the conditions published than the other side violated them. On 26 July, the Soviet leadership learned that Western correspondents accredited in the ČSSR knew where the meeting was going to take place and were preparing to be there. It took an exchange of telegrams and the threat to break off negotiations for the Czechs to regain control of the situation again.[76] The Kremlin's expectations regarding the potential result of the negotiations are most clearly seen in a letter that the Politburo of the CC CPSU dispatched on the eve of the conference, on 27 July, to its four main allies. It stated that the members of the Soviet delegation "were going to aim at ending" the meeting in Čierná nad Tisou no later than 30 July and to issue an invitation for the afternoon of the same day to the participants of the meeting in Warsaw to Moscow to inform them of the results of the negotiations and to discuss with them "the options on how to proceed."[77] It is probable that the Kremlin assumed that the negotiations with the KSČ leadership would end without results as usual and that there was no point in spending time on talks that led nowhere. It is also not difficult to imagine what "options on how to proceed" would have resulted from the discussion with the allies in case the negotiations had ended in an impasse.[78]

Yet against all odds, the meeting turned out prima facie to be a success and went on not for a matter of hours, but for three days. Afterward, the participants went to Bratislava, where they were joined by the remaining participants of the Warsaw meeting. In Bratislava, a joint declaration of the six Communist parties was accepted on 3 August that was intended, despite its formulaic phrases, to speak to the unity of the countries in the Socialist camp and the readiness of the Czechoslovak leadership to adhere to the line of the Soviet Bloc. The basis for the successful conclusion of the negotiations had been the unofficial and rested upon unpublished assurances of the KSČ leadership during talks of teams of two and eight in Čierná nad Tisou.[79] In these assurances, the KSČ leadership committed themselves to ensuring that the presidium of the CC KSČ would establish strict control in the very near future of the mass media and would prevent anti-Soviet and antisocialist material from being published; that the activities of various clubs and organization, including the Social Democratic preparatory committee, would be suppressed; that the Interior Ministry would be reorganized; and, most important of all, that the representatives of "rightist" forces would be removed from positions of power.[80] When Moscow deferred so much to its negotiating partners, it does not seem to have occurred to anyone that Dubček might be making all these promises off the cuff, without the slightest clue about how or when to keep them.[81] At this stage, at least part of the Politburo of the CC CPSU considered the problem at least partly, if not wholly, solved. This was why the question of a military intervention moved to the background for the time being. The majority of the Soviet leadership went off on their holiday, and Moscow viewed the 21 and 22 August requests made by U.S. presidential candidate Richard Nixon during his tour of Europe positively. In the end this visit did not occur.[82]

The "euphoria" occasioned by the results of the negotiations in Čierná nad Tisou and Bratislava disappeared as quickly as it had surfaced. Despite the promises that had been made by the Czechoslovak side, hardly any changes became noticeable in the political life of the ČSSR. Not only did anti-Soviet materials not disappear from the Czechoslovak mass media, they became even more aggressive in tone. Nor did the changes in the party cadres materialize. In the run-up to two sessions of the presidium of the CC KSČ, Dubček told Soviet representatives that he was going to solve this issue; when the sessions began, it was not even on the agenda. The KSČ leadership reacted to all Soviet protests and notes with the same nervousness and agitation and with the repetition of the assurance that everything that was possible was, in fact, being done.[83]

The straw that finally broke the camel's back for Moscow was Brezhnev's telephone conversation with Dubček on 13 August.[84] When the Soviet leader peremptorily insisted on the enforcement of the agreements made at

Čierná nad Tisou, Dubček gave evasive answers and kept on claiming that the situation within the country had changed and that it was impossible to come up with instantaneous answers to all the important questions. What he had promised to accomplish within a matter of days was now adjourned to a relatively distant future ("September," "the end of October"). Even more worrying for the Soviet leaders than the time delays was above all the fact that, as opposed to his assurances at Čierná nad Tisou, Dubček was no longer prepared to guarantee that the promised resolutions were going to materialize at all ("pending the decision of the presidium"). What clinched matters for Brezhnev was the fact that Dubček, who was already confused and a complete wreck owing to the pressure from all sides, mentioned during the telephone conversation his readiness to concur with his own dismissal.[85] This amounted to an admission that he was unable or unwilling (or possibly both) to lead the presidium of the CC KSČ. In this case, all his commitments proved to be no more than "idle talk" since the Kremlin knew only too well what kind of forces would gain power within the KSČ leadership if Dubček were to resign either of his own free will or under pressure. Dubček, who when all is said turns out to have been a very weak political leader, notably in the difficult transition phase the country was experiencing, contributed a great deal to those forces in the "fraternal countries" who had pleaded for a military solution of the "Czechoslovak question" from the beginning finally gaining the upper hand. The Czechoslovak leader kept on repeating either thoughtlessly or dispiritedly the phrase: "Take whatever measures the Politburo of the CC deems necessary." De facto Dubček was asking for himself and his country to be handed down the "sentence" on 13 August.[86]

It is obvious that Soviet leadership, the majority of whom were on holiday in the Crimea, came to the final conclusions two days after the telephone conversation outlined above that it was now time to embark on the military phase of the solution. This marks the beginning of the fourth and last phase.[87] Until 15 August, all the documents and Politburo materials remained within the bounds of the agreements that had been reached in the negotiations with the KSČ. The Politburo, for instance, passed a relatively moderate conclusion on 13 August informing the fraternal parties on the results of the negotiations in Čierná nad Tisou and Bratislava,[88] which underscored both the success of the meetings and the problems, whose solution now depended solely on the Czechoslovak leadership.[89] The text was prepared on 10 August; Brezhnev signed it on the twelfth, Kosygin on 13 August. On the same day, the Politburo of the CC CPSU approved the guidelines for the Soviet ambassador to Czechoslovakia, Chervonenko, regarding his conversation with Dubček and Černik on the antisocialist and anti-Soviet campaign in the Czechoslovak press—the tone was tough, but not threatening.[90] The ambassador was also told to meet President

Svoboda, to thank him, and to ask him for his continued assistance in the struggle against rightist forces.[91]

Up to the middle of August, the Politburo's Commission on Czechoslovakia, which had been put together in May, was busy preparing documents and motions for the session of the Politburo on 15 August. The material included a "Summary of the Material on the Situation in Czechoslovakia of 13 August"[92] as well as the draft of an official memorandum of the Politburo to the Presidium of the CC KSČ, which was rendered more aggressive on 15 August by the insertion of several new demands and an assessment of the latest telephone conversation between Brezhnev and Dubček. It was this very memorandum that subsequently became one of the most important propaganda tools regarding the military intervention.

The fact that the situation changed decisively on 15 August is also vindicated by other clues and documents. After the situation in the ČSSR had been discussed by the inner circle of Politburo members in the Crimea, where most of them were on holiday anyway, a telegram in cipher arrived on the same day from Yalta in Moscow signed by Brezhnev that was to be relayed by Ambassador Chervonenko in Prague to Dubček.[93] However, the cipher telegram contained the directive: "Do not relay to Prague before receiving explicit orders to do so." It was, therefore, held back in Moscow until further notice. The telegram was addressed to Andrei Kirilenko, who was not only "responsible" for the Commission on Czechoslovakia but had also stayed in Moscow during the summer holiday season as the highest ranking Politburo member to do so. On the following day, 16 August, another variant of the document contained in the cipher telegram which was virtually identical with the first one but had now obviously been put to the vote was sent from Yalta to Moscow, this time addressed to Konstantin Chernenko.[94] At the same time, an edited version of the above mentioned Politburo memorandum to the Presidium of the CC KSČ of 15 August arrived from Yalta, which was kept in Moscow. Brezhnev's letter to Dubček was rubberstamped regarding the text and relayed to Prague without further delay.

Brezhnev's letter contained an informative note to the Soviet ambassador which requested him to inform as many members of the CC KSČ as possible who were still considered "healthy forces" by Moscow of the letter and its contents. Because the letter repeated virtually everything that had been said in the telephone conversation between Brezhnev and Dubček on 13 August and because it contained reproaches to Dubček for not keeping his promises, we may assume that it was a move in the political game, namely the opening gambit in a solution of the ČSSR crisis involving the use of force. The "healthy forces" were supposed to inform the KSČ leaders, on the one hand, that Dubček was conducting negotiations with Moscow behind their back—it was obvious that the KSČ leader did not nearly inform even his close collaborators about everything. On the other hand, this was a clear signal to the "healthy forces" that the moment which many of them had been dreaming about and whose advent some had urged the Soviet leadership to move toward was drawing near.[95]

For the world at large, the impending intervention became obvious at the latest when Moscow requested UN Secretary-General U Thant on 16 August to postpone his visit to Prague; the visit was designed to calm the situation down and at least cause a delay of whatever action Moscow was planning. The reasoning behind the secretary-general's trip to Prague, which had been arranged on a short-term basis as an excursion during his stay in Vienna, where he took part in a conference, was that it was extremely unlikely for a serious confrontation to erupt during U Thant's presence in Prague. The hint from Moscow, which was delivered by UN Ambassador Leonid Kutakov, was outspoken enough; U Thant was asked to rethink once more "all aspects of this question" lest he should "find himself in a difficult situation against his will."[96] U Thant saw the light.

At the same time, on 16 August, the top Soviet leadership convened a "big meeting" in Moscow. On 17 August, all members and all candidate members of the Politburo of the CC CPSU, as well as the party leaders of some of the Union's republics who hardly ever took part in sessions in Moscow, assembled. The preparations for the military operation were propelled by a keen sense of purpose, which did not prevent small stumbling blocks from making a nuisance of themselves. What occurred at the time was the rare case of a Politburo resolution that had already been signed (the "signed version") having to be annulled; even Brezhnev's signature had to be crossed out again! The stumbling block took the form of a passage of a text dealing with convening a conference which would involve the party and state leaders of the USSR, Bulgaria, Hungary, the GDR and Poland on 18 August in Moscow. The purpose of the meeting as stated in that first version was the discussion of the "topical issue." This formulation was replaced forthwith[97] by another equally soft one typical of the Soviet party apparatus:[98] the idea of the meeting was "to discuss questions related to joint actions to provide assistance to the Communist Party and the government of Czechoslovakia in their struggle against reactionary and counterrevolutionary forces."[99] The participants of the Warsaw Conference, who had come to Moscow within a few hours, ratified the resolution that had already been passed a long time before on participation in the joint military intervention, even though they needed more time for the detailed formulation in individual documents on which the five countries had agreed; Kádár's last additions were not inserted until the afternoon of 19 August.

Materials were fetched from party safes that had already been prepared around 20 July. Some alterations were made in these materials which had become necessary in view of the changed situation. At Suslov's suggestion, the word "revolutionary" was deleted from the title of the prepared declaration to be delivered by the "Revolutionary Government of the ČSSR"; in the address of the declaration of the five interventionist countries ("Comrades, workers, agricultural laborers, intelligentsia of the people; Czechs and Slovaks, fighters of the people's militia, members of the Communist Party"), the mention of the members of the Communist Party was eliminated. After consulting its allies in the Interventionist Coalition on the topic, the CPSU leadership provided an answer to the question who inside the ČSSR was to be named as allegedly having requested the five countries to undertake a military intervention in the name of protecting the achievements of socialism—from the end of July up to (and including) 18 August several blank lines had marked the place for the insertion of this piece of information.[100] The government of the ČSSR was named as the party responsible for this, even though some documents also contain references to the "majority of the Presidium of the CC KSČ."[101]

Finally, the story of the memorandum that the CC CPSU addressed to the CC KSČ, which had already been written on 15 August, reached closure. Even before it had been delivered to its addressee, it was reedited several times and shuttled around within a few days along the route Moscow–Yalta–Moscow–Prague–Moscow–Prague. The circuitous detour of the document resulted from the fact that, after the text of the memorandum had been finally approved at the Politburo session on 17 August and dispatched to Chervonenko for him to hand it to Dubček, problems surfaced in Prague concerning the document. The Soviet ambassador, having consulted a representative of the "healthy forces" in the Presidium of the CC KSČ, immediately sent back his assessment of the text of the memorandum to Moscow. On the one hand, he suggested several sweeping changes; on the other, he advised handing the document to KSČ leadership not on 18 August (the date specified in the resolution of the CC CPSU), but on 19 August.[102] The ostensible reason given for this change was that 18 August was a Sunday, and it would have been difficult to find any KSČ leader who was on duty. The real reason was that both Chervonenko and the "healthy forces" wanted to reduce the time span between the presentation of the memorandum and the beginning of the invasion as much as possible. An indirect corroboration of this assumption derives from the phrase that

> this opinion [regarding the postponement of the presentation of the memorandum to 19 August] is also shared by our Czechoslovak friends, who would prefer for the memorandum to be handed over as part of routine procedure in order not to attract unnecessary attention or to provoke premature reactions on the part of the right-wing forces.[103]

This resulted in the memorandum being returned to Moscow once more and not getting back to Prague until after last alterations had been made.

The activities in the phase of rising tension in the Politburo of the CC ÇPSU immediately before the beginning of the invasion are characterized by two divergent tendencies. On the one hand, the need to react in operative terms to even the smallest changes in the run-up to the military operation resulted in several resolutions being noted down, as it were, almost on a haphazard basis by a handful of people in pencil on note paper.[104] On the other hand, the most important resolutions were passed immediately in sessions of the Politburo of the CC CPSU by the entire Soviet leadership. Even more remarkable is the fact that even the second names are given in the materials of the CC of those who were directly involved in the formulation of one or the other resolution. As far as the situation that existed at the time is concerned, it is possible to witness a rare picture regarding the Soviet party nomenclature. As regards the most important resolutions, the roll-call of individuals participating in the sessions of the Politburo was almost identical with the roll-call of those who had prepared the resolution. This might of course be interpreted as the realization of the principle of "collective leadership," to which Soviet leaders loved to pay lip service, yet it actually makes a more forceful case for the interpretation that what the CPSU leadership desired was the establishment of a kind of "joint liability," a collective responsibility for the dramatic and politically dubious decisions.

Regardless of all the efforts and the careful preparation of the "military/political operation," the invasion as a whole did not unfold the way the Kremlin had planned it or the way the Soviet leaders would afterwards make the world believe it had unfolded. While the military component unfolded on the whole without a hitch, the political side was anything but satisfactory. Above all, a total fiasco occurred at the beginning of the operation when the "healthy forces" who, not content with being unable to gain control of the country and the party, became pariahs themselves, and had to be shielded and protected.[105] This was obviously linked to the inevitable political "reanimation" of Dubček and his entourage, who were whisked from Uzhgorod, where they were de facto under arrest, to Moscow for negotiations. In the eyes of the Soviets who wanted to restore order in the country with the help of Czechs and Slovaks, there was at the moment no one apart from Dubček who seemed capable of keeping the country in the Soviet camp, even if the name of an alternative candidate had been put forward who commanded a following in the party. During the time that it took to find such a candidate (the choice was soon to fall on the Slovak politician Gustáv Husák), it was not only necessary to keep Dubček in power, but also to make sure he was taking orders from Moscow. This was to be guaranteed by the allied troops stationed in Czechoslovakia and by Dubček's assurances that, after the debacle of Čierná nad Tisou, they were going to be put down in writing in every single case. We may assume that it was thanks to the ineptitude of the "healthy forces" that proved unable to assume power that Dubček was spared the fate of Rákosi, Nikos Zachariadis, or even Imre Nagy.[106]

Another failure for Moscow was the attempt to persuade the president of the ČSSR, Svoboda, to play an active role on its side. Chervonenko had familiarized him with the Politburo missive explaining the inevitability of a military invasion only an hour before the operation began. The Soviet ambassador had also been ordered, should Svoboda "be positively inclined toward the request of the fraternal states," to hand him—"with the tact that the situation requires"—a draft composed in Moscow of the president's address to the Czechoslovak people.[107] It is impossible to tell whether the Soviet Union seriously believed that a man of Svoboda's caliber would consent to such a step. As was to be expected, the attempt failed. Even though the president of the ČSSR took an active part in the ensuing "negotiations" in Moscow and did everything in his power to defuse the situation, it was plain for the USSR to see that he was not positively inclined to what was happening.

The party leaders of the five Socialist countries had clearly misjudged the domestic situation in Czechoslovakia and its development following the invasion, and they openly admitted as much at the meeting in Moscow on 24 August. The intervention had a unifying effect on Czechoslovak society, albeit in an antisocialist and anti-Soviet direction. Under these circumstances, not only the remains of the "healthy forces" but also each ordinary citizen who did not agree with the political line of the KSČ leadership were automatically dubbed "traitors to their native country" and "Moscow's agents." Dubček, Černík, and Smrkovský, who had only shortly before been attacked both from the "Right" and from the "Left" were elevated to "national heroes and martyrs for 'the Idea.'" The troops of the Interventionist Coalition, who had been told prior to the invasion they were being given marching orders at the request of the new state leadership of the ČSSR and of the whole Czechoslovak people found themselves in a situation that was more than ambiguous. There was no new (revolutionary or national) government that had requested military assistance, the Extraordinary 24th Party Conference of the KSČ that had been convened demanded the immediate withdrawal of all foreign troops from the territory of the ČSSR, and the majority of the country's population regarded the foreign military contingents as occupants, not as defenders of socialism.

It is instructive in this context to compare two meetings of the countries participating in the "military-political operation" that took place in Moscow within six days—one three days before the invasion, the other three days after it. On 18 August, the participants were reasonably optimistic in their assessment of the impending operations. Brezhnev pointed out that the "healthy forces" had already united, that they had already demonstrated "unity," and that they were "ready for a decisive battle with the right."[108]

By way of corroboration, details of Chervonenko's latest negotiations with representatives of the "healthy forces" within the KSČ leadership were shared as were their plans for the following days. In addition to this, a letter was read out that a group of leaders of the Slovak Communist Party had handed to Brezhnev already in Bratislava asking for a military invasion. All the other participants at the meeting voiced unanimous agreement with the Soviet leaders, with the sole exception of Gomułka, who tried to make the point that a great deal was going to depend on the domestic situation in the ČSSR: "What the Czechoslovak comrades and the forces on the left will say is of the greatest importance."[109]

The mood was an entirely different one at the consultations on 24 August, when it had become obvious that much of what Moscow had been banking on was simply not going to materialize. In addition to the assessment that the "healthy forces" were failing to deliver ("A number of them took refuge in the embassy and were, therefore, unable to lead propaganda activities," "They got scared," and so forth)—the participants vied with each other in assuring each other that the operation had been justified and inevitable in the prevailing circumstances.[110] Brezhnev tried to convince the allies that the unavoidable negotiations with the interned KSČ leadership did not mean that the USSR did not adhere to the decisions previously jointly adopted.[111] The most controversial issue was how to inform the Czechoslovak public and the world about these negotiations.

Propaganda work during the military invasion was not successful either. In Eastern European countries as well as in the ČSSR, neither the secret agreements struck in Čierná and Bratislava were mentioned, nor was anything about the leaders of the KSČ sabotaging these agreements. It was, therefore, extremely difficult to explain to the world—and above all to the Czechoslovak people—the reasons that had necessitated the invasion only two weeks after the "successful conclusion of negotiations." Such explanations became downright impossible in the wake of the invasion for two reasons. First, all the ČSSR's mass media outlets were in the hands of "rightists"; second, given the outburst of national patriotism that took hold of the public after the invasion, no one would listen to arguments justifying the aggression, no matter how weighty they might have been.

The allies, who had pinned their hopes on the "healthy forces" in the ČSSR, had in addition to all this failed to establish propaganda cadres and to prepare high-quality materials in the Czech and Slovak languages for distribution virtually within hours after the invasion.[112] It was not until 23 August (that is, two days after the invasion) that the hurriedly edited text of the "Address to the Citizens of the Czechoslovak Socialist Republic" in Czech and Slovak was dispatched to Czechoslovakia from Moscow.[113] Access to information for the population of the Socialist countries was also almost nonexistent. In the West, events in Czechoslovakia dominated the headlines, trumping all other news; in the Warsaw Pact countries, citizens were fed the news in tiny doses encrypted in official propagandese. Many critical questions were simply ignored altogether.[114]

A Kremlin analysis of the military operation that was done three months later confirmed that the advance of the troops on Czechoslovak territory took place during the first days in a "propaganda vacuum"; the first leaflets in Czech did not appear until the fifth or sixth day of the occupation, there were no special papers for the occasion, no radio or TV commentaries, and so forth. In Moscow it was conceded, if through clenched teeth, that it had been this "absence of propaganda" in conjunction with the active, goal-oriented activities of "rightist forces" that resulted in the latter de facto securing the lion's share of the Czechoslovaks' sympathy. Soviet troops, according to a Soviet assessment, could act at the beginning of the invasion "with the support and the understanding of roughly 50 to 60 percent of the population"; after the first week, between 75 to 90 percent of the population saw the invasion as an "occupation."[115] It is not surprising that this author did not entertain at least for a moment the possibility that such a massive rejection of the "military-political operation" could have been caused by the national humiliation that had been inflicted on the Czechoslovak people, which was a fact that was not altered by the noble goals that the occupiers claimed to be pursuing. There was a conviction instead that there was a "lesson to be learned for the future" from the events in Czechoslovakia, for imperialism would not desist from its attempts "to use these same means to reverse to its advantage developments in the socialist countries."[116]

This last statement was by no means coincidental. Within the Soviet leadership not the least doubts surfaced as to the justification and the timing of the "military-political operation" either in the summer of 1968 or in later years. The differences of opinion that did exist did not concern questions of principle, but mainly such issues as the pacing and the methods of "regulation" of the Czechoslovak crisis between August 1968 and April 1969, a phase in which Dubček and his comrades-in-arms attempted to keep some elements of their former political line alive. This conviction of the Soviet leaders cannot be explained in terms of their conservative mind-sets or their open fear of an impending collapse of the Soviet camp. A significant role in this concrete case must be assigned to the factors of the Cold War and the bipolar world order. The Brezhnev Doctrine as well as the Sonnenfeld Doctrine, which both concern the definition of the spheres of influence of the two superpowers and which were not frequently cited officially but often applied in practice were most strongly in evidence during the Czechoslovak crisis in the summer of 1968.

The knowledge and analysis of the declassified documents relating to the ČSSR crisis in the context of the time enables us to correct several theses, which have been formulated in recent years regarding the Czechoslovak

crisis, including in particular claims to the effect that events in Czechoslovakia are said to have established the impossibility, in principle, of reforming
the Socialist system.[117] This also applies to the thesis which sees Dubček as
not only engaged in building some kind of a "Utopian society," but also
as someone who was a notoriously more orthodox Marxist in the Socialist sense of the nineteenth century than the Soviet leaders themselves.[118]
It is quite obvious that both postulates are in need of a certain amount of
refinement.

As far as the impossibility of reforming the Socialist system is concerned—
it is a fact that all attempted reforms either ushered in Soviet tanks or a
complete switch to a capitalist system—one must not lose sight of the fact
that this concerned a *Soviet* variant of the Socialist system of which, to use a
contemporary metaphor from genetics, a cloned copy was installed in most
Eastern European countries involving the use of force. Even Vladimir Lenin
admitted repeatedly that there was a huge difference between the proletarian revolution of Marxist theory and what had emerged as a result of the
Russian Revolution. All subsequent statements which claimed that the road
chosen by the USSR was the one and only model to be followed, as well as
the fact that the "progressive" Soviet experiences were forced on the other
countries, were the sole responsibility of the Soviet party functionaries and
ideologues. The result was the inevitable isolation of the Soviet model of
communism in most "people's democracies"—in our concrete case, in
Czechoslovakia. This, in turn, led to the impossibility of reforming the
inadequacies of this model.

Painting Dubček in the role as the last of the Marxist-Leninists is hardly
borne out by the facts. In order to get to the top in a Communist Party
of the Leninist-Stalinist persuasion, which the KSČ was beyond a shadow
of a doubt, one had to have character attributes and capabilities that are
entirely incompatible with the "heroic figure" of a fighter against Soviet
totalitarianism. If there is talk of struggles within the KSČ leadership, it
must not be overlooked that even those who passed in the Soviet Union
for "rightists" were as much representatives of the party nomenclature as
their "leftist" or "conservative" opponents. Many of their activities would
inevitably conform with those rules of the game that had originally been
defined by the circles of the party apparatchiks. Even if they came up with
nice mottos featuring "democratic socialism" or "socialism with a human
face," they themselves had hardly a clue how socialism was to be human-
ized in practice without running afoul of a communism that was prepared
to resort to the use of violence.

This is why the positive action program of the Czechoslovak reformers
was confined in a number of ways to mere words and promises that defied
realization in practice. Their sole use was to fan in the population negative
emotions directed against those that "hindered" Czechoslovakia in the

process of becoming really free and independent—that is, against the USSR, the CPSU, the orthodox faction within the KSČ, and the Slovak nationalists. These external factors, the hotbed from which sprang newspaper headlines, rallies, and demonstrations, worried the Soviet leadership much more and prompted them much more strongly to take aggressive action than the contradictory processes unfolding subliminally inside the Czechoslovak society. Without even a hint of absolving the USSR and the other four countries that became guilty of crass interference in the internal affairs of a sovereign state from their responsibility, one can assume with an increasing degree of certainty that it was also the shortsighted and ill-considered acts of the Czechoslovak reformers, that is, of those in the party elite of the KSČ on the extreme "right," that contributed to the absolutely inadequate, if at the time seemingly inevitable, form that the reaction of the USSR and of the other member countries of the Warsaw Pact culminated in: military invasion.

NOTES

Translated from German into English by Otmar Binder, Vienna.

1. It is owing to this development that over the last few years a large number of documents have been published and many studies have been written which either address the history of the Czechoslovak crisis directly or treat the topic within another context. For details, see Mark Kramer, "The Prague Spring and the Soviet Invasion of Czechoslovakia: New Interpretations, Part 1," *CWIHP Bulletin* 2 (1992): 1, 4–13, and "The Prague Spring and the Soviet Invasion of Czechoslovakia: New Interpretations, Part 2," *CWIHP Bulletin* 3 (1993): 2–13, 54–55. See also R. G. Pikhoya, "Chechoslovakiya, 1968 god," *Novaya i novejshaya istoriya* 6 (1994), 1 (1995); Lutz Priess et al., eds., *Die SED und der "Prager Frühling" 1968: Politik gegen einen "Sozialismus mit menschlichem Antlitz"* (Berlin: Akademie Verlag, 1996); Mikhail Latysh, *"Prazhskaya vesna" 1968 g. i reaktsija Kremlya* (Moscow: Moskva, 1998); R. G. Pikhoya, *Sovetskii Soyuz: Istoriya vlasti, 1945–1991* (Moscow and Novosibirsk: Sibirskii Khronograf, 1998); Jaromir Navrátil et al., eds., *The Prague Spring 1968: A National Security Archive Documents Reader* (Budapest: Central European University Press, 1998); Mark Kramer, ed., "Ukraine and the Soviet-Czechoslovak Crisis of 1968, Part 1, New Evidence from the Diary of Petro Shelest," *CWIHP Bulletin* 10 (1998); Jeremi Suri, *Power and Protest: Global Revolution and the Rise of Détente* (Cambridge, MA: Harvard University Press, 2003); Frank Umbach, *Das rote Bündnis: Entwicklung und Zerfall des Warsaw Pact, 1955 bis 1991* (Berlin: Ch. Links, 2005); Vladislav M. Zubok, *A Failed Empire: The Soviet Union in the Cold War from Stalin to Gorbachev* (Chapel Hill: University of North Carolina Press, 2007).

2. RGANI, F. 3, op. 72, d. 145, pp. 7–8, 12, Politburo resolution of the CC CPSU, "Questions Concerning Czechoslovakia," 25 January 1968; RGANI, F. 3, op. 72, d. 146, pp. 4, 29–30, Politburo resolution of the CC CPSU, "On Functions in Connection with Dubček Visiting the USSR," 29 January 1968; RGANI, F. 3, op. 72, d. 151, pp. 2–12, Politburo resolution of the CC CPSU, "Questions Concerning GKES,

the Gosplan of the USSR and the USSR Defense Ministry." Attachment: resolution of the Council of Ministers of the USSR, "Über die technische Zusammenarbeit der Tschechoslowakei und Polens in der Organisation von Infanteriemaschinen und über den Ankauf solcher Maschinen für die Sowjetunion in der Tschechoslowakei." Attachment nos. 1, 2, 3 to the resolution of the Council of Ministers, 21 February 1968.

3. The attitude of reformist members of the Czechoslovak leadership is illustrated by a statement made by M. Tokar, an attaché at the ČSSR embassy in the GDR, in a meeting with a Soviet diplomat (Tokar was considered to be "pro-Soviet," for he had graduated from the Moscow Institute for International Relations and had married the daughter of Mikhail Men'shikov, who was foreign minister of the RSFSR until August 1968): "In order to be able to solve the political and economic tasks confronting the ČSSR, 50,000 individuals who have held until now key positions in all areas of the political, state and economic administration have to resign from their post or face dismissal." RGANI, F. 5, op. 60, d. 299, p. 155, minutes of a conversation between the first secretary of the Soviet embassy in the GDR, Vsevolod Sovva, with the attaché of the Czechoslovak embassy in the GDR, M. Tokar, 5 April 1968.

4. RGANI, F. 3, op. 68, d. 744, pp. 9–13, an excerpt from minutes of the session of the Politburo CC CPSU, "On the Memorandum of the Politburo CC CPSU to the presidium of the CC," 15 March 1968.

5. RGANI, F. 3, op. 68, d. 744, pp. 5–6, 9–13.

6. RGANI, F. 3, op. 72, d. 155, pp. 9–12, decision of the Politburo of the Central Committee of the Communist Party of the Soviet Union [CPSU], "Regarding the Invitation of the Czechoslovak Communist Party chiefs to spend their vacation in the Soviet Union," addendum to the letter by Leonid Brezhnev to Dubček, 15 March 1968.

7. RGANI, F. 3, op. 72, d. 155, pp. 2–3.

8. After the invasion of the troops on the territory of Czechoslovakia, Brezhnev confirmed that the Soviet Union never tried to protect Novotný: "I did not know a thing then, only said, that if you don't want to make him your president, then don't." RGANI, F. 89, op 38, d. 57, p. 32, stenographic protocol of the negotiations between Brezhnev, Aleksei Kosygin, and Nikolai Podgornyi with the Czechoslovak president Ludvík Svoboda, 23 August 1968, reprinted in Karner et al., *Dokumente*, #108. Indeed, there were grave concerns about Novotný in the Soviet Union; he enjoyed only little control in his country and the party, was unpopular with the Czechoslovak population, was critical about Nikita Khrushshev's firing in 1964, and so forth. However, given the activation of "revisionist forces," Moscow was interested in having even a conservative leader head Czechoslovakia as long as he believed in the ideas of "Soviet socialism." The Soviets took assurances (from Prague) at face value for a while that Novotný's resignation from the position of first secretary of the Central Committee of the Czechoslovak Communist Party was only a means to divvy up the jobs in the party's leadership. The massive attacks on Novotný ensuing soon thereafter, which in the end led to his removal for the post of the presidency, however, were less easily tolerated by the Soviet Union (from a Central Committee of the CPSU resolution a few days after Novotný's removal): "one cannot discount the possibility that those forces who want to remove Czechoslovakia from its So-

cialist path and destroy the fraternal ties between the Soviet Union and the ČSSR, will also put pressure on Novotný to give up his job as President. We believe that General Novotný will have sufficient stamina to obviate those endeavors." RGANI, F. 3, op. 72, d. 155, p. 120, resolution of the Politburo of the Central Committee of the SPSU, P 74 (43), "regarding instructions to the Soviet ambassador to Czechoslovakia," 14 March 1968, reprinted in Karner et al., *Dokumente*, #5.

9. Communist putsch in February 1948, dismissal of twelve bourgeois ministers from their posts by the Communist president, Klement Gottwald, which was a definitive takeover of power by the Communists.

10. RGANI, F. 89, op. 38, d. 60, p. 12, stenographic notes of the negotiations between Brezhnev, Kosygin, and Podgornyi with the party leaders of the ČSSR, 26 August 1968, reprinted in Karner et al., *Dokumente*, #114.

11. *Sasha* is short for *Aleksandr* in Russian. Brezhnev dispensed with all formalities in his conversations with Dubček. For details, see the transcripts of their conversations. RGANI, F. 89, op. 76, d. 75, pp. 1–18, telephone conversation of L. I. Brezhnev with A. S. Dubček, 13 August 1968, reprinted in Karner et al., *Dokumente*, #57; ÚSD, sb. KV ČSFR, 8, Soviet transcript of a telephone conversation of L. I. Brezhnev with A. Dubček on the fulfillment of the agreements of Čierná nad Tisou and Bratislava, 9 August 1968, reprinted in Karner et al., *Dokumente*, #53. Reprinted in English in Navrátil et al., *The Prague Spring 1968*, #77.

12. According to Suri, both Dubček and Brezhnev knew that reforms were overdue in Czechoslovakia, but they did not agree on the timing. The Soviet leader felt it was important to opt for an implementation step by step; Dubček, on the other hand, favored speed. Suri, *Power and Protest*, 200.

13. Moscow was following with a growing sense of unease developments within the Czechoslovak People's Army where, as in all other armies of the Socialist countries, the principle of the leadership of the party and its control over the soldiers was strictly observed. However, in circumstances where the party itself was subject to political erosion, the control exercised by some political organs within the Czechoslovak army had the opposite effect. The political organs in parts of the Czechoslovak People's Army demanded calling an extraordinary party conference, the establishment of trade unions in the army, a review of Czechoslovakia's military strategy, and the country's withdrawal from the Warsaw Pact. Some of these party ideologues were actually advocating ideas that were in direct conflict with the general line that most KSČ leaders still upheld at the time, and by doing so, they created an atmosphere in the army that was hostile to the USSR and to the other Socialist countries.

14. Latysh, *"Prazhskaya vesna" 1968*, 216.

15. RGANI, F. 3, op. 68, d. 744, pp. 15–19, notes for the transcript of the minutes of the session of the Politburo CC CPSU, "On the Politburo CC CPSU Memorandum to the Presidium of the CC," 15 March 1968.

16. "Comrades, Karlovy Vary only serves as a smoke screen!" Brezhnev declared quite openly in a speech in the plenum of the CC CPSU on 17 July 1968. RGANI, F. 2, op. 3, d. 114, p. 28, stenographic notes of the plenum of the CC CPSU. Speech of the secretary-general of the CC CPSU, Brezhnev, "On the Results of the Meeting of the Delegations of Communist and Workers' Parties of the Socialist Countries," 17 July 1968.

17. RGANI, F. 3, op. 72, d. 177, pp. 26–27, Politburo Resolution P 84 (50), "On the Information of the Party Leadership of the BCP, USAP, PVAP and SED with Reference to Kosygin's Trip to Czechoslovakia." Attachment: telegrams to the Soviet ambassadors in Budapest, Warsaw and Sofia, 31 May 1968.

18. See R. G. Pikhoya, *Sovetskii Soyuz: Istoriya vlasti*, 317.

19. RGANI, F. 5, op. 60, d. 266, pp. 27–28, report filed by the correspondent Lukovec to the editor in chief of *Pravda*, Mikhail Zimyanin, on the situation at the Soviet embassy in Prague, 20 May 1968, reprinted in Karner et al., *Dokumente*, #35.

20. RGANI, F. 3, op. 68, d. 820, pp. 52–54, materials for the Politburo resolution of the CC CPSU of 31 May 1968, "On Informing the BCP, USAP, PVAP and SED regarding Kosygin's Trip to Czechoslovakia"; the notes of Konstantin Katushev and Konstantin Rusakov, 27 May 1968.

21. RGANI, F. 3, op. 68, d. 820, p. 54.

22. RGANI, F. 3, op. 72, d. 177, 27 (see note 17).

23. RGANI, F. 3, op. 72, d. 177, p. 27.

24. RGANI, F. 3, op. 68, d. 820, 54 (see note 20).

25. RGANI, F. 3, op. 68, d. 820, p. 56; RGANI, F. 3, op. 72, d. 177, 27 (see note 17).

26. RGANI, F. 3, op. 72, d. 170, p. 3, Politburo Resolution des CC CPSU P 82 (II), "Concerning the Situation in Czechoslovakia," 23 May 1968.

27. RGANI, F. 2, op. 3, d. 114, p. 47, stenographic notes on the session of the plenum of the CC CPSU, speech of the secretary-general of the CC CPSU, L. I. Brezhnev, "On the results of the meeting of the delegations of the Communist and Workers' Parties of the Socialist countries in Warsaw," 17 July 1968.

28. Pikhoya, *Sovetskii Soyuz: Istoriya vlasti*, 309.

29. On 15 March 1968, Dubček tried to conciliate Brezhnev in a telephone conversation by assuring him that "there will be no incidents either in Prague or elsewhere in the country; things are looking bad in Poland right now, and they need help straightaway." Quoted in Pikhoya, *Sovetskii Soyuz: Istoriya vlasti*, 309.

30. Dubček apologized for the "unfortunate article" about Nagy, which had appeared in the periodical of the Czechoslovak writers' association *Literární listy* under the title "One More Anniversary," and assured Brezhnev that the situation after the publication of the article was meanwhile back to normal. "There will be no repetition of this . . . everything is in order now." Quoted in Pikhoya, *Sovetskii Soyuz: Istoriya vlasti*, 324.

31. RGANI, F. 5, op. 60, d. 311, pp. 1–6, report of the military attaché of the Soviet embassy in the ČSSR, Lt.-Gen. Nikolai Trusov, to the CC CPSU on Czechoslovak press reports and radio and television programs on the Warsaw Pact exercises in the ČSSR, 18 July 1968, reprinted in: Karner et al., *Dokumente*, #91; some statements of Czechoslovak leaders concerning the Warsaw Pact further exacerbated tensions between the two countries. In Moscow, the statement of the head of the state administrative department of the CC KSČ, Václav Prchlík, provoked a storm of indignation. Prchlík criticized not only the pact's structure and activities, but in doing so even "allowed," as the document notes, "top secret data to be published." RGANI, F. 3, op. 72, d. 189, pp. 6, 48–52, Politburo Resolution of the CC CPSU P 92 (2), "On the note to the government of the ČSSR." Attachment: note to the government

of the ČSSR, 20 July 1968. The demands for a reform of the Warsaw Pact system and even for a withdrawal option called up new associations in Moscow with Hungary in 1956, with Nagy announcing Hungary's withdrawal from this organization at the climax of the revolution.

32. RGANI, F. 3, op. 68, d. 820, p. 53 (see note 20).

33. RGANI, F. 2, op. 3, d. 114, p. 45, stenographic notes of the session of the plenum of the CC CPSU, speech of the secretary-general of the CC CPSU, L. I. Brezhnev, "On the Results of the Meeting of the Delegations of the Communist and Workers' Parties of the Socialist Countries in Warsaw," 17 July 1968.

34. RGANI, F. 10, op. 1, d. 324, p. 23, minutes of the meeting of the leader of the CC CPSU with the leaders of the Communist parties of Bulgaria, Hungary, the GDR and Poland, 8 May 1968, reprinted in Karner et al., *Dokumente*, #214; RGANI, F. 10, op. 1, d. 324, p. 23, stenographic minutes of the meeting of the Interventionist Coalition in Moscow, 18 August 1968, reprinted in Karner et al., *Dokumente*, #87; Kosygin held the same opinion, particularly after the KSČ leadership had asked the USSR in spring 1968 for a loan of 500 million rubles in gold: "They know that their request will be turned down, that we cannot possibly grant them a loan under the conditions that they are offering—and this is precisely what they are banking on." In Pikhoya, *Sovetskii Soyuz: Istoriya vlasti*, 316.

35. Another difference between the situation in Czechoslovakia and events in Hungary in 1956 was the relationship of the local mass media with the Soviet Union and its politics. In their struggle with their conservative opponents, the Hungarian reformists pointed to the example of Moscow, where, as they thought, the process of "true" de-Stalinization and the democratization of society had set in after Nikita Khrushchev's anti-Stalinist speech at the 20th Party Conference of the CPSU. By contrast, the tide of criticism of the USSR kept on rising in Czechoslovakia during the course of 1968. Even when Moscow attempted to demonstrate a measure of loyalty to and understanding of the specific situation in the ČSSR (as is evidenced above all by the alterations in the *Pravda* print version of large parts of the speech that Dubček gave at the April plenum of the CC KSČ, which concerned all passages that sounded "suspicious" to Soviet ears), no positive reaction was in evidence in the Czechoslovak mass media.

36. RGANI, F. 2, op. 3, d. 114, p. 42, stenographic notes of the session of the CC CPSU plenum, speech of the secretary-general of the CC CPSU, L. I. Brezhnev, "On the Results of the Meeting of the Delegations of the Communist and Workers' Parties of the Socialist Countries in Warsaw," 17 July 1968.

37. RGANI, F. 89, op. 38, d. 57, p. 9, stenographic notes of the meetings of the Soviet leadership with the state president of the ČSSR, L. Svoboda and M. Klusák, 23 August 1968, reprinted in Karner et al., *Dokumente*, #107; RGANI, F. 89, op. 38, d. 57, S. 49, stenographic notes of the meetings of the state president of the ČSSR, L. Svoboda, 23 August 1968, reprinted in Karner et al., *Dokumente*, #108.

38. RGANI, F. 3, op. 68, d. 838, pp. 7–17, 18–22, report by Suslov, Ponomaryov, and Rusakov, "On the Memorandum of the CC CPSU addressed to the CC KSČ," 29 June 1968; draft of a memorandum of the CC CPSU addressed to the CC KSČ, with guidelines for the Soviet ambassador's meeting with Dubček; text of a letter written by Sharaf Radishov from Tashkent, 1 July 1968; Shelepin's report to Brezhnev, 30 June 1968.

39. RGANI, F. 3, op. 68, d. 838, pp. 25–32.

40. RGANI, F. 3, op. 68, d. 838, p. 38.

41. RGANI, F. 3, op. 68, d. 838, pp. 25–32.

42. RGANI, F. 3, op. 68, d. 838, p. 39.

43. Similar cases, in which the Politburo (and/or the Presidium) of the CC CPSU discussed one and the same issue for two days, were limited to the great political crises: Hungary (1956), Cuba (1962), and 1964, when Khrushchev was ousted.

44. RGANI, F. 3, op. 72, d. 183, pp. 3, 5–13, Politburo Resolution of the CC CPSU P 88 (I), "On the Memorandum of the Politburo of the CC CPSU addressed to the Presidium of the CC KSČ," 3 July 1968, reprinted in Karner et al., *Dokumente*, #37.

45. RGANI, F. 3, op. 72, d. 183, pp. 3, 5–13.

46. RGANI, F. 3, op. 68, d. 838, p. 49, stenographic notes of the session of the plenum of the CC CPSU, speech of the secretary-general of the CC CPSU, L. I. Brezhnev, "On the Results of the Meeting of the Delegations of the Communist and Workers' Parties of the Socialist Countries in Warsaw," 17 July 1968.

47. RGANI, F. 3, op. 72, d. 183, p. 4, Politburo Resolution des CC CPSU P 88 (II), "On Organizing a Meeting of the Representatives of the Fraternal Parties," 3 July 1968.

48. RGANI, F. 3, op. 72, d. 183, p. 13.

49. RGANI, F. 3, op. 68, d. 845, p. 15, report on the Politburo Resolution of the CC CPSU, "On Organizing a Meeting of the Representatives of the Fraternal Parties," report by Suslov, Arvīds Pel'she, Shelepin, 3 July 1968.

50. Another member of the Warsaw Pact, Romania, was left out of this meeting owing to the "special" attitude of its leading political figures, who were at pains to flaunt their "independence" of the USSR.

51. The participants declared themselves particularly appalled by the demonstration on 1 May in Prague, where there had not been a single banner in honor of the Communist Party, where sympathizers of previously dissolved and banned organizations had turned up with nationalist catchphrases and even "a U.S. flag," and where all this had been applauded by the Czechoslovak leadership with Dubček at the head.

52. Navrátil et al., *The Prague Spring 1968*, 324–25; RGANI, F. 10, op. 1, d. 235, 27, minutes of the meeting of the head of the CC CPSU with the leaders of the Communist parties of Bulgaria, Hungary, the GDR, and Poland, 8 May 1968, reprinted in Karner et al., *Dokumente*, #77.

53. RGANI, F. 3, op. 72, d. 175, pp. 5–7, Politburo Resolution of the CC CPSU P 83 (37), the "Missive of Comrade L. I. Brezhnev to Comrade A. Dubček on the Question of the Meeting with the Leaders of the KSČ, BCP, USAP, SED, and PVAP on 8 May 1968 in Moscow," 26 May 1968, reprinted in Karner et al., *Dokumente*, #78.

54. RGANI, F. 5, op. 60, d. 308, p. 63, appeal of the Presidium of the CC KSČ to the Politburo of the CC CPSU on the inadvisability of a conference of representatives of the CPSU, KSČ, BCP, SED, USAP and PVAP in the near future, 19 July 1968; for further details, see the following documents: SAPMO-BA, DY 30/3618, 105–7, meeting of the ambassador of the USSR to the GDR, P. A. Abrasimov, with W. Stoph, A. Norden and H. Axen, 10 July 1968, reprinted in Karner et al., *Dokumente*, #79; letter of the Hungarian CP leader, J. Kádár, to L. Brezhnev, 10 July

1968, reprinted in Karner et al., *Dokumente*, #80; RGANI, F. 3, op. 72, d. 186, p. 19, Politburo Resolution of the CC CPSU P 90 (12), "Letter of the Communist Fraternal Parties to the KSČ," 11 July 1968, reprinted in Karner et al., *Dokumente*, #81.

55. RGANI, F. 3, op. 68, d. 852, p. 44, notes for the Politburo Resolution of the CC CPSU, "On the Memorandum of the Politburo of the CC CPSU to the Presidium of the KSČ"; Chervonenko's accompanying letter to the CC CPSU, 18 July 1968; the dissatisfaction of the CPSU leader and of the leaders of the "Big Five" with the course of action taken by KSČ leadership was easy to explain. Moscow dispatched its invitation to Prague as early as 6 July in the name of all participants, the beginning of the conference being scheduled for 10 or 11 July; RGANI, F. 3, op. 72, d. 184, p. 24; RGANI, F. 3, op. 72, d. 185, p. 50, Politburo Resolution of the CC CPSU P 89 (30), "On the Letter of the CC CPSU to Dubček," 6 July 1968. The Czechoslovak side did not only delay the answer for an unreasonably long period, but also informed the public both of the fact that a meeting was scheduled in the near future and of its possible agenda.

56. RGANI, F. 10, op. 1, d. 235, p. 2, minutes of the meeting of the leaders of the CC CPSU with the leaders of the Communist parties of Bulgaria, Hungary, the GDR and Poland, 8 May 1968, reprinted in Karner et al., *Dokumente*, #77.

57. Navrátil, *The Prague Spring 1968*, 218–19.

58. Particularly noteworthy is the passage in the document that says, "We are convinced that a situation has come about, in which the danger threatening socialism in Czechoslovakia jeopardizes the vital interests of the Socialist countries. The peoples of our countries would never forgive us if in the face of such dangers we were to remain indifferent and carefree." RGANI, F. 2, op. 3, d. 110, p. 9, joint letter of the CC BCP, the CC USAP, the CC SED, the CC PVAP and the CC CPSU to the CC KSČ on the results of the Conference of the Communist Parties in Warsaw, 15 July 1968.

59. Navrátil, *The Prague Spring 1968*, 216.

60. SAPMO, DY 30/ 3618, 27, memorandum of the CC SED to the Presidium of the CC KSČ, 4 July 1968.

61. RGANI, F. 2, op. 3, d. 114, 25, stenographic notes of the plenary session of the CC CPSU, words of welcome from the secretary of the CC CPSU, M. A. Suslov, 17 June 1968.

62. First secretary of the CC CPSU Shelest asserted, "The Soviet Union and her allies in the Warsaw Pact will not stand idly by as the counterrevolution attempts to drive a wedge between the Communist Party and the Czechoslovak people; it is legitimate for them to fulfill the obligations that arise from the Pact and to defend the Socialist achievements of the Czechoslovak people." RGANI, F. 2, op. 3, d. 114, p. 61, stenographic notes of the plenary session of the CC CPSU, discussion of the speech of the secretary-general of the CC CPSU, L. I. Brezhnev, "On the Results of the Meeting of the Delegations of the Communist and Workers' Parties of the Socialist Countries in Warsaw," speech of the first secretary of the CC CP of the Ukraine, P. E. Shelest, 17 July 1968. First secretary of the Moscow City Committee of the CPSU, Viktor Grishin explained: "The Politburo of the CC CPSU has to be urged to continue to take all necessary measures in order to support the healthy forces in the KSČ—which also includes the most extreme measures to get the situation in Czechoslovakia back to normal"; RGANI, F. 2, op. 3, d. 114, p. 68, first

secretary of the CC CP of Kazakhstan Dinmukhamed Kunaev said: "If the appeal of the participants in the Warsaw Conference does not suffice to bring the leaders of the KSČ to their senses and if Dubček does not resort to decisive measures to suppress the counterrevolutionary forces in the country, then we have no alternative left but to rely openly on the healthy forces in the KSČ and to channel with their help development again into the direction that is required by us." RGANI, F. 2, op. 3, d. 114, p. 72.

63. RGANI, F. 2, op. 3, d. 114, p. 118, stenographic notes of the plenary session of the CC CPSU, closing speech of the secretary-general of the CC CPSU, L. I. Brezhnev, 17 July 1968.

64. Jitka Vondrová and Jaromír Navrátil, *Mezinárodni souvislosti Československé krize, 1967–1970. Červenec—Spren 1968* (Brno: Ústav pro soudobé dějiny AV ČR v nakl. Doplněk, 1996), 331–33.

65. Pikhoya mentions these resolutions of the Soviet leadership, which were filed in the Politburo "Special Folder," and refers in this context to the Presidential Archive. AP RF, F. 3, op. 91, d. 98, pp. 58–89.

66. RGANI, F. 3, op. 72, d. 189, pp. 2, 4, Politburo resolution of the CC CPSU P 92 (II), "On the Question of the Situation in Czechoslovakia," 20 July 1968.

67. RGANI, F. 3, op. 68, d. 860, p. 83, materials for the Politburo resolution of the CC CPSU, 26 July 1968, "On the Memorandum to the Ambassador of the USA in Moscow on Questions Relating to the Events in Czechoslovakia," Gromyko's report, 24 July 1968.

68. RGANI, F. 3, op. 68, d. 852, p. 15, materials for the Politburo resolution of the CC CPSU, "On the Directives to the Soviet Ambassadors in Connection with the Publication of the Five Communist Parties' Letter to the CC KSČ," 19 July 1968.

69. RGANI, F. 3, op. 68, d. 860, p. 30, materials for the Politburo resolution of the CC CPSU, "On the Information of the Fraternal Parties Concerning Events in Czechoslovakia," 26 July 1968; on this subject, the CC CPSU wrote a special memorandum addressed to the forty-four "fraternal parties" explaining the Soviet policy regarding the situation in the ČSSR. The memorandum contained additional paragraphs written with the Communist parties of Great Britain, India, and Australia in mind, which had shown a particular "lack of understanding" for the USSR's position on the Czechoslovak question; RGANI, F. 3, op. 68, d. 860, pp. 24–25.

70. RGANI, F. 5, op. 60, d. 491, p. 79, Waldeck Rochet's telegram to the 29th CC of the Communist Parties of the European Countries, including the CC CPSU, with the proposal to convene a conference on the events in Czechoslovakia, 17 June 1968.

71. RGANI, F. 3, op. 72, d. 188, pp. 27, 92–93, Politburo resolution of the CC CPSU P 91 (31), "On the Answer to the CC of the Communist Party of France," 18 July 1968, reprinted in Karner et al., *Dokumente*, #165; RGANI, F. 3, op. 72, d. 188, pp. 5, 14–15, Politburo resolution of the CC CPSU P 91 (III), "On the Answer to Comrade W. Rochet," 19 July 1968, reprinted in Karner et al., *Dokumente*, #135.

72. At the October plenary session of the CC CPSU, Brezhnev said that in order to make the position of the USSR clear regarding the Czechoslovak crisis "the members of the Politburo and the Secretaries of the CC CPSU conducted more than fifty meetings and talks with leading figures of the fraternal parties." RGANI, F. 2, op. 3, d. 130, p. 20, from the stenographic notes on the plenum of the CC CPSU. Speech

of the secretary-general of the CC CPSU, Brezhnev, "On the Foreign Political Activities of the Politburo of the CC CPSU," 31 October 1968, reprinted in Karner et al., *Dokumente*, #122.

73. RGANI, F. 3, op. 68, d. 852, p. 23, materials on the resolution of the Politburo of the CC CPSU, "On the Answer to Comrade W. Rochet," 19 July 1968.

74. RGANI, F. 3, op. 68, d. 852, p. 10, materials on the resolution of the Politburo of the CC CPSU, "On the Briefing of the Soviet Ambassadors in Connection with the Publication of the Five Fraternal Parties' Letter to the Central Committee of the KSČ," 19 July 1968.

75. RGANI, F. 3, op. 68, d. 860, pp. 44–45, materials on the resolution of the Politburo of the CC CPSU, "On the Telegram to the Ambassador of the USSR in the ČSSR," 26 July 1968.

76. It took Moscow's threat to move the meeting to Chop, a border town on Soviet territory, for the KSČ leaders to issue a guarantee that the press would be kept away from the negotiations in Čierná nad Tisou. RGANI, F. 3, op. 68, d. 860, p. 97, materials on the resolution of the Politburo CC CPSU, "On the Brief Given to the Ambassador of the USSR in the ČSSR," 26 July 1968.

77. RGANI, F. 3, op. 72, d. 189, pp. 3, 5, Politburo resolution of the CC CPSU P 92 (III), "On the Meeting of the Leaders of the Socialist Countries' Fraternal Parties," 20 July 1968.

78. A good indicator of the mood in which the participants were looking forward to the meeting is the note of the Soviet ambassador to the GDR, Pyotr Abrasimov, to the CC CPSU of 28 July 1968, stating that Walter Ulbricht and his entourage were prepared to be in Moscow "on 30 July at 5 or 6 p.m." for a discussion of options concerning Czechoslovakia, including "a collective strike." Vondrová and Navrátil, *Mezinárodní souvislosti československé krize*, 33–34. An indirect corroboration of the fact that the beginning of the interventions had been scheduled for the end of July or the beginning of August is to be found in a note in Valerij Vartanov, "Die militärische Niederschlagung des 'Prager Frühlings,'" in Karner et al., *Beiträge*, 661–71. Vartanov states that "in the night of 29/30 July 1968, the squadrons of the Soviet air force, which were dispersed across the entire Soviet Union, were unexpectedly ordered, under the pretext of a drill, to leave the barracks and report at the assembly points" (p. 663).

79. In addition to the negotiations between the entire delegations in Čierná nad Tisou, there were other small-scale meetings. Brezhnev talked with Dubček tête-à-tête, and in negotiations with four participants on each side, the teams consisted of Brezhnev, Kosygin, Podgornyi, and Suslov on the Soviet side and of Dubček, Svoboda, Smrkovský, and Černík on the side of the Czechoslovaks. This is corroborated not only by the fact that no minutes of the negotiations in Čierná nad Tisou of any kind are to be found in Russian archives, but also by another piece of evidence, namely that the Soviet leaders subsequently accused Dubček during the negotiations in Moscow of not honoring the obligations into which he had entered, but were unable to produce a single document to prove to the KSČ leader precisely what kind of obligations he had, in fact, assumed.

80. RGANI, F. 2, op. 3, d. 130, pp. 2–3, stenographic minutes of the plenary session of the CC CPSU, speech of the secretary-general of the CC CPSU, L. I. Brezhnev, "On the Foreign Political Activities of the Politburo of the CC CPSU," 31 October,

1968. The most important topics are the dismissals of František Kriegel from his post as a member of the Presidium of the CC KSČ and as chairman of the National Front, of Česimír Císar from his post as the secretary of the CC KSČ, and of Jiří Pelikán from his post as head of the television company.

81. Shortly afterwards, Brezhnev pointed out to Dubček in a telephone conversation that there had been no need for the Soviet delegation during the negotiations in Čierná nad Tisou to raise certain topics themselves: "You raised these questions at the time, without any arm twisting on our part, of your own accord and quite independently, and you yourselves promised to come up quickly with solutions." RGANI, F. 89, op. 76, d. 75, p. 5, Brezhnev on the phone to Dubček, 13 August 1968, reprinted in Karner et al., *Dokumente*, #57.

82. In Moscow, the idea was even floated of inviting Nixon to the Crimea, in case the majority of the Soviet party leaders were still away on holiday at the time.

83. On 9 and 10 August, Stepan Chervonenko was given the order twice by Moscow to pay the Czechoslovak leadership an official call because of the anti-Soviet and antisocialist campaign that continued to be waged in the country. At the same time (on 9 August), Brezhnev talked to Dubček on the phone; the tone was tense but relatively cordial—Dubček promised again he would stand by what he had committed himself to in Čierná nad Tisou, and Brezhnev wished him luck. Vondrová and Navrátil, *Mezinárodní souvislosti československé krize*, 164–66.

84. RGANI, F. 89, op. 76, d. 75, pp. 1–18, transcript of the telephone conversation between Brezhnev and Dubček, 13 August 1968, reprinted in Karner et al., *Dokumente*, #57.

85. "I would dearly love to throw in the towel and return to my former job. . . . At the next plenary session they are going to elect a new first secretary of the CC KSČ . . . I would do any kind of work. I don't like this post. Whoever wants to have it, let him have it, it doesn't matter to me who is going to be the first secretary of the CC KSČ." RGANI, F. 89, op. 76, d. 75, pp. 1–18 (see note 89).

86. The notes that accompany this document, which has been published in Navrátil's volume, *The Prague Spring 1968*, float the idea that Brezhnev may have understood some of Dubček's statements as a signal ("green light") for the interventions to begin (327). Even if one assumes that Dubček did not want deliberately to provoke military measures taken by the Soviet leadership, the line he opted for as the leader of a party and a country that were under the threat of "fraternal military help" from the beginning of 1968 onward was utterly irresponsible in the existing circumstances.

87. This was actually borne out by Brezhnev, who said at the meeting of the five countries taking part in the military intervention on 18 August in Moscow that "the Politburo of the CC CPSU had discussed these questions in detail yesterday, the day before yesterday and three days ago [i.e., on 15 August]." RGANI, F. 10, op. 1, d. 246, p. 22, stenographic minutes of the meeting of the Interventionist Coalition in Moscow, 18 August 1968, reprinted in Karner et al., *Dokumente*, #87.

88. In the original draft of the document, the request addressed to KSČ leadership "to find the strength and the courage to mobilize the party" for the struggle against the counterrevolution was removed as well as remarks on the de facto split of the CC KSČ, and so forth. RGANI, F. 3, op. 68, d. 871, pp. 138–39, materials on the Politburo resolution of the CC CPSU, "On the Information of the Fraternal Par-

ties Regarding the Results of the Meeting in Čierná nad Tisou and the Conference in Bratislava," 13 August 1968.

89. RGANI, F. 3, op. 72, d. 193, pp. 45, 75–80, Politburo resolution of the CC CPSU P 94 (102), "On the Information of the Fraternal Parties Regarding the Results of the Meeting in Čierná nad Tisou and the Conference in Bratislava," 13 August 1968, reprinted in Karner et al., *Dokumente*, #56.

90. RGANI, F. 3, op. 72, d. 193, pp. 45, 71–73.

91. RGANI, F. 3, op. 72, d. 193, p. 74.

92. RGANI, F. 3, op. 68, d. 862, pp. 69–74, materials on the Politburo resolution of the CC CPSU, 16 August 1968, "On the Situation in Czechoslovakia"; Kirilenko's reports, 15 August 1968, with attachment; the materials that had been prepared by the commission were concerned particularly with the inadequacy of Soviet international propaganda concerning the results of the negotiations in Čierná nad Tisou and Bratislava. At the same time, the Czechoslovak diplomats considered the results of these negotiations as a victory for themselves. This assessment was shared by many western Communist parties. The leader of the Austrian CP, Franz Muri, told the bourgeois weekly *Wochenpresse* that the negotiations had shown the Austrian Communist Party's opinion to be correct that the international Communist movement could not be regarded as "a monolithic block." RGANI, F. 3, op. 68, d. 862, pp. 69–74.

93. RGANI, F. 3, op. 68, d. 862, pp. 16–19.

94. RGANI, F. 3, op. 68, d. 862, pp. 13–15. Konstantin Chernenko was chairman of the Presidium of the Supreme Soviet and Soviet president of state from 1984 to 1985.

95. Navrátil, *The Prague Spring 1968*, 324–25.

96. RGANI, F. 3, op. 72, d. 196, pp. 111–12, Politburo resolution of the CC CPSU P 94 (128), "On the Directives to the Vice UN Secretary General, Comrade Kutakov, on U Thant's Planned Trip to Czechoslovakia," 16 August 1968, reprinted in Karner et al., *Dokumente*, #60.

97. RGANI, F. 3, op. 72, d. 197, pp. 3–6, Politburo resolution of the CC CPSU P 95 (I), "On the Question of the Situation in Czechoslovakia," 17 August 1968, reprinted in Karner et al., *Dokumente*, #62.

98. Unintelligible formulations which were designed to keep events shrouded in secrecy as much as possible were not the only means to prevent information about the beginning of the military intervention in Czechoslovakia from spreading. More than seventy staff members of the party apparatus of the CC CPSU, who were involved in varying degrees of intensity in the preparations of the meeting and in the meeting in Moscow, had to formally commit themselves to speak to no one under any circumstances whatever about "what they heard or seen on 18 August in the House of Receptions on the Lenin Hills."

99. RGANI, F. 3, op. 68, d. 874, p. 27, materials on the session minutes of the Politburo of the CC CPSU, 17 August 1968, "On the Situation in Czechoslovakia," draft of a Politburo resolution of the CC CPSU.

100. RGANI, F. 3, op. 68, d. 874, pp. 74, 86.

101. RGANI, F. 3, op. 72, d. 198, p. 18, Politburo resolution of the CC CPSU P 96 (III), 19 August 1968, reprinted in Karner et al., *Dokumente*, #65; RGANI, F. 3, op. 72, d. 198, p. 38, Politburo resolution of the CC CPSU, P 96 (1), 19 August 1968, reprinted in Karner et al., *Dokumente*, #166.

102. Even though changes, such as the classification of the paper *Student* as a rightist publication or the change in the role ascribed to Czechoslovak mass media in the reporting on the meetings in Čierná nad Tisou and Bratislava were really rather minor in character; the request of the "Czechoslovak friends" to delete the phrase "The counterrevolutionary forces are gathering signatures to have the Communist Party liquidated" bear witness to one of two options: one, that Moscow was harboring basic misconceptions as to the situation in the ČSSR; or two, that it was set to fan existing partisanship in order to justify the impending military intervention. RGANI, F. 3, op. 68, d. 874, p. 112, materials on the resolution of the Politburo of the CC CPSU, "On the Telegram to the Soviet Ambassador in the ČSSR," 16 August 1968.

103. RGANI, F. 3, op. 68, d. 874, p. 11, materials on the resolution of the Politburo of the CC CPSU, 16 August, 1968, "On the Telegram to the Soviet Ambassador in the ČSSR": cipher telegram from Chervonenko in Prague of 17 August 1968.

104. Officially, many of these resolutions were passed almost ten days later, on 27 August; in many cases, there were no so-called voting slips, which would make it possible to tell who from the ranks of the senior Soviet leadership had at least seen the document in question.

105. The action plan that the group of "trustworthy persons in the CC KSČ" had committed themselves to fulfill on condition of the guarantee that the invasion of Czechoslovakia was going to take place in the night of 20/21 August and that Brezhnev had reported on in so much detail at the meeting of the Warsaw Five on 18 August, turned out as completely illusory in practice—not a single one of its points was realized. It is obvious that there were several people present at the meeting in Moscow who doubted that everything was going according to plan. Brezhnev himself admitted at the end of the meeting, when he answered a number of questions from Eastern European leaders by saying that "there are several things we do not see clearly either." RGANI, F. 10, op. 1, d. 246, p. 50.

106. Imre Nagy (1896–1958), in October–November 1956, was the head of the revolutionary government of Hungary and of the Politburo of the Central Leadership of the Hungarian Workers' Party (USAP). After the suppression of the Hungarian Revolution in November 1956, he was arrested by the Soviet troops who had occupied Budapest and was sentenced to death in June 1958. Mátyás Rákosi (1892–1971) was a Hungarian politician. He was dismissed in July 1956 from his post of first secretary of the USAP, and he subsequently emigrated to the USSR, where he remained to his death as a political refugee without the right to return to Hungary. Nikos Zachariadis (1903–1973) was a Greek politician. He was secretary-general of the CC of the Greek CP until 1956, then in political exile in the USSR and, like Rákosi, committed suicide in 1973. Both Rákosi and Zachariadis were kept in the USSR against their will, first, because the new political leaders of the Communist parties in Hungary and Greece requested it and, secondly, because Moscow feared the parties might split—the influence and the authority of the two leaders who had fallen from grace remained considerable for a long time. For details, see, for example, Csaba Békés, "The 1956 Hungarian Revolution and World Politics," CWIHP Working Paper 16 (1996); Janós Rainer, *Imre Nagy, Vom Parteisoldaten zum Märtyrer des Hungarian Volksaufstandes, Eine politische Biographie, 1896–1958* (Paderborn: Schöningh, 2006); Jan Foitzik, *Entstalinisierungskrise in Ostmitteleuropa 1953–1956: Vom 17. Juni bis zum Ungarischen Volksaufstand: Politische, militärische, soziale und*

nationale Dimensionen (Paderborn: F. Schöningh, 2001); Erwin Schmidl, ed., *Die Ungarnkrise 1956 und Österreich* (Vienna: Böhlau, 2002); Csaba Békés et al., eds., *The 1956 Hungarian Revolution: A History in Documents* (Budapest: Central European University Press, 2002); Paul Lendvai, *Der Ungarnaufstand 1956: Eine Revolution und ihre Folgen* (Munich: Bertelsmann, 2006).

107. RGANI, F. 3, op. 72, d. 198, p. 8.

108. Navrátil, *The Prague Spring 1968*, 324–25.

109. RGANI, F. 10, op. 1, d. 246, p. 37, "Minutes of the Talks of the CPSU with the Fraternal Parties," 24 August 1968, reprinted in Karner et al., *Dokumente*, #109.

110. The meeting gave rise to a remarkable exchange between Kosygin and Gomułka. In reply to Gomułka's vehemently advanced opinion that the Communist Party had virtually ceased to exist in Czechoslovakia, Kosygin said there must still be such a thing as a Communist Party. To make his point, he resorted to a strange and rather controversial argument: "It is true that we have had a very difficult situation in Czechoslovakia for the past few days—yet the workers in the factories have not stopped working; no one takes to the street. Surely that means that there is someone who still controls the working class; therefore, the Party cannot be said to have virtually ceased to exist in Czechoslovakia." RGANI, F. 10, op. 1, d. 247, p. 30, stenographic minutes of the meeting of the Interventionist Coalition in Moscow, 24 August 1968, reprinted in Karner et al., *Dokumente*, #109.

111. RGANI, F. 10, op. 1, d. 247, p. 30, reprinted in Karner et al., *Dokumente*, #109.

112. The first attempts of the allied armies at broadcasting to a Czechoslovak audience resulted in extremely negative reactions in the ČSSR, even among those who were in favor of the military operation: the commentators' poor command of Czech, their obvious ignorance of daily life in the country, and serious factual blunders caused those who claimed to be acting in the name of the "Czechoslovak patriots and the defenders of Socialism" to unmask themselves.

113. RGANI, F. 3, op. 68, d. 877, p. 173, materials on the resolution of the Politburo of the CC CPSU, "On the Address to the Citizens of the Czechoslovak Socialist Republic"; text of the Proclamation to the Citizens of the Czechoslovak Socialist Republic. When they informed the allies that such a text was being prepared, the Soviet leaders added that "no publication of the proclamation in our press is planned," 22 August 1968.

114. On 28 August alone, forty articles and news items were devoted to Czechoslovakia in the London *Times*, sixty-eight in the Paris *Le Monde*, and forty-eight in the Bonn *Die Welt*. In the USSR, too, a collected volume of documents on the situation in the ČSSR was published in September 1968, which had been compiled from press material by Soviet journalists, *K sobytiyam v Chekhoslovakii: Fakty, dokumenty, svidetel'stva pressy i ochevidtsev*, 1st ed. (Moscow: Moskva, 1968). The small number of copies printed and the late publication date prevented the volume from playing the significant role on which the Kremlin propagandists had counted.

115. RGANI, F. 89, op. 61, d. 6, pp. 2–4, internal order of the departments of the CC CPSU regarding the question of preparing military-political operations on 21 August 1968.

116. RGANI, F. 89, op. 61, d. 6, pp. 1–2.

117. Pikhoya, *Sovetskii Soyuz: Istoriya vlasti*, 342–43.

118. Suri, *Power and Protest*, 200.

6

The KGB and the Czechoslovak Crisis of 1968: Preconditions for the Soviet Invasion and Occupation of Czechoslovakia

Nikita Petrov

Political leaders of the Soviet Union were particularly sensitive to even minor deviations from the ideological concepts and guidelines officially adopted by the USSR by countries of the Socialist Bloc. With regard to Czechoslovak Socialist Republic (ČSSR), the situation was further exacerbated by the fact that the totalitarian system imposed on the country by the Kremlin was experienced as alien and at odds with the historical tradition of pluralism and democracy that was characteristic of Czechoslovakia.[1]

Changes in the political climate and the first stirrings of the civil rights movement can be traced to the end of Antonín Novotný's time in office. After the January plenum of the Central Committee (CC) of the Communist Party of Czechoslovakia (*Komunistická strana Československa* or KSČ) in 1968, the democratization of Czechoslovakia's political system, the process of the revision of antiquated ideological dogmas, and, ultimately, the rehabilitation of the victims of Stalinist repression got off to a good start. This process was diametrically opposed to the domestic politics of the USSR that had been taking shape after Nikita Khrushchev's ousting. Here the process of rehabilitation was shelved completely by the new leadership under Leonid Brezhnev. The Soviet Committee for State Security (KGB) crushed all forms of thought that did not toe the party line and all independent activities in the population. From this point of view, the Kremlin's radical opposition to the political reforms in Czechoslovakia was a foregone conclusion. It is obvious that "the struggle against dissent in Czechoslovakia strengthened the uniformity of official orthodoxy in the USSR."[2]

There was another substantial reason why Czechoslovakia was at the center of the Kremlin leadership's attention. There is plenty of evidence that Brezhnev asked Novotný as early as 1966 to consent to the stationing of Soviet troops on ČSSR soil.[3] Novotný gave his consent to the stationing of rockets, but refused to sanction the presence of Soviet troops on Czechoslovak territory, which irritated Brezhnev considerably, for as he saw it, the implementation of new military strategies in the struggle with the West was imperative. The Kremlin strategists believed it was crucial to have troops in place at the western borders of each satellite state. Czechoslovakia formed a gap between the battle groups in the north, in Poland, and in the south, in Hungary. Aleksandr Mayorov, commander in chief of the 38th Army stationed at the Czechoslovak border, describes in his memoirs how Brezhnev had ordered him to Old Square (*Staraya ploshchad'*), to the CC Communist Party of the Soviet Union (*Kommunisticheskaya Partiya Sovetskogo Soyuza* or CPSU), where the party leader told him: "Our focus must now shift north of Budapest to Prague. . . . And we must have more friends in the Czechoslovak army."[4]

There is also evidence that Brezhnev nursed a grudge against Novotný, who had been one of Khrushchev's protégés. Khrushchev had been especially open toward Novotný and had passed on information to him that he refused to discuss with other Warsaw Pact heads of state. After Khrushchev's fall from power in October 1964 Novotný had a conversation with the USSR's ambassador in Czechoslovakia, Mikhail Zimyanin, in the course of which Novotný mentioned some of the revelations he had received from Khrushchev. Zimyanin reported this to Moscow: "Comrade Novotný said that Comrade Khrushchev had mentioned last year in a conversation that Czechoslovakia was enriching herself at the Soviet Union's expense." During negotiations in Prague, Khrushchev "had also characterized relations between the USSR and the CPSU on the one hand and several fraternal countries and parties on the other—notably the German Democratic Republic (GDR), Poland, and Romania—as well as the political leaders of these parties and countries in a manner that would in all probability—had his utterances been made public—have damaged the interests of the CPSU and the Soviet Union."[5]

The way the Czechoslovak political leaders reacted to Khrushchev's ousting was observed by the KGB representative in Prague. On 15 October, he reported to Brezhnev on his meeting with the minister of the interior, Lubomír Štrougal:

> In a personal conversation Comrade Štrougal told me that the President had been told by Comrade Brezhnev that Comrade Khrushchev had been dismissed on account of mistakes in the field of domestic policy. He also pointed out that there was the danger of an increase of liberalist tendencies and possible demonstrations directed against the Party in Slovakia—inspired notably by Husák and Novomeský. The situation is further exacerbated by the presidential elections that are scheduled for the beginning of November.[6]

. . . The minister underlined that in view of the difficulties experienced in the ČSSR in explaining why Stalin's mistakes had not been recognized as such in time it was presumably going to be even more difficult to explain why Comrade Khrushchev's mistakes had taken so long to be identified. The standing of the KSČ with the masses could easily be undermined by this at least to an extent. This was a subject however that the minister did not return to during our meeting.[7]

However, it appears to have been the case that Czechoslovakia's political leaders were looking for danger in places where there was none. Štrougal, for instance, pointed to "the possibility of nationalistic and 'left-wing' (pro-Chinese) reactions of some elements also within the KSČ."[8] Security arrangements were stepped up in October 1964. According to another report of the KGB representative in Prague, Štrougal convened a meeting of senior cadres at the Ministry for Foreign Affairs on 15 October 1964 to inform them of the dismissal of Khrushchev and the CC of the Presidium of the CPSU. Moreover, he ordered staff to be on twenty-four-hour stand-by duty, and put the police on alert as well as the security details for members of the government according to Line Five of the Czechoslovak Ministry for Foreign Affairs.[9]

THE RISE OF THE KGB'S INFLUENCE IN THE USSR

The internal situation in the USSR after Nikita Khrushchev's ousting may be characterized as a phase of the settling of scores by "moderate" Stalinists and of the consolidation of "dogmatic" positions. The propaganda campaign before the spectacular festivities to celebrate fifty years of Soviet power assumed dimensions that were completely without parallel. Under these circumstances, the Brezhnev regime paid increased attention to suppressing any kind of dissent with or "defilement" of the Soviet ideals. It was obvious for the Politburo that the wave of revelations concerning Stalin's personality cult initiated by Khrushchev was yielding concrete results: people were losing faith in the socialist ideals, a development that was thoroughly unacceptable to the Kremlin.

At the session of the Politburo of the CC CPSU on 10 November 1966, Brezhnev addressed the topic of ideology, which he considered the most important of all:

> In some works, in journals and other publications criticism is being voiced of what people hold most dear, most sacred. It is a fact that some of our writers (who, let me add, subsequently find their way into print) will say for instance that there was no such thing as the Aurora's salvo, that it was no more than a barrel burst, that there were fewer than 28 Panfilov guardsmen or, even more

grotesquely, that the whole story in which Klochkov[10] figures is a fabrication altogether and that he never uttered his famous dictum, "Behind us is Moscow and there is no way we can retreat." This extends all the way to slanderous statements about the October Revolution and other historical stages of the heroic history of our party and of our Soviet people.[11]

The future head of the KGB, Yuri Andropov, registered his total agreement with Brezhnev's point of view and explicitly identified Khrushchev as the source of all evils: "It is a fact that the period before the October plenum of the CC [1964] inflicted considerable damage on both our party and our people in the area of ideological activities."[12]

Six months later, in May 1967, Andropov became head of the KGB. He immediately gave the struggle against "subversion" high priority. As early as July 1967, the Politburo approved Andropov's proposal to add a fifth directorate with five subdivisions to the KGB for the struggle against "ideological diversion." In addition to this, the network of local KGB offices was substantially enlarged. In 200 districts and cities, new KGB branches were installed, which were given the name of District or Municipal Departments of the KGB. This was decreed in a Politburo resolution (P47/97-op), which also provided for the increase of the KGB's overall number of staff to 2,250 (of whom 1,750 were officers, including 100 officers newly appointed to the central apparatus in Moscow's Lubyanka).[13]

Changes also affected other subdivisions of the KGB. The 11th Department of the KGB[14] (which conducted liaison with counterpart services in other Socialist countries) was again made an integral part of the foreign intelligence by a Politburo resolution passed on 4 June 1968 and was now called the 11th Department of the First Chief Directorate of the Committee of State Security (KGB) of the Council of Ministers of the USSR.[15] This was the result of Andropov's explicit request to the Politburo.[16] He wrote that hiving off the 11th Department and setting it up as an independent unit had weakened its "working contacts" with other subdivisions of the security services, which made its work less effective. According to Andropov, the activities of the 11th Department had degenerated in the end to "mere protocolar processing" of hosting state security delegations from other Socialist countries. In the meantime, "the imperialist powers and their secret services are engaging in activities that aim to subvert the unity between socialist countries and the liquidation of their socialist gains."[17]

THE YEAR 1968

The changeover of power in Prague in January 1968 proved decisive in imparting a direction to the development of the Czechoslovak situation that proved unacceptable to the Kremlin. From this point onward, the

Politburo of the CC CPSU regularly received reports from Czechoslovakia that were put on the agenda and required discussion. On 25 January 1968, for instance, a report by the ambassador of the USSR in Czechoslovakia, Stepan Chervonenko, was discussed, and Brezhnev was asked to "inform Dubček of the exchange of opinions in the Politburo."[18] In all discussions on Czechoslovakia, the head of the KGB, Andropov, played a prominent role. He belonged to all the Politburo committees dealing with the ČSSR.

The April plenum of the CC CPSU on 9 and 10 April 1968 contributed decisively to the positions on Czechoslovakia subsequently adopted by the Soviet leadership. Brezhnev delivered his speech "On the Current Problems of the International Situation and on the Struggle of the CPSU for the Unity of the International Communist Movement," and in the ensuing debates, the quality of the ideological work in the USSR was touched upon again and again. Several speakers demanded devoting more attention to this area. The first secretary of the CC of the Communist Party of Belarus, Pyotr Masherov, advocated the extirpation of "ideological weeds"; he felt that literature was being turned into a vehicle for "the libel of all things Soviet" and insisted that it was necessary to strengthen the ideological cadres and to institute "educational measures."[19] First Secretary Radishov of the CC of the Uzbek Communist Party referred to "ideological diversions" and the "subversive influence" of the West in general; he felt that it was this influence to which dissidents owed their existence in the first place: "Such people even appear in the guise of writers, as can be seen from the example of the contemptible dissidents Daniel', Sinyavskii, Ginzburg, Galanskov, Dobrovol'skii, Lashkova and others."[20] Minister of Culture Ekaterina Fursteva used the plenum to voice her criticism of the Taganka Theatre and its director, Yuri Lyubimov. First Secretary Petro Shelest[21] of the CC of the Ukrainian Communist Party criticized Nicolae Ceauşescu for "being heaped with praise"—from the wrong corner. He was particularly scornful of the president of the Council of Ministers of Romania, Ion Gheorghe Maurer, who had visited General C. G. E. Mannerheim's grave while in Finland on a state visit. On this occasion, Shelest said that at the head of the Romanian government was a man who was "at the very least extremely suspect as a communist."[22] Yet the greatest source of anxiety was the situation in Czechoslovakia. First Secretary Sergei Pavlov of the CC Komsomol, speaking of a meeting with Czechoslovak colleagues, said: "We criticized the Czechs" for their lenient attitude toward the mores of Western modernity. Pavlov cited examples such as "the incomprehensible use of stupid Beatles music for advertising purposes, the springing up of so-called Big Beat ensembles all over the place and the massive epidemic of pathological dancing."[23]

Brezhnev had the last word at the plenum and made it clear in his speech that he, too, advocated a course of "putting on the screws." Brezhnev had the example of Czechoslovakia in mind when he said that even a small dose of indulgence and procrastination might be enough to jeopardize Soviet principles: "One has to strengthen discipline in all areas of society and must not be reduced to a situation where one has to resort to extreme measures." The plenum also approved Brezhnev's proposal to enlarge the staff of the secretariat of the CC CPSU by one. Konstantin F. Katushev rose from the post of the first secretary of the Gor'kii Regional Committee to that of Secretary of the CC CPSU. There was no need for Brezhnev to tell the CC members what task the new secretary was going to be assigned because it was obvious to all that the proliferation of differences within the "socialist camp" made filling the vacancy left by Andropov's departure from the secretariat of the CC CPSU a matter of urgent necessity;[24] Andropov had been in charge of the CC CPSU's relations with the "fraternal parties" of the other Socialist countries.

From the spring of 1968 onward, the Kremlin's apprehensions with regard to Czechoslovakia's domestic political situation became ever more urgent. The same was true of the demands presented to Dubček and his government. As a first step, the Politburo nominated a small working group that was to address the situation in the ČSSR. After the group's first briefing at the Politburo session on 6 May 1968, Mikhail Suslov, Pyotr Demichev, Konstantin Katushev, and Konstantin Rusakov were asked to prepare "a proper information sheet on the situation in Czechoslovakia for the party of the CPSU" and to brief journalists on how to present developments in the press and how to account for them to the public.

The USSR Ministry for Foreign Affairs was ordered to prepare a draft for a TASS report to counter the "false rumors with regard to Masaryk's death that were being circulated by the ČSSR's press and radio." It was to contain the information that Andropov had already forwarded in a letter to the CC CPSU on 25 April 1968 stating that the discussion fanned by the Czechoslovak mass media—it was claimed that Masaryk had not committed suicide, as was announced in 1948, but had been murdered by the KGB on Stalin's orders—was based on empty speculations.[25] According to Andropov, it was obvious in the light of new archival research that there was "no connection whatever" between the organs of the Soviet Secret Service (the Committee for Information, KI) and Masaryk's suicide; therefore, the campaign in Czechoslovakia had to stop.[26] However, Section 4 of the Politburo resolution of 6 May is evidence, if veiled in the code of bureaucratic jargon, that this resolution was, in fact, the key to the development that followed and the precondition for the military intervention:

> Comrades Suslov, Andropov, Demichev, Ustinov, Katushev, Ponomaryov, Grechko, Gromyko, Epishev, and Rusakov are to be asked to prepare drafts for the required documents. This also applies to the measures as discussed for the implementation thereof, which will include plans for the concrete steps to be taken according to the situation in the country after the afore mentioned measures have been carried out.[27]

In plain language, this referred to drawing up a plan for the military option, including a time schedule and a detailed listing of all the measures required ("concrete steps") after the invasion ("after the aforementioned measures have been carried out"). At that stage, the purely military aspect had already been resolved. A detailed plan for the invasion of Czechoslovakia by Soviet troops (together with orders for the 38th Army) was presented to Brezhnev on the evening of 11 April 1968 by Minister of Defense Marshal A. Grechko, and by the commander in chief of the Transcarpathian Military District, Mikhail Ivanovich Povalii.[28] All that was needed now was the endorsement of the complex of political measures. Original planning had, of course, provided for the invasion of Czechoslovakia to be carried out using joint "military maneuvers" of the Warsaw Pact countries as a smoke screen.[29]

After the establishment of a permanent ČSSR committee consisting of Nikolai Podgornyi, Suslov, Arvīds Pel'she, Aleksandr Shelepin, Demichev, Andropov, Katushev, Andrei Gromyko, Aleksei Epishev, and Rusakov[30] in May 1968, Andropov, who had a penchant for secretive measures, dispatched his special envoy, the KGB reserve officer Mikhail Sagatelyan,[31] whose official function was that of an assistant editor of the foreign department of the paper *Izvestiya*, to Prague. There he had meetings with a number of ČSSR politicians and submitted his observations in a special report on 4 June 1968. The next day, this secret action plan was forwarded to the Politburo by Andropov (with a note added saying that "in the opinion of the KGB the recommendations contained in this report deserve to be followed").[32]

What Sagatelyan had put into his report did, indeed, deserve the Soviet leadership's undivided attention. During his stay in Czechoslovakia he had managed to establish conspiratorial contacts with several political leaders, notably Deputy Minister of Culture and Information (and CC member) Bohuslav Chňoupek and to receive from him "a number of secret party and government documents." It is evident from the report that Chňoupek engaged in these open talks with Sagatelyan "with Bil'ak's knowledge." The action plan amounted to the following measures. First, a "pro-Soviet faction" was to be created within the Czechoslovak leadership, which would then be instrumental in convening a plenum of the CC KSČ. At that plenum, "the KSČ leadership would be replaced," and Dubček ousted from his job (in Sagatelyan's view "a lesser evil than a military invasion"). Second, the contacts that had been established were to be developed to make sure the flow of information from Chňoupek would be kept up. Third, the Soviet leaders would talk to Vasil Bil'ak, Alois Indra, Dragomír Kolder, and all those who "were named by them as initiated into planning." Fourth, the implementation of these measures was to be entrusted to a KGB operative who was to work "undercover" in the ČSSR for a month or a month and a half. This was due to the fact that according to Sagatelyan "the persons representing the KGB in Prague were well known to the Czechoslovak state security organs and therefore unsuited for such tasks."[33] On reading Andropov's letter and Sagatelyan's proposals, Brezhnev realized their importance and drafted a resolution for the Politburo and the secretariat.[34]

A typescript was found in Brezhnev's desk after his death bearing the title "Notes on the Preparation of the Politico-Military Action on 21 August 1968."[35] Theses notes contain clear and detailed outlines of the planned operations in Czechoslovakia committed to paper shortly before the invasion. The passage dealing with the activities of KGB secret agents embedded in the ranks of the Czechoslovak opposition reads as follows:[36]

> It is imperative for us to add to the military control a political and adminis-trative one. What we are aiming for are massive interferences in the affairs of Czechoslovakia and pressure of all kinds including demands in ultimatum form. . . . The political situation in Czechoslovakia is complicated at the moment and we must make sure it does not get even more complicated. To achieve this goal an extensive plan involving disinformation measures had to be developed. It is crucially important to discredit the right-wing leaders, to compromise them, to strengthen the contacts to those right-wing elements in order to enable the broad masses to charge the right-wing leaders with col-laboration.[37]

The KGB, therefore, carried out so-called special operations in Czecho-slovakia. In April 1968, the KGB operative Vladimir Surzhaninov (active in Prague from 26 April) and two operatives of the "Illegals Directorate" of the First Chief Directorate of the KGB, Gennadi Borzov and V. Umnov, were sent to Prague as undercover agents to reinforce the KGB apparatus in Prague.[38] Their tasks included not only the establishment of working contacts with the pro-Soviet faction within the KSČ, but also secret opera-tions. On the basis of a resolution of the Secretariat of the CC CPSU of 16 April 1968 another two KGB operatives, Georgii Fedyashin and Aleksandr Alekseev, both officially journalists, were sent to Prague.[39]

Its presence in Czechoslovakia having thus been considerably enhanced, the KGB was able to carry out two "special operations" in the country. In the first of these, code-named "Progress," illegal Soviet agents assumed the identity of tourists, business people, or students from the Federal Republic of Germany (FRG), Austria, Sweden, and other Western countries and en-tered Czechoslovakia, where they sought to establish contacts with various oppositional forces and to gather intelligence data and check it for reliabil-ity. If it was deemed necessary, the Soviet agents were also able to influence the activities of the opposition directly. Apart from other aspects, this en-abled them to implicate the Czechoslovak opposition in suspicious Western contacts. The second operation, codenamed "Khodoki" by the KGB, was potentially even more provocative. It assigned illegal Soviet agents the task of fabricating proof that the Czechoslovak opposition was planning an armed counterrevolutionary coup. To this end, the KGB agents built "arms caches," distributed flyers containing appeals to topple the government, and so forth. This was by no means all; the KGB even prepared plans for the murder of Russian women with Czechoslovak spouses. The murders were to be blamed on the "counterrevolutionaries," which would further aggravate the situation.[40] Vladlen Krivosheev, an *Izvestiya* correspondent, recorded an instance of the activities of the KGB agents that were to serve as proof for the "activation of the counterrevolutionary forces." He called them "activities of the Third Force." He was given an assistant, a journalist previously unknown to him, "an expert in international affairs" and, as he did not realize until later, a member of the KGB. When a short time later a "weapons arsenal" was discovered in the western part of Czechoslovakia consisting of a couple of handguns and grenades, Krivosheev remembered that his new assistant had gone there the previous night in *Izvestiya*'s car, a Volga.[41]

A typical example of the disinformation campaign of the Directorate "A" of the First Chief Directorate of the KGB is an article in *Pravda* on 19 July 1968 entitled "The Adventurous Plans of the Pentagon and the CIA."[42] Citing a "strictly confidential operative plan" and documents of the commander in chief of the U.S. Army in Europe, it claimed that the Pentagon and the CIA were playing an active part in Czechoslovakia, engaging in "ideological diversions" and fomenting a "counterrevolutionary coup." This plan, which had supposedly been leaked to Soviet journalists, had, in fact, been fabricated by the KGB.[43]

The oppositional tendencies in Czechoslovakia were grossly exaggerated by Soviet propaganda. The multiplication of civic initiatives and the fact that there was rising criticism of totalitarian dictatorship of the Stalinist type were portrayed as evidence for the disastrous plan "of Czechoslovakia's secession from the socialists camp." All this was valuable only in terms of the USSR's internal propaganda. It is thoroughly typical of the situation that the comprehensive report entitled "On the Activities of the Counterrevolutionary Underground in the ČSSR," which was compiled in October 1968 by the First Chief Directorate of the KGB, devoted no more than a quarter of its text to the "activities of the antisocialist forces before the invasion of the Allied troops in the ČSSR." There is not a word in this section about arms caches or any other tangible underground activities. What featured very prominently were the weakness of the local KSČ organs, the loss of their "leading role," party infighting, chaos in the cadres, the proliferation of oppositional tendencies within society and the mushrooming of all kinds of organized civic groupings, including those of individuals who had been exposed to political repression in the past. There is only one passage that refers to isolated examples of the distribution of flyers and of the use of slogans hostile to the KSČ and the USSR.[44]

The problems that had arisen in connection with events in Czechoslovakia also cropped up on the territory of the USSR. Several Czechoslovak correspondents in Moscow ran afoul of the KGB due to their independent positions and their critical reporting. This was Moscow and not Prague, censorship was totally in effect here, and tolerance of independent judgment was nil. At the instigation of the KGB, which kept the representatives of foreign media under close surveillance, a Politburo resolution was passed on 19 June 1968 entitled "On Anti-Soviet Statements by the Moscow Correspondent of the Czechoslovak Radio, L. Dobrovský."[45] The issue was tricky in that it involved the correspondent of a "fraternal socialists country." The resolution was, therefore, top secret and bears the stamp "Special File." Yet there was no immediate solution to the problem in sight. It was not until after the military invasion that Andropov and Gromyko penned a joint letter on 9 September 1968 proposing Dobrovský "be expelled from the Soviet Union."[46] The proposal was accepted by the Politburo, but the resolution was not officially recorded.[47]

The KGB's secret efforts in the spring and early summer of 1968 provided the Kremlin leadership with the arguments they urgently required to justify the tough line they were taking toward the political leaders of the KSČ. The plenum of the CC CPSU on 17 July 1968 was entirely given over to the developments in Czechoslovakia and the results of the meeting of the Communist and Workers' Parties in Warsaw. Brezhnev gave a speech at the plenum and said that "a carefully camouflaged counterrevolutionary process" was unfolding in Czechoslovakia.[48] There were fourteen speakers at the debate. By way of conclusion at the end of the plenum, Brezhnev announced: "Tomorrow the fraternal parties' letter to the Czechoslovaks will be published."[49]

THE BREZHNEV DOCTRINE

The military action carried out by the Soviet Union and its satellite countries against Czechoslovakia made it plain for all to see how little value was to be attached to the sovereignty of the Warsaw Pact countries. Shortly afterward, a propaganda campaign was initiated in support of the Kremlin's new course. *Pravda* published an article with the programmatic title "Sovereignty and the International Obligations of the Socialist Countries," which caused a sensation.[50] The article presented different aspects of the thesis that the security interests of the entire "Socialist community" were more important than the interests of individual countries within the community. According to the article, it was "inadmissible for the sovereignty of individual Socialist countries to be opposed to the interests of worldwide socialism." As for the military action of the "five allied socialist countries," it was, according to the author of this article, perfectly in keeping "with the basic interests of the Czechoslovak people."[51] The article, signed Sergei Kovalev, contained no additional information as to the author's education or function, so it makes sense briefly to discuss him here.

Sergei Mitrofanovich Kovalyov was known for his tireless struggle against "bourgeois ideology and revisionism."[52] Having been educated at the Moscow Institute of History, Philosophy, and Literature and at the Party University, Kovalev worked at the Department of Propaganda and Agitation of the CC CPSU. One of his first publications bore the title *O natsional'noi gordosti sovetskikh lyudei* (*National Pride and the Soviet Man*).[53] Kovalev quickly rose in the hierarchy and was made director of the state-owned publishing house for political literature in February 1951, where he made the mistake of not realizing in time that political change was in the air. He laid himself open to the charge of having made serious errors in publishing *Istoricheskii materializm* (*Historical Materialism*), which included "mistaken formulations that are in breach of the guidelines of the CC CPSU and harmful to the interest of our state"; Kovalev was dismissed from his post and his file sent to the party Control Committee of the CPSU for inspection.

It took Kovalev a great deal of effort to rehabilitate himself sufficiently to be allowed to work in the field of ideology again. He had learned his lesson and was determined not to forget it. By 1968, his standing was reasonably consolidated again and in June a Politburo resolution assigned him to the group around the Politburo member Andrei Kirilenko, who was due to travel to Italy on a state visit.[54] Then, in September 1968, Kovalev, by then a member of the editorial staff of *Pravda*, published an important article on the extremely sensitive topic of the relations between the Socialist countries. It is hardly conceivable that Kovalev could have written this article without previous briefing by the Kremlin.

The *Pravda* article was immediately spotted by the U.S. State Department and identified as a "new Soviet doctrine." The KGB informed the CC CPSU accordingly in a letter dated 21 October 1968. In the same letter, the KGB also pointed out that in the view of U.S. State Department specialists the "new Soviet interpretation of the issue of sovereignty" contravened the UN Charter, an assessment that was also shared by UN Secretary-General Sithu U Thant. Despite this, Soviet foreign minister Gromyko formally underscored the new Soviet approach to the issue of "limited independence" at the UN Plenary Session.[55]

The new course was developed further at the plenum of the CC CPSU on 30 and 31 October 1968. Brezhnev held a speech on the "Activities of the CC CPSU."[56] He informed the comrades that, at the political level, "the situation in the ČSSR remained precarious even after the military action of 20/21 August." According to Brezhnev, most Socialist countries—and that included Vietnam, Mongolia, North Korea, Cuba—had welcomed the military invasion. Only China and Albania had remained aloof.[57] "What worries us however is the equivocal and far from honest position of several members of the presidium of the KSČ," Brezhnev noted.[58] Yugoslavia, too, was guilty of embracing a "mistaken position," which, according to Brezhnev, had to do with that country's "revisionist tendencies." A similar charge had to be leveled against Romania, even though that country's "position had lately become more moderate." With regard to the general tendencies that were becoming apparent in the assessment of the Soviet invasion, Brezhnev regretted the "unclear positions" held by the French and Italian Communist parties and noted: "What is obvious in the politics of the leaders of several Western European Communist Parties is the deference to the tendencies of the petty bourgeois masses, the abatement of class consciousness and the underestimation of their international obligations."[59] On the whole, Brezhnev could find no fault with the general reactions of the West: "The protests that the governments of these countries registered in their various ways actually had a formal, symbolic character and concerned in no way whatsoever the basis of our interstate and, above all, our economic relationships with these countries." According to Brezhnev, the most important lesson to be drawn from the military action was this, "One thing has been made clear beyond any doubt: the assurances of the CPSU and of the Soviet Union that we will not allow anyone to prize away one single member from the socialist community are no empty propaganda."[60] In this way the doctrine of "limited sovereignty" was given its final touches; it has entered the history books as the Brezhnev Doctrine.

AFTER THE INVASION

Senior representatives of the KGB arrived in Czechoslovakia at the same time as the invasion troops. Their tasks included the organization of operative KGB groups in Prague und Bratislava. At the head of the entire operation were two high-ranking KGB officers: First Deputy of the head of the KGB Nikolai Zakharov and the head of the Second Chief Directorate (Counterespionage) and member of the board of the KGB, Georgii Tsinyov. Aleksandr Yakovlev, who held the post of the First Deputy Director of the CC CPSU Propaganda Department at the time, was sent to Czechoslovakia with a group of journalists on 21 August 1968. Later he told how on his return he had informed Brezhnev of what he had seen: "The KGB generals Zakharov and Tsinyov were spreading fear in our Prague embassy and passing on disinformation to Moscow."[61] Brezhnev simply acknowledged this information without reacting to it or drawing any other conclusion from it apart from asking Yakovlev to keep it from Kosygin.[62]

Brezhnev was convinced that the military action against Czechoslovakia would bear fruit sooner or later. At the plenum of the CC CPSU on 9 December 1968, he had already announced optimistically that the situation in Czechoslovakia was returning to "normal." He also noted that V. Kuznetsov, who had been sent to Prague to assist the Soviet ambassador Chervonenko, "was doing a great job."[63]

In the autumn of 1968, the KGB regularly updated the CC CPSU on events in Czechoslovakia and on events related to the country. Those reports bore the signatures of the first deputy directors of the KGB, Nikolai Zakharov and Semyon Tsvigun, which was presumably due to the fact that Andropov was away on an extended leave beginning 1 September 1968.[64] In report no. 2159-C of 13 September, the KGB informed the CC CPSU of a BBC broadcast in which Moscow writers and their protests against the military invasion of Czechoslovakia had been the topic;[65] a report of 16 October dealt with programs planned by the radio station Svoboda;[66] another report (29 October) centered on one of the editors of the daily *Rudé právo*, Oldřich Švestka, and his comments on the situation in Czechoslovakia and some political leaders of the KSČ;[67] the report of 29 November dealt with the French government's further plans regarding the development of relations between France and the USSR and other Socialist countries;[68] and the report of 27 December 1968 focused on the Italian Communist Party's internal situation and that party's position with regard to the events in Czechoslovakia.[69]

In addition to the problems it had to face in Czechoslovakia, the KGB was also confronted with serious difficulties in the USSR itself. The Soviet propaganda declarations on the "indestructible unity between the party and the people" appeared somewhat discredited after a group of courageous people had dared publicly to register their protest in the Red Square against the occupation of Czechoslovakia. On 25 August, they unfurled banners there with the slogans "Hands off the ČSSR!" and "For your freedom and ours!" Six of the demonstrators were arrested, tried at the Moscow Municipal Court, and sentenced to prison terms ranging from three to five years. Their arrest, its consequences, and the sentences were the subject of no less than three reports to the CC CPSU, by the KGB, the Ministry of the Interior, and the Public Prosecutor's Office respectively.[70]

In the meantime, the Kremlin was undertaking its first move to consolidate the status of the troops in Czechoslovakia and to convert their stationing from a temporary to a permanent one: the Central Group of Forces (CGV) was created. Shortly afterwards, on 17 October 1968, a Politburo resolution of the CC CPSU called into being a special department of the KGB (Osobyi Otgel) and a government communication task force of the Central Group of Forces. For this purpose, new KGB personnel were recruited until a total of 334 officers was reached (its wartime total being 426 officers); of these, 32 officers belonged to Osobyi Otgel of the Central Group of Forces.[71]

All this was contrary to the promises that Brezhnev had previously made to Dubček. The Moscow Protocol of 27 August 1968 contained the explicit provision that the troops would be withdrawn from Czechoslovakia "after the normalization of the situation." This did not happen until 1990.[72]

The operative groups of the KGB stayed put as well. Not until 2 March 1970 did Andropov propose to Brezhnev that the KGB operative groups be withdrawn from Czechoslovakia. Andropov wrote that these KGB groups had been created in connection with the formation of the Central Group of Forces in Prague and Bratislava and "had done a certain amount of positive work since then." Changes in the political situation and the withdrawal of the Soviet troops from these cities had reduced the groups' scope for counterespionage. Andropov added that "their continued activities might be perceived as negative by the Czechoslovak comrades." He therefore proposed that the work of these groups be terminated "in the near future." Andropov's letter bears the inscription: "Agreed. Brezhnev, Podgornyi, Kosygin 3. March 1970" and the remark: "Agreement signaled to Andropov's S[ecretaria]t on 4 March 1970."[73]

The Czechoslovak events led to some rather strange conclusions in the Kremlin. In 1971, the Presidium of the Supreme Soviet of the USSR issued the decree "On the Award of Orders and Medals of the USSR to Members of Soviet Organizations in the Czechoslovak Socialist Republic and to Members of the Staff of the Central Administration."[74] The decree was not designed for publication; contrary to normal decrees concerning the award of distinctions, it bore the stamp "not released for publication." This represented, in a way, the final act of the Czechoslovak drama: the Kremlin was drawing a line and henceforth considered the problem as solved. The text that accompanied the distinctions was fairly basic and put in simple terms: "For the exemplary fulfillment of duties during the events in Czechoslovakia." The men and women awarded high distinctions on this occasion included people from all walks of life—from cooks and chauffeurs at the Soviet embassies and consulates to the USSR's special envoy to Czechoslovakia, Stepan Chervonenko. Yet it was not only diplomatic personnel who were honored, but members of the CC CPSU apparatus as well, such as First Deputy Director of the Propaganda Department Aleksandr Yakovlev and a large number of journalists and newspaper people. The decree reserves a special mention for a group of people whose functions remain unspecified and who are named together with their military rank: members of the

KGB. Ninety people were honored on the occasion, fifty-seven of whom were awarded orders, the rest medals. Of the fifty-seven candidates for orders, as many as twenty were KGB members! The number of high ranking KGB officers included Deputy Director of the KGB Georgii Tsvigun and the director of the KGB's 3rd Directorate (Military Counterespionage), Vitalii Fyodorchuk, who by the time he received this distinction had already advanced to the post of head of the KGB of the Council of Ministers of the Ukraine. The remaining KGB officers, who belonged mainly to the 2nd Directorate (Counterespionage), had formed the bulk of the KGB operative groups in Prague and Bratislava. In addition to these, a number of KGB operatives who worked for the press received distinctions, such as Deputy Director of the Novosti Press Agency Georgii Arsent'evich Fedyashin and Novosti's representative in Czechoslovakia, Aleksandr Ivanovich Alekseev. Of these, Alekseev is especially noteworthy. Having worked for the secret service in Latin America for a long time, he was sent to Cuba in 1959, where he became Fidel Castro's confidante and was made ambassador in 1962. In 1968, he brought his great expertise to the secret operations in Czechoslovakia. On completing his mission in Czechoslovakia, Alekseev was, in an interesting development of his career and again in the guise of a "representative of the Soviet press," sent to parts of the world where the Kremlin sought to step up its influence, namely Chile and Peru.[75]

CONCLUSION

It may be said by way of conclusion that the role played by the KGB in the Czechoslovak events was an extremely important one. In addition to gathering intelligence data on the situation in Czechoslovakia and on the tendencies and activities of the members of the KSČ leadership, the KGB operatives (legal as well as illegal ones) actively influenced developments and sought to guide them into the direction desired by the Kremlin. At first, the Kremlin leaders were more than pleased when Alexander Dubček rose to power: considered to be "his own man," Dubček was fondly referred to in Moscow as "our Sasha." He was presumably expected to be more obliging than Novotný regarding the stationing of Soviet troops, a question that arose as early as 1966. Even though he did not do so explicitly, Brezhnev himself gave his consent at least conditionally to Novotný's dismissal. In December 1967, he referred to the matter in talks with the Czechoslovak leadership with the words "This is nobody's business but yours," presumably in the hope that the new Czechoslovak leadership would be more compliant in the matter of the stationing of troops. Yet subsequent developments took an entirely different turn. The change in the leadership in January 1968 was interpreted by the Czechoslovak people as a defeat of the old totalitarian system and as a summons to start building a civil society. In the end, Dubček was unable to control the liberal forces.

If one takes the medium-term development into account, this turn of events was to the Kremlin's advantage because it was a step in the direction of the ultimate goal: the military action and the stationing of troops in Czechoslovakia. From May 1968 onward, Moscow had deliberately stoked fears of a military invasion. From this perspective, the secret activities of the KGB, which aimed for a destabilization of the situation and general disinformation, are perfectly understandable and so is their overall result. The medium-term goal was achieved: the invasion took place. From a long-term perspective, however, all this resulted in damage to the standing of the Soviet Union. The USSR was saddled with the role of the policeman who makes use of coercive methods, yet in the countries of the Eastern Bloc and later also in the Soviet republics, tendencies toward national liberation had gained a foothold and were on the rise.

NOTES

Translated from German into English by Otmar Binder, Vienna.

1. Zdeňek Mlynář, *Moroz udaril iz Kremlja* (Moscow: Respublika, 1992), 88.

2. Rudol'f G. Pikhoya, *Sovetskii Soyuz: Istoriya vlasti, 1945–1991* (Moscow: Novosibirsk Sibirskii Khronograf, 2000), 293.

3. Mlynář, *Moroz udaril*, 177. Further evidence is found in the reports of a well informed Soviet journalist who worked in Prague between 1965 and 1968. See Vladlen Krivosheev, "*Izvestiya*' i tanki v Prage," *Izvestiya*, 22 August 1998.

4. *Izvestiya*, 21 August 1998.

5. AP RF, F. 3, op. 22, d. 16, p. 35, published in Andrei N. Artizov et al., eds., *Nikita Khrushchev: 1964, Stenogrammy plenumov TsK KPSS i drugie dokumenty* (Moscow: Materik, 2007), 281–85.

6. Underscored by hand in the original.

7. AP RF, F. 3, op. 22, d. 17, pp. 17–20.

8. AP RF, F. 3, op. 22, d. 17, p. 20.

9. AP RF, F. 3, op. 22, d. 17, p. 17. The term "Line Five" apparently alludes to the Fifth Department of the KGB dealing with "ideological diversion."

10. This is a reference to a political activist, V. Klochkov, who fought with the Panfilov division and was killed in 1941 in the defense of Moscow. The myth relating the heroic deeds of the "28 Panfilovci" (Klochkov being one of them) has remained alive to this day in the collective memory of the Russians, notwithstanding the fact that as early as 1948 the USSR's Judge Advocate General's Corps had presented an expert claiming the whole story was the fabrication of one A. Krivickii, a journalist with the paper *Krasnaya Zvezda*. N. Petrov, "O. Edel'man, Novoe o sovetskikh geroyakh," *Novyi mir* 6 (1997): 140–51.

11. *Istochnik* 2 (1996): 112.

12. *Istochnik* 2 (1996): 116.

13. AP RF, F. 3, op. 80, d. 453, p. 17, Resolution No. 676–222 of the Council of Ministers of the USSR, 17 July 1967, published in Aleksandr Kokurin and Nikita Petrov, eds., *Lubyanka: VChK-OGPU-NKVD-NKGB-MGB-MVD-KGB, 1917–1991: Spravochnik* (Moscow: Demokratija, 2003), 711.

14. Prior to this, on 20 October 1966, the department had been spun off from the espionage directorate and made over into an independent subdivision of the central apparatus of the KGB of the Council of Ministers of the USSR.

15. AP RF, F. 3, op. 80, d. 453, p. 70, Politburo resolution of the CC CPSU 84 (91), 4 June 1968.

16. AP RF, F. 3, op. 80, d. 453, p. 71, letter no. 1252-A, Yuri Andropov's letter, 30 May 1968.

17. AP RF, F. 3, op. 80, d. 453, pp. 70–71 (see note 15).

18. RGANI, F. 3, op. 72, d. 145, p. 7, Politburo resolution of the CC CPSU 67 (III), "On Questions Concerning Czechoslovakia," 25 January 1968.

19. See Vyacheslav Selemenev, "Der 'Prager Frühling' und Weißrussland," in Karner et al., *Beiträge*, 929–40.

20. RGANI, F. 2, op. 3, d. 7, pp. 39–40, Stenogramm der Sitzung des Plenums des ZK der KPdSU, 9., 10 April 1968. See Markus Holler, "'Für eure Freiheit und unsere!' Demonstranten am Roten Platz," in Karner et al., *Beiträge*, 849–68; and Vladislav Zubok, "Soviet Society and the Prague Spring," in this volume.

21. See Mark Kramer, "Ukraine and the Soviet-Czechoslovak Crisis of 1968," *Cold War International History Project Bulletin* 10 (1998): 234–47.

22. RGANI, F. 2, op. 3, d. 7, pp. 31–32 (cf. note 20 above).

23. RGANI, F. 2, op. 3, d. 7, p. 53.

24. Until he was made director of the KGB in May 1967, Yuri Andropov was head of the Department for Liaison with Communist and Workers' Parties in Socialist Countries of the CC CPSU from February 1957. After 1962, he was also the secretary of the CC CPSU and, therefore, in charge of these matters.

25. AP RF, F. 3, op. 91, d. 88, pp. 114–21, Document no. 951/A-OP.

26. AP RF, F. 3, op. 91, d. 88, pp. 114–21, Document no. 951/A-OP.

27. AP RF, F. 3, op. 91, d. 90, pp. 7–8.

28. Aleksandr Mayorov, "Esli vy zhivy—prostite . . . ," *Izvestiya*, 21 August 1998.

29. The integrated command exercises and maneuvers "Šumava" ("Bohemian Forest") took place in June and July 1968 with the participation of the operative commands of the Czechoslovak, Soviet, Hungarian, East German, and Polish armies.

30. AP RF, F. 3, op. 91, d. 93, p. 1, Politburo resolution of the CC CPSU, P 82 (II) "On the Question of the Situation in Czechoslovakia," 23 May 1968.

31. Mikhail Rachyanovich Sagatelyan (1927–1988) was an international correspondent of the paper *Izvestiya* from 1968 to 1974 and codirector of the Novosti Press Agency from 1974.

32. AP RF, F. 3, op. 91, d. 94, pp. 27–36.

33. AP RF, F. 3, op. 91, d. 94, pp. 27–36.

34. AP RF, F. 3, op. 91, d. 94, pp. 27–36.

35. "Uroki avgusta 68," *Izvestiya*, 22 August 1995.

36. "Uroki avgusta 68," *Izvestiya*, 22 August 1995.

37. "Uroki avgusta 68," *Izvestiya*, 22 August 1995.

38. Christopher Andrew and Vasili Mitrokhin, *The Mitrokhin Archive: The KGB in Europe and the West* (London: Allen Lane, 1999), 329.

39. RGANI, Archive of the Resolutions of the Secretariat of the CC CPSU, Resolution of the Secretariat, Art. 50/172g-OP, 16 April 1968.

40. RGANI, Archive of the Resolutions of the Secretariat of the CC CPSU, Resolution of the Secretariat, Art. 50/172g-OP, 16 April 1968, 328–34.

41. "'Izvestiya' i tanki v Prage," *Izvestiya*, 22 August 1998.

42. The Directorate "A" of the First Chief Directorate of the KGB at the Council of Ministers of the USSR had the function to carry out "active measures," above all disinformation and moves to discredit Western politicians, the politics of the West, and so forth.

43. Christopher Andrew and Oleg Gordievskii, *KGB: Istoriya vneshnepoliticheskikh operatsii ot Lenina do Gorbacheva* (Moscow: Nota Bene, 1992), 489. See also Donald P. Steury, "Strategic Warning: The CIA and the Soviet Invasion of Czechoslovakia," in this volume.

44. Istochnik, 5–6/1993, 96–118; Istochnik, 1/1994, 62–71.

45. RGANI, F. 3, op. 72, d. 179, 68, Politburo resolution of the CC CPSU 86 (51), "On the Anti-Soviet statements of the Moscow Correspondent of the Czechoslovak Radio, L. Dobrovskii," 19 June 1968.

46. RGANI, File of the Resolutions of the Secretariat of the CC CPSU, Resolution of the Secretariat of the CC no. 2141-A, n.d.

47. RGANI, file of the resolutions of the Secretariat of the CC CPSU, report by Andrei A. Gromyko and Yuri V. Andropov no. 2141-A (vch. 5778), 9 October 1968, "On the Expulsion from the USSR of the Correspondent of the Czechoslovak Radio, Dobrovský." On the report the remark: "Notified of this remark—the assistant of Comrade Andropov, Laptev, and the assistant of Comrade Gromyko, Kovalenko, 18 October '68."

48. RGANI, F. 2, op. 3, d. 8, stenographic minutes of the Plenum meeting of the Central Committee of the Communist Party of the Soviet Union [hereinafter cited as CPSU], 17 July 1968.

49. RGANI, F. 2, op. 3, d. 8, stenographic minutes of the Plenum meeting of the CPSU, 17 July 1968.

50. *Pravda*, 26 September 1968.

51. *Pravda*, 26 September 1968.

52. Sergei Mitrofanovich Kovalev (24 September 1913–7 December 1990) was born in Miloslavichi in the district of Mogilyov and began his studies in 1935 at the Institute of History, Philosophy, and Literature in Moscow, where he graduated after five years and went on to the Higher Party School of the CC CPSU. On graduation, he took up a post in July 1941 in the Propaganda Department of the CC VKP (b). After the war, he was made secretary of the regional committee of the VKP (b) in Kursk. From February 1951, he served as director of Gospolitizdat (a state-owned publishing house for political literature) and a member of the Central Board of the Printing Industry, Publishing and Book Trade of the Council of Ministers of the USSR. In 1954, he defended his thesis on the topic "The Communist Education

of the Workers." In September 1954, he was dismissed from his post of director of Gospolitizdat. From 1960 to 1965, he worked as editor of the periodical *Problemy mira i sotsializma* (*Problems of the World and of Socialism*), from 1965 to 1971 was a member of the editorial committee of the propaganda section of *Pravda*, from 1971 to 1980, acted as first deputy of the editor in chief of the *Great Soviet Encyclopedia*, and from 1980 was a professor at the Academy of Social Sciences of the CC CPSU. His most important publications are the following: *Kommunisticheskoe vospitanie trudyashchikhsya* (1960); *O kommunisticheskom vospitanii* (1966); *O cheloveke, ego poraboshchenii i osvobozhdenii* (1970); *Formirovanie sotsialisticheskoi lichnosti* (1980); and *Samovospitanie sotsialisticheskoi lichnosti* (1986). In September 1973, he was awarded the "Order of the Red Banner of Labor" on the occasion of his sixtieth birthday.

53. Sergei M. Kovalev, *O natsional'noi gordosti sovetskikh lyudei* (Moscow: Gos. izd-vo polit. lit-ry, 1950).

54. RGANI, file of the resolutions of the Secretariat of the CC CPSU, Politburo resolution of the CC CPSU 86 (1), 14 June 1968.

55. RGANI, F. 5, op. 60, d. 469, pp. 94–95, letter of the KGB of the Foreign Ministry of the USSR to the CC CPSU, Nr. 2437-z, 21 October 1968.

56. RGANI, F. 2, op. 3, d. 130, pp. 1–26, speech by L. I. Brezhnev at the session of the Plenum of the CC CPSU, 31 October 1968, reprinted in Karner et al., *Dokumente*, #122.

57. RGANI, F. 2, op. 3, d. 9, p. 139.

58. RGANI, F. 2, op. 3, d. 9, p. 139.

59. RGANI, F. 2, op. 3, d. 9, p. 140.

60. RGANI, F. 2, op. 3, d. 9, p. 141.

61. "Ne zakladyvat' miny," *Izvestiya*, 21 August 1998.

62. "Ne zakladyvat' miny," *Izvestiya*, 21 August 1998.

63. RGANI, F. 2, op. 3, d. 10, stenographic minutes of the Plenum meeting of the Central Committee of the CPSU, 9 September 1968.

64. The resolution to allow Andropov to go on leave from 1 September 1968 was passed on 23 May 1968 by the Politburo CC CPSU (82/XVI).

65. RGANI, F. 5, op. 60, d. 60, letter from Semyon Tsvigun to the Central Committee of the CPSU Nr. 2159-s, 13 September 1968.

66. RGANI, F. 5, op. 60, d. 37, pp. 45–48, Report No. 2404-z.

67. RGANI, F. 5, op. 60, d. 301, pp. 331–33, Report No. 2502-z.

68. RGANI, F. 5, op. 60, d. 492, pp. 158–60, Report No. 2680-z.

69. RGANI, F. 5, op. 60, d. 493, pp. 253–54, Report No. 2848-z.

70. RGANI, F. 89, op. 25, d. 72, pp. 56–60, 62–63.

71. AP RF, F. 3, op. 80, d. 453, Politburo resolution of the CC CPSU 105 (24), 17. 10. 1968.

72. "'Izvestiya' i tanki v Prage," *Izvestiya*, 22 August 1998.

73. AP RF, F. 3, op. 80, d. 453, p. 87. Report No. 534-A.

74. GARF, F. 7523, op. 105, d. 118, pp. 58–65.

75. John Barron, *KGB: The Secret Work of Soviet Secret Agents* (New York: Bantam, 1974), 548; Lutz Priess et al., *Die SED und der "Prager Frühling" 1968: Politik gegen einen "Sozialismus mit menschlichem Anlitz"* (Berlin: Akademie Verlag, 1996).

7

The Moscow "Negotiations": "Normalizing Relations" between the Soviet Leadership and the Czechoslovak Delegation after the Invasion

Peter Ruggenthaler and Harald Knoll

Tuesday, 20 August 1968, at 11 p.m. CET, the Soviet ambassador in Prague, Stepan Chervonenko, called on the president of the Czechoslovak Socialist Republic (ČSSR), Ludvík Svoboda, to inform him that the troops of the Soviet Union, Poland, Bulgaria, the German Democratic Republic (GDR), and Hungary were about to cross the borders of Czechoslovakia. He read out a text prepared by the Politburo of the Central Committee of the Communist Party of the Soviet Union (CC CPSU) and handed the Czechoslovak president an appeal to the people of the ČSSR drafted by the Soviets in Svoboda's name.[1]

Chervonenko said later that, while Svoboda did not welcome the invasion, he at least firmly promised that he "would never sever the links tying Czechoslovakia to the Soviet Union."[2] Before Svoboda was informed of the invasion, Czechoslovak minister of defense Martin Dzúr had been contacted by the Supreme Command of the Warsaw Pact troops involved in the intervention. Instead of immediately informing Prime Minister Oldřich Černík, Dzúr had issued an order to the Czechoslovak People's Army (ČSLA) not to leave their barracks and not only to refrain from offering resistance to the invading troops, but to provide assistance to them if necessary.[3]

To what extent this move was actively supported by Svoboda, the de facto supreme commander of the ČSLA, remained unclear for a long time.[4] Svoboda did, however, give Dzúr the explicit order, independently of Dzúr's own activities, to avoid all bloodshed.[5]

FROM ČIERNÁ NAD TISOU TO THE INVASION

Before the final decision in favor of an intervention was taken by the Politburo of the CPSU, a last attempt was to be made to find a "political settlement" together with Alexander Dubček and the leadership of the KSČ on the basis of the Dresden demands.[6] At the end of July, bilateral negotiations took place in the Slovak town of Čierná nad Tisou near the Czechoslovak-Soviet border and contrary to the expectations of the Kremlin they ended on an upbeat note. We now know that a meeting of the "Warsaw Five" in Moscow had already been in the pipeline during the run-up to the meeting in Čierná nad Tisou. This was cancelled at short notice by the Politburo of the CC CPSU, all of whose members had collectively traveled abroad for the first and only time in the history of the Soviet Union to be present at Čierná nad Tisou.[7] Dubček was given his "very" last chance. Immediately after the bilateral meeting in the east of Slovakia, the "Warsaw Five" met with the KSČ in Bratislava on 3 August. The Soviet leadership considered it imperative, according to Brezhnev, "to enshrine the results of our negotiations with the leadership of the KSČ in a collective document in order to put these results on an international basis. This was done at the conference in Bratislava. In principle . . . the results of the negotiations found their expression in the Declaration of Bratislava."[8]

We may assume with a degree of probability bordering on certainty that there are no official Soviet records of the actual discussion between the Czechoslovak and the Soviet delegations in Čierná nad Tisou. During the "negotiations" after 23 August, Brezhnev merely referred to private discussions, one-on-one talks, and the like. Despite this basic situation, it appears certain today that the Czechoslovak side and most notably Dubček acceded in principle to the Soviet demands for changes in the cadres and for dismissals.[9]

Once the Declaration of Bratislava was signed, the Soviet side had a frame of reference that could be used for the justification of both their further course of action and that of the Warsaw Five. In Bratislava, the last compromise between the parties prior to the occupation of the ČSSR was formulated on the basis of a Soviet draft, which amounted to a legitimation of the "bureaucratic *coup d'état*" that was already being prepared in the presidium of the KSČ by the "healthy forces." In Bratislava, Vasil Bil'ak handed the Soviet delegation the letter that was soon to become notorious, the "invitation by the healthy forces" in the KSČ asking for a "collective rescue operation" by the five interventionist states. The other KSČ leaders were left in the dark with reference to Bil'ak's move.[10]

Dubček's alleged infringement of the Bratislava accord was ultimately used by the Soviet side to justify the invasion. Moscow needed time to organize the "bureaucratic *coup d'état*," which was supposed to take place in the presidium of the KSČ so as to coincide with the invasion. If Dubček failed to honor the accord, which, as he saw it, was a foregone conclusion in any case, the "healthy forces" now had a lever to oust him.

The straw that broke the camel's back in Moscow's eyes was the telephone conversation between Brezhnev and Dubček on 13 August.[11] Dubček was noticeably on edge and offered a string of excuses. The Kremlin's primary interest was the prompt realization of the moves agreed on in Čierná nad Tisou. As it was, neither Jiři Pelikán was relieved of his post as head of TV, nor Zdeněk Hejzlar as head of the Broadcasting Company, nor was the Ministry of the Interior divided into two. This meant that Viliam Šalgovič, who was loyal to Moscow, had to continue in a position that was subordinate to Minister of the Interior Pavel Nowotný.

Three days after this conversation on the phone, on 16 August, Brezhnev addressed a handwritten letter on behalf of the Politburo of the CC CPSU to the KSČ leader.[12] In it, Brezhnev deplored the continued anti-Soviet attacks in Czechoslovakia and Dubček's infringement of his undertakings to divide the Ministry of the Interior into two and to dismiss František Kriegel, Česimír Císař, and Pelikán. This letter was delivered to Dubček by the Soviet ambassador in Prague, Chervonenko. In a postscript to Chervonenko's instructions, the Politburo mandated him to make the contents of the letter known to the "healthy forces" in the KSČ.

Two days later, on 18 August, the Politburo of the CC CPSU addressed another—this time, official—letter to the presidium of the CC KSČ in Brezhnev's name. On page after page, Moscow documented in this "letter of warning"[13] anti-Soviet attacks notably in the Czechoslovak media. In the same Politburo resolution, a letter to Alois Indra and Bil'ak was given the green light as was the draft of a declaration that might come in useful for the "friends" as the basis for an address to the Czechoslovak people after the invasion.

The letter to Dubček could not be delivered to him on 18 August, for he was not in Prague that day; he had gone to meet János Kádár.[14] After consulting Indra and Bil'ak, who were both informed of the letter's substance,[15] Chervonenko advised "headquarters" to have the letter delivered on Monday, 19 August.[16] The Politburo signaled their consent; taking up a suggestion of the "friends," that is of Bil'ak and Indra, they also added to the letter a reference to Brezhnev's letter to Dubček of 16 August.[17] This was done to give Bil'ak and Indra an opportunity to underline Dubček's mistakes and to criticize him for having kept the Kremlin's "warnings" secret from his comrades. In contrast to the letter of 16 August, in which Brezhnev had referred in detail to the one-on-one talks in Čierná nad Tisou and had reproached Dubček with not having solved the "cadre issues," by which he meant that Dubček had not dismissed Pelikán and those of his mind-set, none of these topics were mentioned explicitly in the second letter.

The letter was finally delivered to Dubček by the Soviet ambassador at around 10 p.m. on 19 August. Dubček's failure to respond to the written requests was ultimately to serve the "healthy forces" as a pretext for a motion of no confidence against the KSČ leader in the session of the presidium of the CC KSČ on 20 August. Dubček interpreted the letter as yet another protest or reprimand in the Kremlin's unending series. He failed to see anything new in it. This was also mentioned by Chervonenko when he reported to Moscow on the delivery of the letter.[18]

ON THE EVE OF THE INVASION

On 20 August 1968 at 2 p.m., the presidium of the Central Committee of the KSČ had assembled for a meeting; preparations for the Slovak Party Congress were to have been the most important item on the agenda. However, the real emphasis lay elsewhere. The members loyal to Moscow were planning to engineer a vote of no confidence against KSČ leader Dubček. However, things took a different turn; the session dragged on and on in interminable disputes on matters of procedure. The planning for the "bureaucratic *coup d'état*" started to unravel. No motion of no confidence against Dubček was proposed. The weakness of the forces loyal to the Soviet Union "made . . . an internal coup impossible so that it was the military intervention that ultimately provided the basis required for such an undertaking."[19] Shortly before midnight, Prime Minister Černík announced that he had just been informed by the minister of defense, Dzúr, that Czechoslovakia was at that moment being occupied by socialist "fraternal countries."[20] It was only then that Dubček pulled Brezhnev's last letter of 17 August addressed to him from his briefcase.[21]

At around 12:30 a.m., President Svoboda entered.[22] The members of the presidium had called him asking him for his advice. According to Bil'ak, he was in a good mood; during the discussion of the condemnation of the intervention, he gave no indication as to which way he was inclined. Dubček is even said to have accused Svoboda of having actually called the Soviets.[23]

At 1:30 a.m., the presidium of the CC KSČ approved the draft of a first declaration. It condemned the invasion yet requested the population to maintain calm. The motion was opposed by the Communists loyal to Moscow, Vasil Bil'ak, Drahomír Kolder, Emil Rigo, and Oldřich Švestka. František Barbírek and Jan Piller, who had pledged to support a vote against Dubček, now cast their vote, presumably in the light of the military invasion, in favor of the motion.[24]

After the end of the session, most presidium members remained in the CC building; Černík returned to his official residence, and President

Svoboda to the Hradshin. Two hours later, Černík was arrested. Shortly afterwards, the CC building was occupied. Dubček and other leading functionaries were placed under house arrest. At 6 a.m., Císař was arrested and cross-questioned. On the way to the Soviet embassy, he apparently managed to escape, leaving Prague and going underground for several days.[25]

Early the next morning, the radio station Vltava ["Moldau"] began transmissions from the GDR in Czech and Slovak and presented the rationale behind Czechoslovakia's military invasion by the Five from the invaders' point of view.[26] At 6 a.m. the as yet unoccupied station Czechoslovak Radio broadcast a message from Dubček himself.[27] He appealed to the population not to stay home from work. The Foreign Ministry ordered the broadcasting company to keep on repeating that the occupation of the country was wholly unjustified, and at 8:15 a.m., Svoboda addressed the nation via radio. He appealed to his compatriots to refrain from acting emotionally and to remain utterly calm.[28]

At 9 a.m., the building of the Czechoslovak broadcasting company was occupied by Soviet soldiers, and the same happened a short time later at the editorial offices and the print shop of *Rudé právo*. It proved, however, impossible to silence immediately the Czechoslovak journalists who had acquired a taste for the freedom of the press over several months. "Illegal" radio stations were genuine sources of information for the population for a number of days to come.

At 2 p.m., Dubček and fellow party members Josef Smrkovský, Kriegel, and Josef Špaček were ferried to Prague-Ruzyně airport in an armored personnel carrier and taken to the Soviet Union via Poland.[29] At 6 p.m. CET, Bohumil Šimon was taken to the airport to be followed by Černík in short order.[30]

Dubček was held captive all of Thursday in the Carpathians[31] and was taken to Moscow in the early hours of 23 August.

In the Kremlin, the insight had gained ground in the meantime that Czechoslovakia's future was inextricably tied to Dubček. Ousting Dubček was clearly illusory, for it was obvious that he had popular support.

At 11 p.m., President Svoboda called on the Soviet ambassador in Prague, Chervonenko, requesting his permission to go to Moscow.[32] Svoboda's request was granted, and the allies were informed accordingly. On this occasion, they were also informed to be prepared to leave for Moscow for consultations at short notice.[33]

The next morning, on Friday, 23 August, Svoboda announced in a radio address that he was about to leave for a state visit to Moscow to negotiate a solution for the present crisis with the leadership of the Soviet Union. He had asked the members of the government to authorize him to conduct direct negotiations with the representatives of the USSR. Svoboda was accompanied on this trip by Minister of Defense Dzúr; the members of the presidium of the CC Jan Piller, Bil'ak, Indra; the minister of justice, Bohuslav Kučera, and his own son-in-law, Milan Klusák. Half an hour after Svoboda's radio address, Czechoslovak radio was at pains to emphasize that Svoboda was going to Moscow of his own accord and that he had by no means handed control to a government consisting of "collaborators" loyal to Moscow. At 9:30 a.m. CET, Svoboda's special flight took off from Prague-Ruzyně airport. After a stopover in Bratislava, where Gustáv Husák, the first secretary of the Slovak Communist Party, joined the delegation, the plane took off again for Moscow.[34]

At 11:30 a.m. Moscow time, that is, at the time of Svoboda's departure from Prague, the first "negotiations" between Leonid Brezhnev, Nikolai Podgornyi, Aleksei Kosygin,[35] and Dubček began at an unidentified location.[36] The first round of talks lasted at least an hour and a half and involved, at first, only Dubček. He was later joined by Černík.[37] Brezhnev began the first round with a skillful gambit from his point of view. He proposed that instead of talking about the past they should be acting according to the "principles" of Bratislava. The Czechoslovak government was to abide also in future by the resolutions of the January and May plena of the CC KSČ, in other words, broadly on the basis of the reforms already initiated, but primarily with a view to strengthening socialism in the ČSSR.[38] Brezhnev stepped up the pace by conveying to Dubček that the Soviet side was giving him the benefit of the doubt: they were prepared to believe that the "rightist forces" had become active behind his back: "We don't want to blame you personally, Alexander. You may not have been aware of this." Brezhnev also conveyed to Dubček from the start that while he would continue to count on him, in future he was also determined to put him in his place. Dubček, who had been kept in complete isolation since his arrest and had no information how his comrades had behaved, could easily have felt cornered and could have allowed the conversation to escalate, which he did not. At the same time, he was aware that it was not he who was in a virtually desperate situation, but Moscow and its allies. The obvious lack of coordination regarding his own abduction convinced Dubček that things were not going according to plan for the Kremlin.[39]

Brezhnev proposed to Dubček as the talks continued that they "should keep no secrets from one another." He underscored that Czechoslovakia had, after all, not been occupied. Brezhnev said: "We want the country to be free and that she abide by the socialist cooperation that we agreed on in Bratislava." At the end of his first statement, Brezhnev encouraged Dubček to address "different variants completely freely," not "in a temper" as in Čierná nad Tisou, but "in a controlled manner." Brezhnev wound up emphasizing that Dubček was still "an upright Communist" in the eyes of the Soviet leadership.

In his first reply, Dubček said that he was "in a very difficult state emotionally," but determined nevertheless "to look ahead." He underscored that he was unable to identify with the decision in favor of a military intervention, particularly in light of the fact that preparations had been underway for the Party Conference and for the solution of the cadre issues, in particular for the removal of the "rightist forces." There was no need for Dubček to claim the prophet's role when he told the Soviet leaders that the extreme measures "confronted not only our party and yours, but the entire international Communist movement with the most difficult problem with which this movement has ever had to cope." Dubček underscored the fact that his country looked back on "centuries" of good relations with Russia and accused the Kremlin leaders of having arrived at an assessment of the situation in Czechoslovakia that was out of touch with reality: there was no realistic scenario for a counterrevolution. The result now was a "difficult and tragic situation." Despite his entirely different view of the situation, Brezhnev did not want to pursue this line of argument any further and interpreted Dubček's words as "the wish to find a solution in conjunction with us and with all socialist countries." Brezhnev said to Dubček, "Is that what you're saying, Alexander?" Dubček replied, "Yes, it is."

As part of his next move Brezhnev informed Dubček about how the invasion had gone. Dubček underscored that one of the most important steps of the Presidium of the CC KSČ immediately after the start of the invasion had been to urge the population not offer any kind of resistance. Brezhnev told Dubček that a one-day Party Conference of KSČ had taken place on the previous day which had elected "exclusively people of the extreme right" to form a new CC. Neither Indra nor Bil'ak had been elected into the CC. The new CC did not include a single member of the old one, Podgornyi interjected. In addition to this, it was said that no more than five Slovaks had been present. Then Brezhnev informed Dubček that President Svoboda had asked for permission to come to Moscow to take part in the negotiations and that he had spoken to him repeatedly on the phone, but the connection had been interrupted again and again. As they spoke, Brezhnev said, Svoboda, accompanied by Bil'ak, Piller, Kučera, Ladislav Novák, and Milan Klusák, was "already in the air."

Brezhnev, Kosygin, and Podgornyi repeatedly raised the objection that the Party Conference had been irregular (as there had been virtually no Slovaks present nor any members of the Presidium itself); moreover, recognizing the Presidium of the CC that had, in fact, been elected would mean "that Czechoslovakia was going bourgeois in no time," as Brezhnev put it.

Dubček showed himself broadly in agreement with the line of the Soviet leaders. "We've got to find ways to bring about a certain consolidation of the leading organs of the Party and of the state." Yet he could not help pointing out what it meant "if in Slovakia the Slovaks are taught by the Hungarian army the proper attitude to Socialism and to the Soviet Union . . . and if a Slovak soldier . . . is now being disarmed by a Hungarian soldier." Brezhnev replied laconically that this was the state of affairs with which one had to cope. Dubček replied: "That anybody should take it upon themselves to attempt to teach the Czechoslovaks what socialism is about! German troops invade and we give orders to our population to do their bidding!" Brezhnev did not add then and there the correction that the *Nationale Volksarmee* (NVA) of the GDR had not taken part in the invasion; instead, he chose to reproach Dubček with having sanctioned the meeting of the Sudeten Germans in Cheb.[40] When Dubček denied having done so, this was grist to Brezhnev's mill: "a lot had been happening" behind Dubček's back. In the final analysis, this exchange shows clearly how one-sided and plain wrong a good deal of the information was that the Soviet leadership received.

Once Černík had joined the group at the negotiating table, Brezhnev repeated once again his point of view[41] and underscored that there had been no alternative to "taking this step if the aim was to prevent Czechoslovakia from leaving the path of socialism" and that Svoboda was on his way to Moscow. Before he arrived, Brezhnev said, those present should reassess the situation and think about a government with Černík at the top: "Perhaps we should recognize . . . a government with Comrade Černík as leader." If, on the other hand, the Party Conference was to be considered legal, Czechoslovakia would find herself in the bourgeois camp in a matter of days. This was meant as an *aide mémoire* for Dubček and Černík.

Kosygin finally made the explicit point that the measures for which the participants were casting around and which would ultimately be taken to resolve the crisis would need to find the approval of both Czechoslovakia and the "fraternal countries." Brezhnev continued along the lines of the strategy he advocated and stressed that the top priority at the moment was finding a way out, "It is only after we've managed to do that that we may indulge in mutual recriminations and work out who's made the biggest blunder." Much less conciliatory was the tone chosen by Podgornyi who thought he had understood Dubček as saying there was nothing one could do about the resolutions passed on the previous day at the Prague Party Conference. Černík reputedly tried to calm the situation down,[42] and Kosygin painted once more on the wall the Kremlin's most abhorred bugbear in connection with a recognition of the Party Conference: a bourgeois Czechoslovakia within a month, "perhaps even sooner." At the end of the first round of talks, after about one and a half hours, Podgornyi topped this with another worst-case scenario: "If we do not take appropriate measures, this will lead to civil war—and you will be the ones to take responsibility for it."[43] The meeting was adjourned without any results. The next step was not yet, as Dubček has mistakenly recorded in his autobiography, the meeting with the Svoboda delegation, as this did not take place until late in the evening. The delegation must have been shortly before touchdown in Moscow at this stage, and Brezhnev and the leading Politburo members were getting ready to go the airport to receive Svoboda with pomp and circumstance.

Shortly before 4 p.m. Moscow time, the special flight from Prague via Bratislava touched down at Vnukovo Airport near Moscow.[44] Because Svoboda was on a state visit, he was given the official VIP treatment. Brezhnev, Kosygin, and Podgornyi were all there in person on the tarmac of the air field; then the delegation was escorted to the Kremlin.[45]

At first, Brezhnev, Kosygin, and Podgornyi received only the Czechoslovak president. Svoboda was accompanied by his son-in-law, Milan Klusák, the former Czechoslovak UN ambassador and Svoboda's most important adviser. Brezhnev felt linked to Svoboda by shared memories of front warfare in WWII and had originally staked high hopes on him.[46] However, after the invasion Svoboda did not behave as the Soviet leadership had hoped he would. He did not read out the draft speech in the form in which it had been delivered to him by the Soviet Politburo through the Soviet ambassador to Prague; in Svoboda's eyes, it only offered further proof of how out of touch the Soviets were with the situation on the ground.[47] Such direct words would have painted Svoboda in the eyes of the Czechoslovak public as Moscow's vassal and would have destroyed his authority in the country at one blow. The Soviet leadership had presumably counted on Svoboda finding the right words. This demonstrates again how thoroughly the Soviet leadership misjudged the situation in the ČSSR, a fact for which the pointed disinformation and exaggerations on the part of the Politburo hardliners and, above all, the head of the KGB, Yuri Andropov, must ultimately be held accountable. Andropov was never at a loss in construing all kinds of arguments that were supposed to justify the drastic solution advocated by him.[48]

After the invasion, Svoboda had also rejected a proposal put forward by the Soviet ambassador in Prague, Chervonenko, to the effect of installing a new government comprising the famously "healthy" forces loyal to Moscow.[49] He may have done so less because he was averse to Chervonenko's proposal as such than on the basis of an assessment of the country's situation which was more realistic than that of the Kremlin.

Ultimately, he felt it was more appropriate to discuss the country's future directly with the Soviet leaders, which was, at least from his point of view, the only option that was left. Dubček always felt that Svoboda had sympathized with the ideas of the "Prague Spring."[50]

In his very first statement, Svoboda referred to the above-mentioned "offer" to form a new government, saying, "I received an offer yesterday to form a new government. I think this would constitute a breach of the

Constitution."[51] In what followed, Svoboda seems not to have expressed himself clearly so that Brezhnev had to ask him what point he was making. At this point, the minutes unfortunately do not provide a verbatim record of the talks. According to the recorder's summary of Svoboda's statement, Svoboda appears to have proposed that "Comrade Dubček return to Prague, confess his guilt, and give up his powers." On the other hand, Svoboda is reported to have said that if someone else was going "to be given a turn," then "this was likely to stir popular discontent even more." Asked by Brezhnev who should take over as first secretary of the KSČ if "Dubček were to resign from power," Svoboda replied, "It is obvious you have not really been following me." Presumably Svoboda was simply extemporizing without having a clear idea as to what fate was in store for Dubček at the hands of the Soviet leadership. He had also been left in the dark with respect to how Dubček had been treated so far. Svoboda now enquired about Dubček's whereabouts and Brezhnev replied: "He is well." Svoboda said in response, "We would all benefit if he were to resign from his post. But if he stays on, we can live with that, too. Dubček should address these issues himself but should do so in Prague."[52]

From the start, Svoboda conveyed his readiness to drop Dubček, yet this was not the end of the matter. He underscored with great emphasis this would be the best solution but added that he was not prepared to take the responsibility for this step. Svoboda had betrayed Dubček.

In the course of the talks, Svoboda said that the entire government would remain in office only if Černík was retained as head of government (a point to which the Soviet leadership, as we have already seen, had signaled their approval in principle in the first round of talks at midday involving only Dubček and Černík but this fact had been kept from Svoboda). Bil'ak could not possibly, according to Svoboda, be recycled as head of government, for he was a traitor in the eyes of the people. Subsequently, Brezhnev rehearsed the scenario that was likely to unfold if Dubček were to return to Prague and publicly confess his guilt. Who would then be elected to succeed him, Brezhnev asked, by a party presidium that contained "neither Piller nor Kolder nor Bil'ak nor Indra." It was, therefore, inevitable, Brezhnev continued, for Dubček, Smrkovský, and Černík to declare the Party Conference of the previous day illegal. Klusák then pointed out to the Soviet leadership that a majority of Communists believed "that this CC has been duly elected." "If you declare it illegal . . . then there will be two parties in Czechoslovakia and most people will join the faction that has the new CC on its side." This meant, in other words, that the KSČ was going to be subjected to attrition and that most party members would feel their loyalty lay with the new faction. In dealing with the comrades, it was, therefore, advisable, according to Klusák, not to "tackle this issue in too peremptory a manner." Kosygin objected that given the status of Czechoslovakia as a federation there was no denying that the Slovaks had been underrepresented at the Party Conference. To make matters worse still, the Party Conference had been convened solely by the Prague Municipal Committee, and neither the CC nor the Presidium had been informed. Klusák tried to calm tempers down by emphatically pointing to the situation prevailing in Prague: "You've got to realize that the city is gripped by tumults. You can either prolong these tumults or you can come up with a sensible solution to this problem so that the population understands that quiet has been restored." Klusák's advice was for "these three," namely Dubček, Černík, and Smrkovský, to return to Prague. Svoboda was also emphatic about giving people no pretext to say "that all this has been done on your orders, that we have betrayed the people, and that we have capitulated to you." If they managed to do that, Svoboda felt "positive results were within reach." Then he noted, "Afterwards we can do anything you want."[53] Svoboda was ready to capitulate so that the Czechoslovak-Soviet friendship would be kept unblemished.

Brezhnev insisted on the Czechoslovak leadership collectively declaring the Party Conference illegal; in his eyes, the only question was how to effect this most elegantly. It is crucial to stress here once more that Brezhnev, Podgornyi, and Kosygin understood perfectly well that a recognition of the Party Conference's resolutions was inevitably going to lead to a de facto dissolution of the KSČ and to a loss of the party's monopoly on power, to the transformation of the ČSSR into a "bourgeois" republic and, ultimately, to the country severing its links with the Warsaw Pact. In order to prevent this the Soviet leadership, very much against its original inclination, had to pay the price of leaving Dubček, Černík, and Smrkovský in their posts in order not risk a civil war, which had repeatedly surfaced in the talks as the superlative worst-case scenario. Brezhnev said, "We will not replace Černík, let him keep his post. After some time, he will reshuffle his government. . . . Let Dubček also retain his post. We did not seriously consider removing him. If he then resigns of his own initiative, that's a different matter. And let Smrkovský stay on as well." That is what happened.[54]

Svoboda underscored once more that the formation of a new government that had at first been considered would turn out to be counterproductive ("Then people would spit at me"). Even though he was an old man, there was a lot he "could do to strengthen our friendly ties." Svoboda went on to say, "Given the opportunity I would do anything." Yet he immediately balked at being the first to denounce the Party Conference as illegal and linked this to Dubček's consent ("Pending Dubček's consent and that of other comrades, I will . . .").[55] Brezhnev replied to Svoboda that there was no denying that he was the president and surely entitled in that capacity to voice his opinion. He explained shortly afterwards that the troops would not be withdrawn until there were appropriate formal declarations of commitment, which required moreover the consent of the allies. Klusák inquired whether German soldiers were stationed on Czechoslovak soil. Brezhnev assured him that there were no Germans among the invading troops; they had been "held back." This had caused considerable irritation among the comrades in East Berlin, according to Brezhnev, and a sense that they "were somehow not considered trustworthy."[56]

Svoboda's original planning had provided only for a short visit to Moscow and an early return to Prague immediately after the talks with the Soviet leadership. Brezhnev did not demur, but insisted that the other members of the delegation remain in Moscow for further "negotiations." Svoboda, therefore, wondered whether it would not be best, in case his "influence was going to be needed during the negotiations . . . to schedule another round of talks" while he was still present. Klusák went one better declaring they had better all meet with Dubček, Černík, and Smrkovský "today." Brezhnev signaled agreement and Podgornyi suggested taking a break, after which they would all assemble once more on the same day.

Because the strategy to be adopted was now clear, Svoboda declared that it was now possible for the comrades to join the talks. Brezhnev and Kosygin left the room. In the meantime, Podgornyi talked to Svoboda and Klusák. Summing up developments in Czechoslovakia, he said that the "rightists" had played their cards very cleverly in Czechoslovakia. They had organized everything in a manner that provided no reason for anyone to feel provoked. "They all kept on claiming that they were doing their utmost for the construction of socialism and for friendship, but what they were doing was in fact the exact opposite."[57]

Brezhnev and Kosygin returned shortly afterwards. All the other members of the delegation and the Czechoslovak ambassador in Moscow, Vladimír Koucký, also took part in the meeting. Brezhnev embarked on a monologue explaining that Svoboda had already been approached on the issue of how to find a solution "that will do justice to all sides."[58] He emphasized that the Soviets had never opposed the resolutions of the January and the May plenary sessions of the CC KSČ and had never demanded a change of leadership. There had been a frantic search for a political settlement right to the very end. What was at issue was not whether the "headlong campaign" against the CPSU and the Soviet Union in the media was considered offensive, but that the "whole ideological influence had been one-sided to an extent that endangered the entire system of the state and the cause of socialism in Czechoslovakia."[59] Brezhnev criticized Dubček ("Why has Dubček become the object of a cult to an extent we did not even experience with Stalin?") and told Husák and Bil'ak about the two occasions he had spoken with Dubček from the Crimea, about which Dubček had not even informed the members of his Presidium. He had then sensed, in his own words, "treachery and dishonesty," and it had been obvious that "if one allowed things to continue unchecked and did not take measures to counteract them, the Party Conference was going to pass a resolution that would propel Czechoslovakia along the road leading to the restoration of capitalism." In order to prevent this, a guarantee was needed: "We had one [the agreement of Čierná nad Tisou], but it proved worthless. We don't want to be had a second time."[60]

Brezhnev's monologue amounted to a plea for finding a way to classify the Party Conference as illegal. Brezhnev conceded that this could not possibly be affected by Dubček and Černík from Moscow, so some other way had to be found. Podgornyi spoke next. He noted the necessity of the invasion; otherwise, the "progressive" forces loyal to Moscow would have been blown to smithereens "before the Party Conference or at the Party Conference." Podgornyi continued, "There is no way we can tolerate hostile acts against the socialist community or against the Soviet Union. We will have no truck with such things." According to Podgornyi, the responsibility for the situation that had arisen "lay with all of you," "notably with Comrade Dubček." "War and bloodshed" must not be tolerated.[61]

Now it was Husák's turn. Having expressed his gratitude for being allowed to take part in the meeting, he explained that he understood only too well why the fraternal parties had expressed criticism on account of Czechoslovakia. Everybody was, of course, entitled, according to Husák, "to see things . . . from their point of view." However, he could not help thinking "that the Soviet comrades had overestimated the danger inherent in the given situation and had overreacted" so that in Bratislava, too, the impression had been created "that one was, in fact, confronted with an occupation."

Husák claimed there were only two possibilities for moving forward: either a totalitarian leadership for Czechoslovakia or a "political deal" that created "normal working conditions." Speaking on behalf of the leadership of the Slovak Communist Party and the government of Czechoslovakia, he urged the Soviet leadership "to release the leaders who have been arrested." Husák let it be immediately understood that he felt the Soviet demand for a declaration of commitment was only reasonable "to prevent Czechoslovakia" opting for a development "outside the socialist camp." In addition to this, "the anticommunist and anti-Soviet propaganda must be liquidated." These goals, however, could have been achieved, according to Husák, "without resorting to a military intervention." Husák cemented his position in advance as far as the Party Conference was concerned. He felt it was going to be easy for him "to say that this Party Conference had not been legal," yet one had to allow for the fact that the Party Conference was classified as legal by most of its participants. The situation was extremely difficult, but he was prepared to work for a solution with all his might.

Brezhnev subsequently became visibly aggressive. He and Podgornyi criticized Husák for not having become active—or for having not having become active enough against anti-Soviet and antisocialist propaganda. Brezhnev then changed tack: "Don't let's attack one another! Our talks are difficult enough as it is!" Husák replied that he had always clearly positioned himself at rallies. Podgornyi countered by asking him how much use this had been in his eyes if the media had failed to report it. Podgornyi reiterated once more the danger inherent in the propaganda of the other side. This could "make the cauldron boil over" so that "the result was a real civil war." Brezhnev followed suit: "If you want to speculate on a civil war, then you yourselves will have to shoulder the responsibility." Nowhere in Czechoslovakia, according to Brezhnev, had the military invasion met with resistance apart from Prague, at the moment troops had attempted to bring the mass media under their control. Brezhnev then attacked Husák directly: "If you were really a Communist, a true Leninist, then you would be grateful to us for having gone into Czechoslovakia. We went in to save you—yet you turn this against us."[62]

Finally it was the turn of Bil'ak, one of Moscow's most loyal Communist followers. At the session of the Presidium of the CC on 21 August, he was one of only a handful to openly oppose convening the Party Conference. "They trumpeted that we were traitors and we were unable to shout back resoundingly and unmask them as the real traitors and counterrevolutionaries"; they did not control the media. Bil'ak gave a realistic appraisal of the state of affairs from his point of view and declared that surely President Svoboda was able to report from Moscow that Černík and Dubček had been present at the negotiations. It so happened that in a few days' time the Slovak Communists' Party Conference was due, which according to Bil'ak presented no danger of providing a stage for potentially anti-Soviet agitation. Brezhnev insisted nevertheless on Husák calling his comrades in Bratislava to tell them to abort the Party Conference, which had been scheduled for 24 August.[63]

After the end of the talks, the Soviet leadership acceded to the wishes of the Czechoslovak delegation and had Dubček and Černík, who were put up in accommodations on the Lenin Hills, brought into the Kremlin. There are several clues that seem to suggest that Brezhnev took charge of the two at first and presumably informed them about the attitudes of the delegation's members regarding the 14th Party Conference.[64]

In this briefing, the two must have been confronted with the fact that all members of the delegation had agreed to declare the Party Conference and its resolutions null and void. Immediately afterwards, Dubček and Černík joined Svoboda and the other delegation members. Dubček had expected that Svoboda, "regardless of the pitiable circumstances, would be delighted and relieved" to see him. In light of the newly accessible passages of the minutes from which it follows that Svoboda would have loved to see Dubček ousted from his post, Svoboda's reaction to seeing Dubček does not come as a surprise: "As I stood before him I was shocked to see a look of cold disdain in his eyes. . . . At that moment he seemed almost to radiate enmity, as if something had changed his innermost emotions." Dubček never questioned Svoboda later as to the reasons for his cold reaction.[65] It is possible there was one more meeting between Dubček and Černík and the Soviet leadership, which apparently led to no significant rapprochement between the positions of the two sides.[66]

On the next day, 24 August, Husák announced at 6:20 a.m. on Slovak radio from Moscow that Dubček and Černík were taking part in the negotiations.[67] Ahead of further negotiations, Brezhnev informed the leaders of the "fraternal parties" who had arrived in Moscow in the meantime, Władysław Gomułka, Walter Ulbricht,[68] János Kádár, and Todor Zhivkov, about the state of the negotiations.[69] In this he had the awkward task, as he saw it, of telling the allied comrades that Dubček could not be cast aside. The plan to install a collaborationist government in Prague, which the allies had agreed on in Moscow prior to the invasion on 18 August, had proven impossible to realize. As Brezhnev explained to the leaders of the allied Communist parties, it had not been feasible to begin at once with the political work. "Unfortunately our hopes proved unfounded," Brezhnev said, "that these rascals would get scared and beat the retreat."[70] "Confronted with this mass hysteria, part of the healthy forces took refuge in the [Soviet] embassy and gave up trying to deploy any active propaganda efforts," he continued The forces loyal to Moscow were cowards and were considered traitors in Czechoslovakia. This was the reason, according to Brezhnev, why Dubček, Černík, Smrkovský, Kriegel, Špaček, and Šimon had been interned. He justified the invasion once more, failing which "Czechoslovakia would have become a bourgeois republic in a matter of days." Then Brezhnev informed the allied Communist Party leaders about the "offer" that had been made to Svoboda of forming a new government, which the latter had declined saying that he would be toppled in no time. Svoboda had agreed, according to Brezhnev, to declare the 14th Party Conference illegal, yet he had urged the Soviet leadership "to conduct the negotiations in such a way that the government returning to Prague was a legal one." This meant in plain language "that Černík, Dubček, and Smrkovský were due to return to Prague." Brezhnev summed up the new point of departure succinctly: "We have no new demands in addition to those that we have already formulated in Čierná nad Tisou."

Dubček's attitude was criticized sharply by Brezhnev. Černík was the first, according to Brezhnev, to declare himself prepared to call the Party Conference illegal. Dubček then adopted "this idea," "but not as firmly and with such determination as Černík." There was in Brezhnev's assessment a "certain amount of cunning" on the part of Dubček behind all this. The negotiations had, therefore, not moved beyond an initial phase, but the plan was to let Svoboda fly home ahead of the others and to issue a communiqué saying that the negotiations with the Czechoslovak delegation were being continued. Svoboda had declared he was going to persuade Dubček to resign, but in Brezhnev's eyes, this was simply naive. There is no written evidence for this statement.[71]

While it is impossible to prove that such a conversation did not take place, it appears more plausible that Brezhnev used such words to make it clear that Svoboda was by no means loyal to Dubček; he could, therefore, be regarded as having proven his loyalty to the Soviet Union. However, as one had to take into account Svoboda's position in the ČSSR in the prevailing circumstances, there was no other way out than keeping Dubček and Černík in place for the time being.

Of all the Communist Party leaders of the "fraternal countries," SED leader Ulbricht was the most vehement in his opposition to this. In reply to Ulbricht's interposed question whether it followed from all this that the delegation would return under Dubček's leadership, Brezhnev became again extremely circumstantial, "Do not think for a moment that we are yielding ground by even one step. . . . All we are saying is that the situation is extremely complex." Brezhnev tried to allay the comrades' misgivings. In his assessment, it was crucial for Indra to be the next in line after Dubček. "In this case it would be possible to find some other job for Dubček after a while." Gomułka insisted on the troops stationed in the ČSSR being given new orders for the struggle against counterrevolutionaries, saying, "Let's face the situation with which we're confronted. Czechoslovakia only exists in name. There are isolated communists, but there is no longer a Communist Party. The Communist Party has been transformed into a social democratic party, a party that makes common cause with the counterrevolution, that goes down the same road." Ulbricht subsequently agreed that one had to reach a compromise regarding Dubček, but warned against mentioning him by name in any communiqué. Dubček had cheated on everyone before so often, there was no doubt he would do it again given only half a chance. Zhivkov chimed in in support of Ulbricht. It was his considered opinion that it was possible to "make use" of Černík for a while, but this did not apply to Dubček. Zhivkov said, "We must be on the offensive, Comrade Brezhnev, otherwise things simply go from bad to worse. . . . We must have our sights on the suppression of the counterrevolution. The gangs that are active in Prague must be liquidated," to which Gomułka replied:

> I have no illusions whatsoever, but, the situation being what it is, I still think that Dubček has got to be made use of, if that is possible. Why do we have to make use of him? In order to expose him so that the influence that he still wields is undermined, in order ultimately to send him packing. Dubček must be made to sign something here, something that the counterrevolution simply

cannot accept. . . . How we dispose of him afterwards is a matter that is of no interest at present.[72]

Brezhnev pointed out that Svoboda was going to insist that Dubček's name was inserted in the communiqué. Gomułka came to Brezhnev's aid and underscored that this was needed to appease the population. Ulbricht replied it would have opposite effect. Podgornyi reaffirmed once more that Svoboda would insist on Dubček and Černík being mentioned by name. Brezhnev in the end, resorted to a most drastic formula: "We fully expect a civil war, we reckon with its outbreak. There can be no such thing as capitulation. We count on you. We've got to find a way."[73]

For the afternoon, talks were scheduled between the Soviet leaders and Smrkovský, Špaček, and Šimon. Brezhnev used similar tactics as on the previous day. He said that he was far from blaming what had happened on the Czechoslovak comrades; "maybe all of this happened behind your backs." He again conjured up the worst-case scenario of a civil war in the ČSSR and again explained in detail the significance of the 14th Party Congress and the consequences that would ensue if it was declared to have been legal. Asked by Brezhnev whether he considered the Party Congress to have been illegal, Smrkovský replied: "The Party Congress is as illegal as our own stay here in Moscow." However, if the Czechoslovak people came out in support of the proposal to have the Party Congress reenacted, he was not going to raise any objections. Smrkovský declared he was opposed to bloodshed in his home country and to anything that threatened socialism. Once they were back in Czechoslovakia, they could also declare the Party Congress illegal.

Generally speaking, the dramatis personae have left accounts of the talks in which they are portrayed rebuffing heroically the demands of the Soviet leaders. The minutes of the talks did nothing to preserve the nuances of the wording and were presumably "touched up" in retrospect in any case, so they cannot be used to refute these claims. Podgornyi, for one, was decidedly less than impressed with Špaček's attitude ("I have a feeling that Comrade Špaček is somehow devoid of all enthusiasm"); Brezhnev concurred ("What worries me is that Comrade Špaček is showing so little conviction in his answers"). In the end, after Brezhnev had assured them once more of his unqualified "support" and had requested Comrades Šimon and Špaček to modify their tone, all the people involved declared themselves prepared to have the 14th Party Conference annulled.[74] In the evening, Svoboda informed Prague via the Czechoslovak embassy that the negotiations were set to continue and urged the government" not to interfere in the unsolved problems of the Party."[75] Later that night, Czechoslovak radio broadcast a message from Svoboda saying negotiations were making solid progress, but depended for their outcome on the maintenance of public order in the ČSSR.[76] Shortly afterwards, another message was broadcast that also originated with Svoboda and amounted to less than the truth: Svoboda claimed that he had insisted on Dubček, Černík, and Smrkovský being involved in the negotiations. This was the first step in the genesis of the myth of Svoboda as the savior of Czechoslovakia.

On Sunday, 25 August, Švestka, Josef Lenárt, Milous Jakeš, Barbírek, Rigo, and Zdeněk Mlynař joined the Czechoslovak delegation, which meant that the pro-Soviet wing within the delegation was strengthened.[77] Dubček was ill and in bed,[78] and Indra could likewise not take part in the internal Czechoslovak talks for health reasons. He had had a heart attack and was taken to a Moscow hospital.[79] Even Brezhnev was presumed to have fallen ill and to have spent the whole day in bed.[80] Late in the afternoon, it was, therefore, only Podgornyi, Kosygin, and Arvīds Pel'she who met with the heads of the "fraternal parties." The Soviet leaders informed Ulbricht, Gomułka, Kádár, and Zhivkov about the state of the negotiations.[81]

On 26 August 1968, an "agreement" was finally signed, the so-called Moscow Protocol. It provided the basis for all reforms, resolutions, and staff decisions to be reversed that had been passed during the run-up to the 14th Party Congress of the KSČ as well as for the reintroduction of censorship and the stationing of Soviet troops—initially until the situation had reverted to being "normal" again. The Moscow Protocol was, as the Czechoslovak government committee saw it, a "classic case of a grossly asymmetrical agreement, imposed by force of arms and intimidation."[82] It would be going very far to call the Moscow Protocol the result of negotiations between equal partners.[83]

The only "concession" on the part of the Kremlin was dropping the "charge" of "counterrevolution." Dubček, Černík, and Smrkovský remained in office for the time being, for they were needed to steer Czechoslovakia without bloodshed back on to the path of "normalization."

On 14 and 15 October 1968, the treaty on the permanent stationing of Soviet troops in the ČSSR was signed. This was the end of the chapter in the reform Communist movement that demonstrated the incompatibility of any reforms that went beyond mere cosmetic changes in the makeup of the regime within the Communist system.

SUMMARY

Newly accessible documents, notably the hitherto unpublished parts of the stenographic transcripts of the Moscow "negotiations" from 23 to 26 August 1968, prove that the Soviet leaders were partly clueless how to break the deadlock resulting from the invasion and/or failed to convey to the Czechoslovaks a clear idea of their strategy. The pictures of the military occupation served as a smokescreen for the actual sorry predicament of the Moscow-led interventionist coalition. Politically speaking, the Kremlin had ended up in a cul-de-sac. The plan to install a revolutionary government, which had been legitimated to an extent by "recommendations" given to Bil'ak and the "healthy forces" by the Politburo of the CC CPSU before the invasion, was in tatters.

Given the tense situation in Moscow, President Svoboda, subsequently and for long time to come was celebrated as "Czechoslovakia's savior," even proposed getting rid of Dubček as a political actor. Brezhnev however saw quite clearly that Dubček's dismissal would only have prepared the ground for worse to come. The fact remains that Svoboda would have been prepared to betray Dubček. He dropped him because being in the USSR's good graces was more important to him than continuing to support the reforms of the Prague Spring.

The "negotiations" in Moscow after the military intervention were conducted by the Soviets with the preeminent aim of preventing Dubček from returning to Prague wearing the martyr's crown. In addition to this, the Soviets were determined to deal with the 14th Party Congress of the KSČ, which had elected a new party leadership immediately after the invasion, and to have it annulled. In the eyes of the Kremlin, this was the only alternative to Czechoslovakia's relaunching itself as a western bourgeois republic and presumably turning its back on the Warsaw Pact. A revision of the results of World War II would have been the last thing the Kremlin was prepared to endorse.

Svoboda contributed a great deal to the "normalization" of the situation in the ČSSR; under his aegis, Communist rule was consolidated again. Slovakia's autonomy, which was carefully nurtured by Husák, was one of the levers of this "normalization." Dubček was cunningly exploited and degraded to a tool to further Soviet interests in the country, a role he came increasingly to embrace voluntarily. His successor, Husák, became a replica of János Kádár—with one difference: he did not advance to the post of first secretary of the party in the jaws of the invasion.

NOTES

Translated from German into English by Otmar Binder, Vienna.

1. Jitka Vondrová and Jaromír Navrátil, eds., *Mezinárodní souvislosti československé krize 1967–1970: Červenec—srpen 1968*, vol. 4, no. 2 (Brno: Doplněk, 1996), 211–12; RGANI, F. 3, op. 72, d. 198, pp. 7–11, Politburo resolution of the CC CPSU P 96 (IV), 19 August 1968; Jaromír Navrátil et al., eds., *The Prague Spring 1968: A National Security Archive Documents Reader* (Budapest: Central European University Press, 1998), 405–8.

2. Navrátil et al., *The Prague Spring 1968*, 408. Milan Klusák, Svoboda's son-in-law, was present during the meeting. At the time of the Moscow negotiations, he was head of the First Department of the Czechoslovak Foreign Ministry; until July

1968, he had been the ČSSR's ambassador to the United Nations in New York, and from April 1969 he was deputy foreign minister.

3. Navrátil et al., *The Prague Spring 1968*, 411–13; Jan Pauer, *Prag 1968: Der Einmarsch des Warschauer Paktes: Hintergründe—Planung—Durchführung* (Bremen: Edition Temmen, 1995), 230–31. For details, see Valerij Vartanov, "Die militärische Niederschlagung des 'Prager Frühlings,'" in Karner et al., *Beiträge*, 661–71; on the successful execution of the orders see SAPMO-BA, DY 30/3621, 62–67, "Information der KPdSU an die SED über den Einmarsch in die ČSSR," 22 August 1968, reprinted in Karner et al., *Dokumente*, #104.

4. Pauer, *Prag 1968*, 231.

5. BStU, ZA, SdM 34, 104–9, transcript of the conversation between the minister for national defense of the GDR, H. Hoffmann, with the supreme commander of the Interventionist Alliance, I. Yakubovskii, 29 August 1968, reprinted in Karner et al., *Dokumente*, #100.

6. For details, see Manfred Wilke, "Ulbricht, East Germany, and the Prague Spring" in this volume.

7. RGANI, F. 3, op. 72, d. 192, pp. 18, 30, Politburo resolution of the CC CPSU. P 93/6, 30 July 1968, reprinted in Karner et al., *Dokumente*, #52.

8. RGANI, F. 2, op. 3, d. 130, pp. 1–26, L. I. Brezhnev's speech at the plenary session of the CC CPSU, 31 October 1968, reprinted in Karner et al., *Dokumente*, #122.

9. Cf. Brezhnev's statements that he repeatedly made to Dubček on 23 August in Moscow and in the telephone conversations on 9 and 13 August 1968. There are primay sources on the one-on-one talks between Brezhnev and Dubček. No interpreters were present because Dubček was fluent in Russian. Dubček claimed that no agreements had been reached in Čierná nad Tisou and that in unofficial talks with Brezhnev the upcoming conference in Bratislava had been the only topic. See Alexander Dubček, *Leben für die Freiheit: Die Autobiographie* (Munich: Bertelsmann, 1993), 247–49, here 248. Cf. also the telephone conversations between Brezhnev and Dubček on 9 and 13 August 1968. Vondrová and Navrátil, *Mezinárodní souvislosti československé krize*, 164–67; Navrátil et al., *The Prague Spring 1968*, 336–38; RGANI, F. 89, op. 76, d. 75, pp. 1–18, telephone conversation between L. Brezhnev and A. Dubček, 13 August 1968, reprinted in Karner et al., *Dokumente*, #57; Vondrová and Navrátil, *Mezinárodní souvislosti československé krize*, 172–81; Navratil et al., *The Prague Spring 1968*, 345–56; cf. also Vasil Bil'ak, *Wir riefen Moskau zu Hilfe: Der "Prager Frühling" aus der Sicht eines Beteiligten* (Berlin: Edition Ost, 2006), 119–33.

10. Pauer, *Prag 1968*, 175–94; Lutz Priess, "werten Sie unsere Erklärung als nachdrückliche Bitte und Forderung um Ihr Eingreifen und um allseitige Hilfe," *Darch* 12 (1994): 1252–55; AdBIK, Holdings "Prague Spring," shorthand minutes of the meeting of the Interventionist Coalition in Moscow, 18 August 1968, reprinted in Karner et al., *Dokumente*, #87.

11. For details, see Mikhail Prozumenshchikov, "Inside the Politburo of the CPSU: Political and Military Decision Making to Solve the Czechoslovak Crisis," in this volume.

12. ÚSD, AÚV KSČ, F. 07/15, Zahr. Kor. No. 822. RGANI, F. 3, op. 72, d. 193, pp. 2, 6–8, Politburo resolution of the CC CPSU P 94 (I), "On the Question of the

Situation in Czechoslovakia," 16 August 1968, reprinted in Karner et al., *Dokumente*, #150; Navrátil et al., *The Prague Spring 1968*, 366–67; Pauer, *Prag 1968*, 209.

13. Navrátil et al., *The Prague Spring 1968*, 384–87.

14. For details, see Csaba Békés, "Hungary between Prague and Moscow," in this volume.

15. RGANI, F. 3, op. 72, d. 193, pp. 2, 6–8 (cf. note 12 above).

16. This can be inferred from RGANI, F. 3, op. 72, d. 197, pp. 27, 30, Politburo resolution of the CC CPSU 95 (2), "On the Telegram to the Soviet Ambassador in the ČSSR," 18 August 1968.

17. RGANI, F. 3, op. 72, d. 197, pp. 27, 30.

18. Černík was also present when the letter was delivered. Dubček in retrospect dated the delivery wrongly ("Sunday evening"). Navrátil et al., *The Prague Spring 1968*, 400; Dubček, *Leben für die Freiheit*, 258, 263–64.

19. Pauer, *Prag 1968*, 237.

20. Bil'ak, *Wir riefen Moskau zur Hilfe*, 154; Dubček, *Leben für die Freiheit*, 261; Zdeněk Mlynář, *Nachtfrost: Das Ende des Prager Frühlings* (Frankfurt am Main: Athenäum, 1988), 185–86; Werner Marx and Günther Wagenlehner, eds., *Das tschechische Schwarzbuch: Die Tage vom 20. bis 27. August 1968 in Dokumenten und Zeugenaussagen. Zeitpolitische Schriftenreihe 6* (Stuttgart: Seewald, 1969), 9–13.

21. Dubček, *Leben für die Freiheit*, 258, 263–64.

22. Dubček, *Leben für die Freiheit*, 264; Mlynář, *Nachtfrost*, 187.

23. On this point, the published memoirs of the dramatis personae either contradict one another or differ in the weight they attribute to the controversy between Dubček and Svoboda. Dubček only mentions that Svoboda appeared approximately forty minutes after he first rang him. Neither he nor Mlynář make any mention of the reputedly heated controversy. See Mlynář, *Nachtfrost*, 187, 192; Bil'ak, *Wir riefen Moskau zu Hilfe*, 154–55; Dubček, *Leben für die Freiheit*, 264–66; Pauer, *Prag 1968*, 252–53.

24. Bil'ak, *Wir riefen Moskau zu Hilfe*, 159; Dubček, *Leben für die Freiheit*, 264–65; Mlynář, *Nachtfrost*, 191–93; Pauer, *Prag 1968*, 237–39.

25. Dubček, *Leben für die Freiheit*, 268. It would appear more probable that the security police erroneously discharged him. SAPMO-BA, DY 30/3621, 62–67 (cf. note 3).

26. At 5:22 a.m., Vltava aired the TASS communiqué, and at 5:45 a message to the Czechoslovak People's Army. Both the TASS communiqué and the message to the army are reprinted in *Prager Schwarzbuch* (Bonn: Edition Atlantic Forum, 1969), 22–25.

27. At 7:30 a.m. Czechoslovak radio announced that the station was surrounded by tanks. At 9 a.m., the building of the radio station was occupied by Soviet soldiers.

28. *Prager Schwarzbuch*, 33.

29. Later Dubček learned that in all probability he was made to stop over in Legnica in southern Poland. This is where the headquarters of the allied forces was stationed. Dubček, *Leben für die Freiheit*, 270–71.

30. Dubček, *Leben für die Freiheit*, 269ff; *Prager Schwarzbuch*, 38–39.

31. For details, see above all Pauer, *Prag 1968*, 292.

32. RGANI, F. 89, op. 38, d. 57, pp. 62–110, stenographic transcript of the talks between the Soviet leadership and the first secretary of the KPČ, A. Dubček, and

the president of the ČSSR, O. Černík, 23 August 1968, reprinted in Karner et al., *Dokumente*, #106.

33. RGANI, F. 3, op. 72, d. 199, p. 25, and RGANI, F. 3, op. 72, d. 200, p. 52, Politburo resolution of the CC CPSU P 97 (47), 23 August 1968, reprinted in Karner et al., *Dokumente*, #105.

34. Bil'ak, *Wir riefen Moskau zu Hilfe*, 171–72.

35. Among those present at the time was also Gennadii Voronov, who only spoke once. Brezhnev told Dubček that Svoboda was on his way to Moscow and was "in the air now." Bil'ak, *Wir riefen Moskau zu Hilfe*, 171–72.

36. It has proved impossible to date to ascertain what venue was used for the talks. They did not take place in the Kremlin. In setting the scene, Brezhnev said, "We will conduct the negotiations with Ludvík Ivanovič [Svoboda] in the Kremlin as usual. Secret negotiations will be conducted in this room; as he will be here on an official visit, we will have to make a report. Our meeting will therefore take place where our meetings with statesmen are normally scheduled." RGANI, F. 89, op. 38, d. 57, pp. 62–110 (cf. note 32). The assumption that the Soviet leadership had talked to Svoboda before talking to Dubček is not borne out by the evidence. Dubček himself saw excerpts from the minutes of the talks, which partly jogged his memory, partly confused it. Dubček's version that Brezhnev had used Svoboda to confuse him is most probably due to his reading the minutes after an interval of more than twenty years. Whether Dubček refrained from a reference to his first meeting with the Soviet leaders on purpose is a moot point. We would suggest that Dubček's patchy memories had better be attributed to the ordeal of arrest, abduction, sleeplessness, and impaired health. Dubček, *Leben für die Freiheit*, 276–89.

37. RGANI, F. 89, op. 38, d. 57, pp. 62–110 (cf. note 32).

38. The May plenum of the CC CPČ lasted from 29 May to 1 June 1968. Contrary to the hopes of the "fraternal parties," which had been banking on a decisive victory of the "healthy forces" and the end of the reformist movement, the plenum resulted in a compromise that fell short of the expectations of the "Five." By way of reaction, the political pressure against the CPČ was stepped up. See Lutz Priess et al., *Die SED und der "Prager Frühling" 1968: Politik gegen einen "Sozialismus mit menschlichem Antlitz"* (Berlin: Akademie Verlag, 1996), 156–57. In the Kremlin, expectations during the run-up to the plenum were low. See Prozumenshchikov, "Inside the Politburo," in this volume.

39. See Dubček, *Leben für die Freiheit*, 271.

40. For details, see Dubček's memoirs, where he repeats he was convinced the conference did not take place in the ČSSR. See Dubček, *Leben für die Freiheit*, 282.

41. This is also mentioned by Dubček in his autobiography: "Finally Černík entered the room, and the whole scene had to be repeated for him." See Dubček, *Leben für die Freiheit*, 287.

42. According to Dubček, it was not Černík who had suggested that the 14th Party Congress should be treated as irregular. See Dubček, *Leben für die Freiheit*, 288. The minutes are inconclusive on this point (cf. note 32).

43. Dubček, *Leben für die Freiheit*, 288.

44. Pauer, *Prag 1968*, 288.

45. See *Arbeiter-Zeitung*, 24 August 1968, 1; Bil'ak, *Wir riefen Moskau zu Hilfe*, 172–73; Dubček, *Leben für die Freiheit*, 294.

46. Brezhnev and Svoboda had met at the end of the war. Svoboda was commander in chief of the 1st Czechoslovak Army Corps, which fought side by side with the Soviets. For details, see Michael Morozow, *Leonid Breschnew, Biographie* (Stuttgart: Kohlhammer, 1973).

47. RGANI, F. 3, op. 72, d. 198, pp. 2, 7–11, Politburo resolution of the CC CPSU P 96 (IV), "On the Instructions to the Soviet Ambassador in Prague," 19 August 1968, reprinted in Karner et al., *Dokumente*, #66.

48. See, for instance, his report to the CC CPSU, RGANI, F. 89, op. 61, d. 5, pp. 1–60, "Report of the Head of the KGB, Y. Andropov, to the CC CPSU on the Activities of the Counterrevolutionary Underground in the ČSSR," 13 October 1968, reprinted in Karner et al., *Dokumente*, #121.

49. Pauer, *Prag 1968*, 256–57.

50. "Svoboda and I were linked by years of a cordial relationship and had great respect for one another. We agreed on practically all matters regarding the 'Prague Spring'; Svoboda was an upright supporter of our reforms." Dubček, *Leben für die Freiheit*, 290.

51. RGANI, F. 89, op. 38, d. 57, pp. 1–19, stenographic transcripts of the talks between the Soviet leadership with the president of the ČSSR, L. Svoboda, and M. Klusák, 23 August 1968, reprinted in Karner et al., *Dokumente*, #107 (partially reprinted in appendix 8 of this volume); Pauer, *Prag 1968*, 289. Pauer was not yet able to make use of these stenographic transcripts. In his analysis, he nevertheless came to the correct conclusion that Svoboda considered the Party Congress irregular but wanted this assessment to be validated by the party delegation. Svoboda's role needs to be reassessed in light of the sources now accessible. Up to now it had to be assumed that he was a fervent advocate before the Soviet leadership for Dubček and Černík keeping their posts. This is not borne out by the evidence, as will be shown in greater detail below. It was not until Svoboda had learned from Brezhnev that the Kremlin did not doubt that Dubček was an essential ingredient in the "normalization" of the situation in the ČSSR or that at least normalization could only be achieved at a disproportionately high cost without him that Svoboda began to argue in favor of Dubček and joined the Soviet leaders in the search for the best "solution." Bil'ak, too, seems to have got wind of the idea to oust Dubček during a visit he paid Svoboda and to have come out vehemently against it for the following reasons: Dubček should not be accorded martyr status and he should be "made to face the music." Bil'ak, *Wir riefen Moskau zu Hilfe*, 183. Pauer inferred from the stenographic transcript of Kosygin's talk with the "fraternal parties" that Svoboda had signaled his distrust of Dubček. Pauer, *Prag 1968*, 319.

52. RGANI, F. 89, op. 38, d. 57, pp. 1–19 (cf. note 51).

53. RGANI, F. 89, op. 38, d. 57, pp. 1–19.

54. RGANI, F. 89, op. 38, d. 57, pp. 1–19.

55. RGANI, F. 89, op. 38, d. 57, pp. 1–19; cf. also Pauer, *Prag 1968*, 289

56. RGANI, F. 89, op. 38, d. 57, pp. 1–19 (cf. note 51). See also Rüdiger Wenzke, "Die Nationale Volksarmee der DDR. Kein Einsatz in Prag," in Karner et al., *Beiträge*. According to Gomułka, the NVA, the GDR's National People's Army, was kept back at the express wish of the group around Bil'ak and Indra. Cf. Pauer, *Prag 1968*, 229.

57. RGANI, F. 89, op. 38, d. 57, pp. 1–19 (cf. note 51).

58. RGANI, F. 89, op. 38, d. 57, pp. 19–61, stenographic transcripts of the talks of the Soviet leadership with the president of the ČSSR, L. Svoboda, 23 August 1968, reprinted in Karner et al., *Dokumente*, #108. Only fragmentary excerpts of the transcripts have been available up to now. They were published in Czech in Vondrová and Navrátil, *Mezinárodní souvislosti československé krize*, 250–53; in English in Navrátil et al., *The Prague Spring 1968*, 469–71; Pauer did not even have access to these excerpts. His analyses, therefore, had to make do with the memoirs of Bil'ak and comparable sources. Pauer, *Prag 1968*, 289–91.

59. RGANI, F. 89, op. 38, d. 57, pp. 19–61 (cf. note 58).

60. RGANI, F. 89, op. 38, d. 57, pp. 19–61.

61. RGANI, F. 89, op. 38, d. 57, pp. 19–61.

62. RGANI, F. 89, op. 38, d. 57, pp. 19–61.

63. RGANI, F. 89, op. 38, d. 57, pp. 19–61. This was a risk Brezhnev was not prepared to take. "One had to assume that the right would gain the upper hand there." SAPMO-BA, DY 30/3621, 212–61, minutes of the talks between the CPSU and the "fraternal parties," 28 August 1968, reprinted in Karner et al., *Dokumente*, #109; Bil'ak directed him into the direction desired by the Kremlin. Bil'ak, *Wir riefen Moskau zu Hilfe*, 176–78.

64. Brezhnev mentioned to the representatives of the "fraternal parties" on the following day, 24 August 1968, that he had spoken twice with Dubček and Černík. For details, see below. It may be assumed with a probability bordering on certainty that no minutes were kept during the second conversation—if there was one.

65. Dubček, *Leben für die Freiheit*, 291.

66. The clue is Brezhnev's statement on the following day in his meeting with the CP leaders of the "fraternal countries": "We spoke with them twice yesterday." SAPMO-BA, DY 30/3621, 212–61 (cf. note 63).

67. *Prager Schwarzbuch*, 80.

68. Walter Ulbricht had left Berlin for Moscow around midnight on 23 August 1968 accompanied by Willi Stoph and Erich Honecker. Priess et al., *Die SED und der "Prager Frühling" 1968*, 261.

69. SAPMO-BA, DY 30/3621, 212–61 (cf. note 63); Pauer, *Prag 1968*, 308–10.

70. SAPMO-BA, DY 30/3621, 212–61 (cf. note 63).

71. On this point, see the minutes of the talks between the Soviet leadership and Svoboda on the previous day referred to by Brezhnev in this context, RGANI, F. 89, op. 38, d. 57, pp. 1–19 (cf. note 51).

72. SAPMO-BA, DY 30/3621, 212–61 (cf. note 63). Gomułka used the same argument after his return to Warsaw to explain why Dubček had not been ousted from his post. Pauer conjectures that in Gomułka's thinking his own experience played an important role. Pauer, *Prag 1968*, 311.

73. SAPMO-BA, DY 30/3621, 212–61. The talks ended at 11:50 a.m., almost an hour and a half behind schedule.

74. RGANI, F. 89, op. 38, d. 58, pp. 1–30, stenographic transcripts of the negotiations in Moscow between the leaders of the USSR, L. I. Brezhnev, A. N. Kosygin, and N. V. Podgornyi, and the leaders of the ČSSR, J. Smrkovský, J. Špaček, and B. Šimon, 24 August 1968, reprinted in Karner et al., *Dokumente*, #110. On the talks, see also Pauer, *Prag 1968*, 306; the stenographic transcripts were, however, not accessible to Pauer at the time he wrote his book.

75. A MZV, Tlg. došlé, 7868/1968, telegram of the Czechoslovak ambassador in Moscow, V. Koucký, with a message from L. Svoboda to L. Štrougal, 24 August 1968, reprinted in Karner et al., *Dokumente*, #111.

76. *Prager Schwarzbuch*, 84.

77. For details, see Pauer, *Prag 1968*, 312.

78. Dubček, *Leben für die Freiheit*, 314.

79. Indra did not return to Prague until 28 September 1968, in *Arbeiter-Zeitung*, 29 September 1968, 1; Mlynář, *Nachtfrost*, 284, 297, 309; Pauer believes that the pro-Soviet side may have engineered Indra's disappearance for tactical reasons. Pauer, *Prag 1968*, 306.

80. RGANI, F. 89, op. 38, d. 60, pp. 1–39, 57–58, stenographic transcript of the talks between the delegation of the Politburo CC CPSU and the presidium of the CC KPČ and the president of the ČSSR, L. Svoboda, 26 August 1968, reprinted in Karner et al., *Dokumente*, #114.

81. SAPMO-BA, DY 30/3621, pp. 212–61, minutes of the talks between the CPSU and the "fraternal parties," 25 August 1968, reprinted in Karner et al., *Dokumente*, #113. For details see Pauer, *Prag 1968*, 319–20.

82. Vojtěch Mencl, "Die Unterdrückung des 'Prager Frühlings,'" *Jahrbuch für Historische Kommunismusforschung* (1995): 9–31. The so-called Moscow Protocol has been reprinted several times in the literature, for example in Mlynář, *Nachtfrost*, 342–46.

83. On the "negotiations" from 25 August onward and the differences within the Czechoslovak delegation, see Pauer's extremely well documented analysis: Pauer, *Prag 1968*, 312–26.

III

THE GREAT POWERS AND THE YEAR OF CRISIS IN 1968

8

The Johnson Administration, the Vietnam War, and the American South's Response to the Vietnam War

Mark Carson

"I feel like a hitchhiker in a Texas hailstorm. I can't run. I can't hide. And I can't make it stop."[1] That was how Lyndon Johnson described to press secretary Bill Moyers how troubled he felt while making the agonizing decisions over U.S. involvement in Vietnam. Since ascending to the presidency in 1963 Johnson had solicited the advice of many on Vietnam, and by 1968 the results of the decisions he made over the intervening five years left him frustrated and exhausted. By August 1968, as Soviet tanks rolled into Czechoslovakia, the Johnson administration, although the president himself had already abandoned a reelection bid, found itself in the middle of a floor fight over Vietnam policy at the tumultuous Democratic National Convention in Chicago. The president still held out hope for negotiations with the North Vietnamese, the Vietcong, and an increasingly difficult South Vietnam. Two of the chief architects of his Vietnam policy, Secretary of Defense Robert McNamara and General William Westmoreland, had been relieved. A full 78 percent of Americans believed that the United States was not making any progress in Vietnam.[2] Johnson indeed could neither run nor hide from the Vietnam War, and even though it appeared that negotiations might begin to bear fruit in 1968, he couldn't stop the war.

From 1965 onward, as George Herring and other historians attest, U.S. military policy in Vietnam had been improvised rather than carefully designed. Initially, the administration went to war to prevent the collapse of South Vietnam. From 1965 to 1967, Johnson gradually escalated the bombing of North and South Vietnam and slowly but surely increased the number of ground forces. By 1968 the number of U.S. forces reached well over half a million, and the United States had dropped more bombs on Vietnam than they had on all their enemies in World War II. None of these actions stopped the North Vietnamese from bringing troops into the South or weakened the resolve of the southern-based National Liberation Front, or Vietcong. The increasing bombing of the south and the bloody U.S. strategy of attrition did the opposite of winning the "hearts and minds" of the people the United States was trying to save from communism. Similarly, no amount of military action or monetary aid could create a popular government in Saigon.

Though Johnson did, indeed, improvise in the formulation and execution of his Vietnam strategy, the gradual nature of the president's escalation was deliberate. He always chose a middle course between the military and their champions in and out of Congress, and the political left, who eventually advocated U.S. withdrawal. He did this for a number of reasons. First, Johnson's championing of his Great Society social reforms necessitated limiting the commitment to the war so as not to anger liberals who would support these programs. Second, while keeping the military commitment limited, at the same time he needed to prove to conservatives that he remained committed to decisive military action that would find Ho Chi Minh's "breaking point" so as to not provoke a "right-wing backlash" which also would kill his domestic programs and his presidency. Third, Johnson followed a policy of gradualism in Vietnam because of his fear of provoking the Soviet Union or China into military intervention.[3]

By indirection and public deception, Johnson was able to continue his policy of gradual escalation unabated throughout 1966 and 1967. Even though public discontent grew over these years, resulting in many street protests, the majority of Americans supported the war. Then came the Tet Offensive, which, though militarily disastrous for the Vietcong and North Vietnamese, shattered the illusion broadcasted throughout 1967 by Johnson and Westmoreland that the United States and South Vietnam were on the brink of winning the war. Despite the great American public relations disaster that was the Tet Offensive, Johnson, even after his 31 March speech limiting the bombing and inviting negotiations, kept the pressure on the Vietcong and North Vietnamese, particularly in light of their great losses during Tet. In addition, while welcoming negotiations, Johnson did not initially compromise on fundamental issues once the talks began.

The administration also used every means at their disposal to strengthen the position of South Vietnam during the summer of 1968. While reducing the bombing in the north, Johnson greatly stepped up the air war in the south. Planes attacked infiltration routes, lines of communications, and suspected enemy base camps. The number of B-52 missions tripled, and ground troops conducted the largest search and destroy operations of the war. In addition, the United States and South Vietnam initiated an accelerated pacification plan with such programs as the Chieu Hoi and Phoenix to try to control as much of the countryside as possible. The Americans also aided the South Vietnamese in increasing their force levels. However, all these were long-range undertakings that could not erase years of neglect or mismanagement. None of these measures won many hearts and minds. These efforts certainly weakened, but did not destroy the Vietcong organization or many North Vietnamese main units. Furthermore, the rampant corruption of the South Vietnamese government didn't endear the South Vietnamese to their leaders.[4]

Adding to Johnson's difficulties was the intransigence on both sides of the peace talks in Paris. By August, the time of the tumultuous and divisive Democratic National Convention and the Warsaw Pact invasion of Czechoslovakia, the negotiators in Paris had still not agreed on the shape of the table from which they would negotiate. Though the talks looked increasingly hopeful in the fall, South Vietnam balked at the initial agreement. The Johnson administration failed to get a peace settlement in time to deliver the White House to Democratic presidential nominee Hubert Humphrey.[5] Johnson in his last months in office was a "prisoner of the White House," increasingly isolated and beaten down by dissent from many sources. He had been politically destroyed by Vietnam. Whether or not the United States should have been involved in the war is a matter beyond the scope of this chapter. What is irrefutable is that Johnson's Vietnam policies came under increasing attacks from both hawks and doves.

The president tried not to offend either extreme by choosing a middle course and pleased neither side. And though in America many voices expressed their discontent with Johnson and Vietnam, it was the public opposition of several southern members of the United States Congress, who collectively, in the words of historian John Fry, took "center stage" on foreign policy matters over Vietnam, that both helped influence and also reflected the opinions of a majority of Americans. In congressional hearings and through other acts and statements, southern members of Congress expressed diverse opinions on Johnson and Vietnam. This diversity of opinions among southern leaders in part helped shape the debate over the war and added to the difficulties encountered by the Texas president to prosecute the war.

According to a number of polls, a majority of ordinary Southerners supported a more aggressive military strategy in Vietnam which was more in line with military officials. Southerners supported and southern leaders protected military leaders in part because of the great financial benefit their states enjoyed from military spending. As one scholar described it, "[the South] paid homage to and reaped benefits from the defense establishment." In addition to defense spending, one out of every three soldiers in Vietnam came from the South, a region that represented only 25 percent of the population of the United States. Furthermore, the South had a large share of military retirees as well.[6] Therefore, a significant number of southern legislators became the most fervent hawks on Vietnam, advocating increasingly aggressive measures.

Examples of Southern "superhawks" included Senator J. Strom Thurmond of South Carolina, Representative L. Mendel Rivers of South Carolina, and Senator Russell Long and Representative F. Edward Hebert of Louisiana. All served on the Armed Services Committees of each house, with Rivers and Hebert both serving as chair at various times during the Vietnam War. All of them also consulted regularly with top military brass, who were increasingly frustrated with the limits both Secretary of Defense McNamara and President Johnson put on the U.S. forces in Vietnam. Though many of these leaders were in the loop regarding American military forces and operations, some made irresponsible statements as if they were, in the words of Joseph Fry, "less well informed" on Vietnam.[7] For instance, in 1966 and 1967 Rivers, the chair of the House Armed Services Committee, Hebert, ranking member and later chair, and Thurmond, former member of the reserves, all advocated the use of nuclear weapons if it were necessary to produce victory in Vietnam. "We must stand ready to offer our lives on the altar of freedom," Hebert declared when announcing his support of a possible nuclear attack in Vietnam. "If we do not," he continued, "we are not worthy of being called Americans."[8]

Not all southern hawks made statements that extreme. Senators Russell of Georgia, chair of the Senate Armed Services Committee, and John Stennis of Mississippi, head of the Senate Armed Services Investigating Subcommittee on Military Preparedness, and eventual chair, had agonized privately over Johnson's Vietnam policies before unleashing hawkish public criticisms in 1966 and 1967. In 1954, both Russell and Stennis had spoken out forcefully against U.S. military intervention to try to save the French forces at Dien Bien Phu. Moreover, both made Johnson aware of their hesitation in supporting the escalation of the war early on. Transcripts of Johnson's White House phone conversations in 1964 and 1965 include many heartfelt conversations with Russell over Vietnam, mainly because of the president's long-time association with Russell in the Senate (Johnson considering Russell to be a mentor) and because of Russell's long experience on military and foreign policy matters. There are many quotes suggesting Russell's continuing frustration with the conflict. In a phone conversation with Johnson in mid-1964, Russell declared that the Vietnam conflict was the "damn worst mess I ever saw."[9] From the beginning of U.S. involvement, Russell had little confidence in U.S. military intervention and, at one point in 1965, suggested that the Domino Theory did not apply to Vietnam.[10] Nevertheless, once Johnson committed troops, Russell said U.S. honor was at stake, and he urged Johnson to "go all the way" militarily to win.[11]

Stennis held similar views. Though the Mississippi senator voted enthusiastically for the Gulf of Tonkin resolution in 1964, Johnson's gradual escalation increasingly concerned him. In a joint Senate Armed Services/Foreign Relations Committee hearing in early 1965, Stennis said that the Congress should be consulted before Johnson sent in more troops. However, once Johnson began major escalation of the war, Stennis advocated using "every weapon we have" against the North Vietnamese and Vietcong.[12] Both Russell and Stennis, due to their significant seniority in the Senate and positions of considerable power within the Senate Armed Services Committee, became important spokesmen for the hawks who grew disenchanted with Johnson's gradualism.

At the same time, however, there was a small, less connected, but still influential number of southern members of Congress who served as some of the most prominent congressional doves, questioning the wisdom, legality, and eventually the morality of U.S. involvement in Vietnam. Democratic senator Albert Gore of Tennessee and Republican senator John Sherman Cooper of Kentucky had expressed their doubts to both Kennedy and Johnson through 1965, usually in private, about the wisdom of American involvement in Vietnam. By 1966 and 1967, respectively, these private doubts became public advocacy of withdrawal from Vietnam. Though Gore and Cooper did much to emphasize their dissent over Vietnam, the most influential southern "dove" on Vietnam, arguably the most important "dove" in Congress, was J. William Fulbright of Arkansas, chair of the Senate Foreign Relations Committee.

Fulbright, to his lasting regret, had been Johnson's floor manager for passage of the Gulf of Tonkin Resolution in the Senate. From mid-1964 through early 1966, Fulbright watched as Johnson slowly but surely escalated the war. The Arkansas senator became increasingly concerned that Johnson was leading the United States into a full-scale war to defend a South Vietnamese government that did not have the backing of its own people. As early as December 1964, Fulbright staked out his position on the escalation that at that point was only beginning. The senator, during questioning in Foreign Relations Committee hearings of Maxwell Taylor, then American ambassador to South Vietnam, said in early 1965, "If you want to go to war, I don't approve of it. . . . I am not going to vote to send 100,000 men, or it would probably be 300,000 or 400,000."[13] Over the next year, he continued to voice his concerns as Johnson, his friend and former Senate colleague, increased troops levels and bombing targets. Fulbright greatly angered the president in a foreign policy speech in the Senate on 15 July 1965 in which he proposed that the administration's policy should be to bring an "end [to] the war by seeking a negotiated settlement involving *major concessions on both sides*" (emphasis added).[14]

In January 1966, Fulbright's break with the administration became total when, as chair of the Senate Foreign Relations Committee, in response to a bill providing for a supplemental appropriation to fund the war, he opened full-scale nationally televised Vietnam hearings, in fact debating with Johnson administration officials the wisdom of continuing the war as the war raged on in Vietnam. Fulbright and Gore had been the only southern senators and some of the first legislators in all of Congress to officially break with Johnson over the war. In these hearings, both southern senators grilled Secretary of State Dean Rusk, Ambassador Maxwell Taylor, and others under the lights of the television cameras.

Fulbright began the hearings stating that he and others had been "deeply troubled about our involvement in Vietnam and it seems to us . . . that now is an appropriate time for some examination of our involvement there for the clarification of the people in this country." The committee challenged or questioned almost every aspect of U.S. policy decisions regarding Vietnam. When Rusk suggested that the United States fought in Vietnam to ensure that South Vietnam could make their own decisions regarding their future, Fulbright shot back, "Do you think they can be a completely free agent with our occupation of their land with 200,000 or 400,000 men?" Fulbright and Gore went on to assert that by voting for the Gulf of Tonkin resolution they did not intend to give Johnson a blank check to engage in a full-scale war.[15]

The hearings included experts such as George Kennon, the father of U.S. containment policy, who advocated liquidating the U.S. presence in Vietnam. It also explored such questions as what defines an atrocity and what is an acceptable military action. The hearings also brought out some of the confusion over Johnson's Vietnam policies. When Ambassador Taylor suggested that U.S. military objectives were to convince the North Vietnamese and the Vietcong to stop their aggression in the South, Fulbright responded, "This is just another way of saying 'unconditional surrender' . . . The idea of negotiating a compromise, which is something less than we want, seems to me to be consistent with a limited war. But if they give up and come to our terms, this is what I would call unlimited commitment . . . using whatever we need to bring about the result." He drove the point home in a colorful fashion, "Maybe I'm too stupid to understand what it means when you say, 'We are going to do what it takes to make them come to the conference table.' This to me means they are going to have to, as they used to say in the Ozarks, holler 'Enough' or say 'calf-rope.'"[16]

One of the most controversial debates of the hearings involved the question of what constitutes an atrocity in war. Senator Russell Long of Louisiana, a confirmed hawk, defended the war effort, the U.S. and South Vietnamese military, and the Domino Theory against what he considered unfair attacks that gave aid and comfort to the enemy. While many on the committee took the opportunity to make speeches in front of the television cameras, Long seemed to make more of them than most committee members, save possibly Fulbright.

In a rambling opening statement, Long remarked that Communists, and some senators, had charged that the United States, by its actions in Vietnam, was an "international criminal." The senator appointed himself as defense attorney to "plead my nation Not Guilty." After asking Ambassador Taylor to attest to the excellence of several U.S. military units, he contrasted the U.S. efforts with the brutal tactics of the Vietcong, who he claimed had killed 50,000 civilians, including, "in one year alone, 456 mayors in little villages." Taylor suggested the numbers were probably far higher. Long then challenged the senators and the television audience members to consider "how we would feel if that many mayors or officials in our community had been destroyed."[17]

"War is inherently a rather atrocious activity, is it not?" Fulbright observed when his time came around again to speak. The ambassador agreed. "If we are to talk about such things," Fulbright continued, "we are reminded about air raids on Tokyo, or Hiroshima, or Nagasaki." When Taylor protested, saying that Japan used ruthless tactics treating prisoners and attacking Pearl Harbor, the Arkansas senator observed, "Isn't it true that each country always believes the other one commits the atrocities, and that God is on their side? Isn't this typical of all wars. . . . What difference, really, morally or any other way, do you see between burning innocent little children and disemboweling innocent citizens? Isn't it only the means you use?"

The purpose of his questioning, Fulbright insisted, was not to justify the heinous acts of the Communists. He was attempting to debunk one of the chief tenets of U.S. society, American exceptionalism, that inspired U.S. involvement in Vietnam. "We sometimes think we're the only good people, and I certainly don't think we are bad people. But I don't see any great distinction between using the weapons we happen to have to kill innocent people [when our enemies do the same]. I don't think we should claim great superiority because we happen to have nuclear bombs and other side doesn't."[18]

The 1966 Vietnam hearings solved little, but they still had a significant impact on U.S. attitudes about the war in Vietnam, at least in the short term. After the hearings, Johnson's approval ratings on Vietnam plummeted from 63 percent in January to 49 percent in February. Pat Holt, a Texan and a member of the Foreign Relations Committee staff, believed that, because of the hearings, some Americans realized that "the dissenters were no longer a bunch of crazy college kids invading dean's offices and so on; they were people of substance."[19] Although Americans' public support of the war wouldn't effectively wane until after Tet, the work of Fulbright, Gore, and others in a large sense made Vietnam dissent respectable.

Johnson also responded to the hearings and attempted to steal the thunder of Fulbright by hastily arranging a meeting with the South Vietnamese leadership at a conference in Honolulu. On a few occasions, the networks preempted television coverage of the Vietnam hearings to carry statements from Johnson and South Vietnamese leaders Nguyen Cao Ky and Nguyen Van Thieu. The president also instructed the FBI to monitor all future Foreign Relations Committee hearings to determine if Fulbright, Gore, and other doves were receiving information from Communist sources. He also ordered the Bureau to monitor activities of committee members and record if they made any contacts with foreign, particularly Communist, government officials. In a meeting with Assistant FBI Director Cartha DeLoach, the president belittled Fulbright, his former friend and colleague, saying that he did not "know what the smell of a cartridge is," and that the senator was a "narrow minded egotist trying to run the country."[20]

Fulbright followed up these hearings with several lectures and a book entitled *The Arrogance of Power*, in which he argued that U.S. arrogance led the country's leaders to believe that its military could "go into a small underdeveloped nation and create stability where there is chaos, the will to fight where there is defeatism, democracy where there is no tradition of it, and honest government where corruption is a way of life." Calling upon the region of his birth, Fulbright suggested that the Vietnam War, contrary to the administration's claims, was not unlike the American Civil War. What were the North Vietnamese doing, he wrote, "that is different from what the American North did to the American South a hundred years ago, with results few of my fellow southerners now regret?"[21]

As Johnson continually increased the troop levels and bombing targets, Fulbright, now completely estranged from the administration, did not hold anything back when consulting with the president. In a 25 July 1967 meeting between Johnson and the Senate committee chairs, the president outlined several of the difficulties he faced both on foreign and domestic matters. Fulbright responded bluntly, "Mr. President, what you really need to do is stop the war. That would solve all your problems." Labeling the war as a "hopeless adventure," Fulbright contended that Vietnam was "ruining our domestic and foreign policy." After previously supporting foreign aid measures that facilitated U.S. involvement in Indochina, the foreign relations chairman, a sworn internationalist since the 1940s, insisted he might vote against the legislation "and may try to bottle the whole bill up in committee."

Johnson remained calm and said that if Congress "wanted to tell the rest of the world to go to hell," they could do it. Fulbright stood his ground, "My position is that Vietnam is central to the whole problem. We need a new look. The effects of Vietnam are hurting the budget and foreign relations generally." "Bill," Johnson replied testily, "everybody doesn't have a blind spot like you do. You say don't bomb North Vietnam on just about everything. We haven't delivered Ho yet." Johnson concluded, as he always did when challenged by members of Congress on Vietnam, that Fulbright at any time could introduce a resolution to repeal the Gulf of Tonkin resolution. Johnson, knowing Fulbright had never forgiven himself for acting as floor leader for the resolution, baited him further: "[Y]ou can tell the troops to come home. You can tell General Westmoreland that he doesn't know what he's doing."[22] Fulbright, saddened by the exchange, remained silent. Everyone in the room knew full well that his silence did not mean consent.

The chairman continually fought from 1966 to 1968 for some sort of congressional effort to slow down the pace of escalation. Of major concern to Fulbright and other Southerners, both doves and hawks, was the seeming irrelevance of the legislative branch in determining the course of the war. In late February 1967, the senator supported a nonbinding "sense of the Congress" resolution introduced by Senator Clifford Case of New Jersey that proposed limiting troop levels to 500,000 and stopping the air war unless there was a declaration of war. Fulbright used the measure as another opportunity to debate the war in the Senate, this time with his southern colleague Richard Russell. Though Russell disagreed with Fulbright on Vietnam policy, he did agree that the exercise on executive power in Vietnam, along with the growth of executive power elsewhere alarmed him enough to want to have a "review" in order to "take this country back to the proper separations of powers and the proper weighing of our system of checks and balances." The resolution was later watered down considerably, and despite Russell's eventual opposition, it passed. Though nonbinding, it was the first time the Senate had officially acted to provide a general framework for ending the war and bringing U.S. troops home. It would act as a precedent for later actions.[23]

Fulbright's and Gore's dissent, along with the lack of a coherent military policy in Vietnam, also led to other southern defectors in 1967. In the summer of that year, Congressman Claude Pepper of Florida, a former senator and member of the Foreign Relations Committee in the 1940s, and a former law professor of Senator Fulbright's at the University of Arkansas, withdrew his support for Johnson's Vietnam policy because of the lack of a foreseeable end to the conflict, a refusal of the United States' major allies to help shoulder the burden of war, and the apparent unwillingness of the South Vietnamese army to fight.[24] On 27 July 1967, Republican Senator John Sherman Cooper of Kentucky, the soft spoken, well-respected former U.S. ambassador to India and newest member of the Foreign Relations Committee, advocated publicly the unconditional cessation of bombing in North Vietnam as an incentive to convene a peace conference.[25]

Thruston Morton, the other Kentucky senator, had a much more dramatic change of heart on Vietnam. Morton, a former assistant secretary of state for Congressional Affairs and a former Republican Party national chairman, turned, almost immediately, from a hawk into a dove. As late as June 1967, the junior senator from Kentucky scolded the Johnson administration for not instituting a naval blockade of the port of Haiphong. By August, Morton publicly turned against the war in a speech to the National Committee for Business Executives for Peace in Vietnam. Over the past three years, he began, the United States had "witnessed a disastrous decline in the effectiveness of our foreign policy." The root cause, he asserted, was "the bankruptcy of our policy in Vietnam." In 1965, Morton continued, he supported President Johnson's escalation of the war. The senator paused and added, "I was wrong." Suggesting that the president had been "brainwashed" by the military industrial complex, Morton proposed several options including the cessation of all U.S. bombing of North Vietnam, the end to "search and destroy" missions conducted in South Vietnam by U.S. soldiers, the concentration of U.S. soldiers in coastal and populations centers of South Vietnam, the heightening of pressure on the Saigon government to enter into negotiations and institute internal reforms, the implementation of an internal and regional settlement probably decided by an all-Asian peace conference, and a communication to Hanoi that the United States' "honorable disengagement" deserved an appropriate response. Morton's abandonment of U.S. military action could not have been more complete or stunning in its scope. As one reporter observed, Morton had moved from "the sword to the olive branch."[26] Fulbright, therefore, had some new southern allies in the fight to bring the war to a close.

That month Fulbright again called on his colleague Senator Russell to define further the constitutional responsibilities of the legislative branch in shaping foreign policy. The Arkansas senator asked for Russell's support for another resolution that would assert congressional participation in the making of national commitments. With Russell's promise of support this time, Fulbright proposed a "sense of Congress" resolution that declared it unconstitutional for the executive branch to enter into executive national commitments with foreign nations without some legislative action.[27]

On 16 August 1967, Fulbright opened public hearings to consider the matter. Undersecretary of State Nicholas Katzenbach testified for the administration and against the resolution. Katzenbach aggressively defended Johnson's actions in Vietnam and outraged committee members Fulbright, Gore, and Cooper by stating that, though the Congress still had the constitutional right to declare war, in such a fast moving modern world the term "declare war" was outmoded. He stated that the Gulf of Tonkin Resolution acted as "a functional equivalent of the constitutional obligation expressed in the provision of the Constitution with respect to declaring war."[28] Given the diplomat's reasoning, senators could neither extricate themselves from culpability nor find a way to change the course the administration steered.

The committee, livid at Katzenbach's statement, continued the hearings to highlight what the chairman, Gore, Cooper, and others felt was a constitutional imbalance in foreign affairs. They called upon another long-time southern senator and constitutional scholar, Sam Ervin, chairman of the Judiciary Committee's Subcommittee on the Separation of Powers. Ervin complained of a "marked departure during the last 25 years from the balance struck by the Constitution between the Congress and the Executive branch in matters of foreign policy." He said the trend would have to be "arrested if we are to avoid the fear of the Constitution's framers that unchecked executive power might develop along tyrannical lines and pose the greatest threat to our democratic government and to the liberty of our people." With regard to Vietnam, Ervin repeated the contention that he expressed earlier in the year—the United States had no legal or constitutional authority to intervene militarily in Vietnam. The North Carolina legislator said a distinction should be drawn between offensive and defensive war. The president, he reasoned, could use the armed forces to defend United States territory in the event of a sudden attack on United States territory. Any other use of the armed forces could be taken "only upon congressional authority." The senator also challenged the administration's invocation of the SEATO treaty as justification for intervention. In addition to opposing the Johnson administration's interpretation of the constitution and SEATO treaty, Ervin also rejected the theory of containment. "I have never favored the idea," he declared, "that democracy is so very good that we should try to give it to everybody on the face of the earth, even those people who don't know what democracy is and have no experience in exercising it." Ervin's statement reveals the diversity of opinion of southerners on Vietnam, even among hawks.

Though disavowing the legal and ideological justification for war, Ervin still disagreed with the doves. Like the majority of southerners, he supported fighting the war "with sufficient force to either win it or to bring the enemy to the conference table." After offering his comments, the senator said further that he was unhappy with Johnson's half measures. "I think some in authority would do well to read a little Shakespeare," he mused. "Shakespeare said, 'Beware of entrance to a quarrel, but, being in, bear it, that the opponent may beware of thee.'" The United States, Ervin suggested, ignored the Bard's advice on both counts. It rushed into "quarrels" such as South Vietnam, Korea, the Congo, and Rhodesia. Once in, however, the United States did not make their opponents beware of them. After his eloquent argument, his conclusion echoed a familiar refrain: "I think we ought to turn over the fighting in South Vietnam to the admirals and generals, and see if they can't win the war."

Ervin's hawkish stand seems puzzling in light of his rejection of the administration's justifications for war. He, like other southern congressional hawks, suggested that the time had passed for arguing the wisdom of getting into war in Vietnam. "We are faced with a condition and not a theory," he said, quoting Grover Cleveland.[29] Having rejected the theories that created the condition, however, it seems puzzling that the senator could advocate escalating the war in order to defend both the theories of containment and the belief in the necessity to export the United States' brand of democracy. Perhaps Ervin, also a member of the Armed Services Committee, had been convinced by his southern hawkish colleagues or military officials of the necessity to fight to win in Vietnam. The frustration of the war along with the lack of a cogent "honorable" solution in Vietnam sometimes created strange and conflicted arguments in the halls of Congress. The members of the committee, perhaps sensing their own logic just as tortured in regard to the conflict, did not press the North Carolina senator on the point.

Johnson, though still feeling betrayed by the public dissent of the doves within his own party and region, had said previously that he would be more concerned with the defection of the hawks than the doves. The president, who remembered vividly the disastrous political effects of the right-wing reaction to President Harry Truman's China policies, worried that a similar thing would happen over Vietnam. By 1966 it appeared that the president realized another one of his major fears.

As the number of U.S. casualties grew significantly, southern hawks became increasingly impatient with Johnson's gradual escalation. In the 1966 Vietnam hearings, Russell Long expressed discontent with the fighting of a "limited war" in Vietnam that resonated throughout the South. An opinion poll in June 1966 revealed that southern whites and, to a somewhat lesser extent, southern African Americans, were more inclined to believe that the United States would secure an "all out victory" in Vietnam.[30] Long, in his 1966 comments in the Vietnam hearings, concluded with a warning to the Johnson administration: "If the 1st Division has to pull Old Glory down on a flagpole it is going to be because somebody over here made a mistake not somebody over there."[31] Increasingly for southerners, those "somebodies" were Lyndon Johnson and his chief Vietnam advisor up to that time, Robert McNamara.

McNamara prompted the sharpest criticism among southern hawks. It did not sit well with Russell, Stennis, Thurmond, House Armed Services Committee Chairman Mendel Rivers and ranking member F. Edward Hebert, and several less prominent legislators that a civilian systems analyst wanted not only to revamp the Defense Department, but also, in reality, served as the architect of Vietnam military polices. Southerners on both House and Senate Armed Services committees detested McNamara's perceived arrogance and his attempts to quantify every military question in his management of the war and the Defense Department. Rivers went out of his way to rankle McNamara, instructing his committee's chief council to get Navy workmen to make a plaque and place it in the front of the rostrum where it would face the secretary. The plaque read:

> U.S. Constitution—Art. 1—Sec. 8—The Congress shall
> Have the power . . . To raise and support Armies . . . provide
> And maintain a Navy . . . make rules for the Government
> And Regulation of the land and naval forces.[32]

Stennis was not prone to personal attacks, but he was no less disturbed by McNamara and his prosecution of the war. He called for an "all-out assault" by air on strategic targets in North Vietnam. Russell agreed.[33]

In August 1967, just as Fulbright convened hearings on his commitments resolution, John Stennis of Mississippi held hearings of his own to suggest more hawkish policy alternatives. In August 1967, Stennis, chairman of the Senate Armed Services Preparedness Investigating Subcommittee, convened seven hearings to discuss conflicting reports between civilian and military authorities as to the effectiveness of the bombing campaign. The prime "target" of these hearings was, predictably, Robert McNamara. The defense secretary had just sent a memorandum to Johnson suggesting no amount of bombing would force the North Vietnamese to negotiate. Members of the Joint Chiefs, who consulted regularly with Stennis and other military commanders, completely disagreed with the secretary, and the Mississippi senator set out to hear their side of the story. As historian Michael Scott Downs asserts, the hearings "had all the quality of a wild west lynching party, with Robert McNamara as a guest of honor."[34] Besides the defense secretary, only one nonmilitary man, a retired general, testified.

The hearings began with testimony by several top military officials who were allowed to make a formidable case against the administration's bombing policies. They revealed that sharper more effective air attacks had been refused by the administration. They also asserted that any reduction of or suspension of the bombing would increase U.S. casualties and also result in the deployment of additional combat troops. On the other hand, the military officials concluded that if the administration allowed the Air Force to bomb Hanoi, Haiphong, and all the restricted targets, the North Vietnamese would surrender. The committee treated the military with the utmost respect when they testified.[35]

The attitude of the senators changed when the troubled McNamara sat down to testify before the committee on 25 August 1967. The secretary had to endure a six-hour grilling from a hostile subcommittee. Thurmond, as usual, attacked the secretary in the most strident fashion. He suggested that the secretary cared more about North Vietnamese civilian casualties than U.S. casualties in South Vietnam. He also accused the secretary of placating and appeasing the Communists. "It is a statement of no win," he continued.

"It seems to me that if we follow what you have recommended that we ought to get out of Vietnam at once, because we have no chance to win, and I deeply regret that a man in your position is taking that position today."[36]

In the end, the subcommittee report, which Chairman Stennis quickly made public, made explicit both his and his constituents' frustration with the concept of limited war:

> The cold fact is that this policy has not done the job and has been contradictory to the best military judgment. What is needed now is the hard decision to do whatever is necessary, take the risks that have to be taken, and apply the force that is required to see the job through. . . . It is high time to allow the military voice to be heard in connection with details of military operations.[37]

The president did add a number of bombing targets during the hearings to thwart the publicity of the hearings. Overall, however, he did not fully follow the advice of the subcommittee. Nevertheless, Stennis did illustrate the increasing divide between Johnson and the hawks, and in so doing, he expressed the opinion of, if not a majority of Americans by 1968, at the very least a majority of his fellow Southerners.

Despite the mounting criticism from congressional and other sources, the president, Secretaries McNamara and Rusk, and General Westmoreland had convinced most Americans that U.S. forces would prevail soon. The Tet Offensive in late January 1968 changed considerably both the course of the war and the length of Johnson's presidency. On 31 January during a bombing halt to mark the Vietnamese Tet holiday, the Vietcong attacked almost every major city and provincial capital in South Vietnam, including Saigon. In the capital city they assaulted both General Westmoreland's headquarters and, as U.S. television cameras recorded the event, the American embassy in Saigon. Though the Vietcong lost every battle, Tet shattered the illusion of the immanent victory that Johnson and the military had preached for quite some time. In the wake of Tet, Johnson's approval rating on Vietnam dropped to 26 percent.[38]

Southern members of Congress, as always, did not speak with one voice in response, but most believed that changes needed to be made in Johnson's policies. "How is it that the Viet Cong [*sic*] could mount such a series of co-ordinated attacks against American bases and provincial capitals?" queried Senator Harry Byrd Jr. of Virginia. "Is it now not time," he continued "for a reappraisal of our policies and procedures for obtaining our objectives?"[39] Richard Russell, while publicly calling for increased attacks on the Vietcong and approval of additional bombing targets in North Vietnam, privately communicated to the administration his doubts on continuing the war. Hearing of Westmoreland's pending request of up to 200,000 more troops, the Georgia senator advised the president that he should not grant the request "until there was a complete reappraisal of Vietnam, primarily on the will and desires of the people of South Viet Nam." His comments centered mainly on his doubts of the will of the South Vietnamese to fight. "If they did not show more interest to defend [South Vietnam] we should consider getting out."[40]

Even southerners who had enthusiastically supported Johnson's prosecution of the war harbored doubts after Tet. In a presidential briefing of some leaders of Congress on 6 February 1968, Senator Robert Byrd of West Virginia charged that the administration had poor intelligence and was not prepared for the attacks. Furthermore, he felt the Americans both underestimated the "morale and vitality" of the Vietcong and "overestimated the support of the South Vietnamese government and its people." When Johnson disagreed and insisted that the administration knew the Vietcong had been planning a general uprising, Byrd did not back down. "I have never caused you any trouble on this matter on the Hill," he reminded the president. "But I do have serious concerns about Vietnam." Johnson continued his denials, saying that he did not underestimate North Vietnamese and Vietcong strength. "Something is wrong over there," Byrd accurately observed and pointed out that the Vietcong had achieved their objective. The Communists wanted "to show that they could attack all over the country and they did." Johnson still dismissed Byrd's criticism and said that he took more stock in the opinions of the military and diplomatic men than congressional carping. "Anybody can kick a barn down," he said, quoting former Speaker of the House Sam Rayburn from Texas. "It takes a good carpenter to build one." Byrd stood his ground. "I do not want to argue with the President," he said. "But I am going to stick to my convictions."[41]

The Tet offensive marked the final straw for Stennis. Though, like Russell, he had publicly called for increased efforts to win the war, he had never attacked Johnson's overall policy. In the aftermath of the Vietcong offensive, the Mississippi senator made a final break with the administration. Under Johnson's policies, Stennis observed, the U.S. action was contained "by the boundaries of Laos, Cambodia, and North Vietnam." At the same time, the enemy used the port of Haiphong and several other ports restricted from U.S. bombs to resupply and rearm its troops. Under those circumstances, Stennis reasoned, the United States could expect to wait a long time and lose more men in order to "force an honorable and effective solution" to the conflict. With the realization that after years of war Vietnam was no nearer to an acceptable settlement, Stennis posed a question: "Is it more men that we need for the present policy? Or is it more men that we need for a new policy? . . . In short, it is clear to me that we are now compelled to choose between a hard-hitting war or no war at all."[42]

To southern doves, Tet stood as further proof of Johnson's duplicity and the moral bankruptcy of U.S. policy. Gore repeated calls for a negotiated settlement and posited that the war had both drawn Russia and China together and increased the danger of Chinese intervention. Cooper captured the attitude of a growing number of Americans when he questioned the purpose of the United States' utter destruction of South Vietnam as a result of the war. The Kentucky senator quoted reporter James Reston, who questioned how the United States could win a military victory in South Vietnam without "destroying what we are trying to save." Cooper continued, "Is it not time for us to ask whether we are crossing that line, when South Vietnam's major cities, such as Hue and parts of Saigon, are systematically reduced to rubble and dust?"[43]

In the aftermath of Tet, William Fulbright continued to push for a clarification of the administration's objectives. On 5 February, he put into the record an article by columnist Tom Wicker on the differences between the statements of the U.S. military and civilian officials in Vietnam, who were encouraged to be optimistic, and the more realistic accounts of the reporters who traveled with ordinary troops. A few days later, the Foreign Relations Committee voted to ask the president again, as they had over the past few months, to allow Secretary of State Rusk to testify publicly in order to explain the current situation in Vietnam. In a letter to the president, Fulbright observed that some members, presumably including the chairman himself, "felt strongly that what is now at stake is no less urgent a question than the Senate's constitutional duty to advise, as well as consent, in the sphere of foreign policy."[44]

While waiting on a response, Fulbright convened hearings to study the incidents that prompted the passage of the Gulf of Tonkin resolution. Since early 1966, Fulbright, in light of other inconsistencies in Johnson's statements, had begun to question the administration's conclusions about what happened in the Gulf of Tonkin in early August 1964. He had never consulted the logbooks of either the *Maddox* or *C. Turner Joy*, but a retired navy admiral had commented to him that the events "sounded unrealistic." In the wake of Undersecretary of State Nicholas Katzenbach's insistence that the chairman knew the full implications of the 1964 resolution when he convinced questioning senators to vote for it and the undersecretary's characterization of the resolution as a "functional equivalent of a declaration of war," Fulbright instructed his staff to investigate the Gulf of Tonkin incidents. They uncovered several facts inconsistent with Defense Secretary McNamara's explanations in August 1964. The South Vietnamese "OPLAN-34" raids on the North Vietnamese coasts, and the U.S. "Desoto patrols" had been related. In other words, the U.S. ships had acted provocatively and almost invited attack. In addition, doubt still remained as to whether the second incident, in which the *Maddox* was allegedly attacked, had ever occurred. Fulbright called for hearings. McNamara, now out of office and by some accounts at the point of a nervous breakdown, reluctantly agreed to testify.[45]

The former secretary continued to claim that the *Maddox* and *C. Turner Joy* had no knowledge of the OPLAN-34 attacks. Fulbright then read a cable sent from the *Maddox* at the time that referred to the operations. McNamara's response seemed like pure nonsense. "We can find no basis," he declared, "for the commander making that statement." Eventually McNamara confirmed the commander actually sent the cable, but he disagreed with its conclusions. Fulbright quoted another cable from a naval commander who reviewed the second incident and cast doubt on whether the North Vietnamese ever fired torpedoes at the *Maddox*. McNamara stood by his convictions, saying he was convinced the attack had taken place.

Fulbright could not contain his contempt and despair. He exclaimed that if he had knowledge of the full story he would not have pushed for quick passage of the resolution. "We accepted your statement [in 1964] completely without doubt":

> I went on the floor to urge passage of the resolution. You quoted me, as saying these things on the floor. . . . All my statements were based on your testimony. I had no independent evidence, and now I think I did a great disservice to the Senate. I feel very guilty for not having enough sense at that time to have raised these questions and asked for evidence. I regret it. . . . I regret it more than anything I have ever done in my life.[46]

McNamara, in response to the hearings, released a twenty-one page statement saying that Johnson and he had acted responsibly in August 1964. It further condemned Fulbright, Gore, and others for impugning his and his administration's integrity. Fulbright retaliated. He insisted that the administration misled Congress in 1964 and continued to cover up its duplicity. He revealed that when a navy commander contacted the committee in November 1967 to provide information on McNamara's lack of candor immediately after the Gulf of Tonkin incidents, Pentagon officials confined him to a mental ward for a month. Fulbright, to complete the public humiliation of the administration, released the full transcripts of the hearings. Americans now knew that their president had lied to them about Vietnam.[47]

The president himself, though publicly declaring throughout February and March that the United States would win in Vietnam, began to doubt the prospects of continuing to fight to win the war or to extend his presidency. The war, the sluggish economy, and the riots in the cities also diminished his personal approval rating to the all-time low of his presidency. An unexpectedly strong showing by Democratic presidential candidate Eugene McCarthy in the New Hampshire primary and the subsequent entry of his old nemesis Robert Kennedy into the race added to his personal pressures. Senator Russell, his close confidante throughout his presidency, dreaded meeting with Johnson during this period because the president often cried uncontrollably. Having also lost key hawks such as Stennis on the war, Johnson gradually came to the conclusion that he should begin a de-escalation of the conflict. On 31 March 1968, he proposed a halt in the bombing of North Vietnam north of the Demilitarized Zone. The president would not grant Westmoreland's request—he would only send 13,500 more troops over the next five months. Johnson also promised to reduce "substantially the present level of hostilities." The president hoped that the moves would encourage the North Vietnamese to begin peace negotiations. At the end of the speech, he dropped a bombshell—in order to concentrate on ending the war he would not seek or accept the Democratic nomination for president. About a month later formal peace negotiations between U.S. and North Vietnamese officials began, which were to bog down a few weeks before the November general election.[48]

One of the last public debates the Johnson administration had to endure over Vietnam came at the tumultuous Democratic National Convention in Chicago in August 1968. As usual, southern legislators commanded the spotlight. As Mayor Richard Daley's police force attacked protesters outside the convention hall, a ruinous and vitriolic debate erupted on the floor over Vietnam policy. On one side stood the chairman of the Platform Committee, House Majority Whip Hale Boggs of Louisiana, a staunch Johnson ally. Predictably, Boggs followed the administration's line of continuing the fighting and bombing as well as peace talks. On the other side, Tennessee senator Gore, the maverick Democrat who a growing number of Tennesseans considered too liberal for the state, helped lead a spirited fight to adopt a more dovish Vietnam plank within the Democratic platform. Gore took the podium and proposed a Vietnam platform that advocated an unconditional ending to the bombing of Vietnam, a mutual phased withdrawal of U.S. and North Vietnamese troops, and direct negotiations between Saigon and the National Liberation Front. In an impassioned speech, he also criticized the continuation of the status quo as represented in the administration's Vietnam platform proposal and lamented the result of what he considered the United States' tragic involvement in Vietnam:

> What harvest do we reap from this gallant sacrifice? An erosion of the moral leadership, a demeaning entanglement with a corrupt political clique in Saigon, disillusionment, despair here at home, and a disastrous postponement of imperative programs to improve our social ills.
>
> The American people, in my opinion, and overwhelmingly in that regard, think that we made a mistake. And yet, read the proposed platform. We're called upon not only to approve the disastrous policy, but even applaud it. I wonder if the American people are applauding it—they want to change it.

His state's representatives at the convention, however, did not agree. The *Nashville Tennessean* reported that while he received "rousing cheers from other delegations, his own was silent during this appearance on the platform." In fact, they voted against Gore's proposal, forty-nine to two.[49] Since the senator would not face reelection until 1970, he may have figured that he could recover whatever ground he might lose by his participation. He never did.

With the election of the new Republican president in November 1968, the United States had thoroughly rejected Lyndon Johnson's Vietnam policies. The attitudes of southerners who voted to repudiate Johnson had been greatly influenced by the hawks. Despite the efforts of Fulbright and Gore in particular, southerners still supported the move for a military victory, as evidenced by their enthusiastic support of George Wallace for president. Southern hawks, on the other hand, by their refusal to actively support Humphrey, enabled Nixon's victory.

Johnson's rejection also had much to do with the "middle course" he steered in Vietnam between hawks and doves. He stood more with the former, wanting to escalate the war enough so that the North Vietnamese would surrender. He was more influenced by his old friend Richard Russell, and his former colleagues John Stennis and Mendel Rivers, as evidenced by his approval of additional bombing targets as the air war hearings began. Though he viewed his "former friend" William Fulbright's dissent as more a nuisance than a threat, he could not ignore the mounting criticism and "responsible" protests which the Vietnam hearings had, in part, inspired. The strength of the antiwar movement, as evidenced by the early success of dovish candidate Eugene McCarthy, played a part in Johnson's decisions to refuse renomination and to halt the bombing of North Vietnam. As he left office, the proud but broken Texas politician still harbored resentment for the Arkansas senator. They never reconciled.

The debates that raged within Congress did not fully change Johnson's mind, but they did add to his difficulties in prosecuting the war. The president left office, in one sense, a casualty of the war his administration escalated beyond anyone's anticipations. The year 1968 became his administration's breaking point, and southern members of Congress, though not the first to publicly break with Johnson's Vietnam policies, lent credence, weight, and influence to the many voices of dissent. Johnson's preoccupation with Vietnam and its dissenters possibly could have limited his attention to the August 1968 Soviet invasion of Czechoslovakia. That invasion came during a Democratic Convention that showed the political leaders of Johnson's region, Johnson's party, and the United States in general at one of its most divided and preoccupied periods in history.

NOTES

1. "LBJ Goes to War (1964–1965)," *Vietnam: A Television History*, 1983, American Experience Series, Corporation for Public Broadcasting, http://www.pbs.org/wgbh/amex/vietnam/104ts.html (accessed 14 June 2008).

2. Joseph Herring, *America's Longest War: The United States and Vietnam, 1950–1975*, 4th ed. (Boston: McGraw Hill, 2002), 243.

3. Several sources describe both Johnson's strategy as "improvised" and provide reasons for the stated reasons for his gradual escalation. See Herring, *America's Longest War*; James Olson and Randy Roberts, *Where the Domino Fell: America and Vietnam, 1945–1990* (New York: St. Martin's, 1991); William Conrad Gibbons, *The U.S. Government and the Vietnam War: Executive and Legislative Roles and Relationships, Part IV: July 1965–January 1968* (Princeton, NJ: Princeton University Press, 1995); and many others.

4. Herring, *America's Longest War*, 252–59.

5. Herring, *America's Longest War*, 262–68. See also Olson and Roberts, *Where the Domino Fell*, 199–206.

6. "Southern Militarism," *Southern Exposure* 1 (Spring 1973): 60–62. Bruce J. Schulman, *From Cotton Belt to Sunbelt: Federal Policy, Economic Development, and the Transformation of the South, 1938–1980* (New York: Oxford University Press, 1991), 146.

7. Joseph Fry, *Dixie Looks Abroad: The South and U.S. Foreign Relations, 1789–1973* (Baton Rouge: Louisiana State University Press, 2002), 285.

8. Mark D. Carson, "F. Edward Hebert and the Congressional Investigation of the My Lai Massacre" (master's thesis, University of New Orleans, 1993), 6.

9. Michael Beschloss, ed., *Taking Charge: The Johnson White House Tapes, 1963–1964* (New York: Touchstone, 1997), 363.

10. *Face the Nation*, Transcripts of Television program, Columbia Broadcasting System, 1 August 1965, Richard Russell Senatorial Papers, hereafter referred to as Russell Collection, Richard B. Russell Library, Series, Athens, GA, IIIZ, Box 84.

11. Robert Mann, *A Grand Delusion: America's Descent into Vietnam* (New York: Basic Books, 2001), 480.

12. Congress, Senate, Committee on Foreign Relations (hereafter referred to as SFRC), vol. 17, *The Situation in Vietnam*, 89th Cong., 1st Sess., 2 April 1965, 366–67, 393–403.

13. SFRC, vol. 16, *The Situation in South Vietnam*, 88th Cong., 2nd Sess., 3 December 1964, 369–70.

14. Congressional Record (hereafter referred to as CR), 89th Cong., 1st Sess., 15 June 1965, 13656–58.

15. SFRC, Senate, Foreign *Supplemental Foreign Assistance Fiscal Year 1966—Vietnam*, 89th Congress, 2nd Sess., 28 January 1966, 9, 14–15.

16. SFRC, Senate, Foreign *Supplemental Foreign Assistance Fiscal Year 1966—Vietnam*, 90th Congress, 2nd Sess., 17 February 1968, 454–55, 496–98, 545.

17. SFRC, Senate, Foreign *Supplemental Foreign Assistance Fiscal Year 1966—Vietnam*, 90th Congress, 2nd Sess., 462–66.

18. SFRC, Senate, Foreign *Supplemental Foreign Assistance Fiscal Year 1966—Vietnam*, 90th Congress, 2nd Sess., 498–99, 544–45.

19. Mann, *Grand Delusion*, 497.

20. Mann, *Grand Delusion*, 496.

21. William J. Fulbright, *The Arrogance of Power* (New York: Vintage, 1966), 15, 18, 106–8.

22. David M. Barrett, ed., *Lyndon B. Johnson's Vietnam Papers: A Documentary Collection* (College Station: Texas A&M University Press, 1997), 451–53.

23. CR, 90th Cong., 1st Sess., 28 February 1967, 4715–16, 4718. See also Gibbons, *The U.S. Government and the Vietnam War, Part III*, 585–602.

24. "Pepper Stands Up—Any One Else Care to Be Counted?" *Miami News*, 9 August 1967, 16A.

25. CR, 90th Cong., 1st Sess., 27 July 1967, 20379–81.

26. William Greider, "Morton Modifies Vietnam War Views: 'I Was Wrong,'" *Courier-Journal & Times Bureaucrat*, 8 August 1967, John Sherman Cooper Collection (hereafter referred to as Cooper Collection), The Wendell H. Ford Research Center and Public Policy Archives, University of Kentucky, Lexington, KY, Box 548. See also "Address of Senator Thruston B. Morton, R.-KY before the National Committee of Business Executives for Peace in Vietnam," Cooper Collection, Box 569

27. Gibbons, *The U.S. Government and the Vietnam War, Part III*, 808–11.

28. SFRC, U.S. Commitments to Foreign Powers, 90th Congress, 1st Sess., 16, 17, 21, 23 August and 19 September 1967, 79–81, 89–90.

29. SFRC, U.S. Commitments to Foreign Powers, 90th Congress, 1st Sess., 16, 17, 21, 23 August and 19 September 1967, 189–95, 197–99, 205.

30. Fry, *Dixie Looks Ahead*, 269, 279.

31. SFRC, *Supplemental Foreign Assistance Fiscal Year 1966—Vietnam*, 598.

32. Will Huntley, "Mighty Rivers of Charleston" (Ph.D. diss., University of South Carolina, 1993), 264.

33. William Peart, "Stennis Says Army Doesn't Have 'Green Light' to Win," *Jackson Daily News* (Jackson, MS), John Stennis Collection, Mitchell Memorial Library, Mississippi State University, Starkville, MS, vertical file, Stennis Collection. See also "Senator Russell on Vietnam: Go in and Win or Get Out," *U.S News and World Report*, 2 May 1966, pp. 56–57.

34. Michael Scott Downs, "A Matter of Conscience: John C. Stennis and the Vietnam War" (Ph.D. diss., University of Mississippi, 1989), 87.

35. Senate, Armed Services Committee (hereafter referred to as ASC), Preparedness Investigating Subcommittee, *Air War against North Vietnam, Part 1*, 90th Congress, 1st Sess., 23 August 1967, 57–65.

36. Senate, Armed Services Committee, Preparedness Investigating Subcommittee, *Air War against North Vietnam, Part 4*, 90th Congress, 1st Sess., 25 August 1967, 294–97.

37. Downs, *Matter of Conscience*, 93.

38. Mann, *Grand Delusion*, 570–75.

39. Speech before Marian, VA, Chamber of Commerce, 8 February 1968, Harry Byrd Jr. Papers (hereafter cited as Byrd Jr. Papers), Special Collections, University of Virginia, Charlottesville, VA, Box 55. See also "The Mood of Virginians," transcript of senate speech, Box 55, Byrd Jr. Papers.

40. Notes of conversation between Richard Russell and Robert McNamara, 12 February 1968, Russell Collection, Box 200.

41. Barrett, *Lyndon B. Johnson's Vietnam Files*, 584.

42. Downs, *Matter of Conscience*, 100.

43. CR, 90th Congress, 2nd Sess., 7 February 1968, 2445–47, 2494.

44. CR, 90th Congress, 2nd Sess., 5 February 1968, 2080–85. See also J. William Fulbright to Lyndon Baines Johnson, 7 February 1968, J. William Fulbright papers, University of Arkansas, University Libraries Special Collections, Fayetteville, AR Series 1:1, Box 4:1.

45. Mann, *Grand Delusion*, 577–79.

46. SFRC, *Gulf of Tonkin, The 1964 Incidents*, 90th Congress, 2nd Sess., 20 February 1968, 53–53, 76–80, 101–2.

47. Mann, *Grand Delusion*, 580–81.

48. Mann, *Grand Delusion*, 600–604.

49. Robert Clyde Hodges, "Senator Albert Gore, Sr., and the Vietnam War" (master's thesis, University of Kentucky, 1989), 83–85.

9

"No Action": The Johnson Administration and the Warsaw Pact Invasion of Czechoslovakia in August 1968

Günter Bischof

The United States did not directly intervene during any Cold War crises in the Eastern Bloc after Soviet military actions in its sphere of influence. In spite of President Dwight D. Eisenhower and John Foster Dulles's vigorous "liberation of captive peoples" rhetoric, Washington reluctantly refrained from supporting the people's uprisings in the German Democratic Republic and Hungary in 1953 and 1956. The administrations of President Lyndon B. Johnson and Ronald Reagan also remained passive militarily, following the Warsaw Pact invasion of Czechoslovakia in 1968 and the turmoil produced by the labor union Solidarity in Poland 1980–1981. While Washington supported the East Germans with food parcels and encouraged the rebels with vigorous U.S. propaganda campaigns in Hungary as well as Poland, Washington refrained even from a crusading propaganda campaign in the case of the invasion of Czechoslovakia. While the Central Intelligence Agency (CIA) was active in 1953, 1956, and 1980–1981, it maintained more of a role of distant analytical observer in 1968. During the Hungarian crisis in 1956 and the Czech crisis in 1968, Washington's arms were tied. Moreover, by having to deal with parallel crises in Suez and Vietnam respectively, as well as presidential election contests at home during those crisis years, chances for a U.S. intervention were minimal.[1]

This then raises the question: why was the Johnson administration so passive after the Warsaw Pact intervention, which stopped the flowering of a daring Communist reform movement during the "Prague Spring"? Was it the fear of going down the escalatory ladder toward nuclear war in case of a U.S. military response to the invasion as in Hungary 1956? Was it the reluctance of committing to a second military conflict given the full U.S. military engagement in the deepening Vietnam quagmire? Did Johnson's "bridge building" policies vis-à-vis Eastern Europe and his vigorous search for détente with the Soviet Union prevent him from reacting more strongly to the Warsaw Pact invasion? Was it the deepening domestic turmoil at home, spawned by broad popular resistance to the Vietnam War, the assassination of leaders such as Martin Luther King Jr. and Robert Kennedy, and the contentious presidential election campaign of 1968, which bogged down the Johnson administration?[2] Or was it all of the above? This chapter will try to provide some answers to these significant historical issues concatenating during the global crisis year of 1968.

When the Johnson White House heard about the Warsaw Pact invasion of Czechoslovakia in the evening hours of 20 August, its crisis management team sprung immediately into action and worked in high gear during the last ten days of August 1968.[3] By early September, however, it had become clear that the United States would do no more than protest meekly in the United Nations and deter a spillover of the crisis to Moscow's Warsaw Pact ally Romania, and potentially even to Yugoslavia, Austria, and Germany. Washington diplomacy engaged in a frustrating campaign to stop accusations both in East and West of prior "collusion" with the Soviet Union based on respecting "spheres of influence" agreements going back to Yalta in 1945. Washington shrewdly utilized the Czech crisis to both strengthen the floundering North Atlantic Treaty Organization (NATO) alliance and alleviate the pressure from the U.S. Congress to withdraw American troops from Western Europe. The skilled crisis management machinery of the Johnson administration operated smoothly in August 1968. Four days after the invasion, the president went on his scheduled vacation to his beloved Texas Ranch, and by late September the crisis mood had largely dissipated. When Richard Nixon entered the White House in January 1969, he quickly resumed Johnson's détente policies that had to be discontinued due to the invasion of Czechoslovakia. In the end, the larger mid–Cold War agenda of growing superpower cooperation, bridge building, and peaceful coexistence would not be sacrificed to a crisis within the Soviet Bloc.[4]

THE JOHNSON ADMINISTRATION'S RESPONSE TO THE INVASION OF THE WARSAW PACT IN CZECHOSLOVAKIA[5]

In early May 1968, Eugene V. Rostow, the undersecretary of state, recommended to Secretary of State Dean Rusk to send a strong deterrent signal to Moscow not to intervene in Czechoslovakia. Rostow reasoned: "In retrospect, our failure to deter the Communist takeover of Czechoslovakia in 1948 was one of the most serious mistakes of our foreign policy since the war." He added: "Firm diplomatic action then—a period of our nuclear monopoly—could well have prevented the Cold War." Similarly, stating in public that the United States would not intervene during the Hungarian crisis in 1956 "gave the Soviets full license." What was at stake now was "the process of movement toward detente." Rostow sternly admonished the secretary of state that the Russians were hesitating: "The moment to give them a deterrent signal is therefore now." Once they crossed the border it would be too late. Rusk wrote two words on top of the one-page memorandum and initialed them with "DR": "*No action.*"[6] Rusk's minimal comment indeed characterized the entire response of the Johnson administration to Warsaw Pact pressure and later military aggression against Czechoslovakia during the summer of 1968. Rosy CIA analyses about the Prague Spring tended to predict moderate Soviet behavior in response to the Czechoslovak reform agenda of the Prague Spring. Moscow merely had decided "to do some saber-rattling in order to influence the Czechoslovaks to put a brake on their democratization."[7]

The State Department expected a Soviet intervention all along and began to coordinate serious contingency planning with the Pentagon in May 1968 by instituting a "EUR[opa] advisory group" under the leadership of Malcolm Toon, the director of Soviet affairs in the State Department.[8] In June, Secretaries of State Rusk and Defense Clark Clifford both agreed that they wanted "to stay out" of the Czech crisis, hoping that Prague could resolve their differences with Moscow directly. Rusk, like the CIA, was still hopeful that the Czechoslovaks might "get away" with their reform agenda—the U.S. did not intend "tinkering with it in any way."[9] Next to the Vietnam conflict, Clifford's main worry at this time were the efforts by powerful Senators Mike Mansfield, Stuart Symington, and Henry Jackson to withdraw American forces from Europe to limit defense expenditures.[10] Only on 22 July did Rusk warn Soviet ambassador to the United States Anatolii Dobrynin for the first time. Rusk noted that "the USA has been against interference in the affairs of Czechoslovakia from the very start." In the message summarizing this conversation that Dobrynin sent to the Politburo, Rusk apparently said: "*This is a matter for the Czechs first and foremost. Apart from that, it is a matter for Czechs and other nations of the Warsaw Pact*" (emphasis added).[11] Did Rusk mean to indicate that this was entirely an internal affair in the Soviet Bloc? According to Dobrynin, then, Rusk seems to have indicated that he respected the Soviet sphere of interest in Eastern Europe. Kremlin leaders (especially KGB chief Andropov) took this as a "green light" to the Kremlin to go forward with their plans for intervention.[12]

In spite of a growing number of signals of impending Warsaw Pact action in August, the Johnson administration did not anticipate direct Soviet intervention in Czechoslovakia. A daring reform agenda by the Czechoslovak Communists such as allowing free speech and a refining of Czech historical memory by openly criticizing the Stalinist purges of the early 1950s became increasingly intolerable to the Warsaw Pact allies as these changes threatened to spill over into the Bloc and initiate an undermining of their own regimes.[13] President Johnson himself seems to have recognized the imminent threat of "falling dominoes" in the Soviet Bloc when he wrote in his memoirs in his typically hyperbolic rhetorical style: "If the fire was not stamped out quickly, they might soon face a holocaust."[14] Warnings about impending Soviet action were coming in from NATO headquarters in Belgium.[15] CIA chief Richard Helms warned the president also on 18 August that something was brewing in Moscow. Helms's futile warnings met with no success in moving the president toward action (it was like "peeing up a rope," noted Helms later).[16] The principal reason for this lackadaisical response in the White House clearly was the fact that the United States *"obviously was not prepared to intervene militarily"* (emphasis mine) in case of a Soviet intervention. All the United States could do was try to intimidate the Soviets by whipping up world public opinion, mobilizing Western European Communist parties to warn Moscow not to interfere "in internal affairs of a brother Communist Party and nation," and involving the United Nations, noted the Eastern Europe expert Nathaniel Davis. He warned, however, not to make the mistakes of Hungary 1956 again, namely "in creating expectations we are not prepared to follow through on."[17]

The surprising events of 19 to 21 August placed the president on a veritable roller-coaster ride. When the invasion of as many as half a million Warsaw Pact troops finally came during the night of 20/21 August, President Johnson initially refused to accept it. It instantly squashed his ambitious agenda for accelerating détente with the Soviet Union. Soviet Ambassador Anatolii Dobrynin, himself most likely ignorant of the impending invasion,[18] presented a handwritten note to the White House on 19 August for the public announcement the following morning of a summit meeting between President Johnson and the Kremlin leaders in Leningrad in early October.[19] After the signing of the Nonproliferation Treaty in early July, this summit was scheduled to begin talks on Strategic Arms Limitation and the Limitation of Anti-Ballistic Missile Systems. Progress in such negotiations was expected to be the culmination of Johnson's détente efforts.[20] During the regular Tuesday lunch on 20 August, Johnson served a glass of sherry to his principal advisers and toasted the impending summit. He boasted: "This could be the greatest accomplishment of my administration." Yet the dark clouds gathering over Czechoslovakia were discussed also. CIA director Helms thought that a hastily called meeting of the Central Committee in Moscow indicated Soviet action soon. His gloomy warnings were prophetic.[21]

The evening of 20 August brought shocking news to the White House. At 7:05 p.m. that evening, Ambassador Dobrynin made a rare direct call to the president to ask him for a meeting right away. An hour later, the Soviet ambassador informed the president that the invasion of Czechoslovakia by

Warsaw Pact troops was already underway. The intervention was designed to stop the "domestic and international conspiracy" against Czechoslovakia. President Johnson kept blabbering about the summit meeting and seems to have failed to register the full meaning of the dire invasion news. It appears that an embarrassed Walt W. Rostow, Johnson's national security advisor, set the president straight after Dobrynin's departure.[22]

Rostow and Rusk set the gears of the White House crisis management team into motion and called for an emergency meeting of the National Security Council at 10:15 p.m. Clark Clifford noted in his memoirs how different Johnson's mood was compared to the giddy lunch meeting earlier that day. Johnson felt doubled-crossed by the Kremlin leaders and reluctantly agreed to cancel the summit meeting. Secretary of State Dean Rusk averred that the United States could do little to help Prague—the Czechs had to help themselves. General Earle G. Wheeler, the chairman of the Joint Chiefs of Staff, made it abundantly clear that a military U.S. response was out of the question and insisted: "We do not have the forces to do it." Wheeler confirmed what Rusk had observed after the U.S. invasion of the Dominican Republic in 1965: the United States did not have the military capability to respond to two major international crises at the same time. Vice President Hubert Humphrey, who right away sensed the repercussions of the Czech crisis on his presidential run in 1968, also counseled caution. All that could be done was "giving the Russians hell" by castigating their intervention in the United Nations and registering a formal protest via the Soviet ambassador with the Kremlin.[23] Rusk proceeded to do this by calling Dobrynin to the State Department before midnight. Rusk told him "the Soviet action was like throwing a dead fish in the president's face." He told him to call Moscow immediately and cancel all preparations for the planned summit meeting since the United States did not want to condone "the Soviet march into Czechoslovakia."[24] During the same night, the State Department activated a special "Czechoslovakia Task Force" to monitor the Czech crisis and coordinate the crisis response with NATO and principal U.S. allies.[25] Bonn was asked to closely observe its borders with Czechoslovakia yet prevent border incidents. The governments of the Federal Republic and Austria were called upon to help refugees coming across the borders.[26]

On Wednesday 21 August, the president handled the Czech crisis as part of his daily routine. The president got up at 8 a.m. after only three hours of sleep and began working the phones to draft an official statement on the invasion. Since the crisis so far had not been a "sanguinary" one, this statement should not be an "inflammatory" one; he sincerely bemoaned this step backwards after all the progress in East-West relations in recent months. CIA and State Department analysts zoomed in on the repercussions for U.S. and Western European détente efforts.[27] George McGhee, who had just finished his tour as U.S. ambassador to West Germany a few months earlier, insisted that the United States must not give the impression that it accepted the status quo and Moscow's sphere of influence in Europe. He observed prophetically that the Warsaw Pact invasion gave the United States a unique opportunity to strengthen NATO and stop Congressional efforts to withdraw U.S. forces from Europe.[28] In a briefing for NATO ambassadors by Charles Bohlen, the undersecretary of state for European affairs, West German ambassador Knappstein expressed his fear that the Soviets might also intervene in Berlin (the West's "testicles" that could be squeezed at any time, as Nikita Khrushchev had once observed).[29] As Melyn Leffler has recently demonstrated again, the divided Germany was still considered the most intractable Cold War issue in the 1960s by both superpowers.[30] Johnson read his official statement on the invasion at noon and then proceeded to take his usual hour-long afternoon nap after lunch. He then worked the phones for the rest of the day, keeping the most important members of Congress informed.[31]

After his 21 August statement to the American and world public, the president needed to brief his government and further consult with his advisers about the Czech crisis. He called a meeting of his cabinet for the afternoon of Thursday, 22 August, and left no doubt about his profound disillusionment with the Kremlin. The entire détente agenda was in question, and it was clear that the "Cold War was not over." The Pentagon's Clifford and the president agreed that the United States had no obligation to intervene militarily to help the people of Czechoslovakia, who did not seem to demonstrate a strong will for resistance. Rusk made it crystal clear that "if there were military intervention, there would be world war." The secretary of state expressed his frustration with perceptions around the world that perceived superpower interventionism in Czechoslovakia and Vietnam to be the same thing. Washington continued to show grave concern over the repercussions of the invasion on West Germany and Berlin.[32]

On the next day, Friday, 23 August, discussions continued with the president's principal foreign policy advisers. Secretary of Defense Clifford noted that the Soviet military action was well planned and efficiently executed, yet politically disastrous. CIA director Helms expressed his concern that the crisis could spill over into Romania. The State Department advised putting pressure on Moscow via the United Nations (UN) and not NATO. NATO action would merely confirm the Soviet propaganda line of both NATO and a West German conspiracy against Czechoslovakia.[33] In a meeting with Dobrynin, Rusk calmed him down with the observation that "in the atomic age the President is doing everything possible to diminish the potential for conflict."[34] Discussions in the Pentagon came back to the major conclusion that the Soviet action confirmed the importance of the U.S. presence in Europe. It killed all Congressional efforts to withdraw American forces and offered an opportunity to strengthen NATO. In the Pentagon's analysis, the Warsaw Pact invasion of Czechoslovakia offered a great opportunity to strengthen the U.S. hegemonic position in Europe and improve NATO military force structures for future negotiations from strength—surely not what the Kremlin had envisioned as the U.S. response.[35]

"No action"—Rusk's earlier advice to Eugene Rostow's entreaties to send warnings to Moscow—also defined the basic posture of the Johnson administration vis-à-vis the Warsaw Pact intervention in Czechoslovakia. Within forty-eight hours it was clear that the Johnson administration would not respond militarily to the renewed rape of Czechoslovakia. Washington never contemplated a military response for just one second and was forced to freeze—quite reluctantly—the entire spectrum of "bridge building" and détente activities with Moscow and the entire Soviet Bloc. Washington had learned the tough lessons of "Hungary 1956," namely not to encourage premature rebellion with a propaganda onslaught to encourage senseless resistance by the Czechs and the Slovaks against overwhelming odds of crushing military power. Neither was the unleashing of covert operations seriously contemplated. The only pressure that could be exerted on the Soviets was via condemnation by the United Nations Security Council. The Johnson administration was quick to jump on the sudden opportunity to stop all Congressional talk of defense savings via American troop withdrawals from Europe and strengthen NATO and its crisis response scenarios. Washington's main worry, however, became a possible spillover of the crisis to Romania, and maybe even Yugoslavia and farther into Central Europe.

WASHINGTON'S FEARS OF CZECH CRISIS SPILLOVER

Starting on 23 August, Washington's growing anxiety that Romania might be next on the list of Soviet interventions captivated policymakers and diplomats for the next week. Nicolae Ceauşescu's Romania had become a thorn in Moscow's flesh with his growing emancipation from Kremlin control. Romania did not participate in the invasion of the "Warsaw Pact Five" (Soviet Union, Poland, Bulgaria, Hungary, German Democratic Republic); its official protest launched against its allies' invasion of Czechoslovakia was even more galling.[36] On 23 August, CIA director Helms warned against a Soviet troop buildup on Romania's borders. Rumors of an imminent Soviet invasion seemed to have mainly originated from Romanian sources. The U.S. military attaché in Hungary visited the border areas and could not detect any massive troop build-ups vis-à-vis Romania or Yugoslavia.[37] Soviet expert George Kennan, vacationing in Scandinavia, commented on the stark difference between Czechoslovakian and Romanian behavior: while the Czechs had been faithful to their alliance commitments, the Romanians had abused them.[38]

Secretary of State Rusk worried greatly about an escalating threat toward Romania. He did not want to take any chances and ordered his "Czecho-slovakia Task Force" to initiate contingency planning for Romania as well. NATO headquarters, too, monitored Warsaw Pact troop movements toward the Romanian borders and Yugoslavia's mobilization of reservists carefully.[39] Rusk also issued repeated warnings to Ambassador Dobrynin. He warned him that an invasion of Romania would have devastating consequences for U.S.-Soviet relations and world politics. Dobrynin pooh-poohed all the unsubstantiated rumors flying around Washington about Soviet threats toward Romania. On 29 August, Rusk again called in Dobrynin to the State Department after the plot of Soviet troop movement toward and border incidents vis-à-vis Romania seemed to thicken. He warned the Soviet am-bassador that an intervention in Romania would produce "incalculable risks" in world politics. Rusk added: "Any move against Berlin would be '*of utmost gravity*'" (emphasis mine).[40] W. W. Rostow summarized State Depart-ment and CIA analyses of a threat to Romania for the vacationing president in Texas. The State Department resident Soviet expert Charles Bohlen and U.S. ambassador in Moscow Llewelyn Thompson calculated that chances for a Soviet invasion were 30 percent for and 70 percent against. The CIA presented an "inconclusive" general picture.[41] President Johnson still took the opportunity to send a clear warning to Moscow in a speech the next day in San Antonio, Texas. He obliquely warned against the prospect of aggres-sion against Czechoslovakia being repeated elsewhere in Eastern Europe, yet put Moscow unmistakably on notice: "*So, let no one unleash the dogs of war*" (my emphasis). Dobrynin quickly reassured Rusk again that Moscow had no military plans vis-à-vis Romania.[42] Johnson's warning clearly regis-tered in the Kremlin. Even though rumors about Soviet movement vis-à-vis Romania continued to persist throughout the entire month of September, frequently stoked by Romanian diplomats, the danger slowly abated in the course of the fall.

Wild rumors also circulated about a Soviet threat toward Yugoslavia at the same time.[43] Josip Broz Tito's Yugoslavia had also officially condemned the Warsaw Pact action against Czechoslovakia and allowed thousands of Czechoslovak vacationers on the Adriatic beaches to stay, some of them free of charge. Soviet counter-propaganda produced "a full-blown war scare" in Yugoslavia. Tito ordered some defensive measures, but did not alarm the world with a general mobilization. Rusk asked the Yugoslav ambassador to keep him informed about Soviet maneuvers and castigated Soviet "black propaganda." He expressed regrets over the damage done to détente and bridge-building in Eastern Europe by the Warsaw Pact intervention. Rusk assured Ambassador Crnobrnja that unlike Hungary 1956, the CIA had not unleashed any covert military infiltration in Czechoslovakia. Clearly, unlike President Eisenhower's overheated rhetoric of "rolling back" communism, the Johnson administration practiced a traditional containment policy and respected the Soviet sphere of influence.[44]

The Austrian political class suffered from a bad case of jitters, too.[45] From Vienna, Austrian minister of defense Georg Prader spread the rumor that Warsaw Pact troops on the Austrian border enabled it to unleash military action against Romania, Yugoslavia, and Austria. Prader expected an invasion of Romania in the week of 2 to 8 September. Unless the West protested such a likely intervention vigorously, an attack on Yugoslavia and an ultimatum against Austria could be next. U.S. ambassador to Austria Douglas MacArthur III felt that Prader's alarmist defense ministry experts argued from a "visceral feeling," while Socialist critics like opposition leader Bruno Kreisky saw such Soviet actions as "remote." The Austrian government was angling for discrete U.S. and NATO guarantees to protect Austria's vulnerable neutrality.[46] President Johnson did warn members of Congress that after cleaning up in Romania and Yugoslavia, Austria could be next: "The next target might be Austria."[47] The State Department did not want to take any chances and initiated contingency planning for Austria as well.[48] The Austrian government also had to contend with Soviet black propaganda about harboring U.S. "green berets" in eastern Austria preparing for covert military action into Czechoslovakia.[49]

SUPERPOWER COMPLICITY? THE MYTH OF PRIOR U.S.-SOVIET AGREEMENT

President Charles de Gaulle unleashed a wave of attacks against the Johnson administration that the United States colluded with the Soviet Union not to intervene in case of Soviet invasion of Czechoslovakia.[50] Like the Johnson administration, De Gaulle's government published a communiqué, too, on 21 August. The French statement related the Czech events back to the great spheres of influence agreement at the Yalta Conference in February 1945: "The armed intervention of the Soviet Union in Czechoslovakia is evidence of the fact that the Moscow Government has not abandoned the policy of power blocs imposed upon Europe by the effect of the Yalta Agreements. That policy is incompatible with the right of peoples to self-determination." De Gaulle was quick to point out that France did not take part in the Yalta Agreements and regretted that the invasion impeded East-West détente. The French insisted that Eastern Europe belonged to the Soviet sphere of influence, but blamed Yalta and Anglo-American complicity for those spheres.[51]

Dean Rusk and the State Department were quick to reject such notions of prior U.S.-Soviet agreements as preposterous, "malicious and totally without foundation":

The U.S. government has never entered into any "sphere of influence" agreements or understandings with anyone anywhere in the world. There has been no discussion of any such idea in connection with recent developments in Czechoslovakia nor has any government attempted to elicit from the U.S. government any such understanding.

Rusk reminded U.S. missions around the world that Yalta dealt with zones of occupation in Germany and Austria, but not with spheres of influence in Eastern Europe. In a poignant history lesson for the French president, Rusk noted that at Yalta, in fact, France was granted a zone of occupation and postwar representation on the Allied Control Council in postwar Germany. As a final clincher, Rusk wanted to remind the world that the "Declaration of Librated Europe" tried to secure free elections in the countries liberated by the Red Army in Eastern Europe—exactly "the opposite of [a] spheres of influence" agreement.[52] Rusk also resented being constantly needled by the French with the analogy of the U.S. invasion of the Dominican Republic in 1965 and the Soviet invasion of Czechoslovakia and strongly reprimanded French ambassador Lucet over such an unfriendly equivalency.[53]

In a speech in Connecticut a couple of weeks later, Rusk came back to denying emphatically any charges of "complicity" with the Soviet Union. He reminded the world that it was the Soviets that divided Europe "in violation of its Yalta pledge." It was the Soviet Union that "used force and the threat of force from its occupying armies to impose Communist regimes on Romania, Bulgaria, Poland, Hungary, Czechoslovakia, and the Soviet zone of Germany." It was the Kremlin, Rusk insisted, that "established and maintained by force in Eastern Europe a sphere—not of influence but of dominance." NATO had been established as a defensive pact not to establish a "sphere of influence" in Western Europe, but to protect Western Europeans against the threat of Soviet aggression. When France withdrew its forces from the NATO command in 1966, Rusk reminded de Gaulle, the fourteen NATO members withdrew their military headquarters quickly from France.[54] Yet in spite of these strong official rejoinders, the intellectual debate about Yalta and spheres of influence continued. While the official news media supported de Gaulle's position, the eminent political scientist Raymond Aaron upbraided de Gaulle for his myth-making. While de Gaulle accepted the division of Europe when he sent a representative to the Communist Lublin government in Poland in the fall of 1945, Yalta was the final attempt to prevent a division of Europe. Aaron admonished de Gaulle that he was in no position to preach to the Anglo-Americans on this matter.[55]

Alas, charges both in Western and Eastern Europe about U.S.-Soviet "collusion" and U.S. "complicity" in the intervention did not go away. The Viennese press interpreted Washington's failure to protest the invasion sharply as a tacit agreement between the superpowers. Austrian foreign minister

Kurt Waldheim felt that East and West had clearly marked their respective spheres of interest, and Socialist Party boss Bruno Kreisky commented in a similar vein that the superpowers wanted to see their mutual spheres of influence respected. The daily *Arbeiterzeitung* noted that the United States had lost the moral high ground in Vietnam. Western cries of outrage about the Soviet invasion, noted the Socialist daily, could easily be dismissed by cynics with the counterpart of U.S. interventions in Southeast Asia and Latin America.[56] The West German press was full of charges of "spheres of influence agreements" as well. President Johnson's weak response to the Warsaw Pact action against Czechoslovakia undermined his leadership role in the Western world. A National Security memorandum summarized West German public opinion: "the German press is heavy with charges of 'superpower complicity' in the Czechoslovak crisis and expressions of uneasy doubt of the ability of the U.S. and other of Germany's allies to stand up to the Warsaw Pact."[57]

In Czechoslovakia, too, the rumor mill of conspiracy theories about prior U.S.-Soviet complicity was churning. Zedněk Mlynář, a prominent member of the Alexander Dubček regime and intellectual force behind the reforms of the Prague Spring, prominently insisted on explicit prior agreements in his memoirs *Nightfrost*. Mlynář mentions that Leonid Brezhnev received the confirmation from President Johnson on 18 August that the United States respected the Yalta and Potsdam Agreements. The Soviet leader allegedly took this as a clear signal from Washington that the United States would not react to a Soviet intervention.[58] No "smoking gun" was ever found in the Soviet or U.S. archives that confirmed such a clear-cut explicit prior agreement.[59] The most that can be said of Rusk's policy of nonintervention, as apparently pronounced to Ambassador Dobrynin on 22 July, was the U.S. policy of "hands off" from internal affairs in the Eastern Bloc—a policy that by and large had been practiced during the Soviet interventions in East Germany in 1953 and Hungary in 1956 as well. The obvious historical analogy with the Soviet invasion of Hungary in 1956—unleashed by Moscow to stop satellite dominoes from falling as well as the U.S. failure to intervene—was, indeed, regularly made in analyzing the Czech crisis.

UNINTENDED CONSEQUENCES: THE INVASION OF CZECHOSLOVAKIA AND THE STRENGTHENING OF THE NATO ALLIANCE[60]

Ever since de Gaulle's withdrawal of French forces from the military command of NATO in 1966, the Western alliance seemed floundering in a state of crisis. In 1967 the "Harmel Report" was published, ostensibly giving NATO a larger role in European efforts toward détente. In the midst of the growing U.S. engagement in Vietnam and the mushrooming costs of that war, tensions were further aggravated by pressure on West Germany and the NATO allies to assume more of the costs of Western defense. A reluctant West Germany agreed to buy more arms from the United States and, thus, help to assuage the U.S. balance of payment deficits with such massive "offset payments." The resistance of NATO allies to aid the U.S. war effort in Vietnam with troops led Senate leaders to demand the withdrawal of sizable numbers of U.S. forces from Western Europe. American troop withdrawals could help save costs and remind Western Europeans that the presence of American forces on the continent never was intended to be a permanent feature of Western European defense, but only a temporary fix.[61] The Warsaw Pact invasion of Czechoslovakia brought an unusual clarity to many of these contested issues of Western defense. Warsaw Pact aggression and the Brezhnev Doctrine dramatically demonstrated that Moscow was still the same wolf in sheep's clothing. The role of NATO for the defense of Western Europe suddenly seemed more vital than ever, and the Czech crisis gave a new lease on life to NATO.

Vojtech Mastny posits that NATO's response to the 1968 crisis "was on the whole calm, reasonable, and ultimately effective." Harlan Cleveland, the shrewd and experienced U.S. ambassador to NATO in Brussels, recognized the repercussions of the "Czech affair" right away. With the "forward capacity" of Warsaw Pact forces on the German border of Czechoslovakia, NATO's crisis preparedness was gravely challenged. For one, the rapid response time for NATO forces was shorter.[62] Yet the Pentagon told the supreme commander, Allied Forces Europe (SACEUR) that "NATO should not regard Soviet recent military movements as directed essentially against the West." As a consequence, in spite of the obvious change in the alert and readiness status of Soviet and Warsaw Pact forces in Eastern Europe, the SACEUR did "not put into effect any of the formal measures of military vigilance for which he has existing authority." However, the NATO intelligence effort was intensified following the invasion. Elements of twenty-six divisions on Czechoslovak territory, Cleveland reminded Washington, represented a "military shift" that "while not evidently directed against NATO, considerably increases military uncertainties faced by NATO." Cleveland reported from NATO Headquarters that there was "an instinctive shift to NATO" among allies. Since nobody in the West was thinking about militarily supporting Czechoslovakia, NATO could turn its gaze inward and assess the vital issues of military preparedness and alliance solidarity, as well as the alliance's political goals. After all, NATO was never created to save the Eastern European satellites, Cleveland reminded Washington. The Warsaw Pacts destroyed with a single blow—which was militarily effective but politically counterproductive—NATO's recent turn toward détente and the chance for mutual balanced force reductions and a final European peace order.[63]

What would be the right Western diplomatic maneuver to counter the Warsaw Pact invasion of Czechoslovakia? To reenter the limelight of great power diplomacy, the French predictably pleaded for a Western summit of the United States, United Kingdom, and France. Yet it was West Germany that had been the United States' most reliable continental ally for some time. Chancellor Kurt Georg Kiesinger pushed the idea of following the Warsaw Pact intervention with a NATO summit meeting to arrest the erosion of the troubled alliance. West German diplomats soon dismissed Kiesinger's radio interview, in which he called for a NATO summit, as a typical "holiday talk." Washington, however, reacted very cautiously to any suggestions for summitry, for a Western summit of any type might confirm Moscow's propaganda line that there was a NATO and/or West German "conspiracy" afoot against Czechoslovakia and the Soviet Bloc. Any move that smacked of Western military intervention or escalation of the crisis needed to be avoided. Moscow must not be "stigmatized" in terms of the traditional Cold War context, concluded the State Department. Such caution, then, effectively meant a NATO "hands off" policy as well in response to the Warsaw Pact intervention.[64]

U.S. views quickly gained a foothold to take the invasion of Czechoslovakia as a starting point for a comprehensive NATO defense review. NATO force levels and overall strategy should be thoroughly reassessed. After all, a crisis *within* the Eastern Bloc was something very different from a direct confrontation between NATO and the Warsaw Pact. NATO needed to rethink its entire crisis management procedures as well as the future of détente. Moreover, weapons systems, troop training, and logistics needed to be reviewed as well. Cleveland pleaded for "striking a viable transatlantic defense bargain," namely a better mobilization of Western European reserve forces, along with a strengthening of U.S. force levels.[65] Washington thus utilized the Czech crisis to place greater pressure on the Western European allies to increase their defense budgets and military posture. With plenty of hyperbole, President Johnson reminded Kurt Birrenbach, Chancellor Kiesinger's emissary to Washington: *"While Rome is burning, the Europeans are asleep"* (emphasis mine).[66] At the same time, the Czech crisis stopped all talk in Congress that called for a withdrawal of U.S. forces from Europe. At the end of September, Rusk smugly reported in a cabinet meeting that a number of critical NATO allies such as Germany and Norway had agreed to increase their defense budgets while all talk in the Senate about troop withdrawals from Europe had been stopped. Saki Dockrill is correct in noting that as far as the reinvigoration of the NATO alliance was concerned, the Czech crisis was a "blessing in disguise."[67] At the same time, bickering did not stop among the Western European allies about whether the Czech crisis showed a weakening of U.S. leadership in the alliance. Washington was called upon to show a more robust engagement with European affairs.

CONCLUSION

"The brutal disillusionment over overoptimistic interpretations of trends in détente" in Europe, was one of the principal consequences of the Czech crisis, noted Ambassador McGhee quite rightly. The presence of Soviet troops in Czechoslovakia improved the balance of power in Europe in favor of the Soviets. McGhee still advocated a pragmatic continuation of détente policies as soon as possible in order to secure the progress that had already been made.[68] A basic National Security Council paper came to the same conclusions in early September when it recommended a return to détente policies "in due course."[69] President Nixon would, indeed, sign a major agreement on strategic arms limitations—also resulting from the negotiations the Johnson administration wanted to move forward in the summit of October 1968 "that never was"—as a major foreign policy initiative before his first term was over. The new German chancellor Willy Brandt had already begun pushing his ambitious *Ostpolitik* in 1969. Johnson never wanted a rupture in his détente policies with Moscow; thus his ambitious agenda was put on hold only temporarily. The Warsaw Pact invasion of Czechoslovakia was a very inconvenient bump on the road to détente. Secretary of State Rusk's "hands off" policy made sure that East-West tensions would not escalate so that a return to détente would be possible. Vojtech Mastny asserts that the 1968 crisis over Czechoslovakia ironically "fostered the budding détente" since both NATO and the Warsaw Pact "at the moment of truth . . . both showed a prudent disposition to underestimate their own strength and overestimate the strength of the adversary." Their 1968 crisis performance led them "to the sobering conclusion that the war they had been preparing for was wrought with so many uncertainties that it could not be planned with any reliability." After 1968, Mastny concludes about the larger significance of the Czechoslovak crisis for Cold War strategies, "neither side courted a disaster in Europe deliberately."[70]

Johnson's desire for a summit was motivated by more than a simple improving of his image at home and abroad, as Jeremi Suri has suggested. A summit in 1968 might have frozen the arms race in intercontinental missiles and resulted in nuclear parity. Instead, the arms race continued, and the ICBMs were upgraded with MIRV technology, notes John Prados.[71] One of the consequences of the continued arms race was the rise of the neocons and their critiques of Soviet superiority in the arms race and the entire détente agenda. This brought Ronald Reagan to the White House and the resumption of the Cold War. The setbacks of 1968 may have been the year when the United States entered a declining trajectory in its position of global hegemony.[72] Indeed, as the West Europeans frequently noted in the course of the Czech crisis, during the dual crisis of Vietnam and the Warsaw Pact intervention in Czechoslovakia, American leadership was lackluster.

ACKNOWLEDGMENTS

For help in preparing this chapter, I am grateful to the archivists and librarians at the Lyndon B. Johnson Library and the National Archives and Records Center in College Park, Maryland. Scott Manguno has assisted me with research, and Peter Ruggenthaler has been a valuable reader and sympathetic critic. From Mark Kramer and Thomas Schwartz's work I have learned enormously over the years. Vladislav Zubok has also helped clearing up some points.

NOTES

1. See the unpublished paper by Günter Bischof, "Respecting Cold War Boundaries: U.S. Responses to the Soviet Invasions of East Germany (1953), Hungary (1956), Czechoslovakia (1968)," lecture delivered in the conference in honor of Charles S. Maier, *Crossing Boundaries: International History in a Global Age*, American Academy, Berlin, Germany, 7 June 2008.

2. On the crisis year 1968, see Mark Kurlanski, *1968: The Year That Rocked the World* (New York: Ballantine, 2004); Ronald Fraser, ed., *1968: A Student Generation in Revolt* (New York: Pantheon, 1988); for the larger context of the 1960s, see Terry H. Anderson, *The Movement and the Sixties: Protest in America from Greensboro to Wounded Knee* (New York: Oxford University Press, 1995); David Bruner, *Making Peace with the 60s* (Princeton, NJ: Princeton University Press, 1996); Arthur Marwick, *The Sixties: Cultural Revolution in Britain, France, Italy, and the United States, c. 1958–c. 1974* (Oxford: Oxford University Press, 1998).

3. On the Johnson presidency, see Robert Dallek, *Lyndon B. Johnson, Portrait of a President* (Oxford: Oxford University Press, 2004); Randall Woods, *LBJ: Architect of American Ambition* (New York: The Free Press, 2006); Bruce J. Schulman, *Lyndon B. Johnson and American Liberalism: A Brief Biography with Documents*, 2nd ed. (Boston: Bedford/St. Martin's, 2007); John L. Bullion, *Lyndon B. Johnson and the Transformation of American Politics* (New York: Pearson Longman, 2008).

4. The secondary literature on these events is considerable. Among the most important publications are Thomas Alan Schwartz, *Lyndon Johnson and Europe: In the Shadow of Vietnam* (Cambridge, MA: Harvard University Press, 2003); Jeremi Suri, *Power and Protest: Global Revolution and the Rise of Détente* (Cambridge, MA: Harvard University Press, 2003); Vladislav M. Zubok, *A Failed Empire: The Soviet Union in the Cold War from Stalin to Gorbachev* (Chapel Hill: University of North Carolina Press, 2007); Mark Kramer, "The Czechoslovak Crisis and the Brezhnev Doctrine," in *1968: The World Transformed*, ed. Carole Fink et al., Publications of the German Historical Institute, Washington, DC (Cambridge: Cambridge University Press, 1998), 10–71; H. W. Brands, ed., *The Foreign Policies of Lyndon Johnson beyond Vietnam* (College Station: Texas A&M University Press, 1999); H. W. Brands, *The Wages of Globalism: Lyndon Johnson and the Limits of American Power* (New York: Oxford University Press, 1995); Robert A. Divine, "Lyndon Johnson and Strategic Arms Limitations," in *The Johnson Years*, vol. 3, *LBJ at Home and Abroad*, ed. Robert Divine (Lawrence: University of Kansas Press, 1994), 239–79; Mitchell B. Lerner, ed., *Looking Back at*

LBJ: White House Politics in a New Light (Lawrence: University of Kansas Press, 2005); Warren I. Cohen and Nancy Bernkopf Tucker, eds., *Lyndon Johnson Confronts the World: American Foreign Policy 1963–1968* (Cambridge: Cambridge University Press, 1994); Lawrence Kaplan et al., eds., *NATO after Forty Years* (Wilmington, DE: Scholarly Resources, 1990); Vojtech Mastny, "Was 1968 a Strategic Watershed of the Cold War," *Diplomatic History* 29, no. 1 (2005): 149–77; Mitchell Lerner, "Trying to Find the Guy Who Invited Them: Lyndon B. Johnson, Bridge Building and the End of the Prague Spring," *Diplomatic History* 21, no. 3 (2008): 77–103; Hal Brands, "Progress Unseen: U.S. Arms Control Policy and the Origins of Détente, 1963–1968," *Diplomatic History* 30, no. 2 (2006): 253–85; John C. McGinn, "The Politics of Collective Inaction: NATO's Response to the Prague Spring," *Journal of Cold War Studies* 1, no. 3 (1999): 111–38; A. Paul Kubricht, "Confronting Liberalization and Military Invasion: America and the Johnson Administration Respond to the 1968 Prague Summer," *Jahrbücher fur Geschichte Osteuropas* 40, no. 2 (1992): 197–212; Andreas Daum et al., eds., *America, the Vietnam War, and the World: Comparative and International Perspectives*, Publications of the German Historical Institute, Washington, DC (Cambridge: Cambridge University Press, 2003); Alexandra Friedrich, "Awakenings: The Impact of the Vietnam War on West German–American Relations in the 1960s" (Ph.D. diss., Temple University, 2000).

5. The sources for this chapter come from three major documentary collections: the National Security Council files and other file collections in the Lyndon Baines Johnson Presidential Library in Austin, Texas (LBJL), as well as two collections in the National Archives and Records Administration in College Park, Maryland (NARA); first, the documents in the file collection "POL 27-1 COM BLOC-Czech" (hereafter abbreviated as POL-27) and "POL Czech—USSR DEF 4 NATO" (hereafter abbreviated as POL Czech), "Central Foreign Policy Files 1967–1969 [CFPF]" in Record Group 59, the General Records in the Department of State; secondly, the "Czech Crisis Files" (Lot 70 D 19) (hereafter abbreviated as CCF) in the Office of the Executive Secretariat of the Department of State, also in RG 59. I have contributed U.S. documents to the collection of Karner et al., *Dokumente*. U.S. documents reprinted in the basic collection of the Department of State, *Foreign Relations of the United States*, vol. 17, *Eastern Europe 1964–1968* (Washington, DC, 1996), are hereinafter abbreviated as FRUS, unless another volume from this series is specifically referenced. Johnson's official public statements and speeches are conveniently reprinted in Lyndon B. Johnson, *The Public Papers of the President of the United States, 1968–1969*, 2 vols. (Washington, DC: Office of the Federal Register, National Archives and Records Service, General Services Administration, 1970) (hereafter abbreviated as PPP). Frequent references will be made to the massive volume of essays by Karner et al., *Beiträge*.

6. "Soviet threat to Czechoslovakia," Rostow to Rusk, 10 May 1968, Folder "6/1/68," Box 1558, POL-Czech, RG 59, NARA (reprinted in appendix 3 of this volume).

7. "Saber-Rattling," in CIA memorandum "The Czechoslovak Situation," 9 May 1968, Folder 6, and "Present USSR Attitude toward Czechoslovakia," Folder 3, both Box 179, NSC Country Files Czechoslovakia, LBJL; see also the chapter by Donald P. Steury in this volume.

8. Memorandum, "Pressures on Czechoslovakia," Walter J. Stoessel Jr. to Mr. Read, 9 May 1968, and Lawrence Eagleburger to Stoessel, 10 May 1968, both in Folder 6, Box 179, NSC Country files Czechoslovakia, LBJL. Walter J. Stoessel Jr., who was the deputy assistant secretary of state for European and Canadian Affairs in May and who assumed the post of ambassador to Poland right around the time of the intervention, had expected an intervention throughout the Prague Spring crisis months: *"'We' had expected it so often over the duration of the crisis, and it had NOT transpired so often, that by the time it happened 'we' were indeed surprised"* (my emphasis). This is how Stoessel summarized State Department expectations vis-à-vis Tom Simons when he arrived in Warsaw for embassy duty. Personal e-mail communication from Ambassador Thomas W. Simons Jr. to author, October 22, 2008. Like the War Department in 1941 in the Pacific, the State Department anticipated an intervention throughout the spring and summer of 1968. This had a "lulling effect" (Simons) on Foggy Bottom. When the attack finally occurred it came as a shock to officials and people.

9. "Memorandum of Conversation" with Sir Patrick Dean, 17 July 1968, Folder "POL US—USSR 1/1/68," Box 2665, CFPF, RG 59, NARA.

10. Minutes, secretary of defense staff meeting, 29 July 1968. Box 18, Papers of Clark Clifford, LBJL (reprinted in appendix 9 of this volume).

11. Rusk's statement is reported in a Central Committee resolution of 26 July 1968, reprinted in Karner et al., *Dokumente*, #191 (for a translation of this document see appendix 5 of this volume). In the State Department memorandum of conversation of the 22 July meeting with Dobrynin, Rusk's message is less clear and direct than in the one Dobrynin sent to Moscow—the Warsaw Pact is not mentioned and Rusk refers to the "bridge building" policies of the Johnson administration with Eastern Europe: "He said we had not wished to involve ourselves directly in this matter, that the U.S. had been attempting to develop better relationships with Eastern European countries as well as with the Soviet Union." FRUS, 212–14 (here 213); see also Matthew J. Ouimet, *The Rise and Fall of the Brezhnev Doctrine in Soviet Foreign Policy* (Chapel Hill: University of North Carolina Press, 2003), 34.

12. Michael Prozumenshchikov argues that Rusk's message, as reported by Dobrynin, "virtually gave [the Soviets] the green light for their planned moves in Czechoslovakia"; see his chapter in this volume. Ouimet, however, stresses the point that in the absence of more documentary evidence this cannot be construed as a "green light" to the Soviets, see *Rise and Fall of the Brezhnev Doctrine*, 32–34.

13. See also the Wilke chapter in this volume.

14. Lyndon Baines Johnson, *Vantage Point: Perspectives of the Presidency, 1963–1969* (New York: Popular Library, 1971), 486.

15. Ginsberg Memorandum for W. W. Rostow, 15 August 1968, Folder 3, Box 179, NSC Country File, Czechoslovakia, LBJL.

16. Ginsberg Memorandum for W. W. Rostow, 15 August 1968; for Helms citation, see Bennett Kovrig, *Of Walls and Bridges: The United Sates and Eastern Europe* (New York: New York University Press, 1991), 114.

17. Nathaniel Davis Memorandum "Czechoslovak Contingencies" (no date, but located in documents prior to the invasion), Folder 5, Box 179, NSC Country File, Czechoslovakia, LBJL (reprinted in appendix 6 of this volume).

18. Rusk thought so, since Dobrynin had assured him only three weeks earlier that no invasion was planned; see Dean Rusk as told to Richard Rusk, *As I Saw It* (New York: W. W. Norton, 1990), 351.

19. Handwritten "Message by Soviet Ambassador Dobrynin and delivered 19 August 1968, the day before the invasion of Czechoslovakia," Folder 1, Box 57, Special Head of State Correspondence, NSF, LBJL, reprinted in Karner et al., *Dokumente*, #192.

20. For a fine summary of Johnson disarmament efforts, see John Prados, "Prague Spring and SALT: Arms Limitation Setbacks in 1968," in Brands, *Foreign Policies of Lyndon Johnson*, 10–36 (esp. 24f).

21. Citation from Clark Clifford (with Richard Holbrooke), *Counsel to the President: A Memoir* (New York: Random House, 1991), 559; Johnson writes that opinions were divided about Soviet moves against Czechoslovakia "and I was not completely optimistic," see *Vantage Point*, 487; W. W. Rostow's Czech agenda item for the meeting is mentioned in John Prados, *Keepers of the Keys: A History of the National Security Council from Truman to Bush* (New York: William Morrow, 1991), 194.

22. Daily diary, 20 August 1968, Box 16, the President's Daily Diary 1963–1969, and Dobrynin's official note with the Kremlin's public explanation for the invasion in appointment file (diary backup), Box 108, both in Papers of LBJ, LBJL; "Meeting Johnson," Rostow with Dobrynin in Cabinet Room, 20 August 1968, FRUS, 236–41, reprinted in Karner et al., *Dokumente*, #193. See also Anatolii Dobrynin, *In Confidence: Moscow's Ambassador to America's Six Cold War Presidents* (New York: Times Books, 1995), 179f; Johnson, *Vantage Point*, 486; George W. Ball, *The Past Has Another Pattern: Memoirs* (New York: W. W. Norton, 1982), 440. For a good summary and Johnson's obliviousness, see Schwartz, *Johnson and Europe*, 216–20.

23. Notes of emergency meeting of the National Security Council, 20 August 1968, 10:15 p.m., in FRUS, 236–41; also reprinted in Jaromír Navrátil et al., eds., *The Prague Spring 1968* (Budapest: Central European University Press, 2006), #109.

24. Rusk, *As I Saw It*, 351.

25. Katzenbach memorandum for the president, 21 August 1968, Folder 6, Box 3, CCF, RG 59, NARA.

26. Department of State, Czech Task Force, 21 August 1968, Folder State Situation Papers, Box 182, NSC Country File, Czechoslovakia, LBJL; Rusk telegrams to embassies in Bonn and Vienna and all US NATO missions, 21 August 1968, Folder "8/21/68," Box 1993, POL 27-1, RG 59, NARA.

27. W. W. Rostow memorandum for the president, 21 August 1968, Folder 3, Box 182, NSC Country File, Czechoslovakia, LBJL; CIA memorandum, "The Soviet Decision to Intervene," and Thomas L. Hughes memorandum, "Impact of Soviet Move on Western Europe—First Thoughts," both 21 August 1968, Folder 3, Box 182, NSC Country File, Czechoslovakia, LBJL.

28. McGhee memorandum for Rusk, 21 August 1968, Folder 1, Box 1, CCF, RG 59, NARA (reprinted in appendix 7 of this volume).

29. "Bohlen Briefing on Czech Situation," Rusk to all NATO Headquarters, 22 August 1968, Folder 1, Box 1, CCF, RG 59, NARA. Rusk had reminded his colleagues of this colorful metaphor in the emergency NSC meeting on 20 August, namely that

"Khrushchev called Berlin the testicles of the West and when he wanted to create pressure he squeezed there," FRUS, 243.

30. The centrality of the German question and Soviet fears of a resurgent Germany throughout the Cold War is a surprisingly persistent theme in Leffler's *For the Soul of Mankind: The United States, the Soviet Union, and the Cold War* (New York: Hill and Wang, 2007).

31. White House press release at 12:15 p.m., 21 August 1968, appointment file (diary backup), Box 108, LBJ Papers, LBJL; reprinted in PPP, 1968, II, 905.

32. For complete transcript, see notes of cabinet meeting, 22 August 1968, Folder "8/22/68," Box 14, Cabinet Papers, LBJL; for summary notes, see FRUS, 48–49. Johnson's presentation to the full cabinet is based on W. W. Rostow's memorandum, "Czechoslovakia—Talking Points for Today's Cabinet Meeting," 22 August 1968, Folder "8/68," Box 179, NSC Country File, Czechoslovakia, LBJL, reprinted in Karner et al., *Dokumente*, #203. Rostow wanted to maintain the chance for détente and wrote: *"The Cold War is not over,* but we should also understand that we cannot simply return to it" (my emphasis). Johnson changed the second half of the sentence to "our relations with the Soviets are in transition."

33. Summary of meeting, 23 August 1968; see also minutes of secretary of defense staff meeting, 26 August 1968, Box 18, Clifford Papers, LBJL.

34. Memorandum of conversation (Rusk, Dobrynin, Thompson), 23 August 1968, Folder "23/8/68," Box 1994, POL 27-1, CFPF, RG 59, NARA.

35. Minutes of the secretary of defense meeting, 26 August 1968, Box 18, Clifford Papers, LBJL. The Germans were pushing the strengthening of NATO above all else; see the memoranda of conversation between Chancellor Kiesinger and Henry Cabot Lodge, the U.S. ambassador in Bonn, 5 and 18 September 1968, in *FRUS 1964–1968*, vol. 15, *Germany and Berlin* (Washington, DC: GPO, 1999), 733–37, 743–46, as well as summary of Lodge for the president, 28 September 1969, in *FRUS 1964–1968*, vol. 15, *Germany and Berlin*, 750–51. The best discussion of the declining trajectory of the U.S. hegemonic position as result of the Vietnam War is George C. Herring, "Tet and the Crisis of Hegemony," in Fink et al., *1968: The World Transformed*, 31–53.

36. See also Mihail Ionescu, "Rumänien und die Invasion der 'Bruderstaaten,'" in Karner et al., *Beiträge*, 605–16.

37. CIA memorandum, "Possible Soviet Threat to Rumania," 23 August 1968, Folder "Cables 10/66–1/69," Box 204, NSC Files, LBJL; Hillenbrand (Budapest) to Rusk, 28 August 1968, Folder 5, Box 2, CCF, RG 59, NARA.

38. George Kennan's views on Czech intervention, Hilton memorandum, 29 August 1968, Folder 9, Box 179, NSC Country File, Czechoslovakia, LBJL.

39. Rusk Memorandum, "Expansion of Czechoslovakia Task Force to Include Romanian Contingency," for president, 29 August 1968, Folder 9, Box 179, NSC Country File, Czechoslovakia, LBJL; NATO #04389, Cleveland to Rusk, 26 August 1968, Folder 5, Box 2, CCF, RG 59, NARA.

40. Memorandum of conversation (Rusk, Dobrynin, Thompson), 23 August 1968, FRUS, 256; Rusk to Cleveland (NATO mission), 31 August 1968; "Oral Communication from Ambassador Dobrynin of the USSR to Secretary Rusk," 30 August 1968, both Folder "9/20/68," Box 1997, POL 27-1, RG 59, NARA.

41. The "top secret" memorandum W. W. Rostow cabled to the president at the ranch in Texas on 30 August 1968 is more informative than the brief report Rusk sent to the NATO mission (see previous note), Folder 9, Box 179, NSC Country File, Czechoslovakia, LBJL.

42. "Remarks in San Antonio at the Annual Convention of Milk Producers," 30 August 1968, Johnson, PPP, 1968, II, 917–20 (quotation 920); see also Kovrig, *Of Walls and Bridges*, 114; Dobrynin's throwing water on the Washington rumor mills is mentioned in memorandum of conversation (Rusk and Norwegian ambassador Gunmeng), 11 November 1968, Folder 6, Box 3, CCF, RG 59, NARA.

43. See also the Jakovina chapter in this volume.

44. Thomas L. Hughes memorandum for Rusk, "Yugoslav Support of Czechoslovakia Persists Despite Scare over Soviet Aggression," 28 August 1968, Folder "8/28/68," Box 1995, POL 27-1, RG 59, NARA; Memorandum of conversation (Rusk, Ambassador Crnobrnja), 29 August 1968, Folder 6, Box 3, CCF, RG 59, NARA; for a summary of this conversation by Crnobrnja from the Serbian archives, see Karner et al., *Dokumente*, #147.

45. See also Peter Ruggenthaler, "Die Neutralität verplichtet: die sowjetisch-öster reichischen Beziehungen 1968," in Karner et al., *Beiträge*, 993–1006.

46. Vienna #06326, MacArthur to Rusk (and Department of Defense), 30 August 1968, Folder "Vol. I 7/64 1/69," Box 163, NSC Country File Austria, LBJL.

47. Brands, *Wages of Globalism*, 119.

48. "Austrian Contingency Arrangements: Information Memorandum," Leddy to Rusk, 29 August 1968, Folder "9/20/68," Box 1997, POL 27-1, RG 59, NARA.

49. Vienna #06276, MacArthur to Rusk, Folder 5, Box 2, CCF, RG 59, NARA; Austrian ambassador Wodak in Moscow was directed by the Ballhausplatz in Vienna to register a sharp protest in the Kremlin against these rumors, see Vienna #06275, MacArthur and Rusk, 29 August 1968, Folder 5, Box 2, CCF, RG 59, NARA; a similar protest by Bohlen is mentioned in Rusk to MacArthur, 28 August 1968, Folder "8/28/68," Box 1995, CFPF, RG 59, NARA, reprinted in Karner et al., *Dokumente*, #180; the Moscow story of "green berets" in Austria also was included in the "Daily Situation Report" on 28 August of the Czech Task Force in the State Department; see Folder 5, Box 2, CCF, RG 59, NARA. About Austrian foreign minister Kurt Waldheim's and Chancellor Josef Klaus's protests with the Soviet ambassador in Vienna of 29 and 31 August, see Karner et al., *Dokumente*, #181 and #182; see also the Ruggenthaler chapter (note 45).

50. The only authors who cover de Gaulle's curious "politics of history" in the Czech crisis are Kubricht, *Confronting Liberalization and Military Intervention*, 208–21, and Ouimet, *Rise and Fall of the Brezhnev Doctrine*, 32–34.

51. De Gaulle's translated communiqué was quickly cabled back to the State Department on 21 August, see Folder "8/21/68," Box 1993, POL 27-1, CPF, RG 59, NARA, reprinted in Karner et al., *Dokumente*, #198. See also Frédéric Bozo, *Two Strategies for Europe: De Gaulle, the United States, and the Atlantic Alliance*, trans. Susan Emanuel (Lanham, MD: Rowman & Littlefield, 2001), 223ff, and the Soutou chapter in this volume.

52. State #226360, Rusk to all diplomatic missions, 23 August 1968, Folder 4, Box 2, CCF, RG 59, NARA, reprinted in Karner et al., *Dokumente*, #204; the embassy

in Vienna also presented this declaration to the Foreign Ministry. Ivan Pfaff has soundly rejected the myth of the "division of Europe" at Yalta and places the Soviet advances into Central Europe at the end of the war in the larger context of geostrategic developments; see "Die Legende von Jalta," *Forum für osteuropäische Zeitgeschichte* 8, no. 2 (2004): 53–112.

53. Memorandum of conversation (Rusk, Luce, et al.), 26 August 1968, Folder 6, Box 3, CCF, RG 59, NARA.

54. Excerpts of Rusk speech before the Connecticut Manufacturers' Association, 12 September 1968, Folder State Department [1 of 2], Box 64, NSC, Agency File, LBJL.

55. Paris #20083, Shriver to Rusk, 28 August 1968, Folder 5, Box 2, CCF, RG 59, NARA.

56. Vienna #06262, MacArthur to Rusk, 29 August 1968; Waldheim's views in Vienna #06253, MacArthur to Rusk, 28 August 1968, both Folder 5, Box 2, CCF, RG 59, NARA.

57. Bonn #16394, Lodge to Rusk, 4 September 1968, Folder "9/1/68," Box 1996, POL 27-1, CFPF, RG 59, NARA; this conversation is documented from the German side in Karner et al., *Dokumente*, #211; see also NSC Paper "The United States, Europe, and the Czechoslovakia Crisis" (n.d.), FRUS, 271.

58. Zedněk Mlynář, *Nightfrost in Prague: The End of Humane Socialism*, trans. Paul Wilson (New York: Karz, 1980), 241.

59. See Ouimet, *Rise and Fall of the Brezhnev Doctrine*, 33–34. This author set out on his archival visits with the goal on finding such a "smoking gun"; like Ouimet, he was unsuccessful.

60. In his final analysis for the Kremlin leaders of the Czech crisis, Dobrynin also came to the conclusion that the Czech Crisis strengthened NATO, see "Die USA propagieren die Stärkung der NATO," 3 October 1968, reprinted in Karner et al., *Dokumente*, #217

61. For this larger context overshadowing the Czech crisis, see Schwartz, *Johnson and Europe*, 187–222; Schwartz, "Lyndon Johnson and Europe: Alliance Politics, Political Economy"; Schwartz, "'Growing Out of the Cold War,'" in Brands, *Johnson's Foreign Policies*, 37–60; Friedrich, "Awakenings"; Frank Costigliola, "Lyndon B. Johnson, Germany, and 'the End of the Cold War,'" in Cohen and Bernkopf Tucker, *Lyndon Johnson Confronts the World*, 173–210; Bozo, *Two Strategies for Europe*, 187–218; Grosser, *Das Bündnis*, 293–358; Richard Barnett, *The Alliance America-Europe-Japan: Makers of the Modern World* (New York: Simon and Schuster, 1983); and various essays in Kaplan et al., *NATO after Forty Years*. The "dollar crisis" is keenly analyzed in Hubert Zimmermann, "Who Paid for America's War? Vietnam and the International Monetary System, 1960–1975," in Daum et al., *America, the Vietnam War, and the World*, 151–73. The enormous anxiety about Congressional pressure to reduce U.S. forces in Europe and thereby weaken the Western defense posture comes through strongly in the weekly staff meetings of the Department of Defense, see appendix 9 of this volume.

62. Mastny, "Was 1968 a Strategic Watershed of the Cold War?" 174; NATO #04388, "NAC Discussion of Warsaw Pact Threat to NATO," Cleveland and Rusk, 26 August 1968, and NATO #04375, Cleveland and Rusk, 26 August 1968, both Folder 5, Box 2, CCF RG 59, NARA.

63. NATO #04447 Cleveland to Rusk, 29 August 1968, Folder 5, Box 2, CCF, RG 59, NARA.

64. The transcript of the Kiesinger radio interview is in Bonn #15990, Lodge to Rusk, 25 August 1968, Folder 4, Box 2, CCF; see also NATO #04379, Cleveland to Rusk, 26 August 1968, Folder 5, Box 2, CCF; Kiesinger's foreign policy adviser Oster-hammel told the Americans that the chancellor's idea of a summit meeting for the revitalization of NATO originated with the U.S. expert on Eastern Europe Zbigniev Brezinzki, see Bonn #15996, Lodge to Rusk, 26 August 1968, Folder 5, Box 2, CCF, all RG 50, NARA.

65. NATO #04427, "NATO Post-Czech Reassessment Program," Cleveland to Rusk, Folder 5, Box 2, CCF, RG 49, NARA.

66. Memorandum of conversation (Eugene Rostow, Birrenbach et al.), 10 Sep-tember 1968, Folder 6, Box 3, CCF, reprinted in Karner et al., *Dokumente*, #214; LBJ citation in Schwartz, *Johnson and Europe*, 220; the importance of the invasion for NATO is also discussed in memorandum of conversation (Birrenbach, Rusk et al.), 9 September 1968, in *FRUS 1964–1968*, XV, 737–40. The effect of the Czecho-slovak crisis on NATO and on Congress in terms of strengthening NATO defenses and ending all talk of American troop withdrawals from Europe in Washington, is a persistent theme in Clifford's weekly staff meetings in the Pentagon (see appendix 9 of this volume).

67. Minutes of cabinet meeting, 18 September 1968, Folder "9/18/68 [1 of 3]," Box 15, Cabinet Papers, LBJ Papers, LBJL; see also the chapter by Saki Ruth Dockrill in this volume.

68. McGhee memorandum for Rusk "New Situation for U.S. created by Czech Crisis," 4 September 1968, Folder 6, Box 3, CCF, RG 59, NARA. Given that McGhee had served as U.S. ambassador in Bonn until the spring of 1968, it does not come as a surprise that he advocated a leadership role for West Germany in NATO; see George McGhee, *At the Creation of a New Germany: From Adenauer to Brandt. An Ambassador's Account* (New Haven, CT: Yale University Press, 1989).

69. NSC Paper, "The United States, Europe, and the Czechoslovak Crisis" (n.d.), FRUS, 266.

70. Mastny, "Was 1968 a Strategic Watershed of the Cold War?" 176–77.

71. Jeremi Suri, "Lyndon Johnson and the Global Disruption of 1968," in Lerner, *Looking Back at LBJ*, 53–77 (here 66); Prados, "Prague Spring and SALT," 32–33.

72. Herring, "Tet and the Crisis of Hegemony," 31–53, see also Brands's conclu-sions, "Hegemony's End," in his *Wages of Globalism*, 254–64.

Tanks in the streets of Prague. The Soviet tanks are marked with a white cross.
Courtesy of Ústav pro soudobé dějiny Akademie věd České republiky

Buses and trams are used to build barricades.
Courtesy of Ústav pro soudobé dějiny Akademie věd České republiky

Buses and trams are used to build barricades.
Courtesy of Ústav pro soudobé dějiny Akademie věd České republiky

Solidarity among protesters.
Courtesy of Ústav pro soudobé dějiny Akademie věd České republiky

Soviet tanks are burning!
Courtesy of Ústav pro soudobé dějiny Akademie věd České republiky

A Soviet tank is captured at the Wenceslas Square.
Courtesy of Ústav pro soudobé dějiny Akademie věd České republiky

The first casualties (victims) of the invasion.
Courtesy of Ústav pro soudobé dějiny Akademie věd České republiky

Devastated streets.

Courtesy of Ústav pro soudobé dějiny Akademie věd České republiky

21 August 1968: Austrian tanks.

Source: Bundesministerium für Landesverteidigung/Heeresbild-und Filmstelle
Courtesy of the Ludwig Boltzmann-Institut für Kriegsfolgen-Forschung

21 August 1968: Austrian soldiers await their orders.
Source: Bundesministerium für Landesverteidigung/Heeresbild-und Filmstelle
Courtesy of the Ludwig Boltzmann-Institut für Kriegsfolgen-Forschung

Humanitarian aid for Czechoslovak refugees.
Source: Wiener Stadtund Landesarchiv
Courtesy of the Ludwig Boltzmann-Institut für Kriegsfolgen-Forschung

Jan Palachs' self-immolation shocks the world.
Courtesy of Ústav pro soudobé dějiny Akademie věd České republiky

Remembrance turns into protest!
Courtesy of Ústav pro soudobé dějiny Akademie věd České republiky

10

Strategic Warning: The CIA and the Soviet Invasion of Czechoslovakia

Donald P. Steury

As is well known, the origins of the Czech crisis and the so-called Prague Spring lay in the election of Alexander Dubček to the post of first secretary of the Communist Party of Czechoslovakia (*Komunistická strana Československa* or KSČ) on 5 January 1968.[1] Dubček replaced the moribund Antonin Novotný, first secretary since 1957.

Dubček's election was greeted with enthusiasm both in Czechoslovakia and in Moscow—at least initially. Novotný had presided over the decline of the previously efficient Czech economy and apparently was regarded in the Kremlin as something of a "neo-Stalinist nuisance." Dubček, at forty-six, was young, energetic, and—in Moscow's eyes—reliable, having been educated in the Soviet Union and lived some seventeen years there. In the Soviet Committee for State Security (KGB) he was known as "our Sasha." In December 1967, the Soviet Communist leader Leonid Brezhnev made an unscheduled visit to Prague during which he made clear to Novotný that he had lost Moscow's backing—thus effectively paving the way for Dubček's election.[2]

Despite this apparent stamp of approval from Moscow, Dubček proved to be anything but reliable. From his election onward, the Czech Communist leadership embarked on a program of dramatic liberalization of the Czech political economic and social system, including the overhaul of the KSČ leadership, freedom of speech, surrender of authority to the Czech National Assembly by the Communist Party, real elections at local and national levels, and even the suggestion of legalizing noncommunist political parties.

All this alarmed Moscow and the leadership of the Warsaw Pact, but throughout the Prague Spring, Dubček went out of his way to demonstrate

237

his personal loyalty to Moscow and Prague's intention to remain firmly within the Warsaw Pact military alliance. How sincere he was in these protestations is difficult to say, but Dubček and his allies clearly feared a repetition of the Hungarian uprising of 1956, bloodily crushed by Soviet and Warsaw Pact troops.

These fears were mirrored in Washington and, to a certain extent, even in Moscow. Certainly the Kremlin, under the nearly comatose leadership of Leonid Brezhnev, had no desire to provoke a crisis, while any disturbance anywhere was seen as a threat to the increasingly ramshackle stability of the Soviet Bloc. There was, moreover, a general tendency—at least in the West—to view some kind of internal reform as a necessary precondition for the stability of the Warsaw Pact.

Although the Warsaw Pact had been created in 1955 as a "paper organization" to counter the rearming of West Germany and the cooperative effort of the western Allies in the North Atlantic Treaty Organization (NATO), by the early 1960s, the Warsaw Pact gradually was acquiring more form and substance as a military alliance. Under Nikita Khrushchev, the pact had become the mechanism by which Moscow could introduce large-scale troop reductions, principally in conventional forces deployed to Europe.[3] With substantially fewer forces on the ground in Eastern Europe, Moscow had more at stake in making the alliance work. Thus, although the non-Soviet members of the Warsaw Pact had had little choice in joining the organization, once they were members of an alliance with the Soviet Union, they found they had a relatively greater voice in ordering their own affairs.[4]

By 1965, the Warsaw Pact was becoming a framework in which the nations of Eastern Europe could exercise a growing level of relative autonomy. General disenchantment with Marxist economics and Soviet-style politics and the growing attraction of the West were giving the states of Eastern Europe "both the incentive and the opportunity for striking out on their own"; "[t]he Soviets," noted ONE, will find it difficult to arrest the process; "though crises are an ever-present danger, we believe that these countries will be able successfully to assert their own national interests gradually and without provoking Soviet intervention."[5] The Prague Spring thus seems to have been evaluated as part of a broader reform movement within the Warsaw Pact as a whole. There was the cautious belief that Sasha Dubček—if he were very careful and very, very lucky—just *might* pull it off.[6]

Agency analysis in the Prague Spring focused on two critical factors. The first of these was the importance of the Czechoslovak armed forces to Warsaw Pact military planning. In a war with NATO, the Czechoslovakian army would have formed the first echelon of a Warsaw Pact attack into southern Germany, intended to outflank any NATO effort to defend the inner-German border and, ultimately, to drive across Bavaria and Baden-Württemberg to the Rhine.[7] The Czech military leadership was given command of this front and would have retained command of its armed forces in wartime—which put Czechoslovakia, alongside Poland, in a privileged position in the Warsaw Pact hierarchy.[8] The reduction of Soviet ground forces in the early 1960s had only increased Czechoslovakia's importance to Soviet/Warsaw Pact war planning.[9]

The second was the importance of the Czech economy. Czechoslovakia was among the most industrially developed of the Warsaw Pact countries, yet it had suffered the most from twenty years of Communist rule. In 1948, Czechoslovakia was better off than West Germany. By 1968, per capita output was about two-thirds that of the Federal Republic, quite apart from major differences in quality. Moscow was aware that popular opinion in Czechoslovakia blamed the old-line party hierarchy for its relative decline.[10] "Economic pressure is a major force for political change in Eastern Europe," noted one U.S. Central Intelligence Agency (CIA) memorandum; without meaningful reform, Czechoslovakia's problems "may become acute in the next two or three years. . . ."[11]

To the CIA, the Czech economic crisis meant that the Soviet leadership was concerned with the stability and reliability of the Czech military contribution to the Warsaw Pact. The Soviets thus were likely to be receptive to anything that promised a solution to Czechoslovakia's internal problems. They also realized that the first result of a premature attempt to intervene decisively in Czechoslovakia would likely be the demoralization of the Czech military. At the same time, they were concerned that the "contagion" of Czech democratization not spread and that the Czechs themselves would go too far in creating an open society. All these factors seemed to add up to a Soviet decision to watch, wait, and hope for the best, while preparing for the worst.[12]

As the snows of winter melted, it became possible to hypothesize that Dubček's "socialism with a human face" would find a place in the Warsaw Pact. On 23 March, Czechoslovakia was the main topic of discussion at a Warsaw Pact summit in Dresden. The CIA reported that Moscow had used the occasion to put a limit on how far Dubček could go, but that

> [i]f the new leadership in Prague proceeds carefully and step-by-step good progress can be made. . . . [I]n view of its political economic and military importance to the USSR and the Soviet bloc, the CSSR cannot start an anti-socialist or anti-Soviet policy. The USSR would not allow this . . . [but] there [is] no anti-socialist or anti-Soviet movement involved in the new political evolution of the CSSR . . . only a strong movement for democratization and liberalization of the system.[13]

Consequently, the Soviet leadership "did not consider Dubček as someone willing to start an anti-Soviet line."[14]

This conclusion was supported by the KSČ Party Action Program, published on 10 April. The CIA noted that it was "restrained in tone, realistic and relatively free of cant . . . disappointing to the radical reformers in some aspects."[15] Armed with this evidence of Dubček's moderation and the Kremlin's tolerance, by the end of April, the CIA had concluded that the leaders of the Soviet Union appeared to have "grudgingly accepted" the Czech reforms. The only limits placed on Czech reforms were the continued primacy of the KSČ and Czechoslovakia's honoring its military and economic commitments to the USSR.[16] An unsigned CIA memorandum argued that the Soviets could have applied economic pressure had they wanted to halt Dubček's reforms and cited as evidence a Czech radio broadcast:

> Let us not forget that . . . our cars run on Soviet gas, two out of three rolls are baked from Soviet flour, and our gigantic metallurgical combines would come to a standstill within a few days after Soviet ore shipments stopped. Nothing of the sort is happening here, as is common knowledge: cars are running, rolls are baked, and so forth.[17]

In general, the CIA's analysis seems to have accurately characterized attitudes inside the Soviet Politburo. Correctly deducing that the Soviet leadership was split over the need for intervention, the Agency reported that—at least for the time being—the Kremlin had accepted the Czech reforms as the lesser of two evils.[18] Although there was strong evidence of Soviet "anxieties" over the Czech reforms, Dubček continued to prove himself to be adept at balancing reforms inside Czechoslovakia with continued adherence to doctrines of communism and pledges to uphold Czechoslovakia's military commitments to the Warsaw Pact.[19] There thus seemed reason to hope that, although Soviet pressure on Czechoslovakia would increase over "the long hot summer," the Soviets "will take no 'harder,' i.e., military measures."[20]

What could not be known was that the Politburo's confidence in Dubček was being eroded from within. As the Mitrokhin Archive makes clear, KGB chief Yuri Andropov was playing a growing role in the decision-making process over Czechoslovakia. Andropov was not a voting member of the Politburo and is not even mentioned in some studies of the Czech crisis.[21] But Andropov's position as head of the KGB gave him a powerful voice inside the Kremlin. Andropov cared little for Dubček's protestations of solidarity or (one suspects) even for Prague's expressions of continued loyalty to the Warsaw Pact. To Andropov, an open society anywhere would serve as a conduit for penetration by Western intelligence services. He thus flooded Czechoslovakia with KGB agents tasked with active measures designed to discredit the Dubček regime and with the fabrication of evidence showing a counterrevolutionary conspiracy. This material was both fed back to Politburo members to goad them into action and put forward as justification for the application of "extreme measures."[22]

At least in part because of Andropov's effort to marshal support for direct military intervention, relations between Moscow and Prague deteriorated steadily over the next few months. The Politburo remained reluctant to sanction military action, but late in April, the CIA reported that "[d]evelopments since the Dresden meeting indicate that the Russians and the Eastern Europeans were dissatisfied with the results of the conference and remained concerned about Czechoslovakia's course."[23] By mid-June, Czechoslovakia was reported to be in an "uneasy truce" with Moscow.[24] Dubček reportedly was now playing for time, hoping that he could implement enough reforms quickly to present the Kremlin leadership with a fait accompli. Nonetheless, "[a]t some stage in the game," the Agency reported, "the Soviets will . . . become aware that their earlier hopes for a return to anything like the status quo ante in Czechoslovakia were without foundation. It is the Czech hope that this realization will have come too late and that the Soviets' reactions will be minimal."[25]

It was now clear to Agency analysts that the Politburo viewed developments in Czechoslovakia with growing dissatisfaction.[26] Indecision still reigned in Moscow, but the only thing now preventing the Soviet Union from intervening militarily was concern over the broad impact of yet another violent repression of an Eastern European bid for autonomy.[27] On 17 July, the Office of National Estimates (ONE) warned the director of Central Intelligence: "We know of no way of foretelling the precise event in Czechoslovakia which might trigger . . . extreme Soviet reaction, or of foreseeing the precise circumstances which might produce within the Soviet leadership an agreement to move with force."[28] But the Soviets believed that Communist authority in Czechoslovakia was seriously threatened.[29] "The possibility will exist for some time that the Soviets will choose to intervene rather than permit Czechoslovakia to . . . move decisively toward . . . an open disavowal of Communism or of the Warsaw Pact."[30] Still the Soviet leadership had not decided what to do.[31] Very much still depended on Dubček and Czechoslovakia. "Some appropriate concessions" from Dubček would remove the need for military action. So would a conservative overthrow of Dubček.[32]

The crisis seemed to have reached a climax at the end of July when Soviet leaders journeyed to Čierná nad Tisou, on the Czech border, to meet with the Czech Politburo. The bilateral negotiations were covered by a blanket of secrecy, but on 31 July, TASS reported that the talks at Čierná had an atmosphere of "frankness and comradeship,"—this, reported the CIA, was Soviet code for tough talk but no action.[33] Ominously, however, that same day Dubček's family was reported as leaving Czechoslovakia for Yugoslavia.[34]

The Čierná conference concluded on 1 August and was almost immediately followed by a general Warsaw Pact summit at Bratislava. Two days later, the only written statement to emerge from either of these conferences was produced. This was little more than a statement of alliance solidarity, combined with an affirmation of the principles of Marxism-Leninism. With this, the crisis seemed to be over. The Czech leadership apparently had mollified its Soviet and Warsaw Pact allies, at least for the time being. Dubček seemed to have won.

Not three weeks later, the Soviet Union invaded Czechoslovakia.

CIA military reporting closely paralleled Agency political analysis. As a member of the Warsaw Pact, Czechoslovakia was perforce under a fairly high level of routine surveillance. As tensions heightened over the spring and summer of 1968, so did the attention paid to Czechoslovakia by U.S. and NATO intelligence services.

The full panoply of sources available to Western intelligence included photo-reconnaissance satellites; covert intelligence collection performed by U.S. Air Force (USAF) aircraft transiting the Berlin traffic corridors, as well as by SR-71 reconnaissance aircraft along the inner German border, if required; SIGINT collection sites in southern Germany and on the Teufelsberg in occupied Berlin; and—particularly important during the Czech crisis— observations by the Allied military missions in East Germany.[35] There also seems to have been some agent reporting available.[36]

Military tension ratcheted up in the last half of March as the USSR concentrated troops along the Czech–East German border in the period leading up to the Warsaw Pact summit in Dresden.[37] This was judged to be a prophylactic measure, but on 9 May, the CIA reported that Soviet troops in Poland had been seen south of Krakow moving in the direction of Czechoslovakia.[38] Noting that the Soviets had a total of thirty-nine divisions available should they decide to intervene militarily, the CIA concluded, "It would appear that Moscow has decided to do some saber-rattling in order to influence the Czechoslovaks to put a brake on their democratization."[39]

The next month, the Soviet Union began a series of Pact-wide military exercises designed to mask the build up of forces against Czechoslovakia. These included

- Šumava or Böhmerwald: over 20–30 June, a command post and communications exercise involving Soviet, East German, Czech, and Polish troops in Czechoslovakia;[40]
- Neman: from 23 July to 10 August, a rear-services exercise; and
- Skyshield: an air defense exercise, conducted over 11–20 August.[41]

Of the three, Neman was regarded as the most ominous, since it involved recalling reservists, requisitioning transport from the civilian economy, and mobilizing forces from Latvia to Ukraine—measures which obviously could be designed to cover the mass movement of troops against Czechoslovakia.[42] Nevertheless, although the CIA warned that these exercises could well be signs of military intervention, most analysts in the U.S. intelligence community continued to believe that the Soviet Union would exercise restraint.[43]

The situation grew more ominous during July. Late in the month—just prior to the bilateral talks at Čierná nad Tisou—reports poured in of large troop movements in East Germany, southern Poland, and the parts of the USSR along the Czech border.[44] On 22 July, the British Military Mission (BRIXMIS) reported that the Soviet 71st Artillery Brigade and 6th Motorized Rifle Division had vacated their barracks at Bernau, while the East German army barracks at Halle was empty.[45] On 26 July, the CIA reported that the Polish government was under great pressure to prepare for an invasion. The Soviet 32nd Army in Poland had mobilized, as had a large number of forces in East Germany. Five Polish divisions in the Silesian Military District were at a high state of readiness.[46] That same day, substantial elements of three East German divisions, including, most probably, the 7th Armored Division and the 11th Motorized Rifle Division (MRD) moved into restricted areas seventy-five miles south of Berlin.[47] To find out more, USAF SR-71s flew along the inner German border, from where they could monitor developments up to 100 kilometers inside East Germany. Meanwhile, on 29 July, BRIXMIS saw the Soviet 19th MRD deploying from its barracks.[48]

At the end of the month, most of the Soviet troops in Czechoslovakia were withdrawn, but they remained just outside the country, and Western observers noted that the route signs leading into Czechoslovakia for the military movements had been left in place.[49] Four Soviet divisions in Hungary were reported moving into the field, roadblocks were set up, and convoys were seen moving in the direction of Czechoslovakia.[50] On 31 July, the Soviet air force was detected making contingency preparations for operations in Czechoslovakia, while high-level military officials in Moscow were reported operating on an indefinite alert status.[51] Three days later, the CIA's Office of Strategic Research (OSR) warned, "It would appear the Soviet High Command has in about two weeks time completed military preparations sufficient for intervening in Czechoslovakia, if that is deemed necessary by the political leadership."[52]

Over the first three weeks of August, the CIA was forced to function without the support of its principal collection asset, photo-reconnaissance satellites. The film-return systems in use at the time lacked the flexibility to respond to the rapidly changing situation in Czechoslovakia. A KH-4B satellite was in orbit, but its canister was not recovered until after the invasion, and when it was, the film showed Soviet forces deployed to invade: airfields packed with aircraft and Soviet military vehicles painted with white crosses to distinguish them from identical Czech equipment.[53]

By this point in time, however, overhead reconnaissance was not really necessary: there already was ample intelligence from other sources to show that, by the end of July, the Warsaw Pact was mobilized for an invasion of Czechoslovakia. The next two weeks or so were something of an anticlimax, for the simple reason that the Soviets themselves had not decided to intervene.

This hesitation gave some reason to hope that an intervention was not forth-coming, but, with nearly forty Soviet divisions on the move, it was clear that the Soviet alert was continuing.[54] When, on 18 August, the Soviets did decide to intervene, it was announced by SIGINT reporting of a Soviet military com-munications blackout all over Central Europe.[55]

Two days later, on the morning of the invasion, Director of Central Intel-ligence Richard M. Helms met with the Bruce Clarke, the director of Stra-tegic Research, and Richard Lehman, the director of Current Intelligence. Lehman relayed a wire service report that Soviet leaders had been sum-moned to Moscow for an urgent Politburo meeting—which, in fact, had occurred on 18 August. This was unusual in itself: Soviet leaders normally spent August entrenched in their dachas, and only a crisis would serve to get them out. Clarke, Lehman, and Helms agreed that, taken together with the military alert in Central Europe, the emergency Politburo meeting was a sure indicator something was about to happen, most probably the invasion of Czechoslovakia. Helms was already scheduled to meet with President Lyndon B. Johnson and decided to convey the information personally. Remarkably, Johnson rejected that conclusion, saying, "Dick, that Moscow meeting is to talk about us." What Johnson knew, and Helms did not, was that the Soviet Union and the United States were due to make a joint an-nouncement on 21 August concerning the planned strategic arms limita-tion talks. Not unreasonably, but unfortunately, Johnson believed that to be the subject of the meeting in the Kremlin.[56]

The president and his advisors soon were disabused of that notion. At 11:00 p.m. on 20 August, a Soviet Spetznz battalion landed at and occupied Prague airport.[57] At 11:11 p.m., NATO radar monitors reported that the air space around Prague was covered with artificial "snow," blanking out radar screens and preventing observation of what was happening.[58] Just a few hours later, at 2200, Washington, DC, time, Helms was summoned back to the White House for an emergency meeting. The invasion of Czechoslova-kia was underway.[59]

Given the swiftness of events, it is hard to see how Johnson could have received more warning than he did. Official Washington was holding its breath in August 1968, waiting to see what the Soviets would do. Ample, precise, and accurate strategic warnings concerning events in Central Eu-rope had been pouring in all summer. The August calm before the storm may have meant that much of the intelligence community was surprised by the invasion when it occurred, but there had been no indication that the Soviets had stood down in Central Europe, nor had strategic warnings ever been withdrawn.

A CIA memorandum prepared immediately after the event noted that the decision to intervene must have come very late in the game.[60] Exactly how and when Moscow's forbearance "became unraveled" was something of a mystery. To CIA analysts, however, it was clear that the decision had come some time after the Čierná nad Tisou and Bratislava conferences. The time that elapsed, the scattering of the Soviet leadership to their dachas for the August holidays, the attitude of the Soviet press, and the anodyne communiqués that were issued after each meeting all were indicators that the Dubček government was being given more time—to do what was not clear.[61] "The most likely explanation," Agency analysts concluded, "appears to be that, under the impact of internal pressures within the leadership and of importuning from its anxious allies in Eastern Europe . . . the fragile balance in the Soviet leadership which produced the Čierná agreement has, in the space of less than three weeks, been upset in favor of those who may all along have wanted the toughest kind of policy. . . ." With the political scales in Moscow in such precarious balance, "it would not have needed a great shock to upset them."[62]

So, on the morning of 21 August, Czechoslovakia was invaded from the north, east, and south by twenty Warsaw Pact divisions totaling some 250,000 men. At the same time, the positions vacated by these units were backfilled by ten Soviet divisions. Once strategic points in Czechoslovakia were occupied, most of these forces redeployed into western Czechoslovakia, restoring the front against NATO.[63] There they were backed by the full might of the Warsaw Pact, including thousands of nuclear weapons targeted against Western and Central Europe. Nothing short of a world war was likely to get them out. In 1938, the Western powers had responded to threats against Czechoslovakia by backing down, rather than face a Nazi Germany they falsely believed was ready for war. In 1968, they had no choice.

NOTES

1. All statements of fact, opinion, or analysis expressed are those of the author and do not reflect the official positions or views of the Central Intelligence Agency (CIA) or any other U.S. government agency. Nothing in the contents should be construed as asserting or implying U.S. government authentication of information or CIA endorsement of the author's views. This material has been reviewed by the CIA to prevent the disclosure of classified information.

2. Christopher Andrew and Vasili Mitrokhin, *The Sword and the Shield: The Mitrokhin Archive and the Secret History of the KGB* (New York: Basic Books, 1999), 250.

3. NIE 12-65, "Eastern Europe and the Warsaw Pact," 26 August 1965, Doc. Nr. 273191, 1, 3–4. This and all other CIA primary source documents cited herein are available online from the *CIA Freedom of Information Act Electronic Reading Room*, http://www.foia.cia.gov (accessed 14 September 2008).

4. NIE 12-65, "Eastern Europe and the Warsaw Pact," 5.

5. ONE Special Memorandum 10-65, "Prospects for Independence in Eastern Europe," 18 February 1965, Doc. Nr. 427965, 1.

6. NIE Special Memorandum 1-68, "Czechoslovakia: A New Direction," 12 January 1968; Doc. Nr. 608720, 14; CIA intelligence information cable, "Political Events and Personnel Changes in Czechoslovakia," 27 March 1968, Doc. Nr. 242352, 7; unsigned CIA memorandum, 8 April 1968, Doc. Nr. 119580, 1–2.

7. Office of Strategic Research (OSR) intelligence memorandum, "Warsaw Pact War Plan for Central Region of Europe," 18 June 1968, Doc. Nr. 969832, 5.

8. OSR intelligence memorandum, "Warsaw Pact War Plan," 1.

9. OSR intelligence memorandum, "Warsaw Pact War Plan," 1.

10. ER IM 68-33, "Economic Pressure for Change in Eastern Europe," (27) March 1968, Doc. Nr. 427962, 2.

11. ER IM 68-33, "Economic Pressure for Change in Eastern Europe," 1, 4.

12. Unsigned CIA memorandum, 8 April 1968, Doc. Nr. 119580, 1–2.

13. CIA intelligence information cable, "Political Events and Personnel Changes in Czechoslovakia," 27 March 1968, Doc. Nr. 242352, 7–8.

14. CIA intelligence information cable, "Political Events and Personnel Changes in Czechoslovakia," 7–8.

15. CIA, "Weekly Summary," 19 April 1968, Doc. Nr. 44603, 13.

16. DI Intelligence Memorandum 0658/68 (OCI), "Czechoslovakia in Transition," 23 April 1968, Doc. Nr. 608719, 2.

17. Unsigned CIA memorandum, 8 April 1968, Doc. Nr. 119580, 1.

18. ONE memorandum for the director, "Subject: The Czechoslovak Crisis," 17 July 1968, Doc. Nr. 242346, 5.

19. Unsigned CIA memorandum, "Subject: The Czechoslovak Situation (as of 1200 hours)," 9 May 1968, Doc. Nr. 262105, 3; ONE Special Memorandum 12-68, "Subject: Czechoslovakia: the Dubček Pause," 13 June 1968, Doc. Nr. 95035, 1.

20. CIA intelligence information cable, "Present USSR Attitudes toward Czechoslovakia," 10 May 1968, Doc. Nr. 242350, 2.

21. For example, Jiri Valenta, *Soviet Intervention in Czechoslovakia, 1968: Anatomy of a Decision* (Baltimore: Johns Hopkins University Press, 1991).

22. Andrew and Mitrokhin, *Sword and Shield*, 250–57.

23. DI Intelligence Memorandum 0658/68 (OCI), "Czechoslovakia in Transition," 23 April 1968, Doc. Nr. 608719, 12.

24. ONE Special Memorandum 12-68, "Subject: Czechoslovakia: the Dubček Pause," 13 June 1968, Doc. Nr. 95035, 1.

25. ONE Special Memorandum 12-68, "Subject: Czechoslovakia: the Dubček Pause," 16–18.

26. ONE Special Memorandum 12-68, "Subject: Czechoslovakia: the Dubček Pause," 4.

27. ONE Special Memorandum 12-68, "Subject: Czechoslovakia: the Dubček Pause," 5, 9.

28. ONE memorandum for the director, "Subject: The Czechoslovak Crisis," 17 July 1968, 7.

29. ONE memorandum for the director, "Subject: The Czechoslovak Crisis," 4.

30. ONE memorandum for the director, "Subject: The Czechoslovak Crisis," 6–7.

31. ONE memorandum for the director, "Subject: The Czechoslovak Crisis," 5.

32. ONE memorandum for the director, "Subject: The Czechoslovak Crisis," 6.

33. CIA intelligence memorandum, "The Situation in Czechoslovakia as of 4:00 PM EDT," 30 July 1968, Doc. Nr. 265449, 1.

34. CIA intelligence memorandum, "The Situation in Czechoslovakia as of 4:00 PM EDT," 2.

35. James Bamford, *Body of Secrets: Anatomy of the Ultra-Secret National Security Agency, from the Cold War to the Dawn of a New Century* (New York: Random House, 2001), 152; David Miller, *The Cold War: A Military History* (New York: St. Martin's, 1998), 38; Curtis Peebles, *The Corona Project: America's First Spy Satellites* (Annapolis, MD: U.S. Naval Institute, 1997), 235; Jeffrey T. Richelson, *The Wizards of Langley: Inside the CIA's Directorate of Science and Technology* (Boulder, CO: Westview, 2001), 170.

36. See, for example, CIA intelligence information cable, "Preparations for Military Intervention in Czechoslovakia," 26 July 1968, Doc. Nr. 96552.

37. CIA intelligence information cable, "Political Events and Personnel Changes in Czechoslovakia," 27 March 1968, Doc. Nr. 242352, 7.

38. Unsigned CIA memorandum, "Subject: The Czechoslovak Situation (as of 1200 Hours)," 9 May 1968, Doc. Nr. 262105, 4.

39. Unsigned CIA memorandum, "Subject: The Czechoslovak Situation (as of 1200 Hours)," 2–3, 4.

40. Miller, *The Cold War*, 38, and Cynthia M. Grabo, "Soviet Deception in the Czechoslovak Crisis," *Studies in Intelligence* (Spring 1970): 29.

41. Miller, *The Cold War*, 60.

42. Grabo, "Soviet Deception," 29.

43. ONE Special Memorandum 12-68, "Subject: Czechoslovakia: the Dubček Pause," 13 June 1968, Doc. Nr. 95035, 2, and Richelson, *Wizards of Langley*, 170.

44. Miller, *The Cold War*, 38.

45. Miller, *The Cold War*, 38.

46. CIA intelligence information cable, "Preparations for Military Intervention in Czechoslovakia," 26 July 1968, Doc. Nr. 96552, 1.

47. CIA intelligence memorandum, "The Situation in Czechoslovakia as of 4:00 PM EDT," 30 July 1968, Doc. Nr. 265449, 1, and CIA intelligence memorandum "The Situation as of 4:00 PM EDT," 26 July 1968, Doc. Nr. 265446, 2.

48. Miller, *The Cold War*.

49. Miller, *The Cold War*.

50. CIA intelligence memorandum, "The Situation in Czechoslovakia as of 4:00 PM EDT," 30 July 1968, Doc. Nr. 265449, 1.

51. CIA intelligence memorandum, "The Situation in Czechoslovakia as of 4:00 PM EDT," 31 July 1968, Doc. Nr. 265448, 2.

52. Richelson, *Wizards of Langley*, 169.

53. Richelson, *Wizards of Langley*, 170.

54. Miller, *The Cold War*, 39.

55. Miller, *The Cold War*, 38.

56. Richard M. Helms, *A Look over My Shoulder: A Life in the Central Intelligence Agency* (New York: Random House, 2003), 340–41.

57. Miller, *The Cold War*, 60.

58. Miller, *The Cold War*, 38.

59. Helms, *Look over My Shoulder*, 342.

60. CIA intelligence memorandum, "The Soviet Decision to Intervene in Czechoslovakia," 21 August 1968, Doc. Nr. 326291, 3.

61. CIA intelligence memorandum, "The Soviet Decision to Intervene in Czechoslovakia," 1–2.

62. CIA intelligence memorandum, "The Soviet Decision to Intervene in Czechoslovakia," 2.

63. Miller, *The Cold War*, 61.

11

Defense and Détente: Britain, the Soviet Union, and the 1968 Czech Crisis

Saki Ruth Dockrill

In late October 1968, that is, over two months after the Soviet and War-saw Pact invasion of Czechoslovakia (20/21 August 1968), the Foreign and Commonwealth Office was sending its instructions to Her Majesty Government's major overseas missions about "Czechoslovakia: East-West Contacts."[1] The gist of the message was that the critical period was now over, and the missions could return to business as usual. Britain, along with the rest of its allies, would, therefore, continue to pursue its existing policy "based on both Defense and détente" vis-à-vis the Eastern Socialist Bloc. But there was a caveat in the above-mentioned telegram, "While showing willingness to do official business with them, you should avoid public expression of goodwill." This probably meant that it would be better not to smile widely, or not to shake hands vigorously with Eastern Bloc officials, particularly in front of the media. Doing so would be playing into the hands of Soviet propaganda, for Moscow was already suggesting that the East-West relations were back to normal, implying that "nothing important has happened."[2]

This is not to suggest that avoiding "the public expression of goodwill" was as far as the British could go in the form of protest against the Czecho-slovakian invasion. The United States, too, remained cautious, urging its allies to engage in "quiet diplomacy."[3] The North Atlantic Treaty Organiza-tion (NATO) was not prepared to do anything militarily which might pro-voke the Soviet Union during the Czech crisis. For the United Kingdom, the crisis underlined Soviet weakness as much as the importance of maintain-ing the solidarity of the Western alliance, and this chapter explains why.

THE EVOLUTION OF BRITAIN'S POLICY
TOWARD EUROPE AND THE SOVIET UNION

Despite the relatively low level of interest Whitehall had shown toward Eastern European countries during the Cold War, it must not be forgotten that it was the European theatre to which Whitehall gave first priority from the point initially of its strategic and defense importance to Britain after 1950. By that time, the Cold War had become a fact of life; the Iron Curtain had descended on Central Europe; and the North Atlantic Alliance had come into being. In March 1950, the Cabinet Defense Committee agreed that holding the Soviets "East of Rhine" was now "vital" to the defense of Britain. This entailed an important shift in Britain's global strategy from the Middle East to Western Europe. With the shock of the Korean War, Britain increased its defense contribution to NATO even further, while launching an ambitious rearmament program.[4]

This priority given to Europe coincided with Britain's other and equally important decision. That was to seek multilateralism in fighting the Cold War in Europe, along with the United States, and within the framework of the North Atlantic Alliance. This was not to say that Britain's Atlanticism came naturally after the end of the Second World War. In the immediate postwar years, the wartime special relationship with the United States was replaced by a rather more uneasy partnership. Following the abrupt ending by Congress of Lend Lease in August 1945, Britain began difficult negotiations with the United States for a loan. The passage of the McMahon Act through Congress in 1946 was another blow to Britain's close atomic relations with the United States. It was only the growing pressures of the Cold War, as well as the West's fear of Soviet expansionism in the Mediterranean, the Middle East, and Europe that helped to draw the United States and Britain closely together in establishing the North Atlantic Alliance.[5] In the case of London, this was motivated by a practical, but nonetheless serious, consideration of what Britain could do on its own in keeping Soviet-led communism at bay in Europe. It is interesting to find how candidly this feeling of the limitations of Britain's capacity to defend itself was expressed officially at one of the Cabinet Defense Committee (consisting chiefly of cabinet ministers of overseas and defense departments plus the chancellor of the exchequer, and the representatives of the chiefs of staff, chaired by the prime minister) meetings in the summer of 1949. It affirmed that "[we] have reached a stage where we can no longer avoid stating our intentions to Western Union. We know for certain that without United States active and early support the defense of Western Union is not practical unless or until a period of full scale rearmament is embarked upon."[6]

Since then, Britain's policy for the defense of Europe remained remarkably consistent. Throughout the Cold War and beyond, London remained a

keen supporter of the transatlantic alliance, although it preferred to be seen
to be an "influential" member of that organization. At no time did Britain
try to go it alone in Europe as General Charles de Gaulle's France had done
by withdrawing from NATO's integrated military command in 1966. This
is worth noting, for Britain was more independent in its formulation of
the nation's global policy outside Europe, where Britain, in the 1950s and
1960s, still held considerable responsibilities for ensuring the stability and
peace of many countries and protectorates, such as in East Africa, the Persian Gulf, and Southeast Asia. During Harold Wilson's Labour government
years, the Lyndon Johnson administration wanted the United Kingdom to
send troops to Vietnam and/or to retain its military presence East of Suez as
long as the United States was fighting in Southeast Asia. The U.S. requests
were, of course, discussed and considered at cabinet level, but Britain did
not feel able to comply with either of these pleas. Britain chose the timing
and manner in which it would retreat from Singapore, Malaysia, and also
from the Persian Gulf in 1967 and 1968 even if this meant doing so at the
cost of upsetting Washington.[7]

When turning to Europe, Britain found such independent action unthinkable. NATO continued to be seen to be a "vital element" and was
"cardinal to the security of Britain."[8] This stance can be understood when
viewed against Britain's perceptions of the Soviet Union and of the Eastern
European countries. The Foreign Office's Permanent Undersecretary's Committee (PUSC, comprising its highest officials) set out, in January 1952,
Britain's long-term policy toward the Soviet Union. It appreciated that the
USSR's objective was the spread of communism worldwide under Moscow's
leadership, but at the expense of Western interests. The paper asserted that
the present Soviet leadership was inspired not only by "traditional Russian
ambitions but also by a fanatical and dynamic revolutionary spirit which
utterly rejects the very idea of a lasting settlement with the non-communist
part of the world."[9] Under the circumstances, Britain could only contain
Soviet "encroachment by active and ceaseless vigilance over a long period
of time, backed by armed strength." The final and lasting settlement after
this "uneasy absence of war" with the Soviet Union was likely to "follow a
substantial modification in the outlook and structure of the present Soviet
régime." That is, regime change was the sine quo non for the end of the
Cold War.[10]

Referring to the liberation of the Eastern European countries, the document recognized the possibility that the satellites could be detached with
Western help "from the Soviet Bloc by a series of ostensibly spontaneous
uprisings." As happened in Yugoslavia, the PUSC continued, "[T]he psychological effect of the liberation of any satellite from the Soviet yoke would . . .
be far reaching throughout the Soviet orbit, and indeed, in the free world."[11]
These ideas were somewhat similar to the subsequent U.S. Republican policy

of liberating captive peoples in Eastern Europe; however, it was important to note that the PUSC saw little prospects for any successful liberation by Eastern European resistance groups unless they were backed up by Western armed forces. In fact, the committee foresaw quite accurately that "with the possible exception of Albania" (who would leave the Warsaw Pact in 1968), none of the satellite countries would, in the foreseeable future, be able to depart from the Soviet camp "unless the Western Powers were able to neutralize the Soviet army either by armed intervention on a sufficient scale or by diversionary action elsewhere or by the possession of such preponderant strength that the Soviet government would be unwilling to incur the risk of a general war." In the committee's view, therefore, the liberation of Eastern Europe could not be successful without substantial Western help, but none of the Western powers were ready to provide this at the cost of confronting the Soviet Union.

Indeed, the subsequent crisis in Hungary in 1956 brought the severe limitations of U.S. liberation policy home to the White House. The revolutionary Hungarian government led by Imre Nagy proclaimed Hungary's withdrawal from the Warsaw Pact and appealed to the United Nations for help in defense of Hungarian neutrality. These developments placed the West in a moral quandary about what steps they should take toward Hungary. While President Dwight Eisenhower was clear that "it has never been our policy to incite captive peoples," U.S. support for the liberation of Eastern Europe was greatly exaggerated worldwide, resulting in mounting criticism of U.S. and Western inaction over Hungary.[12] The lesson learned from the 1956 Hungarian crisis was, in the words of Permanent Undersecretary David Gore-Booth (1965–1969), "not to offer false expectations."[13]

THE EMERGENCE OF DÉTENTE WITH THE EAST BETWEEN 1963 AND 1968

After the Cuban Missile Crisis and the successful conclusion, in August 1963, of a limited test ban treaty outlawing nuclear testing in the atmosphere, in outer space, and under water, a significant step by the three major nuclear powers toward managing and controlling nuclear weapons, East-West relations seemed to move toward détente, which was defined in the West as "the search for secure and peaceful East-West relations leading in time to a European security settlement."[14] The UK Joint Intelligence Committee (JIC)[15] in 1964 noted that the Soviet Union, too, wanted a respite from the Cold War because of the economic strain of waging it, the costly arms race with the United States, growing difficulties with Communist China, and a lack of any "gains by their tough tactics in Berlin and Cuba." However, the committee astutely observed that Soviet interest in détente was a matter of tactics rather than the reflection of a fundamental change in its basic policy. Thus the détente will be "subjected to interruptions," concluded the committee, "whenever they [the Soviets] consider that their purposes can best be served by raising tension."[16]

For Britain, too, détente cut both ways: it was welcomed as far as it would make Europe a safer place by making its opponent more predictable, would help to reduce NATO's defense expenditures, and would increase business and trade with the Eastern Bloc. However, détente could also work against the interests of Britain. It might threaten the solidarity of the NATO alliance, dividing the pro-Atlanticists and pro-Europeanists, while détente might lead the U.S. Congress to demand the return of U.S. troops from Europe. After 1965, U.S. national security interests gravitated toward the conflict in Vietnam, away from a relatively calmer Europe. The German question might also raise its ugly head when West Germany felt free to pursue its own national goals.[17]

Despite these limitations, détente, if successful, was a much better alternative to the high Cold War of the previous decades. It was, therefore, British policy to seek détente and negotiations with Moscow when any opportunity arose, and this was certainly part of the vision embraced by the incoming Labour government led by Harold Wilson after October 1964. At the age of forty-eight, Wilson was a determined, pragmatic, and astute politician, with twenty years of experience in politics. Like his predecessors Winston Churchill and Harold Macmillan, Wilson, too, wanted to play a major role in trying to prevent a superpower conflict and to secure a "friendly understanding" with Moscow.[18] On the surface, the new prime minister had more than sufficient experience in dealing with the Soviet Union. As president of the Board of Trade between 1947 and 1951, Wilson was already known to the Soviet Committee for State Security (KGB) as a politician enthusiastically promoting trade with the USSR. In the 1950s, he continued to be a strong advocate of encouraging trade with Moscow and was the first visitor in May 1953, in the aftermath of Josef Stalin's death, to the capital from the British political establishment. When he became shadow prime minister, he visited the Soviet Union twice, once in 1963 and again in 1964, and presented his idea of convening regular summit talks with Moscow, along with the United States and, possibly, France. According to the Mitrokhin Archive, the KGB once attempted to convert Wilson into a Soviet agent. Perhaps more damaging to him was an unfounded rumor circulated in the U.S. Central Intelligence Agency (CIA) and the British Security Services (MI5) that Wilson was, indeed, a Soviet mole.[19]

As the new Labour prime minister, he continued to aspire to a better relationship with the USSR, although his interests remained largely in the field of trade and technology. In reality, Britain was not able to exercise much influence on the Soviet Union. A number of attempts Wilson initiated to bring about a negotiated settlement in Vietnam in cooperation with the Soviet Union did not secure a sympathetic ear in Moscow. In February 1966, the British prime minister proposed the setting up of a hotline between London and Moscow, but this did not materialize until October 1967. By then, however, Charles de Gaulle's France had already established a similar communication link with the Kremlin.[20] The Anglo-Soviet summit talks in February 1967 began with negotiations for an Anglo-Soviet friendship treaty. The treaty was intended to "regulate commercial, cultural, educational and scientific exchanges," but the negotiations soon became stalled in early 1968.[21]

The timing coincided with Britain's devaluation of sterling in the autumn of 1967 and its subsequent announcement of an accelerated withdrawal from East of Suez in January 1968.[22] Reporting to London, the British ambassador to Moscow, Sir Geoffrey Harrison, expressed his amazement at the bad press Britain was receiving in Moscow over its East of Suez decision. Great Britain was described by the Soviet press as a country going through a period of "profound malaise and disillusionment" in 1967, and warned that 1968 would be even worse for Britain.[23] The problems, they analyzed, were due to Britain's dire dependence on the United States. The Foreign Office suspected that these were the usual Soviet tactics of trying to drive a wedge between the two Anglo-Saxon countries.[24] Behind the façade of peaceful Anglo-Soviet relations, the Soviet Union in the aftermath of Britain's retreat from East of Suez quickly projected its naval power into the Indian Ocean. Prior to July 1967, there had been no permanent Soviet naval presence in the Indian Ocean, but by 1974, the number of Soviet warships in the ocean rose to more than 10,000.[25] The Kremlin optimistically saw the fragmentation of American society after Vietnam as a sign of the failure of the Western capitalist system. There was rising confidence in Moscow that the Soviet Union, and not the United States, was "becoming the dominant actor" in the world.[26]

Just as Britain thought that the real solution to the Cold War required a drastic change in the Soviet system, Moscow's condition for any improvement on Anglo-Soviet bilateral relations would be for Britain to sever its relations with the Western alliance, especially the United States. One can see that there was, therefore, little room for the two governments to cultivate any real friendship beyond certain trade and cultural exchanges. This, in turn, implies the severe limitations Britain and the West would face in exercising any influence over the Soviet Union and its policies, such as over Czechoslovakia in 1968.

All was not well in the Western Bloc, either. The emergence of détente resulted in differing approaches in the West to the security of Western Europe. In the mid-1960s, many observers on both sides of the Atlantic raised serious concerns about the possible collapse of NATO, which was seen to be in deep crisis. The role of the United States as the ultimate nuclear guarantor was becoming increasingly questionable, since the superpower nuclear arms race now produced a balance of terror in Europe. The John F. Kennedy administration's solution was to enhance the conventional capabilities of European powers to meet a less serious military threat. This meant that European NATO allies had to raise the nuclear threshold, making U.S. nuclear deterrence less credible to military conflicts in Europe, and increasing the risk of conventional limited wars occurring there.[27] Moreover, the question of NATO's nuclear sharing, especially that of meeting West Germany's aspirations for an equal status in NATO's nuclear policy, required skilful diplomacy. The idea of creating the Multilateral Nuclear Force (MLF) proposed during the Kennedy years had, however, never become a serious proposition for the Europeans, and by 1964, West Germany and the United States were the only countries who supported the scheme.[28]

General Charles de Gaulle, the president of the French Republic, became increasingly irritated by what he perceived to be Kennedy's intention of dominating European NATO, and the relaxation of East-West tensions prompted the general to embark on an East-West rapprochement "from the Atlantic to the Urals" outside the framework of the transatlantic alliance. In July 1966, France withdrew from NATO's integrated military structure and asked NATO to withdraw its staff and institutions from France by April 1967. The emerging East-West détente was by no means accepted by all the NATO powers at this time. Those countries close to the Iron Curtain (West Germany, Turkey, and Norway) took the growing Soviet military capability more seriously than did other European countries, and Bonn was, in any case, unlikely to be drawn into a premature détente unless it embraced the reunification of Germany.[29]

Not only did France withdraw from NATO's military command, but the two other major powers, the United States and Britain, also revived their long-term grievances about NATO. They felt that their initial troop commitment to Europe, which had been forced upon them when the Cold War was at its height in 1949–1950, should now be reduced. London and Washington were united in maintaining that the other European allies, especially the Federal Republic of Germany, should pull their weight by contributing more resources to the defense of Western Europe now that their economies had become prosperous.[30]

For Britain, some defense cuts in a relatively peaceful Europe proved to be possible when the Labour government embarked on a series of defense reviews after 1964. The United States became heavily involved in the war in Vietnam with over half a million troops fighting there. U.S. involvement in the war in Vietnam was regarded in Europe as a diversion of attention and resources from the defense of Western Europe. The United States, on the other hand, was displeased with a lack of support from its European allies to the cause of Asian containment, and in August 1966, Congress began to call for a substantial reduction in U.S. troops in Europe unless the Europeans were prepared to resolve the "dollar gap" in the foreign exchange. The subsequent tripartite negotiations between the United States, Britain, and West Germany about Anglo-American troop reductions demonstrated how difficult it was to overcome the differences between these three Western countries.[31]

In order to overcome NATO's mid-life crisis, Whitehall had plenty to worry about and to do to maintain the cohesion of the Western alliance. In the end, however, the alliance survived de Gaulle's challenge reasonably well. NATO resolved the question of nuclear sharing by setting up the Nuclear Planning Group (December 1966), accepted in 1967 the new strategy of flexible response, which included options preferred by both Europe and the United States, and agreed to adopt the Harmel Report (December 1967) calling for détente and defense, a strategy which served to increase Western Europe's pressure for détente in the 1970s. All of these were, in fact, in line with the national interest of the United Kingdom, and it welcomed the fact that détente was now part and parcel of NATO's objective, a slap in the face to de Gaulle's solo pursuit of détente.

By contrast, the UK's interest in Eastern Europe remained unremarkable. While it agreed to start negotiations on what became known later as the Mutual and Balanced Force Reductions (MBFR) Talks with the Warsaw Pact, Whitehall did not make much effort to promote cultural exchanges or contacts at ministerial levels either. The prime minister focused heavily on improving Anglo-Soviet relations. The Foreign Office gave only a grudging approval of change in "the atmosphere and mechanics" of the relationship with Moscow, but reported that the two powers were not any closer on "fundamentals."[32] There was also the problem of a large expansion of Soviet and Eastern Bloc intelligence activities in England after 1964. Following the arrest of a British citizen, Gerald Brooke in Moscow in 1965, V. A. Drozdov (a third secretary in the Soviet embassy in London) turned out to be a spy and was sent back to Moscow in 1968 after he was caught collecting top secret official information from a so-called dead letter-box in London.[33] The Foreign Office's prescription was that Britain should be firmer and more realistic in dealing with the Soviets and avoid "running after them."[34]

THE WEST'S INTELLIGENCE FAILURE, OR DEALING WITH AN UNPREDICTABLE KREMLIN? FROM THE PRAGUE SPRING TO THE SOVIET/WARSAW PACT INVASION

In the East, things were not working according to the theories of Marxism-Leninism. It was clear by the middle of the 1960s that the Socialist economic system had seen better days. The major Eastern European countries were struggling with severe economic problems. The Kremlin (then led by Nikita Khrushchev) had encouraged gradual and limited political and economic reforms because it believed that these might ignite the economic dynamism needed for the economic recovery of these countries. Czechoslovakia, under a conservative Stalinist ruler, Antonin Novotný, was compelled to introduce a degree of relaxation, moving away from the Stalinization of the past. Reforms soon strengthened the hands of the anticonservative section of the party and made Novotný's position difficult. In January 1968, he was replaced by a moderate and populist figure, Alexander Dubček.[35] In effect, Dubček became instrumental in promoting "socialism with a human face," a precursor of Eurocommunism in the 1970s. By the summer of 1968, the Czechoslovakian perestroika (restructuring) and glasnost (openness) were gaining their own momentum, and pressures for change spread to nearly every corner of the country. Dubček sought to reform Czechoslovakia, but he had no intention of breaking away from the Soviet Union. However, other Czech reformist party officials were willing to go further by reducing party control over the church, parliament, censorship, and the economy as was to happen later in Mikhail Gorbachev's perestroika. The dilution of the party's role in Czech social, political, and economic affairs became the mainstay of the Prague Spring.[36] Indeed, the Prague Spring looked as if it might be spreading to other Eastern European countries.

In May 1968, the Foreign Office set up a conference of British ambassadors to Eastern European capitals, which discussed the implications of the Prague Spring. An important question, initially, was how the Soviet Union and other Eastern European countries would react to the Prague Spring, but with less attention given to the relevance of the Prague Spring to Western Europe. Permanent undersecretary at the Foreign Office, Booth felt that the West had no power to control or influence the events which were taking place in Czechoslovakia, and that in any case, it would not be in the West's interest to increase Soviet "difficulties" by interfering in what was perceived to be its internal affairs. The ambassador to Moscow, Sir Geoffrey Harrison, also predicted that the Prague Spring would not affect Anglo-Soviet relations in any serious way. But Harrison believed that the turmoil in Czechoslovakia must have "serious implications" for the USSR and wondered how this would affect the Kremlin's foreign policy toward the West. If Czechoslovakia succeeded in establishing its own distinctive version of socialism at home and such reform started spreading to other Warsaw Pact countries, Harrison suspected that the Kremlin might "crush" the Prague Spring, or conversely let the reforms in Czechoslovakia continue, but limit any damage caused to the Kremlin's leadership in Eastern Europe. The most optimistic speculation was that the Kremlin might even go along with the Czech movement as part of the current détente. The conference did not

reach any definite conclusion, but suggested that there was some consola-
tion to be extracted from the Soviet Union's current preoccupation with
Eastern Europe, for Moscow's interference in other theaters, such as the
Middle East and Far East, would be reduced at a time when British interests
there were threatened.[37]

The result of this conference was developed into the UK's official policy,
which was circulated by Foreign Secretary Michael Stewart to the cabinet
in mid-June 1968. What is worth highlighting here is a new effort to link
the events taking place in Eastern Europe to the interests of the West. This
may have been the result of taking into consideration the views expressed
by UK ambassadors serving in Eastern Europe. They were dissatisfied with
Britain's neglect of that part of the world, and asked King Charles' Street
to be more constructive in its policies toward Eastern Europe. The official
memorandum therefore appreciated that most East European countries
retained a degree of Western democratic traditions, and that, as a result,
they would be more susceptible to modernization, liberation, and other
democratic changes. Not only the reforms in Czechoslovakia, the documents continued, but other more modest economic and social reforms in
Hungary and Poland might gather momentum and might, in turn, lead to
a more independent Eastern Europe. Thus the document admitted that "the
desire of the East European countries for greater individual independence is
also in the interests of the West generally." In order to encourage this trend,
Britain should increase "substantially" its contacts with Eastern Europe in
terms of official visits as well as cultural and business associations.[38]

This was as far as the Foreign Office would go, since its hard-line analysis
of the Soviet Union remained much the same as before. That country, after
its abandonment of the "more brutal features of Stalinism" had still not
completely escaped from "the grip of the old system."[39] While current moderate economic reforms might "in the very long run cause radical changes,"
any reform would require some loosening of central control which might,
however, threaten the stability of the existing Soviet system, a dilemma
Gorbachev later encountered in the 1980s. Otherwise, Moscow continued
to believe in its mission to spread communism worldwide, maintained a
hostile stance toward Western democratic countries, and was anxious to
undermine the relationship between the United States and Western Europe. The last thing that Britain and its Western allies wanted was to rock
the boat in the Eastern Bloc, such as by driving wedges between the Eastern European countries and the Soviet Union. Instead, the Foreign Office
recognized that what the West could do to help Eastern European reforms
such as the Prague Spring was extremely limited, while London assumed
that the Eastern European countries should generally continue to support
Soviet foreign policy, either because it suited their national interests or for
"tactical reasons."

Overall, the Foreign Office produced a generally hopeful, but pragmatic, and sometimes farsighted, analysis of the Soviet Union and Eastern Europe. Meanwhile, the ferment in Czechoslovakia increasingly worried the Kremlin and the other Warsaw Pact countries. In May, the Warsaw Pact powers began to deploy their troops close to the Czechoslovak borders under the guise of Warsaw Pact military exercises, but, in fact, the redeployment was meant to serve as a threat to the pro-reform Czechs.[40] Walter Ulbricht of East Germany and Władysław Gomułka of Poland grew frustrated by the inability of the Dubček regime to control the pace and degree of the reforms in Czechoslovakia.[41] The country was a major producer of advanced weapons and uranium for Moscow's military-industrial complex and as such was too important to be allowed to leave the Soviet orbit. Nevertheless, Brezhnev was reluctant to resort to repressive measures against Prague, which might, he feared, provoke the West into war against the Soviet Union. Soviet foreign minister Andrei Gromyko, and chief of the KGB Yuri Andropov, both apparently persuaded an indecisive Brezhnev to make the decision to intervene. There was also the fear that once Czechoslovakia fell into the hands of "counterrevolutionaries," the rest of the Warsaw Pact powers might follow suit. It was important for Moscow to nip "the Prague Spring" in the bud.[42] We now know that it was a difficult decision to make, but the decision was made nonetheless.[43]

On the night of 20/21 August 1968, the Soviet Union, with the help of other Warsaw Pact countries (the German Democratic Republic, Poland, Hungary, and Bulgaria), mounted a huge military operation, twice as large as Moscow's intervention in Hungary in 1956, and with it the Prague Spring ended abruptly. Twenty-nine army divisions, 7,500 tanks, and more than 1,000 aircraft were sent to "a Defenseless country which had not even mobilized." The Soviet military intervention shocked Dubček and other Czechoslovakian reformers, and they were reluctantly forced to accept that Marxist-Leninist theory was, in fact, "incompatible with a genuine, modern, democratic, economic and political system" and even worse, the system was not "even open to reform."[44]

The August invasion caught the Western leaders off-guard. This was not because the Western intelligence communities failed to detect massive troop movements on the border areas of Czechoslovakia in the summer. Indeed, June and July were the months when Western intelligence officials were most acutely concerned about the risks of a Soviet military intervention in Czechoslovakia.[45]

Partly because of this heightened sense of danger, NATO governments, led by the United States, had deliberately kept a low profile. The White House was decidedly against any move which might provoke the Soviet Union at this difficult time. In the United Kingdom, the foreign secretary told Parliament on 18 July that every country had its own right to determine its own domestic affairs, which could be taken as a veiled warning to Moscow, but Whitehall, too, avoided giving any impression that the United Kingdom was interfering in the Soviet Union's sphere. In June, NATO showed an interest in discussing with the Warsaw Pact countries the Mutual Balanced Reduction Forces. The implications were that if the Soviet Union went ahead with the use of force, détente would then be in jeopardy, which, the West believed, would make the Soviet Union think twice before it used force against Czechoslovakia.[46]

Apart from this soft approach to Moscow, the West did not have any strategy to deal with what turned out to be an escalation of the Czech crisis, for few in Western capitals really believed that the Soviet Union would resort to force to restore stability and order in Czechoslovakia. Thus the crucial point of this analysis must focus on the question of interpretations and, ultimately, the judgments by senior ministers and officials on the basis of the information collected, rather than on the technical accuracy of such information that influenced the UK and West's attitudes toward the Soviet Union and its intentions toward Czechoslovakia.

In hindsight, it was ironic that the Harold Wilson government had undertaken a series of reforms of the UK intelligence community, for he thought the community's credibility had been reduced in recent years by numerous Soviet spy cases, the difficulty of collecting information from within the Ian Smith regime in Rhodesia, and the failure to predict unrest in Ghana and in Nigeria.[47] Like the Eisenhower administration's centralization of the numerous U.S. intelligence agencies in the 1950s, the Labour government introduced measures which were intended to enhance the efficiency and accuracy of the intelligence community, including the appointment (in the spring of 1968) of an intelligence coordinator operating from the cabinet office. The reformed intelligence system ignominiously failed to pass the first big test over the Soviet invasion of Czechoslovakia in August. Sir Percy Cradock, a former Foreign Office official, recalled that the Federal Republic of Germany's intelligence community got it right, more or less, in terms of the likelihood of military invasion, but those Western intelligence officers who believed that there might be a Soviet armed invasion thought that this would be after the Czechoslovakia Party Congress on 9 September, and not before.[48]

According to recently declassified documents in the United Kingdom, the JIC maintained throughout the crisis that the Soviet Union was not going to invade Czechoslovakia in defiance of world opinion and détente. UK intelligence officials were aware of two large military exercises taking place between 11 and 20 August, but these were interpreted as part of "the psychological warfare" against Prague and not a preinvasion move, which was what they turned out to be. How could this military training maneuver involving a total of twenty-nine divisions around the Czech border area be dismissed as a mere show of force? The line of argument by the intelligence community was that if intervention was on the agenda then the military build-up would be kept secret where possible, and not be as openly conducted as it was prior to the invasion.[49]

The Foreign Office, too, was aware of the risk of invasion, but it thought that the Soviets would do everything—"bully and cajole, bribe and threaten"—to the Czechs, except embark on a military invasion. This feeling was somewhat strengthened by another mistaken belief that the heightened tension between the Soviet Union and Czechoslovakia had been largely resolved during their bilateral meetings at Čierná nad Tisou between 29 July and 1 August and also at Bratislava on 3 August.[50] As a result of this estimate, the Joint Intelligence Committee "in consequence sat on the fence."[51]

Why did the United Kingdom and the West so misjudge Soviet intentions? One can, of course, legitimately argue that this was because the Kremlin itself did not reach a final decision to intervene until late July. However, while there were frequent and massive military exercises by the Warsaw Pact countries from the summer onwards, the West, including the United Kingdom, continued to dismiss the thought of Soviet invasion, assuming that the Kremlin should not, or would not, do things which might affect the development of détente with the West. Why? This was probably because it was the desire of the Western leaders to maintain détente with the Eastern Bloc, which resulted in not fully appreciating the strategic priorities from the Soviet Union's point of view and that of other conservative Eastern European leaders who were desperate to hold Eastern Europe together under the Kremlin leadership for the sake of their countries' stability and interests. Michael Stewart gave what he meant to be a veiled warning to the Soviet Union when he met M. Smirnovsky, the Soviet ambassador to Great Britain, at the end of July: "[I]f events went badly over Czechoslovakia, the opportunities for increasing understanding between us would be frozen."[52] Hence, "too much thinking in Western terms" led to misjudgements about what was to happen in Prague.[53]

UK POLICY AFTER THE INVASION

When the invasion actually took place, most cabinet ministers were away on their summer vacations, and only a few (including the prime minister, the foreign secretary, and the defense secretary) attended a hastily arranged emergency cabinet meeting on 22 August.[54] The invasion was condemned by Yugoslavia, Romania, and many other Western governments, including Great Britain. Whitehall was concerned that the Soviet Union might also use force against Romania or Yugoslavia. Denis Healey, returning home after cutting short his family holiday in Switzerland, felt it important to warn Moscow that NATO would not stand aside if a neutral country, like Yugoslavia, was attacked. Later in November, NATO publicly urged the Soviet Union "to refrain from using force and interfering in the affairs of other states," and repeated this warning later in April 1969 at the end of the NATO's Council meeting in Washington, DC.[55]

The August cabinet meeting was also reminded that soon after the invasion, the Soviet government made painstaking efforts to convey a message to the United Kingdom and other NATO governments to the effect that its invasion was limited in nature and scale and that Moscow had no intention in harming any other states. In the case of the United Kingdom, Moscow hoped that its bilateral relationship with London would not be affected by this incident. It was also confirmed at this cabinet meeting that there seemed to be no other threats in the European theater. The prime minister promised at the end of the cabinet meeting that if, in the meantime, there was any urgent development which might require the UK's action, this would be considered by himself in consultation with the foreign secretary, suggesting that no full cabinet meetings would be necessary for the time being.[56] Nevertheless, Wilson called for an emergency sitting of Parliament for two days toward the end of August. The pro-Wilson minister of health and Social Security, Richard Crossman, thought it was "right" for Wilson to arrange this, which brought nearly three hundred members of parliament back from their holidays. Having said that, Crossman soon found the debate rather depressing because "everyone now knows that Britain could do nothing to help the Czechs."[57]

That the crisis had no serious implications for the United Kingdom had, of course, to do with the low priority accorded to Eastern Europe in its global policy, and this was also generally true for most NATO countries (with a possible exception of the Federal Republic of Germany). President Johnson, anxious to outmaneuver Republican presidential candidate Richard Nixon's informal overtures to Moscow, was keen to persuade the Kremlin to agree to start arms negotiations talks before he ended his term as president in January 1969. This almost blinded him to what was going on in Czechoslovakia on 20 August. On that early Sunday evening in Washington, DC, the Soviet ambassador read to the president a message from Moscow. Johnson did not seem to react in any adverse way to the invasion. On the contrary, and to the surprise of Anatolii Dobrynin, the president was anxious to move on to a different subject, that is, a possible beginning of the Strategic Arms Limitations Talks (SALT) with Moscow as though seven thousand Soviet tanks rolling into Czechoslovakia had nothing to do with the United States.[58] Similarly, the British prime minister concentrated his attention on the next summit talks with Moscow. Within NATO, the main task in 1968 was a series of studies developing the Harmel Report into practical policies.[59] This lack of attention to the Czech liberation movement in the West was facilitated by the fact that, unlike the Hungarian uprising in 1956, the Dubček government did not try to break away from the Kremlin's tutelage or from the Warsaw Pact. This situation saved the West from the moral dilemma about what action to take in the face of the unfolding tragedy in Czechoslovakia.

The first major postinvasion analysis of Britain's relations with the Soviet Union in late September was subdued, but not wholly pessimistic. The invasion was considered to be a setback (but not a serious one) for the West in pursuing détente with the East. Whether Moscow's use of force in Czechoslovakia marked any change of approach by the Soviet Union to NATO and the West generally remained to be seen, but the JIC did not expect that it would lead to any danger of Moscow's going to war with the West because of the Czech crisis.[60] In terms of the East-West military balance, and especially in relation to the long border with West Germany, the JIC recognized that Soviet armed forces deployed in Czechoslovakia meant that the Eastern Bloc had increased its military capabilities (although the eleven existing Czech divisions would not now be regarded as trustworthy by the Kremlin), which would enable it to mount a surprise attack on the NATO forward areas. But again, the Cabinet Defense and Overseas Committee was not convinced that the Czech crisis increased Soviet readiness to use force against the West, and the paper concluded that NATO still expected "substantial political warning of a change in this direction."[61]

Outside the NATO area, the committee examined the Far East and the Middle East, where the British government had recently announced its decision to retreat from East of Suez. Their findings concluded that there would be no change in Soviet strategies in these theaters which would require any urgent revision of UK global policy.[62] Despite the crisis, there was no evidence that the Soviet Union would pose a more serious threat to NATO than before. The committee, however, believed that the Czech crisis revealed that the Soviet Union was "willing to act violently and to use massive force in complete disregard of world opinion where she considers that her fundamental interests are at stake."[63] Later in November, these sentiments were codified in a public statement by Brezhnev in Poland, known in the West as the Brezhnev Doctrine.

For the West, the crisis provided NATO with an opportunity to renew its purposes and commitments. The secretary of defense reminded the cabinet in late September that prior to the crisis, there had been some worrying signs in NATO: following France's withdrawal from the command structure, the United States was also demanding some U.S. troop reductions in Europe. But the crisis demonstrated that de Gaulle's independent move toward détente outside the North Atlantic Alliance carried little weight. From the British point of view, the crisis could be seen as a blessing in disguise.

Whitehall could now turn this into an opportunity to strengthen Britain's links with Europe and NATO. The idea was well received in Washington, which had long insisted that the European powers should do more to assist in the defense of Western Europe. The Ministry of Defense was already considering a number of measures (but not at the cost of increasing defense expenditures) to reinforce NATO's defensive power.[64]

While ministerial visits to the Eastern Bloc were put on hold as part of the West's protest against the Soviet use of force in Czechoslovakia, normality slowly returned by the summer of 1969 when official contacts with the Soviet Union were resumed. In the United States, as a result of the invasion, SALT had been postponed, but only for a short period. Nixon invited the Soviet Union to the opening of arms limitations talks in June 1969, and in November, the talks began in Helsinki between officials of the two superpowers. The election of Willy Brandt as the next chancellor of the Federal Republic of Germany in 1969 removed the remaining obstacle to détente. The United Kingdom fully supported Brandt's *Ostpolitik*, which was to accept the existence of Eastern Germany, and from then on, détente demonstrated genuine possibilities for increasing contacts between both sides. In other words, despite the setback caused by the Czechoslovakian crisis, UK policy toward the Soviet Bloc did not change significantly and would continue to be based on "defense and détente."

CONCLUSION

While the Soviet Union may have won a tactical victory over the West with its surprise invasion of Czechoslovakia, the death of the Prague Spring marked the decline of the legitimacy of Communist rule throughout Eastern Europe. The Soviet Communist Party had lost its appeal to its fellow Communists in Western Europe. The younger generation of Eastern European intellectuals began to search for a "European" identity as an alternative to subordination to Moscow, although many of their rulers had no choice but to return to conservatism (or "normalization") by closing the doors to the modernization of the Communist socioeconomic systems, a situation which persisted into the middle of the 1970s.[65] The Kremlin, having found that there had been no violent reactions from the West to its crushing of the "Prague Spring," became more confident about the ability of the Soviet Union to defend its own interests. This sense of confidence was reinforced by growing Soviet military and nuclear strength, which had been built up in the latter half of the 1960s. The Soviet Union was now ready to enter into more peaceful international relations, despite the remaining ideological differences with the Western Bloc. Détente was simply for Moscow the

West's recognition of the Soviet Union's equality with the United States in terms of power and influence in the world.[66]

For Britain, détente meant more contacts with the Eastern Bloc through trade and scientific and cultural exchanges, rather than a break from the Cold War. However, because of the UK's long history of interactions with Russia and the USSR, the United Kingdom was a tad more suspicious about Soviet intentions than was any other NATO power. Thus the right balance between defense and détente needed to be struck if the West was ultimately to win the Cold War by changing the Soviet system. The Czech crisis provided the opportunity to strengthen NATO and helped the UK to reinvigorate its efforts to maintain NATO's political cohesion.

In other aspects, the crisis also exposed how Britain's détente policy was not always consistent, and sometimes not even coherent. Post-1945, prime ministers often sought summit meetings with Kremlin leaders, which they believed might lead, almost magically, to the end of the Cold War. Wilson was no exception, but the Foreign Office regarded the prime minister's dealings with the Soviet leaders as too soft and even pedantic. This was particularly so, given the unvarying hostility expressed by the Soviet Union toward Britain (London was often singled out by the Soviet Union as a hard-line country anxious to exploit Moscow's weaknesses). The more enthusiastic the West became about détente (which might provide the West with an opportunity to penetrate the Eastern Bloc), the more suspicious the Kremlin became. As Geraint Hughes argues, this vicious circle may have tipped the balance in Moscow in favor of the use of force against Czechoslovakia.[67] On the other hand, British ambassadors in Eastern Europe felt that UK policy for Eastern Europe lacked initiative and inspiration. They believed that pursuing détente with a heavy focus on the Soviet Union, while neglecting British relations with Eastern Europe, was a foreign policy weakness, but this too, could now be reexamined thanks to the Czechoslovak crisis and the subsequent slow progress of détente.[68]

In the final analysis, the following three points are important in understanding the UK's attitude toward the crisis. First, the UK government regarded the crisis as a misfortune for the Soviet system. At a Defense and Oversea Policy Committee (OPD) meeting in late September, Denis Healey stated that he found the Soviet's action significant because force was used "to maintain the status quo, not to change it."[69] Thus, instead of exploiting this misfortune to the full, the United Kingdom chose to keep a low profile (in line with the rest of the NATO powers) in order not to make things more difficult for the Kremlin. The other side of the coin was not to give Moscow any propaganda opportunity to accuse the West of provoking Moscow into resorting to force over the Prague Spring. Second, London thought that it was right for NATO to stick to the noninterference policy. The Ministry of Defense explained this in cut and dried terms just a few days after the invasion: NATO was "never designed to protect any War-saw Pact country from Soviet intervention" because it was "an essentially integrated organisation with a single military purpose, namely to protect its members from outside attack by positing an effective deterrent." Thus, while the crisis was unfolding in Eastern Europe, Britain's main task was to observe that there was no threat to Western Europe. When British post-invasion analyses showed that this really was the case, as far as the United Kingdom and NATO were concerned, the crisis was over.

The final point was about the importance of Western Europe for the United Kingdom, which has been explained fully in the earlier part of this essay. This remained unchanged throughout the Cold War years. Because of this importance, the United Kingdom wanted to make sure that the United States and European NATO powers were working closely together and was conscious of the fact that Moscow was aware that the United Kingdom had significant influence, especially in Washington.[70] This role could only be played effectively so long as the United Kingdom worked as part of the multilateral organization in dealing with the Soviet threat in the primary theatre of Europe. Thus, what the foreign and commonwealth secretary minuted in February 1969 is worth citing here, "An independent power acting alone, we cannot achieve much vis-à-vis the Soviet Union: as an influential member of the Alliance and in due course of a united Western Europe, we have a very considerable part to play."[71] Thus, the assumption that the Czechoslovakian crisis had huge implications for the future fate of the Soviet Eastern European empire, the conviction about what NATO was for, and the belief in multilateralism, these three factors defined, shaped, and characterized Britain's policy toward the Prague Spring and the Soviet invasion in August 1968.

NOTES

1. The Foreign Office and the Commonwealth Relations Office were amalgamated and became the Foreign and Commonwealth Office (FCO) from 17 October 1968.

2. Michael Stewart to certain missions and dependent territories, guidance telegram, no. 264, 29 October 1968, *Documents on British Policy Overseas Series III*, vol.1, *Britain and the Soviet Union, 1968–1972* (London: The Stationery Office, 1997), 85–86 (hereafter cited as DBPO).

3. John G. McGinn, "The Politics of Collective Inaction: NATO's Response to the Prague Spring," *Journal of Cold War Studies* 1, no. 3 (Fall 1999): 127.

4. Cabinet Defense Committee Meeting, DO (50) 20, 20 March 1950, Cabinet 131/9, the National Archives, England (hereafter cited as TNA).

5. Saki Ruth Dockrill, *Britain's Retreat from East of Suez: The Choice between Europe and the World?* (Basingstoke, UK: Palgrave Macmillan, 2002), 11–12.

6. Cabinet Defense Committee Meeting, DO (49) 45, 17 June 1949, Cabinet, CAB131/17, TNA; see also John Baylis, *The Diplomacy of Pragmatism: Britain and the Formation of NATO, 1942–1949* (London: Macmillan, 1993), 76–91.

7. For Anglo-American relations and Britain's decision to withdraw from Singapore, see Dockrill, *Britain's Retreat from East of Suez*.

8. Cabinet Defense and Overseas Policy Committee memoranda, DO [O][S][64] 29, 2 October 1964, Cabinet, 148/9, TNA.

9. "Future Policy toward Soviet Russia," PUSC (51) 16 (final), 17 January 1952, Foreign Office, FO 371/125002/4, TNA.

10. "Future Policy toward Soviet Russia," PUSC (51) 16 (final), 17 January 1952.

11. Annex B. Liberation of the Satellites to PUSC (51) 16 (final), 17 January 1952.

12. MacArthur II to Hoover (minute), 13 November 1956, *Foreign Relations of United States 1955–1957*, vol. 25, *Eastern Europe* (Washington, DC: Government Printing Office, 1990), 435 (hereafter cited as FRUS).

13. Paul Gore-Booth, *With Great Truth and Respect* (London: Constable, 1974), 386.

14. Enclosure, "The Longer Term Prospects for East-West Relations after the Czechoslovak Crisis," in Mr. Stewart to HG ambassador to Moscow (Sir D. Wilson), RS 3/2, 15 May 1969, DBPO, 151.

15. The Joint Intelligence Committee (JIC), created in 1936, is composed of the representatives of numerous intelligence agencies as well as the major departments, including the Foreign Office, the Ministry of Defense, the Home Office, and the Treasury. For the history of the JIC, see Percy Cradock, *Know Your Enemy: How the Joint Intelligence Committee Saw the World* (London: John Murray, 2002), 7–49ff.

16. JIC (63) 85, 3 March 1964, CAB148/4, TNA.

17. R. Gerald Hughes, *Britain, Germany and the Cold War: The Search for a European Détente, 1949–1967* (London: Routledge, 2007), 155.

18. For Harold Wilson's personalities and his government, see Dockrill, *Britain's Retreat from East of Suez*, 46–49.

19. Christopher Andrew and Vasili Mitrokhin, *The Mitrokhin Archive: The KGB in Europe and the West* (London: Allen Lane, 1999), 528–29. See also, John Young, *The Labour Governments, 1964–1970: International Policy* (Manchester, UK: Manchester University Press, 2003), 14–16.

20. Andrew and Mitrokhin, *The Mitrokhin Archive*, 129.

21. Geraint Hughes, "Giving the Russians a Bloody Nose: Operation Foot and Soviet Espionage in the United Kingdom, 1964–1971," *Cold War History* 6, no. 3 (May 2006): 233.

22. The January 1968 announcement was based on the decision in July 1967 to withdraw from East of Suez by the middle of 1970s. See Dockrill, *Britain's Retreat from East of Suez*, 193–208ff.

23. G. Harrison to Mr. HFT Smith (Head of the Northern Dept.), Foreign Office, 17 January 1968, *DBPO*, 6.

24. Hayman (asst. undersecretary of state) to Harrison, Moscow, NS 3/18, *DBPO*, 26–27.

25. Robert G. Patman, *The Soviet Union in the Horn of Africa: The Diplomacy of Intervention and Disengagement* (Cambridge: Cambridge University Press, 1990), 80–87.

26. Neil S. MacFarlane, "Successes and Failures in Soviet Policy toward Marxist Revolutions in the Third World, 1917–1985," in *The USSR and Marxist Revolutions in the Third World*, ed. Mark N. Katz (New York: Woodrow Wilson International Centre for Scholars, 1990), 35; Odd Arne Westad, "The Fall of Détente and the Turning Tides of History," in *The Fall of Détente: Soviet-American Relations during the Carter Years*, ed. Odd Arne Westad (Oslo: Scandinavian University Press, 1997), 11–19.

27. Lawrence S. Kaplan, *NATO and the United States* (New York: Twayne, 1994), 82–84; Lawrence S. Kaplan, *The Long Entanglement: NATO's First Fifty Years* (Westport, CT: Praeger, 1999), 99–111; Helga Haftendorn, *NATO and the Nuclear Revolution: A Crisis of Credibility, 1966–1967* (Oxford: Clarendon Press Oxford, 1996), 1–11.

28. Christoph Bluth, *Britain, Germany and Western Nuclear Strategy* (Oxford: Clarendon Press Oxford, 1995), 95–104; Saki Dockrill, "Britain's Power and Influence: Dealing with Three Roles and the Wilson Government's Defense Debate at Chequers in November 1964," *Diplomacy & Statecraft* 11, no. 1 (March 2000): 227–34.

29. Frédéric Bozo, *Deux Stratégies pour l'Europe: De Gaulle les États-Unis et L'alliance Atlantique, 1958–1969* (Paris: Plon, 1996), 72–77, 102–32, 133–66; Haftendorn, *NATO*, 13.

30. Simon W. Duke and Wolfgang Krieger, eds., *U.S. Military Forces in Europe: The Early Years, 1945–1970* (Boulder: Westview, 1993); Olaf Mager, *Die Stationierung der britischen Rheinarmee-Großbritanniens EVG-Alternative* (Baden-Baden: Nomos, 1990); Saki Dockrill, "Retreat from the Continent? Britain's Motives for Troop Reductions in West Germany, 1955–1958," *Journal of Strategic Studies* 20, no. 3 (September 1997): 45–70; Saki Dockrill, "No Troops, Please. We Are American—the Diplomacy of Burden Sharing in the case of the Radford Plan, 1956"; Hand-Joachim Harder, *Von Truman bis Harmel: Die Bundesrepublik Deutschland im Spanningsfeld von NATO und europäischer Integration* (Munich: Oldenbourg, 2000), 121–31; Hubert Zimmerman, "The Sour Fruits of Victory: Sterling and Security in Anglo-German Relations during the 1950s and 1960s," *Contemporary European History* 9, no. 2 (2000): 225–43.

31. Kaplan, *Long Entanglement*, 139, 152; Dockrill, *East of Suez*, 165.

32. Sir D. Greenhill (deputy undersecretary of state at Foreign Office) to Gore-Booth, 29 January 1968, Prime Minister's Office minutes, PREM13/2402, TNA; See also Young, *The Labour Governments*, 129.

33. Gerald Brooke (a British citizen) was tried by a Moscow court and was sentenced to one year in prison followed by four further years serving in a labor camp, for "importing bibles" into the USSR. The case was not resolved until 1969 when the Wilson government decided to exchange Brooke with two U.S. intelligence agents who were spying for the Soviet Union and were arrested in the United Kingdom in 1961. See Young, *The Labour Governments*, 129; see also Harrison (Moscow) to H. F. T. Smith, Foreign Office, NS 3/3, 17 January 1968, *DBOP*, 7.

34. Cabinet Defense and Overseas Policy Committee memoranda, OPD (68) 45 "Relations with the Soviet Union and Eastern Europe," 17 June 1968, CAB 148/37, TNA.

35. Ben Fowkes, *The Rise and Fall of Communism in Eastern Europe* (Basingstoke, UK: Macmillan, 1995), 121–22; R. J. Crampton, *Eastern Europe in the Twentieth Century and After* (London: Routledge, 1997), 315–19.

36. Crampton, *Eastern Europe*, 326–40.

37. "Record of the 9th meeting of the Conference of Her Majesty's Representatives in Eastern Europe," 10 May 1968, *DBPO*, 45–48.

38. OPD (68)45, 17 June 1968, CAB 148/37, TNA (see note 34).

39. OPD (68)45, 17 June 1968, CAB 148/37, TNA.

40. McGill, "The Politics of Collective Inaction," 124.

41. Wilfried Loth, "Moscow, Prague and Warsaw: Overcoming the Brezhnev Doctrine," *Cold War History* 1, no. 2 (January 2001): 105–6.

42. Vladislav Zubok, "The Brezhnev Factor in Détente, 1968–1972," in *Cold War and the Policy of Détente: Problems and Discussions*, ed. N. I. Yegorova (Moscow: Russian Academy of Sciences, Institute of Universal History, 2003), 291–92; Andrei Gromyko, *Memories* (London: Hutchinson, 1989), 232–33; Mark Kramer, "Ideology and the Cold War," *Review of International Studies* 25, no. 4 (October 1999): 545.

43. Loth, "Overcoming the Brezhnev Doctrine," 108; Anatolii Dobrynin, *In Confidence: Moscow's Ambassador to America's Six Cold War Presidents* (New York: Random House, 1995), 184.

44. Crampton, *Eastern Europe*, 336, 337–40.

45. Cradock, *Know Your Enemy*, 241, 249.

46. See the editors' (Gill Bennett, Keith Hamilton, et al.) comments, *DBPO*, 65.

47. Young, *Labour Governments*, 14–16.

48. Cradock, *Knowing Your Enemy*, 252.

49. Redacted version of the "Nicoll Report: The JIC and Warning of Aggression in May 2007," in Michael S. Goodman, "The Dog That Didn't Bark: The Joint Intelligence Committee and Warning of Aggression," *Cold War History* 7, no. 4 (November 2007): 537–38; see also Tom Bower, *The Perfect English Spy: Sir Dick White and the Secret War, 1935–1990* (London: Mandarin, 1996), 362–63.

50. Cradock, *Know Your Enemy*, 251; Loth, "Overcoming the Brezhnev Doctrine," 107.

51. Cradock, *Know Your Enemy*, 249.

52. Stewart to Harrison, Moscow (letter), 24 July 1968, *DBOP*, 68.

53. Cradock, *Know Your Enemy*, 252.

54. Young, *Labour Governments*, 133.

55. Cabinet memoranda, CC (68) 38, 22 August 1968, CAB 128/43, TNA; OPD (68)17th mtg., 25 September 1968, CAB 148/35, TNA; Denis Healey, *The Time of My Life* (London: Michael Joseph, 1989), 320; Anthony Howard, ed., *The Crossman Diaries, 1964–1970* (London: Hamish Hamilton & Jonathan Cape, 1979), 466–68; Foreign and Commonwealth Office (FCO) to certain diplomatic missions, tel. 86 guidance, 18 April 1969, PREM 13/2553, TNA.

56. CC (68) 38, 22 August 1968, CAB 128/43, TNA.

57. Howard, *Crossman Diaries*, 467–68.

58. Dobrynin, *In Confidence*, 185.

59. McGill, "The Politics of Collective Inaction," 132.

60. OPD (68) 58, 20 September 1968, CAB 148/38, TNA.

61. OPD (68) 58, 20 September 1968, CAB 148/38, TNA.

62. OPD (68) 58, 20 September 1968, CAB 148/38, TNA.

63. OPD (68) 58, 20 September 1968, CAB 148/38, TNA; see also OPD (68) 63 (Joint memorandum by Michael Stewart and Denis Healey), 28 October 1968, CAB 148/38, TNA.

64. OPD (68)17th mtg., 25 September 1968, CAB 148/35, *NSA*; OPD (68)63, 28 October 1968, CAB 148/38, TNA.

65. Loth, "Moscow, Prague and Warsaw," 108; Odd Arne Westad, introduction in *The Soviet Union in Eastern Europe, 1945–1989,* ed. Odd Arne Westad et al. (Basingstoke, UK: Macmillan, 1994), 5.

66. Raymond L. Garthoff, *Détente and Confrontation: American-Soviet Relations from Nixon to Reagan* (Washington, DC: The Brookings Institution, 1994), 40, 41–57.

67. Young, *Labour Governments,* 135; Hughes, "Giving the Russians a Bloody Nose," 235–36.

68. Geraint Hughes, "British Policy toward Eastern Europe and the Impact of the Prague Spring, 1964–1968," *Cold War History* 4, no. 2 (January 2004): 133–35.

69. OPD (68) 17th meeting, 25 September 1968, CAB 148/35, TNA.

70. OPD (68) 45, 17 June 1968, CAB 148/37, TNA.

71. OPD (69) 8 by Michael Stewart on "The long term prospects for East-West Relations after the Czechoslovakian Crisis," 18 February 1969, CAB 148/91, TNA.

12

Paris and the Prague Spring

Georges-Henri Soutou

The invasion of Czechoslovakia by Warsaw Pact troops on 20 August 1968 spelled the end for de Gaulle's policy of détente, which had been predicated on the Eastern Bloc's increasing de-ideologization and on its growing independence from Moscow. Many observers have come to the conclusion that, in the wake of these events, government circles in Paris vacillated between disappointment and indifference, yet in view of what we know today, historians are less likely to arrive at such a straightforward picture. What did the policy of détente actually mean to Paris? How was the Soviet invasion assessed? What lessons did the French government draw from it? The archives that have now become accessible enable us to piece together a picture that is both telling and complex. The leading government circles saw the August crisis as proof rather than a refutation of their previously held views, even if this was not in keeping with the majority view at the time.

DE GAULLE'S *OSTPOLITIK* AND HIS POLICY TOWARD GERMANY PRIOR TO THE CZECHOSLOVAK CRISIS

From 1964 to 1965, Paris was engaged in developing a genuine political dialogue with Moscow. The driving forces were, on the one hand, disappointment with the Federal Republic of Germany (FRG) arising from the inefficacy of the Elysée Treaty of 1963 and, on the other, a fear that rapprochement between Washington and Bonn might go too far and enable the FRG to take part in the decision-making process concerning nuclear armament.[1] Furthermore, there was the will to build a counterweight together

271

with the Soviet Union to the FRG in Europe and, on a global scale, to the United States.[2]

Because of the split between Beijing and Moscow (which became obvious in 1964 and was beyond repair) and the resulting weakening of the global standing of the Soviet Union, Charles de Gaulle came to the conclusion that the time was now ripe for his great plan. He considered the de-ideologization of Eastern Europe and a rebirth of independent nations free from Soviet tutelage a genuine possibility. There was in Paris in 1964 the perception that such a development was already discernible.[3] It would, therefore, soon be possible for France, once the so-called Yalta gap had been addressed, to pursue a new European policy. The first objective of this political realignment was to be a solution of the German question within a European security framework led by Moscow and Paris. At the same time, on the strength of interstate cooperation within the European Economic Community, France would become Western Europe's leading power and would ensure a balance of power vis-à-vis the Soviet Union.[4]

In this overall concept of a new European security system, the German question played a key role in de Gaulle's eyes, albeit not without a certain ambiguity. On 18 May 1968, he told Nicolae Ceauşescu that the German two-state solution was "temporary and artificial" and that there was only "one German people."[5] However, this statement did not entail a demand for reunification.

During his visit to the Soviet Union in June 1966, de Gaulle told the Soviet party leader Leonid Brezhnev that he was "neither very keen" on German reunification, nor in any great hurry. In any case, Germany would have to offer security guarantees, which meant above all foregoing the possession of atomic, biological, and chemical (ABC) weapons and accepting the borders of 1945.[6]

De Gaulle had presumably other forms of rapprochement and/or collaboration between the two German states in mind. In December 1967, an article in *Foreign Politics* (*Politique étrangère*) caused a stir with its analysis of potentional European security systems. Entitled "European Security Models" ("*Modèles de sécurité européenne*") and listing its authors simply as a "research group," the article was, in fact, based on a study by the Franco-German Research Committee (*Comité d'études et de recherches franco-allemand* or CERFA),[7] which was run in close collaboration with the Elysée as well as with West German experts.[8] The authors did not envisage reunification for Germany; they preferred the model of the German Union (*Deutscher Bund*) of 1815: "Over more than 50 years this Union safeguarded [Germany's] internal stability and a European balance of power." The article described a potential variant of such a union, which would have included the creation of joint agencies headquartered in Berlin, in which the two German states would be represented on equal terms; both the Bundeswehr and the *Volksarmee* were to be preserved if only in a reduced form and linked to one another through a liaison staff. In this way, a European security system guaranteed by the United States, the Soviet Union, Great Britain, and France might be a way of overcoming Europe's division by reversing the division of Germany within that pan-European security system.

As late as May 1968, de Gaulle still believed that the FRG would prove amenable to the realization of this overall concept. He told Ceauşescu on 18 May he wanted to encourage Bonn to enter into negotiations with Eastern European countries, including the Czechoslovak Socialist Republic (ČSSR). His relationship with the West German foreign minister Willy Brandt was sufficiently good to warrant such ideas.[9] The new European security system whose creation the general had in mind would be taking shape, if necessary, without the involvement of the United States, which tallied well in principle with Soviet intentions.[10] The salient point here was that Paris and Moscow would have assumed a dominant position in Europe with Germany under their control. The continuity of de Gaulle's policy from his journey to Moscow in 1944 to the Franco-Soviet Treaty and the years 1966/1968 has quite rightly been remarked on repeatedly.[11]

THE PRAGUE SPRING IN THE REPORTS OF THE FRENCH EMBASSIES IN PRAGUE, MOSCOW, AND WARSAW

The reports coming from the French embassy in Prague during Czechoslovakia's invasion by the Warsaw Pact states were extremely patchy. The embassy had next to no contacts in the population. There were rather pathetic predictions of an early end to Alexander Dubček's "moral resistance."[12] The embassy in Prague discounted the possibility of a long-term determination on the part of the people to resist the occupation. In psychological and historical terms this was portrayed as proof of the Czechs' putative pliability that had been in evidence since 1938—an attempt, one might say, to get rid of France's co-responsibility for the Munich Agreement of 1938. According to this interpretation, the Soviet invasion was not based on ideological but on geostrategic reasoning. The long-term strategic goal, in the words of Ambassador Roger M. Lalouette on 17 September, was the advance to the Mediterranean and the annexation of Czechoslovakia by the USSR.[13] His report was given the derisive nickname "the Anschluss telegram" at the Quai d'Orsay. Robert Morisset, active as an embassy inspector at the time and formerly accredited himself at the Prague embassy at the end of the 1950s, made a trip to Prague in September on a tour of inspection of the embassy and its activities.

The first thing he noted was that the embassy had failed to cultivate contacts with the population. He himself talked to ordinary citizens and to intellectuals; in doing so he noticed how deeply rooted in people's minds was the tendency to advocate liberation, at least as a theoretical possibility.[14]

The French embassy in Moscow was more accurate in its assessment of the situation. It was headed by two outstanding personalities: Ambassador Olivier Wormser and Minister Henri Froment-Meurice. The two nurtured no illusions regarding a so-called liberalization of the Soviet Union, nor did they entirely toe the line of de Gaulle's foreign policy.[15] They were well aware of the difficulties Moscow was up against: on 21 August 1968, their analysis of TASS's announcement of "fraternal assistance" had already led them to the conclusion that the Soviet government was not going to mount a serious attempt to justify its decision by citing an "invitation" issued by the Czechoslovak government or the party leadership.[16] On 23 August, they mentioned in a telegram on the occasion of an international scientific meeting in Moscow the openly displayed despair of the Soviet intelligentsia.[17] The conclusion they expressed in an internal telegram on 27 August was a very cautious one: Moscow's reactions were defensive and hesitant; the invasion had been carried out to silence internal criticism which was aimed at the leadership's lack of response to developments in Czechoslovakia. On 5 September, they registered their disagreement with a view that was repeatedly voiced in the West, namely that the USSR was entering into a new expansionist phase. In the view of the two French diplomats, Soviet policies were generally defensive in character also vis-à-vis Bucharest or Belgrade.[18] The Kremlin, as they saw it, was above all concerned with defending its *cordon sanitaire* in Eastern Europe. It was also unacceptable for Moscow that reforms should progress more quickly in Eastern Europe than in the USSR itself.

On 14 September, the French embassy noted in its internal communications that Moscow was attempting to shift responsibility for the Czechoslovak crisis to Bonn, which constituted a crucial change in the overall assessment and had far reaching effects on Paris, as will be shown below. The significance of the Brezhnev Doctrine of "limited sovereignty" within the "socialist camp" was fully understood from the beginning both at the Moscow and the Warsaw embassies, which reported extensively on the matter and on the basis of reliable information.[19] The message of the events was clear for most diplomats and observers: de Gaulle's notion of a de-ideologization within the Eastern Bloc and the rebirth of the nations was either mistaken or premature at the very least.[20]

THE QUAI D'ORSAY'S ASSESSMENT OF THE SITUATION

The assessment of the situation by the Quai d'Orsay coincided largely with that of the Moscow embassy and was, on the whole, correct. Already on 11 July 1968, the Eastern Europe Department had concluded that after the hardening of Moscow's attitude at the beginning of July an invasion could no longer be excluded, even if grave consequences should be attached to it. Moscow would not tolerate liberalization in Czechoslovakia, even with the proviso that the country would remain inside the Communist fold and a member of the Warsaw Pact, for this would be too dangerous for the maintenance of the status quo in the USSR itself.[21] After the invasion, the fact that liberalization in Eastern Europe had been stopped for good was used to justify the invasion. The USSR had given precedence to shoring up its sphere of influence in Eastern Europe at the expense of East-West détente and had been motivated to adopt this course of action by the fear of escalating reform pressure within the USSR itself. This development spelled the end of the optimism that had been prevalent above all between 1964 and 1966 at the Quai d'Orsay as to the reformability of the Soviet system.[22] It should also be noted that no one at the Foreign Ministry thought the FRG was to blame for developments in the ČSSR.[23] This charge was first formulated by the ambassador in Bonn, François Seydoux, and was taken up above all by the top representatives of the state and by leaders of the Gaullist Party. Those diplomats who had studied the Soviet Union and the Communist system most closely concluded that a liberation of Eastern Europe was impossible at the time (the Prague Spring was perceived by hardly anyone as a harbinger of things to come); the politics of détente played a subordinated role for Moscow, and the Kremlin evinced no interest in the security model for Europe favored by France, which had Germany's neutralization at its center. Instead, it concentrated on maintaining the ideological and power political status quo in Eastern Europe.

PUBLIC REACTIONS OF THE FRENCH GOVERNMENT

The French government condemned the invasion immediately and unequivocally, demanded the prompt withdrawal of troops, and restated its aversion to "bloc" politics.[24] Paris equated the invasion of Czechoslovakia with the landing of U.S. troops in the Dominican Republic in 1965.[25] The example of the ČSSR was viewed in Paris as a corroboration of the French policy which was aimed at reducing the role of the two hegemonic powers and/or blocs.

This policy was also considered the only possible solution for Europe on a larger scale. It was, therefore, only logical for Paris to assert that France intended to pursue its policy of "détente, understanding and cooperation" with regard to the East as far as possible. Outwardly, Paris demonstrated restraint as to possible consequences of the invasion. Before the Foreign Policy Committee of the National Assembly, Foreign Minister Michel Debré referred to the invasion as "a traffic accident on the road to détente," which caused a certain amount of consternation.[26]

De Gaulle saw his views vindicated. He emphasized in a press conference on 9 September 1968 "Soviet hegemony" and praised the Czechoslovaks' resistance and the courage they had shown in confronting the occupiers. Embodying "the character of Europe," they were also living proof how sound the foundations were on which French policy was based.

Vehement public criticism of the FRG came from Michel Debré because the FRG refused to accept its Eastern frontiers and was trying to expand eastward economically. It now became apparent that Paris was attempting to blame the crisis in Europe on the FRG. Once the Soviet-Czechoslovak treaty of 15 October 1968 on the stationing of Soviet troops in the ČSSR had been signed, France stopped pressing for a withdrawal of Warsaw Pact troops in their meetings with Soviet diplomats. By December 1968, this U-turn in French policy had become impossible to overlook. From January 1969, it was business as usual in this respect in Paris, and the crisis was noticeably downgraded. The weightiest argument that remained and was repeatedly formulated in the public debate was that the invasion had vindicated the French policy of détente as the only possible option.

THE FRENCH GOVERNMENT'S INTERNAL INTERPRETATION

In its internal assessment, the French government showed great restraint and caution. A circular note to the embassies of 31 August contained the following guidelines: there would be no change in economic and cultural matters in France's attitude toward the countries of the Eastern Bloc; politically a "certain temporary distance" was to be observed.[27] In a number of meetings with representatives of other countries on 10 and 12 October, 15 November, and notably with U.S. representatives 19 November, leading French politicians asserted that the Soviet Union's stance was a purely defensive one, which was exclusively oriented to preserving the status quo and that the fear of more of the same (directed against Yugoslavia or Romania) was almost certainly unfounded.[28]

In de Gaulle's view, the crisis had no bearing on France whatever. On 3 December, he told the French ambassador in Moscow, Wormser, "What we have here is a communist family quarrel. Under these circumstances, dear Ambassador, you will understand that I don't care a fig about Czechoslovakia" ("*La Tchécoslovaquie, dans ces conditions, je m'en bats l'oeil*").[29] The meaning of this statement, couched in the humoristic musketeer language characteristic of de Gaulle, and expressed as an answer to Wormser's discreetly diverging views, was obvious: the invasion did not call the overall plan of French foreign policy into question. The time for this plan was simply not yet ripe because there were no serious liberalizing tendencies discernible in Prague, nor a genuine striving for national independence and de-ideologization.

In de Gaulle's view, it was not Prague that spelled danger for détente, but Vietnam and the Middle East, by which, of course, he alluded to U.S. foreign policy.[30] With reference to Germany, he now thought—as opposed to earlier statements—that the country had to remain divided under all circumstances and that it must not be allowed to form any kind of political alliance either because this would spark a war with the Soviet Union.[31] The real cause of the crisis and the purpose of the invasion, as the French president saw it, lay in the Soviet Union's resolution to intimidate the FRG, which would ensure its back was covered for the confrontation with China. De Gaulle saw no reason for a change of strategy, nor did he seek a rapprochement with the United States and/or the North Atlantic Treaty Organization; he continued to stand by the strategy of nuclear deterrence, which was predicated on decisions taken in 1967 and tallied with the premises of his foreign policy.[32]

THE SALIENT POINT: THE GERMAN QUESTION

The Prague crisis highlighted a central tenet of French politics according to which the greatest source of danger for peace was not the Soviet Union, but Germany. This is evidenced notably by the fact that both internal meetings of the leading political circles and talks with foreign diplomats and politicians in the weeks before and after the invasion were dominated by references to World War II. All the charges against Bonn that had accumulated since the beginning of the 1960s were again stated and widened in scope: the FRG had not observed due care in its dealings with Prague;[33] it was not prepared to recognize the Oder-Neisse border; it was nursing ambitions to obtain nuclear armaments, and after the project of the Multilateral Force had been abandoned,[34] Bonn had consistently tried to introduce a "European clause" into the Nuclear Nonproliferation Treaty in order to keep open the back door for the Bundeswehr being given nuclear potential.[35]

The great currency crisis of 1968—the FRG stubbornly resisted the appreciation of the *Deutschmark* and, consequently, a depreciation of the French *Franc* appeared imminent, which was unacceptable to de Gaulle for reasons of national prestige—led to relations between the two countries coming under serious strain. The *Bild-Zeitung*'s notorious banner headline—"Again Number One" (*"Wieder Nummer Eins!"*)—was by no means helpful. In the margin of a report about a derogatory remark made by the German ambassador in Paris, Foreign Minister Debré made the note on 21 November: "Germans will be Germans" (*"Les Allemands seront toujours les Allemands"*).[36] Great political significance attached to the currency crisis. The French public got the impression that Germany was trying to throw its economic weight around on the political stage. Debré was very reserved in all his dealings with Germany. During the crisis, he was torn between two contradictory fears. On the one hand, he felt that the FRG's attitude vis-à-vis the Soviet Union was incautious and provocative; on the other, he feared Central Europe would be carved up on the sly between Bonn and Moscow.[37] De Gaulle, whose foreign policy included a rapprochement with the FRG and reconciliation with Germany as cornerstones, appeared disillusioned and pessimistic. On 27 September, he told Federal Chancellor Kurt Georg Kiesinger in a tense conversation that the invasion of Czechoslovakia had its causes in the policies of the FRG. The Germans would be well advised, according to de Gaulle, to adopt a "very humble" attitude toward the East, in particular with regard to the border question, to its economic policy, and also in its relations with the German Democratic Republic (GDR).[38]

RELATIONS TO THE SOVIET UNION: TURNING OVER A NEW LEAF TO BRING ABOUT RAPPROCHEMENT AND THE FORMATION OF A STRATEGIC COUNTERWEIGHT

As had already been repeatedly the case in the Fifth Republic, Moscow was the most important partner for Paris with regard to its German policy. On 24 August 1968, the Quai d'Orsay's secretary-general, Hervé Alphand, told the Soviet ambassador in Paris, Valeriyan Zorin, that Paris condemned the invasion and demanded the withdrawal of troops from Czechoslovak territory.[39] One week later, on 2 September, Debré told Zorin that even though France demanded a withdrawal of troops, Soviet-French cooperation was the only policy capable of putting an end to "German militarism."[40] His Soviet counterpart, Andrei Gromyko, received assurances from Debré on 5 October that Paris was intent on continuing the policy of détente.[41]

Initially, de Gaulle's diction in his dealings with the Soviets was more forceful than that of Debré. He told Ambassador Zorin as late as 19 November that the policy of détente was now in danger and that the cause was not Germany, but the Soviet Union. Nevertheless, Paris wished to return to the policy of détente and was ready for talks on Vietnam and the Middle East, but not on Europe. De Gaulle, however, agreed to continue bilateral negotiations.[42]

However, the overall situation was about to change dramatically very shortly. Between 21 and 24 November, the currency crisis and the resulting tug-of-war between Paris and Bonn reached their climax; de Gaulle unexpectedly came down against the depreciation of the Franc, which the government was preparing to adopt. On 28 November, Zorin, speaking on behalf of Soviet Premier Aleksei Kosygin, offered France assistance in dealing with the currency crisis; Kirilin, the head of the Soviet delegation in the Great Committee, the body dealing with Soviet-French economic cooperation, would shortly be dispatched to Paris. Deals worth billions of Francs to the French economy were on the horizon.

De Gaulle welcomed Kirilin's prompt visit and the fact that the session of the committee was moved forward; it had actually been scheduled to take place several months later.[43] The Great Committee was convened in Paris in January 1969 and decided to intensify trade relations between the two countries. At the meeting, Debré told Kirilin with his eye on Germany: "Let's hope Moscow and Paris will never forget the lessons that history and geography can teach us and let's hope they will always assist one another. Peace in Europe depends on it."[44]

SUMMARY

De Gaulle and Foreign Minister Debré both undoubtedly responded with regret to the fact that Soviet hegemony continued and became even more deeply entrenched in Eastern Europe. De Gaulle, however, remained faithful to his perspective of bilateral détente between Moscow and Paris and even felt vindicated by the crisis, for "bloc politics" was incompatible in his eyes with a new order in Europe. Yet the crisis did affect his policy of détente in that it shifted the focus of his attention from ideology, that is, from the de-ideologization of the Eastern Bloc, to power aspects. It was no longer the national rebirth of the Eastern European countries and the decline of communism that served as key concepts, but a play of balance and counterweights. The policy of détente was continued, and the liberation of Eastern Europe was downplayed. With reference to Germany there was an unmistakable hardening in de Gaulle's attitude. Earlier on, his views on reunification were, if ambiguous, at least not negative in principle. Now Paris rejected this possibility out of hand. The crisis had laid bare the latent animosities and misgivings that Paris harbored against Bonn.

As for the future of Czechoslovakia, de Gaulle on occasion took an optimistic view (as at a press conference in September), on other occasions also a pessimistic one (as vis-à-vis Ambassador Wormser). A view that interpreted the Prague Spring as a harbinger of things to come (also regarding a potential transformation within the Communist system) was not in evidence. The only way of overcoming communism, according to de Gaulle, was the resuscitation of a national consciousness. Seen from Paris, there was no third way: there was either communism or the traditional national consciousness. This is the real meaning of de Gaulle's "je m'en bats l'oeil" ("I couldn't care less"). The opportunity of understanding the developments of 1968 as a point of departure for later transformation in the East that transcended the old demarcation lines went unclaimed.[45]

NOTES

Translated from German into English by Otmar Binder, Vienna.

1. On 22 January 1963, Federal Chancellor Konrad Adenauer and President Charles de Gaulle signed a treaty on Franco-German cooperation at the Elysée Palace.

2. AN, 5AG3/858, historical introduction to the notes of the director of the European Department, Jacques Andréani, 2 February 1979.

3. Georges-Henri Soutou, "De Gaulle's France and the Soviet Union from Conflict to Détente," in *Europe, Cold War, and Coexistence, 1953–1965*, ed. Wilfried Loth (London: Frank Cass, 2003), 173–89.

4. Georges-Henri Soutou, *L'Alliance incertaine: Les rapports politico-stratégiques franco-allemands 1954–1996* (Paris: Fayard, 1996), 281–82; Georges-Henri Soutou, "La France et la défense européenne du traité de l'Elysée au retrait de l'OTAN 1963–1966," in *Crises and Compromises: The European Project, 1963–1969*, ed. Wilfried Loth (Brussels: Bruylant, 2001).

5. MAE, *Secrétariat général*, vol. 34.

6. Private holdings, minutes of the meeting of de Gaulle and Brezhnev in June 1966.

7. CERFA was founded on the basis of an intergovernmental agreement in 1954 as a platform for political-scientific exchange between Paris and Bonn.

8. For the genesis of this article, see Walter Schütze, "Vingt deux ans après: Un concept français pour un règlement panallemand dans le cadre européen," *Politique étrangère* 3 (1989).

9. Maurice Vaïsse, "De Gaulle et Willy Brandt: Deux non-conformistes au pouvoir," in *Willy Brandt und Frankreich*, ed. Horst Möller and Maurice Vaïsse (Munich: R. Oldenbourg, 2005).

10. MAE, Secrétariat général, vol. 34. Minutes of the meeting with Brezhnev in June 1966 and of the meeting between the head of the Political Department, Beaumarchais, with his Soviet counterpart, Oberenko, on plans concerning a European security conference with the United States, 15 May 1968.

11. Pierre Maillard, *De Gaulle et l'Allemagne* (Paris: Plon, 1990), 241, 247–52.

12. MAE, Europe 1960–1970, Tchécoslovaquie, vol. 243, report of 16 October 1968.

13. MAE, Tchécoslovaquie, vol. 243.

14. Private holdings, letter written by Morisset to Jean-Marie Soutou (then inspector general of embassies), 20 September 1968.

15. Olivier Wormser, "L'occupation de la Tchécoslovaquie vue de Moscou," *Revue des Deux Mondes* (June/July 1978): 590–605, 30–45; Henri Froment-Meurice, *Vu du Quai: Mémoires, 1945–1983* (Paris: Fayard, 1998).

16. MAE, Tchécoslovaquie, vol. 245.

17. MAE, Tchécoslovaquie, vol. 245, telegram of 23 August 1968.

18. MAE, Tchécoslovaquie, vol. 245, telegram of 23 August 1968.

19. MAE, Tchécoslovaquie, vol. 245, report from Moscow, 23 August 1968; MAE, Tchécoslovaquie, vol. 245, report from Warsaw, 25 August 1968.

20. Raymond Aron, "D'un coup de Praguee à l'autre," *Le Figaro* 2 October 1968, reprinted in Raymond Aron, *Les articles de politique internationale dans Le Figaro de 1947*

à *1977*, vol. 3, *Les Crises février 1965 à avril 1977: Présentation et notes par Georges-Henri Soutou* (Paris: Éditions de Fallois,1997), 561–64.

21. MAE, Tchécoslovaquie, vol. 244.

22. Soutou, "De Gaulle's France."

23. De Gaulle mentioned this in a meeting with Federal Chancellor Kiesinger. Debré shared his opinion; Prime Minister Maurice Couve de Murville did not.

24. MAE, Tchécoslovaquie, vol. 315.

25. See the statements de Gaulle made at a press conference on 9 September 1968; Charles de Gaulle, *Discours et Messages* 5, 1966–1969 (Paris: Plon, 1970), 332–33; for details, see the article by Günther Bischof, "'No Action': The Johnson Administration's Response to the Czech Crisis of 1968," in this volume.

26. Michel Debré, *Gouverner autrement: Mémoires 1962–1970* (Paris: Albin Michel, 1993), 259.

27. MAE, Tchécoslovaquie, vol. 242.

28. MAE, Secrétariat général, vol. 35.

29. Wormser, "L'occupation de la Tchécoslovaquie vue de Moscou," 45.

30. See his letter to President Johnson, 3 January 1969, in Charles de Gaulle, *Lettres, Notes et Carnets, Juillet 1966–Avril 1969* (Paris: Plon, 1987), 273.

31. MAE, Secrétariat général, vol. 35, de Gaulle's conversations with Senator Scranton, 20 September 1968, and with U.S. ambassador Robert Sargent Shriver Jr., the brother-in-law of the assassinated John F. Kennedy, 23 September 1968.

32. Georges-Henri Soutou, "La menace stratégique sur la France à l'ère nucléaire: Les instructions personnelles et secrètes de 1967 et 1974," *Revue Historique des Armées* 236 (2004); de Gaulle's speech at the Institut des Hautes Etudes de Défense nationale, 25 January 1969 in De Gaulle, *Lettres, Notes et Carnets*, 284.

33. This is also the gist of Debré's no-compromise speech before the UN General Assembly on 7 October 1968. MAE, Tchécoslovaquie, vol. 245.

34. The MLF was a proposal floated by the United States dating back to 1963, which provided for a fleet consisting of U.S. submarines and twenty-five NATO country warships equipped with multiple nuclear-armed Polaris ballistic missiles (with a range of 4,500 km). The rockets and warheads were to form the joint property of the NATO countries involved. The fleet would have operated under NATO command. This was supposed to give the nonnuclear members of the alliance, which included Germany, access to and control of a nuclear strike capability. After lengthy discussions within NATO, the proposal was abandoned because no countries except the FRG and the United States were prepared to make substantial contributions to its finances.

35. MAE, Secrétariat général, vol. 35, meeting between Debré and Rusk, 4 October 1968.

36. MAE, Secrétariat général, vol. 34.

37. Debré, *Mémoires*, 257–58.

38. MAE, Secrétariat général, vol. 34.

39. MAE, Secrétariat général, vol. 245.

40. MAE, Secrétariat général, vol. 244.

41. MAE, Secrétariat général, vol. 35.

42. MAE, Secrétariat général, vol. 35.

43. MAE, Secrétariat général, vol. 35.

44. Debré, *Mémoires*, 261.

45. At the Quai d'Orsay, Robert Morisset appears, in his letter to Jean-Marie Soutou quoted above, to have been the only one who believed that such a development was possible.

13

France, Italy, the Western Communists, and the Prague Spring

Alessandro Brogi

Most Western European Communists loved Marilyn Monroe. They especially loved her dead, for they valued all her tragic contradictions. Her life, the leading Italian Communist review *Rinascita* commented after her death, "was enlightened by her efforts to be accepted for what she was, and not as a product of a consumerist society." The actress represented the fundamental contradiction of a "society that knows how to unleash the vitality of its components only to engage them in a violent struggle which leads to its own destruction." Monroe epitomized the isolation and sense of alienation that Paul Goodman detected in a society in which "human nature could not fully develop or even exist." For the French Communist critics, Marilyn the icon was also the iconoclast. There was a beautiful inconsistency in her sexual rebellion against a puritanical and conformist society because it made eroticism familiar and spontaneous for every conformist as well. But her "spontaneous defiance" finally "devoured her." Such comments did not go without resistance within the French and Italian Communist parties (*Parti communiste français* or PCF and *Partito Comunista Italiano* or PCI, respectively), and there was an intense polemic between new and old intellectuals, new and old guard within each party, with the older generation being accused of "intellectual snobbery" toward the cultural ferment in the United States.[1]

Undoubtedly, the Western Communists, while always irredeemably anti–United States from an ideological standpoint, also nurtured ambivalence toward the pluralism of U.S. society. This ambivalence was particularly heightened in the immediate post–World War II period and in the 1960s. The centrality of themes of dissent and the intellectual magnetism for the European Left of characters such as Walt Whitman, Ernest Hemingway, William Faulkner, Jack Kerouac, Bob Dylan, or even contradictory ones such as Marilyn Monroe or James Dean, informed the cultural and political debate among French and Italian Communists, even as they, and particularly *when* they, confronted themselves with the emerging dissent or antiestablishment developments in Eastern Europe. It is on the intersection between their adaptation to neocapitalism and their continued temptation to rebel against the establishment, whether in the West or the East, that this chapter focuses. The Prague events, together with the student movement, intensified both the French and Italian Communist parties' dilemma about how best to overcome the Cold War policy *and* politics of the two blocs that constrained their power: to what extent could they reconcile their effort to become accepted by the establishment with their eagerness for renewal on the Left which embraced rebellion both at home and elsewhere directed toward international socialism? Ultimately this dilemma, if not their whole Cold War experience, was determined more by their cultural and political confrontation with the West than by their issues of allegiance with the East.

BRAVE NEW WORLDS

According to negative *topoi* fully formed by the 1920s, modern capitalism, in its managerial, "Americanized" form, subsumed a mechanized world immersed in materialism, consumerism, and mass culture, all together projecting the worst visions of a homogeneous, conformist, spiritually and intellectually hollow society.[2] Italian and French Communists, while echoing and amplifying those fears, also portrayed the Soviet model of modernization as the alternative, serving instead of enslaving humanity.

But idealism also meant discerning what *both* "young countries," the United States and the Soviet Union, could offer to those whose expression had long been repressed (under Fascist Italy) or stifled (in both France and Italy during the interwar period). From the 1920s onward, that offer consisted of the two emerging superpowers' nature as dynamic masters of technology, architects of a brave new world distinguished from stagnant, decadent Western Europe.[3] That was how PCI founder Antonio Gramsci first analyzed the United States in his essays on Fordism and Americanism: as the place of the most advanced technological *and* societal experimentation.[4]

Youthfulness and informality were also the main strengths of American literature, a powerful response to the elitist, rigid academic nature of Europe's bourgeois culture. In the words of intellectual and novelist Italo Calvino, to many Western European Communists until the late 1940s,

Hemingway was "a sort of God," and jazz was a "banner of untamed cosmopolitanism."[5] Traveling to the United States in 1946, French Communist author Claude Roy became captivated by the America *on the road*, where "the individual himself becomes the road," and where "the road can become a drug, flavorless like *marihuana*." America, he added, was a genuine "rebellion of the spirit," a land of "infinite possibilities." These possibilities could go either way, for America's "pride [was] sometimes tragic and menacing," and "sometimes attractive."[6] For Italian writer Cesare Pavese, America was "an immense theater where our common drama was played out with greater frankness than elsewhere." Party leader Pietro Ingrao remembered that in the 1930s the American novel "gave us the image of a society where contradictions openly erupted."[7] All these observations displayed far more than fascination with the enemy. They also reflected Communist hopes that the radical, experimental America would prevail over the conservative, philistine, imperialist United States. They were hoping that this vibrant and youthful America would somehow rub off on themselves, too.

The ensuing condemnation of the United States by these same intellectuals was just as revealing. Having nurtured hopes about democratic America, they felt betrayed by the Cold War United States, above all because the "New World" had ceased to be new. Instead of helping to bring liberation to Europe, it imitated and allied itself with Europe's most conservative, stifling political and cultural elements. Pavese best expressed this disillusion: Americans had turned bad only in part because, in their Cold War retrenchment, they now appeared closer to traditionalist American values; actually, their main fault was that they had "undergone a process of spiritual Europeanization," losing "a large part of the exotic and tragic directness that was their essence."[8] Thus disenchanted, French and Italian intellectuals were just waiting, if not wishing, to be proven wrong. The United States could, perhaps, again help them spearhead their war against philistine provincialism. Dismissive as leftist thinkers might be in their condemnation of U.S. politics and society, their set of attitudes, especially their reconciliation of subjectivity and social commitment, was bound to make connections with radical thought in the United States, starting from the late 1950s and culminating in the late 1960s. The result would deeply affect the French and Italian Communist parties.

In part, the two superpowers were presumed to "deprovincialize" Europe. What a dream it would be if in the East, too, the contradictions of the human condition were fully displayed, but with the basic difference that, in the East, the oppressed would both express and overcome those contradictions! It would have made the Soviet Union look more human than utopian—utopian with all the meaning of the word, including the dangers associated with being a "brave new world" above human condition. Even before the 20th Congress of the Communist Party of the Soviet

Union (*Kommunisticheskaya Partiya Sovetskogo Soyuza* or CPSU) and Nikita Khrushchev's denunciation of Stalinism, members of the PCF and PCI already nurtured the illusion that the Soviet Union was well on its way to perfecting its social and cultural experience through *constant* debate and *open* exchange of ideas. The PCI's Cultural Commission, in its report of November 1953, noticed that while debates on ideology and culture were stalling in the Italian Left, lacking "enough self-criticism," in the "country where Marxist-Leninist theory has been tempered by thirty years of experience . . . our comrades liberally and animatedly discuss everything." On the other hand, the United States, in the throes of McCarthyism, was rapidly "decaying toward authoritarianism." Indeed, "having ended the common struggle against fascism," the head of the Cultural Commission, Carlo Salinari, observed, "that is, without the progressive thought embodied in some of its traditions, America, no matter how many skyscrapers, and automobiles, and military [technologies] it produces, will no longer be the vanguard of mass culture. Without its struggle for progress, it will in fact risk surrendering to fascism, even in the name of its best traditions."[9] By 1956, while through de-Stalinization the Soviet leadership was "admitting its own mistakes," in Italy the Communists had seen no reprieve from McCarthyism, still represented there by the obstreperous U.S. ambassador, Clare Boothe Luce.[10]

By the early 1960s, the effects of the "economic miracles" in both countries and the first Marxist analyses of the resilience of neocapitalism somewhat mitigated the Western Communist image of an imperialist and irreparably declining United States. Among French and Italian workers, the prospect of individual, not collective, improvement was now captivating. The working class—and even Communist activists in both countries—craved higher individual living standards. Lotteries were becoming the "new opium of the poor." Small Fiat or Deux Chevaux Citröen cars, or even the Lambretta scooters may have been poor matches to what U.S. workers could afford, yet even at those modest levels, they were luxuries worth many months of the average Italian or French worker's paycheck. Nevertheless, their number rose by the millions. Films and television celebrated this newfound freedom and way of life. The PCI's Giorgio Amendola, who distinguished himself for his economic expertise and political moderation, and Luciano Romagnoli, who directed the party's propaganda section, were among the first to recognize that "higher standards of living" were "genuine developments toward a more democratic society"; they also felt more compelled than ever to rouse the "workers' class conscience." The party, as Enrico Berlinguer exhorted, would not allow "American ideology" and "modernity" to weaken "the sort of political and moral tension, the sort of human spirit without which there cannot be revolutionary action."[11]

For the PCF, it was easier to find a culprit outside the mechanisms of neo-capitalism: Gaullist charisma. The party's political bureau recognized that the "grand illusions [of welfare inspired by the president] are the greatest obstacle against the unity of the working class." The PCF's persistent *ouvriérisme* not only alienated potential new social strata; it also weakened the very counter-cultural society the party was striving to maintain among workers, for, indeed, sectors of increasingly affluent workers did not resist the lure of consumerism. As it has been widely recognized, "the traditional, closed world of the worker, which reinforced an identification with the PCF . . . slowly dissolved." The new urban landscape, with its anonymous high-rises, privileging "family, personal space, and 'modern' communications (principally television)—in a word 'individualism'—usurped the place of the locality and the party." As in the United States, people gradually began to shed their workers' identity, aspiring to a middle class status and comforts.[12]

A persistent anti-U.S. prejudice was matched by a renewed faith in Soviet progress, nurtured by the dream of plenty revived by Khrushchev. In the late 1950s, the Soviet leader launched the slogan "'catch up and surpass America' as the cornerstone of the construction of communism over the next twenty years." His predecessors had never allowed communism to be judged other than through its own criteria. Now the peoples of the Soviet Union and Eastern Europe began to compare their standards of living with those of the Americans.[13] Did Khrushchev's revolutionary romanticism affect the French and Italian Communists? Maybe not on nuclear issues, given the two parties' continued reliance on pacifism to extend their popular appeal, but on the competition with capitalism, most evidence shows that it did. The press from both parties kept repeating like a mantra that, as Pierre Lefranc put it, "we are approaching the moment of truth, when the first Socialist country is going to catch up and overtake the first capitalist country." New discoveries in the field of automation also revived the contrast between the job-killing machines in the capitalist West versus technology placed at the workers' service in the Soviet dreamland. In a system not subordinate to the law of profit, the two parties' economic experts argued, unemployment was virtually impossible, and automated factories brought material *and* cultural improvement to the masses. Soviet workers benefited from higher productivity, growing salaries, and opportunities in technical education. Even the Vatican's 1961 encyclical *Mater et Magistra*, calling for greater social welfare and deploring the arms race and economic disparities among nations, had mainly one significance for both parties: it was a serendipitous admission of capitalism's shortcomings and an implied concession to the superiority of the Soviet system.[14]

By the end of the decade, socialism with a human face at first appeared to be the true fulfillment of the Gramscian dream of cultural hegemony, of the organic intellectual truly undistinguished from the forces of the proletariat, truly bringing about the classless society. It could also be a special validation of the intellectual correctness of the Italian vision of socialism, not just the Italian path to socialism. So admission of failure in the Soviet camp, in this vision, would actually restore the credibility of Western communism and its mixture of parliamentary and insurrectionary tactics.

But both the French and Italian Communist parties miscalculated not only on the Soviet side, thinking that socialism could be reformed from above, but also on the side of protest at home, failing to comprehend the antiestablishment spirit from below. At the time of the events in Hungary in 1956, PCF and PCI leaders had come across as defenders of authoritarianism. In 1968, they simply looked old, a group quickly aging, in every sense, just like Charles de Gaulle or the old guard Christian Democrats. Youthful rebels and the new extraparliamentarian Left saw the PCF as a bureaucratized apparatus that compromised with the Soviet Union, which, in turn, had compromised with de Gaulle; in the case of the PCI, its own left wing disconcerted the new rebels once it began its slow approach to Catholic groups, though not the Catholic establishment.

THE PCF, PCI, AND THE SOVIET SCRIPT

Significant differences divided the two parties, and they have been amply examined and reassessed. For the sake of brevity, the most significant difference is summarized in historian Marc Lazar's quip that the more thoroughly Bolshevized PCF followed the Soviet script in *allegro vivace* whereas the PCI did it in *allegro moderato*.[15] Although recent research has revealed that the Italian Communists maintained as strong an intimacy with Moscow as their French comrades, at least until 1956, it remains indisputable that the PCI's reference to Stalin was less obsessive than that of the PCF.[16] To some extent, this difference reflected the respective political traditions of Italy and France. In the former, where the state's weakness remained endemic, "partitocracy," or rule by parties, undermined a strong executive—with the notable exception of the discredited fascist years—and also favored the search for constant mediation and even "transformism"; the Communists reinforced their tendency to assimilate and compromise.[17] In the latter, where the state was strong and centralized and societal conflict more inscribed in its evolution and even enshrined in the French Revolution, unassailable ideological faith could be more easily conflated with national identity.[18] The PCI's long experience as a clandestine group under fascism also kept its cadres alert to the danger of being ostracized again.[19]

The prominence of intellectuals was notable in both parties. Nevertheless, the PCI fielded a more highly educated leadership than the PCF. As historian Stephen Gundle has noted, the PCI's "well-directed strategy aimed at achieving a hegemonic position within national thought and culture was virtually without precedent in the history of the European working-class movement." The French Communist leaders brandished their modest backgrounds as badges of honor, but also retained less control of fellow-traveling intellectuals. This was potentially and ironically one of the PCF's major weaknesses.[20]

ESTABLISHMENT VERSUS ANTIESTABLISHMENT

By the mid-1960s, after almost twenty years in opposition, both parties were trying to form alternative government coalitions. The PCF did so by relaunching the cooperation of the Left with the Socialists, starting with the presidential elections of 1965. The PCI debated whether it should break the center-left coalition by seeking cooperation with the Socialists or by reaching out to Catholic workers.[21] All these tactics required détente at home and an implied accommodation with the rapprochement between the establishment forces in the West and the establishment forces in the Soviet Union. In France, this meant endorsing to a certain extent the efforts of President de Gaulle of using détente to distance himself from Washington, while also drawing a distinction between that effort and a more thorough connection to the East proposed by the Left.

At the same time, both parties tried to co-opt the movements on their Left, endorsing some of their antiestablishment tactics. Paradoxically, that was especially true for the more parliamentarian of the two parties, the PCI. The cooperation between labor and student movements was more intense there because of the rapid, hence problematic, transition to modernity for Italy. In an interview with *Rinascita* in December 1968, PCI secretary Luigi Longo went as far as arguing that insurrection was an option, especially if youth and labor demonstrations continued to be met with violent repression.[22] But both parties' main efforts were directed at harnessing the antiestablishment forces. When the PCF proposed a government of popular democratic unity following the May 1968 events, it was not acting in a revolutionary way, but was channeling the revolutionary tide toward the rather limited goal of unseating de Gaulle.[23]

The Prague events intersected with this contradiction because they contained a disruptive potential for the détente that was the premise for the two parties' access to the government and because they also contained a potential for their genuine emancipation from Moscow and even for a rejuvenated or new kind of revolutionary spirit in the West. Philosopher Jean-Paul Sartre, in a rather unusual defense of the establishment in 1956, had described Hungary's revolution as infected by a "rightist spirit." Hungarian refugee François Fejtö rebutted that the Stalinists were the right-wing reaction to an experiment to improve communism from within.[24] Few French radical intellectuals would question the latter's interpretation during the Prague Spring of 1968.

REACTION TO THE EVENTS IN PRAGUE

Prague was the second chance for the greater autonomy of Western Communists as well. Each time a crisis had arisen in the East, the two parties, the PCI especially, tried to relaunch their own initiative in the West. The first of such attempts at coalition building among Western Communist parties was a conference in San Remo, Italy, in May 1956. Palmiro Togliatti's speech on polycentrism came right after the publication of Khrushchev's report in June. A key part of that speech, even more than its claim of greater autonomy from Moscow, was the assertion that the path to socialism could occur without the Communist parties being the leading ones in a coalition. This was the first genuine step toward a reformed socialism incorporating some social democratic forms.

The PCI reiterated its principle of unity within diversity after the repression in Hungary. French and Italian Communists concurred in denouncing the "imperialist plot" in Hungary, but only the PCI also admitted the mistakes made by the Hungarian Communists. The French Communists clashed with their Italian comrades more in 1956 than in 1968, accusing Togliatti of revisionism (at the world conference of sixty-eight parties in November 1957). It should be noted, though, that the PCI remained more loyal than the PCF to Khrushchev, for the Soviet leader was for a while seen as an agent of social renewal at home. In this sense, the French Communists, pledging loyalty to Stalinism, asserted their nationalist position more strongly than the Italian Left. In 1956, intellectuals started a slow hemorrhage in the PCF, and a more abrupt withdrawal from the PCI, with a famous document signed by one hundred intellectuals specifically addressing the issue of democratization in the East. Most of that group defected by the end of the year.[25]

A major reason for both parties promoting a sharper break with Moscow in 1968 was the pursuit of internal legitimacy. They both had to demonstrate that their own brand of communism was compatible with the democratic process. The electoral situation had favored this moderation for the PCI, but not as much for the PCF. With national elections held in May 1968, the PCI actually gained votes, proving it had, in part, channeled the radicalism of students and workers. In the French elections of the following month, the PCF lost one-tenth of its electorate, showing above all its inability to harness the youth movement.

The PCF's support of Alexander Dubček's reforms was very *"temperé."* In July, Waldeck Rochet warned the Czech leader of the dangers of counter-revolution, so strongly that Dubček wondered whether the warning came from the PCF or the USSR. There is no conclusive evidence of Moscow's success in using the PCF as mediator. But a big scandal erupted in France in 1970 after it was revealed that the French Communist leadership had given the "normalized" Czech government documents from the exchange between Rochet and Dubček, which resulted in trials of several members of the dissident group Club 231. The PCI was more ostensibly sympathetic to the winds of change in Prague, but Luigi Longo in July asked his party's political bureau to warn Dubček that there were "dangerous positions within the movement (of the Prague Spring) . . . that threaten[ed] the very basis of socialism" and against which it was "necessary to fight."[26] Both parties condemned the joint intervention of the Warsaw Pact powers in August. Notable dissidents included Jeannette Thorez-Veermesch, Emilio Colombi, and Pietro Secchia on the "orthodox" side, and Roger Garaudy, Umberto Terracini, and the PCI's Manifesto group further breaching the wall of party orthodoxy.[27]

Reconciliation for the PCF with the USSR came as early as 3 November 1968. The French party accepted normalization. Although it also endorsed the summoning of a conference of Communist parties in Moscow the next June, the PCF rejected any formal international agency along the lines of the previous Cominform. The PCI refused to sign the common declaration (it approved only the document condemning imperialism). Also, the Italian Communists condemned the normalization and upheld the notion of "pluralism," though only within a Socialist framework. The party leadership, however, still expressed solidarity with the world of socialism and the Soviet Union.[28]

The crushing of the Prague Spring was, however, traumatic for the leadership of both Western parties. This impact was, perhaps, best exemplified by the similar passionate reactions of the two party secretaries, Rochet and Longo. Consternated by the Soviets' conduct, they both fell ill soon after the invasion of Czechoslovakia. The simultaneous deaths of Togliatti and Thorez in 1964 had not led to significant transformations in the two parties. Instead, the new leadership emerging in the late 1960s further explained the two parties' increasingly diverging paths. Georges Marchais was, in many respects, more orthodox than Rochet, and Berlinguer was considerably more flexible than Longo. The Italian leader had already anticipated his departure from the bond with Moscow, predicting immediately after the invasion of Czechoslovakia that the "USSR suffer[ed] from an ideological retrenchment"; therefore, it was likely that the Western Communists would "engage in a political confrontation with the Soviet comrades."[29]

Several reasons dictated a moderate response by the two parties to the Soviet repression of the reform movement. Concisely, they can be ascribed to their leaders' concerns about various possible domino effects should they actually fully express their criticism.

1. *Fear of Domino Effects in the East:* French and Italian Communist leaders upheld the connection between détente and "controlled" Socialist reform: the radical forces from below, or, after Nixon's visit to Beijing in 1972, from China, could be upsetting in the West, but they could be devastating in the East. For both parties, the choice of muffling the antiestablishment pressures (from any direction) reflected their slogan of "neither orthodoxy nor heresy."[30]

2. *Fear of Domino Effect One in the West:* Moderation was also dictated by the fear that an ideological domino effect originating from the discredited East might easily affect the Western Communists as well. An utter condemnation of Moscow could have meant a loss of credibility for socialism altogether, argued the most orthodox members in both parties.[31]

3. *Fear of Domino Effect Two in the West:* The domino effect could also come from the extreme Left. The PCI in part balked because of the position of the Manifesto group within the party and of other extraparliamentarian groups that favored China over the Soviet Union. So pressures from radicalism reinforced a tactical orthodoxy.[32]

4. *Fear of Political Domino Effects at Home:* A moral equivalent between the United States and the Soviet Union might force the PCI and especially the PCF to compromise at home with the Socialists, or with regard to their own practice of "democratic centralism." A break with the Soviet Union, PCF leaders admonished Garaudy in January 1969, would only serve the cause of Western imperialism. By the end of 1969, Marchais condemned Garaudy after the publication of his book *Le grand tournant du socialisme* because its denunciation of totalitarian excesses included all of Eastern Europe and even Latin America's Marxist movements "so bravely fighting their own bourgeoisie and American imperialism." Garaudy's book was also censured for its acceptance of the "Marcusian" argument that after the working class had been "integrated" into the "consumer society" it had lost its role as the guide to revolution, which was now waged by the still "excluded" students and other "social or intellectual outcasts."[33]

Correlated with these fears were other concerns. Once the PCF found full reconciliation with Moscow, the Italian Communists worried about their own isolation in the Western Communist movement.[34] Concerns about grassroots connections also haunted the leadership of both parties; steeped in Soviet myths, the parties' rank and file had more trouble than their leaders with estrangement from Moscow. But above all, the political advantages of the emerging détente seemed to command a moderate response to the Soviet Union. Even the PCI in the end informally recognized normalization, in part out of fear that the forces of radicalism or Chinese intransigence would freeze détente in Europe and leave no room for maneuvering for the party's possible rapprochement with social democratic forces in the West. Maintaining détente meant keeping close relations with Moscow.[35]

INTERNATIONALISM AND CONTINENTAL INTEGRATION

In 1968, however, French and Italian Communists were still excluded from domestic politics. So they aimed at regaining some exposure by giving priority to foreign policy issues. The two parties' internationalism was, in part, predicated on their belief that they could preserve a role in the West if they could act as mediators in the East. This had been the case since the Moscow meeting of the eighty-one Communist parties in November–December 1961. On that occasion, both the French and the Italian parties sought to revive their international credentials by trying to cushion the impact of the Sino-Soviet split. Throughout the following decade, the PCI was quieter than the PCF on this issue. But its own concern about balancing détente with Sino-Soviet reconciliation was finally emphasized in the meeting Giancarlo Pajetta and Carlo Galluzzi held in Moscow with Andrei Kirilenko and Mikhail Suslov in July 1968.

More importantly, by the mid-1960s, the two parties practiced a "new internationalism," as the Italian Communists called it. The core elements of this policy were the virtually unconditional support of North Vietnam in its fight against "imperialism" and the effort to reestablish relations with the European Left—as the PCI did at the end of the decade by endorsing Willy Brandt's *Ostpolitik*.

Protesting the Vietnam War gave the parties control of the streets and the propaganda battle. It also established their strongest connection with the youth movement. During the summer of 1968, the PCF's political bureau decided to increase aid to North Vietnam and to create various committees supporting not just peace, as before, but victory for the Vietminh and Vietcong forces. Even more so now, the political bureau argued in August 1968, given the bourgeois attacks on socialism following the Czech events, the party needed to call the public's attention to the "struggle for freedom" in Vietnam. The constant parallel between Vietnam and Czechoslovakia, under the rubric of "freedom and independence," PCF's Roland Leroy told the leader of the *Mouvement de la Jeunesse Communiste Française* Roland Favaro, drowned the anti-American tradition into anti-Soviet animosity.[36]

But it was through a reevaluation of Western European integration that French and Italian Communists could get recognition and more control in parliament. For the PCI especially, this "Europeanism" reflected its effort to transform détente into a vehicle for European emancipation from *both* superpowers.

During the development of events in Prague, the PCF in July first proposed a meeting of the European Communist parties aimed at averting the Soviet action. It was a way for the PCF to establish its mediation role, but also to reassert the status of the Western parties. Moscow ignored that proposal. Indeed, for both Italian and French Communists, the main goal was to coalesce the Left in the West to better combat Western (U.S.) imperialism more than Moscow's control. The Soviet intervention in Czechoslovakia gave them the pretext to further their attempt to overcome the "politics of the two blocs." For the PCI's main champion of an acceptance of the European Economic Community (EEC), Giorgio Amendola, the Prague events would help prompt a campaign for the "withdrawal of [both] imperialist forces from occupied Europe . . . and the achievement of a real "European unity."[37] This position, prevalent in the PCI, actually favored utter condemnation of the Czech invasion, setting the tone against those who feared that an ideological domino effect would follow the party's reprobation of Soviet conduct. Denouncing Moscow, this argument went, could, in fact, give the party more power within the Socialist movement. Also, if Moscow's interference in the East was not rejected, the West could justify counter-coups against socialism in the West.[38] That was how the PCI saw the events in Chile five years later, or the so-called strategy of tension at home, which started with Fascist terrorist bombings in December 1969.

The risk of an escalating aggression from *both* superpowers in Europe was highlighted in a Mediterranean conference in April 1968, the first Cold War general Western Communist gathering to be organized separately from Moscow. The meeting, held in Rome, discussed geopolitical scenarios in the region after the Arab-Israeli War of June 1967. The delegates concluded that the situation "created the threat of 'aggressive Atlantic-American imperialism' and threatened to transform the Mediterranean into a potentially explosive new front or scene of dangerous confrontation between the U.S. Sixth Fleet and the newly introduced Soviet naval units."[39]

Just as the impact of the Hungarian events in 1956 was mitigated by the imperialist venture at Suez and the follow-up of the Eisenhower Doctrine, so the repression in Prague twelve years later was counterbalanced by a persistent anti-Americanism centered on a campaign against the Vietnam War. That campaign had actually contributed to reinserting the two Communist parties into a general national consensus opposing the war. Significant for the dialogue between Communists and Catholics, early in 1966 Pope Paul VI had established an informal diplomatic contact with North Vietnam through Berlinguer and other party leaders.[40] Moreover, the anti-Sovietism unleashed by the events in Prague in most respects prompted both the PCI and the PCF to intensify their anti-Americanism, almost as an instinctive reaction: their main reproach was that the ruling parties, enslaved to the United States through the North Atlantic Treaty Organization (NATO) and the EEC, could not "afford to lecture" the two Western Communist parties or the Soviet Union.[41]

For the older generation of World War II Communist resistors, the Soviet myth, combined with a vision of capitalist decline, persisted, even after de-Stalinization and Western economic miracles. The fact that large sectors of the working class, especially in Italy, were still excluded from consumption, economically justified the continuing myth and resulted in improved electoral results for the PCI in the 1970s. That myth also ascribed to the Soviet Union a sincere desire for détente, as opposed to a relentless imperialist drive from the United States.[42] But as officials from the U.S. embassy in Rome predicted as early as September 1968, the invasion of Czechoslovakia might have induced the PCI to begin reevaluating its denial of Soviet expansionism and to seek shelter in the Western alliance for its own brand of socialism, which is what Berlinguer did gradually by balking at the campaign to prevent the renewal of the NATO treaty in 1969, by accepting NATO in 1974 in front of the political bureau, and by publicly announcing this turn in June 1976.[43]

For the PCF, anti-Americanism remained a *raison d'être*, not only because of its orthodoxy, or because of its tactics to harness the youth movement, but also because de Gaulle himself had shifted direction. After recognizing that "with [the] Soviets on [the] warpath this is not time to be feuding with [the] U.S.," the French government took the role as host to Vietnam negotiations "in part due to the evident unpopularity of 'way out' anti-U.S. rhetoric."[44]

If the PCI and PCF had some room to maneuver in international politics, it was also, in part, because of Moscow's diminished interest in them. Soviet money now primarily went to Vietnam, Cuba, and the Arab countries; the two parties' protest against repression in Czechoslovakia also deprived them of a lot of money, but not of their autonomy. In fact, financing from Moscow resumed in the early 1970s after a brief break.[45] This renewed funding corresponded to the Soviets' own redefinition of national security. The Western parties had ostensibly received more autonomy in the immediate aftermath of the 1956 events. A decade later, for the USSR, national security became more tightly dependent on ideological cohesion, *anywhere*, because of the increasing ideological permeability of its Eastern satellites. It is no accident that the PCI's reform leader Amendola in 1971 first suggested the end of Soviet funding as a means to gain more autonomy in international politics.[46]

Financial matters were not the only barometer of this increasing autonomy. The crisis of 1956, together with other events, had moved the main international focus to the emerging Third World. The year 1968 was a different story: it restored hopes among Western European Communists that revolution was possible in Europe and in the West, too.

THE MEANINGS OF EUROCOMMUNISM

It is now widely accepted that for both the PCF and (especially) the PCI, the decline of the Soviet model began in 1968, and both parties fully acknowledged that decline only by the mid-1970s. Until the mid-1970s, Italy's Communists still analyzed world politics through Soviet lenses: the United States was in decline and power was shifting to the Soviet side. What the PCI seriously questioned from the late 1960s onward was the bipolarity implied in the détente process—or in the constant Soviet demonizing of the United States—as well as the internal practices of the Soviet camp.

After a meeting with a Soviet delegation in Budapest in November 1968, Berlinguer rejected his counterparts' suggestion to intensify anti-NATO propaganda, as the PCF had done after its encounters with the CPSU of a few weeks earlier. Those pressures for tactical anti-Americanism, Berlinguer told Boris Ponomaryov, were unacceptable.[47] It was the first time that the Italian Communists diverged from the Kremlin on anti-American propaganda.

By the mid-1970s, realizing that communism was no longer expanding, that Angola, and later, Afghanistan, were illusions, the Berlinguer leadership redefined the Soviet model from the geopolitical standpoint as well. In positioning itself as the middle path between social democracy and communism and in favor of European interdependence, Eurocommunism strove to deny both blocs. In January 1973 at a party meeting, Berlinguer defined a policy that would be "neither anti-Soviet nor anti-American."[48] In fact, with its anti-U.S. accents, its anticonsumerist ethic (all the campaigns for austerity and for a moral cleanup of Italian politics of the late 1970s and 1980s), it continued to favor a catastrophic vision of capitalist decline, thus reemphasizing its identity as the genuine harbinger of a reformed Eastern Bloc, as if the Prague Spring could be revived from the West. Faith in this capacity was essential; otherwise, Western communism would have been just another social democracy.[49]

The paradox was that only under the Atlantic umbrella, Berlinguer thought by 1974, could Western communism be free to advance the true "socialism with a human face."[50] The PCI increasingly saw NATO as a vehicle of peace and détente: once détente was achieved, then emancipation from NATO would be possible.

Eurocommunism enjoyed a brief season of hope and moderate success. It is beyond the scope of this chapter to narrate its developments. It will suffice here to mention the milestones of this design orchestrated mainly from

Rome. The theme was first addressed at a meeting between Marchais and Berlinguer in May of 1973, which also paved the way for the conference of the Western Communist parties held in Brussels the following year. Eurocommunism became the main banner of the ensuing meetings between Marchais and Berlinguer in November 1975, the PCF summit of a few days later with the Spanish Communists (PCE), renewed encounters between the French and Italian leaders in Paris in June of 1976, and, finally, the summit of the three leaders, including Santiago Carillo, in Madrid in March of 1977. The plenary conference of all European Communist parties, held in Berlin in June 1976, gave the three parties the chance to present their autonomous views within the Communist movement. Besides upholding their open cooperation with the Socialist and Social Democratic parties, the Western Communists abided by the declaration signed by Marchais and Berlinguer at their 1975 meeting, which supported the promotion of basic rights and freedom in Socialist societies.[51]

In the end, Eurocommunism had a minimal impact on politics in the West; it did not significantly lift the U.S. veto on a Communist sharing of power. But it did have a subversive impact on the East, for it drew the attention of East Germans, Romanians, Poles, and Yugoslavs. The Soviet Union became hostile because of this "magnetism" and because of its own fear that Eurocommunism, with its increasing acceptance of NATO, would ultimately favor the militarization of Western Europe.[52] Interestingly, from the other side, U.S. secretary of state Henry Kissinger also opposed the Eurocommunist idea because he thought that the PCI's experimentalism would weaken Western resolve and work its subversive way through to dominate Italian politics. In this case, for the realist Kissinger, ideology and the struggle for the minds and hearts did matter.[53]

What was most remarkable for both parties was that, although they ostensibly waged their main actions internationally, they both claimed their independence from Moscow first in their internal affairs, from as early as the mid-1960s.[54] Embracing interdependence did not mean excluding a nationalist outlook. In fact, years after the Prague events, both parties continued to define the defense of national autonomy as the main achievement of the reform movement in Czechoslovakia. They shared an utter rejection of a restored Cominform under any disguise.[55]

Again, traditions of nationalism and the nation-state, and even the nationalist belief that revolution had its roots in France, contributed to making the PCF more impervious than the PCI to any transnational option. The PCI was nationalist only intermittently and, like other Italian parties, looked at Europe as an instrument for the country's emancipation from the Cold War.[56]

But the emancipation from the blocs was also inherent in the PCF's internal choice of siding with the establishment represented by François

Mitterrand. Internal détente in France clashed with the external one, where the Soviet Union favored the ostensibly anti-Atlantic de Gaulle and his successors on the Right to a presumed pro-Atlanticist Mitterrand. It became an essential tactic for the Communists to have electable candidates.[57] After a narrow loss by Mitterrand in the presidential elections of 1974, which was actually welcomed in the Left as an unexpected success, the PCF had to become the suitor in the relationship and part of the system. But when the common program with the French Socialists (*Parti Socialiste* or PS) temporarily foundered in 1977, the Communists in most respects reverted to orthodoxy on matters of détente and European integration.[58]

For the PCI, Eurocommunism also meant the beginning of the Historic Compromise with the Christian Democrats, an external support to the ruling party first proposed by Berlinguer in three famous articles in the party's magazine *Rinascita* in the issues from October through December 1973. The main aim was that of eventually entering and transforming the government coalition. This was more of an anti-U.S., rather than an anti-Soviet, move. Following the coup in Chile against Salvador Allende, the Historic Compromise proposal was, in part, designed to prevent a similar scenario, invoking the common struggle against fascism, as in the postwar coalition of all democratic parties.[59]

While accepting Europe as a genuine third force between the two superpowers, Eurocommunism never truly coalesced with the forces of social democracy. The PCI's contacts with Brandt or Olav Palme were confined to issues of nuclear proliferation and aid policies for the southern hemisphere. Berlinguer's strategy consisted of finding a legitimate insertion in Western democracy, while remaining an ideological bridge between East and West. It was a tough balancing act that would have required truly overcoming the Cold War. The "Europeanization" of the PCI, it has been noted, was "never a choice of civilization." It was a *"Westpolitik,"* as PCI intellectual Sergio Segre put it in 1974. It was focused on détente rather than pluralism and democracy. This focus on international matters was chosen in order to keep the more orthodox PCF and the more radical Communist Party of Spain (*Partido Comunista de España* or PCE) tied to the project. In part it also stemmed from the fear of alienating the Soviet Union with a radical departure from democratic centralism.[60]

Actually, the French Communists became more antiestablishment than their Italian counterparts with regard to détente. They espoused, earlier than the PCI, the campaign for human rights in the East. A series of articles in the party's newspaper *L'Humanité* in October 1975 condemned the incarceration of high profile dissenters, mathematician Leonid Plyushch above all. But this criticism was still based on the belief that Soviet repression was merely a remnant of Stalinist distortions of socialism and national security. That's why a notable exception was the more thoroughly dissenting

Aleksandr Solzhenitsyn: against his *Gulag Archipelago* the PCF mounted a virulent campaign.[61] In the following years, the attacks against the Soviets' shabby human rights record and against totalitarianism of all colors came not only from the militant group of the New Philosophers led by Bernard Henri-Levy and the reviews *Les Nouvelles Littéraires* and *Le Nouvel Observateur*; former Communists, such as Jean-Marie Domenach, Pierre Daix, and Paul Vercors echoed those voices and denounced orthodox Marxism as scholastic.[62] But the French Communists continued to oppose détente as the validation of the status quo in the West, resenting its mitigating effect on their anti-U.S. campaigns.[63] In the final analysis, Eurocommunism for the PCF was a mere temporary expedient and even less of a choice of civilization than for the PCI.

The main question for both the Italian and the French Communists, in light of the protest movements in the East and the West, was whether it was possible to build a European identity outside the two superpowers. The mass movements from both sides and their stress on participatory democracy made this impossible. They made it impossible to break loose from the influence of U.S. mass culture, not from the extreme Left that had apparently commanded the rebellions of the late 1960s.

THE PATH TO AMERICA . . .

The impact of the events in Prague in August 1968 on the French and Italian Communists cannot be fully comprehended without including the events of Paris in May 1968. French intellectual and student activist Régis Debray ten years later quipped, "The French path to America passed through May '68." While much of the youth movement rebelled against the materialism and consumerism of the U.S. way of life, it also followed trends and a redefinition of oppression based on the ethical, individualistic modes of American radicalism rather than the Marxist script or the "French-style revolutionary sensibility."[64] Much has been said about the Italian and especially the French Communists' ineptitude in absorbing these movements. Suffice here to underline how their dilemmas between establishment and antiestablishment broadly affected their reactions to the Prague Spring.

The pressures of the antiestablishment from both sides of Europe ultimately undermined the ideological tension that the two parties formulated in strictly Cold War terms. As U.S. deputy assistant secretary of state for European affairs George Springsteen observed to French conservative leader Raymond Barré, the generation gap in Eastern Europe meant that the youth were not interested in ideology. In the West, the two concurred, all the revolutionary romanticism sounded like a triumph of ideology and like a "virus" causing contagion from France to the rest of Europe, but, in fact, if "no system of spiritual, political and social values [was] immune," then it meant that the post–World War II generations had no reference at all, or even that their "real problems [could] spread into other areas and provide the foundation for frivolity."[65]

Sir Isaiah Berlin described the 1960s movements as "the rebellion of the repentant bourgeoisie against the complacent and oppressive proletariat." Both the PCF and the PCI appeared insulted and worried by this new development. The French Communists' reaction to the youth movement is often exemplified by Marchais' *Humanité* article that lambasted Daniel Cohn-Bendit as an anarchist and the movement as bourgeois.[66]

While the PCI developed a strategy of "attention" toward the youth movement, even a moderate such as Amendola lamented the "resurgence of extremist infantilism," and an anarchic tendency that equated criticism of the Soviet Union to that of American imperialism. In the secret debate within the party's political bureau in June, Amendola waxed confident about absorbing a diversified extreme Left and not "repeating the same errors as the PCF"; but he also worried that the students, rather than advancing Maoist sectarianism, might instead, with their defiance "against all intellectual heritage," feed the theories on "the end of ideologies." In much harsher tones poet and movie-maker Pier Paolo Pasolini excoriated the students for their fascination with the counterculture: "the Americans," he pointed out in a controversial poem addressed to the students, "with their stupid flowers, are inventing a 'new' revolutionary language, for their own! . . . But you cannot do it because in Europe we already have one: can you ignore it? Yes you want to ignore it. You ignore it by 'going more to the left' . . . you set aside the only instrument that truly threatens your parents: communism." Earlier, just as significantly, Pasolini had denounced the "beatnik Stalinism" of the Italian New Left.[67]

To paraphrase historian Jeremi Suri, the two parties in the end sided with power more than with protest.[68] They feared being outflanked on the left and from below. They wanted détente and, possibly, a restoration of security into European hands, which was to their internal advantage because it would open a path to the government.

In Czechoslovakia, the disjunction between workers and intellectuals also evoked the emerging split in the West. The country was very egalitarian by the 1960s, and Stalinism had repressed the intellectual elites the most. So with the first signs of liberalization from above, it was the intellectuals who began to clamor for more. Czechoslovakia was also the first country in Eastern Europe to have a student revolt, in October 1967 at Prague's Technical University. When Italian students sang, "We are not with Dubček; we are with Mao," a major miscommunication between East and West was revealed: for many students in Rome, Paris, and Berlin, "pluralist democracy was the enemy," whereas for the Czech students "it was the goal."[69]

Another way in which Prague was connected with the student revolt in the West was by challenging democratic centralism. It was Achille Occhetto, as one of the leaders of the Italian Communist Youth Federation (*Federazione Giovanile Comunista Italiana* or FGCI), who most explicitly invited "in Italy a new socialist experience, in which . . . next to the socialization of the means of production there will be a socialization of the power system" with a "mixed system of delegated democracy and participatory democracy." Party secretary Longo recognized that the youth movement was "a struggle against authoritarianism . . . for greater participation of the masses in decision making . . . both in capitalist and in socialist countries [where] the bureaucratic structure of power tends to suffocate and exclude the single as well as the group."[70]

To be sure, the student movement, especially in Italy, saw this change as the precursor of true socialism. But in denying the party its function of guide in favor of that of mere "coordination" of factory and student counsels, it was, in fact, undermining its Marxist-Leninist essence.[71] In the end, democratic centralism could not be given up because with a genuine internal debate the PCI and PCF would have become as factionalized as the other parties. Even the FGCI gave priority to the struggle for unity with the proletariat, gaining members in the following years, but at the price of its *ideological* cohesion.

The intellectual diaspora was also more consequential for both parties in 1968 than in 1956 because of the combined effect of the youth rebellion, the increasing gap between intellectuals and the "complacent proletariat," and the events in Prague. Attention to dissent had started earlier in France, with Communist intellectual Pierre Daix prefacing the first French edition of Solzhenitsyn's *One Day in the Life of Ivan Denisovich* in 1963. The journal *Les Lettres Françaises* accepted dissident contributors beginning in 1965, and its director Louis Aragon shed all his remnant orthodoxy and called the Soviet intervention in Czechoslovakia a "Biafra of the spirit." Roger Garaudy was expelled from the party after a critical speech at the 19th Party Congress in 1970.[72] For Jean-Paul Sartre, 1968 actually changed the role of the intellectual altogether: the existentialists took an active part instead of just being moral supporters. This change was inspired in part by the Chinese model, but it ended up encouraging the individualist implications of the youth rebellion. Sartre's condemnation of the PCF's handling of the student movement matched his condemnation of Prague: "today the Soviet model," he sentenced, "smothered as it is by a bureaucracy, is no longer viable."[73]

In part because of the influence of Sartre and Existentialism and in part because of economic conditions, the countercultural aspects of the youth rebellion held a broader appeal on the French Left than on the Italian Left. With its individualist pathos, the French cultural scene fielded several intellectuals who waged with fervor human rights campaigns against the Soviet

Union. But the PCI had also better absorbed the intellectual dissent: the Yalta Memorandum had called for more freedom in intellectual life. The party's Cultural Commission had been phased out in 1962 and absorbed by the more liberalized Gramsci Institute.[74]

What was characteristic of left-wing intellectual autonomy in both countries was an amalgam of, on the one hand, efforts to "create a more direct and unmediated contact with the people" using such dated instruments as the wallpaper or the improved *Festival de l'Unità* (the annual fund-raising fair of the PCI) and, on the other hand, the triumph of the media intellectual distilling the debate, but also highly "mediating" it for the masses. The two parties' cultural profile was raised by the apparent dialogue established with the new forms of protest that criticized Western models of development, as well as by their coming to terms with an increasingly individualized Western culture that was repelled by totalitarianism. In fact, French and Italian Communists faced two far more insidious and, for that reason, insurmountable challenges: that from consumerism and the apparently opposite one from the theories of alienation against the consumerist society which, however, turned upside down the conventional Marxist understanding of revolution in a socioeconomic sense. It was at this time that the young Marx was "exhumed," the one with an accent on psychological more than social repression. The new generations took that philosophical turn to justify their emphasis on private desires over collective struggles. Both challenges reflected the "individualist sensibilities of the age."[75]

The U.S. culture of dissent, with its emphasis on existential problems and issues of individual expression—namely cultural alienation, women's emancipation, the generation gap, and gay rights—subverted the economic discourse that had informed Marxist doctrines and established a transatlantic dialogue between the younger generations. In dealing with these developments, the French and Italian Communist leadership showed either rigidity (especially in the PCF) or flexibility (in the PCI) to the point of losing their ideological and political consistency altogether.

Furthermore, the United States' self-perception had changed by the late 1960s to be less exceptionalist, less naïvely optimistic, and more vulnerable in every way, showing the superpower's true weaknesses, but also highlighting its pluralistic and multifaceted character. It thus inspired further adaptations and permutations of Communist anti-Americanism in France and Italy. It also reignited a subtlety and ambivalence in the Communists' assessments of the United States that resumed and refined their equivocations of the immediate postwar period.

The ambivalence of America begat the ambivalence of anti-Americanism: as early as March 1966, *Rinascita*'s correspondent to the United States, Gianfranco Corsini, with an opening article in an issue of *Il Contemporaneo* dedicated to the "America of dissent," reflected that there was "an America that does not dwell in complacency, and that prefers to pose the most daring questions, rather than remaining bound to an immutable belief system"; because of the "tight cultural interdependence of our time," Corsini concluded, "these [American] debates can help us understand ourselves better in a moment in which we try to interpret and correctly evaluate (without any prejudice) other peoples' troubles."[76] The Writers Union of the PCF took a little longer to fathom the value of U.S. counterculture, but by 1971, it drafted a memorandum questioning whether it was a temporary phenomenon or the beginning of a genuine cultural revolution in the West spearheaded by the U.S. "underground" movement. "Would you pay," the Union asked the party leaders,

> considerable interest to what in the United States they now call the "hip culture," or do you dismiss it as a passing phenomenon, maybe even a backward one? What significance do you attribute to developments such as the pop music, the new shows inspired by the "happening," the wall literature, the theater without script, the papers or films underground—in short, to all this movement that we should call "cultural" and that is developing outside the traditional circles and in opposition to them?[77]

These assessments reflected the United States' own ambivalence, proved its cultural dominion, and confirmed its role as harbinger of Europe's future.

The PCF remained unable to address the new problems of education, individual liberties, and sexual liberation. In the 1960s, it still defined birth control as a product of reactionary Malthusianism inspired by imperialist capitalism. The PCI, despite its tentacular reach into all new cultural developments, especially through its cultural recreation organization ARCI, also failed to fully grasp the redefinition of oppression by women's and youth groups. In its attempt to establish a Historic Compromise with the Christian Democrats, it muffled its leadership in causes such as the divorce and abortion referenda of the mid-1970s and early 1980s. Feminism was at first dismissed as an "heir to the youth movement and its errors" and as "more an expression of social unease than a social movement."[78]

At the same time, the PCI remained more Eurocentric than did Communist and radical French intellectuals. From the time Pope Paul VI issued his encyclical *Populorum Progressio* in 1967, which upheld the theories of modernization, Italian Communist leaders kept fearing that the main global focus of change and progress might switch from the developed countries to the developing ones and that, therefore, the Chinese interpretation of revolution might prevail.[79] Modernization theories, on the other hand, connected new French and American sociological theories, adding luster to France's intellectual heritage.

It should also be noted that part of the modernist assumptions, which gave so much credit to neocapitalism, prompted PCI leaders to further expand their own notions of "socialism with a human face." The NATO umbrella to which Berlinguer referred was not only a protection in terms of security, but also in economic and social terms. According to Communist intellectual Franco Rodano, Italy could spearhead the transformation of Europe through the use and diversion of a consumerist economy, shifting its dimension gradually from private to "public" or "social consumption."[80] In other words, a more affluent Europe, made possible by its permanence in NATO, would ultimately emancipate Europe socially and geopolitically from U.S. control.

The 1960s movements in both Europe and the United States that "purported to despise and abhor 'consumer culture' were from the outset an object of cultural consumption, reflecting a widespread disjunction between rhetoric and practice." As Tony Judt has best noted, the effects of both revolts in the East and the West were limited: "in the East the message of the Sixties was that you could no longer work within the 'system'; in the West there appeared no better choice." So much of the fervor and antiestablishment of the 1960s was the "swansong" of Europe's "revolutionary tradition."[81] It was the second major step toward ending ideological politics in Europe. The first one had an economic dimension, the "politics of productivity," as pointed out by Charles Maier and others in reference to the effects of the Marshall Plan. This second one ultimately went deeper, favoring the private sphere over collective struggles, or as Maier again noticed, 1968 transformed the social, technological, and cultural bases of the "imperial rivalry" between the two superpowers, and ended the "controlled conflictuality" of bipolarism and the Cold War.[82]

CONCLUSION: REFLECTIONS ON THE
U.S. CONFRONTATION WITH WESTERN COMMUNISM

The main key to understanding the tension between establishment and antiestablishment pressures within the French and Italian Communist parties lies in their perceptions of and interactions with U.S. influence. The U.S. response was also significant. Throughout the Cold War, the United States only gradually evolved toward exhibiting the necessary flexibility in confronting left-wing anti-Americanism.[83] After placing much confidence in economic determinism during the early phases of the Marshall Plan, the U.S. foreign policy establishment reached the conclusion that communism in the West did not thrive only in poverty. An Intelligence Report of December 1952 described the situation of the previous years in France, where the living standards were relatively high while the social gaps did not appear to diminish, but to widen. The study pointed out that "only a rough correlation exists between poverty and adherence to the French Communist Party.

What is true, rather, is that the party rallies those who are discontented with their present living standards, which may not necessarily be the lowest in the country, that they are convinced that only thoroughgoing changes in the social and economic order could possibly improve things for them."[84]

The resilience of both the PCI and PCF, despite their strong identification with the Soviet Union and in face of the two nations' economic growth, induced the Truman and Eisenhower administrations to refine their own instruments of psychological warfare and also to wage a "cultural cold war" to defuse many of the Western Europeans' assumptions about the United States' cultural shallowness. Psywar consisted above all of repressive actions geared to reduce the institutional power and mass appeal of the two Communist parties. Those actions yielded only short-term results. The U.S. cultural cold war institutional framework also had relative success in the 1950s and 1960s, but in 1967 was discredited by revelations of CIA backing.[85]

All the refinement of these propaganda battles are rather significant for the gradual, long-term effects they had on U.S. leadership itself. In 1949, George F. Kennan was in a relative minority as he observed that in the West, the Communist appeal was "emotional" more than economic. This induced the architect of containment to stigmatize some "fundamental flaws" within the "complicated civilization" of the West. He regretted the disappearance of the sense of organic community in modern U.S. society. Instead, he noted, the individual found solace in a culture of media, consumerism, and hedonism. The result of all this was "a gradual paralysis of the sense of responsibility and initiative in people. . . ." "Not being the masters of our own soul," Kennan concluded, "are we justified in regarding ourselves as fit for the leadership of others? All our ideas of 'world leadership,' 'the American century,' 'aggressive democracy', etc. stand or fall with the answer to that question." Almost ten years later, President Dwight D. Eisenhower also mused over the insecurities of the Western man and the conditions of atomized passivity and confided to his speechwriter Emmet J. Hughes that he felt "the need to assert American purposes, before all the world, in terms more proud, and in measures less mean, than sheer material might."[86]

At the onset of the youth rebellion and anti-Vietnam protest in both Europe and the United States, most U.S. officials feared that the most insidious forms of left-wing anti-Americanism on both sides of the Atlantic could be mutually nurtured.[87] This did happen, but in the end, as we have seen, to the detriment of Communist orthodoxy and even power in France and Italy. It is no accident that Senator J. William Fulbright, who best grasped the importance of U.S. soft power, during the Vietnam war argued that the "self-critical, generous America," should eventually prevail over the "egotistical . . . self-righteous" one. As late as 1977, at the peak of the Eurocommunist experiment, Secretary of State Henry Kissinger reflected that "the spread of

Marxism" in Western Europe "[could] be one of the profound problems of the modern period, namely the alienation of the population from the modern industrial state, that in the modern industrial state no matter how it is governed the people feel that they have no influence over the real decisions, and if you couple that with certain left wing traditions in Italy and France you can see why it spreads."[88] Analyses such as these deeply informed the U.S. response to pluralism in the West and to Eurocommunism: they had the peculiar quality of synthesizing realism, a cultural understanding of certain exceptions in Western European politics, and an understanding of the limits of traditional Marxism in those contexts.[89]

Washington's response to the Communist threat in France and Italy, and even the effects of Americanization altogether, were strongest when the United States married its own "psychological warfare" to a subtle use of diplomatic actions that only indirectly helped modify the political balance within each of the two allied countries. Making diplomatic concessions to the French and Italian governments throughout the Cold War helped raise their profile against the Communist opposition. Moderately accommodating President de Gaulle on certain international issues helped muffle the anti-Americans on the left in France. Eisenhower's Atoms for Peace campaign won over important sectors of public opinion in France and Italy and in only a few other countries. The diplomacy of détente, both in the late 1950s and in the Nixon-Kissinger era helped not only harness the voices of pacifism and protest in the Western world, but also check Communist pressures within NATO. U.S. diplomacy in the Middle East from the mid-1950s, allowing indirectly a U.S. dialogue with the center-left in Italy, helped isolate that country's extreme Left.

The years 1975 to 1977 proved to be crucial in this particular respect: facing the threat of reformed Western communism, U.S. diplomacy renounced direct confrontation and instead adopted its most subtle approach to date, drawing, through the emerging G-7 summits, a concert of powers aimed at forging a socioeconomic consensus around the restoration of laissez-faire principles. This included the cooption of social democratic forces in France, Germany, and Italy. Both the French and the Italian Communists for the most part continued to rely on neo-Keynesian recipes. While this confirmed their cultural and economic adaptation to neocapitalism, it also showed their detachment from the realities of international economics and diplomacy that took shape under the influence of Kissinger and German chancellor Helmut Schmidt.[90] A restored laissez-faire policy, while temporary, was the dream of neither the Prague nor the Paris rebels. Most of Italy's Communists, converging into the establishment of the new Party of the Democratic Left at the end of the Cold War, at best strove for a capitalism with a human face.

NOTES

1. Gianfranco Corsini, "Marilyn tra mito e verità," *Rinascita*, 11 August 1962; Jean-Marc Aucuy, "Hommage a Marilyn Monroe ou le decolonisation par l'erotisme," *Nouvelle Critique* 140 (November 1962); Gianfranco Corsini, "Marilyn e gli intellettuali," *Rinascita*, 8 September 1962; see also "'Miller: Mia moglie è geniale; Marilyn: mio marito è matto': Intervista con i due," *Vie Nuove*, 23 April 1960.

2. For background, see especially Philippe Roger, *The American Enemy: The History of French Anti-Americanism* (Chicago: University of Chicago Press, 2005); Jessica C. E. Gienow-Hecht, "Always Blame the Americans: Anti-Americanism in Europe in the Twentieth Century," *American Historical Review* 111, no. 4 (October 2006): 1067–91; Herbet J. Spiro, "Anti-Americanism in Western Europe," *Annals of the American Academy of Political and Social Sciences* 497 (May 1988): 120–32; David W. Ellwood, "The American Challenge Renewed: U.S. Cultural Power and Europe's Identity Debates," *Brown Journal of World Affairs*, Winter/Spring 1997; Federico Romero, "Americanization and National Identity: The Case of Postwar Italy," in *Europe, Its Borders and the Others*, ed. Luciano Tosi (Napoli: ESI, 2000); David Strauss, *Menace in the West: The Rise of French Anti-Americanism in Modern Times* (Westport, CT: Greenwood, 1978); *Nemici per la pelle. Sogno americano e mito sovietico nell'Italia contemporanea*, ed. Pier Paolo D'Attorre (Milan: F. Angeli, 1991).

3. Cf. Ilya Ehrenburg, "Non potete capirci niente se dimenticate che è un paese giovane," *L'Unità*, 18 August 1946; Italo Calvino, "Petrov e Ilf in America," *L'Unità*, 23 March 1946; Marcello Flores, *L'immagine dell'URSS: L'Occidente e la Russia di Stalin (1927–1956)* (Milan: Il Saggiatore, 1990), 343–48.

4. Antonio Gramsci, "Americanism and Fordism," in *Selections from the Prison Notebooks*, ed. and trans. Quintin Hoare and Geoffrey Nowell Smith (London: Lawrence and Wishart, 1971); see also Antonio Gramsci, *Note sul Machiavelli, sulla politica e sullo stato moderno* (Turin: Einaudi, 1955), 329–40.

5. Quoted Calvino, "Hemingway e noi," *Il Contemporaneo*, 13 November 1954, pp. 3, 5; cf. Nello Ajello, *Intellettuali e PCI, 1944–1958* (Bari: Laterza, 1979), 14; Patrick McCarthy, "America: L'altro mito della cultura comunista," in D'Attorre, *Nemici per la pelle*, 222–23.

6. Claude Roy, "Le ciel est ma frontière," *Les Lettres Françaises*, 1 November 1946.

7. Cesare Pavese, *La letteratura americana, e altri saggi*, 3rd. ed. (Turin: Einaudi, 1959), 194; see also Elio Vittorini, *Diario in pubblico*, 2nd ed. (Milan: Bompiani, 1957), 234; Michele Bottalico, "A Place for All: Old and New Myths in the Italian Appreciation of American Literature," in As *Others Read Us: International Perspectives on American Literature*, ed. Huck Gutman (Amherst: University of Massachusetts Press, 1991). Ingrao qtd. in McCarthy, "America: L'altro mito," 223.

8. Pavese, *La letteratura americana*, 196.

9. Report Commissione Culturale Nazionale, November 1953, 5; and Report Salinari, in Report Commissione Culturale Nazionale, November 1953, 33, Commissione Cultura, Archivio del Partito Comunista Italiano, Istituto Gramsci, Rome, Italy (hereafter APCI).

10. Quoted Mtg. Direzione, 20 June 1956, Verbali Direzione (hereafter VD), mf 198, APCI. On Clare Luce in Italy, see also Mario Del Pero, "American Pressures and Their Containment in Italy during the Ambassadorship of Clare Boothe Luce, 1953–56," *Diplomatic History* 28, no. 3 (June 2004): 407–39; and Alessandro Brogi, *L'Italia e l'egemonia americana nel Mediterraneo* (Florence: La Nuova Italia, 1996), chaps. 2, 3, and 4.

11. Quoted Stephen Gundle, *Between Hollywood and Moscow: The Italian Communists and the Challenge of Mass Culture, 1943–1991* (Durham, NC: Duke University Press, 2000), 90 (Berlinguer also qtd. ivi; see also 80); quoted Amendola and Romagnoli in Mtg. Direzione 28 February 1962, VD, APCI.

12. Decision Bureau Politique (hereafter Dec. BP) 24 May 1962, Archives du Parti Communiste Français, Seine-Saint-Denis, Paris, France (APCF). Quoted D. S. Bell and Byron Criddle, *The French Communist Party in the Fifth Republic* (Oxford: Oxford University Press, 1994), 220; cf. Marc Lazar, "Le Réalisme socialiste aux couleurs de la France," *L'Histoire* 45 (March 1982): 60ff; Roger Martelli, "De Gaulle et les communistes entre traditions et modernité," in *50 ans d'une passione française: De Gaulle et les communistes*, ed. Stephane Courtois and Marc Lazar (Paris: Balland, 1991).

13. Quoted John L. Gaddis, *The Cold War: A New History* (New York: Penguin, 2005), 77; quoted Eric Shiraev and Vladislav Zubok, *Anti-Americanism in Russia from Stalin to Putin* (New York: Palgrave, 2000), 13–14.

14. Lefranc, "Le nouveau nouveau monde," *Democratie nouvelle* (March 1961): 74; Jacqueline Vernes, "Les USA face au défi économique de l'URSS," *Democratie nouvelle* (July 1960): 54–61; Jean Bruteau, "Problemes de l'automatisation," *La Nouvelle Critique* (September/October 1957): 21–34; Nicola Sarzano, "Siamo tutti Rockefeller," *Vie Nuove*, 5 March 1964; Carlo Marcucci, "Le quattro lezioni dei giochi," *Vie Nuove*, 17 September 1960; Antoine Casanova, "La doctrine sociale de l'Eglise et le marxisme," *La Nouvelle Critique* 141 (December 1962). Attributing a corporatist outlook to Catholic reformism, see Bruno Trentin in meeting 28 February 1962, VD, APCI; see also Alfredo Reichlin a Segreterie, Federazioni e Comitati Regionali, 22 August 1962, Sezione Stampa e Propaganda (hereafter SSP), MF 494, APCI.

15. Marc Lazar, *Maisons rouges: Les Partis communistes français et italien de la Libération à nos jours* (Paris: Aubier, 1992), 73, see also 18–27, 329–40. Cf. Elena Aga Rossi and Gaetano Quagliarello, *L'altra faccia della luna: I rapporti tra PCI, PCF e Unione Sovietica* (Bologna: Il Mulino, 1997), 51–78. Cf. traditional accounts emphasizing differences, especially Thomas H. Greene, "The Communist Parties of Italy and France: A Study in Comparative Communism," *World Politics* 26 (October 1968): 4; Donald L. M. Blackmer and Sidney Tarrow, eds., *Communism in Italy and France* (Princeton, NJ: Princeton University Press, 1975), especially the chapter by Sidney Tarrow, "Communism in Italy and France: Adaptation and Change." See also Cyrille Guiat, *The French and Italian Communist Parties: Comrades and Culture* (London: Frank Cass, 2003).

16. See essays in Aga Rossi and Quagliarello, *L'altra faccia della luna*; Valerio Riva, *Oro di Mosca: I finanziamenti sovietici al PCI dalla Rivoluzione d'Ottobre al crollo dell'URSS* (Milan: Mondadori, 1999); Gianni Donno, *La Gladio Rossa del PCI, 1945–1967* (Soveria Mannelli: Rubbettino, 2001); Pietro di Loreto, *Togliatti e la "doppiezza": Il PCI tra democrazia e insurrezione, 1944–1949* (Bologna: Il Mulino, 1991); Elena Aga Rossi and Victor Zaslavski, *Togliatti e Stalin: Il PCI e la politica estera*

staliniana negli archivi di Mosca (Bologna: Il Mulino, 1997); for balanced accounts on this issue, see Silvio Pons, "L'URSS e il PCI nel sistema della guerra fredda," in *Il PCI nell'Italia repubblicana, 1943–1991*, ed. Roberto Gualtieri (Rome: Carocci, 2001); Marcello Flores, *Sul PCI. Un'interpretazione storica* (Bologna: Il Mulino, 1992), 68–82.

17. On how the war experience worsened the already poor "state vocation" of the Italians, the best sources are Ernesto Galli della Loggia, *L'identità italiana* (Bologna: Il Mulino, 1998), 59–84, and Silvio Lanaro, *L'Italia nuova: Identità e sviluppo, 1861–1988* (Turin: Einaudi, 1989), 221–27.

18. On how the sense of statehood enhanced the sense of nationhood in France, see especially studies by Pierre Nora, Robert Gildea, Rogers Brubaker, and, most recently, Michael Kelly, *The Cultural and Intellectual Rebuilding of France after the Second World War (1944–1947)* (New York: Palgrave Macmillan, 2005).

19. On PCI's lesson from Fascist totalitarianism and meanings of *Partito nuovo* see also Palmiro Togliatti, *Opere, 1944–1955*, vol. 5 (Rome: Ed. Riuniti, 1955), 80–108.

20. Gundle, *Between Hollywood and Moscow*, 12; Lazar, *Maisons rouges*, 333–34; cf. Jean-Paul Molinari, *Les ouvriers communistes: Sociologie de l'adhésion ouvrière au communisme* (Thonon-les-Bains: L'Albaron, 1991); on intellectual influence in both countries, see also the works by Marcello Flores, Nello Ajello, Albertina Vittoria, David Caute, Herbert Lottmann, Dominique Desanti, David Drake, Tony Judt, Pascal Ory, and Jean-François Sirinelli.

21. Research memo by George C. Denney Jr. to acting secretary of state, "Socialist-Communist Collaboration in France: A New 'Popular Front'?" 6 August 1963, POL 12-1 France, Record Group (RG) 59, National Archives, College Park, MD (NARA); Intervention by Waldeck-Rochet at Mtg. Bureau Politique, in Dec. BP, 2 December 1965, APCF; Stephane Courtois and Marc Lazar, *Histoire du Parti communiste français*, 2nd ed. (Paris: PUF, 2000), 335. Regarding the contrast following Togliatti's death in 1964 between the PCI's right-wing led by Amendola and favoring the cooption of Socialist forces away from the center-left government, and the left wing, led by Pietro Ingrao, which viewed the Socialists as integrated into neocapitalist developments, and favored an anticapitalist coalition involving a possible alliance with Catholic forces, see especially Giorgio Amendola, "Il socialismo in Occidente," *Rinascita*, 7 November 1964; Pietro Ingrao, "Un nuovo programma per tutta la sinistra," *Rinascita*, 25 December 1965; cf. Grant Amyot, *The Italian Communist Party: The Crisis of the Popular Front Strategy* (New York: St. Martin's, 1981), chaps. 3 and 10; Carlo Galluzzi, "I comunisti e il centro-sinistra," *Critica marxista* 5 (1972): 93–109.

22. *Rinascita*, 28 December 1968; see also Luigi Longo, "Il movimento studentesco nella lotta anticapitalistica," *Il Contemporaneo*, 3 May 1968; cf. Alexander Höbel, "Il PCI di Longo e il '68 studentesco," *Studi storici* 45, no. 2 (2004): 435–43; Jean-Jacques Becker, *Le Parti communiste veut-il prendre le pouvoir?* (Paris: Seuil, 1981).

23. Lazar, *Maisons rouges*, 129.

24. Tony Judt, *Postwar: A History of Europe since 1945* (New York: Penguin, 2005), 426; cf. François Fejtö, *The French Communist Party and the Crisis of International Communism* (Cambridge, MA: MIT, 1967).

25. Palmiro Togliatti, "La via italiana al socialismo," report to CC of 24 June 1956, in Palmiro Togliatti, *Opere*, vol. 6; Donald L. M. Blackmer, *Unity in Diversity: Italian Communism and the Communist World* (Cambridge, MA: MIT, 1968), 125; Velio Spano, "Origini e lineamenti della nostra politica," *Rinascita*, January–February 1957; Lazar, *Maisons rouges*, 90–106; Hélène Carrère d'Encausse, *1956. La déstalinisation commence* (Brussels: Complexe, 1984). The best recollections on the intellectual defection among PCI member are the memoirs of Antonio Giolitti, *Lettere a Marta: Ricordi e riflessioni* (Bologna: Il Mulino, 1992). See also Nello Ajello, *Intellettuali e PCI, 1944–1958* (Bari: Laterza, 1979), 401–13.

26. Quoted Courtois and Lazar, *Histoire du Parti communiste français*, 353. Cf. Dec. BP 27 August 1968, and letter Garaudy to Rochet, 2 September 1968, in Idem, APCF. On scandal, see PCF: Watson to State Dept., 16 May 1970, POL 12 FR, RG 59, NARA. Longo in mtg. Direzione 17 July 1968, mf 020, APCI.

27. Garaudy to Rochet, 2 September 1968, cit.; Courtois and Lazar, *Histoire du Parti communiste français*, 355; Colombi in Mtg. Direzione, 23 August 1968, mf 020. G. Marini, "La repressione della primavera cecoslovacca: dal 'grave dissenso' alla 'riprovazione,'" in *Luigi Longo: La politica e l'azione*, ed. Giuseppe Vacca (Rome: Editori Riuniti, 1992), 120; Alexander Höbel, "Il PCI, il '68 cecoslovacco e il rapporto col PCUS," *Studi Storici* 4 (2001): 1149 and 1164–65; see also Alexander Höbel, "Il contrasto tra PCI e PCUS sull'intervento sovietico in Cecoslovacchia: nuove acquisizioni," *Studi Storici* 2 (2007): 523–50.

28. Mtg. Direz. 31 October 1968, mf 020, pp. 1085–86, APCI. Berlinguer in VD, 20 June 1969, mf 006, pp. 1722–29, Fondo Berlinguer, fasc. 81, APCI; Carlo Galluzzi, *La svolta. Gli anni cruciali del Partito comunista italiano* (Milan: Sperling and Kupfer, 1983), 211–14. Höbel, "Il PCI, il '68 cecoslovacco," 1168; Lazar, *Maisons rouges*, 144–47; Lilly Marcou, *Le mouvement communiste international depuis 1945* (Paris: PUF, 1980), 81–88.

29. In Mtg. Direzione 18 September 1968, mf 020, p. 939, APCI; see also Report Berlinguer to Political Bureau in Mtg. Direzione 16 November 1968, mf 020, p. 939, APCI. Based on newly released Soviet documents, Victor Zaslavsky has analyzed the postinvasion reaction of the Communist Party of Italy (PCI) on the relationship of the PCI and the Communist Party of the Soviet Union (CPSU) as part of the Boltzmann Institute's international research project on the Prague Spring. Zaslavsky's essay is hitherto only published in German. He comes to the conclusion that on the basis of the new perspectives it is necessary to correct our view of the relationship between the Communist Party of Italy and the Communist Party of the Soviet Union after the invasion of Czechoslovakia in 1968. The PCI's demonstrative protest against the invasion and its search for a "third way" strained its relationship with the CPSU. Italian Communists, like the Soviets, saw Communist identity grounded "in anti-capitalism and in demonizing social democrats." Still the PCI did not see "the source and the epicenter" of the crisis in Moscow. Even the most liberal of Italian Communists had a hard time criticizing the Soviet view of the sovereignty of states. After all, such a critique would only have supported "deviationist forces on the right" and undermined détente policies. There was also a contradiction here in the recognition of the rights of oppressed peoples. Whereas the PCI and the global communist movement demanded the right of independence for peoples of the "Third World," even including armed struggle, Zaslavsky contends that they denied

the same right to the "victims of Soviet aggression." See Victor Zaslavsky, "Die italienischen Kommunisten zwischen Widerstand und Resignation," in Karner et al., *Beiträge*, 531–47. The author would like to thank the editors for this reference.

30. Dec. BP 14 August 1968, APCF; Höbel, "Il PCI, il '68 cecoslovacco," 1150–51; Silvio Pons, *Berlinguer e la fine del comunismo* (Turin: Einaudi, 2006), 11.

31. See, for example, Colombi in Mtg. Direzione 23 August 1968, mf 020, APCI; cf. Giuseppe Boffa, "La crisi cecoslovacca," in *Luigi Longo*, cit., 114; Jeannette Vermeersch in Comité Central (hereafter CC), 20–21 October 1968, Ivry sur Seine, transcripts of audio CD n. 41 and 42, Cote AV: 4AV10/151, APCF.

32. Berlinguer in Mtg. Direzione, 18 September 1968, cit. 939. Sergio Dalmasso, *Il caso "Manifesto," e il PCI degli anni '60* (Turin: Cric, 1989), 69–70.

33. Marini, "La repressione della primavera," 123–24; Dec. BP, 17 January 1969, APCF; letter Marchais to BP, 18 December 1969; quoted Philippe Fuchsmann, "Karl Marx, notre contemporain," *Cahiers du communisme* 45, no. 2 (February 1969); see also "Communiqué du Bureau Politique sur un nouveau livre de Roger Garaudy," *Cahiers du communisme* 46, no. 1 (January 1970).

34. Amendola in Mtg. Direzione 7–8 May 1969, VD, mf 06; cf. Ufficio Segreteria, 2 September 1968, 1488, mf 020, APCI.

35. See, for example, Bufalini in Mtg. Direzione 18 September 1968, mf 020, APCI; cf. Pons, *Berlinguer e la fine del comunismo*, 9; Giorgio Amendola, "Il nostro internazionalismo," *Rinascita*, 6 September 1968. Giorgio Napolitano in Mtg. Direzione, 8 November 1968, 1123, mf. 020, APCI. Report Billoux to Bureau Politique, in Dec. BP 7 August 1969, APCF.

36. Letter Charles Fourniau to Secretariat, 4 April 1968, Fonds Gaston Plissonnier 264 J, Box 2, and Dec. BP 14 August 1968, APCF; memo conversation Leroy-Favaro, 16 September 1968, Fonds Roland Leroy, 263 J 65, box 37, APCF; Tel. A-1564 U.S. embassy to the Department of State, 1 March 1968, POL 12 FR and Reinhardt to State Deptartment, 20 May 1965, POL 12 IT, RG 59, NA.

37. Amendola intervention at Central Committee PCI, in *L'Unità*, 28 August 1968.

38. Cf. Giorgio Amendola, "Il nostro internazionalismo," *Rinascita*, 6 September 1968; on Amendola's pro-EEC choices cf. Roberto Gualtieri, "Giorgio Amendola dirigente del PCI," *Passato e Presente* 24, no. 67 (2006). On PCF's persistent skepticism see Charles Fiterman, "Pour une Europe indépendante, démocratique et pacifique," *Cahiers du communisme* 44, no. 2 (April 1968): 14–26. On U.S. fears of conflict with Moscow see Günter Bischof, "'No Action': The Johnson Administration and the Warsaw Pact Invasion of Czechoslovakia in August 1968," in this volume.

39. Special Report CIA: "Italian Communist Party Draws Further Away from Moscow," 25 October 1968, FRUS, 1964–68, XII: doc. 144.

40. On Paul VI, see Enzo Roggi, "Una pagina di storia rivelata: 'Così Paolo VI scrisse a Ho Chi Minh,'" *Circolo Partito Democratico RAI—Comunicazione*, http://www.dsrai.it, accessed March 2008.

41. Luca Pavolini, "Autonomia e internazionalismo," *Rinascita*, 26 July 1968.

42. Gundle, *Between Moscow and Hollywood*, 133; Pons, *Berlinguer e la fine del comunismo*, 13.

43. Ackley to State Department, 13 September 1968, POL 12 It, RG 59, NA; Berlinguer in Mtg. Direzione 5 December 1974, VD, mf. 073, APCI.

44. Tel. Paris embassy to Department of State, 10 October 1968, FRUS 1964–68, XII: doc. 84.

45. In general, on this topic see Valerio Riva, *Oro di Mosca. I finanziamenti sovietici al PCI dalla Rivoluzione d'ottobre al crollo dell'URSS* (Milan: Mondadori, 1999).

46. On redefinition of Soviet national security, see Matthew J. Ouimet, *The Rise and Fall of the Brezhnev Doctrine in Soviet Foreign Policy* (Chapel Hill: University of North Carolina Press, 2003). Amendola in Mtg. Direzione 8 January 1971, mf 017, APCI; cf. also for follow-up in the late 1970s toward more autonomy for the PCI: Gianni Cervetti, *L'oro di Mosca* (Milan: Baldini & Castoldi, 1993).

47. Berlinguer in Mtg. Direzione 16 November 1968, VD, mf 020, APCI.

48. Berlinguer in Mtg. Direzione 31 January–1 February 1973, VD, mf 041, 420–23; Nota Riservata Sergio Segre to Berlinguer, 12 March 1976, VD, mf. 239, Pajetta in Mtg. Direzione 18 July 1977 (afternoon), VD, mf. 299, Amendola in Mtg. Direzione 20 February 1979, 8, VD, mf. 7906, APCI.

49. On this point in general, see especially Pons, *Berlinguer e la fine del comunismo*, passim, and Gundle, *Between Hollywood and Moscow*, 158–64.

50. See for best archival record, Berlinguer in Mtg. Direzione 5 December 1974, cit.

51. Cf. Claudio Terzi, "The PCI, Eurocommunism, and the Soviet Union," in *The Italian Communist Party: Yesterday, Today, and Tomorrow*, ed. Simon Serfaty and Lawrence Gray (Westport, CT: Greenwood, 1980); François Hincker, *Le parti communiste au carrefour* (Paris: Albin Michel, 1981), 166ff; Jean Fabien, *La guerre des camarades* (Paris: Olivier Orban, 1985).

52. See Pons, *Berlinguer e la fine del comunismo*, 37; Irwin Wall "L'amministrazione Carter e l'eurocomunismo," *Ricerche di storia politica* 1 (August 2006): 181–96. On contrasts between the PCF and PCI, see Amendola and Galluzzi in Mtg. Direzione 13 October 1977, VD, 273, 276, mf 304, APCI.

53. See, for example, Henry A. Kissinger, "Communist Parties in Western Europe: Challenge to the West," in *Eurocommunism: The Italian Case*, ed. Austin Ramney and Giovanni Sartori (Washington, DC: American Enterprise for Public Policy Research, 1978), 183–96; and Mtg. of Sec. Henry A. Kissinger with representatives of foreign service class, 6 January 1977, Kissinger TelCons, 1973–77, Nixon Presidential Materials Staff, NARA.

54. Cf. tel. A-183 report by Shriver (Paris embassy), "The French Communist Party in Mid-1969," 29 July 1969, POL 12 FR, RG 59, NARA.

55. See Longo in Mtg. Direzione 7–8 May 1969, VD, mf 006, APCI; Dec. BP 15 July 1972, APCF.

56. On this point, see in particular Federico Romero, "L'Europa come strumento di nation-building. Storia e storici dell'Italia repubblicana," *Passato e Presente* 13, no. 36 (1995): 19–32; Bernard Brunetau, "The Construction of Europe and the Concept of the Nation State," *Contemporary European History* 9, no. 2 (2000): 245–60.

57. Dec. BP 12 November 1970, APCF; cf. Thomas Gomart, "Le PCF au miroir des relations franco-soviétiques (1964–1968)," *Relations Internationales* 114 (Summer 2003): 249–66.

58. Gino G. Raymond, *The French Communist Party during the Fifth Republic: A Crisis of Leadership and Ideology* (London: Palgrave-McMillan, 2005), 60–63, and

Alistair Cole, *François Mitterrand: A Study in Political Leadership* (London: Routledge, 1994), 74.

59. See the interventions by Pajetta and Berlinguer in Mtg. Direzione 12 September 1973, VD, mf 041, APCI; Antonio Rubbi, *Il mondo di Berlinguer* (Rome: Roberto Napoleone, 1994), 53–57; Agostino Giovagnoli, *Il Caso Moro: Una tragedia repubblicana* (Bologna: Il Mulino, 2005), 9–13.

60. Pons, *Berlinguer e la fine del comunismo*, xxi, see also 52–60 (Segre qtd. ivi 55).

61. Courtois and Lazar, *Histoire du Parti communiste français*, 380–82; David Drake, *Intellectuals and Politics in Postwar France* (London: Palgrave, 2002), 148–50; Jean Elleinstein, *L'histoire du phénomène stalinien* (Paris: Grasset, 1975); cf. the seminal book, Alexander Adler et al., *L'URSS et nous* (Paris: Editions sociales, 1978).

62. Drake, *Intellectuals and Politics*, 150–52; S. Khilnani, *Arguing Revolution: The Intellectual Left in Postwar France* (New Haven, CT: Yale University Press, 1993), 151–53; cf. in general Arthur Marwick, *The Sixties: Cultural Revolution in Britain, France, Italy, and the United States, 1958–1974* (Oxford: Oxford University Press, 1998); Carole Fink et al., eds., *1968: The World Transformed* (Cambridge: Cambridge University Press, 1998).

63. See, for example, the intervention by Jean Kanapa in Comité Central 18–19 January 1974, transcripts from CC du PCF, Année 1974, CD 8, track 3, APCF.

64. Both quotes from Roger, *The American Enemy*, 405.

65. Memo conversation Raymond Barre (vice president of Commission of European Communities) with George S. Springsteen (deputy assistant secretary for European affairs), Abraham Katz, Director's Office of OECD, European Community and Atlantic Political-Economic Affairs, 5 June 1968, FRUS, 1964–68, XIII: 699–705.

66. Georges Marchais, "De faux révolutionnaires à démasquer," *L'Humanité*, 3 May 1968; Rochet report "Les événements de mai-juin 1968," CC 8–9 July 1968, Nanterre, Cote 4AV10/128, transcript from CD n. 18, APCF; cf. Annie Kriegel, *Les communistes français* (Paris: Seouil, 1985), 317–42; Roger Martelli, *Mai 68* (Paris: Messidor/Editions Sociales, 1988); for connection with Prague Spring and Soviet influence on the PCF's perceptions of May events cf. Gael Moullec, "Mai 1968, le PCF et l'Union Sovietique: Notes des entretiens entre les dirigeants du PCF et l'ambassadeur soviétique en France," *Communisme* 53–54 (1998): 151–64.

67. Giorgio Amendola, "Necessità della lotta sui due fronti," *Rinascita*, 7 June 1968; Amendola in meeting Direz. 6 June 1968, VD, mf 020, APCI; Pier Paolo Pasolini, "Il PCI ai giovani!" (October 1968), in *Empirismo eretico* (Milan: Garzanti, 1981), 151–59, also highlighted in Höbel, "Il PCI di Longo e il '68 studentesco," cit., 442. On "strategia dell'attenzione," see Luigi Longo, "Il movimento studentesco nella lotta anticapitalistica," in *Rinascita-Il Contemporaneo*, 3 May 1968. In general, see Sidney Tarrow, *Democracy and Disorder: Protest and Politics in Italy, 1965–1975* (Oxford: Clarendon, 1989); Robert Lumley, *States of Emergency: Cultures of Revolt in Italy from 1968 to 1978* (London: Verso, 1990); Paul Ginsborg, *A History of Contemporary Italy: Society and Politics, 1943–1988* (London: Penguin, 1990), chap. 9; and Luisa Passerini, *Autobiography of a Generation*, trans. Lisa Erdberg (Hanover, NH: University Press of New England, 1996).

68. Jeremi Suri, *Power and Protest: Global Revolution and the Rise of Détente* (Cambridge, MA: Harvard University Press, 2003). On de Gaulle in this sense see Georges-Henri Soutou, "Paris and the Prague Spring," in this volume.

69. Quoted Judt, *Postwar*, 421. Cf. Gerd-Rainer Horn, "The Changing Nature of the European Working Class: The Rise and Fall of the 'New Working Class' (France, Italy, Spain, Czechoslovakia)," in Fink et al., *1968*.

70. Occhetto in Direzione nazionale della FGCI, "Atti del convegno nazionale degli studenti universitari comunisti: Firenze, Palagio di Parte Guelfa, 17-18-19 marzo 1968," in *Nuova Generazione*, 6 July 1968, pp. 63–66; also in Höbel, "Il PCI di Longo" (Longo quoted ivi 438).

71. Achille Occhetto, *A dieci anni dal '68*, interviewed by Walter Veltroni (Rome: Editori Riuniti, 1978), 90–94.

72. Courtois and Lazar, *Histoire du PCF*, 355–56; cf. Pierre Grémion, *Paris/Prague: La gauche française face au renouveau et à la régression tchéchoslovaques, 1968–1978* (Paris: Julliard, 1984); "Communiqué du Bureau Politique sur un livre de Roger Garaudy," *Cahiers du communisme* 46, no. 1 (January 1970): 117–18.

73. Quoted in Drake, *Intellectuals and Politics*, 135; cf. Ian H. Birchall, *Sartre against Stalinism* (New York: Berghahn, 2004), 199–220.

74. Giuseppe Vacca, "Politica e teoria nel marxismo italiano degli anni sessanta," in *Il marxismo italiano degli anni sessanta: La formazione teorico-politica delle nuove generazioni*, ed. Istituto Gramsci (Rome: Editori Riuniti-Istituto Gramsci, 1972); Albertina Vittoria, *Togliatti e gli intellettuali: Storia dell'Istituto Gramsci negli anni cinquanta e sessanta* (Rome: Editori Riuniti, 1992).

75. Quoted Judt, *Postwar*, 403, and Raymond, *The French Communist Party during the Fifth Republic*, 159. Cf. Fuchsmann, "Karl Marx, notre contemporain," cit., 78–88; cf. Bernard Brillant, "Intellectuels: Les ombres changeantes de Mai 68," *Vingtieme Siecle* 98 (2008): 89–99; Gramsci, Lukacs, and Luxemburg were also rediscovered in the 1960s; they all disagreed with most Leninist practices.

76. Gianfranco Corsini, "L'America del dissenso," *Il Contemporaneo/Rinascita*, March 1966.

77. Memo by Union des Ecrivains (to Cultural section BP), "À Propos de la Politique Culturelle," 2 February 1971, drafted by Bernard Pingaud, Fonds Roland Leroy, 263 J 65, APCF.

78. On the PCF and "Malthusianism," see adoption Resolution Veermesch in Decisions BP, 13 April 1956; see also Dec. BP, 30 November 1961, APCF; cf. Yvonne Dumont, "Les femmes, leurs problèmes et leurs luttes," *Cahiers du communisme* 44, no. 1 (January 1967): 75–84; last quotation from Gundle, *Between Hollywood and Moscow*, 150.

79. See, in particular, comments by Sereni and Amendola in meeting Direzione 5 April 1967, VD, APCI.

80. Quoted in Pons, *Berlinguer e la fine del comunismo*, 43–44.

81. Judt, *Postwar*, 447–49. For a recent similar view see also the thorough analysis by Michael Seidman, *The Imaginary Revolution: Parisian Students and Workers in 1968* (New York: Berghahn Books, 2004); for a different view, see Kristin Ross, *May '68 and Its Afterlives* (Chicago: University of Chicago Press, 2002). Ross and Seidman, however, concur on the importance of the transformative power that the media and the intellectual debate attributed to those events, regardless of their actual effects on French and Western life. See also, for most recent debate, Xavier Vigna, "Clio contre Carvalho. L' historiographie de '68," *RILI* 5 (May–June 2008); Kristin Ross, Nicolas Hatzfeld, Antoine Artous, "Mai '68: Le débat continue," *RILI* 6 (July–August 2008).

See also Robert Gildea, "1968 in 2008," *History Today* 58, no. 5 (2008): 22–25, and Gian Carlo Marino, *Biografia del sessantotto: Utopie, conquiste, sbandamenti* (Milan: Bompiani, 2004).

82. Charles S. Maier, "The Politics of Productivity: Foundations of American International Economic Policy After World War II," *International Organization* 3 (1977); David Ellwood, "The American Challenge and the Origins of the Politics of Growth," in *Making the New Europe: European Unity and the Second World War*, ed. Peter M. Smith and M. L. Stirk (London: Pinter, 1993), 183–94; Richard F. Kuisel, *Seducing the French: The Dilemma of Americanization* (Berkeley: University of California Press, 1993), chap. 4; Bryan Angus McKenzie, *Remaking France: Americanization, Public Diplomacy, and the Marshall Plan* (New York: Berghahn Books, 2003); Charles S. Maier, "The Cold War as an Era of Imperial Rivalry," in *Reinterpreting the End of the Cold War*, ed. Silvio Pons and Federico Romero (London: Frank Cass, 2005).

83. On U.S. reactions to Communist politics and propaganda in France and Italy and for the comments in the following paragraphs, I am referring to Alessandro Brogi, *Confronting Anti-Americanism: The United States' Cold War against the Communists in France and Italy*, forthcoming from the University of North Carolina Press.

84. Intelligence Report no. 6140, "The French Communist Party: Its 1952 Record and Prospects for 1953," 30 December 1952, Office of Intelligence and Research, RG 59, NARA.

85. On these aspects, besides my forthcoming book, see also Kenneth Osgood, *Total Cold War: Eisenhower's Secret Propaganda Battle at Home and Abroad* (Lawrence: University Press of Kansas, 2006); and Volker R. Berghahn, *America and the Intellectual Cold Wars in Europe: Shepard Stone between Philanthropy, Academy, and Diplomacy* (Princeton, NJ: Princeton University Press, 2001).

86. Kennan to Hooker, 17 October 1949, George F. Kennan Papers, box 23, Seeley J. Mudd Library, Princeton University, Princeton, NJ; Emmet J. Hughes, *The Ordeal of Power: A Political Memoir of the Eisenhower Years* (New York: Atheneum, 1963), 275–81.

87. See the documents cited in notes 53, 54, and 65 above.

88. J. William Fulbright, *The Arrogance of Power* (New York: Random House, 1966), 245–46; Meeting Kissinger with Representatives of Foreign Service Class, 6 January 1977, cit.

89. For a similar approach, see also the memoirs of President Carter's ambassador to Italy, Richard N. Gardner, *Mission Italy: On the Front Lines of the Cold War* (Lanham, MD: Rowman & Littlefield, 2005).

90. On these diplomatic maneuvers see Brogi, *Confronting Anti-Americanism*; cf. argument in broader context in Alessandro Brogi, *A Question of Self-Esteem: The United States and the Cold War Choices in France and Italy, 1944–1958* (Westport, CT: Praeger, 2002). On G-7 and anticommunist strategy see also Duccio Basosi and Giovanni Bernardini, "The Puerto Rico summit of 1976 and the end of Eurocommunism," *The Crisis of Détente in Europe: From Helsinki to Gorbachev, 1975–1985*, ed. Leopoldo Nuti (London: Routledge, 2008).

IV

EUROPEAN NEIGHBORS DURING THE PRAGUE SPRING

14

The USSR, the Federal Republic of Germany, and the Czechoslovak Crisis of 1968

Aleksei Filitov

This chapter answers three basic questions regarding how the Prague Spring crisis in Czechoslovak Socialist Republic (ČSSR) affected relations between the Soviet Union and the Federal Republic of Germany (FRG). First, how did Soviet interpretations of the FRG's politics concerning Czechoslovakia come into being, and to what extent did they correspond to reality? Second, on what did Czechoslovakia—in the eyes of the Soviets—base its relations with the FRG? Finally, what effects did the Czechoslovak crisis and its outcome ultimately have on USSR-FRG relations?[1]

The Politburo Resolution of the Central Committee of the CPSU ("Information for Fraternal Parties on the Current Situation in Czechoslovakia") of 28 October 1968 contains the following passage:

> Reactionary Western circles actively support the rightist forces in Czechoslovakia. As is known from a reliable source, the USA, England, the FRG and Italy, acting on a US government initiative, reached an agreement at the beginning of July, which provides for these countries to pursue a common course with regard to Czechoslovakia. This course concerns above all political and economic measures designed to weaken Czechoslovakia's ties to other Socialist countries, notably the Soviet Union. *It was also agreed for the Federal Republic of Germany to play the key role in the deployment of Western influence on developments in Czechoslovakia.* (Emphasis added)

In March 1968, Franz Josef Strauss stated in a meeting with senior West German Christian Democratic Union (CDU) functionaries that the U.S. and the German governments had invested a great deal of work in order to compromise the Communist Party of Czechoslovakia (KSČ) leadership in the eyes of the Czechoslovak public. According to Strauss, the Western world was, therefore, supposed to make "sensitive and prudent" use of all channels of ideological and economic influence in order further to weaken the KSČ's clout in the country and "gradually to prise away Czechoslovakia from the USSR."[2]

SOURCES FOR THE SOVIET INTERPRETATION OF THE FRG'S POLICY CONCERNING THE ČSSR

It has proved impossible to identify the source from which the Soviet leadership could have obtained this information. Leaving the authenticity issue aside, we may note that in this concrete case, mention is made of plans and intentions on the part of the West to interfere in Czechoslovak affairs, yet there are no facts to document any kind of actual interference. These are referred to in the next paragraph of the document, in which charges are leveled not at West German, but at Austrian politicians, those in Austria's Socialist Party (SPÖ), to be precise.

An examination of the files of the Soviet press and of TASS results in a corroboration of the Austrian role in events in Czechoslovakia, which is even stronger and more accentuated than the West German one. The *Literaturnaya Gazeta* of 28 August 1968[3] published an article entitled "Green Berets Again" about the transfer of "arms and saboteurs" from the FRG to Czechoslovakia across Austrian territory, whereas *Pravda* wrote about the transfer of "22 West German radio transmitter stations"—again across Austrian territory.[4] According to these incriminatory articles, the Soviet propagandists blamed Czechoslovakia's two "Western" neighbors in equal measure. In the secret TASS material, Austria's role is underlined more strongly and in a more "aggressive" diction, as a glance at some of the headlines of these information bulletins[5] conveys: "Austria's radio transmits Czech language broadcasts on developments in the ČSSR" and "The Vienna unit of Austria's Military Secret Service focuses its activities on Czechoslovakia."[6]

It has to be borne in mind that we are talking here of the time after the invasion of the ČSSR by the troops of the Warsaw Pact. While the crisis was still brewing, the main target for all incriminations regarding "interference" was clearly the FRG. It is obvious that propaganda came in different degrees of intensity. Judging by the dossier "Czechoslovakia and the FRG," which was put together in 1968 at the Soviet Foreign Ministry from TASS material, statements of FRG politicians, which were full of exhortations to use caution in exploiting the new situation in the ČSSR for German purposes, were the first focus of interest. A Deutsche Presse-Agentur (DPA) report of 1 April reported that

Ernst Majonica, a CDU member of the *Bundestag*, warned against rushing through an initiative concerning the re-establishment of diplomatic relations between the Federal Republic and Czechoslovakia. Majonica: We do not want to put the government in Prague on the spot by pressurizing them. It will be advisable to exercise restraint in making comments on developments in Prague, as our comments are liable to have repercussions on the Federal Republic's relations to Moscow. . . . Any West German eastern policy is doomed to fail if it is anti-Soviet in character.[7]

It took some time for annoyance with the FRG to surface in comments in connection with the events of the Prague Spring. Reporting in the West German media on events in the ČSSR triggered the first sharp reaction. On 25 May the regular edition of the TASS Report[8] published an article entitled "Libelous article in the weekly *Der Spiegel* on the developments in Czechoslovakia" (referring to the article "Zu Europa" in the edition of 13 May). Soon afterwards, the visits of members of the FRG's political and economic elite in the ČSSR were given top priority in the TASS Report. Of particular interest to the Soviet Foreign Ministry were the almost simultaneous trips— on 12 and 13 July—of two representatives of the Free Democratic Party (*Freie Demokratische Partei* or FDP), Hans-Dietrich Genscher and Walter Scheel, and of the president of the Bundesbank, Karl Blessing.[9] On 16 July, TASS published an article entitled "UPI on the Relations between the FRG and Czechoslovakia" ("UPI zu den Beziehungen zwischen der BRD und der Tschechoslowakei") by the correspondent of the U.S. news service in Bonn, Wellington Long, which contained the following statement:[10]

> West Germany has begun building a political bridgehead in Czechoslovakia. A first "on-the-spot inspection" was carried out at the end of last week by the party leader of the opposition FDP, Walter Scheel, and by the CEO of the Bundesbank, Karl Blessing. . . . The institute that Blessing heads is an issue bank and the Federal Reserve Bank. He does not grant or underwrite loans yet he can certainly offer his services as a go-between and has no doubt done so. A word from Blessing uttered in the right place can work wonders in Germany.

It appears that the idea of Czechoslovakia receiving economic aid from the FRG rather rattled the Soviet leadership—a flashback to Josef Stalin's reaction to the Czech government's resolution in 1947 to accept aid under the Marshall Plan. However, given the state of affairs in the latter half of the 1960s, it was clearly unrealistic to follow in Stalin's actions in order to solve the problem, that is, to order the Czechoslovak leadership to Moscow and dress them down. The only channel that remained open was propaganda. The task consisted in showing that, while the FRG was ostensibly offering talks on economic aid, it was, in fact, planning a military intervention. Soviet press reports began to announce the discovery of arms caches on

Czechoslovak territory that had been deposited there by West German *re-vanchistes* close to the *Landsmannschaft der Sudetendeutschen*, the association of Sudeten Germans. TASS published an announcement from the Reuters News Agency to the effect that "the Sudeten German refugees have rejected Soviet charges today as the products of 'pure fantasy.'"[11] The announcement also quoted the chairman of the *Sudetendeutsche Landsmannschaft*, Walter Becher, accusing the USSR of doing "their utmost to create an atmosphere which made Russian interference in Czechoslovak affairs appear called for"—which was actually the case. At the same time, it becomes quite obvious from the Reuters correspondent's interview with Becher that the latter did not deny the existence of the arms caches: "These weapons are, as Dr. Becher explained, quite obviously leftovers from the American postwar occupation of this region."

The activities of the Sudeten German organizations and the statements of its president proved a boon to Soviet propaganda, particularly as Becher also belonged to one of the parties represented in the FRG's coalition government of the day. In an interview for *Der Spiegel* of 29 July, Becher quite openly advocated "the return of Sudeten German experts to federal Czechoslovakia, to the federal Bohemian, Moravian, and Slovak state."[12] Because such a program obviously existed, the thesis of *revanchiste* expansionism and of a threat to the Socialist construction—or even of the already existing statehood—of the ČSSR did not seem utterly absurd any longer.

Becher was planning to expound the rationale behind his program at a projected gathering of 25,000 Sudeten Germans on 24/25 August, the so-called Pear Sunday weekend, in Schirnding close to the Czech border. Planning for this gathering acquired ominous overtones when it was linked directly to plans concerning *Bundeswehr* maneuvers which were also due to take place in the ČSSR border region. When the *Der Spiegel* correspondent mentioned the possibility of a link between the two developments, Becher replied:

> All the chickens at the Bohemian-Bavarian border will burst their sides with laughter when they hear that a perfectly innocuous holiday of the inhabitants of the Egerland is linked to maneuvers entitled "Black Lion." Personally, I regret the whole kerfuffle surrounding these maneuvers. It might be a good idea either to give them a different name or to hold them somewhere else.[13]

"Kerfuffle" was presumably Becher's term for the acrimonious polemics that had erupted in FRG political circles around these maneuvers. The FRG press reported at length on the differences of opinion within the ruling coalition on this subject, namely between Minister of Defense Gerhard Schröder and the Social Democrats. This was also documented in some detail in TASS Reports. On 22 July, a report in the "Breaking News" section noted that "the FRG government had decided to either hold the 'Black Lion' maneuvers, which had been planned for the autumn, either at a different location or at a different time." However, this information was not taken up by the press.

As opposed to the "Black Lion" maneuvers, the gathering at Schirnding was not adjourned. In a reaction to this development, the FRG ambassador to the USSR, Helmut Allardt, told the head of the 3rd European Department of the USSR Foreign Ministry, Garal'd Gorinovich, on 31 August that the FRG government had "implemented measures designed to reduce in size the gathering of Sudeten Germans in Schirnding at the border with the ČSSR. What eventually took place there was no more than a religious service for Sudeten Germans."[14] These "measures" neither made it into the press nor the materials of TASS. It appears that the difficult relations between FRG government circles and the *Landsmannschaften* received scant attention in Western media. The precise timing of the implementation of these so-called measures remains unclear. If they took place after 21 August, it indirectly corroborates the interpretation transported by Soviet propaganda that the military action of the Warsaw Pact countries "caused a certain disillusionment among West German *revanchistes*."

Soviet propaganda, incidentally, was directly affected both by what FRG politicians said and did not say and by material lifted from West German media. It is characteristic that the TASS Report memorably entitled "Bonn's Subversive Tactics against the ČSSR" repeats almost the entire *Der Spiegel* article.[15] It should be noted that *Der Spiegel* was used in this concrete case as a source of non-partisan, objective information, even though the weekly had exclusively been characterized in extremely negative terms in the past. The report reported that "the West German Secret Service recruits its agents from among FRG citizens traveling to the ČSSR, according to the latest edition of the periodical *Der Spiegel*." The weekly reported that West German border police keep tabs on the names, car registration plates, and addresses of those West German citizens who crossed the border from the FRG into the ČSSR. "The data on these persons are then forwarded to the staff headquarters of the West German Secret Service in Munich. On the basis of these data, individuals are selected who are capable of working as agents and informants for the federal Intelligence Service."

TASS also noted that the police activities mentioned above had been questioned by Werner Porsch, one of the FDP members of the *Bundestag*, and that the reason given for them by the Bavarian Ministry of the Interior was "considerations of state security." The communiqué winds up in a manner that makes it difficult to tell whether the concluding remarks are based directly on the *Der Spiegel* article or on the TASS correspondent's judgment: "The registration procedure at the border does not serve the purpose of uncovering agents of the East but of recruiting agents for the West. This is how, according to the periodical, the principle of 'strict non-interference' in internal affairs proclaimed by the Chancellor is put into practice."

It must be said that some of the statements made by FRG politicians on this "principle" were, indeed, highly ambiguous. One of the editions of TASS rendered an interview that Willy Brandt had granted a German TV station in which he "advocated not only as Foreign Minister but also as a representative of SPD restraint and strict non-interference in the developments in Czechoslovakia."[16] He "emphatically" declared on the same occasion: "I would like to state with complete candor that this does not come easily to me. It weighs on me that there are people we cannot receive, that there are many one would like to see and to talk to if there were the time to do so. Yet here we have to submit to a higher law."

ESTABLISHING CONTACTS BETWEEN BONN AND PRAGUE

Brandt's afterthought could be interpreted as referring to contacts that had already been established in secret with Prague and to attempts on the part of Prague to upgrade these contacts to a higher level, which would, however, have to wait. Such an interpretation obviously presupposes a certain measure of distrust or even suspicion regarding the intentions and activities of the Prague reformers. Both were present in generous measure in the minds of the Soviet leadership. The question that is interesting in this context is whether these were justified.

The first foreign political activities of the new ČSSR leadership could not give rise to further distrust or suspicion, at least as far as relations with the FRG were concerned. The memorandum "Reactions in the most important Czechoslovak papers to the resolutions of the January plenum of the CC KSČ" (Central Committee of the Communist Party of Czechoslovakia), whose author was the second secretary of the Soviet embassy in Prague, Yuri Zhuravlev, mentions the fact that "on 10 January, the KSČ's central organ, *Rudé právo*, published a foreign political commentary which unmasks the fabrications and speculations of the bourgeois propaganda with reference to the changes that are supposed to have taken place in the ČSSR's foreign policy in the wake of the January plenum." It goes on to give a detailed summary of the most important points of this article, in particular the passage that deals with the ČSSR's relations with the two German states:

> Czechoslovakia will steadfastly adhere to its traditional political course in the German question. The alliance the ČSSR has entered into with the German Socialist state, the GDR, is a fixed and unalterable element of Czechoslovakia's international position as is also the ČSSR's attitude regarding West Germany. In addition to this, neither the class character nor the political system of the

FRG will impede per se the development of legitimate economic or even diplomatic ties. The main reason why relations between the ČSSR and the FRG have not yet been normalized are aggressive demands for a revision of the results of the war within Europe.

The Soviet diplomat referred to an isolated lapse from correct political behavior by noting that "the imperialist aggression in the Middle East [was] not going to be considered."[17]

On the day of the publication of this article in *Rudé právo*, a declaration of the Czechoslovak government on the activities of neo-Nazi and *revanchiste* forces in West Germany was also published. The declaration sharply criticized not only the *Sudetendeutsche Landsmannschaft* and the National Democratic Part of Germany (NDPD), but also the federal government and the governments of "several" NATO countries.[18] Both the content and the tone of the declaration were completely in accordance with the "tough stance" vis-à-vis the FRG that had been agreed upon at the 1967 Warsaw Pact Conference in Karlovy Vary.

On the following day, 11 January, a condensed version of the declaration was published in *Rudé právo*.[19] The paper's version admittedly differed somewhat from the original government declaration in that it was more laconic in tone; the demands to the FRG government were less specific, and the criticism of other Western governments and of NATO was omitted altogether. A feature common to both the declaration and the *Rudé právo* article was the explicit provenance of the facts documenting *revanchiste* and right-wing extremist activities in the FRG from documents of the country's Ministry of the Interior and the SPD-associated Friedrich Ebert Foundation. These documents contained outspoken condemnations of these activities, which did not corroborate the thesis that the activities were carried out "with the government's consent." On the contrary, in this manner the position at least of the junior partner in the coalition, the Social Democrats, was vindicated, if indirectly.

Soviet diplomats could not have cared less for such nuances at the time. One can form some idea of the position they held from the following passage in the transcript of a conversation between the Soviet ambassador to the FRG and his Dutch colleague, de Beys, on 26 January 1968:

> De Beys asked me about our assessment of political developments in the FRG, notably of the FRG coalition government's so-called "*Ostpolitik*" (Eastern Politics). I stressed that the policies pursued by the Kiesinger and Brandt government had unfortunately brought no changes and had basically remained the same as those of Adenauer and Erhard. As far as the principled positions vis-à-vis the Socialist countries were concerned, the FRG government continues to embrace unrealistic positions by ignoring the changes that are taking place in Europe. All this makes one cautious with regard to the true objectives of the FRG government.[20]

One should beware, however, of exaggerating the importance of the contradictions between the Soviet and the Czechoslovak assessments of the party political situation in the FRG during the first phase of the Prague Spring, lasting roughly to March 1968. At the time, Prague's ideological attitude aimed at avoiding an exclusive reliance on the leadership of the SPD; instead, it reached out also to "leftist," "progressive" forces within this party; these were going to become steadily more important in proportion to the progress of democratization in Czechoslovakia. In a report compiled by the 4th European Department of the Foreign Ministry of the USSR on reactions of the Western press to the developments in Czechoslovakia, the following passage from *Rudé právo* of 19 March was reprinted without comment:

> The unfolding of events in the ČSSR gives rise to certain fears in West Germany's Social Democratic circles, particularly among right-leaning leaders. These are aware that a successful conclusion of the process that is now unfolding in Czechoslovakia could lead to some of the more conservative positions held by the Social Democrats being seriously called into question, which would result in a shift to the left of the entire SPD.[21]

This is followed by a report on reactions in the Czechoslovak press. Under the heading of 16 April, a statement is quoted from a speech given by Hessian Minister of Economy and Transport Rudi Arndt at the opening of the "Czechoslovak Days in the FRG": "In the FRG, we, too, should be working toward such a progressive development as is now underway in Czechoslovakia." The editors of the compilation work note that "these words were put in bold print in the *Prace*."[22]

Such emphasis is perfectly understandable. Arndt's statement underlines the prognosis that the Czechoslovak model will have a positive effect on the West. Whether this corresponded to the truth is another matter, yet it is probable that it made people think, including those in Moscow. The question that the Soviet envoy to the FRG, Semyon Tsarapkin, put in the course of a conversation on 14 March 1968 to someone whose competence and influence particularly in the FRG's leftist circles was beyond doubt, namely the head of the Metal Workers Trade Union, Otto Brenner, was a well considered one. Tsarapkin asked about people "belonging to the left wing of the SPD leadership." The answer was a thoroughly discouraging one from the Soviet viewpoint, "Brenner declared that the left wing of the SPD leadership was non-existent, despite the fact that leftist tendencies were prominent in grassroots organizations." Brenner's ensuing remarks painted an even more downbeat picture: "In the FRG, a new generation of 'young careerists' is about to assume political power." Within the SPD leadership, a group of "young careerists" prominently including Helmut Schmidt, an opportunist in Brenner's eyes, was "getting thoroughly entrenched."

At the end of the conversation, Brenner passed a sort of verdict on the very party on which the Czechoslovak reformers were pinning their hopes: "As the SPD no longer considers itself as a workers' party but as a party for everyone, the Trade Unions are called upon to assume the role of the proponent of the interests and views of the working class—not only in the economic but the political arena as well."[23]

If no perspective whatsoever was in sight that the SPD might eventually identify with the ideas of the Prague Spring, the opposite view was gaining in strength, namely that the KPČ would be unable to resist the influence of the West.

In TASS correspondence from Bonn on the event that was also at the center of the Foreign Ministry report of 16 April, this information was relayed in a tone that might be called anxious rather than neutral:

> From 31 March to 10 April the "Czechoslovak Days" took place in Frankfurt am Main. They were organized by the German-Czechoslovak Society that is based in the FRG. . . . At the opening of the "Czechoslovak Days," the director of the Institute for Politics and Economics in Prague, Prof. Šnejdarek, delivered an address. According to the *Frankfurter Allgemeine*, Šnejdarek has been active over the past few years as covert promoter of a gradual *raprochement* between the German and the Czechoslovak viewpoints. The subject Šnejdarek chose for his address in Frankfurt was the Munich Agreement. Commenting on the address, the *Frankfurter Rundschau* writes: "He went so far as to say that the Czechs thought the statements of Brandt and Kiesinger on the Munich Agreement sufficient." Politically speaking, this of course means turning over an entirely new leaf.[24]

An interview of the head of the Economics Department of the same Prague Institute, Karl Tauber, with the radio station Deutschlandfunk was linked by the DPA to the following day. In it, Tauber "advocated a speeding up of the establishment of diplomatic relations between Czechoslovakia and the FRG" and also referred to the ČSSR's "interest to obtain loans from the FRG." He also noted certain reservations on the Czech side: "Tauber declared that what Czechoslovakia was waiting for before diplomatic contacts could be established was a clear and unequivocal statement that the Munich Agreement was invalid from the beginning. In addition, it was desirable for the Federal Republic to turn over a new leaf in its attitude to the other part of Germany."[25]

There is no doubt that this bit of news had the potential to alarm those who read it in the USSR. Czechoslovakia could potentially go down the road of Romania, particularly as the "reservations" that were quoted were extremely weak. The Romanian analogy, incidentally, was extremely topical with regard to the ČSSR at the time and was frequently discussed in European circles. A characteristic example is taken from a conversation between

the Soviet ambassador to Austria, Boris Podtserob, and his Czech colleague
Pavel Novotný on 26 February 1968. The transcript contains the following
passage:

> Austria's political leaders evince considerable interest in their talks with No-
> votný in the changes that have recently taken place in the Czechoslovak party
> leadership. They seem to assume that changes are unfolding in Czechoslovakia
> that will result in the country taking up a position comparable to Romania.
> This, however, will not be the case, said Comrade Novotný, as Czechoslovakia
> will abide by its course of lasting friendship and close cooperation with the
> USSR and the other Socialist countries.[26]

The publication of "Apropos Foreign Politics" by Šedivoj in *Literární noviny* of 18 April 1968 and "Should We Negotiate with the FRG?" by Henzel
in *Lidová demokracie* of 24 April bore witness to changes in exactly the direction that Podtserob's interlocutor had ruled out as impossible. The more
detailed assessment of these articles in the files of the Soviet embassy undertaken for Moscow's information was already couched in a deliberately
disapproving tone.[27]

It was not only on the level of theoretical disquisitions of individual journalists that a new course was steered on the basis of unilateral activities that
had not previously been discussed with the Warsaw Pact allies. Developments at the ČSSR-FRG border made headlines in the Western media, from
where the news gradually seeped through to the Soviet decision-makers
through TASS, that is, through nonpublic channels. On 3 April, the Reuters
News Agency, citing the Bavarian Ministry of the Interior, reported that
"today Czechoslovak soldiers have removed the triple barbed-wire barrier
at the West German border." This was followed by an "expert" explanation:
the border installations "have become redundant as a new barrier is being
erected about a kilometer further inland on Czechoslovak territory."[28] After
a two-week silence, the ČTK News Agency, citing *Práce*, came up with its
own version:

> As we have gathered from the commanding officer of the border police in the
> region of Chodský, repair works on the barrier are underway at those sections
> of the barrier that have either been damaged over time or that have been
> moved too far inland. There are several stretches where the triple barrier is too
> far away from the actual border, so much so that the intervening space is being
> used for agriculture or forestry. . . . Instead of the barrier that has now been
> removed new ones will be built at the border that are technologically up-to-
> date and more effective.[29]

The contradiction between the two versions—the first one claimed that the
barrier was going to be moved farther inland, whilst according to the second,
more authoritative one it was a matter of making the barrier identical with

the border—was not difficult to notice. It necessarily led to the conclusion that until such time as the "other barrier was being built" there would be no barrier at all. It was precisely this (logical) reasoning that led to Aleksei Kosygin's well known letter to the first minister of the ČSSR, Oldřich Černik, in which he stated that "owing to the overindulgence of the Czechoslovak authorities involved, the borders of Czechoslovakia are virtually open."[30]

This accusation was repeated in a more pointed form in the note of 20 July sent by the Foreign Ministry of the USSR to the ČSSR embassy, which stated that "the situation at the Western borders of the ČSSR has not only not improved after the receipt of the Czechoslovak side's answer but work at the border has actually slowed down."[31] In the reply to this note, the Czechoslovak embassy in Moscow duly denied this accusation, adding that "the new Czechoslovak government has introduced a number of measures since May in order to ensure a stricter border management regime also for foreigners." The note cited as proof above all that "during the recent maneuvers of the Allies, members of the Warsaw Pact High Command, with Soviet Marshal Ivan Yakubovskii at the head, visited a border post" and had "voiced their satisfaction with the measures, efforts and means that were being deployed in the defense of the Czechoslovak border."[32]

It would be tempting to accept the Czech line of argumentation if it were not obvious that the Western borders of the ČSSR had indeed been "open" in 1968, which was, in fact, due to the visa regulations that were in force. The ČSSR's reply to the Soviet note, incidentally, gave an answer to a question that had not been asked by stating that the issue of visas to "members of the Armed Forces of NATO countries" had been stopped. This measure, however, was insufficient to rebut the charge referring to the possibilities that "were immediately exploited by imperialist intelligence services, particularly of the FRG and the U.S. These services sent spies and 'diversants' to the ČSSR, who were outwardly indistinguishable from ordinary tourists, in order for them to engage in subversive activities against the leadership in Czechoslovakia as well as against that in other Socialist countries."[33]

It is conceivable that the Soviet side did not want to be painted as a sponsor of the Iron Curtain or to reveal information it had received through secret channels. However, it did not take long for openly accessible information to emerge. In addition to the episode mentioned above concerning Porsch's query that was commented on by *Der Spiegel*, there was an article three days later in the *Neue Rhein-Zeitung* of 7 August entitled "Queuing up for Visas to Czechoslovakia." It stated, among other things, that the ČSSR Military Mission in West Berlin was "literally being flooded with visa applications." Because these applications were processed inside one day, the result was that "in the first seven months of this year, more than 152,000 visas have been issued to German citizens." This article also soon found its way into the TASS Report.[34]

The TASS files already mentioned on "Bonn's subversive activities directed against Czechoslovakia" quoted an even higher number of West German visitors to Czechoslovakia, "The West German Intelligence Service has a considerable potential for recruiting agents to spy on the ČSSR. According to press reports, *368,000 German citizens* have entered Czechoslovakia in the first half of this year alone" (emphasis added).[35] It goes without saying that such a massive influx of Western tourists could not possibly be adequately monitored, even if one accepts the most conservative estimate of their number. This inevitably posed certain security problems for the Warsaw Pact countries.

Shortly prior to the beginning of the invasion, new reports on economic contacts between the ČSSR and the FRG surfaced. An announcement issued by Agence France-Presse (AFP) in Frankfurt/Main on 14 August stated that "a group of Czechoslovak finance experts are due to arrive here for talks with the Deutsche Bundesbank."[36] The talks were officially classified as "technical"; loans were explicitly excluded from the agenda, and the precise topics of the talks remained unspecified. It is understandable that such reports could only increase the suspicions Moscow harbored toward the plans of the Czechoslovak reformers, particularly if they were not offset by official information.

A comparable lack of information also prevailed regarding the visits of West German politicians to the ČSSR. It was even the case that the country's diplomats were not informed in time, which led to bizarre incidents. One example concerns the ČSSR ambassador to Austria, Novotný, who was showing considerable irritation with Austria's media during a conversation with his Soviet colleague, Podtserob, on 22 July, at the peak of the crisis in Czechoslovakia. The media, according to Novotný, "spread all kinds of lies and try thereby to influence politics in Czechoslovakia and the country's relations with the Socialist countries." From the transcript of the conversation, it is apparent to what the envoy of the ČSSR was referring. "Austria's media are carrying reports on a visit of the leader of the West German FDP, Scheel, to Czechoslovakia. This report is a pure and unmitigated fabrication."[37] However, the news of Scheel's visit had already been published by TASS on 13 July, and on the day of the conversation between Podtserob and Novotný, it was published by ČTK, which added that the visit was a nonofficial one. The result was that the ambassador was forced to retract his words the following day. The problem of the relationship between leading exponents of the ČSSR's foreign politics and the country's diplomats is beyond the scope of this article, but the above example shows very clearly that not all was well in this respect. This placed an additional burden on the Soviets in forming an objective, unbiased assessment of the Prague reformers and their political and foreign political goals. It was very difficult not to lose one's bearings given this mêlée of reports, rumors, retractions, and the like.

So far this chapter's discussion has only concerned image questions. But what were the actual stages in the development of Soviet–West German relations? What role did the events in Czechoslovakia play in this development?

THE REPERCUSSIONS OF THE ČSSR'S CRISIS ON RELATIONS BETWEEN BONN AND MOSCOW

As far as the relations between Bonn and Moscow were concerned, the year 1968 began with the jarring, tough-worded diplomatic note of 6 January 1968 on the topic of West Berlin, in which the Soviet government expressed its vehement disapproval of FRG policy. Bonn's reply, handed to Soviet Ambassador Tsarapkin by Chancellor Kurt Georg Kiesinger on 1 March, limited itself to expressing "surprise" at "the accusations filed by the government of the USSR"; it made no constructive contribution.[38] West Germany's reaction on 15 January to a Soviet proposal (made as early as 15 August 1967) concerning the establishment of a direct airlink between the USSR and the FRG was more satisfactory in operational and constructive terms. This positive reaction was obviously part of the policy of "small steps," the essence of Bonn's Eastern politics, and a kind of hallmark of the Great Coalition. Unsurprisingly, Bonn's diplomats in their reply hewed to West Germany's claim to sole representation; they even managed to ascribe this position to the Soviet side. In concrete terms, the reply stated that the FRG government "welcomed the Soviet proposal to start talks involving the relevant ministries of both countries on the establishment of a direct German-Soviet airlink." The Soviet proposal had, of course, referred to this goal as the establishment of "direct flights between the Soviet Union and the Federal Republic of Germany." A positive Soviet reply did not arrive until the end of the year, a development that figures into the chain of events discussed later in this article.

In many talks on both official and unofficial levels, FRG representatives affirmed their wish for the USSR to demonstrate a modicum of acceptance of the FRG and its politics; this was accompanied by denials of the existence in the FRG of *revanchism*, a neo-Nazi threat, and so forth. The USSR reacted to this by repeating the same catalogue of demands: the existing borders had not yet been recognized; the other German state had not yet been recognized; there were unwarranted claims on West Berlin; the development of neo-Nazism did not meet with an adequate response; the country was banking on nuclear energy; the country was evading the issue of the Munich Agreement; and the country was preparing "extraordinary legislation."

The Soviet side supported the strict measures taken against *revanchistes* by the GDR, as is evidenced by a conversation between the Polish ambassador

to Moscow, Paszkowski, and the head of the 3rd European Department of
the Foreign Ministry of the USSR, Anatolii Blatov, on 17 April 1968.[39] At the
same time, care was taken at the Soviet Foreign Ministry not to demonstrate
too much solidarity with their GDR comrades:

> As regards the missive of the ambassador of the USSR to the GDR, Comrade
> Pyotr Abrasimov, on the revelations of the FRG's *revanchiste* and expansionist
> legislation, we want to make the following statements:
>
> 1. The announcement of the GDR government concerning this topic was
>   published in the GDR on 20 February this year. On 21 February, the
>   *Pravda* carried an article entitled 'The Taming of the *Revanchists*' com-
>   menting on this announcement.
> 2. At the beginning of March, several GDR experts on International Law were
>   in Moscow to discuss with Soviet colleagues the text of a joint declaration
>   formulated by International Law experts from a number of Socialist coun-
>   tries concerning the GDR law dating from 3 August 1967 . . . a delegation
>   is expected on 4 April to vote on the draft document.
>
> For the time being, we consider a declaration supporting the announcement
> of the GDR government concerning several new laws passed in the FRG inop-
> portune.[40]

The most important topics in the talks held between staff members of the
3rd European Department and FRG diplomats, namely Ambassador Allardt
and the embassy's two ministers, Sante and Rudolf Wolff, were problems
related to the FRG's position on the Nuclear Nonproliferation Treaty and
to its renunciation of the use of force. The discussion of the two problems
proved fraught with difficulties, but was not hindered by polemics.

The situation in Czechoslovakia was not touched upon in these talks, as
this author can testify. The same can be said of talks of the Soviet ambassador to the FRG, Tsarapkin, with politicians and representatives of public
life in the FRG. These revolved around domestic issues of the FRG: neo-
Nazism, extraordinary legislation, the student movement, and so forth. The
only mention of events in Czechoslovakia in the documents that have been
examined is in connection with the federal minister for Scientific Research
in the FRG, Gerhard Stoltenberg, in the course of a talk with the Soviet
ambassador on 18 July 1968:

> Concerning the situation in Czechoslovakia Stoltenberg said that the Euro-
> pean nations were spellbound by the changes occurring in Eastern Europe.
> Important and irreversible developments are unfolding in Czechoslovakia
> that will have a great impact on the entire situation in Europe. These changes
> are, of course, occurring within the framework of Czechoslovakia's Commu-
> nist regime. Stoltenberg conveyed that the FRG government was not going to

make radical alterations with reference to its *Ostpolitik* until the outcome of the Czechoslovak developments was beyond dispute.[41]

One interpretation of this deliberately vague statement is that the West German minister had a compromise in mind: further steps away from Adenauer's old *Ostpolitik* would be possible, provided the USSR acknowledged the irreversibility of the developments that originated in Czechoslovakia and were now affecting all of Eastern Europe. If this interpretation hits the mark, a new set of possibilities for decoding the statement becomes available. Was this an inadmissible attempt to blackmail the USSR, or a well-meaning attempt to warn those in charge against taking violent action? The answer will depend on the viewpoint of whoever is interpreting the statement. Whatever the result, Stoltenberg's attempt has to be called a failure at least on account of the date of 18 September 1968 that the minutes of the meeting bear; in addition to this, it was not received by the Soviet Foreign Ministry until much later. Such a delay between an actual talk and its record being committed to the ambassador's official log is rather unusual. Again, a range of different explanations is possible, one of them being that Soviet diplomats in third countries were loath to address topics on which they felt out of their depth and which they assumed were also causing unease in Moscow. An indirect corroboration of this explanation derives from the fact that the ambassador added no comment of his own to his interlocutor's statement quoted above.

The conversation, however, took place at a time when the crisis that was brewing in the relations between Czechoslovakia and most of the other Warsaw Pact countries and its fallout, which would also affect Soviet-German relations, was approaching its climax. Almost simultaneously, the Soviet government dispatched strongly worded notes to the Czechoslovak government and a memorandum to the government of the FRG. In the latter the FRG was taken to task for making public the contents of the documents concerning a bilateral exchange of opinions on the topic of the renunciation of the use of force—notwithstanding the fact that at the same time the contents of these documents had been published in their entirety in the Soviet press. It has to be borne in mind that when Tsarapkin explained the purpose of the Soviet action to the Dutch ambassador, he did not mention Czechoslovak affairs with a single word. He confined himself to the remark that the action had been a "retaliatory measure" because the West German side had ignored the confidentiality principle in the dialogue. A further passage that is of interest in Tsarapkin's minutes of this brief conversation on 16 July is the one where he describes the reaction of his interlocutor and his own answer to his colleague's by no means trivial question: "The Dutch ambassador declared himself to be in agreement with my arguments and asked whether I concurred in thinking that the publication of the documents by both sides spelled the end of negotiations. I replied that the door to a continued exchange of opinions had not been closed."[42]

A comparable position was the one held by the 3rd European Department. In a memorandum dated 22 June and addressed to Andrei Gromyko by Anatolii Kovalev and Garal'd Gorinovich, the minister is given the advice to receive Ambassador Allardt and to inform him that the government of the USSR "is ready for a further exchange of opinions on the topic of the renunciation of the use of force." The memorandum also noted that "it is presumably helpful to raise the issue of the FRG's accession to the Nuclear Non-Proliferation Treaty in order not to provide a basis for the other side to claim the Soviet Union is bringing pressure to bear in some way."[43]

By now, the FRG had already shifted the polemical exploitation of the Czechoslovak question to an official intergovernmental level. The declaration of the FRG's government spokesman, Günther Dill, which was issued on 18 July 1968, must be considered the first "broadside" that was fired in this campaign. In it, he gave short shrift to the Soviet government's declaration of 5 July and noted that the details of this note "suggested the presence of pitch black humor" and that confidence in Moscow had thereby "been seriously undermined."

The exchange of protest notes between the Foreign Ministry of the FRG and the Soviet embassy in Bonn, which was to follow two weeks later, was the next step. It has proven impossible for this author to locate Soviet documents about this episode; the only document available is a version of a DPA report, which may, however, be considered reliable. It was in any case published without commentary in the daily edition of TASS under the title "On the Relations between the USSR and the FRG."[44] The following text is a translation from the Russian version: "Despite the federal government's protests, the Soviet Union remains convinced that 'certain circles' within the Federal Republic are meddling in the events in Czechoslovakia and want to exert 'hostile' influence on the relations between Moscow and Prague."

On the following day, Bonn filed a protest against such accusations; a day later, on a Thursday, the Soviet embassy in Bonn issued a communiqué to the effect that Ambassador Tsarapkin rebutted the protest "in the most categorical terms." In its rebuttal, the embassy referred to a talk that had taken place between Undersecretary Georg-Ferdinand Dukwitz and the Soviet ambassador at the Foreign Ministry on Wednesday. On that occasion, Dukwitz had registered a protest against the Soviet accusations and deplored the campaign that was being waged against the Federal Republic in the Soviet press.

In the communiqué based on this talk, the ambassador emphatically sided with the Soviet press with regard to the accusations against the FRG. The ambassador could not but rebuff the protest because "the evidence used by the Soviet press is based on facts amounting to proof that certain circles in the FRG are determined to interfere in a number of ways in the relations pertaining between the USSR and the ČSSR as well as in the internal affairs of the ČSSR." The interference was undertaken with the "express purpose of undermining Soviet-Czechoslovak relations."

The communiqué went on to say that Soviet-Czechoslovak relations and the situation in Czechoslovakia were not on the agenda in talks with the Federal Republic.

According to diplomatic observers, the Soviet-German "controversies" about putative German interference signaled Moscow's increasingly rigid attitude toward Bonn during the escalation of the situation in Czechoslovakia. This can also be inferred from the federal government's white book, which was published after negotiations with Moscow on the renunciation of the use of force stalled unexpectedly on 11 July.

The white book is significant in several ways. First, it provides definitive proof for the hypothesis that it was, in fact, the West German side that initiated official polemics centering on the Czechoslovak question. Second, the controversy followed a trajectory that was highly unusual given the traditional relations between the USSR and capitalist countries. Normally, the Soviet side would protest diverse articles published by the Western press; this drew a routine answer to the effect that the government involved in the matter, being unable to interfere in the affairs of independent media, was unable to assume responsibility. In the case under discussion, it was the other way round. Third, the Soviet side did not resort to the argument it habitually used on other, rare occasions when it was confronted with claims on the basis of positions put forward by Soviet media. It tacitly admitted that in this case the viewpoints of the Soviet press and the Soviet government were identical. This transformed the accusations leveled against the FRG by the press into a kind of official intervention. Fourth, in this case, accusations were not leveled against the government, but against "certain circles" in the FRG, which is indicative of Soviet diplomats' determination to minimize the conflict. Finally, the main thrust of the Soviet counterprotest was no more than an explication of the Brezhnev Doctrine.

It is difficult to ascertain what the actual objective of the FRG's intervention was. The government must have been aware that a change in the tune of Soviet propaganda was not in the cards. If the point of the exercise was to continue to expose propaganda for what it was, it would have been more logical to analyze the Soviet counterprotest and to expose the weaknesses of the Soviet position. However, Bonn came up with an entirely different reaction. According to the UPI Press Agency on 2 August, the FRG Foreign Ministry confined itself "to rebuffing the accusations of the Soviet ambassador, Tsarapkin, which centered on the claim that 'certain circles' were meddling in the internal affairs of Czechoslovakia" and stated "that the Foreign Ministry had no intentions of discussing this issue any further."[45]

By 21 August, USSR-FRG relations were smoother, if not entirely back to normal. On 20 August, literally on the eve of the invasion of the ČSSR by Warsaw Pact troops, a meeting took place between the head of the 3rd European Department, Gorinovich, and the ambassador of the FRG, Allardt, who signed, on behalf of the federal government, an international agreement on the Rescue of Astronauts, the Return of Astronauts, and the Return of Objects Launched into Outer Space. In the minutes of this meeting, Gorinovich writes: "I welcomed Allardt and expressed the hope that the next international agreement would be the one on Nuclear Non-Proliferation. The ambassador replied that this was by no means impossible."

Allardt inquired about the state of affairs concerning the direct airlink between the Soviet Union and the FRG because the FRG was still awaiting a reply to its note of 15 January. Gorinovich answered evasively: "The project is still being evaluated."[46]

Public reaction in the FRG to the invasion of the ČSSR by troops of the five Warsaw Pact countries was extremely negative. Protest demonstrations outside the buildings of the USSR's embassy and trade delegation escalated into riots. Bonn's official position was more restrained, if not downright apologetic. On 31 August, another meeting took place between Gorinovich and Allardt, which Allardt used to register a protest. However, his protest did not concern the events of 21 August, but a comment made in a German-language program of Radio Moscow to the effect that Chancellor Kiesinger's statement on 25 August "could be interpreted as a declaration of war and that the Warsaw Pact countries would draw their own conclusions from it." The Soviet side denied, of course, that it had the intention of starting a war with the FRG, and at the end of the meeting, the ambassador had to tender an apology for what had happened outside the Soviet embassy.

Kiesinger himself was even more obliging toward the USSR in a meeting with Tsarapkin on 2 September 1969. This author has already written extensively on this topic, yet one characteristic detail can now be added: the West German ambassador had confined himself to asserting that his government had never interfered in the internal affairs of the ČSSR and would certainly not do so in future.[47] At the same time, he conveyed that the FRG could not remain indifferent to the events unfolding in a neighboring country. The chancellor went definitely further than this. According to the minutes that were made on Tsarapkin's behalf, "he underscored . . . that the government of the FRG had never tried to interfere in security matters concerning Socialist countries or in their internal affairs or *in their mutual relations*" (emphasis added). As far as the past was concerned, this statement was less than candid; as an assurance concerning the future, it sounded decidedly attractive in Soviet ears.

An anecdote may be helpful in illustrating the mood at the time. On 7 September, Berthold Beitz, a member of the board of directors of the Krupp conglomerate, called on the Soviet ambassador in Bonn. He told the diplomat he had received an invitation to go hunting in Romania and was wondering "whether this trip might not provoke criticism in view of the existing circumstances." An indulgently inclined Tsarapkin gave his permission: "It was up to [Beitz] where and when he chose to go hunting."[48] Before 21 August, such an answer would have been unthinkable.

The FRG's reactions were not limited to exceptional demonstrations of respect for the Soviet state and to official declarations of the same effect. In bilateral relations, the "business as usual" mode soon began to reassert itself and included an initiative to intensify contacts that originated with the FRG. As early as 5 September, the West German side contacted the Foreign Ministry of the USSR to inquire whether a delegation of the Ludwigsburg-based Central Office of the State Justice Administration for the Investigation of National Socialist Crimes was welcome in the USSR. A positive answer was given on 9 September. On 20 September, the second secretary at the FRG embassy, Diepgen, told Ivan Sorokoletov, an official at the 3rd European Department, that the visiting group "was making good progress" and that the members of the group were "very in good spirits."[49] Otto von Stempel, the acting plenipotentiary, hinted in a meeting on 7 October with the new head of the 3rd European Department, Valentin Falin, that the FRG might conceivably be having second thoughts on its formerly adamant position regarding trade and cultural exchange agreements. He also raised the question again as to when the FRG could expect an answer on the direct airlink issue. This time, the Soviet reaction was less evasive than in the Gorinovich-Allardt meeting on 20 August: Falin assured his interlocutor that "an answer might well be forthcoming any time soon"—and "soon" it was to be: on 21 October the Air Ministry signaled its approval to the start of negotiations and these kicked off on 9 October 1968 in Bonn.[50] The crisis between the USSR and the FRG had been overcome and soon gave way to normal relations.

It is to be deplored that this happened after a demonstration of its power by the USSR; in a way, one could even say this happened because of it. This was not setting the best of examples for the future.

NOTES

Translated from German into English by Otmar Binder, Vienna.

1. The sources used here are above all the files of the Archive of Foreign Policy of the Russian Federation from the holdings F. 138a (Czechoslovak Desk), F. 757 (FRG Desk), F. 553 (Desk of the Soviet embassy in the FRG), F. 66 (Austrian Desk), and F. 56 "b" (holdings of the Press Department—TASS files), as well as the files of the former Archive of the CC of the CPSU.

2. RGANI, F. 3, op. 72, d. 214, 61, Politburo resolution of the CC of the CPSU P 106 (10), "On the memorandum addressed to the fraternal parties on the current situation in Czechoslovakia," 18 October 1968.

3. See also the chapter by Günter Bischof, "'No Action': The Johnson Administration and the Warsaw Pact Invasion of Czechoslovakia in August 1968," in this volume.

4. This was one of the issues the Soviet ambassador to Austria, Boris Podtserob, addressed on 31 August 1968 in his conversation with Austria's chancellor, Josef Klaus. AVP RF, F. 66, op. 47, 100, d. 6, pp. 179–83, official log of the USSR ambassador to Austria, Podtserob, reprinted in Karner et al., *Dokumente*, #182.

5. This refers to a reprint of an article first published in *Volksstimme*.

6. TASS, 28 August 1968, 4-AD, and TASS, 30 December 1968, 16-VE.

7. TASS, 2 April 1968, 11-BE.

8. TASS-Report, 1-4-AD.

9. TASS, 13 July 1968, 29-BE, 41-BE.

10. TASS, 16 July 1968, 19–20-BE.

11. TASS, 20 July 1968, 6-AD.

12. The said interview was also published in the TASS edition of 2 August 1968, 15–19-BE.

13. TASS, 2 August 1968, 17–18-BE.

14. AVP RF, F. 757, op. 13, 84, d. 13, p. 47, transcript of the conversation between the FRG ambassador to Moscow, H. Allardt, and the head of the 3rd European Department of the Soviet Foreign Ministry, G. Gorinovich, on 31 August 1968.

15. TASS, 5 August 1968, 34–35-BE.

16. TASS, 3 August 1968, 16–18-BE.

17. AVP RF, F. 138a, op. 49, 148, d. 16, p. 27, report of the second secretary of the Soviet embassy in Prague, Y. Zhuravlev, to the Soviet Foreign Ministry.

18. AVP RF, F. 138a, op. 49, 147, d. 12, pp. 1–4.

19. AVP RF, F. 138a, op. 49, 148, d. 16, pp. 2–4.

20. AVP RF, F. 757, op. 13, 84, p. 2, transcript of a conversation between the Soviet ambassador to Bonn, S. Tsarapkin, and his colleague, the Dutch ambassador to Bonn, de Beys, 26 January 1968.

21. AVP RF, F. 138a, op. 49, 148, d. 16, pp. 85–86, report of the 4th European Department of the Foreign Ministry of the USSR, 25 March 1968.

22. AVP RF, F. 138a, op. 49, 148, d. 16, p. 160, report of the 4th European Department of the Soviet Foreign Ministry, 16 April 1968.

23. AVP RF, F. 757, op. 13, 84, d. 14, pp. 12–13, transcript of a conversation between the Soviet ambassador to Bonn, S. Tsarapkin, and the head of the Trade Union of Metal Workers, O. Brenner, 14 March 1968.

24. TASS, 11 April 1968, 35–36-BE.

25. TASS, 12 April 1968, 18-BE.

26. AVP RF, F. 66, op. 47, 100, d. 6, p. 45, transcript of a conversation between the Soviet ambassador to Vienna, B. Podtserob, and his colleague, the Czechoslovak ambassador to Vienna, P. Novotný, 26 February 1968.

27. AVP RF, F. 138a, op. 49, 148, d. 16, pp. 120, 223–24, report of the Soviet ambassador to Vienna, B. Podtserob, to the Soviet Foreign Ministry, April 1968.

28. TASS, 4 April 1968, 6-AD.

29. TASS, 17 April 1968, 40-BE.

30. AVP RF, F. 138a, op. 49, 147, d. 1, p. 23, quoted according to the text of the Soviet note of 20 July 1968.

31. AVP RF, F. 138a, op. 49, 147, d. 1, p. 25.

32. AVP RF, F. 138a, op. 49, 147, d. 2, pp. 14–15, text of the Czechoslovak note.

33. AVP RF, F. 138a, op. 49, 147, d. 1, p. 24.

34. TASS, 8 August 1968, 14-BE.

35. TASS, 5 August 1968, 34-BE.

36. TASS, 15 August 1968, 18-BE.

37. AVP RF, F. 66, op. 47, 100, d. 6, p. 155, transcript of a conversation between the Soviet ambassador to Vienna, B. Podtserob, and his colleague, the Czechoslovak ambassador to Vienna, P. Novotný, 22 July 1968. In addition to this, Novotný passed on another piece of information to Podtserob: the West German ambassador, Josef Löns, had assured him that the last thing the FRG wanted was to interfere in the course of events in Czechoslovakia. In Bonn's leading circles, the question of granting a loan to Czechoslovakia had been discussed. The idea was dropped, Löns said, because no one wanted to be accused of meddling in Czechoslovakia's internal affairs. Comrade Novotný, however, added it was all very well for Löns to say this; the ruling circles in the FRG were in fact acting differently.

38. AVP RF, F. 757, op. 13, 85, d. 19, pp. 8–12, note of the government of the FRG, 1 March 1968.

39. AVP RF, F. 757, op. 13, 84, d. 13, p. 13, transcript of a conversation between the Polish ambassador to Moscow, Paszkowski, with the head of the 3rd European Department of the Soviet Foreign Ministry, A. Balatov, 17 April 1968.

40. AVP RF, F. 757, op. 13, 85, d. 19, p. 19.

41. AVP RF, F. 757, op. 13, 84, d. 14, p. 34, transcript of the conversation between the Soviet ambassador to Bonn, S. Tsarapkin, with the federal minister of Scientific Research, G. Stoltenberg, 18 July 1968.

42. AVP RF, F. 757, op. 13, 84, d. 14, p. 31, transcript of a conversation between the Soviet ambassador to Bonn, S. Tsarapkin, with the Dutch ambassador, de Beys, 16 July 1968.

43. AVP RF, F. 757, op. 13, 85, d. 19, p. 36, report written by A. Kovalev, A. Gromyko, and G. Gorinovich, 22 June 1968.

44. TASS, 2 August 1968, 14–15-BE.

45. TASS, 3 August 1968, 7-BE.

46. AVP RF, F. 757, op. 13, 84, d. 13, pp. 40–41, transcript of a conversation of the FRG ambassador to Moscow, Allardt, with the head of the 3rd European Department of the Soviet Foreign Ministry, 20 August 1968.

47. See N. I. Egorova and A. O. Čubarjan, eds., Cholodnaja vojna i politika razrjadki: Diskussionnye problemy (Moscow: Moskva, 2003), 181–82.

48. AVP RF, F. 757, op. 13, 84, d. 14, p. 45, transcript of the conversation between the Soviet ambassador to Bonn, S. Tsarapkin, with Berthold Beitz, a member of the board of directors of the Krupp conglomerate, 7 September 1968.

49. AVP RF, F. 757, op. 13, 84, d. 13, p. 55, transcript of the conversation between the second secretary of the FRG embassy in Moscow, Diepgen, with Ivan Sorokoletov, an official of the 3rd European Department of the Foreign Ministry, 20 September 1968.

50. AVP RF, F. 757, op. 13, 84, d. 13, pp. 57–58. AVP RF, F. 757, op. 13, 84, d. 13, pp. 61–62.

15

Ulbricht, East Germany, and the Prague Spring

Manfred Wilke

THE POWER QUESTION

In early 1968, the Czechoslovak Communists surprised their sister parties in the Soviet Empire with their plans for reform. Relations with the ruling Communist parties were the job of the respective party leaders. Walter Ulbricht, the first secretary of the Central Committee of the Socialist Unity Party of Germany (*Sozialistische Einheitspartei Deutschlands* or SED), was full of mistrust toward this "Prague Spring." The changes interested him above all from a political angle: did they serve the Communist Party of Czechoslovakia's (*Komunistická strana Československa* or KSČ) monopoly on power or not? As the reforms of the KSČ pertained to the political system and the central administrative economy of the country, they did indeed affect core areas of its monopoly on power.

It was already clear to the SED leadership in March 1968 that these reforms were leading to a "counterrevolution." This keyword was used by Communists to characterize a change of system in a Socialist society. In order to avoid such a change in the Czechoslovak Socialist Republic (ČSSR), the SED took an active part in the Soviet politics of intervention to restore the dictatorship.

This chapter focuses on the political decision process in the SED party leadership and their actions in the interventionist coalition against the reformist Communists in Prague. The activities of the Ministry for State Security (MfS) and the National People's Army (NVA) in connection with preparations for an invasion of Warsaw Pact troops in August are handled by other authors in this volume.[1]

The SED itself acted in close coordination with the Communist Party of the Soviet Union (*Kommunisticheskaya Partiya Sovetskogo Soyuza* or CPSU). This corresponded to its self-conception and the status of the German Democratic Republic (*Deutsche Demokratische Republik* or GDR) as a satellite state of the Soviet Union. In 1968, the CPSU pursued first and foremost a political aim regarding the ČSSR: to restore the Communist Party of Czechoslovakia's monopoly on power which was being eroded by the reforms. From the Soviet point of view, it was not a question of occupying the country, but only of protecting socialism in a "sister state." Soviet general secretary Leonid Brezhnev had already articulated this aim to Alexander Dubček at the Dresden meeting in March. In the notorious "letter of invitation" from Vasil Bil'ak and four other members of the Presidium of the KSČ from August to Brezhnev, this aim is precisely and openly formulated: "The very being of socialism in our country is in danger." With this phrase, the Communist Party's monopoly on power was rewritten, which the reformers in the Party consciously wanted to renounce. In order to sustain its monopoly on power, the dogmatic wing of the Party required assistance from abroad: "Only with your help can we rescue the ČSSR from the impending counterrevolution."[2]

This political aim also explains the procedure of coordination regarding the decisions of the CPSU with four of her "sister parties" and the function of the internal conferences. It was imperative to organize and demonstrate closeness in the Warsaw Pact. For the impartial viewer, this is a contradiction in terms; the policies and the military measures decided on were directed against a member state; one of them, Romania, did not participate in these interventionist politics.

By 1968, Moscow was no longer the undisputed leadership center of all Communist parties. Above all, there was the dispute with the Communist Party of China and the two largest western European parties in France and Italy. The response in the Communist world movement to the attempts at reform in Prague was divided. In April, the SED had already specified the differences between the Communists on this matter.[3]

The chosen position of the SED regarding the "Czechoslovak events" came about without losing sight of the Moscow line and the internal coordinating conferences. They constituted the breaks during the course of the crisis between the individual phases of its progress.

In Dresden in March, the "Warsaw Five"—the CPSU, the SED, the Bulgarian Communist Party (BCP), the Polish United Workers' Party (PUWP), and the Hungarian Socialist Workers' Party (HSWP) who would intervene in Czechoslovakia—brought to an end the phase of interpreting the reforms in the ČSSR as an impending "counterrevolution." They confronted the delegation of the KSČ with this result. In Moscow in May, the Warsaw Five were concerned with increasing external pressure on the leadership of the KSČ in order to force the abandonment of the reforms. Then, in Warsaw in July, the basic decision to intervene was up for discussion. In Moscow, a few days before the invasion, Walter Ulbricht, Todor Zhivkov, Władysław Gomułka, and János Kádár signed the commitment to involve their states in the intervention. Following the invasion, the politics of restoration and the stationing of Soviet troops in the ČSSR were negotiated in Moscow between the CPSU and the KSČ and voted on by the CPSU in the context of the Warsaw Five.[4]

"COUNTERREVOLUTION" IN PRAGUE?

As the year 1968 dawned, First Secretary of the Central Committee of the SED Walter Ulbricht was at the zenith of his power. The borders of the GDR, closed since the construction of the Berlin Wall in 1961, provided for economic planning security; the mass exodus to the West was eliminated. The SED discussed a reform of the direction of the planned economy and a new constitution. The latter was to emphasize inwardly and outwardly the independence of the SED state. The "leading role" of the SED in the GDR received constitutional status and, thus, had to be respected by all citizens and social institutions. The constitution did not give up on the prospect of a united Germany and identified the GDR as the Socialist core state that was to demonstrate to a united Germany what its future development would look like.

With regard to foreign affairs, the GDR had received support at the 1967 conference of twenty-five European Communist parties in Karlovy Vary/ Karlsbad for its demand for international recognition as the second German state. In the West and in the noncommitted states, the Federal Republic had prevented this recognition since its founding in 1949. In Karlsbad, the SED received the assurance that in the future no Socialist state would enter into diplomatic relations with the Federal Republic before the latter had recognized the GDR. This agreement was a direct response to Romania entering into diplomatic relations with the Federal Republic.[5]

With the support of the CPSU, the SED gained a foreign affairs victory. This support foiled the intention of the new eastern policy of the great coalition in the Federal Republic to isolate the GDR within the Socialist camp.

The change from Antonín Novotný to Dubček at the head of the KSČ in January 1968 did not yet disconcert the SED. The demand made by Ota Šik to introduce a new criterion for legitimating the rule of the Communist Party was presented quietly and did not immediately make it beyond the Czechoslovak border. He demanded in the future "the creation of better living conditions and the solution of the new social contradictions," and, if the party did not bring this about, the danger existed "that the people would begin to turn their backs on socialism." In order to prevent this, he demanded that "the Party should give up its monopoly on power" and fundamentally alter the style of party work: "Under current circumstances, it is not possible and also not necessary that the Party directs and controls the entire power and leadership apparatus in detail."[6] With this, he formulated the fundamental idea of the reformers: in the future, the Leninist conception of the party should not legitimate the power of the party; rather, the living conditions of the people under socialism should constitute in the future the yardstick by which its actions would be judged.

The SED leadership did not become alarmed until the developments of the following months: the personnel changes on all levels of the party organization, Novotný's resignation as state president, the debate on the rehabilitation of the victims of repression at the beginning of the 1950s, and above all the abolition of censorship and, with it, the party's control over the media.

An important building block for the first chosen positioning of the Central Committee apparatus of the SED in March was the report of the GDR ambassador in Prague. Peter Florin reported the following to East Berlin:[7] "The activity of the opposing forces has intensified over recent days and assumes increasingly open counterrevolutionary characteristics."[8] The press, radio, and television were largely in "opposition hands," and the media were becoming in this way organizers of "counterrevolution."[9]

The keyword for the Marxist-Leninist perception of the dangerous character of the Prague reform politics had been spoken. It was a phrase with a meaning that provided direction. The first sentence of the Soviet black book from August 1968, with which the intervention was justified, was: "The counterrevolutionary line amounted to liquidating the leading role of the KSČ."[10] For the SED ideologues, counterrevolutionary processes in Socialist states under the circumstances of systemic confrontation between socialism and imperialism were always an interaction between "imperialist aggression" from the outside and the emergence of "hostile forces" within the Socialist society. The ideological struggle against the ruling Communist Party was among the most important instruments of "counterrevolution."[11] At the meeting in Dresden, Ulbricht delivered a presentation on the causes of the Czechoslovak crisis with the KSČ delegation in mind. Using the example of the current discussion surrounding freedom in the ČSSR, he lectured on the interplay between the internal and external factors of a counterrevolutionary process. He stressed that the administrative errors made by the KSČ in the past had not been corrected in the framework of the politics of a Marxist-Leninist party, but rather under the slogan of absolute freedom, the transition from dictatorship to freedom, etc. However, dear friends, you are not alone in Europe. On the western border you have German imperialism. Absolute freedom brings with it several difficulties for you. The opponent is waging psychological warfare. At this moment in time, it would be very costly for you to proclaim absolute freedom.[12]

From this point of view, the main "counterrevolutionary" attack was always directed against the Communist Party's monopoly on power. The GDR ambassador's report contained a message that was particularly unsettling for the SED leadership: unity within the KSČ leadership no longer existed; an "open" and an "illegal center" were active within it.

The term "center" had a bloody meaning in the party language of the Communists. The accused during the Moscow show trials that took place in Moscow from 1936 onwards were defined according to "centers." The first show trial against the old Bolsheviks was directed against the "Trotsky-Zinoviev center"; in January 1937, the "illegal so-called Soviet-hostile Trotskyist parallel center" was condemned.[13]

The composition of the "illegal center" in Prague in 1968 was unknown to Florin in terms of its personnel. The "open center" consisted of the economic reform planner Šik, the director of television Jiří Pelikán, the chairman of the Writers' Association Eduard Goldstücker, and the author Pavel Kohout. The differences in the new KSČ leadership were expressed by Florin in the conspiracy constructions of the Stalinist show trials. The victims of the show trials in Prague at the beginning of the 1950s were to be rehabilitated at that precise moment.

On 15 March, Soviet general secretary Brezhnev invited Dubček to Dresden for an economics conference of the ruling Communist parties.[14] The Central Committee of the SED met prior and parallel to the Central Committee of the CPSU in order to establish their position.[15] The report of the Central Committee apparatus on developments in the ČSSR was regarded internally as prescribed terminology and named critical points of the reform process in the neighboring country: the removal of censorship and the publicly recognizable differences within the party leadership. Josef Smrkovský, Šik, and Goldstücker were characterized as revisionists. According to comments he made in an interview with WDR, Smrkovský's stated goal was to unite democracy and socialism. For the SED, the demand for "democratization" was the banner under which the antisocialist forces were to be gathered; a tactical concealment of the actual aim, that is, the overthrow of socialism. Prior to Dresden, the SED was already convinced that in Prague the old social democratic revisionism was ideologically and politically stepping out in new clothes.[16] Two days before the 5th Central Committee Congress, Rudolf Helmer[17] had already communicated to a counselor from the Soviet embassy in East Berlin an event that was important for Moscow, which the counselor noted as follows: "He stressed that they have no secrets from their Soviet comrades and that, as he was aware, the principal judgment and the access to events in the ČSSR on the part of the leaderships of the CPSU and the SED were consistent with each other."[18]

Ulbricht used this Central Committee Congress to evaluate the SPD's new eastern policy and to link it with the changes in Prague. For the SED boss, this new eastern policy was a strategy of ideological "maceration of the socialist countries with new methods and demands and that under the slogan of security in Europe, the slogan of the 'new eastern policy.'" For Ulbricht, the Social Democratic Party of Germany (*Sozialdemokratische Partei Deutschlands* or SPD) sought with this policy to find "ways of infiltrating the GDR, of unrolling the GDR from within, in order to transfer the West German system of state monopoly capitalism with its Federal Armed Forces to the whole of Germany"; the aim of German unity was for him "the main point of difference with the Social Democrat leadership."[19] Ulbricht mistrustfully recorded all contact between the SPD and KSČ during the spring.

THE DRESDEN TRIBUNAL IN MARCH 1968

The intervention in August began with a confrontation in March in Dresden. The leadership of the CPSU, the PUWP, the Hungarian Socialist Workers' Party, the BCP, and the SED reproached the delegation of the KSČ, led by Dubček, that a counterrevolutionary process had been established in the ČSSR. The Communist Party of Romania was consciously not invited. Dubček accepted the invitation, knowing in advance what the topic would be, but the other KSČ officials traveling with him were under the mistaken impression that the conclave would deal with economic issues.[20] Ulbricht as host then announced the real topic of the conference.[21] He requested of Dubček information regarding the plans of his Central Committee and the preparation of the KSČ's Action Program. He stressed the self-evident right of every Communist Party to determine its own policies, but his party was entirely isolated. "Thus, developments in a socialist country and the resolutions of a sister party can have far-reaching consequences for every other party and also the situation in Europe. Our mutual mortal enemy, imperialism, does not sleep." Before entering into the order of business, Brezhnev declared: "The discussion will be very serious; . . . I would, therefore, suggest not keeping the minutes." Dubček agreed, but Ulbricht allowed a record to be made.

For the time being, Dubček had to explain the policies of his party without any preparation.[22] Following his comments, the confrontation began. Brezhnev presented his assessment of events in the ČSSR and explained bluntly that the meeting in Dresden was not about discussing reforms with the KSČ, but about coordinating a mutual evaluation of developments in the ČSSR. Four parties toed the line laid down by Brezhnev. The question posed to the KSČ delegation was would it yield to this verdict and alter its course?

Brezhnev's keyword in describing the situation in the ČSSR was "counterrevolution," which was organized by "an entire group or entire center" in public life in the ČSSR. He asked Dubček directly what he understood "democratization" or "liberalization" to mean. "Have you not had democracy thus far?" For him, the "main processes" of the preceding few weeks were: "Public attacks against the Central Committee" and "defamation" of all the "achievements" of the previous twenty-five years "that will be printed in West Germany, in America, in Austria, everywhere." "Attacks against the leading cadre of the Party, against the government, against the Ministry of Defence, against the Ministry of the Interior. . . . It's all being denigrated." He demonstrated what the consequences might be by citing Foreign Minister Václav David: "For twenty years he led the struggle against imperialism in alliance and agreement with us . . . but he was also pelted with dirt in order to create a basis for the 'independent foreign policy.'"

The antisocialist background to all these campaigns seemed for Brezhnev to be no secret: he saw this in the tendencies of a "Czech socialism." In order to emphasize this judgment on the danger of a domestic system change, he followed on with the question, "Yes, what will come next?"

What did the enemy want? That was the key question in the struggle against "counterrevolution." The "enemy acted skillfully, very tactfully and organized. We cannot claim that one single center is being established today in Czechoslovakia. Perhaps there are several centers."[23] But all events—this must be stressed—are consummated in intellectual circles, in youth circles, but not in the sphere in which one could find strong support for the Presidium and the Central Committee, in order to fight against the counterrevolution. That is, namely, the working class.[24]

The concern over the potential change of sides on the part of the ČSSR, which was already hinted at in the question regarding an autonomous foreign policy, was repeated as a question pertaining to the Warsaw Pact. Why was the view being disseminated: "Our people do not know what the contents of the Warsaw Pact are, but if our people did know it, our people would very quickly withdraw from the treaty. As though it was a gagging treaty in the event of a war."

In the Dresden debate on the autonomy of Socialist states and their Communist parties as well as on how binding the Warsaw Pact was, Soviet prime minister Aleksei Kosygin positioned himself unequivocally. The discussions in the Czechoslovak media on the role of the Communist Party and relations with the Soviet Union were not only followed worldwide, they "not only concern the entire socialist camp," but affected the whole Communist movement. With this, Kosygin formulated the keynote of the

later so-called Brezhnev Doctrine of the limited sovereignty of the Socialist states. For him, the Dresden meeting served to support the KSČ in the
struggle against the "counterrevolution." Addressing Dubček directly, he
said that here "the support for Czechoslovakia in the struggle for a Socialist
and Communist Czechoslovak country was forged, . . . for the business of
Czechoslovakia is our mutual business and we do not surrender this business to our enemy, whatever it might cost us!" Brezhnev's comments on
the—from the point of view of the Communists—negative reports in the
ČSSR media were accentuated by Kosygin: they found themselves "in the
hands of the enemy."

Brezhnev personalized the term "counterrevolution" and mounted a
massive attack on Josef Smrkovský.[25] His list of transgressions began with
the interview on West German Radio (WDR). Brezhnev quoted him: "We
are convinced that that which we are undertaking will set an example for
the comrades of other socialist countries. That's what he said! He assured
the Federal Republic that that which they are doing will set an example for
everyone. We will do and achieve that, and believe that it will be interesting for both German socialists and the socialists of other western countries,
he said." Addressing Dubček directly, the Soviet party leader commented
"[and you] give him a good appraisal, honest etc." Using the example of
Smrkovský, he demonstrated at the same time the leadership weaknesses of
the KSČ Presidium and Central Committee: "In Party practice it is not common that some coal minister or forestry minister replaces the Central Committee and gives interviews to the Federal Republic, indeed an anti-socialist,
anti-communist interview for which one could pay millions of dollars. . . .
How is it that the Central Committee did not know that such an interview
exists?" Brezhnev's next charge was Smrkovský's relationship with the Soviet
Union. "The same Smrkovský says: Oh well, what does it mean if the Soviet
Union has lost 100,000 soldiers, but the Czechs have also lost, and why?
The Party has made so many mistakes." Again addressing the KSČ delegation, he passed judgment: "That means, dear comrades, behind your back
this highly praised politician of yours carries out his anti-socialist, anti-Party
activities." Once more he quoted the WDR interview. From Brezhnev's point
of view, Smrkovský answered the question as to what was to be done in the
ČSSR with a challenge: "Perhaps something that no communist party has
done, namely the combining of socialism with freedom." Brezhnev clarified
that the CPSU regarded the events in the ČSSR not as an "experiment" but
as a "premeditated scheme" to bring about a change of system. This view
became very clear at the end of his speech:

> We have the authorization of our Politburo, to express the hope to you who
> are seated here today that you at the top will be in a position to alter events and
> prevent a very dangerous development. We are prepared to give you moral,

political and democratic assistance. I would be very pleased and happy—and so would our Party—if I could at the same time express the support of all other parties present here.

He remarked threateningly:

> If that should not be possible, however, or if you consider that to be incorrect, then we are nevertheless unable to remain detached toward developments in Czechoslovakia. We are united with one another by means of friendship, by means of international commitments, by means of the security of the socialist countries, by means of the security of our states.

The KSČ's political goal was formulated as follows: the KSČ should assert its monopoly on power in Czechoslovakia and strike down the "counter-revolution" using its own power. In order to achieve this aim, it could count on the assistance of the CPSU. In order to achieve it ultimately without and against the KSČ, the invasion of Warsaw Pact troops took place on 21 August. The restorative aim had already been formulated in Dresden.

What everyone expected from Dubček was repeated by Gomułka as head of the Polish delegation: "We are of the opinion that it is today still possible to face these dangers, I would say, to face these dangers in a peaceful way, nonetheless with an energetic counteroffensive that must in our opinion be undertaken by the leadership of the Communist Party of Czechoslovakia against the counterrevolutionary forces."

Dubček immediately received pledges of assistance from the PUWP, the SED, the HSWP, and the BCP. In addition, each of the parties communicated specific messages to the KSČ. The minutes convey the impression of a well thought-out performance. It began with the "confession" of the accused Dubček, the "plea" by Brezhnev, to which the SED, the BCP, the PUWP, and the HSWP acquiesced and with which a united course was constituted; it became the binding frame of reference. The PUWP and the HSWP then reminded the KSČ of the lessons of the counterrevolutionary experiences of the year 1956. Hungary's party leader János Kádár delivered a historic analogy in order to underline Brezhnev's judgment: "[T]his process is extremely similar to the prologue of the Hungarian counterrevolution at a time when it wasn't yet a counterrevolution. This means that is the process that took place in Hungary from February 1956 to the end of October. And we ask that you give that some thought."

The SED undertook to demonstrate by means of the German example the interaction between western interference and the stance of the internal "enemy" and to recall the struggle of the Socialist camp against imperialism. Ulbricht began with the special situation of the GDR and the ideological threat posed by West German reporting on events in the ČSSR. He spoke of the "heating up of the psychological war" and referred explicitly to Brezhnev's remarks on Smrkovský's WDR interview. The praise of the Czechoslovak press association (ČTK) for the politics of the SPD in their report on the SPD's Nuremberg party congress was, for Ulbricht, interference in the domestic affairs of the GDR; on top of everything he saw in this report the "representation of the ideology of West German imperialism." He announced to the KSČ that the SED would no longer remain silent regarding these things, but would publicly "refute the opposing arguments." Following a lesson on the causes of the current situation, which he sought in the failure of ideological work within the KSČ, he described how the West was currently benefiting propagandistically from developments in the ČSSR: "In a situation where we are all interested in the Socialist camp and the Warsaw Pact states acting unanimously, now, where U.S. imperialism is in a difficult position with its global strategy, in this of all situations you start to discriminate against your own party, you give the enemy material for its campaign against Socialist countries, and West German imperialism naturally exploits that and conducts a massive campaign." In his analysis of the new tactics of the enemy—he claimed to have learned from the failure of the Hungarian "counterrevolution"—he dealt with the importance of future developments involving freedom of the press. If freedom of the press existed as in the ČSSR, where a "platform for counterrevolution at the current stage" could be publicized unimpeded without this being prevented, then the freedom of the press would lead directly "to counterrevolution."[26]

Ulbricht demanded from Dubček that the KSČ in their Action Program "state concretely what happened in the past, what must be corrected, how the situation is assessed, and what dangers have arisen as a result of the revisionist approach of certain intellectuals. The Party leadership should turn to the workers." Dubček and his leadership should say openly "which dangers exist." He provokingly accentuated the question: "Will you also have the courage to say that there are counterrevolutionary forces under Western influence who are attempting to do their business?" With the accentuation on block loyalty and the conflict of systems, Ulbricht intrinsically represented the political interests of the SED relating to Germany and also attempted in this way to preclude special negotiations on the part of the ČSSR with the Federal Republic on the normalization of state relations.

The Dresden conference set the course for the further development of the Czechoslovak crisis. With the claim that the main tendency of developments had been leading since the KSČ's January plenum to "counterrevolution," the CPSU made their assessment of the situation. Supported by the SED, the PUWP, the BCP, and the HSWP, they demanded from Dubček and his leadership the restoration of the KSČ's monopoly on power and with it the abandonment of the reform course, which was stigmatized in the person of Smrkovský. This political aim was never subsequently revised. Once the "healthy forces" within the KSČ could no longer realize this on their own, external military intervention was affected. In each phase, the SED executed this Soviet policy of intervention without restrictions.

THE SED INTERVENES

Until mid-March, the GDR press remained silent on events in its neighboring country, although the issue increasingly attracted interest in the media of the Federal Republic, and the GDR population was also informed by means of electronic media as a result. The SED assessed these reports as part of the Federal Republic's psychological war against the GDR. As Ulbricht had announced in Dresden, open polemics against the Prague reform Communists began at the end of March. Kurt Hager[27] openly attacked Smrkovský at a convention of philosophers in the GDR and reproached him for his criticism of the KSČ being exploited by the Western media.[28] Until 25 March 1968, an unwritten law between the Communist parties in power was in force: no public interference in the affairs of other Socialist states. The publication of Hager's attack on Smrkovský in *Neues Deutschland*, the central organ of the SED, broke this rule. In his report on the speech, the Soviet ambassador in the GDR, Pyotr Abrasimov, announced tactical doubts about the date, yet the speech was, in fact, given on the eve of the Central Committee plenum of the KSČ.[29] Its effect in the ČSSR was counterproductive for the intentions of the SED. The Czechoslovak media was outraged. In Berlin, the Czechoslovak ambassador appealed to the GDR foreign minister Otto Winzer.[30] Winzer rejected the protest and explained to the ČSSR ambassador Václav Kolář in plain words the specific position of the GDR: "There is a West Germany, but no West Hungary, no West Bulgaria, and no West Czechoslovakia."[31] If, therefore, Czechoslovak politicians or authors made appearances in West German media in order to discuss the democratization of socialism in Prague, they were—in Winzer's opinion—interfering in the domestic affairs of the GDR. As a result of this, the SED had to defend itself against "West German propaganda" directed at the GDR; this, therefore, amounted to no interference in the domestic affairs of the ČSSR.

Ulbricht reproached the Czechoslovak ambassador Kolář with the public rehabilitation of victims of repression supplying the "Western press" with material "for the struggle against the socialist world system. Why must you dig up the dead?"[32] The demand made by the SED leadership that the number of "Western journalists" in the ČSSR be restricted and Czechoslovak citizens prevented from making unauthorized appearances in the media of the Federal Republic, was ignored there.

At the "April plenum" of the KSČ, the Action Program was passed and the attacked Smrkovský elected to the Presidium of the Central Committee of the KSČ.[33] Dubček had kept his silence in Prague regarding the conference in Dresden;[34] the results of the Central Committee plenum were now the opposite of that which the "sister parties" had demanded from him there: the position of the reformers within the party leadership was strengthened; the Action Program, the content of which had been devised by him, was passed.[35] A public statement from the SED regarding the Action Program "Czechoslovakia's Path to Socialism" did not exist. Internally, however, the Central Committee apparatus had analyzed the program and understood its character to be a compromise between the two wings of the party. The most important point for the SED was the statement on the leading role of the KSČ. They now no longer presented themselves as "the conscious and organized vanguard of the workers and negated Marxism-Leninism as science."[36] The SED expected hefty internal conflicts within the KSČ when it came to the implementation of the action program. Following the press campaign, the next stage of interference in the internal affairs of the ČSSR began: the SED strengthened the "healthy forces" in the KSČ and conducted to this effect "educational work on the ground" by means of delegation trips. In this relationship, the SED cadre in the ČSSR often did not have to search for long; they found conservative KSČ functionaries who supplied them with unsolicited information.[37]

At the end of April, the Bulgarian Communist Party passed on their assessment of the state of the KSČ leadership to the general secretaries of those parties present at the Dresden conference, and attempted to arrange, according to personnel, the different opposing centers operating within the leadership.[38] Ulbricht saw in this report a confirmation of his own analysis. Toward the Bulgarian ambassador in Berlin, he initially advanced the Dresden line: "We must win Dubček and help him to take measures in order to obtain control over the press, the radio and television; that is very important."[39] To a statement in the Bulgarian report to the effect that in Prague "no conclusions were drawn from the meeting in Dresden," Ulbricht responded, "In all probability, a second Dresden consultation is unavoidable."

MOSCOW, 8 MAY 1968: MILITARY PRESSURE AND THE QUESTION OF "HEALTHY FORCES"

The second "Dresden" took place on 8 May directly after the discussion between the CPSU and the KSČ in Moscow.[40] The two most important results for the CPSU leadership were that the Czechoslovak delegation agreed to Warsaw Pact maneuvers in their country and that the differences in the Presidium of the KSČ became visible.[41] This time, the Warsaw Five met without the KSČ. By the end of their conference, the building of an interventionist coalition had been decided. At Brezhnev's suggestion, a "hotwire" was set up between the five parties. The CPSU, like the SED, set up a special task force in its Central Committee in order to prepare analyses of the developments in the ČSSR.[42]

In Moscow, Brezhnev demanded that the "sister parties" sign a joint communiqué with a clear warning to Prague. Its core statement should be that the KSČ was not alone and could not decide on its course of action independently of the five parties. This, however, they had just done with their Action Program, in which Gomułka saw the "general line of counter-revolution" and which Brezhnev did not want to publish.

In contrast to Dresden, the military card was now openly brought into play. There was unanimity that the maneuvers agreed on between the High Command of the Warsaw Pact and the ČSSR would have to begin soon. The SED had insisted in advance to the still hesitant Soviet side that the National People's Army (*Nationale Volksarmee* or NVA) should take part in these maneuvers.[43] Ulbricht combined the maneuvers with the aim of strengthening the position of the "healthy forces" in the KSČ with a demonstration of power.

The main problem for the Warsaw Five was still who within the KSČ party leadership should become their partner. During deliberations between the CPSU and the KSČ, Bil'ak alone from the Czechoslovak delegation had accepted the Soviet criticism. Ulbricht demanded, even when it was "only a minority group in the Presidium of the KSČ that advances the correct line, then I am in favor of us helping this minority group." Opinions on Dubček were divided in this context; above all Kádár and Brezhnev had not yet given up on him. Both called attention to the popularity that Dubček enjoyed not only nationwide, but also internationally. As such, the question as to who in the KSČ leadership would be prepared to take on the struggle for the restoration of the Party's monopoly on power was still open for the Warsaw Five. While Ulbricht suggested relying on the right wing of the KSČ—which ultimately happened—Brezhnev hoped until into August that Dubček could be won over to the idea of taking on this role himself.

At the end of the conference, Brezhnev drew the conclusion that was to become known as the Brezhnev Doctrine of limited sovereignty of the Socialist states: "By defending Czechoslovakia, we are defending the entire socialist camp, the entire international Communist movement. We must recognize our strengths and become active." Toward Dubček and his delegation, the same message read as follows: "We are ready to give you help, if this becomes necessary. We are ready to do this, and in awareness of the mood of Comrades Gomułka, Ulbricht, Zhivkov and others, I can say that such a readiness is also at hand from them."[44]

Ulbricht demanded in Moscow a concerted international campaign against the "revisionism" in Prague, as part of which it should be openly said "that there is counterrevolution in the ČSSR." He repeated his thesis, according to which the main thrust of this counterrevolution was directed against the GDR. The SED could no longer accept that the GDR would be taken in a political pincer attack: on the one hand from the new eastern policy of the Federal Republic and on the other hand from the reformers in Prague. The first secretary of the SED was concerned that both events could contribute to the erosion of the SED's monopoly on power in the GDR.

This fear was not unfounded. Both events elicited hope for change in the GDR. The new Bonn eastern policy opened up the prospect of an improvement in German internal relations and the reforms in Prague awoke the hope among Socialists for analogous improvements in the GDR. The Leipzig historian Hartmut Zwahr noted in his diary, "Beneath the surface, a wave of sympathy is rolling; a large proportion of the youth is trembling with the Czechs."[45]

The SED confronted the danger of the Czech infection in the GDR with campaigns and prescribed ideological terminology. "With the power of the apparatus and of the entire state, the Party establishes Party opinion, the 'orientation': before it all public discussions fell silent. A new taboo is created."[46] Not everyone fell silent; Robert Havemann gave an interview to a Czech magazine.[47] Turning to the reformers, he said, "[S]ocialists and communists across the world are following political developments in the ČSSR with genuine sympathy and filled with great hopes."[48] He stressed the self-assessment of the reform Communists, that they attempted for the first time to reconcile socialism and democracy. He was concerned with Stalinism being overcome.[49] Havemann was able to publish his German text in the Federal Republic, but not in the GDR. A Danish journalist who published this interview in Copenhagen was identified on Ulbricht's direct orders. The MfS received the directive to intensify the surveillance on Havemann and his circle of friends. The distribution of the German-language *Prager Volkszeitung* (*Prague People's Newspaper*) was prohibited in the GDR.

In the KSČ, the May plenum (29 May until 1 June) was supposed to set the course; it decided to convene the 14th Party Congress in September. The party had in the meantime split into two wings: the conservatives and the reformers. Dubček constituted the integrating clip between them. In the resolution accepted by the plenum, the Soviet criticism was absorbed. Both wings agreed on the struggle against the counterrevolutionary danger. The KSČ's claim on the leading role in the political system was strengthened.[50] Initially, it looked as though the resolutions and decisions of the May plenum had consolidated the position of the leadership in order that they could prepare for the Party Congress in peace.[51] This proved to be a fallacy in terms of both domestic and foreign policy. Thus Florin reported from Berlin that at the plenum no "debate was conducted with those revisionist views strongly represented among those persons active in the cultural sector and the middle-class intelligentsia, above all with regard to the leading role of the Communist Party in society."[52] It was precisely this that the Warsaw Five expected from Dubček.[53] The SED's skepticism as to whether the necessary turnaround in the KSČ's politics would come about was also demonstrated by the prognosis of the ambassador regarding the probable result of the 14th Party Congress: "During the preparation of the Party Congress, the Party will as hitherto lose itself in a general discussion and questions on the new composition of the Central Committee will take center stage. The danger exists that the KSČ will take a social democratic development on the basis of the Action Program."[54] The Soviet ambassador in Prague personalized the consequences that "the healthy forces will disintegrate at the Party Congress" and the party would split. It was now already clear that Drahomír Kolder, Alois Indra, Bil'ak, and others would not be elected as members of the Central Committee and, perhaps, not even as delegates to the Party Congress. Should this situation be consolidated, the party would be led across to the right at the Party Congress.[55] Neither ambassador allowed himself to be deceived by the resolution. While Florin stressed the change in character of the KSČ, his Soviet college had the "cadre question" in mind, without which the monopoly on power of the Party in the ČSSR could not be restored.[56] Mikhail Prozumenshchikov has dealt with the consequences that Dubček's politics had for the Soviet leadership, concluding: "To a certain extent, Dubček himself with his constant promises to improve the situation (which were not, however, fulfilled) also contributed to the increase within the Russian leadership of the number of those who advocated a solution of the problem by force."[57] A party reform requires an alteration in its statute. Florin did not, however, address the draft of the new party statute, although the text would have confirmed his prognosis, for he envisaged an extension of membership rights as well as the secret ballot for leadership functions and a protection of minorities.[58]

The election of delegates in July led to a change in generations and resulted in a clear majority of 80 percent for Dubček and the reformers.[59] In Moscow, Ulbricht had realistically estimated the balance of power in the KSČ: the "healthy forces" were a minority.

The Šhumava (Bohemian Forest) maneuver was set to end on 30 June. The Soviet Army used it to prepare undercover the occupation of the ČSSR.[60] The military demonstration and the political pressure of the Warsaw Five aroused in the ČSSR not only fear, but also resistance. This resistance was articulated in the "2,000 Words," written by Ludvík Vaculík.[61] He called upon the citizens to take the initiated democratization of their country into their own hands, to support the progressive wing of the Communists in view of the election of delegates, and not to allow a restoration. In his report of 3 July, the GDR ambassador recorded very precisely the contradictory response at the conferences of delegates to the "2,000 Words."[62] Two days after its appearance, Ulbricht received an estimate from the GDR ambassador in Prague. Florin presented a piece of "evidence": "This document is a call for counterrevolution, which bears programmatic character and contains the methods for the implementation of the counterrevolutionary intentions."[63]

This corresponded to the meaning of the "2,000 Words" for the CPSU, who also expressed this in its letter of 4 July to the Presidium of the KSČ.[64] The SED received the letter at the same time as Prague did. The handwritten underlining on the German translation—presumably marked by Ulbricht himself—is important for understanding the position of the SED in its own letter to the KSČ. The underlining relates to a series of passages, above all those in the Soviet letter that concern the ČSSR's relationship with West Germany and in which the CPSU assumes the position of the SED. The following was underlined: the "decisive question . . . as to whether Czechoslovakia should be socialist or not"; the behavior of the KSČ toward the "anti-socialist forces," against whom no "effective blow" had so far been dealt; the passage on the revisionists in the party and on the intention to "legalize factions and groups" within the KSČ; and finally the questions of missing party control over mass media and the exploitation of events in the ČSSR by the "enemies of socialism [for] comprehensive ideological diversion." Reflected in this underlining is the keyword that gave direction to the SED leadership's perception of the "Prague Spring": counterrevolution.

Following receipt of the CPSU letter, the Politburo of the SED convened for an extraordinary session with just one item on the agenda: the situation in the ČSSR. The committee approvingly took note of the letter from the Kremlin and finalized the text of its own letter to the KSČ.[65]

The letter ended, like the Moscow original, with an "offer of assistance." In contrast to the nonspecific "promise of help" from Moscow, the SED stated the basis of its willingness more precisely by making reference to the corresponding agreements between the Warsaw Pact states and the spirit of "socialist internationalism," while at the same time narrowing them down. This offer related only to such decisions made and steps taken by the KSČ that were suitable for strengthening the position of socialism in the ČSSR.[66] All these letters by the Warsaw Five were supposed to warn Dubček to take the criticism and demands of the Warsaw Pact states seriously.

WARSAW, 15 JULY: THE DIE IS CAST!

The "2,000 Words" became in "many respects the turning-point in Soviet-Czechoslovak relations and characterized the beginning of the third stage, during which the better part of the Soviet leadership psychologically came to terms with the necessity of a military solution to the problem," according to Prozumenshchikov.[67]

The CPSU resolved to convene a new conference of the "Five" and the KSČ in Warsaw. Under pressure from large municipal associations, Dubček cancelled his participation in the meeting and proposed instead bilateral negotiations with the individual parties.[68]

In Warsaw, the die was cast for an effort of collective assistance for the protection of socialism in the ČSSR, though not yet for the decision to intervene. The Soviet general secretary came to Warsaw with the draft of a letter endorsed by his Politburo.[69] It was to be sent to the Presidium of the KSČ as a joint warning and at the same time legitimate externally the collective action. The letter was approved and passed on to Prague; in it, the most important parts of the existing letters were repeated. It instructed the KSČ in a threatening tone: "We, therefore, think that the decisive repulse of attacks by the anti-communist forces and the resolute defense of the socialist order in Czechoslovakia are not only your task but also ours."[70] The joint letter gave the interventionist coalition its name Warsaw Five.

The papers of the party leaders all had the character of a general reckoning with the developments of the previous months in the ČSSR. All of them emphasized the broken promises of the KSČ leadership since Dresden.[71] In the assessment of the situation, all were in agreement: in the ČSSR, a change of system loomed. The Polish party head, Gomułka, precisely formulated this theory: in Czechoslovakia, "a peaceful process of change from a socialist state . . . to a republic of middle-class character is taking place." This was, for him, an event that threatened "to turn into a weakening of our bloc." His reasoning considered that, because at that moment all political problems were decided on a global scale, the action in Czechoslovakia meant a weakening of socialism "as represented by us." Neither the Poles not the GDR were the decisive problem for imperialism; for him, the Soviet Union and its nuclear potential counted above all; it was the decisive force that held the "imperialist world" at bay. The Czech comrades were in the process of altering the European balance of power with their course. In order to do that, they had "already broken their bond with us. They have broken our bilateral and multilateral resolutions. They do not consult with us in significant matters." Gomułka advocated "practical measures" to restore the closeness of the Bloc and "a unified line in the main issues"; this was, for him, "our unity toward the imperialist camp."

Ulbricht likewise addressed the Bloc confrontation; he combined the theory of peaceful system change, as formulated by Gomułka and with which he agreed, with western, imperialist politics toward the Socialist states. For him there was no doubt that the organizers of the "counterrevolution" were located in Washington and Bonn.[72] He apodictically declared:

> The current measures and the appearance of counterrevolution in Czechoslovakia are part of the strategy of the U.S. and West German imperialism in the struggle for hegemony in Europe. Comrade Gomułka is right when he says it is not a question of whether businesses remain owned by the people or are transferred to private ownership. A state capitalist Czechoslovakia . . . can also come completely under the command and control of the World Bank and the West German Bundesbank; completely, even under the enterprise of socialism, the new socialism.

For Ulbricht, it was not the property question that was the decisive one; rather, "political power is what it's about."

Brezhnev himself shared this view and emphasized: "There is no example where socialism has been victorious and is firmly established, of capitalist circumstances triumphing anew. That does not exist and we are convinced that it also never should and also never will."

The invocation of socialism and internationalism and the references to the existing treaties among the Socialist states already served to legitimize the imminent "collective action" in Czechoslovakia. Brezhnev justified at length why it did not represent interference in the internal affairs of a sovereign state. Prior to the decision on this "collective assistance" for socialism in Czechoslovakia, Brezhnev asked once more: Would the KSČ leadership have the courage to take resolute measures "to topple the reaction, to rescue the position of socialism?"

If it did not do this, the downfall of socialism loomed, which the Five could not allow! Therefore, it remained necessary "to support" the "healthy forces" in the KSČ. Moreover, the "sister parties" must be ready at the "first call of the Czechoslovak comrades to arise or, in the event that the circumstances required such an appearance and if the Czechoslovak comrades were having difficulties, to turn to us for assistance." The new keyword for the intervention was "assistance."

The Bulgarian party leader Zhivkov translated what this word really meant in the context of July 1968. He began solemnly, explaining that prior to the 14th KSČ Party Congress, which should never have taken place, the Five had had a "historic task" to fulfill: "There is only one way out, namely for the socialist countries, the Communist Parties and the Warsaw Pact to provide decisive assistance to the ČSSR." The "inner forces of the ČSSR" could no longer be entrusted with rescuing socialism. "We can address diverse appeals and letters to them, of course, but unfortunately at present there are no such forces in the ČSSR that could assume the task mentioned in the letters. Czechoslovakia must be supported by the assistance of the socialist countries and the Communist Parties, by the assistance of the Warsaw Pact, primarily by the armed forces of the Warsaw Pact. First of all, the dictatorship of the proletariat must essentially be resurrected there."

This demand did not yet, however, answer the question as to who in the ČSSR should restore the dictatorship and rebuild the KSČ. The "collective assistance," should it fulfill its political aim, required party followers in the ČSSR who were to assume the task of restoring the monopoly on power into their own hands.

In his report on the Warsaw meeting before the plenum of the Central Committee of the CPSU on 17 July, General Secretary Brezhnev fell back on the suggestion from Ulbricht in May in Moscow in order to find a solution to these questions: "When we see that the leadership of the KSČ does not wish to adhere to our considerations, one must pursue efforts to promote other healthy forces in the Party and search for the opportunity to turn to these forces in the Party, which perhaps emerge with the initiative in the struggle for the restoration of the leading role of the KSČ and for the normalization of conditions in the country."[73] In order to organize this, there must be a meeting at which "representatives with the initiative group empowered by us . . . who represent the healthy forces in the Presidium of the Central Committee of the KSČ and convey our position to the political stage, on the basis of whom one can consolidate the Party, issue a rebuff to the anti-socialist elements and above all declare our readiness to provide our necessary support." Then he repeated the passage from his speech in Warsaw, in which he had called on the "sister states" to look out for the first call for help from Prague. The Central Committee approved the report, and with this the Politburo was given a free hand.

On 22 July, the Soviet foreign minister, Marshal Grechko, was commissioned by the Politburo "to take measures." At the same time, documents were drawn up in Moscow, "which had supposedly been written by the future leadership of the ČSSR, who should displace the current leaders."[74] At the July plenum of the Central Committee, Brezhnev had devised the contours of the Soviet approach during the action of collective assistance. In the event of doubt, an "initiative group" of "healthy forces" in the Presidium of the Central Committee of the KSČ would solicit assistance from abroad for the protection of socialism in the ČSSR. This "appeal" was the indispensable political prerequisite for the implementation of the military operation. In this way, as Brezhnev evidently hoped, the "measures" could be legitimized and lose their character of an intervention in the affairs of a sovereign state.

On 18 July, the GDR ambassador Florin announced from Prague that the Presidium of the KSČ had substantiated its "negative attitude" to the Warsaw Letter with the "principle of personal responsibility for domestic developments." The course of the session had shown that the "Party leadership is still not prepared to engage in an energetic struggle, supported by the sister parties, against the counterrevolutionary activities."[75] In view of the approach of the Czechoslovak leadership, collective action became more and more probable. The SED began to prepare itself. The first measure was a resolution from the SED Politburo on 19 July to install a radio transmitter in the region of Dresden, which was to broadcast political information mornings and evenings in Czech and Slovak. As the technical equipment of GDR Radio was not sufficient, the mobile transmitter of GDR-*Ferienwelle* (GDR Holiday Wave) was used for this purpose.[76]

The military preparations were complete.[77] On GDR territory alone, 650,000 soldiers were mobilized. "Overall, the military concentration of the troops of the five 'fraternal armies' reached its highpoint on the borders of the ČSSR on 29 and 30 July. The intervention had become militarily possible; the Soviet generals awaited the political approval of the CPSU leadership."[78] The GDR was also prepared. On 29 July, the National Defense Council (NVR) had convened and received reports on the status of military preparations and those from the Interior Ministry and the MfS.[79] When the Presidium of the KSČ met with that of the CPSU on 29 July in Čierna nad Tisou, the SED had completed the political and military preparations for the intervention in the ČSSR, but the SED like the Soviet generals also had to wait for the order to deploy.

The political preparation for the "collective actions" was significantly more complicated. The KSČ had a leadership chosen by the relevant party bodies and its reform program was widely approved within the Czechoslovakian population, including its insistence on barring interference from the Warsaw Five in the internal affairs of the ČSSR. A further problem for the Soviet leadership was that Dubček agreed internally with the criticism on the part of the CPSU of the approach of the "antisocialist forces," but did not proceed against them. In short, the intervention required a political justification; it was most elegant when Dubček publicly committed himself to an agreement with the Warsaw Five and then failed to abide by it. When one takes all the CPSU's points of criticism of developments in the ČSSR since January 1968 together, it was also clear to Brezhnev by the meeting in Warsaw at the latest that Dubček and his leadership would not bring about a change in the "counterrevolutionary process" on their own initiative. It seems, however, also to have been important to the CPSU general secretary to demonstrate this to the Communists in the ČSSR, in the Socialist states, and in the global movement. Perhaps he also still hoped to induce Dubček to "take the leap" in order to utilize his popularity for the politics of restoration—as indeed happened after the intervention.

There were thus reasons enough for his plan of continuing to want to search for a "political solution" with which he concluded his report to the Central Committee on 17 July. He affirmed that "before we resort to extreme measures," the leadership at a bilateral meeting with the KSČ would still attempt to resolve this political solution. Its contents were known to Dubček and his Presidium since the Dresden meeting; the letter from the Warsaw Five had updated them.

The meeting began on 29 July;[80] the Czechoslovakian railway border crossing to the Soviet Union, Čierna nad Tisou, had been selected as the venue. The Soviet Politburo met for the first time outside its national boundaries. The gathering lasted several days. In the end, the SED, BCP, PUWP, and HSWP were invited on 2 August by the CPSU to a meeting with the KSČ in Bratislava on the next day. During the negotiations, the CPSU had forced a series of conditions on the Czechoslovakian side in order to regulate the political issues: they were to win back control over the mass media and to prevent the activity of political clubs outside the National Front, as well as attempts to reestablish the Social Democratic Party. The changes in the cadre were serious: in the Presidium and the Central Committee, secretariat Česimír Císař and the chairman of the National Front, František Kriegel, were to lose their posts, as well as Interior Minister Josef Pavel and the director of state television, Jiří Pelikán. Viliam Šalgovič was again to assume leadership of state security. "Brezhnev insisted on these commitments and threatened, if they were not complied with, 'we will come to your assistance'—evidently militarily."[81]

The gathering in Bratislava had one single aim: for the Warsaw Five and the KSČ to adopt a joint communiqué. Dubček accepted the Soviet draft as a basis for negotiations.[82]

With regard to the future foreign policy of the ČSSR, the KSČ had prepared the formula of "exclusive responsibility of each country for socialism in their own country" for the 14th Party Congress, and with it justified the rejection of the letter of the Warsaw Five.[83] In contrast, in Bratislava the KSČ signed a very different formula, namely that of the "mutual duty of all socialist countries to defend socialism. The Soviet side did not even allow the basic principle of non-intervention guaranteed by the bilateral alliance treaties."[84] Before the Central Committee of the SED, Hermann Axen, Central Committee Secretary for International Affairs, assessed it as a great success that the term nonintervention called for by the Czechoslovakian delegation was not included in the communiqué.[85] As a member of the editorial commission, Ulbricht spoke out vehemently against the Czechoslovakian conception of the SPD as a "progressive force" in the Federal Republic and got the formulation accepted into the communiqué "that promised above all support to the [Communist Party of Germany, *Kommunistische Partei Deutschlands*] KPD, which was banned in the Federal Republic."[86] Hence, in Bratislava the KSČ had agreed in the joint communiqué both to Socialist internationalism and to the renunciation of an individual path to socialism. If in the view of the Kremlin, the KSČ should break the agreements made, it had itself signed the political basis on which the "collective action" or the "brotherly assistance" could be legitimized.

On the fringes of the conference in Bratislava, the "initiative group" of the "healthy forces" announced by Brezhnev to his Central Committee, which was indispensable for the political justification of an intervention and for the day after, also finally made an appearance. Jan Pauer writes, "During the course of the Bratislava meeting, a plea, a letter was passed to the Soviet comrades, in which several members of the Presidium of the Central Committee of the KSČ and the government requested help from the Soviet leadership. It was stated in the letter that 'should the situation continue to deteriorate and the accepted commitments not be fulfilled—the undersigned comrades would see no other option than international assistance from the allies, because we won't get out of there on our own steam and there won't be any more time for new negotiations.'[87] The letter was signed by five members of the KSČ Presidium and Secretariat, who took part in the negotiations in Čierna nad Tisou themselves.[88]

With that, the political problem of collective action appeared for Brezhnev to be solved. Should Dubček, as expected, not adhere to the agreements, there was now an alternative. A few days later, an SED delegation traveled to Karlsbad for bilateral discussions with Dubček.[89] The situation seemed to ease up, but Ulbricht was, in fact, implementing an exploratory mission for the Politburo of the CPSU. He wanted to examine how the agreement of Čierna nad Tisou was put into practice. Two points were particularly important: (1) "[m]easures for controlling the media" (Ulbricht for this reason dug his heals in toward Dubček during a joint press conference) and (2) whether or not the activity of the Social Democratic Party would be prevented and the clubs disbanded.

The content of the report to Moscow is not known, but under the circumstances Ulbricht could only confirm that party control over the media had not yet been reestablished.

THE SOVIET UNION ACTS

The period of joint debates was over.[90] On 16 August, the Politburo of the CPSU established that the KSČ had broken the agreements of Čierna nad Tisou. The CPSU listed in detail which ones in their letter to the Presidium of the KSČ from 17 August, at which time it decided to respond to the "call for help" from Prague. The Soviet ambassador in Prague was at the same time instructed to hand the draft of a "Declaration of the Presidium of the Central Committee of the KSČ and the Government of the Czechoslovakian Socialist Republic" to Bil'ak and Indra.[91] The draft was to serve as the political foundation for their bureaucratic putsch plan, the carrying out of which they had promised the Soviet leadership for the Presidium session on 20 August.[92] The Politburo transferred the military high command to Grechko, the Soviet defense minister, and it decided to call a further meeting with the "Warsaw Five" in Moscow for 18 August with a single point on the agenda. The four parties were to assume uncritically the decisions made for their parties and countries and with it guarantee their participation in the "collective action." The assent of the SED was a simple "yes" from Ulbricht, which he reinforced with his signature beneath the minutes. Brezhnev demanded silence regarding this session, including toward the respective national party leaderships. The first secretaries of the four parties had to sign a set of minutes that stayed in Moscow.[93] Ulbricht's "yes" remained in force; the GDR supported the intervention and helped in forcing through the "normalization" in the ČSSR, with which the restoration of the monopoly on power of the Communist Party and its cleansing of "revisionists" was party-officially rewritten.[94]

1988: A SPIRIT IS ABROAD IN THE SOCIALIST CAMP

The suppression of Communist self-reform in the ČSSR in 1968 was a Pyrrhic victory for the Warsaw Five. They did not succeed in enduringly securing the Communist Party's monopoly on power in Czechoslovakia and in their own states.

Twenty years after the violent suppression on 21 August 1968 of the democratization of the Communist dictatorship in Czechoslovakia emanating from the KSČ, the spirit of reformist communism was abroad anew.[95] One year before peaceful revolutions in the GDR and Czechoslovakia ended their rule, two protagonists of the restoration of the Communist Party's monopoly on power in Czechoslovakia from 1968, Bil'ak and Erich Honecker, spoke in East Berlin full of concern for their own power about the new evaluation of the history of Communist rule taking place in the Soviet Union. It concerned the debate on Stalin in the Soviet Union. In 1968, Bil'ak had belonged to the "healthy forces" within the KSČ who had "solicited" the intervention of the "five sister states" for the protection of socialism in the ČSSR. As then Central Committee secretary for security in the SED Politburo, Honecker had unreservedly supported the intervention policy of the SED.

Now, in view of the Soviet policy of reform, they were haunted by the memories of the crimes in the history of communism, to which the suppression of the "Prague Spring" doubtlessly belonged. In 1988, the memories had a name for Honecker and Bil'ak: Mikhail Gorbachev. The general secretary of the CPSU pursued a policy of democratization; Stalin's victims were rehabilitated and censorship abolished. Soviet historians spoke and wrote openly about the Terror of the 1930s and asked what part Stalin's politics had in Adolf Hitler's seizure of power.[96]

According to the SED's memorandum on the discussion, Bil'ak complained about the dangerous political consequences that could arise from the Soviet history debate.

> The Soviet comrades would rather not admit that nasty developments can take place. He, Comrade Bil'ak, has explained to them: "If one hits a rabbit over the head, it is dead; if that befalls a bear, nothing happens. We, however, are a rabbit." An enormous pressure developed in the direction of a destabilization of the Socialist countries. For this reason, he, Comrade Bil'ak, also asked the Soviet comrades whether they realize that the attacks against Stalin ultimately—as in 1968 in the ČSSR—target the party? They are supposed to call into question the legitimacy of the Party of the Bolsheviks.[97]

Bil'ak was dismayed about the presence of the history of the Prague Spring in the Soviet reform debate. He reported "some Soviet representatives demanded that the events of 1968 be re-evaluated. The First Secretary of the Communist Party of Estonia had advised this internally; Comrade Gorbachev also advanced that the events must be re-evaluated, but the Czechoslovakian comrades are not prepared to do that."[98] To Honecker, Bil'ak expressed the feeling of losing his "hinterland."

These quotations prove that, for the leaders of the ruling Communist parties, the history of their own rule primarily served the historical legitimization of their own power. The question to which historians are bound, namely that of the historical truth regarding the methods with which power was gained and held, always turned from this point of view into an attack on the dictatorial power of the Communist Party. Only from this perspective can the significance of the "Prague Spring" in the history of the Soviet Empire also be explained. It was no coincidence that the Soviet reformers of 1987–1988 contemplated a "reevaluation" of these Czechoslovakian reforms: the Prague reform Communists were their forerunners. Precisely because of its violent ending, the history of the "Prague Spring" remained politically current and was one of the causes of the peaceful revolutions in Eastern and Central Europe and in the GDR in 1989. Robert Havemann predicted this at the end of 1970, in order to encourage himself and others to continue the struggle with this hope in mind: "It is in the long run quite inevitable that the ideas of the KSČ precisely as a result of the intervention will also spread within the countries of the interveners. Freedom is the disease from which Stalinism will die."[99]

NOTES

Translated from German into English by Alex Kay, Berlin.
1. On this, see the texts from Rüdiger Wenzke, "Die Nationale Volksarmee der DDR. Kein Einsatz in Prag," 673–86, and Thomas Großbölting, "Die Niederschla-

gung des 'Prager Frühlings' und das Ministerium für Staatssicherheit der DDR," 807–22, both in Karner et al., *Beiträge*.

2. Lutz Prieß, "Der 'Einladungsbrief' zur Intervention in der ČSSR 1968," *Deutschland Archiv* 12 (1994): 1253; RGANI, F. 3, op. 72, d. 197, pp. 3–14, Politburo resolution of the Central Committee of the CPSU P 95 (I), 17 August 1968, reprinted in Karner et al., *Dokumente*, #62.

3. SAPMO-BA, DY 30/3616, pp. 182–207, report of the Department for International Ties, "Zur Reaktion in der kommunistischen Weltbewegung auf die Ereignisse in der ČSSR," to the office of W. Ulbricht, 11 April 1968, reprinted in Karner et al., *Dokumente*, #162.

4. The name originated in July when the CPSU, the BCP, the PUWP, the HSWP, and the SED sent a joint letter to the KSČ following the Warsaw Conference.

5. Hermann Wentker, *Außenpolitik in engen Grenzen: Die DDR im internationalen System 1949–1989* (Munich: Oldenbourg, 2007).

6. Zdenek Hejzlar, *Reformkommunismus: Zur Geschichte der Kommunistischen Partei der Tschechoslowakei* (Cologne: Europäische Verlagsanstalt, 1976), 146.

7. Peter Florin, born 1921, was of the "Moscow cadre" and son of Wilhelm Florin (KPD). In 1935 he emigrated to the Soviet Union, in 1942 completed an apprenticeship at the School of the Communist International, in 1943/1944 was a partisan in Belarus, in May 1945 returned to Berlin, from 1952 to 1966 served as head of the Department for Foreign Affairs in the Central Committee of the SED, and from 1958 to 1989 was a member of the Central Committee of the SED.

8. SAPMO-BA, DY 30/3616, pp. 52–57, report of the GDR ambassador in the ČSSR, P. Florin, on the situation in the country, 10 March 1968, reprinted in Karner et al., *Dokumente*, #3 (reprinted in appendix 1 of this volume).

9. *Rudé pravo*, report of the Central Committee of the KSČ regarding the alteration of the authority of the Central Publication Administration, 6 March 1968, reprinted Karner et al., *Dokumente*, #2.

10. *Zu den Ereignissen in der Tschechoslowakei: Tatsachen, Dokumente, Presse- und Augenzeugenberichte* (Moscow: Pressegruppe Sowjetischer Journalisten, 1968), 3.

11. "Defamation of the revolutionary power as a 'totalitarian dictatorship' and the related demand for 'pluralism' and the 'democratization' of power under socialism serve them as the main means for the ideological preparation and implementation of counter-revolution." Rudolf Dau et al., eds., *Wörterbuch des wissenschaftlichen Kommunismus* (East Berlin: Dietz, 1982), *Stichwort: Konterrevolution*, 216. Further keywords, which are characteristic for "counterrevolution" are anticommunism, anti-Soviet, and nationalism. Anticommunism: "Wesenszug und Grundtendenz der gesamten Ideologie und Politik des Imperialismus im Kampf gegen den Sozialismus, gegen die revolutionäre Arbeiterbewegung und den Marxismus-Leninismus, gegen die Friedensbewegung und alle anderen demokratischen Kräfte" (*Stichwort: Antikommunismus*, 26). Anti-Soviet: "dominierendes Kennzeichen des Antikommunismus. Er richtet sich gegen die Sowjetunion, gegen deren führende Kraft—die KPdSU—, gegen Politik, Wirtschaft, Ideologie und Kultur des sowjetischen Staates. Der Antisowjetismus entstand als konterrevolutionäre Reaktion auf die Entstehung des ersten sozialistischen Staates in der Welt. Er zielt auf die Diskreditierung und Vernichtung der sowjetischen Gesellschaft" (*Stichwort: Antisowjetismus*, 30). Nationalism: "ist eine 'bürgerliche Ideologie,' im Zusammenhang mit dem Ost-West-Kon-

flikt bekommt er eine spezifische Bedeutung: Mit Hilfe des Nationalismus sollen die politisch-ideologischen Grundlagen des Sozialismus in einzelnen Ländern untergraben, die Einheit der sozialistischen Gemeinschaft und der kommunistischen und Arbeiterparteien durch die Leugnung allgemeisngültiger Gesetzmäßigkeiten, die Überbetonung nationaler Besonderheiten und nationalistischer Ideen zerstört werden" (*Stichwort: Nationalismus,* 270–71).

12. SAPMO-BA, DY 30/11834, pp. 1–271, stenographical record of the consultation of the five "sister parties" with the KSČ in Dresden, 23 March 1968, reprinted in Karner et al., *Dokumente,* #75.

13. A. J. Wyschinski (Vyshinsky), *Gerichtsrede* (East Berlin: Dietz Verlag, 1952), 545, and Wladislaw Hedeler, *Chronik Moskauer Schauprozesse 1936, 1937, und 1938* (Berlin: Akademie Verlag, 2003).

14. RGANI, F. 3, op. 72, d. 155, p. 5, Politburo resolution of the Central Committee of the CPSU P 74 (II), 15 March 1968, reprinted in Karner et al., *Dokumente,* #73.

15. RGANI, F. 3, op. 72, d. 157, pp. 6 and 15–19, Politburo resolution of the Central Committee of the CPSU P 76 (12), 23 March 1968, reprinted in Karner et al., *Dokumente,* #30.

16. On this, see Lutz Priess et al., *Die SED und der "Prager Frühling"* (Berlin: Akademie Verlag, 1995), 63–64.

17. Rudolf Helmer, KPD member since 1931, since 1959 served as head of the Department for Neighboring Countries of the Ministry for Foreign Affairs of the GDR.

18. RGANI, F. 5, op. 60, d. 299, pp. 108–13, taken from the official diary of the embassy counsel of the USSR in the GDR, V. P. Grenkov, 19 March 1968, reprinted in Karner et al., *Dokumente,* #6.

19. Quoted from Priess et al., *Die SED und der "Prager Frühling,"* 172–73. On this, see also Békés, "Hungary and the Prague Spring," in this volume.

20. RGANI, F. 3, op. 72, d. 154, p. 2, Politburo resolution of the Central Committee of the CPSU P 73 (1), 11 March 1968, reprinted in Karner et al., *Dokumente,* #72; RGANI, F. 3, op. 72, d. 155, p. 5, Politburo resolution of the Central Committee of the CPSU P 74 (II), 15 March 1968, reprinted in Karner et al., *Dokumente,* #73. On this, see also Békés, "Hungary and the Prague Spring," in this volume.

21. RGANI, F. 3, op. 72, d. 154, p. 2 (see note 20) and SAPMO-BA, DY 30/11834, S. 1–271 (see note 12); all quotes that follow are from these minutes.

22. Jan Pauer writes about how Dubček and his delegation dealt with the confrontation in Dresden: "Neither the Party leadership nor the public learnt anything about the conflict and about possible verbal undertakings on the part of the KSČ delegation to the effect that they wanted to bring developments more in line with Soviet intentions." Jan Pauer, *Prag 1968, Der Einmarsch des Warschauer Paktes: Hintergründe—Planung—Durchführung* (Bremen: Ed. Temmen, 1995), 43–44.

23. SAPMO-BA, DY 30/3617, pp. 17–19 and 26–32, internal Bulgarian information passed on to the GDR and other participants at the Dresden meeting, 30 March 1968, reprinted in Karner et al., *Dokumente,* #21.

24. SAPMO-BA, DY 30/3617, pp. 17–19 and 26–32.

25. SAPMO-BA, DY 30/3616, pp. 1–16 and 46, text of the speech of Comrade Josef Smrkovský on the plenum of the Central Committee of the KSČ, 1 February 1968, reprinted in Karner et al., *Dokumente,* #1.

26. This is a reference to a survey by the *Literární listy* on basic questions relating to current affairs, on the importance of free elections, a functioning parliament, an opposition, and active neutrality. Ulbricht commented on the last point with the statement "no more Warsaw Pact then."

27. Kurt Hager (1912–1998) was a participant in the Spanish Civil War, in 1955 was secretary of the Central Committee of the SED for Culture and Science, was a 1958 nominee, and from 1963 until 1989 served as a member of the Politburo.

28. See Priess et al., *Die SED und der "Prager Frühling,"* 81–94.

29. RGANI, F. 5, op. 60, d. 299, pp. 298–307, report of the Soviet ambassador in the GDR, P. Abrasimov, to the departmental head of the Central Committee of the CPSU, K. V. Rusakov, "Zur Frage der Beziehungen zwischen der SED und der KPČ, der DDR und der Tschechoslowakei," 19 April 1968, reprinted in Karner et al., *Dokumente*, #16.

30. Otto Winzer (1902–1975) was in 1925 a KPD member, a member of the Comintern, emigrated to the Soviet Union, in 1945 returned to Berlin as a member of the "Ulbricht Group," and from 1965 to 1975 served as foreign minister of the GDR.

31. SAPMO-BA, DY 30/316, memorandum on a discussion between the minister for foreign affairs of the GDR, Winzer, and the ambassador of the ČSSR in the GDR, Kolář, on 1 April 1968.

32. SAPMO-BA, DY 30/3616, pp. 235–41, memorandum on a discussion between the first secretary of the Central Committee of the SED, Walter Ulbricht, and the ambassador of the ČSSR in the GDR, Kolář, 16 April 1968, reprinted in Karner et al., *Dokumente*, #15.

33. The "April plenum" took place from 28 March 1968 until 1 April 1968.

34. From the record of the information provided orally by Dubček and other members of the Czechoslovak delegation regarding the meeting of the Communist parties in Dresden, 23 March 1968, reprinted in Karner et al., *Dokumente*, #76.

35. See Priess et al., *Die SED und der "Prager Frühling,"* 95–110; ÚSD, sb. KV ČSFR, D IV/25, extract from the Action Program of the Communist Party of Czechoslovakia, 5 April 1968, reprinted in Karner et al., *Dokumente*, #13.

36. Information no. 23/68, see Priess et al., *Die SED und der "Prager Frühling,"* 104.

37. SAPMO-BA, DY 30/3616, pp. 221–24, information from the GDR embassy in Prague regarding a discussion with the director for fiction in the party's publishing house "Svoboda," J. Hájek, 5 April 1968, reprinted in Karner et al., *Dokumente*, #14.

38. SAPMO-BA, DY, 30/3617, pp. 17–19 and 26–32 (see note 23).

39. A MVnR, op. 5 sh, a. e. 516, 112, coded telegram from the Bulgarian ambassador in Berlin, Daskalov, to the Bulgarian Foreign Ministry, 30 April 1968, reprinted in Karner et al., *Dokumente*, #20.

40. AdBIK, holding "Prager Frühling," minutes of the discussion between the heads of the Central Committee of the CPSU and the heads of the Communist parties of Bulgaria, Hungary, the GDR and Poland, 8 May 1968, reprinted in Karner et al., *Dokumente*, #77; SAPMO-DA, DY 30/11835, pp. 1–48, notes made by Ulbricht on this discussion, 8 May 1968; the subsequent verbatim quotes from Priess et al., *Die SED und der "Prager Frühling,"* 118–32.

41. Pauer, *Der Einmarsch des Warschauer Paktes*, 45–62.

42. On this, see also the chapter by Mikhail Prozumenshchikov, "Inside the Politburo of the CPSU: Political and Military Decision Making to Solve the Czechoslovak Crisis," in this volume and Priess et al., *Die SED und der "Prager Frühling,"* 158.

43. On this, see also the text from Rüdiger Wenzke, "Die Nationale Volksarmee der DDR: Kein Einsatz in Prag," in Karner et al., *Beiträge*, 673–86.

44. Pauer, *Der Einmarsch des Warschauer Paktes*, 58.

45. Hartmut Zwahr, *Die erfrorenen Flügel der Schwalbe: DDR und "Prager Frühling"* (Bonn: Dietz, 2007), 81.

46. Zwahr, *Die erfrorenen Flügel der Schwalbe*, 75.

47. Robert Havemann (1910–1982) was in 1943 sentenced to death by the *Volksgerichtshof*, but the physicist/chemist survived by carrying out research in jail; in 1950 he was a member of the SED and professor at Berlin's Humboldt University; in 1964 he lost his professorship, was ejected from the SED, and was the voice of opposition in the GDR until his death.

48. Quoted from Priess et al., *Die SED und der "Prager Frühling,"* 139.

49. "Stalinism is the system of distrust and hypocrisy; democracy is that of trust and the free and critical expression of opinion. In Stalinism, the state has the citizens; in democracy, the citizens have the state." Priess et al., *Die SED und der "Prager Frühling,"* 140.

50. On this see also the text from Vondrová, "Der 'Prager Frühling' 1968 und Moskau," in Karner et al., *Beiträge*, 171–204.

51. Vondrová, "Der 'Prager Frühling' 1968 und Moskau," in Karner et al., *Beiträge*, 171–204.

52. SAPMO-BA, DY 30/3617, p. 9, embassy in Prague, 13 June 1968, assessment of the May plenum by the Central Committee of the KSČ (29 May–1 June 1968).

53. SAPMO, DY 30/3618, p. 6, in a letter from the CPSU to the Presidium of the KSČ from 4 July 1968, it says: "The offensive announced at the May plenum of the Central Committee of the KSČ against the right-leaning and anti-socialist forces was neither ideological, nor political, nor organizationally secured; it simply didn't take place" (extract from the German version).

54. SAPMO, DY 30/3618, p. 17.

55. On this, see also Vondrová, "Prag und Moskau," in Karner et al., *Beiträge*, 171–92.

56. At the 14th Party Congress conducted underground on 22 August 1968, these persons were indeed not elected to the Central Committee: Jiři Pelikán, ed., *Panzer überrollen den Parteitag, Protokoll und Dokumente des XIV: Parteitags der KPČ am 22 August 1968* (Vienna: Europa Verlag, 1969).

57. On this, see also Prozumenshchikov, "Inside the Politburo of the CPSU," in this volume.

58. Hejzlar, *Reformkommunismus*, 194–200; the draft of a new party statute is printed in Pelikán, *Panzer überrollen den Parteitag*, 143–84.

59. Hejzlar, *Reformkommunismus*, 179-80.

60. BA-MA, VA-01/12826, pp. 115–18, report of the operational group of the NVA from the operational headquarters of the supreme commander of the Unified Forces of the Warsaw Pact in Legnica, 25 July 1968, reprinted in Karner et al., *Dokumente*, #92.

61. SAPMO-BA, DY 30/3617, pp. 169–79, 28 June 1968. The manifesto of the "2,000 Words," 28 June 1968, is reprinted in Karner et al., *Dokumente*, #28.

62. SAPMO-BA, DY 30/3618, pp. 14–21, report of the GDR ambassador in the ČSSR, Peter Florin, regarding the preparations for the extraordinary 14th Party Congress of the KSČ, 3 July 1968, reprinted in Karner et al., *Dokumente*, #29.

63. Priess et al., *Die SED und der "Prager Frühling,"* 177.

64. RGANI, F. 3, op. 72, d. 183, pp. 3–17, Politburo resolution of the Central Committee of the CPSU P 88 (I), 3 July 1968, reprinted in Karner et al., *Dokumente*, #37.

65. See Priess et al., *Die SED und der "Prager Frühling,"* 180–86.

66. Priess et al., *Die SED und der "Prager Frühling,"* 182.

67. On this, see also Prozumenshchikov, "Inside the Politburo of the CPSU," in this volume.

68. On this, see also Vondrová, "Prag und Moskau," 171–92.

69. RGANI, F. 3, op. 72, d. 186, p. 19, Politburo resolution of the Central Committee of the CPSU P 90 (12), 11 July 1968, reprinted in Karner et al., *Dokumente*, #81.

70. SAPMO-BA, DY 30/3618, p. 8, letter from the "Warsaw Five" to the Central Committee of the KSČ, 15 July 1968. The "Warsaw letter" is reprinted in Karner et al., *Dokumente*, #45.

71. SAPMO-BA, DY 30/11836, 1–116, stenographical record of the meeting of the interventionist coalition in Warsaw, 14 and 15 July 1968, reprinted in Karner et al., *Dokumente*, #82.

72. On the politics of the United States and the Federal Republic, see the articles from Horst Möller, "Die Bundesrepublik Deutschland und der 'Prager Frühling,'" in Karner et al., *Beiträge*, 549–58; and Udo Wengst, "Die bundesdeutschen Parteien und ihre Reaktionen auf den Einmarsch," in Karner et al., *Beiträge*, 559–70; as well as Günter Bischof, "'No action': Die USA und die Invasion in die Tschechoslowakei," in Karner et al., *Beiträge*, 319–54.

73. RGANI, F. 2, op. 3, d. 114, pp. 27–54, speech of the general secretary of the Central Committee of the CPSU, L. I. Brezhnev, 17 July 1968, reprinted in Karner et al., *Dokumente*, #38.

74. On this, see also Prozumenshchikov, "Inside the Politburo of the CPSU," in this volume.

75. Telegram from the ambassador of the GDR in Prague, 18 July 1968, SAPMO-BA, DY 30/ 3618, p. 1.

76. Priess et al., *Die SED und der "Prager Frühling,"* 206–9.

77. Rüdiger Wenzke, *Forschungen zur DDR-Geschichte*, vol. 5, *Die NVA und der Prager Frühling 1968: Die Rolle Ulbrichts und der DDR-Streitkräfte bei der Niederschlagung der tschechoslowakischen Reformbewegung* (Berlin: Ch. Links, 1995).

78. Wenzke, *Forschungen zur DDR-Geschichte*, 5:211–12.

79. Wenzke, *Forschungen zur DDR-Geschichte*, 5:202; on this see also the protocols of the NVR from the year 1968, *Bundesarchiv*, 2008 http://www.bundesarchiv. de/fb_daofind/Zdaofind_DVW1_NVR/mets/NVR_39490/index.htm (accessed 21 June 2008).

80. On this, see also Prozumenshchikov, "Inside the Politburo of the CPSU," in this volume and Vondrová, "Prag und Moskau," 171–92.

81. Priess et al., *Die SED und der "Prager Frühling,"* 213.

82. Pauer, *Der Einmarsch des Warschauer Paktes*, 173.

83. Pauer, *Der Einmarsch des Warschauer Paktes*, 174.

84. Pauer, *Der Einmarsch des Warschauer Paktes*, 174.

85. Hermann Axen (1916–1992): 1932 member of the Communist Youth Organization; imprisoned after 1933, inc. in Auschwitz concentration camp; 1945 KPD; 1970–1989 member of the Politburo of the SED, Central Committee secretary for international affairs.

86. Priess et al., *Die SED und der "Prager Frühling,"* 215.

87. Pauer, *Der Einmarsch des Warschauer Paktes*, 175.

88. RGANI, F. 3. op. 72, d. 197, pp. 3–6, Politburo resolution of the Central Committee of the CPSU P 95 (I), 17 August 1968, reprinted in Karner et al., *Dokumente*, #62.

89. SAPMO-BA, DY 30/3621, pp. 57–61, minutes of the discussion between members of the delegations of the SED and the KSČ, 13 August 1968, reprinted in Karner et al., *Dokumente*, #86; RGANI, F. 89, op. 76, d. 73, pp. 1–2, Politburo resolution of the Central Committee of the CPSU P 94 (82), 10 August 1968, reprinted in Karner et al., *Dokumente*, #54.

90. On the significance of this discussion for the forming of opinion in the Central Committee apparatus of the CPSU, see also Prozumenshchikov, "Inside the Politburo of the CPSU," in this volume.

91. RGANI, F. 3. op. 72, d. 197, pp. 3–6 (see note 2).

92. Pauer, *Der Einmarsch des Warschauer Paktes*, 228–62.

93. On this, see Manfred Wilke, "Protokoll der 47: Sitzung der Enquete-Kommission: Der Prager Frühling 1968 und Solidarnosc 1980/81," in *Materialien der Enquete-Kommission der 12. Wahlperiode des Deutschen Bundestages*, vol. 1, ed. Der Deutsche Bundestag (Baden-Baden: Nomos, 1995), 170; AdBIK, holding "Prager Frühling," stenographical record of the meeting of the interventionist coalition in Moscow, 18 August 1968, reprinted in Karner et al., *Dokumente*, #87.

94. Priess et al., *Die SED und der "Prager Frühling,"* 226–84, and Pauer, *Der Einmarsch des Warschauer Paktes*, 283–391.

95. SAPMO-BA, DY 30/11836, pp. 1–116 (see note 59).

96. Boris Meissner, *Die Sowjetunion im Umbruch* (Stuttgart: Deutsche Verlags-Anstalt, 1988).

97. Memorandum on a discussion between the general secretary of the Central Committee of the SED and chairman of the State Council of the GDR, Comrade Erich Honecker, and the member of the Presidium and secretary of the Central Committee of the KSČ, Comrade Vasil Bil'ak, on 24 November 1988 in the offices of the Central Committee, SAPMO-BA, DY 30/2439, p. 3.

98. SAPMO-BA, DY 30/2439, 5.

99. Robert Havemann, *Fragen Antworten Fragen: Aus der Biographie eines deutschen Marxisten* (Munich: R. Piper, 1970), 59.

16

Hungary and the Prague Spring

Csaba Békés

The reform movement in the Czechoslovak Socialist Republic (ČSSR) that began in January 1968 coincided with the introduction of the "new economic mechanism" in Hungary.[1] The Hungarian leadership saw three possible scenarios on which to base a prognosis regarding the potential consequences of the events in Prague on Hungary. In the best-case scenario, the Czechoslovak reforms would remain moderate; they would, if reluctantly, be accepted by the Soviets in a development that was analogous to that in Poland in October 1956. In this case, Hungary and Czechoslovakia, the two leading reformist countries within the Soviet Bloc, would be able to support each other and serve as an example to the other countries. This would echo the first half of the 1960s, when Hungary and Poland had played a leading role in de-Stalinization.

In a second, much more probable scenario, the Czechoslovak reforms, which were above all political in nature, would sooner or later—perhaps even contrary to the original intentions of their initiators—move beyond the limits set by the Soviet leadership. This would ultimately lead to an armed intervention on the pattern of Hungary 1956 and could seriously jeopardize all initiatives and reforms in the Soviet Bloc that deviated from the Soviet model, including the Hungarian economic reforms.

In the third scenario, the far reaching political reforms in Prague might prove unacceptable to Moscow, which could lead to Hungary's course of moderate restructuring, which did not threaten political destabilization, being given a green light as the lesser of two evils. A comparison of the two processes, which differed in their objectives, might even awaken a certain amount of sympathy on the part of the Soviet leadership for the downright moderate Hungarian reforms, which only aimed at improving economic efficiency and indirectly also served Soviet interests. It was, in fact, this third scenario which was turned into reality in 1968 and the ensuing years. The Soviet leadership, after being rather tolerant at the beginning, exerted substantial pressure on the Hungarian leadership in the early 1970s to prevent the reforms from leading to the country's destabilization, and they made sure that the leading reformists were removed. János Kádár himself was not removed, however, whereas Władysław Gomułka and Walter Ulbricht were both forced to resign from their posts during those years; the most important measures of the Hungarian economic reform were allowed to remain in place.

Since the beginning of 1968, it was quite clear that there was only one objective for Kádár and the Hungarian leadership: to do everything in their power to make the first scenario come true. Failing that, the next one in order of preference was the third one; the second one, discrediting all reforms, was to be avoided at all costs. This determination was the driving force behind Kádár's repeated attempts to persuade the Czechoslovak leaders to be cautious, to slow down the pace of reform, to acknowledge realities while he worked hard up to the middle of July, and even after that to convince the Kremlin and the other Soviet Bloc leaders to muster more understanding and patience because the cause of socialism was not yet critically endangered there.

It is important to make it quite clear from the outset that the difference of opinion between Kádár and the Soviets and/or the other Socialist leaders did not concern the question whether the Soviet Union and the member states of the Warsaw Pact were entitled to intervene if a restoration of capitalism was to be attempted in Czechoslovakia. Kádár had given an unequivocal answer to that question at the session of the Central Committee of the Hungarian Socialist Workers' Party (HSWP) held on 19 and 20 June 1968:

> If we conclude that this is a counterrevolution and that the counterrevolution is gaining the upper hand, then, quite frankly and if truth be told here among us, one has to go to the limit, and I would raise both my hands in favour of those Warsaw Pact countries that are prepared to do so occupying Czechoslovakia. This is what has to be done because the socialist world cannot afford to lose Czechoslovakia.[2]

This statement showed Kádár running true to form. This was, after all, the same man who accepted the leadership of the countergovernment in 1956 and went on to suppress brutally the Hungarian Revolution with the help of the Red Army. He was even the only political leader in the entire Eastern Bloc to have overseen a "rescue operation" of the Communist system in a serious crisis.[3] So the difference was not one in the degree of loyalty to the Communist system, but in the assessment of the situation, that is, in choosing the right moment once it was obvious that there was no longer the chance of a political settlement and that Czechoslovakia could only be kept within the Socialist camp through a military invasion. Yet in this question he stubbornly clung to the formula that was for him a tried and proven one on the basis of his own experience: armed intervention was the method of choice only once the counterrevolution had already gained the upper hand. If this undesirable development did indeed come to pass, then the Soviet Union was in a position to restore order and the Communist system in a matter of a few days. This was the reason why at the beginning there was so much emphasis on the Hungarian assessment of developments in Czechoslovakia, particularly regarding the fact that despite negative tendencies there was as yet no counterrevolutionary danger; the goal was merely the correction of earlier mistakes.

By early May 1968 Kádár, too, saw the danger of a counterrevolution and the seriousness of the situation and modified his position accordingly. From that point on, he underlined that at least the counterrevolution had not yet been victorious. At the Warsaw meeting of the "Five" in July, Kádár endorsed the plan of a joint invasion *in principle* and declared Hungary to be prepared to participate, but he continued to do everything to prevent a drastic solution from happening.[4] In the end, he bowed to the inevitable, and Hungary took part in the military action on 21 August. Even then Kádár rather curiously refused to give up his theoretical point of view. In mid-August, in the days immediately preceding the intervention, he told Leonid Brezhnev that the Czechoslovak developments had their closest parallels not to the Hungary of 1956, but to Poland. The Soviets nevertheless opted for the "Hungarian solution."[5] Kádár maintained that Czechoslovakia, as opposed to Hungary in 1956, had not yet reached the counterrevolutionary phase in August 1968. He remained true to himself when he felt that the intervention had been premature.

In this case, however, Kádár's assessment of the situation was mistaken. In 1956, Gomułka had got the measure of Soviet tolerance and its limits and was able to contain developments within boundaries that were acceptable to Moscow. Czechoslovakia, on the other hand, had undergone a process of democratization by August 1968 that could not be arrested without the use of force, either internally or from outside and that, in fact, recalled two developments in Hungary.

First, the process occurring between February and November 1956 brought about, by the time of the second Soviet intervention on 4 November, a situation in which Communist power had ceased to exist;[6] the general elections, which were due to be held shortly, would most certainly have resulted in the establishment of a bourgeois democratic system.

At first sight, a comparison of the two crises seems to show up significant differences, the chief one being that there was no armed uprising in

Czechoslovakia. Yet a closer look will reveal that such developments as the extraordinarily fast decay of the Communist Party's self-confidence resulting from the freedom of the press and the societal pressure it generated, the evaporation of its legitimation, its erosion and subsequent dissolution would have taken place within a very short time in Czechoslovakia as well. In Hungary, these developments unfolded step by step in the half year leading up to the revolt and at an accelerated pace during the two weeks of the revolution.[7]

Secondly, the regime change in Hungary in 1988/1989 highlights in an extremely instructive manner how the Communist Party attempted at that time, in a transitional situation similar to the one in Czechoslovakia in 1968, to take into account society's changed interests to a larger extent than had previously been the case in order to revitalize its legitimation. From a starting point of accepting pluralism within the party, it was propelled by pressure both from radicals in the party and in society very quickly to the nominal acceptance of a multiparty system, which the party envisaged as coexisting with its dominant role remaining intact within an overall framework of regulated power sharing. This "new model of socialism" evolving from the middle of 1988 was, in fact, very similar to Alexander Dubček's vision of "socialism with a human face." By May 1989, however, once the danger of a Soviet intervention had gradually receded into the background, this position swiftly gave way to the party's *voluntarily* accepting the idea of genuine free elections. The subsequent Round Table talks resulted in September in an agreement between the party and the opposition on holding free elections the next spring, and in early October, the HSWP itself morphed into a social-democratic party.[8]

In Soviet, Polish, East German, and Bulgarian prognoses, it was precisely these fears that were expressed in the summer of 1968 with reference to the developments in Czechoslovakia, and for this there was good reason. The free press, the foundation of political clubs (that were clearly proto-opposition parties), the preparations for a relaunch of the Social Democratic Party, the "2,000 Words" manifesto and the reception it met with in public opinion, and societal demands of increasing radicalism all concurred in underlining that the Czechoslovak society, which had a powerful streak of nostalgia for the parliamentary democracy of the interwar years, would not have limited its political goals to the acceptance of a reformed Socialist system if it had not been for a military intervention from outside. There is no doubt that the reform movement that was underway in Czechoslovakia in the summer of 1968 gradually but rather quickly progressed from visions of a reformed Socialist model toward a nontotalitarian system and would ultimately have reached the modern variant of such a system, that of parliamentary democracy; this is indeed what happened in 1990 without pressure from outside in a matter of months.

The Dubček leadership, which was at least in nominal control of developments until the military intervention in August, had two options in this situation. The first one was to restrict liberalization to below the Soviet threshold of tolerance (the Gomułka model of 1956). In this scenario, the gradual relaxation since January 1968 and the freedom of the press would have resulted in a serious conflict between the established power of the state and society so that the increasing societal resistance would probably have had to be dealt with domestically by the use of force (Jaruzelski model of 1981). Yet Dubček, like Hungary's Imre Nagy or Poland's Stanisław Kania, belonged to the "soft" type of Communist leader who was neither willing nor capable of using brute force against society in a crisis to suppress the process of democratization. In this sense, Kádár, who as leader of Hungary's "soft" dictatorship was regarded as a liberal Communist in the West, clearly belongs with Communists of the "hard" type. Another notable representative of this type was Josip Tito, whose independent foreign policy line was highly appreciated in the West while the Yugoslav political and economic model was the most serious deviation from the Leninist-Stalinist-type Communist model. Moreover, he was also lucky for not having had to face and handle a serious internal crisis during his reign. Nevertheless, when Nikita Khrushchev and Georgi Malenkov secretly visited him before the Soviet intervention to crush the Hungarian Revolution in November 1956, Tito not only agreed that intervention was necessary to save the Communist system there, but also promised to help eliminate his virtual allies—Prime Minister Imre Nagy and his adherents—from political life.[9]

The second option—and this is the one that both Nagy in 1956 and the Prague leaders in 1968 chose—consisted of attempting to avoid the conflict with society and yielding gradually to societal pressures. At the same time, it was necessary to convince the Soviets that the political reforms, no matter how far reaching they might appear, were still within the framework of the Socialist system. The Czechoslovak leadership did not accede to the Soviet demands contained in the agreement of Čierna nad Tisou in August 1968 because they understandably concluded that this would be interpreted by the people as a betrayal of the cause of the Prague Spring and provoke determined resistance.[10] The Soviets in their turn viewed the inactivity of the Prague leadership as irrefutable proof of their inability and their unwillingness—which was even worse—to channel developments into the direction of Soviet expectations.

In view of an unreliable party leadership and an increasingly free press, Moscow had by early August also lost confidence in the Czechoslovak security services and in the country's military leadership, as they, too, seemed loyal not to the Soviet Union, but to the Prague leadership.

It was the same four factors as in Hungary in 1956 that were interpreted as symptoms of a deep crisis in Czechoslovakia in 1968, and this realization propelled Moscow toward the military intervention that spelled the end for the Prague Spring.[11]

In moral terms, the two actions constituted blatant interferences in the internal affairs of nominally independent allies, yet in terms of realpolitik, the Soviet Union, having its own imperial interests at heart, was making rationally justifiable decisions.[12]

KÁDÁR MEDIATES BETWEEN BREZHNEV AND DUBČEK

On taking office as leader of the Communist Party of Czechoslovakia (KSČ), Alexander Dubček held his first international negotiation with János Kádár. Having received an official invitation to Moscow on 10 January, Dubček confidentially asked the Hungarian party leader for a secret meeting before his trip to Moscow.[13] Kádár was an obvious choice for the Czechoslovak leader. De-Stalinization, which had been carried out successfully in Hungary in the early 1960s, and the reformist élan of the leadership made the Hungarian party automatically a potential ally of the Prague reformers and one to which they were looking for support of their policies.

Dubček was of course well aware that the Soviets would learn of the meeting, yet he possibly banked on the meeting being legitimized in the Kremlin's eyes by an—ultimately unrealized—move that Leonid Brezhnev had suggested during the crisis of a month before, in December 1967, which would also have involved a mediating role for Hungary.

During his trip to Moscow in November, Antonín Novotný had invited Brezhnev to Prague without informing the leadership of the KSČ; he hoped that the presence of the Soviet leader would bolster his own weakened position. In a move unusual even by the standards of Soviet Bloc practice, Brezhnev made Novotný also invite Kádár to Prague, again without informing the KSČ. The Soviet leader had obviously concluded that Kádár's international standing and his "experience" in dealing with domestic crises and in the consolidation of a difficult situation might help persuade the disgruntled members of the Prague leadership to defer Novotný's ousting. As the Hungarian party leader shared this view regarding Novotný at the time, he signaled his willingness to accept the invitation.[14]

The following incident is evidence of the dramatic pace at which the Czechoslovak developments were unfolding. In a telephone call on 13 December 1967, Brezhnev attempted to motivate Kádár to undertake the trip to Prague, which was then only three days away, by saying that the Czechoslovak leaders were impatiently looking forward to his arrival—only to be told by Kádár that Novotný had withdrawn the invitation on that very day.[15]

The meeting between Dubček and Kádár, which also included a hunting expedition, took place on 20 and 21 January 1968 in Polarikovo and Topol'čianky in Slovakia. The two leaders had known each other for a long time, which gave the meeting an amicable atmosphere. This is also evidenced by Kádár's greeting, which was not what one might call a standard formula: "Congratulations—and my most sincere condolences!" With this unusual phrase, he signaled that he was only too familiar with the Czechoslovak problems.[16] "The atmosphere was excellent, Comrade Dubček even said that for obvious reasons there was hardly anyone apart from Kádár with whom he could have talked about those topics in the same manner."[17]

Dubček gave Kádár a detailed report on the causes of the Czechoslovak crisis and mentioned the mistakes that had been made since the 1950s in a historical retrospective. He also spoke about the circumstances of Novotný's removal and his own election. Kádár admitted openly that Brezhnev and he had felt in December that Novotný should have been removed at a later date. Kádár knew intuitively that Dubček had actually sought the meeting in the hope of being given friendly advice, and he was unlikely to disappoint him. Kádár therefore advised restoring unity in the party leadership and tackling the problems methodically, calmly, and patiently. He also told Dubček that he must on no account embark on an "offended" political course and that he had to put up with other fraternal parties not being happy about the changes in Prague.[18] "Tell yourself that they are only insufficiently aware of the circumstances and of your own point of view. They will become more aware of the actual situation before long and revise their assessment accordingly."[19]

These encouraging words reflect Kádár's initial optimism. They also proved to have been a prophesy which was soon to come true—if in a way that was disastrous for the Czechoslovak leaders. Kádár also mentioned that he deemed secret meetings inadvisable. It was agreed that the Czechoslovak leaders were to come to Budapest in late March or early April for a friendly visit, on which they would report. In retrospect, Kádár called the meeting "an open, straightforward private conversation" and Dubček a "sane, sober-minded communist motivated by a sense of responsibility and also struggling with problems."[20]

The next meeting between Dubček and Kádár took place before March as developments were picking up momentum not only in Prague and Moscow, but also in East Berlin and Warsaw, where leaders were becoming increasingly concerned about the situation in Prague.[21] The Czechoslovak leaders' trip to Moscow took place earlier than originally planned, at the end of January. A meeting with Gomułka was arranged for 10 February.[22] An invitation to the German Democratic Republic (GDR) had also arrived. Therefore, it became important for Dubček, once he had completed his introductory visit to Moscow, to schedule the first official negotiations with one of the countries of the Soviet Bloc. This first country was to be Hungary, which was considered a close ally, a fact that Dubček openly addressed in the letter of 27 January to Kádár containing the invitation.[23] The hectic pace of developments in Prague becomes apparent from the fact that Dubček originally planned to go to Budapest on 5 February; the information was accordingly conveyed to the Hungarian embassy in Prague. A few minutes later, Dubček himself called the ambassador and asked him to make arrangements for a meeting in Komárno on 4 or 5 February instead.[24]

In order to underline the official character of this meeting, which took place on Czechoslovak soil in Komárno, the list of participants included the foreign policy secretaries of the two parties, Vladimír Koucký and Zoltán Komócsin, as well as Hungarian deputy foreign minister Károly Erdélyi.[25] Dubček reported on the Action Program that was going to be submitted to the session of the Central Committee scheduled for March, and mentioned that "they did not want to tackle too much at once."[26] For the time being, priority was given to solving the most important problems. The necessity of drafting a document that dealt in detail and from a long-term perspective with the problems confronting the party, the state, the economy, and society, which would have to be passed by the KSČ's Central Committee, was not mentioned by anyone. Kádár expressed his concerns with regard to the Czechoslovak developments extremely diplomatically when he said: "Mark my words: now everyone is at work there on their own Action Program."[27]

At the Politburo session of the HSWP on 6 February, the Hungarian leader formulated this concern much more pointedly. According to information he had received two days before the meeting in Komárno, things had taken a turn in Czechoslovakia

> that made one's hair stand on end. In a number of different areas all kinds of twelve-point programmes are formulated and submitted to the Central Committee. Their tenor is not hostile or directed against the party but the initiative has been taken out of the hands of the Central Committee and some proposals go beyond the CC's presently held position. They contain such issues as whether Novotný could be allowed to continue as President.[28]

At the meeting, Dubček painted his visit to Moscow as a great success. He said that Brezhnev and the other Soviet leaders had assured him of their assistance. He underlined that he had explicitly made the point that he wanted to solve all problems in close cooperation with the Soviet Union. Dubček and Kádár agreed in their assessments of the international situation across the board (Middle East, Vietnam, the issue of the Budapest Conference of the Communist and Workers' Parties, and so forth). The most interesting discussion was the one regarding relations with the Federal Republic of Germany (FRG). Kádár noted with relief that the Czechoslovak and Hungarian points of view were identical and felt sure he had found an ally in the Czechoslovak leadership in a question that was crucially important to the Hungarian economy. The secret protocol that had been endorsed under Polish and East German pressure by the Conference of Foreign Ministers in February 1967 in Warsaw made it impossible, after Romania's earlier unilateral move, for Bulgaria, Czechoslovakia, and Hungary to enter into diplomatic relations with the FRG even though the Bonn government had extended this offer to all four countries.[29] Kádár and Dubček welcomed the fact that diplomatic relations had been reestablished in the meantime between West Germany and Yugoslavia. There were now three Socialist countries (the Soviet Union, Romania, and Yugoslavia) that had official relations with the FRG. The fact that Dubček agreed with him that this created an entirely new situation made Kádár hope that with help from the Czechoslovak leadership the time might come for the Warsaw directive to be reviewed. Kádár used open, flexible language to describe his point of view to Dubček:

> We have accepted this agreement and stand by it without any emotional involvement either way. It came into being under adverse circumstances. The position it creates is a rigid one and the six points [of the Warsaw protocol] create an impression as if we expected the FRG to proclaim itself a Soviet republic. The conditions are over the top and too rigid. I said that we were of course going to stand by the agreement but afterwards we informed all the parties concerned that this was a question that was not going to go away. It continues to be on the agenda. The situation must be reviewed constantly—and the same applies to what needs to be done about it. It's not one of those problems that can be dealt with once and for all. And we cannot afford not to be able to come up with political answers to political questions.

Dubček and Koucký found themselves in complete agreement with the Hungarian leader.[30] That Kádár pinned his hopes of bringing about a review of the Warsaw Pact's attitude toward the FRG to Dubček's help appears to be an important clue in any attempt to understand why he insisted for so long that Czechoslovakia's consolidation according to the interests of the Soviet Bloc be carried out with the Dubček leadership rather than with the "healthy forces" backed by Moscow.

The meeting also produced an agreement on a continued development of bilateral economic and cultural relations. At Dubček's request, Kádár was willing to consider that the friendship treaty between the two countries that had been concluded for twenty years in February 1949 should be renewed a year before its termination, with a clearly demonstrative purpose in the summer of 1968.

The next meeting between Kádár and Dubček also took place earlier than had originally been planned, at the anniversary of the Communist takeover in Czechoslovakia in February 1968. Initial planning had provided for the invitation of delegations from the "fraternal countries" headed by one Politburo member, yet in mid-February Dubček, citing "domestic and foreign policy reasons," requested in no uncertain terms that the Soviet delegation be led in person by Brezhnev.[31] According to the ritual of "imitation," which was well established in the Soviet Bloc, it now became imperative for all other countries to be represented on the occasion by their party leaders as well. In Prague, Kádár had his most important conversation curiously enough not with Dubček, but with Novotný. The Hungarian leader was not only interested in Novotný's views on the developments in Czechoslovakia, but he also tried to persuade the deposed politician not to be swayed by injured pride and not to block reform. A positive outcome was dependent on a unified leadership, Kádár told Novotný, and advised him "to work for a solution of the problems alongside the comrades."[32]

In March, the news from Czechoslovakia that reached the countries of the Soviet camp became more and more perturbing. After the abolition of censorship, ever more radical views found their way into the media. Novotný's suggested removal from the post of president, for instance, did not even make it into the list of the particularly courageous "proposals." The Soviet leaders therefore concluded that a meeting must be called immediately to enable leaders of "fraternal countries" to offer Dubček and his comrades Communist assistance in the task of consolidating the situation.

The story of the meeting in Dresden on 23 March 1968 and Kádár's role as a mediator are sufficiently well known. What is less well known is the precise role Kádár played in the run-up to the meeting, which, generally speaking, was the result of agreements involving Brezhnev, Gomułka, and Kádár. During the Czechoslovak crisis, Brezhnev was in regular contact by telephone with the leaders of the five other countries of the "Six"; he was also regularly in touch with Kádár for purposes of sharing information and consultation. On average, he spoke to Kádár at least once a week, with occasional peaks of twice a day.

Wishing to provoke Kádár into speaking his mind, Brezhnev told him on 11 March that Gomułka and Todor Zhivkov, who were both deeply worried about the Czechoslovak developments, had suggested a meeting in Prague in that very week, if possible. Because Dubček himself had suggested at the March meeting of the Warsaw Pact Political Consultative Committee in Sofia that the members should meet more frequently at top level to discuss issues of economic cooperation, this meeting was to be advertised as one devoted to economic consultations, which meant that, in addition to the party heads and prime ministers, the leaders of the state planning boards would have to be invited as well.

Kádár's reaction to the proposal was far from enthusiastic, yet he did not think it prudent to reject it out of hand. He suggested holding the meeting in Uzhgorod rather than in Prague "so that things were less obvious." He also objected to painting the meeting as something different from what it was actually going to be: "Comrade Dubček must be told the truth whole and unabridged." He also suggested that participation in the meeting should be confined to the party heads of four countries, namely the Soviet Union, Czechoslovakia, Poland, and Hungary. Because Kádár knew the points of view of each of the respective leaders, he concluded that a smaller forum, excluding Bulgaria and the GDR, was going to provide more opportunity for offering the KSČ genuine constructive advice and assistance and at same time reduce the probability of it ending in outright condemnation of the Prague leadership's erroneous ways.[33]

On 12 March, Brezhnev took the "initiative" out of the hands of "mediators." He was now saying that dangerous tendencies were becoming apparent in Prague that were spreading to the military as well and that this made a meeting necessary. At first, Gomułka was in favor of inviting Novotný and suggested Moravska Ostrava as a possible venue for the meeting, yet after learning about Kádár's proposal, he, too, favored a reduction of the number of participants; he would even have agreed to limiting the invitation to the Soviet Union, Hungary, and Czechoslovakia.[34] On the next day, Brezhnev announced that he had spoken to Dubček on the phone and had mentioned the proposal of a meeting. Dubček had reacted positively, saying he would give his answer later. Brezhnev told Kádár that the Soviet leadership was examining a variety of moves, among others also inviting Dubček to Moscow, and signaled that "certain other measures would be taken as well," which he was not prepared to discuss on the phone, even if it was supposedly tap-proof. This meant, in other words, that preparations for a military solution were underway.[35] On 16 March, Brezhnev told Kádár that Dubček still welcomed the idea of a meeting, but had as yet been unable to commit himself to any details. He had, however, mentioned that he was going to speak to Kádár and perhaps even to travel to Hungary for discussions with him. Brezhnev noted that "it was obvious that Dubček was eagerly looking forward to meeting Comrade Kádár; the relationship is a very good one and marked by complete trust." Brezhnev was trying to curry favor with Kádár for a good reason: mutual trust would stand him in good stead in the realization of their common goal. He signaled approval of the idea; in a bilateral meeting, Kádár would be able to address their common worries and problems and prepare the ground for the four-party meeting.[36]

Dubček, however, changed his mind in the meantime, abandoned the idea of going to Hungary, and informed Brezhnev on 19 March that he was ready for a meeting. He named Dresden as a possible venue because he had never been to the GDR and considered Dresden neutral territory. In light of the GDR leadership's point of view,[37] Dubček's proposal does not really make sense in retrospect. What is even more curious is the fact that in the meantime Dubček had even adopted Brezhnev's idea of the smoke screen; he suggested making the meeting appear like an "economic forum," which would necessitate including the heads of the planning boards.[38] What he was probably hoping for from this solution was that it might make it easier for him to ward off both international and national criticism of the Czechoslovak leadership's decision to take part in a meeting whose main topic was bound to be an assessment of the situation in Czechoslovakia. In the literature on the Prague Spring, the myth, born in 1968 and still generally surviving, suggests that the Czechoslovak delegation was ensnared in Dresden only to realize the true nature of the meeting after its opening. Now it is obvious, however, that Dubček was aware of the situation from the outset and it was precisely him, who "forgot" to inform his colleagues. Thus the rest of the Czechoslovak delegation was sincerely shocked when they recognized the trap.

Brezhnev had, therefore, achieved his goal. All that remained to be done for him was to ensure that the Bulgarians were going to take part. To "soften up" Kádár, he told him that Gomułka had already agreed in principle.[39]

The same day also saw a session of the Politburo of the HSWP. Several members of that body viewed the meeting with considerable anxiety; they were worried that it might be construed as a clear case of interference in the internal affairs of Czechoslovakia and, therefore, inflict unnecessary political damage on the Prague leadership. The proposal was floated to hold the meeting in Budapest. Quite a few asked Kádár to advise the Czechoslovak leaders not to go to Dresden on account of the dangers lurking for them there.

Kádár had not anticipated such a critical attitude on the part of his Politburo. The thought that, in a situation where Brezhnev had finally succeeded in persuading Dubček to attend the meeting, it might fall to him to "abort" the plan quite obviously rattled him. Political maneuvering, manipulation, and the untiring search for compromise formulas were definitely Kádár's strong points yet it was unthinkable for him to thwart openly Brezhnev's intentions. He therefore told the Politburo in a long argumentation that there was simply no way the meeting could now not take place. He did not even shirk from using arguments the implausibility of which he himself was perfectly aware. For instance, he wound up his speech by saying that "it was possible for the meeting to have no other result than to convince us, the others, of the necessity to support wholeheartedly the concept of the Central Committee of the Czechoslovak Party." He then added in a more realistic vein, signaling his own doubts: "If this becomes apparent there, then that in itself would be no mean result."[40] Kádár telephoned Moscow on the same day to inform the Soviets about the positive result of the Politburo session, yet he added that this body "had reacted to the proposal with mixed emotions because they did not expect much good to come of it and they foresaw a negative echo both inside and outside Czechoslovakia."[41]

In Dresden, Kádár attempted to divide his efforts out of genuine conviction evenly between the two goals he had set himself: to assure the Czechoslovak leaders of his unqualified support and, at the same time, to point out to them emphatically the dangers inherent in the present situation. In his speech, he underlined the Hungarian leadership's solidarity with the KSČ; what was happening in Czechoslovakia had to be considered an internal affair of that country in which no one was entitled to interfere. He urged solving the present problems in a manner that would result in a strengthened Socialist system. He also pointed out that the leadership was not unified and that there could be no successful conclusion to the present troubles without unity. A second precondition for victory, according to Kádár, was a recognition of the necessity to wage consistently a two-front war to fight for the correction of mistakes that had been made in the construction of socialism prior to January 1968 and to fight antisocialist phenomena and tendencies. Kádár spoke at length on his view that Czechoslovakia had not yet—contrary to the assertions of Brezhnev and Gomułka—reached the stage of counterrevolution; there was, however, that danger because the present situation resembled in a number of ways the one that preceded the Hungarian "counterrevolution" of 1956. He expressed the hope that the outcome would be different in Czechoslovakia. The most effective argument that Kádár advanced was that the people who had brought about the Hungarian crisis had not been ardent counterrevolutionaries either. Rather, they had been a confused lot without firm convictions, who had rallied to the cry of putting the resolutions of the 20th Party Congress of the Communist Party of the Soviet Union (CPSU) into practice and had caused tremendous damage without intending to do so: they had opened the gates of the Socialist fortress to the class enemy. In case this was not yet powerful enough as a warning note, Kádár added for good measure: Imre Nagy had not been a conscious counterrevolutionary aiming for regime change; he was carried away by the events of 25 and 26 October and made common cause with the class enemy. Finally, Kádár said quite bluntly to the Czechoslovak delegates: "These events can turn any one of you into an Imre Nagy."[42] Because Kádár was the only representative of the five parties openly to support the Dubček leadership and to maintain that the solution of the Czechoslovaks' problems was exclusively their own concern, his speech was the most liberal at the meeting in Dresden. Conversely, it must be said that his remarks about Nagy were by far the bluntest reference to a worst-case scenario; everyone knew that Nagy had been executed.

The Hungarian leaders came to play an important role in drafting the final communiqué. The Soviets had originally proposed to itemize in detail the tasks and obligations of the Czechoslovak leaders in the communiqué. Because this would have constituted a blatant interference in the internal affairs of Czechoslovakia, it was unacceptable for the Hungarians.

During a break at the close of the meeting, Prime Minister Jenő Fock told the Czechoslovak delegation that a communiqué of this sort might have disastrous consequences for the Prague leaders and that they must on no account allow that to happen. Drahomir Kolder felt that mentioning all these points in the communiqué would be tantamount to a death sentence for all of them. Kádár, the master of compromise, insisted that at least mention must be made of the discussion of these points in the course of the negotiations "for if we don't mention that, the world will make fun of us for not having discussed the situation in Czechoslovakia at this juncture." Dubček signaled his agreement to the communiqué mentioning that the KSČ had informed the other parties about the situation in their country. Then Brezhnev entered and announced that a new text was being drafted in which Czechoslovakia was not mentioned. The Hungarians said they had just struck a compromise with the Czechoslovaks. Thus the final draft of the communiqué was written by a Soviet-Czechoslovak-Hungarian "ad hoc committee."[43]

FROM DRESDEN TO WARSAW: "IN CZECHOSLOVAKIA THE COUNTERREVOLUTION HAS NOT YET GAINED THE UPPER HAND"

The meeting in Dresden fell short of rea"ching its aims. Despite the "fraternal" parties' warnings, the Czechoslovak leadership failed to halt democratization and attempted to paint the whole process as a renewal of socialism. In a manner that was actually rather naïve, they continued to believe that this was not going to endanger the position of the Communist Party.

In view of the latest developments, Brezhnev summed up his assessment of the situation in a conversation with Kádár on 16 April: "We are about to lose Czechoslovakia." He hinted at the necessity for the fraternal parties to meet again in secret very soon to discuss the situation; this time without the KSČ. Kádár signaled his readiness to attend this meeting. However, as he sensed that the handling of the crisis was about to undergo a drastic qualitative change, he demurred that "he could not envisage discussing [the Czechoslovaks'] fate in their absence."[44]

In spite of Kádár's doubts, this undesirable situation materialized very soon, and at the Moscow meeting on 8 May the only option left to the Hungarian party leader was an attempt to convince his comrades that the present Czechoslovak leadership only needed sufficient support in order to get the situation back under control. However, the representatives of the other parties who had assembled in Moscow saw the situation as indisputably counterrevolutionary and the KSČ leaders as incapable of consolidating it. From this date onward, the idea was gaining ground that consolidation through political means was to be achieved by "healthy forces" seizing power internally. Kádár acknowledged in his statement that there was rampant anarchy in Czechoslovakia and that this fact was being exploited by antisocialist forces. The leadership was weak, divided, and unable to control state or society. There was, however, no doubt that it was engaged in a two-front struggle. This was to be welcomed, and there was no alternative in any case. He called the KSČ's Action Program a "big zero" because it could be interpreted at will either as a defense of socialism or as its abandonment. What it meant depended on what people wanted to read into it. So the situation was indeed dangerous, but counterrevolution had not yet gained the upper hand in the country.[45] Kádár therefore proposed that in assessing the situation simplistic schemata should "be replaced by societal analyses, by the analysis of necessities." To illustrate the point he was trying to make, he chose examples that cannot have been to the Soviets' or any of the others' liking, for he appeared to caricature the simplifications endemic to the Eastern Bloc: "For instance, if you call Mao Tse-tung and his clique insane, Castro a petty bourgeois, Ceauşescu a nationalist, the Czechoslovaks crazy, you have not actually done anything to deal with the underlying problems."[46] After that, he emphasized that "the struggle would ultimately be decided in Czechoslovakia, in the party, by the working class, by the people. This sets out clear boundaries for our actions: to do everything on the one hand to make a communist solution to this difficult situation possible and on the other to do nothing that might give comfort to our enemies."[47] He was certain that there would be those that advocated a military solution, so he closed with a plea for restraint, saying that he, too, was in favor of using military maneuvers as a means to exercise pressure on both the Czechoslovak leadership and on the people, yet "the problem cannot be solved by military means alone; the political issues are too complex for that." He used a curious example to illustrate that point: "One should bear in mind for instance that Soviet troops were stationed in Hungary in 1956 and that it was their deployment that served as a pretext for the counterrevolution."[48] He was trying to make the others, most notably Brezhnev, understand that there was an enormous difference between the stationing of Soviet troops and their deployment to restore order, and that the latter could easily backfire.

In this speech, Kádár did no less than rewrite history, at least for the benefit of those who were present, by fundamentally reinterpreting the causes of the "counterrevolution" that had officially been diagnosed in December 1956: the mistakes of the Rákosi-Gerő group, the treachery of the Nagy group, and the disruptive and destructive influence of internal and external reactionary forces. What he was actually saying amounted to a claim that the intervention of the Soviet troops, whose aim had been the restoration of order following the outbreak of the armed revolt on 23 October, had caused the escalation of the revolution and of the anti-Soviet freedom struggle. This assessment of the sequence of events is indeed borne out by the latest research.[49] Through this interpretation, Kádár was indirectly blaming the Soviet Union for the consequences of the revolution of 1956.

Kádár was soon given an opportunity to play again the role of mediator that he had assumed from the beginning: he was asked to influence Dubček. The visit of the Czechoslovak leaders that had originally been planned for March finally took place on 13 and 14 June, and a delegation consisting of party and government representatives left Prague for the Hungarian capital.[50] In order not to leave anything to chance, Brezhnev telephoned Kádár on the previous day and urged him to help Dubček understand "the dangers that are threatening the KSČ, socialism and himself." If they wanted to count on Soviet support, then the least they had to do was get the mass media under their control and detach and distance themselves from the revisionist group.[51] After the Moscow meeting of the "Five," this visit had something of a demonstrative character anyway, which was further enhanced by the renewal for another twenty years of the Treaty of Friendship, Cooperation, and Mutual Assistance between the ČSSR and the People's Republic of Hungary. In public, Kádár assured the Czechoslovak leadership of his support for their efforts to consolidate the situation. In private, however, he sounded a note of warning. The Hungarian experiences of 1956 showed that it was necessary to curb democratization and to draw an unmistakable line against deviations and hostile tendencies; otherwise, the party was bound to lose control. Dubček replied in a self-confident vein:

> If the antisocialist forces were to become so powerful as to endanger the socialist system, they [Dubček and the other leaders] would not hesitate to confront them and neither their hands nor their knees would be trembling as they did so. They were powerful enough to call those who were scheming against the socialist system to account, even if there was the threat of external interference.[52]

This determination began to sound increasingly hollow to Moscow, and the news from Prague was ever more worrisome. An article published by *Literární Noviny* on the tenth anniversary of the execution of Imre Nagy, which called him wrongfully executed and a martyr, caused indignation in Budapest as well as in Moscow. Kádár considered this as sniping that was taking aim at him personally and at his support for the Prague leadership. What he found particularly galling was the fact that the leadership of KSČ did not react unequivocally to this provocation. The "2,000 Words" manifesto, which was published on 27 June, was counterrevolutionary in the eyes of the Hungarian leadership, and they expected it to draw a number of resolute administrative responses. In a letter to Dubček of 5 July, Kádár outlined in detail his utter condemnation of the two documents. Whereas in his reply Dubček classified the article on Nagy as a provocation, he defended the KSČ's attitude concerning the "2,000 Words" by pointing out that the manifesto had produced no tangible result.[53] It is important to declare that contrary to previous interpretations, neither the Nagy article nor the "2,000 Words" manifesto was a turning point in the policy of the Hungarian leadership, since the HSWP's position remained to avoid a military solution at all costs, even in the middle of July.

Toward the end of June, Kádár traveled to Moscow at the head of a party delegation. Brezhnev painted a somber picture of the ČSSR: Dubček was gradually drifting to the right, the right was growing in strength, Czechoslovakia was getting ever closer to going down the road of Yugoslavia, and its further trajectory might even take it into the bourgeois camp.[54] Brezhnev announced that Moscow was planning two moves: first, a letter to the KSČ and, second, another meeting with those of its allies who had been present in Dresden. Kádár agreed in principle, but remembering the negative Czechoslovak echoes of the meeting of the "Five" in Moscow in May, he underlined the crucial importance of allowing Czechoslovakia to participate in the meeting. The Hungarian leadership itself differed at that time from the Soviet line on a number of issues, such as economic relations with the West in general and relations with the FRG in particular, so it seemed important to maintain the goodwill of the Soviet leadership. Kádár presumably felt that the time had come to make it quite clear that, while the Hungarian party favored a political solution for the Czechoslovak crisis in principle, it would support a military intervention as a measure of last resort if a political settlement could not be achieved and the continued existence of the Socialist order was in danger. This had been his point of view all along yet from what he had said so far, the Soviets could not be sure. This is why his "declaration of loyalty" was so important. Kádár did not want to irritate Moscow with aberrations of which he was not guilty. The minutes of the meeting of the Politburo of the CPSU of 3 July 1968 contain Brezhnev's take on the topic: "In expounding his thoughts on the Czechoslovak situation, Cde. Kádár said it was obvious that an occupation of Czechoslovakia was inevitable. 'If this should become necessary, we will vote in favour of this move.'"[55] In the version of the report prepared for the Politburo of the HSWP, this pledge is not mentioned. Nevertheless, we may follow Tibor Huszár in believing that Kádár actually made some similar statement, provided we assume that it was made in the dialectical form outlined above in which military intervention was seen as a measure of last resort.

Brezhnev distorted Kádár's statement to foreground the part that he himself played and to be able to present it as evidence of an important political victory he had gained by forcing a wavering ally back into line with the rest of the Soviet camp. This was certainly the interpretation that the members of the Politburo of the CPSU made of it.[56] It was by no means Brezhnev's first "distortion" of Kádár's point of view: in the meeting of the Central Committee of the CPSU on 17 July 1968, he claimed that in their assessment of the Czechoslovak situation at the Moscow meeting of the "Five" on 8 May there had been "unanimous agreement," even though Kádár had put forward a point of view there that differed sharply from that of the others.[57]

Kádár also came to play an important role in preparing the meeting of the "Warsaw Five" on 14 and 15 July in Warsaw. Brezhnev had informed the others on 9 July that the Presidium of the KSČ had on the previous day declined at short notice the invitation to another meeting of the six "Dresden" allies. Kádár was taken aback by the reaction of the KSČ, for during his visit to Budapest, Dubček had voiced his dissatisfaction with the fact that in May the "Five" had met for consultations in Moscow without the Czechoslovaks. This is why Kádár proposed a meeting between representatives of the KSČ and the CPSU within a day or two, which would be followed in seven to ten days' time by a meeting of the six allies. This would allow the leaders from Prague sufficient time to do their homework. If they were to decline this invitation as well, then the meeting would have to go ahead without them.[58] On the next day, Presidium member Oldřich Švestka, òne of the representatives of the "healthy forces" told János Gosztonyi, editor-in-chief of the HSWP's daily who had been sent by Kádár on a secret mission to Prague to gather firsthand information, that the Presidium of the KSČ had come out unanimously against the proposal. Kádár therefore, echoing Švestka, told Brezhnev that the Warsaw meeting was making the situation of the left more difficult by shifting the center to the right.[59] Vasil Bil'ak, another representative of the "healthy forces," had been in Budapest a few days before; in his talks with Kádár and György Aczél, he had repeatedly stressed that Czechoslovakia was capable of solving its problems on its own and needed no help from outside.[60] Kádár therefore suggested to Brezhnev wording the letter to the KSČ in a tone that would make the Czechoslovaks' participation possible. He added for tactical reasons that the topic of the talks had better not be the situation in Czechoslovakia; each party was to be asked to report on its own situation.[61]

In this difficult situation, Dubček asked Kádár urgently to meet him in secret. The meeting took place on 13 July on Hungarian soil, in Komárom. Yet the hopes of Dubček and his companion Černík were disappointed. Instead of offering assurances of continued support, Kádár and Fock severely criticized them for declining to take part in the Warsaw meeting. Kádár told them not only that this had been their worst mistake since January, but that they had also reached a point of no return, which meant "that we have parted ways and will be fighting on opposing sides."[62]

When Kádár set out for the meeting in Warsaw on 14 and 15 July he did so equipped with a resolution of the HSWP Politburo that continued to call for a political settlement for Czechoslovakia and that was designed to keep the leaders of the "fraternal parties" from opting for a "military solution."

In Warsaw, Kádár stuck to his brief in his first speech. He reported on the meeting in Komárom and underlined the danger inherent in the country's situation, which had, however, not yet reached the stage of counterrevolution. In the debate, Ulbricht and Zhivkov allowed themselves to be carried away in the moment for which there had been no parallel up to then: they not only resolutely and openly condemned Kádár's point of view, but added (the former overtly, the latter indirectly) that it might well be the case for Hungary's internal problems to be next in line for a solution at a comparable meeting of the "fraternal parties."[63] This was evidence for the emergence of a dangerous tendency that entitled "fraternal parties" to act as joint trouble shooters not only in crucial crises, but also in the context of developments or reforms that did not endanger socialism as such but were considered undesirable by the others. There was no doubt that Hungary was a case in point at that time.[64] Kádár therefore thought it advisable to repeat in front of the present company the "declaration of loyalty" he had issued two weeks before in Moscow in order to calm everyone down. He unexpectedly rose to his feet a second time and announced: "We unreservedly agree with the explanations and conclusions of our Soviet comrades and are prepared to take part in any joint action."[65] Although this was a serious violation of the HSWP's resolution, taking this step was arguably facilitated for Kádár by Brezhnev's making it clear in his speech that despite pressure from the others no final decision would be reached at the meeting itself. Kádár was, therefore, still free, even though he had "publicly" committed himself to agreeing in principle to an ultimate military solution, to work toward a political settlement in the background. Yet the chances for such a settlement were dwindling.

FROM WARSAW TO MOSCOW: KÁDÁR'S LAST EFFORTS FOR A POLITICAL SETTLEMENT

After the Warsaw meeting, Kádár concentrated on persuading Brezhnev to make one more effort, to stage one more Soviet-Czechoslovak meeting in order to make it quite clear to Dubček and his comrades that in case they continued to do nothing to stop a development that bore all the hallmarks of total disintegration, there would have to be outside intervention to save the Socialist system. Kádár had the impression that he had succeeded in frightening Dubček and Černík in Komárom; at the end of the meeting, when they realized the danger they faced, both men burst out crying.[66] He hoped that a last warning to the leadership by the Soviets would prove effective and trigger at long last the administrative measures required for a consolidation of the Communist system. The Soviet-Czechoslovak meeting in Čierna nad Tisou at the end of July was mainly the result of Kádár's tireless efforts at mediation. At the ensuing meeting in Bratislava, Kádár confronted Dubček quite openly with the alternatives the KSČ had to choose between: either they themselves used force to stop certain tendencies or force would be applied from outside. He illustrated this with his own example and underlined that in 1956 it had been necessary to use deeply unpopular measures to save the Communist system in a context that was much more difficult; yet he had done what had to be done.[67]

At Brezhnev's invitation, Kádár went to Yalta on 15 August. During the ensuing negotiations, everyone knew that a decision in favor of a military solution was in the offing. Kádár now concentrated on the time after the intervention. The situation being as it was, he consented to the military solution, yet he emphasized that, in the long-term, only a political settlement can ensure success. The struggle for the correction of the mistakes made before January 1968 had to be continued, and the KSČ must not relinquish its two-front struggle. Kádár felt that the difficult situation the Soviets were in might provide him with an opportunity to criticize the policy of the CPSU in a constructive manner. He said the Soviet leadership had been impatient in its dealings with the Czechoslovak party and that this impatience had been a key factor in the escalation of the crisis; a more patient approach might have rendered military intervention unnecessary. In this context, he formulated a question that rose far above the present context: "When the CPSU is perceived as rigid by the world, by the global communist movement, who is going to play the role of the standard bearer in the global communist movement?"[68] He praised Soviet policy after 1956 and said the Soviet leadership had then shown trust in the Hungarian and Polish party leaders and had allowed them to seek new solutions. This had brought a handsome dividend, for they were able to consolidate the situation in their countries.[69] With these lessons from history Kádár was pursuing two goals. He was first of all trying to make sure that postinvasion Czechoslovakia would be allowed to reestablish order with minimum interference from the Soviets; second, he was trying to broaden with these arguments the maneuvering space in terms of domestic policies in the states of the Soviet Bloc.

In Yalta, Brezhnev entrusted a last mediation mission to Kádár, saying that the Hungarian party was the only one in addition to the CPSU to which Dubček might be prepared to listen. The meeting took place in Komárno on 17 August. It made one thing abundantly clear: the Czechoslovak leaders seemed completely unaware that they were sitting in a train that was heading for the abyss. Even if they suspected their predicament, they preferred resignedly to wait for the catastrophe; none of them had the courage to pull the emergency brake. It is little wonder that Kádár, who was notorious for his pragmatism, described the meeting as "embarrassing, ill tempered, sterile, pointless."[70]

After the invasion on 21 August, an unexpected opportunity arose for Kádár to influence the course of events positively. On the first day of the crisis management negotiations of the "Five," which took place parallel to the Soviet's talks with the captive Czechoslovak "delegation" between 24 and 26 August in Moscow, he was a fervent advocate of the need to find a compromise with the legitimate Czechoslovak leadership. In order to give emphasis to this Hungarian point of view, he first submitted it to the Soviets in writing.

Ulbricht and Zhivkov clearly advocated a dictatorial solution, the formation of a revolutionary government of workers and peasants in keeping with the Hungarian model of 1956. Gomułka, who was apparently completely out of his depth, went as far as to claim that the situation in Czechoslovakia was much worse than the one in Hungary at the time of the "counterrevolution."[71] In view of the fact that there were a number of influential supporters of a radical solution among the Soviet leaders themselves, Kádár, with his plea for Dubček and his comrades, came down clearly on the side of the realistic solution also favored by Brezhnev and Aleksei Kosygin. He thereby contributed in the end to a political compromise being hammered out that involved the legitimate Czechoslovak leaders and culminated in the signing of the Moscow Protocol.

NOTES

Translated from German to English by Otmar Binder, Vienna.

1. For an overview of the history of the Prague Spring, see H. Gordon Skilling, *Czechoslovakia's Interrupted Revolution* (Princeton, NJ: Princeton University Press, 1976); Karen Dawisha, *The Kremlin and the Prague Spring* (Berkeley: University of California Press, 1984); Jaromír Navrátil et al., eds., *The Prague Spring 1968* (Budapest: Central European University Press, 1998); Kieran Williams, *The Prague Spring and Its Aftermath: Czechoslovak Politics, 1968–1970* (Cambridge: Oxford University Press, 1997). On Hungary's economic reform in 1968, see Ivan T. Berend, *The Hungarian Economic Reforms, 1953–1988* (Cambridge: Oxford University Press, 1990).

2. Magyar Országos Levéltár [Hungarian National Archives] (hereafter cited as MOL) M-KS-288, F. 4/92, minutes of the meeting of the HSWP CC, 19–20 June 1968.

3. While in the Soviet Bloc, there had been two other serious crisis situations as well, the local leaders did not have to play a similar role in those cases. In June 1953 while crushing the Berlin uprising, the Soviet military commander directed operations, and Ulbricht and his comrades returned from hiding only after order

was restored. In October 1956 during the Polish crisis, Gomułka did not have to save the Communist system, but avoid a Soviet military intervention which he did and consequently emerged from the crisis as a most popular leader.

4. For the role of the Hungarian army in the invasion of Czechoslovakia, see Iván Pataky, *A vonakodó szövetséges: A Magyar Népköztársaság és a Magyar Néphadsereg közreműködése Csehszlovákia 1968. évi megszállásában* [*The Wavering Ally: The Participation of the Hungarian People's Republic and the Hungarian People's Army in the Occupation of Czechoslovakia in 1968*] (Budapest: Zrínyi Kiadó, 1996).

5. MOL, M-KS-288, F. 5/467, minutes of the meeting of the HSWP CC, 20 August 1968.

6. For details on the Hungarian Revolution in 1956, see Csaba Békés, et al., eds., *The 1956 Hungarian Revolution: A History in Documents* (Budapest: Central European University Press, 2002).

7. For a comparative analysis of the two crises, see Csaba Békés, *Európából Európába: Magyarország konfliktusok kereszttüzében 1945–1990* [*From Europe to Europe: Hungary in the Crossfire of Conflicts, 1945–1990*] (Budapest: Gondolat, 2004), 223–36.

8. For details of the Hungarian party's policy at the time of regime change, see Melinda Kalmár, "From 'Model Change' to Regime Change: The Metamorphosis of the MSZMP's Tactics in the Democratic Transition," in *The Roundtable Talks of 1989: The Genesis of Hungarian Democracy*, ed. András Bozóki (Budapest: Central European University Press, 2002).

9. Csaba Békés, *The 1956 Hungarian Revolution and World Politics*, Cold War International History Project, Woodrow Wilson International Center for Scholars, Washington, DC, September 1996, Working Paper No. 16, http://cwihp.si.edu.

10. For details see the chapter of Harald Knoll and Peter Ruggenthaler, "The Moscow 'Negotiations,'" in this volume.

11. See Békés, *Európából Európába*, 233.

12. For details on Hungary's policy with reference to the Czechoslovak crisis, see Tibor Huszár, *1968, Prága, Budapest, Moszkva: Kádár János és a csehszlovákiai intervenció* [*1968, Prague, Budapest, Moscow: János Kádár and the Intervention of Czechoslovakia*] (Budapest: Szabad Tér, 1998).

13. MOL, M-KS-288, F. 5/444, minutes of the meeting of the HSWP Politburo 23 January 1968.

14. MOL, M-KS-288, F. 47/743, memorandum of conversation between Kádár and Dubček, 22 January 1968.

15. Navrátil et al., *Prague Spring 1968*, 22.

16. MOL, M-KS-288, F. 47/743, memorandum of conversation between Kádár and Novotny, 26 February 1968.

17. MOL, M-KS-288, F. 5/444 (cf. note 13 above); Huszár, *1968, Prága, Budapest, Moszkva*, 15.

18. MOL, M-KS-288, F. 47/743 (cf. note 14 above).

19. MOL, M-KS-288, F. 5/444 (cf. note 13).

20. MOL, M-KS-288, F. 47/743 (cf. note 14).

21. For details, see the article by Manfred Wilke, "Ulbricht, East Germany, and the Prague Spring," in this volume and Paweł Piotrowski, "Polen und die Intervention," in Karner et al., *Beiträge*, 447–60.

22. The meeting was later moved forward to 8 February and finally took place on 7 February.

23. MOL, M-KS-288, F. 47/743 (cf. note 14).

24. MOL, M-KS-288, F. 47/743, memorandum on Dubček's message to Kádár, 29 January 1968.

25. After the end of the negotiations, Dubček and his comrades paid a half-hour visit to Komárom on the Hungarian side of the border at Kádár's request. Komárom was originally one town, located on both sides of the Danube that was cut in two by the Trianon Peace Treaty of 1920.

26. MOL, M-KS-288, F. 47/743, memorandum of conversation between Kádár and Dubček in Komárno, 5 February 1968.

27. MOL, M-KS-288, F. 5/445, minutes of the session of the HSWP Politburo, 6 February 1968.

28. MOL, M-KS-288, F. 5/445, minutes of the session of the HSWP Politburo, 6 February 1968.

29. For details on the Soviet Bloc's FRG policy, see Csaba Békés, "The Warsaw Pact and the Helsinki Process, 1965–1970," in *The Making of Détente: Eastern and Western Europe in the Cold War, 1965–1975*, ed. Wilfried Loth and Georges-Henri Soutou (London: Routledge, 2008), 201–20 and Douglas Selvage, "The Warsaw Pact and the German Question, 1955–1970," in *NATO and the Warsaw Pact: Intrabloc Conflicts*, ed. Mary Ann Heiss and S. Victor Papacosma (Kent, OH: Kent State University Press, 2008).

30. MOL, M-KS-288, F. 5/445 (cf. note 27).

31. MOL, M-KS-288, F. 47/743, memorandum of a telephone conversation between Kádár and Brezhnev, 13 February 1968.

32. MOL, M-KS-288, F. 47/743, memorandum of conversation between Kádár Novotný, 26 February 1968.

33. MOL, M-KS-288, F. 47/743, telephone conversation between Kádár and Brezhnev.

34. MOL, M-KS-288, F. 47/743, telephone conversation between Kádár and Brezhnev.

35. MOL, M-KS-288, F. 47/743, telephone conversation between Kádár and Brezhnev.

36. MOL, M-KS-288, F. 47/743, telephone conversation between Kádár and Brezhnev.

37. For details on this, see Wilke, "Ulbricht, East Germany, and the Prague Spring," in this volume.

38. MOL, M-KS-288, F. 47/743, memorandum of a telephone conversation between Kádár and Brezhnev, 19 March 1968.

39. MOL, M-KS-288, F. 47/743, telephone conversation between Kádár and Brezhnev.

40. MOL, M-KS-288, F. 5/451, minutes of the session of the HSWP Politburo, 19 March 1968.

41. MOL, M-KS-288, F. 47/743, memorandum of a telephone conversation between Kádár and Brezhnev, 19/2 March 1968.

42. SAPMO BA, ZPA, IV 2/201/778, minutes of the Dresden meeting, 23 March 1968, reprinted in Karner et al., *Dokumente*, #21.

43. MOL, M-KS-288, F. 5/452, minutes of the session of the HSWP Politburo, 2 April 1968.

44. MOL, M-KS-288, F. 47/743, memorandum of a telephone conversation between Kádár and Brezhnev, 16 April 1968.

45. Navrátil, *The Prague Spring 1968*, 138.

46. For Kádár's entire speech at the meeting of the CPSU leadership with the leaders of the Communist parties of Bulgaria, Hungary, the GDR, and Poland on 8 May in Moscow, see AdBIK, holding "Prague Spring," minutes of the meeting of the leaders of the CPSU CC with the leaders of the Communist parties of Bulgaria, Hungary, the GDR, and Poland, 8 May 1968, reprinted in Karner et al., *Dokumente*, #77. The quotation as cited above is a translation from the report compiled by Károly Erdélyi, MOL, M-KS-288, F. 5/455, cited in Huszár, *1968, Prága, Budapest, Moszkva*, 86.

47. Navrátil et al., *Prague Spring*, 139.

48. AdBIK, Holdings "Prague Spring," minutes of the meeting between the leaders of the CPSU CC with the leaders of the Communist parties of Bulgaria, Hungary, the GDR, and Poland, 8 May 1968 (cf. note 46). The quotation as cited above is a translation from the report compiled by Károly Erdélyi, MOL, M-KS-288, F. 5/455, cited in Huszár, *1968, Prága, Budapest, Moszkva*, 88. According to the Russian document, Kádár confined himself to saying how good it had been that there were Soviet troops in Hungary in 1956 because they were at hand to save Hungary, and he mentioned the problem of an intervention from outside only in the context of Czechoslovakia. However, there is good reason to believe that the statement cited here, which is found only in the Hungarian version of the report, expresses Kádár's concerns about the deployment of foreign troops in a more precise and more complex manner.

49. See Csaba Békés, *Az 1956-os magyar forradalom a világpolitikában* [*The 1956 Hungarian Revolution and World Politics*] (Budapest: 1956-os Intézet, 2006), 85–86.

50. The Czechoslovak delegation consisted of Alexander Dubček, Oldřich Černík, Vasil Biľak, and Jiří Hájek.

51. MOL, M-KS-288, F. 47/743, memorandum of a telephone conversation between Kádár and Brezhnev, 12 June 1968.

52. Huszár, 1968, *Prága, Budapest, Moszkva*, 117.

53. Huszár, 1968, *Prága, Budapest, Moszkva*, 138.

54. Huszár, 1968, *Prága, Budapest, Moszkva*, 135.

55. Huszár, 1968, *Prága, Budapest, Moszkva*, 145.

56. Huszár, 1968, *Prága, Budapest, Moszkva*, 145.

57. Navrátil, *Prague Spring*, 251.

58. MOL, M-KS-288, F. 47/743, memorandum of a telephone conversation between Kádár and Brezhnev, 9 July 1968.

59. MOL, M-KS-288, F. 47/743, Kádár's letter to Brezhnev, 10 July 1968; MOL, M-KS-288, F. 47/743, János Gosztonyi's minutes of a conversation with Oldřich Švestka in Prague, 11 July 1968.

60. MOL, M-KS-288, F. 47/743, minutes of the conversation between György Aczél and Vasil Biľak in Budapest, 6 July 1968; MOL, M-KS-288, F. 47/743, minutes of the conversation between Biľak and Shelest, 20 July 1968. Biľak was in Hungary

again on 20 July at Brezhnev's behest to organize a secret meeting with Petro Shelest, a member of the Politburo of the CPSU.

61. MOL, M-KS-288, F. 47/743 (cf. note 58).

62. MOL, M-KS-288, F. 4/93, minutes of the meeting of the HSWP CC, 7 August 1968; Huszár, *1968, Prága, Budapest, Moszkva*, 163.

63. Navrátil et al., *Prague Spring*, 218, 220–21. Kádár's entire speech is reprinted in Karner et al., *Dokumente*, #77.

64. This threat could in no way be regarded as a merely theoretical possibility as indeed, there had been such a precedent not so long ago. Following the failed Hungarian Revolution in 1956, at the Communist summit on 1–4 January 1957 in Budapest, the Soviet, Czechoslovak, Bulgarian, and Romanian leaders forced the Hungarian party to make serious concessions concerning the political development of the country, including vetoing the introduction of a limited pseudo-multiparty system akin to the Czechoslovak model. The same forum also decided on the initiation of a court procedure against members of the Imre Nagy group. Békés et al., *The 1956 Hungarian Revolution*, 485–95.

65. Navrátil et al., *Prague Spring*, 229.

66. Navrátil et al., *Prague Spring*, 216; MOL, M-KS-288, F. 5/462, minutes of the meeting of the HSWP Politburo, 15 July 1968.

67. Huszár, *1968, Prága, Budapest, Moszkva*, 228.

68. MOL, M-KS-288, F. 5/467, minutes of the meeting of the HSWP Politburo, 20 August 1968.

69. MOL, M-KS-288, F. 5/467, minutes of the meeting of the HSWP Politburo.

70. MOL, M-KS-288, F. 5/467, minutes of the meeting of the HSWP Politburo.

71. For details of the negotiations of the "Warsaw Five" between 24 and 26 August 1968, see Navrátil et al., *Prague Spring*, 474–76; MOL, M-KS-288, F. 4/95, minutes of the meeting on 27 August 1968; Huszár, *1968, Prága, Budapest, Moszkva*, 272–74.

17

Tito, the Bloc-Free Movement, and the Prague Spring

Tvrtko Jakovina

CHANGES IN 1960

In the U.S. National Intelligence Estimate on Tito's Yugoslavia written in April 1967, all U.S. intelligence organizations concluded that Yugoslavia "is a Communist state in name and theory, but in practice it is a fully independent country which has rejected most of the 'Socialist' experience of other states, including the USSR and which is deliberately removing its economy from centralized controls and freeing its people from arbitrary authority."[1] In the foreign psolicy domain, the Yugoslav goal was to retain independence at any cost. The Socialist Federal Republic of Yugoslavia (*Socijalistička Federativna Republika Jugoslavija* or SFRY) was a "model of nonaligned socialist enterprise" achieving goals by "shrewd compromise" and "clever improvisation." Although still a defender of the Communist creed, Josip Broz Tito, the undisputed leader of Yugoslavia since 1945, became a model for national-istic Communists who seemed to be appearing in different quarters of the world. The Yugoslav economy was socialist, to be sure. However, in 1965 re-forms and decentralization, the lessening of central control in the decision-making process, was taking Yugoslavia toward "market socialism." The Soviet Union was Yugoslavia's largest single trade partner, but the country stayed free from dependence on the *Lager*. The SFRY's foreign trade share with Western and nonaligned countries was 68 percent.[2] Nevertheless, the U.S. estimate was probably too rosy. Yugoslavia was full of problems. Ups and downs are a constant feature of any country's development, but Tito had "[o]ver the years . . . responded to this debate with revisions and reforms designed to satisfy at least some of the people some of the time."[3] Yugo-slavia, with its many disparate elements and ethnic groups was interesting and dynamic, but far from the best example to emulate. However, Yugoslav achievements in some fields were very attractive. Some in the Third World and those in the Socialist world who were eager to become more independent, could, nevertheless, find Belgrade leadership inspirational. If such was the impression of the brightest experts in the U.S. intelligence community, why deny that there was a certain appeal for the Socialist leaders squeezed by the Soviets? Ever since the break with Joseph Stalin in 1948, Yugoslavia had been closely observed by the *Lager* countries. Some were envious, some scared by the heretical socialism supported by the West, but a few Socialist leaders concentrated on the autonomy the Yugoslavs were enjoying. Yet deep-seated political and economic problems did not evaporate after the split with the Soviets, despite positive U.S. estimates to the contrary.[4]

Both Yugoslavia and Czechoslovakia were founded after World War I and had enjoyed friendly relations ever since. For a few months during 1912, Tito had worked in Čenkov, a town in the central part of Bohemia. His visit to Prague in 1965 was historic for many reasons. It had been almost two decades since Tito's previous visit to Czechoslovakia. Comrade Antonín Novotný was Tito's host in Prague, Alexander Dubček in Bratislava.[5] In Čenkov, Tito gave a speech in which he praised the Socialist system and his comrade, also a former metal worker, Novotný, "You are happy today just like our people, our working man, are happy. Since they are themselves governing factories, land, and everything they need."[6] Before World War II, Czechoslovakia was much more sophisticated and developed than Yugoslavia. But now Belgrade was constantly experimenting, trying to overcome economic weaknesses, national antagonisms, and political factionalisms, developing quickly and successfully.[7] Czechoslovakia and Yugoslavia were both complex countries, and similarities between them abounded. In 1966, Slovak linguists in Smolenice had a conference on "Theses Concerning Slovak" that stressed the representational function of the language. In March 1967, the Declaration on the Name and Position of the Croatian Literary Language was signed in Zagreb by many intellectuals, including members of the Communist Party and some members of the Central Committee.[8] Intellectuals in Czechoslovakia were becoming more and more vocal in criticizing the Communist Party of Czechoslovakia's (*Komunistická strana Československa* or KSČ) leader Antonín Novotný. The Yugoslav reforms that began in the mid 1960s gained momentum, especially after the deposition of Alexander Ranković, the strongest Serbian politician in the postwar Yugoslavia. Head of the secret police and minister of the interior and, after Tito, the strongest politician in the party hierarchy, Ranković was deposed as a symbol of the conservative, unitarist forces. Sometimes those forces were using him, sometimes hiding behind him. Although he was not aligned against Tito personally, Ranković became the main obstacle to modernization and reforms. Since his power base was primarily Serbian, he by default antagonized other nationalities.[9] After 1966 and his replacement, constraints in Yugoslavia were lessened and liberal changes speeded up in different parts of the SFRY. For example in Mostar, the capital of Herzegovina, an advisory party meeting was held at which secret police measures taken against the population were condemned and the belief that Herzegovians ought to be much more included in the party and state positions in Bosnia and Herzegovina advanced.[10] Reform of the economy, issues between different nationalities, and international position (that is, independence) were the most obvious topics connecting Yugoslavia and Czechoslovakia.[11]

At the plenary session of the Central Committee (CC) of the KSČ in late 1967, Alexander Dubček asked for the democratization of inter-party relations. He also called for a new party program.[12] In January 1968, Novotný was replaced as the first secretary of the KSČ by "our Sasha," as an initially happy KGB was calling Dubček.[13] Things started to change rapidly. During Tito's week-long visit to Czechoslovakia in 1965, politicians who had accompanied the Yugoslav leader during his brief visit to Bratislava reported how his host, Sasha Dubček, was radiating pleasure. Judging from future developments, he had sincerely admired Tito and was not just being polite. For Moscow, even the remote possibility of being inspired by the Yugoslavs was scary.

After the loss of Albania in 1961 and Romania's policy that was increasingly independent of Moscow, the Soviets were getting nervous.[14] Since the early 1960s, the Chinese had been trying to foment discord within the *Lager*. Although Beijing's efforts in Europe as well as in the Third World were unsuccessful, problems facing the Soviets did not evaporate.[15] With the increasingly disturbing developments in Czechoslovakia—groups who were asking for the revival of the multiparty system and voices who were talking of the Little Entente, a prewar grouping of Czechoslovakia, Romania, and Yugoslavia—danger for Moscow in the ideological and geopolitical realm was still acute.[16] All three Eastern European countries were Socialist. Two were members of the Warsaw Pact, but only Prague was vital in the military considerations for the Soviet Union. Yugoslavia was nonaligned and outside Moscow's orbit. Taking into account the positive impressions Americans had of Yugoslavia, the liberalization in Czechoslovakia, and the independent attitude of Romania, one could expect Washington to be interested in the further liberalization of those countries. As it turned out, because improved relations between Moscow and Washington occurred at a time when the USSR was becoming its approximate equal and the United States was in crisis, the existence of a peaceful environment in the buffer countries between the West and the East turned out to be much more important to the United States than supporting liberalization in Eastern Europe.[17]

YUGOSLAVIA AND CZECHOSLOVAKIA
(JANUARY TO AUGUST 1968)

For the Yugoslavs, the 5 January change in Prague was something they had been anticipating since the Hungarian Revolution of 1956. János Kádár, the Hungarian Communist Party boss, stressed at the session of the CC in June 1968 how Belgrade, although not revisionist and not for the counterrevolution in Prague, was supporting developments there in the same way as in Hungary a decade ago. Tito's final goal, Kádár concluded, was to see these developments fully approach a "Yugoslav type of socialism."[18] During the mid-1960s, reforms and decentralization of the economy were undertaken in several eastern countries, including the notoriously Soviet-subservient Bulgaria.[19] Hungary was cautious enough to avoid using "Yugoslav terminology," but in a report written by Kiro Gligorov, the vice president of the Yugoslav government after his April visit, Hungarian hosts were stressing "similarities of their reform, with ours and Czechoslovakia's."[20] Although Dubček and his allies immediately stressed how no changes in foreign policy were to be expected, many politicians in the *Lager* were unhappy with the developments in Prague, including Leonid Brezhnev and Mikhail Suslov, as were others in Berlin, Warsaw, and Bulgaria.[21] Reforms in and of themselves were, of course, not problematic, but those with the hint of Yugoslav revisionism, especially if conducted by the Soviet-dominated Socialist country, were.

If the Yugoslav example was inspirational for Dubček, it was observed from far and not followed closely. Bilateral cooperation between the Yugoslav League of Communists and the KSČ in the first half of 1968 was nonexistent. Although agreed upon in early February 1968 and despite Czechoslovakia stressing how an exchange of experience was essential, until mid-July none of the agreed upon visits were realized, and all were postponed until the second half of the year.[22] On the state level, however, the Yugoslavs were asked to advise their Czechoslovak colleagues on different foreign policy and European issues. Marko Nikezić, state secretary for foreign affairs, was invited to visit Prague in mid-May.[23] Shortly after him, Kiro Gligorov and Marin Cetinić, representatives of the Federal Executive Committee, also paid a visit to Prague. Gratitude for the Yugoslav support was always stressed, but both teams could report only on the numerous possibilities for undertaking cooperation in many fields.[24] Still, cooperation remained cautious, more friendly than deep. Probably the Czechs and the Slovaks were unwilling to show any connection with the Yugoslavs, in order to avoid provoking the Soviets.

Tito, however, did a lot. Issued an invitation to visit Moscow while in Japan and Mongolia in April 1968, Tito had agreed to pay a short visit to the Kremlin where he met Leonid Brezhnev, Aleksei Kosygin, Nikolai

Podgornyi, and Andrei Gromyko at the very end of April 1968.[25] Brezhnev harshly criticized the situation in Prague. Antisocialist elements, foreign influences, restoration of capitalism, and a revival of the bourgeoisie were all at work in Czechoslovakia, the Soviet leader stated.[26] Tito's opinion was totally the opposite: their Czechoslovak comrades were capable of controlling the situation. The only thing they needed was brotherly help. Probably some unfriendly elements existed in Prague, but the Communists in charge were not counterrevolutionaries.[27] Tito even recalled his own experiences from Čenkov in 1912. In his opinion, it was unlikely to see the counterrevolutionary forces overwhelming the working class who possessed as glorious a tradition as the Czechoslovaks had. Brezhnev was annoyed by Tito's comments. He cut the Yugoslav leader short, saying how in his country developments similar to those in Czechoslovakia existed:[28]

> In Socialist countries there are questions that are general and common. If our destiny is connected in a joint effort of building socialism, it is natural to be interested in your developments and vice versa. . . . We are worried whether you will be able to fulfill your own goals. As you see, we are asking all these questions and someone might see this as an interference [in your interior affairs]. But we are sincere and doing this with pain in our soul.

Tito's reaction to the words that later became known as the Brezhnev Doctrine was harsh. The Soviet leader was, as always, negotiating with a stick and carrot in his hands. Brezhnev asked Tito to talk with Dubček in order to influence him not to be overtaken by liberalism. A few weeks later in the spring of 1968, the secretary general of Tito's office, Vladimir Popović, had directed all employees to observe the situation in Czechoslovakia with particular care. A special meeting for the Yugoslav ambassadors in Eastern Europe was organized by the Federal Secretariat for Foreign Relations on 24 June. Dubček was described as progressive, striving toward greater democracy within the Bloc.[29] The Yugoslavs were to support Dubček unconditionally. In the light of the recently begun maneuvers of the Warsaw Pact countries (without Romania) in Czechoslovakia (22–30 June), the Yugoslavs' decision to support Dubček was significant.[30]

The Yugoslav ambassador in Czechoslovakia during 1968 was Trpe Jakovlevski. For being one of many middle-ranked party and state officials with no previous diplomatic experience posted in one of the East European capitals, he did his job rather well.[31] On 10 July 1968, Minister F. Vlasak informed the Yugoslav ambassador how the Soviet troops had entered the Czechoslovak territory and refused to withdraw.[32] Only one day later, on 11 July 1968, Slavik, a member of the Secretariat of the CC KSČ, had informed the Yugoslavs of the conversation between Dubček and Brezhnev. Dubček declined the invitation to participate in the multilateral meeting of the Communist parties in Warsaw, ignoring letters from Sofia, Berlin,

Budapest, Warsaw, and Moscow (3 July) advising him to attend.[33] On 12 July 1968, Czechoslovak minister of foreign affairs Jiří Hajek informed Jakovlevski that bilateral meetings in Czechoslovakia should include both the Yugoslavs and the Romanians. Therefore, he was, without previous consultations, asking whether Tito would be ready to pay a visit to Dubček although it was not his turn to come on a state visit.[34] Jakovlevski's answer was positive. After expressing his gratitude, Hajek tried to explain why bilateral relations between the two countries had to have such a low profile. Since the Soviet Union was interpreting developments in Czechoslovakia as being inspired by Yugoslavia, as stated by Andrei Gromyko, with the goal of forming one of the new models of socialism and nonalignment, Prague was very cautious not to behave in a way that supported such an opinion. Nevertheless, it must be clear to Belgrade, Hajek said, that nonalignment had never been an option for Prague.[35] Hajek did not fear direct military intervention from the USSR because the Soviets had no forces in Czechoslovakia on which they could rely. The importance of Tito's help was stressed several times.[36] On 14 July 1968, secretary of the president of the Czechoslovak Assembly J. Smrkovský asked Yugoslav ambassador Jakovlevski for Tito to send his letter to the "Five" in Warsaw.[37] After the meeting in Poland on 14 July was over, a joint message was sent to the Czechoslovaks.[38] For János Kádár, the Hungarian leader, that was the point when he, allegedly, gave up. Dubček, in his opinion, took the same road as Imre Nagy in 1956.[39] The two leaders met in Komarno on 13 July. Only one day later, Tito received a message from Jakovlevski based on his conversation with Smrkovski about how Kádár was ready to oppose an already planned intervention. He did not know by then or was deliberately avoiding information that Dubček was almost crying while watching his Hungarian ally change sides.[40]

The letter from Poland published on 17 July 1968 represented the culmination of foreign pressure on Prague. It was addressed to the Central Committee, not the presidency of the KSČ, obviously hoping to cause a rift between them. The "progressive" part of the Czechoslovak leadership was determined to continue with the reforms, but became more vigorous in "visibly decreasing extremist views, liberal and anti-socialist elements," the Yugoslav ambassador reported to Belgrade.[41] Czechoslovaks were asking comrade Tito to influence Nicolae Ceauşescu of Romania and Italian Communist leader Luigi Longo to do the same.[42]

As agreed, Dubček had mailed Tito on 15 July 1968 to set up a personal meeting in the shortest time possible.[43] In the meantime, an answer to the letter received from Moscow was being written in Belgrade. On 19 July 1968 it was published in Yugoslav newspapers, repeating the well-known Yugoslav position. The working classes in Czechoslovakia were being led in the right direction. Each party was responsible for its own politics, and it was the international duty of other parties to support their efforts. Everything else, especially interference in the internal business of independent countries, would be damaging for the overall cause of world communism, went the Yugoslav letter. References to the Belgrade and Moscow Declarations from the mid-1950s were stressed. Even more bluntly, in an interview given to *Al Ahram*, Tito had expressed his hope that no one in the Soviet Politburo was so short-sighted as to use force in Czechoslovakia.[44] A few days later, on 30 July 1968 in the Parliamentary Committee on Foreign Policy, State Secretary for Foreign Affairs Marko Nikezić went even further. Pressures on Prague, in his opinion, were similar to the pressures put on Yugoslavia in 1948 by the Informburo.[45]

Alexander Dubček's space for maneuvering, always limited, was becoming painfully narrow. Tito, however, had visited Prague from 9 to 11 August 1968. The bilateral meeting started at 6:45.[46] In Tito's notes prepared for the meeting, the only concrete proposal was to found a joint Yugoslav-Czechoslovak Bank.[47] Everything else was political: full independence, cautious approach to the West, more rights for those who work. That was "far more important and significant" than the "freedom of press" and other "classical political freedoms" read Tito's notes on the Yugoslav document. Playing with the multiparty system destroyed Nagy. That should be suppressed and a Peoples Front enforced instead.[48] Federalization and full equality between Czechs and Slovaks was essential. That problem should be solved "definitely" since only then would and could it not be used by "big powers."

Tito's treatment in Prague was glorious, comparable only with his first visit in 1946.[49] Media coverage was big, the reactions of common people fantastic.[50] Taking into account how organizers wanted to avoid mass gatherings since they could have evolved into anti-Soviet demonstrations and, therefore, did not publicize the times and routes of Tito's entourage, the number of people on the streets was huge. The U.S. weekly *Time* magazine reported how Tito's proposal for economic cooperation was discussed. His idea was for Yugoslavia and Czechoslovakia to create a "sort of two-country common market that will enable each country to draw on the other's investment capital, labor pool, and special industrial talents."[51] However, the Yugoslavs did not have any intention of (or possibility for) substituting the Czechoslovak-Soviet cooperation. They were happy to see how Dubček was trying to mend fences and talk. Czechoslovak media analysts were stressing the "calming effect" of the visit in contrast to the dynamic events of recent weeks.[52] *Mladá Fronta*, a Czechoslovak daily, nevertheless discouraged those who were seeing parallels between Yugoslavia in 1948 and the Prague Spring. However, Změdělské noviny clearly wrote that the Yugoslav exclusion from the Information Bureau of the Communist and Workers' Parties, informally known as Cominform, gave them the right to and the possibility for understanding what was going on in Prague.[53] *Lidová demokracie* stressed how each country had to determine its own path. The

Czechoslovak's road was agreed upon in January 1968. Therefore, it had to be followed vigorously, relying on those who were open-minded when talking of democracy and socialism. From Prague, Tito had returned to Pula and his summer residence on the Brijuni Islands. The most important goal of the visit—the visible support for Dubček—had been achieved.

A few weeks earlier, Tito's state secretary for foreign affairs, *Marko Nikezić*, during a closed session with Serbian journalists had stressed how, in the Soviet's opinion, Yugoslavia was a country with the most "concentrated revisionist" party program.[54] In his opinion, developments in Czechoslovakia were contributing significantly to the consolidation of everything already achieved in Yugoslavia. No democratization should ever be expected from Moscow. Therefore, small steps forward in different Socialist countries should be supported in order to achieve democratization, ease tensions, and create a new environment in Europe.[55] Bearing that in mind, it was clear why the Yugoslavs were so eager to help Dubček. A few days after Tito's stay in Prague, Nicolae Ceauşescu of Romania followed. We know now that on 17 August, the day of the last meeting between Kádár and Dubček, the Soviet Politburo gave the final go-ahead for the invasion. Zdeněk Mlynář claims that Kádár, unable to change Dubček's mind, had asked almost desperately, "Do you really not know the kind of people you're dealing with?"[56]

HOW CAN WE HELP YOU, MRS. DUBČEK?

Mrs. Ana Dubček came to Rijeka on 2 August 1968 with two children and a personal driver. She called on the harbor authorities and asked for permission to board the Czechoslovak ship *Gojnice*. Her oldest son was supposed to get some world experience while traveling along the Mediterranean and working onboard.[57] Her trip had not been previously announced to the Yugoslav authorities. Only after Radio Prague had asked Radio Zagreb colleagues to do a story on the first lady's trip had Jože Smole, head of Tito's office, asked the Croatian police to check her whereabouts. Tito's personal wish was to have a member of the Croatian authorities pay her a visit. Ana Dubček was one of 50,000 Czech and Slovak tourists who had decided to spend their summer holidays along the Adriatic coast that year. Ota Šik, the vice president of the government, and Minister of Foreign Affairs Hajek were the most prominent among them. Ana Dubček stayed in Crikvenica, a summer resort in the northern part of the country as a guest of the director of the port of Rijeka. She was probably preparing to go to bed when, on 20 August 1968 at 11:40 p.m., Florian Siwicki, the Polish general in charge of the Silesian Military District, received an order to start operation "Danube" from the north.[58] His colleagues from Hungary and Bulgaria received similar orders from the Soviet general, as agreed in Moscow on 18 August.[59] From a military standpoint, the occupation of Czechoslovakia was achieved brilliantly.[60] Savka Dabčević-Kučar, president of the executive council of the government of the Socialist Republic of Croatia, together with Miko Tripalo, member of the highest party organs in Yugoslavia, and Dragutin Haramija, major of Rijeka, went to see her.[61] Mrs. Dubček was depressed, but calm. She did not ask for any help.

General Zlatko Rendulić, commander of the technical service of the Yugoslav Air Force, was near Orebić in southern Croatia when the Warsaw Pact countries invaded Czechoslovakia. He, like all of his colleagues, was called to report to his military unit instantly. First he went to Belgrade, then to the northern city of Sombor. Armed soldiers who were waiting for the Soviets to attack surrounded the large military airport there. Some soldiers were even trying to escape. News came from Subotica, a city at the Hungarian-Yugoslav border, that Soviet tanks were already entering the city. Eventually, it was revealed that the Soviet tanks purchased by the Yugoslavs before the Prague Spring were loaded on the Soviet train. They were waiting for clearance to be shipped to Yugoslavia. It could have been only a coincidence or a sign that in spite of everything, nothing was to change between Moscow and Belgrade.[62]

At the time of the invasion, Josip Vrhovec, a journalist at *Vjesnik*, a leading Croatian daily newspaper, but soon-to-become an ideological czar of the Croatian Communists, was with his family in Prague. Leaving Czechoslovakia proved to be tricky. Czechs were changing and replacing road signs to make the Soviet advance more difficult. However, many of the common people in small towns and villages were eager to help people driving Yugoslav cars get back home. Some, seeing Yugoslav license plates, were yelling at the drivers not to forget them, to tell the world what had happened in Czechoslovakia.[63]

The hottest activity was on the Brijuni Islands. As soon he received news of the invasion, Tito summoned leading politicians from all parts of Yugoslavia.[64] Also invited were the vice-premier of Czechoslovakia, Ota Šik, State Secretary Hajek, and two other ministers and high party and state officials from Czechoslovakia. All were depressed and scared, but allowed to continue with political work as part of the legal Czechoslovak government.[65] During the day, a note on the conversation between the U.S. *chargé d'affaires* in Belgrade with Deputy State Secretary Mišo Pavićević was delivered to Tito. The Yugoslavs were informed about the Soviet ambassador in the United States Anatolii Dobrynin's conversation with the U.S. president Lyndon Johnson and Secretary of State Dean Rusk. Probably the Soviets' position, which stressed how no "state interests of the U.S. or any other country" were to be endangered by the "fraternal" intervention of five countries in Czechoslovakia, garnered significant attention.[66] What the Yugoslav leading politicians probably did not know was how almost indifferent President Johnson's reaction to Dobrynin's message was. Johnson had promised to study the paper, immediately changing the conversation to the arms control talks.[67] Tito had opened the emergency joint session of the presidency and the Executive Committee of the CC of League of Communists of Yugoslavia by saying how a public demonstration must be made, and it was! The very next day, Mijalko Todorović Plavi, secretary of the Executive Committee of the CC League of Communists of Yugoslavia (*Savez komunista Jugoslavije* or LCY) addressed 250,000 people in Belgrade. During his speech, he used a phrase which eventually became quoted relatively often. The "most glorious flag of world communism," muddied in 1948, has now fallen.[68] Tito, who was addressing the gathered delegates on the Brijuni Islands, repeated that there were no reasons for the intervention because West Germany was not threatening Czechoslovakia, and socialism there was not endangered from within:

> The case here is not only Czechoslovakia. As a matter of fact it is about us. We are the real opposition to the Soviet leadership with our internal development, with our determination not to allow interference in our internal issues. It is understandable; an attack on Czechoslovakia does not mean that one day we might not be attacked, too.[69]

On 23 August 1968, the party CC met in Belgrade. Before his comrades had a chance to say anything, Tito stressed that the news from Czechoslovakia had made him dizzy.[70] Later that day, he met Bruce Elbrick, the U.S. ambassador to Yugoslavia.[71] The purpose of the "occupation of Czechoslovakia" was to undermine the Socialist development based on the democracy, Tito concluded. Aware that Yugoslav-Soviet relations would not stay as good as they were, Tito was clear-minded regarding how global considerations this time were much more important for the Yugoslavs, which was why Yugoslavia would stay firm on the position of independence, equality, and noninterference.[72] If relations between the Socialist countries were not based on equality, how could they ask for equal treatment from the capitalist countries, asked Tito. State Secretary for Foreign Affairs Marko Nikezić was more direct in his conversation with the U.S. ambassador a few days later. He reminded Elbrick of their conversation in July when the American had stated how Washington's goal was not to complicate further the Czechoslovaks' situation. At the same time, they were not ready to endanger relationships with their "big partner."[73] Closer negotiations between Moscow and Washington were positive, but not at the expense of the small and weak, the Yugoslav secretary concluded.

Less than twenty-four hours later on August 24, on the Romanian's initiative, Tito met Ceaușescu in Vršac, Vojvodina.[74] The Romanian dictator had informed Tito about the founding of the Patriotic Guard which was tasked with defending the independence of their "Socialist motherland." Ceauşescu went further, asking whether the Yugoslavs would have allowed armed Romanian forces to occupy Yugoslav territory, if they were not planning on shooting at the Soviets if attacked. The Yugoslav leader had promised to receive only un-armed individuals or to disarm soldiers before they crossed the border.[75] In the report given to the Soviets by the Hungarian diplomats in Belgrade, Tito was very depressed during the meeting. "The good atmosphere we had been creating for years, has suddenly gone," Tito said.[76] Moreover,

> American Cold War policy brought the USA to isolation. The foreign policy of France had undermined the unity of the imperialist countries. There was a crisis in NATO. Socialism was a general tendency in the developing countries. There was a growing tendency to democratization in the Socialist countries. That has all changed now. The only side benefiting from this was the United States and reactionary forces. The root of evil is in the Soviet leadership.[77]

The Soviets were, as always, unwilling to admit any mistake, which was part of how they suppressed the independence of other countries. As well as the Romanians, Yugoslav politicians were ready to maintain good relations with the Soviet Union. The Yugoslavs were, nevertheless, determined to fight, but not to continue with their provocations. They were aware of the differences between the "Five." As a matter of fact, the Yugoslav diplomats in Prague were informed of the same. Polish diplomat Stičinski, who was far from friendly when Dubček became the first secretary, had admitted that he was to defend the opinion of his government in spite of the "huge loss of prestige of all Warsaw Pact countries."[78] It was impossible to prove or disprove that counterrevolution was taking place in Prague. Certainly, there was no invitation sent to invade Czechoslovakia. Propaganda preparation was bad, and Radio Vltava horrible, Stičinski said.

On 31 August 1968, Tito was back on the Brijuni Islands. Ivan Benedik-tov, the Soviet representative in Belgrade, came to deliver his demarche pro-testing the anti-Soviet propaganda. Benediktov was cold and professional. His presumptuous way of talking and the information he shared about the mistreatment of Yugoslavs in Moscow had annoyed Tito. He was interrupt-ing the Soviet ambassador, saying many undiplomatic things. The Kremlin was listening to Walter Ulbricht and Todor Zhivkov, rather than Tito. Lyn-don Johnson was probably the only one happy with the intervention, Tito said to the Soviet ambassador. The Soviets were spreading "obvious lies" when talking about Yugoslavia.[79] Sergei Astavin, head of the Fifth Division in the Ministry of Foreign Affairs of the Soviet Union, while complaining to the Yugoslav diplomats in Moscow about the harsh reactions from Bel-grade, expressed his surprise. The Yugoslavs, he said, "were informed" of the Soviet intention to use troops in Czechoslovakia.[80]

Belgrade was determined to resist. The Americans and the British were ready to help, at least to a certain extent. On 27 August 1968, Ivo Sarajčić, the Yugoslav ambassador in London, had approached the British authorities. If the decision was not to interfere in the *Lager*, what would be the policy toward the states outside the blocs, he asked?[81] Only one day later, Sarajčić was approached by the former British Foreign Office boss George Brown. He wanted Sarajčić to inform Belgrade how any threat to Yugoslav security would be responded to in kind. He was clear that Britain would threaten with force all those who would dare to do the same to Yugoslavia. The Yugoslav ambassador in the United States, Bogdan Crnobrnja, had approached Dean Rusk, the U.S. secretary of state, on 29 August with no particular requests to make, only stressing his country's determination to fight back if attacked.[82] The Western countries had promised to help Belgrade in the event of a Soviet military intervention. The "occupation of Yugoslavia or Austria would have a particularly serious effect on NATO interests and it follows from this that any threat to or attack upon either of these countries would create a tense political atmosphere," said the Chiefs of Staff Committee of the Defense Policy Staff in London.[83] Dean Rusk even stressed how the eventual Soviet presence on the Adriatic "was of vital concern to the entire Western world."[84] There was a panic in Belgrade and on the Brijuni Islands for a few days. As soon as it became clear how firm the guarantees from the West were and how small the Soviet interest to intervene, big changes began to take place in Yugoslavia.

THE U.S. COMMUNIST ALLY—FOR A SECOND TIME?

After the initial fear and insecurity, a few days after the invasion the Yugoslavs were convinced that their independence still mattered to the world. Early in September 1968, the British Foreign secretary and secretary of defense had agreed that a Soviet attack on Yugoslavia was unlikely. The Prague Spring had been "designed to maintain the status quo," not to change radically the conservationist policy of the Warsaw Pact.[85] Anyhow, an invasion of Yugoslavia would change the balance of power on the Old Continent. Therefore, during the meeting with the Americans, the British government concluded: "It should be made clear to the Russians that any attack on Yugoslavia would have the same effect as one on a member of NATO."[86] "The occupation of Rumania, serious though it would be, would not in itself touch upon vital Western security interests, but the invasion of Yugoslavia would be quite another matter."[87] The U.S. ambassador in Belgrade, Elbrick, after the interview with President Johnson on 14 October, once more stressed how "[t]he President cited our long tradition of assistance to Yugoslavia and expressed his admiration for the Yugoslav people and their dedication to freedom. The President made very clear his continuing interest in that country's independence, sovereignty, and economic development."[88]

Since the break with Stalin in 1948, Yugoslavia had sometimes been called an "American Communist Ally." The West tried to support Yugoslavian-style communism and to widen the wedge between countries in the Socialist world. If possible, the aim was to develop trends in Eastern Europe detected in the National Intelligence Estimate on Yugoslavia in 1967. However, by the time that things started to change in Czechoslovakia, the overall political environment had already been changed. "[D]espite setbacks to our expectations for détente, the search for secure and peaceful East-West relations leading in time to a European security settlement is the only political goal consistent with Western values," the British were reporting.[89] That goal could have been achieved only with cooperation from Moscow. No one in the West was willing to start an even bigger quarrel with the Soviets, let alone serious fighting.[90] The strategy of driving a wedge between the satellites and Moscow and establishing regimes like Tito's was an old and unsuccessful plan.[91]

In February 1948, Czechoslovakia was the last country in Europe to become Communist and a member of the Soviet Bloc. In June 1948, Yugoslavia was the first Socialist country to change sides, keeping the Socialist regime, but leaving Moscow. In 1956, Hungary was the first Bloc country to try to emulate the Yugoslav example. In 1968, Dubček seemed to be doing the same in Czechoslovakia. The Yugoslavs were helpful to both countries, although far less directly in 1968. Western propaganda was very outspoken during the Hungarian Revolution. One decade later, there was almost a silence. Although the "reawakening of political life" in Czechoslovakia was "obviously" in U.S. interests, as Western observers reported, a policy of nonaction carried the day.[92] The West Germans, who were in charge of Radio Free Europe and Radio Liberty, chose to seem disinterested in the liberal developments in Czechoslovakia, in a move intended to avoid provoking the Soviets[93]: "There is absolutely no evidence that either the State Department or the CIA took any measures to use the Prague Spring as a means of destabilizing or subverting the Soviet Bloc, in spite of constant Soviet propaganda about the sinister efforts of Western imperialism to do so."[94]

Enver Hoxha, the Albanian dictator and one of Tito's archenemies, softened his position. Tirana had described the intervention in Prague as the "aggression of the Soviet revisionists."[95] The anti-Yugoslav campaign was stopped. Semiofficial signals from Tirana aimed at the improvement of relations between the two countries became numerous. Hoxha was afraid of the Soviets, especially since Bulgarians were printing maps of Greater Bulgaria with the San Stephan borders from 1878.[96] Although the positive trend in Yugoslav-Albanian relations did not last for long, there were some lasting positive improvements. For example, ambassadors were exchanged in February 1971.[97]

Once the Prague Spring was crushed, the Bulgarians, the most bellicose of all neighbors, refused to return the Yugoslav Army missiles they were supposed to mend. The Soviet Army was still on the very edge of the Pannonian Plain. Huge ferries, allegedly for the Soviet tourists, were being built in Odessa.[98] Some of the most pessimistic analysts were thinking how the Soviets were aiming at creating a Greater Bulgaria at the Albanian and Yugoslavs' expense.[99]

The answer to the diplomatic problems was to start with an ambitious diplomatic game. The initiative from Addis Abeba to convene a conference of "peace-loving" countries in Belgrade and to condemn the Soviets was politely refused, though. Serious splits among the nonaligned countries had to be ironed out first.[100] The Arabs were pro-Soviet because the Soviets were helping them in the Middle East.[101] To revive the nonaligned countries' unity and to avoid alienating them in the process became a new major task of the Yugoslav diplomacy. The Soviets were aware of the Yugoslavs' attempts. Therefore, Soviet diplomats were informed of the "active anti-Socialist and anti-Soviet" Yugoslav politics in Asia and Africa. The Soviets were to confront the "antisocialist" Yugoslav diplomats because advocating nonalignment, especially among the Socialist countries, was in their opinion nothing but an imperialist strategy aimed at harming the unity of the Socialist world.[102] Only one year before the Prague Spring was crushed, Tito was in Moscow attending an advisory meeting of the Eastern European countries (minus Romania) which was coordinating the Yugoslav assistance to the militarily defeated Egypt in the Six Days War.[103] After August 1968, Tito was, for a while, traveling only to the West, including an important trip to the Vatican.[104] The (re)imposition of the rigid Communist regime in Prague showed the continuing importance of Yugoslavia for the West.

Dubček was probably inspired by Belgrade's independence, but he was not directly influenced or led by Tito. Tito and Ceaușescu were eager to help the Czechoslovaks achieve not greater liberalism, but their independence form Moscow. While in Bulgaria the reforms of the 1960s were stopped, in Yugoslavia, they were sped up.[105] After the end of the Prague Spring, Tito continued with a program of reforms in order to satisfy different nationalities. The Yugoslav People's Army went though the most elaborate change. Ivan Gošnjak, ideologically rigid and fully devoted to Tito as commander in chief, was replaced.[106] Territorial units were introduced, and each Socialist republic of Yugoslavia became partially responsible for its own protection.[107] Some of the Marxist dissidents in Yugoslavia saw in the Czechoslovak events "the hope that the evolution they had argued for was now within their grasp. . . . Tito's support for Dubček . . . permitted some of them to predict a second Yugoslav revolution."[108] Federalization and decentralization of the country led to the so-called Croatian Spring of 1970–1971. When Tito and his number two in the nomenclature, Edward Kardelj, were talking about the reformers they considered too liberal in the second-largest republic (and among some other politicians in all parts of SFRY), they would often call them "Dubček-ites" adding how they would rather see Russian tanks in Zagreb than tolerate their "Dubček-ism."[109] Yugoslav leadership was quick to forget how pro-Dubček they had been only a few years earlier and even more eager to adopt the Soviet language. With the crash of the Yugoslav "Dubček-ites," it was all over. That's when Yugoslavia actually died.

NOTES

1. U.S. National Intelligence Estimate (hereafter NIE) 15–67, "The Yugoslav Experiment," 13 April 1967.

2. NIE 15–67, "The Yugoslav Experiment," 13 April 1967. Commercial exchange with the *Lager* countries was 33 percent, with Western Europe 38 percent, and 10 percent with the United States. A respectable 19 percent was foreign trade with the nonaligned countries. In 1966, the Socialist Federal Republic of Yugoslavia signed the General Agreement on Tariffs and Trade (GATT), a move which emphasized Yugoslav dependence on Western markets.

3. NIE 15–67, "The Yugoslav Experiment," 13 April 1967.

4. NIE Memo, "The Yugoslav Succession Problem," 10 March 1969.

5. Blažo Mandić, *Tito u dijalogu sa svijetom* (Novi Sad: Agencija "MiR," 2005), 193–202.

6. *Vjesnik*, 11 August 1965 ("Words of Comrade Tito"); "S Titovim drugom iz Čenkova" ["With Tito's Comrade in Čenkov"], *Borba*, 11 April 1965.

7. NIE Memo, "The Yugoslav Succession Problem," 10 March 1969.

8. R. J. Crampton, *The Balkans since the Second World War* (Harlow, UK: Longman, 2002), 131.

9. On Ranković and his fall many books were written, some with a visible bias. See, for example, Savka Dabčević-Kučar, *'71-hrvatski snovi i stvarnost* (Zagreb: Interpublic, 1997), 82–85; Dennison Rusinow, *The Yugoslav Experiment 1948–1974* (Berkeley: University of California Press and Royal Institute of International Affairs, 1977), 184–91.

10. Dušan Bilandžić, *Propast Jugoslavije i stvaranje moderne Hrvatske* (Zagreb: AGM, 2001), 227.

11. KPRI-2, 63/J:1107–12, Br.kutije 82, bilateral cooperation between the Savez komunista Jugoslavije (League of Communists of Yugoslavia, LCY) and the Communist Party of Czechoslovakia (KPČ) in 1968. Produced in the Central Committee of the League of the Communists of Yugoslavia (hereafter CK SKJ), 18 August 1968.

12. Julius Bartal et al., eds., *Slovak History: Chronology and Lexicon* (Bratislava: Slovenske Pedagogicke nakladitelsvo, 2002), 156; and Tony Judt, *Postwar: A History of Europe since 1945* (London: Pimlico, 2005), 439–40.

13. Christopher Andrew and Vasili Mitrokhin, *The Mitrokhin Archive, The KGB in Europe and the West* (London: Penguin Books, 2000), 327. In February 1968, Mišo Pavićević, deputy state secretary for foreign affairs, was informed of the changes in Prague by Ladislav Šimovič, Czechoslovak ambassador in Belgrade. In the ambassador's opinion, Novotný's misunderstanding of the mentality of Czechs and Slovaks, his personality, and the methods he used, as well as his relationship with the Slovaks, caused the changes in Prague. KPR I-5-B Čehoslovačka (hereafter KPR) I-2, 63/J:1107–12, Br.kutije 82, from the note on the meeting between the deputy secretary on Foreign Affairs, Ambassador M. Pavićević, with the ambassador of the ČSSR, L. Šimovič, 17 February 1968.

14. See, for example, Mark Kramer's discussion of this in his articles "Moldova, Romania, and the Soviet Invasion of Czechoslovakia," *Cold War International History Project Bulletin* 12, no. 13 (Fall/Winter 2001): 326–33 and "Ukraine and the Soviet-Czechoslovak Crisis of 1968 (Part 2): New Evidence from the Ukrainian Archives," *Cold War International History Project Bulletin* 14, no. 15 (Winter 2003/Spring 2004): 273–368.

15. John W. Young and John Kent, *International Relations since 1945: A Global History* (Oxford: Oxford University Press, 2003), 310.

16. Rusinow, *Yugoslav Experiment*, 240.

17. Thomas Alan Schwartz, *Lyndon Johnson and Europe, in the Shadow of Vietnam* (Cambridge, MA: Harvard University Press, 2003), 218–22.

18. KPR I-2, 63/J:1107–12, Br.kutije 82, Kádár on Yugoslav and Romanian views regarding developments in the ČSSR.

19. Crampton, *The Balkans*, 172–73.

20. KPR I-2, 63/J:1107–12, Br.kutije 82, visit of the vice president of the Federal Executive Committee (SIV, Savezno izvršno vijeće, that is, the Yugoslav government) Comrade K. Gligorov to the Peoples Republic of Hungary. Kiro Gligorov later became the first president of an independent Macedonia; Roger Gough, *A Good Comrade: János Kádár, Communism, and Hungary* (London: I. B. Tauris, 2006), 153.

21. KPR I-2, 63/J:1107–12, Br.kutije 82, the Bulgarian military attaché in Belgrade was openly criticizing the changes in Prague, noting how revisionism was penetrating some Communist Party of Czechoslovakia members (*Komunistická strana Československa* or KSČ).

22. KPR I-2, 63/J:1107–12, Br.kutije 82, bilateral cooperation SKJ-KPČ in 1968. Prepared in the Department for International Relations, 18 August 1968.

23. KPR I-2, 63/J:1107–12, Br.kutije 82, from the note on the talk between the advisor of the state secretary, Ljubo S. Babić, with the ambassador of the ČSSR, L. Šimovič, 9 May 1968.

24. KPR I-2, 63/J:1107–12, Br.kutije 82, visit of the State Secretary of Foreign Affairs M. Nikezić to Czechoslovakia.

25. Mandić, *Tito u dijalogu sa svijetom*, 290.

26. Dabčević-Kučar, *'71-hrvatski snovi i stvarnost*, 97; Marko Vrhunec, *Šest godina s Titom (1967–1973): Pogled s vrha i izbliza* (Zagreb: Nakladni zavod Globus/Adamić, 2001), 57; Mandić, *Tito u dijalogu sa svijetom*, 291. Blažo Mandić, head of the press office in Tito's cabinet, was less descriptive of Brezhnev's comments on Dubček. Savka Dabčević-Kučar, at the time head of the Executive Committee of the Socialist Republic of Croatia, had also accompanied Tito to Japan and Moscow. She wrote

how Brezhnev had used words like "putsch," "attempt to destroy communism," "wild counterrevolution," and the like.

27. KPR 1.2. SSSR, *Put Josipa Broza Tita u SSSR*, 28–30, April 1968, minutes of the talk between the chairman of the SFRJ and the chairman of the SKJ, Comrade Josip Broz Tito, and the Yugoslav members of the state party delegation with the Soviet state and party leadership in Moscow, 29 April 1968. "Regarding the situation in Czechoslovakia, we think that their leadership, if fully supported, will manage to reduce the influence of the reactionaries, which are, and here I agree with you, numerous. . . . [our] Czech comrades need our full support to keep things developing in the right direction," Tito said to Brezhnev. Dabčević-Kučar, *'71-hrvatski snovi i stvarnost*, 96.

28. Dabčević-Kučar, *'71-hrvatski snovi i stvarnost*, 96.

29. Vrhunec, *Šest godina s Titom*, 58.

30. Andrzej Paczkowski, *Pola stoljeća povijesti Poljske, 1939–1989* (Zagreb: Profil/ Srednja Europa, 2001), 295.

31. Jakovlevski's biography prior to his ambassadorial career was not especially exciting. He was a middle-ranked official in Macedonia. After his tour of duty in Prague, he became a member of the Federal Executive Council, the Yugoslav government in Belgrade. His conduct in Prague was, obviously, regarded as fair. Ranko Petković, *Subjektivna istorija jugoslovenske diplomatije 1943–1991* (in cyrillic) (Belgrade: Službeni list SRJ, 1995), 175.

32. KPR I-2, 63/J:1107–12, Br.kutije 82, Sveska II, Information on some aspects of the situation in the ČSSR, 10 July 1968.

33. Gough, *A Good Comrade*, 166–67; Judt, *Postwar*, 443.

34. KPR I-2, 63/J:1107–12, Br.kutije 82, information on the situation in the ČSSR given by Minister Hajek to Ambassador Jakovlevski, 12 July 1968.

35. KPR I-2, 63/J:1107–12, Br.kutije 82, information on the situation in the ČSSR given by Minister Hajek to Ambassador Jakovlevski, 12 July 1968.

36. KPR I-2, 63/J:1107–12, Br.kutije 82, Sveska II, Information on several aspects of the situation in the ČSSR, 10 July 1968.

37. KPR I-2, 63/J:1107–12, Br. kutije 82, Sveska II, Information on several aspects of the situation in the ČSSR, 14 July 1968. From the talk between Ambassador Jakovlevski with Smrkovský, 13 July 1968.

38. KPR I-2, 63/J:1107–12, Br.kutije 82, Sveska I, osnovni materijal, estimation of Ambassador Jakovlevski on the situation in the ČSSR after the "Warsaw letter" by the five fraternal parties, 17 July 1968.

39. KPR I-2, 63/J:1107–12, Br.kutije 82, Sveska I, osnovni materijal.

40. Gough, *A Good Comrade*, 167.

41. KPR I-2, 63/J:1107–12, Br. kutije 82, Sveska I, osnovne informacije, short overview on the development of the situation in the ČSSR made in the State Secretariat for Foreign Affairs (that is, the Ministry of Foreign Affairs), 19 July 1968.

42. Marcus Wolf, *Čovjek bez lica, Šef špijuna u tajnom ratu* (Zagreb: Golden marketing Tehnička knjiga, 2004), 145. The East German secret police were reporting on contacts between the liberal circles in Prague with the Western circles, especially social democrats in Germany and Eurocommunists in Italy.

43. KPR I-2, 63/J:1107–12, Br.kutije 82, full text of the letter sent by the first secretary of the CC KSČ to Comrade Tito, 15 July 1968.

44. Zdravko Vuković, *Od deformacija SDB do maspoka i liberalizma: Moji stenografski zapisi 1966–1972 godine* (Belgrade: Narodna knjiga, 1989), 202.

45. Vuković, *Od deformacija SDB do maspoka i liberalizma,* 203; Jože Pirjevec, *Jugoslavija: Nastanek, razvoj ter razpad Karadjordjevičeve in Titove Jugoslavije* (Koper: Založba Lipa, 1995), 275. After the publication of the letter of "Five," the Belgrade daily *Politika* published it in an article entitled "Informbiro 1968."

46. KPR I-2, 63/J:1107–12, Br.kutije 82, records of the conversation between Tito with Dubček, 9 August 1968 (handwritten by Jože Smole).

47. KPR I-2, 63/J:1107–12, Br.kutije 82, reminder for the talks in Prague.

48. KPR I-2, 63/J:1107–12, Br.kutije 82, censorship of press and electronic media was formally abolished on 26 June 1968. Judt, *Postwar,* 441.

49. AJ, 507, III/134, records of the XI joint meeting of the presidencies of the Executive Committee and the presidency of the CK SKJ, 21 August 1968, Brioni, 8 p.m.

50. *Vjesnik,* 13 August 1968 ("Pleasure with the visit of Tito to Prague"); *Vjesnik,* 10 August 1968 ("Welcome Yugoslav friends"). A personal dossier prepared for Tito before the trip even included letters from common people who were thanking him for not forgetting the Czechoslovaks. Allusions to the treason of 1938 were made all the time.

51. "Prague's Purposeful Hospitality," *Time International,* 23 August 1968. The phenomenon of "guest-workers" was acute in Yugoslavia; hundred of thousands were migrating to West Germany, Austria, and France, among other countries, to find jobs. Although this flood of workers painfully showed how the Socialist economy was not working, their migration was allowed to continue. Since there was a need for masons in Czechoslovakia, it was agreed to allow "tens of thousands" of Yugoslavs to migrate to Czechoslovakia. Since the standard of living in Czechoslovakia was lower than that in Yugoslavia at the time, the big question was how and who would force potential workers to go there? "Tanjugov bilten, Put predsednika Tita, zapadnoeruopski izvori," *Vjesnikova Novinska Dokumentacija* (VND), Zagreb, Croatia, 12 August 1968.

52. *Vjesnik,* 13 August 1968 ("Contribution to the strengthening of Socialism").

53. Tomislav Buturac, "Praško proljeće: dvadeset godina poslije," *Danas,* Zagreb, Croatia, 26 January 1988, p. 4. A series of articles in this leading Yugoslav weekly was written by Buturac, Croatian correspondent from Prague from 1968 to 1970.

54. Vuković, *Od deformacija SDB do maspoka i liberalizma,* 199.

55. Vuković, *Od deformacija SDB do maspoka i liberalizma,* 200. Nikezić probably also referred to the April conversation between Tito and Brezhnev in Moscow. The Soviets then stated that there was "no reason to change a system which had been effective for 50 years."

56. Gough, *A Good Comrade,* 171.

57. KPR, I-2, 63/J:1107–12, Br.kutije 82 (No title; letters signed by Jože Smole, head of Tito's office to Croatian police and Spoljnoplitička služba G.S.P.R.).

58. Paczkowski, *Pola stoljeća povijesti Poljske,* 295; Wolf, *Čovjek bez lica,* 149.

59. Gough, *A Good Comrade,* 171; Judt, *Postwar,* 444.

60. NARA, secretary of defense staff meeting, 26 August 1968.

61. Dabčević-Kučar, *'71-hrvatski snovi i stvarnost,* 98–99. Dragutin Haramija, president of the Parliament of the Council of Rijeka, that is, mayor, was soon to become

president of the Executive Council of Croatia (Government), while Savka Dabčević Kučar became president of the CC of the League of Communist of Croatia. Tripalo was one of the most prominent younger politicians in Yugoslavia at the time.

62. Zlatko Rendulić, *General Avnojske Jugoslavije, sjećanja* (Zagreb: Golden Marketing/Tehnička knjiga, 2004), 280–81.

63. Oral history interview, Olga Vrhovec, Zagreb, 19 October 2007.

64. AJ, 507, III/134, records of the XI joint meeting of the presidencies of the Executive Committee and the presidency of the CK SKJ, 21 August 1968.

65. Miko Tripalo, *Hrvatsko prolječe* (Zagreb: NZMH, 2001), 115. Minister Hajek left for New York shortly after the intervention. Both he and Šik were meeting with their Yugoslav hosts as members of the Czechoslovak government, not as representatives of the government in exile. Some Soviets officials tried to impute how it was no coincidence that Šik and Hajek were on holidays along the Adriatic Sea. At the very end of August, Hajek was allowed to return first to Belgrade and then, together with Šik and the rest, to Prague. They were received by the vice president of the Yugoslav Executive Council Kiro Gligorov and left for Czechoslovakia. KPR I-5-b, Br. Kutije 236, Czechoslovakia; Conversation between the chairman of the Republic with U.S. Ambassador to Yugoslavia B. Elbrick, 23 August 1968; bulletin on the developments in ČSSR, br.1, 24 August 1968; Iljičov, deputy minister of the Foreign Affairs of the USSR; Yugoslavia and the developments in the ČSSR; minutes on the talk of the Deputy State Secretary M. Pavićević with the ambassador of the ČSSR to Belgrade, 29 August 1968.

66. KPR, I-2, 63/J:1107–12, Br.kutije 82.; Pavićević to the cabinet of the chairman of the Republic and the State Secretary for Foreign Affairs, Brioni. Almost the same message was delivered orally by Ambassador Smirnovsky to the British prime minister at 1:30 a.m. on 20 August 1968: "Our actions are not directed against any European State and in no way infringe upon anybody's state interests, including the interests of Great Britain. They are dictated entirely by the concern for strengthening peace in the face of a dangerous growth of tension, which left no choice to the Socialist countries," National Archives, London, UK, Public Record Office (hereafter PRO), Foreign and Commonwealth Office (hereafter FCO) 28/68.

67. Thomas Alan Schwartz, *Lyndon Johnson and Europe, in the Shadow of Vietnam* (Cambridge, MA: Harvard University Press, 2003), 217.

68. Pero Simić, *Tito, svetac i magle: Tito i njegovo vreme u novim dokumentima Moskve i Beograda* (in cyrillic) (Belgrade: Službeni list SCG, 2005), 212. Todorović was in Prague together with Tito from 9 to 11 August. In a speech, Norbert Weber, a member of the Central Committee of the Yugoslav League of Communists and a long-time manager of a large metallurgic complex in Sisak, a city fifty kilometers south of Zagreb, said: "Yugoslavia is today exactly what it was in the year 1941 when all of Europe looked to her as she resisted a much stronger enemy; today the international worker's movement of the world gathers around and looks up to her, because Yugoslavia shows the path which should be taken, Yugoslavia reveals that it is not socialism which the Soviet Union presents with the occupation of Czechoslovakia. Therefore it must be understood that today socialism is much broader . . . we must once again raise the shaken belief in socialism." HDA Sisak, Records of the municipal conference of the Savez komunista Hrvatske (League of Communists of Croatia, or SKH), Sisak, 10 September 1968. The Soviets were furious about the meeting in

Belgrade. The Yugoslav military attaché in Moscow was verbally attacked by Astavin, head of the Fifth Department of the Soviet Ministry of Foreign Affairs. He expressed his surprise regarding the Yugoslavs' overall attitude, which was not neutral at all.

69. AJ, 507, III/134, records of the XI joint meeting of the presidencies of the Executive Committee and the presidency of the CK SKJ, 21 August 1968 (Brioni, 8 p.m.).

70. Simić, *Tito, svetac i magle*, 212.

71. AJ, 507, III/135, conversation of the president of the republic with the U.S. ambassador to Yugoslavia, B. Elbrick, 23 August 1968.

72. AJ, 507, III/135, Conversation of the president of the republic with the U.S. ambassador to Yugoslavia, B. Elbrick, 23 August 1968.

73. AJ, 507, III/135, minutes of the talk of the State Secretary for Foreign Affairs M. Nikezić with U.S. ambassador to Yugoslavia B. Elbrick in Belgrade, 30 August 1968. U.S. secretary of defense Clark M. Clifford explained: "[T]he best policy is to permit the Soviets and the Czechs to adjust their differences. We have a number of items going with the Soviet Union and it would be an exceedingly unfortunate time to get involved." NARA, secretary of defense staff meeting, 15 July 1968.

74. Pirjevec, *Jugoslavija*, 276; AJ, 507, III/134, Romanian position; excerpts from the conversation of Ambassador Petrić with the member of the Executive Committee and the secretary of the CK KPR, in Bucharest, 30 August 1968.

75. Tripalo, *Hrvatsko proljeće*, 123; Stephen Clissold, ed., *Yugoslavia and the Soviet Union, 1939-1973: A Documentary Survey* (London: Oxford University Press for the Royal Institute of International Affairs, 1975), 81; Pirjevec, *Jugoslavija*, 276.

76. Russian State Archives for Contemporary History, Moscow (hereafter RGANI) F. 5, op. 60, d. 271, 4 September 1968. (Report from the embassy of the People's Republic of Hungary on the meeting between Tito and Ceaușescu on 24 August 1968). Hungarians got the report from Romanian sources, while the Soviets were informed through the Hungarian Ministry of Foreign Affairs.

77. RGANI, F. 5, op. 60, d. 271, 4 September 1968.

78. KPR, I-2, 63/J:1107-12, Br.kutije 82, excerpts from the conversation with the Polish chargé Stičinski, Prague, 29 August 1968.

79. Simić, *Tito, svetac i magle*, 212-13; Vuković, *Od deformacija SDB do maspoka i liberalizma*, 222-23. For example, Ambassador Dobriovje Vidić was stopped by the Soviet police on his way to Kaluga on 17 August 1968. He was kept for forty minutes without explanation and then ordered to return to Moscow. Yugoslav journalists in Moscow were asked to stop reporting on 23 August. KPR, I-2, 63/J:1107-12, Br.kutije 82, conversation between Babić and Benediktov, 24 August 1968.

80. KPR, I-2, 63/J:1107-12, Br.kutije 82, bulletin on the developments in the ČSSR, br.1, 24 August 1968.

81. PRO, PREM 2638 (Foreign Policy), 5 September 1968.

82. PRO, PREM 2638 (Foreign Policy), 31 August 1968.

83. PRO, FCO 46/262, "Chiefs of Staff Committee, Defense Policy Staff, Allied Reactions to Possible Soviet Moves in Eastern Europe," 27 August 1968.

84. PRO, FCO 28/560, "Yugoslavia: Defense: Security against External Aggression," 15 October 1968.

85. PRO, FCO 28/559, Downing Street 10, 6 September 1968 and PREM 2638 (Foreign Policy), 5 October 1968.

86. PRO, FCO 28/559, 5 October 1968.

87. PRO, FCO, 28/559, 23 September 1968

88. PRO, FCO 28/560, "Yugoslavia: Defense: Security against External Aggression," 15 October 1968.

89. PRO, FCO 49/240, "Permanent Undersecretary's Planning Committee: Long-term Prospects for East-West Relations after the Czechoslovak Crisis."

90. PRO, FCO 49/240, "Permanent Undersecretary's Planning Committee." "In the light of all the trends of the last eighteen months or so it seems clear that the main objective of the Soviet leaders will be the maintenance of their own model for Communism in the Soviet Union itself and in Eastern Europe. They will prefer to do so without embroiling themselves in a major quarrel with the West."

91. Charles Gati, *Failed Illusions: Moscow, Washington, Budapest, and the 1956 Hungarian Revolt* (Washington, DC: Woodrow Wilson Center/Stanford University Press, 2006), 70. Although there were some similarities between Yugoslavia and Albania, Tirana represents another, and different, Stalinist aberration.

92. Schwartz, *Lyndon Johnson and Europe*, 214.

93. Gati, *Failed Illusions*, 6. That line was especially visible vis-à-vis Hungary in 1956.

94. Schwartz, *Lyndon Johnson and Europe*, 215. As written in Jaromir Navratil et al., *The Prague Spring, 1968* (Budapest: CEU, 1998). For different view, see, for example, Andrew and Mitrokhin, *Mitrokhin Archive*, 322–41.

95. Paulin Kola, *The Search for Greater Albania* (London: Hurst, 2003), 128–32.

96. PRO, FCO, "Yugoslav/Albanian Relations" (UK Ambassador Julian Bullard i Jakša Petrić, assistant state secretary at the Foreign Ministry), 27 January 1971; AJ 507, III/136, stenographic notes of the XIII joint meeting of the presidencies of the Executive Committee and the presidency of the CK SKJ, 14 November 1968.

97. PRO, FCO 28/2122, "Yugoslav/Albanian Relations," 21 May 1971; Crampton, *The Balkans*, 162–63.

98. Vuković, *Od deformacija SDB do maspoka i liberalizma*, 546.

99. Rendulić, *General Avnojske Jugoslavije*, 283, 288–89; Vuković, *Od deformacija SDB do maspoka i liberalizma*, 526, 542.

100. AJ, 507, III/135, initiative of Ethiopia for an extraordinary conference on the ČSSR, 28 August 1968.

101. AJ, 507, III/135, "Position of the Government of United Arab Republic—Excerpts of Our Chargé in Cairo with the Undersecretary in the Ministry of Foreign Affairs," UAR, 28 August 1968.

102. RGANI, F. 3, op. 72, d. 215, pp. 50–52, Politburo decision of the CC CPSU P 106 (48), "To all Soviet ambassadors, to the Soviet representative in Wellington, to all representatives of the USSR at international organizations," 23 October 1968, reprinted in Karner et al., *Dokumente*, #171.

103. KPR I-2; 54/j:1050–55; Br. kutije 73, note on the meeting of the leaders of the KP and heads of states or governments of the socialist countries held in Moscow on 9–10 June 1967, 91. Mandić, *Tito u dijalogu sa svijetom*, 293–444; Vjekoslav Cvrlje, *Vatikanska diplomacija: Pokoncilski Vatikan u međunarodnom odnosima* (Zagreb: Školska knjiga/Kršćanska sadašnjost, 1992), 116–26.

104. Mandić, *Tito u dijalogu sa svijetom*, 293–444; Vjekoslav Cvrlje, *Vatikanska diplomacija: Pokoncilski Vatikan u međunarodnom odnosima* (Zagreb: Školska knjiga/ Kršćanska sadašnjost, 1992), 116–26.

105. Mandić, *Tito u dijalogu sa svijetom*, 173.

106. AJ 507, III/135, authorized stenographic notes from the XII joint meeting of the presidencies of the Executive Committee and the presidency of the CK SKJ, 2 September 1968.

107. The change in the defense doctrine turned out to be essential for the break up of Yugoslavia two decades later. However, similar ideas with the armed people were adopted in Albania and Romania at the same time. Crampton, *The Balkans*, 162. Mark Kramer, in his paper "The Soviet-Romanian Split and the Crisis with Czechoslovakia: Context, Reverberations and Fallout," presented at the conference in Dobiacco, Italy (26–28 September 2002), talked of the doctrine of "Total People's War for the Defense of the Homeland."

108. CIA intelligence report, 20 November 1970. Dabčević-Kučar, *'71-hrvatski snovi i stvarnost*, 600.

109. See Dabčević-Kučar, *'71-hrvatski snovi i stvarnost*.

18

Austria and the End of the Prague Spring: Neutrality in the Crucible?

Stefan Karner and Peter Ruggenthaler

The situation with which Austria found itself confronted in 1968 recalled in an uncanny way the one that had prevailed after the crushing of the Hungarian uprising. Even though the Soviet Union had respected Austria's neutral status in 1956, fears arose again in 1968 that the invasion of the Warsaw Pact troops might not be limited to Czechoslovakia and could spill over to Yugoslavia and Romania, with collateral damage being inflicted on Austria. It became obvious again how close Austria was to the fault lines created by the Cold War. The military invasion of Czechoslovakia took place against a political and economic backdrop that was characterized in Austria by the country's increasingly successful efforts to intensify its economic contacts with Comecon countries. These efforts were due in part to the way Austria's negotiations for membership in the European Economic Community (EEC) developed or rather failed to develop: Rome blocked any progress because of the persistent South Tyrolean problem. Central and Eastern Europe played an increasingly important role in the economic policy of the Austrian federal government. On 1 June 1968, Austria became the first Western country to clinch a long-term deal with the Soviet Union regarding gas supplies; a pipeline via Bratislava was scheduled to come online on 1 September 1968 and to pump natural gas to Austria and the West across the Iron Curtain, which had shown its first signs of being lifted during the "Prague Spring." The invasion of the Warsaw Pact troops put the policies of détente and rapprochement to the test and awakened in Austria memories of the country's Soviet occupation (1945–1955).[1] At the same time, Austria had to fulfill its self-imposed duties of playing host to Czechoslovak refugees and informing the world via its media about the events in the neighboring country. This was the backdrop for Austria's policies in 1968.

At 7 a.m. on 21 August 1968, a few hours after the troops of the "Warsaw Five" had invaded Czechoslovakia, Josef Klaus, Austria's federal chancellor at the head of an ÖVP single-party government since 1966, issued a communiqué on the tragic events that were unfolding in the country with which Austria shares a border in the north and northeast. Klaus lost no time; in the very first sentence, he underlined Austria's commitment to a policy of neutrality and independence, which rightly served as the basis of "the trust in Austria of all the four signatories of the State Treaty as well as . . . of the trust of its neighbors."[2] The chancellor went on to say that the country was "far from indifferent to the fate of other nations and peoples." These words were attuned almost perfectly to the occasion. On one hand, Klaus had to bear in mind, in the interest of his country, that sending a wrong signal or striking—in Moscow's ears—a wrong note might cause the crisis to leap over Austria's border; on the other, his words were an unambiguous token of empathy with the Czechoslovak people, even though they stopped short of condemning the invasion as such.

A few hours later, at 12:30 p.m., the Soviet ambassador in Vienna, Boris F. Podtserob,[3] called on the chancellor in his capacity of representative of the Soviet government in Austria to explain the reasons for the invasion of Czechoslovakia by Warsaw Pact troops.[4] The ambassador stated that the turn events had recently taken in Czechoslovakia had impinged on "vital interests of the Soviet Union" and "the threat to the construction of the Czechoslovak state jeopardized at the same time the principles of European peace and international security." Using the Kremlin's official diction, the ambassador interpreted the invasion as no more than the Soviet reaction to the calls for help that had come from Czechoslovak comrades loyal to Moscow.[5] Podtserob ended his remarks to the Austrian chancellor with the assurance that the invasion of Czechoslovakia was not going to reflect adversely on Soviet-Austrian relations. Podtserob said:

> We want the Chancellor to be quite clear about what is happening. Our actions are not directed against any state and do not violate any state interests. They are dictated solely by the desire to safeguard peace in the face of a dangerous rise in tensions that left the Socialist countries with no alternative. We take it for granted that these events will not in any way damage Soviet-Austrian relations, whose cultivation continues to be of great importance to the Soviet government.[6]

The Austrian federal chancellor responded to this by saying that "Austria was committed to unambiguously abiding by its policy of neutrality, as it had been in the past; however, Austrians were not indifferent to the fate of their neighbors."[7] Klaus went on to say:

On the basis of reports by the Federal Chancellor and the Federal Minister for Foreign Affairs, the Federal Government has formulated a declaration in an extraordinary session of the Council of Ministers that it will strictly observe the commitment to neutrality it entered into of its own accord in 1955. In the same manner the Austrian government will observe its obligations in the area of asylum law, as it has always done.[8]

Klaus also pointed out that Austria "had no intention of interfering in the internal affairs of other sovereign nations, for the simple reason that we ourselves would have to reject most categorically any such attempt, should it be forthcoming. As a small neutral country, Austria is particularly sensitive in matters concerning sovereignty and non-interference."[9] Klaus asked Podtserob to make sure Austrian tourists were free to leave Czechoslovakia as they saw fit and also brought the border violations by Soviet aircraft to the ambassador's attention without, however, protesting them. Podtserob entered the following note in his official log:

During last night and this morning there were several incidents in which Soviet aircraft and helicopters violated Austrian airspace in a minor way. The Chancellor suggested that there were technical reasons for these incidents and he was trying to prevent these violations from being made public. He was, however, quick to modify this statement by adding that this was rather difficult to do, given the constraints imposed by democracy. He urged the Soviet Military Command to make sure such violations did not occur again.

The Soviet ambassador assured Klaus that "his statement" would duly be passed on to the Soviet government and expressed his regret at the violation of Austria's airspace by Soviet forces. He added "that these incidents had not been intentional." At the end of the fifteen-minute conversation, the Soviet ambassador asked the head of the Austrian government to discourage potentially violent demonstrations outside the offices of Soviet diplomats, which Klaus agreed to do.[10]

Shortly afterwards, the Council of Ministers was convened for another extraordinary session at the Chancellery,[11] in which Klaus informed the members of his government about his meeting with the Soviet ambassador.[12] This meant that within hours after the invasion it was clear that the events in Czechoslovakia were not going to affect Austria directly. The Kremlin was not going to call the country's neutrality into question; there was no immediate danger. During the day, several more violations of Austria's airspace occurred; over the following days, the incursions began increasingly to look like reconnaissance flights.[13] On the evening of 21 August, Minister for Foreign Affairs Kurt Waldheim asked the Soviet ambassador to call on him. He, too, pointed out the violations of Austrian airspace but, like Klaus before him, did not enter a formal protest. Speaking in the name of Austria's federal government, Waldheim expressed "his concern" at the incidents and requested that "the Soviet side undertake all measures to prevent future violations of Austria's borders." If there were no end to the incursions, which Waldheim also presumed to be due to "technical reasons," the Austrian government would be forced to lodge a formal protest.[14] Ambassador Podtserob assured Waldheim that planning did not include further incursions. Waldheim for his part informed Moscow's representative "that according to a decision taken by the Austrian government today" there would be "a troop redeployment with a view to strengthening the garrisons north of the Danube."[15] Waldheim was astonishingly frank in explaining the rationale behind this decision: "This redeployment of troops did not mean that troops were amassed near the border; the sole objective was to reassure the population." Podtserob took note of Waldheim's statement and assured him that Moscow would be duly informed.[16]

Waldheim also cautiously signaled to the Soviet ambassador the Austrian government's lack of information on the actual position of the Czech government because contradictory statements were emerging from Prague. Podtserob pointed out that official statements were often made by people who were not authorized to do so.[17] In the evening, the Czechoslovak ambassador, Pavel Novotný, called on Waldheim and informed the Austrian minister for foreign affairs of the positions of the Central Committee of the Communist Party of Czechoslovakia and of the Presidium of the National Assembly. Novotný subsequently reported to Prague that "the Austrian population" had expressed "concern and sympathy for us in general terms."[18]

In an Austrian Television (ORF) evening news bulletin, Federal Chancellor Klaus stated once again that "the State Treaty and the Neutrality Law . . . are the unalterable foundations on which our state rests" and that "we . . . will not meddle in the internal affairs of other states."[19] This was the end to an eventful day that had had a hectic beginning for the Austrian federal government. It was the holiday season, and the federal chancellor had been staying at his house in Wolfpassing, which was not even connected to the telephone network. The armed forces, meanwhile, followed a coordinated contingency plan that had already been worked out on 23 July together with the Ministry for the Interior and were ready for deployment within hours; the first meeting at the Chancellery did not start until 7:45.[20]

"A SERIOUS SETBACK FOR DÉTENTE": WHAT ELSE?

On the morning of 22 August, Minister for Foreign Affairs Waldheim gave the Austrian Press Agency an assessment of events in Czechoslovakia. He referred to what the federal chancellor had already said on the subject and explained:

The Austrian people have reacted to events in Czechoslovakia with dismay. Developments over the past few weeks have been followed with a great deal of concern, and we had hoped it would be possible to settle differences at the negotiation table. We deeply regret that this has come to naught—and we regret this all the more since the Austrian government has always advocated the peaceful development of interstate relations and will continue to do so. The latest events certainly constitute a ~~serious~~ setback[21] for the process of détente, which we have always upheld and which has fortunately[22] made such progress over the last few years. It is still too early to say how the situation will develop from here. All we can do is to hope that a normalization that takes into account the wishes of the long-suffering population[23] will take place in our neighboring country, which we feel connected to by untold ties of friendship and blood.

On the evening of the same day, Federal Chancellor Klaus addressed via TV the Austrian people with remarks made in a similar vein. Klaus assured his audience that the government had taken measures that "reflect our unique vital interests as a permanently neutral state." In more concrete terms, he mentioned stepping up the protection of the borders and preparations for the reception and accommodation of refugees, the need for which was a distinct possibility. Klaus criticized the invasion of Czechoslovakia indirectly as a "blow to the policy of détente of the last few years, to peaceful coexistence, and to the development of amicable relations between the peoples of Europe." He wound up by expressing the hope that "all possibilities will be used that may exist even at this late hour in order to bring about a normalization of the situation in Czechoslovakia."[24]

FLIGHT TO AUSTRIA

As opposed to Hungary in 1956, the Warsaw Pact troops had received orders this time not to prevent people from leaving Czechoslovakia. On 18 August, Leonid Brezhnev told the Communist leaders of the "fraternal states" not to stop "defectors wishing to depart for the West. We herd these renegades together, and then we don't know what to do with them. Should we sentence them to imprisonment, hang them, or let them go? After all, no upright guys will want to flee anywhere and if they're counterrevolutionaries, let them go."[25]

When a large number of Czechs turned up at the Austrian embassy on the morning after the invasion to apply for visas, the Ministry for Foreign Affairs in Vienna was contacted for guidelines. A day later, on 22 August, a directive arrived from the Ministry of the Interior: "The embassy building is to be locked . . . and access to be granted only to Austrian passport holders. Czechoslovak citizens who are inside the building at this stage are to be informed that the embassy is reserved for the exclusive use by Austrians, and they are to be persuaded to leave the building of their own accord."[26] When Austrian Ambassador Rudolf Kirchschläger returned to Prague on 22 August, he decided to ignore this order: "I must confess that I would end up in the most dreadful moral quandary if I were to carry out this directive." When a cache of 10,000 blank ČSSR passports was found, another security directive arrived from Vienna on 25 August that remained similarly unheeded: no more visas for Czech passport holders. Kirchschläger cabled to Vienna on 30 August: "There is widespread apprehension and despair here, which is reflected in the rising number of applications for visas: 2,006 have been issued today and the number is still rising." The number of refugees was to rise to 208,000 by the end of 1968.

After 30 August, the number of refugees was augmented by the 50,000 or so Slovak and Czech holidaymakers who had been vacationing on the shores of the Adriatic or the Black Sea and were caught unawares by the invasion. The wife of Czech leader Alexander Dubček, who was one of them, was offered protection by President Josip Broz Tito of Yugoslavia, which she declined.[27]

Vienna and Lower Austria bore the brunt of coping with the influx of refugees with help from the United Nations (UN). According to the UN High Commissioner for Refugees, approximately 70,000 Czechoslovak citizens were in Austria between 26 August and 6 September, most of whom were refugees.[28] Of these, 53,314 were put up in temporary housing, 1,650 in private homes, 5,074 in hotels in Vienna, and another 10,737 outside of Vienna, mostly in Lower Austria. The majority of refugees were young, talented, and well educated. Quite a few decided in the end to remain in Austria, including people of the caliber of Karel Krautgartner, Zdeněk Mlynář, and Pavel Kohout.

VIOLATIONS OF AIRSPACE AND NO END IN SIGHT

No end was yet in sight for the violations of Austria's borders. In the first days after the invasion of Czechoslovakia, several incidents took place. On 23 August, a Soviet helicopter gunship landed near Unterretzbach, and two Soviet jets penetrated approximately ten kilometers into Austrian airspace near Altnagelberg. Yet these and other comparable incidents still failed to draw protests from the Austrian government. In the manner that had already become almost a routine, the Soviet ambassador was, in his own words, "invited" to the Austrian Foreign Ministry.[29] That day, at 10:45 a.m., the Foreign Ministry general secretary, Wilfried Platzer, acting at Waldheim's behest, handed the Soviet diplomat a list of the border incidents. He explicitly stated that "this was not to be interpreted as a note"; the Austrian purpose was to inform the Soviets as to the precise timing and location of the incidents.[30] Podtserob once again expressed "regret at the violations of Austria's borders," adding "that these were not intentional." He renewed his assurance to "inform Moscow so that adequate measures would be taken."[31] In the further course of the meeting, the Soviet diplomat also mentioned the Austrian chancellor's televised address of the previous night. He asked Platzer whether it was the chancellor's intention "to call Austria's policy of neutrality into doubt."[32] In his reply, Platzer averred that "reducing tensions and enhancing security and cooperation in Europe were longstanding political objectives of the Austrian government" and "that Austria is committed to a policy of neutrality and determined not to be deflected from this course." Platzer also assured Podtserob that he was going to discuss this issue with Chancellor Klaus. At the end of the conversation, Platzer thanked Podtserob for the fact that Austrians were free to leave Czechoslovakia without permission or hindrance and that Austria's ambassador to the Czechoslovak Socialist Republic (ČSSR), Rudolf Kirchschläger, had likewise been enabled to return safely to Prague by car.[33]

After this meeting between Ambassador Podtserob and General Secretary Platzer, a certain amount of hectic activism seems to have taken hold of the Ballhausplatz. Foreign Minister Waldheim repeatedly tried in vain to reach the Soviet ambassador on the phone. His failure was due to the fact that the diplomat had left the meeting at the Foreign Ministry to attend a function at the Romanian embassy on the occasion of Romania's National Day. On his return to the Soviet embassy, Podtserob was informed of Waldheim's urgent wish to speak to him. In the phone call that followed, Waldheim once more underscored the statements made by Chancellor Klaus in his televised address and Platzer's assurances as to Austria's commitment to neutrality. Waldheim added that Austria was going to "adhere to its course of neutrality and would not consider other options under any circumstances." The Austrian Foreign Minister made it explicitly clear that his statement was official in character.[34]

In this way, positions were made quite clear immediately after the invasion of Czechoslovakia. Moscow had informed Vienna of the reasons that had motivated it to make this move and had given assurances that Austria was not going to be affected by it in any way. Vienna, in turn, had explicitly repeated its commitment to a strict course of neutrality several times vis-à-vis the Soviet Union in the days following the invasion of Czechoslovakia.

VIENNA LODGES A PROTEST AFTER ALL: DIPLOMATIC SPARRING WITH CONSEQUENCES?

All the clarifying talks with the Soviet ambassador notwithstanding, the Austrian government mandated its envoy to Moscow, Walter Wodak, on the same day, 23 August, "to register formal protest with the Foreign Ministry on account of repeated violations of Austrian sovereignty."[35] It is said to have taken Wodak three days before he was granted an appointment at the Soviet Foreign Ministry. Waldheim was also mandated to protest formally on behalf of the federal government to the Soviet ambassador, but, as Waldheim put it in an interview later, the latter "did not turn up at my office for three days—under the pretext of having fallen ill."[36] For this reason, the official protest was not entered until 26 August. The Soviet Foreign Ministry representative is said to have expressed regret at the border incidents and to have asserted that care would be taken "to prevent a repetition of such incidents."[37]

Three days later, the tone on the part of the Soviet embassy became much more direct. In a démarche made by the Soviet embassy counselor, the diplomat conceded on one hand that "the Soviet Union was gratified to take note of the official statements issued by the Austrian federal government" but criticized the fact that "the Austrian press as well as radio and TV had shown themselves to be partisan in a thoroughly non-objective and tendentious manner, which was incompatible with the standards of a neutral country. They had in fact become mouthpieces of the counterrevolution in the ČSSR."[38] Ambassador Podtserob had been informed two days before by the president of Parliament, Alfred Maleta, that "there [was] going to be a meeting involving the Federal Chancellor, the Vice-Chancellor, the Minister for the Interior, and [ORF] Program Director Gerd Bacher." The Soviet envoy conveyed to the Ballhausplatz that the Soviet Union was aware of the concept of freedom of the press; at the same time he made it clear, if almost apologetically, how important it was for the Austrian government to keep an eye on the "line taken by the mass media."[39]

The Ballhausplatz reached the conclusion that the démarche was not meant "as a protest against Austria's state authorities" and that it was obvious that the Soviet side "had been intent from the start to avoid any hostility or acrimony in their dealings with Austrian authorities." This was also the reason why Austria had deliberately waived the opportunity to focus on negative reports on Austria that were appearing in the Soviet press.[40]

In the afternoon of the same day, Kurt Waldheim invited the Soviet ambassador to the Foreign Ministry, where they discussed a recent *Literaturnaya Gazeta* article in which Austria was accused of turning a blind eye to the presence of North Atlantic Treaty Organization special commandos on its territory.[41] Waldheim had been alerted to the article only a few days before by the U.S. ambassador.[42] He assured Podtserob once more that Austria was not tolerating any activities on its soil that were incompatible with its neutrality. Austria, as Waldheim told the diplomat, "appreciated friendly relations with the Soviet Union very much and was doing its utmost to keep them from being tarnished."[43] In the conversation he repeatedly queried the purpose of the *Literaturnaya Gazeta* article. Podtserob replied that the journal apparently had contact to credible sources and added that the *Gazeta* was published by the Union of Soviet Writers, which was neither the mouthpiece of a party organization, nor of any other state institution of the USSR. As opposed to reports in Austria's media on the Soviet Union, the article in question had been "a very moderate reaction." Waldheim subsequently repeatedly clapped his hands together and remarked that its freedom made the press immune against government influence. Off the record, he confided to the Soviet ambassador "that he had repeatedly talked to newspaper editors . . . and had instructed them to take into account in their reports on events in Czechoslovakia the limits imposed by Austria's neutrality. These people, however, were not accountable to the Austrian government; they were *de facto* independent." Waldheim agreed with Podtserob "that the actually existing freedom of the press had limits, which were imposed by Austria's obligations resulting from the State Treaty." It is not surprising that the Soviet sources contain no clues as to whether the Soviet ambassador actually submitted an apology to Waldheim for the conduct of the Soviet government.[44]

VIENNA AS A SECRET SERVICE HUB

The Soviet Committee for State Security (KGB) leveled a great number of charges against Austria in 1968: twenty-two radio transmitters, arms, and money had been smuggled into Czechoslovakia from Austria, sometimes in ambulances; German and U.S. elite commandos (Green Berets) had stopped off at Salzburg's Schwarzenberg Barracks before being smuggled into the ČSSR in the guise of tourists; 500 Austrian plainclothes policemen were active in Czechoslovakia; Austrian agents had infiltrated the ČSSR People's Army; Western intelligence services had made Vienna their base for operations directed against the Eastern Bloc; since the Prague reformers opened the borders with the Federal Republic of Germany (FRG) and Austria, there was a daily influx of up to 40,000 so-called tourists; there had been more than 370,000 in spring 1968, many of whom, according to an angry Brezhnev, undertook liaison missions.[45]

The KGB took for granted the active role played by the Austrian secret service in countermeasures against the invasion of the ČSSR. From the end of World War II, Eastern and Western secret services had been using Austria as a hub for their operations; in 1968, there was a significant increase in their activities, notably on the part of the KGB, which was tracking and observing more and more Austrians. A case in point is Simon Wiesenthal, who had blown the cover of several ex-Nazis working in German Democratic Republic (GDR) government agencies. The Soviet news agency TASS claimed that the Austrian military secret service was active, primarily against the ČSSR. These claims were rebutted by Federal Chancellor Klaus and Foreign Minister Waldheim.[46]

How important Vienna was as a secret-service hub in 1968, particularly for Eastern secret services, is demonstrated by the high degree of infiltration of Austria's secret services.[47] Forty-seven members of the *Staatspolizei* were suspected of engaging in espionage on behalf of foreign secret services, and many arrests led to convictions. The first to be arrested were Josef A., Johann A., and Norbert K. Josef A., an editor of the Federal Press Agency, had been recruited in Vienna by a Prague secret service officer and correspondent of the ČSSR news agency ČTK. Private detective Johann A., a former civil servant, had passed on the records of the interrogations of Czechoslovak refugees to a Communist Party organization. All three were sentenced to long terms of imprisonment. The same was true of the press spokesman for the minister of the Interior Franz Soronics, Alois E., who had spied both for the German *Bundesnachrichtendienst* and for the Czechoslovak secret service. A parliamentary commission of inquiry was set up to shed light on his connections, and he was sentenced to three and a half years of hard labor in 1969.

Much information came from a very dubious source: Major Ladislav Bittman, employed at the Czechoslovak embassy in Vienna since 1966 and formerly of the disinformation department of the ČSSR secret service.[48] Many of Bittman's pieces of information, which were taken at face value in 1968, turned out to be false. On 7 September 1968, for instance, more than a fortnight after the invasion, the head of the Military Secret Service, Peterlunger, informed Federal Chancellor Klaus on the basis of information passed on by Bittman on the intention of the Soviet Army to blockade the Austrian-Czechoslovak border in order to dislodge armed ČSSR troops and push them onto Austrian territory. An outbreak of hostilities was to serve as a pretext for the occupation of eastern Austria. The so-called Polarka plans, which were supposed to serve the Soviet army as it crossed eastern Austria en route to Yugoslavia, also belonged under the heading *"Deza"* (disinformation).

MOSCOW CHARGES AUSTRIA WITH BREACHING ITS NEUTRALITY

On 31 August 1968, the Soviet ambassador paid a call on Josef Klaus at his country refuge in Wolfpassing near Vienna in order to hand him a note from the Soviet government. The note repeated that the invasion of Czechoslovakia was "an act of fraternal help to the Czechoslovak people that would have suffered no delay" and that the intervention was not directed against any other state.[49] The Soviet envoy informed Klaus on the conclusion of the "negotiations" a few days earlier between the government delegations of Czechoslovakia and the Soviet Union. After a lengthy explanation of the agreement achieved on the "normalization" of the situation in Czechoslovakia, the Soviet envoy launched into an open criticism of Austria. Previously, as we have already seen, it was reporting in the Austrian media that had provoked Soviet criticism; now Podtserob openly accused the Austrian government of having breached the country's policy of neutrality. The fact that "Austrian TV, which was state controlled, as well as the Austrian press" had become vehicles of an anti-Soviet and antisocialist position was in "direct and open contrast to Austria's status as a neutral country. . . . This could not but damage Austria's foreign policy."[50] The Soviet ambassador, however, also stressed that the USSR had taken note of Austria's repeated official statements affirming its neutrality and pointed out that it was in Austria's interest "that the policy of European states be built on the unshakable acceptance of existing borders in Europe and the rejection of attempts to undermine the principles of European security." Klaus affirmed again in his reply that Austria was irrevocably committed to its neutrality policy. "Having said that," Klaus added, "it is equally clear that the Austrian government cannot remain indifferent to the fate of a neighboring country that Austrians feel close to on account of historical and kinship grounds. This is the reason why Austria, motivated by purely humanitarian considerations, has provided material help to those Czechoslovaks who are at present on Austrian soil due to the recent developments."

The federal chancellor rebutted the Soviet ambassador's charge that the press was under the control of the government, saying that "in view of the legal situation . . . the government . . . was unable to control the press," despite the fact that he had recently been holding "almost daily meetings with the heads of radio and TV" in order to "instruct them to take the government's neutral position as the basis from which to report on events in Czechoslovakia." Klaus committed himself to continuing to exert this kind of influence on the media and shared with the Soviet ambassador the story of how he himself had become the butt of criticism in a recent *Presse* editorial, even though he had been on friendly terms with the writer of the article for twenty years. The federal chancellor also addressed the topic of Soviet press reports on Austria—without explicitly mentioning the *Literaturnaya Gazeta* article—and called them devoid of any factual basis.

Klaus explicitly mentioned the Soviet charges that Austria had supported "counterrevolutionary forces" in the ČSSR with radio transmitter stations and stated emphatically "that the government was not aware of any actions whatsoever that might have infringed Austria's neutrality and the State Treaty." The Soviet ambassador, who had been prepared for this reply as part of his briefing by the Politburo of the Central Committee (CC) of the Communist Party of the Soviet Union (*Kommunisticheskaya Partiya Sovetskogo Soyuza* or CPSU), was quick to use this cue and suggested that the Austrian government might possibly "not be aware of such developments even though they did exist." There might, after all, be "dishonest individuals among Austrian customs officials."[51] Klaus took this as a facetious remark.[52]

Generally speaking, the Soviet ambassador's call on Chancellor Klaus fell short of a downright "protest" on the part of Moscow against the course taken by the Austrian government. On the previous day, the Moscow Politburo had charged Soviet ambassadors all over the world to communicate clearly the Soviet point of view "regarding the latest developments centering on Czechoslovakia." Some indication of how important it was in Moscow's eyes that Austria should maintain its neutral position in 1968 derives from the fact that in the distribution schedule of this brief, which comprised dozens of countries, Austria ranked in fifth place, after the United States, France, Great Britain, and West Germany.[53]

NO DAMAGE DONE TO SOVIET-AUSTRIAN RELATIONS

Austria's avowals of intending to keep to a strictly neutral course amounted to more than empty words during the following weeks. At the UN Conference of Nuclear-Free States in Geneva, Waldheim reiterated on 6 September 1968 that "Austria has always asserted its special interest in the creation of a climate of détente and international cooperation that is free from the dangers of armed conflict and confrontation." "Austria," Waldheim went on to say, "deplores any acts of violence as they jeopardize the order which is the foundation of security for all of us. We condemn these acts in the most categorical manner."[54] Diplomatic words like these were apt to meet with all around approval. In the West, they could be interpreted as a condemnation of the invasion of Czechoslovakia, even though Waldheim was not explicitly referring to the Czechoslovak crisis, and there was no need for Moscow to feel incriminated since the Soviet government was painting the invasion as a means of enhancing security in Europe. A "counterrevolutionary" victory would have endangered that security by impinging on the USSR's vital interests. Waldheim was already positioning himself for the role of UN secretary-general, the post that he assumed on 1 January 1972, and was able in this manner to grow in stature in the Kremlin's eyes. That Waldheim managed in this crucial phase of Austrian foreign politics to build a good relationship with the Soviets without having much explicit knowledge of internal Soviet deliberations that have only recently become apparent and intuitively to steer the correct course—correct also in light of the principles of Austrian neutrality which were not even hammered out yet—is evidenced by the confidential talk he had with the Soviet ambassador on 28 September, immediately before his trip to Yugoslavia as a member of the entourage of Federal President Franz Jonas.[55] Waldheim explained to Podtserob that the forthcoming visit was a purely ceremonial one and only served for Vienna to reciprocate Tito's visit.[56] Podtserob, in turn, professed that while the peoples of the USSR entertained special feelings for the peoples of Yugoslavia on account of the war in which they had fought side by side against National Socialism and while Moscow was interested in good relations with Belgrade, these feelings only made sense on a basis of reciprocity. Waldheim, appearing immediately to have spotted a role for himself as a mediator, underlined the significance of his partner's utterances, particularly because "rumors were being circulated by the media as regards Soviet military measures against Yugoslavia."[57] The Soviet ambassador disclaimed any such rumors. He and Waldheim agreed that it must be Yugoslavia that was spreading such rumors. Waldheim also mentioned the report circulated by the Deutsche Presse Agentur about a hypothetical demand put forward by Moscow to be granted the right to march through Austria to Yugoslavia. He claimed he had denied the existence of such a demand in the strongest of terms, which had even provoked the expression of a certain uneasiness toward him on the part of several West German politicians.

The extremely conciliatory course that Waldheim opted for in his encounter with the Soviet ambassador made the latter remark that the reporting on developments in Czechoslovakia in Austrian media, above all in the ORF, had become less partisan.[58] The state visit of the Soviet minister for the gas industry, Aleksei Kortunov, in Austria had contributed noticeably to a consolidation of Soviet-Austrian relations.[59] Podtserob thanked Waldheim for the hospitality with which Minister Kortunov and his entourage had been met in Austria and "for the amicable atmosphere." Waldheim replied by expressing the hope that it would be possible to continue intensifying the economic ties between Austria and the Soviet Union, and somewhat bluntly pointed out to the Soviet diplomat that such a development might strengthen the position of the Austrian government, which was facing increasing pressure to secure the country's accession to the European Communities (EC) at the earliest possible date.[60] According to the ambassador's notes, Waldheim said, "Some people vociferously complain that the end of Austria's industry is imminent in case the country does not join the EC. The development of economic ties with the Soviet Union and other Eastern European countries would deal a blow to these critics." In this way, Waldheim clearly conveyed the impression to Moscow that EC accession was not a top priority of the Austrian government for the time being and that, as far as the economy was concerned, Austria was prepared to cooperate more closely with Eastern Europe.[61] Finally Waldheim also addressed the issue of South

Tyrol and informed the ambassador of the latest developments. He did so presumably in the hope that the Soviet Union's position on this issue might change one day. Having pointed out that the South Tyrol issue was, after all, a product of World War I, he added that Italy had been allotted South Tyrol for strategic reasons ("The Brenner Pass is now in Italian hands"). Podtserob asserted that the Soviet Union did not want "this controversy to be exploited for objectives that were at odds with the interests of peace in Europe."[62] In this way, the postponement of the trip to the Soviet Union of the president of the Austrian Parliament, Alfred Maleta, was Austria's only concrete reaction to the invasion of Czechoslovakia.[63] Even accusations against Austria in KGB reports that look bizarre in retrospect and that surfaced in part in the "White Book" published in the autumn of 1968 remained without impact on the bilateral level.[64]

CONCLUSION

In his study on the foreign policy of Austria's Second Republic, Michael Gehler concludes that the hesitant, tactically motivated way in which the Austrian government reacted to the invasion of Czechoslovakia led to a sense of bewilderment in the population and ultimately to a loss of stature for the Klaus government. Whether Austria's politicians really felt out of their depth is another matter. Yet Gehler is no doubt right when he asks whether history would have taken a different course if the Austrian government had managed to appear more sure of itself and more resolute.[65]

Austria's cautiousness with regard to the invasion of the troops of the Warsaw Pact's pro-interventionist coalition may ultimately be explained by the absence of a U.S. security guarantee. In 1956, just such an explicit guarantee had existed. At that time, Washington would not have tolerated an infringement of Austrian sovereignty. In the crucial days of August 1968, no such guarantee materialized, presumably because the U.S. government took it for granted that the Warsaw Pact military action was going to remain confined to Czechoslovakia. Austrian diplomats are said to have lobbied for a U.S. guarantee; it is unlikely, however, that in this matter they got much support from the foreign minister. The assessment of the newly created situation that Waldheim made was a sober and unexcited one, and he attempted to make the most of it for Austria. The crisis in Hungary, which occurred barely a year after Austria declared everlasting neutrality, tested that neutrality to the full on the stage of world politics. In 1968, the situation was entirely different. Not only was Austria's interpretation of neutrality "more comprehensive and more consistent than in 1956," but the country in general and the Klaus government in particular were pursuing their own interests.[66] The intensive shuttle diplomacy between Austria and the countries of the Eastern Bloc was beginning to bear fruit, which exposed the government to opposition criticism for its "Eastern bias." From a purely economic perspective, Austria could easily have ended up in a cul-de-sac if it had behaved differently toward Moscow. Closing the gap that separated the country from accession to the EC remained a dubious undertaking on account of the issue of South Tyrol.

Against this backdrop, it is understandable that in November 1968 Waldheim, in a diplomatically brilliant, indirect manner, rebutted in Brussels the statement of U.S. secretary of state Dean Rusk that Austria and Yugoslavia touched on U.S. security interests. He did so by pointing out that safeguarding Austrian independence and territorial integrity was an obligation shared by all four signatories of the State Treaty. Waldheim's words were ultimately greeted with approval in the Soviet press.[67]

After the Warsaw Pact invasion of 1968, Austria followed lines similar to those of the major powers in its reactions. Priority was given to avoiding anything that might provoke the "Russian bear." For this reason, the army was stationed thirty kilometers away from the Austrian border, and units that had originally been deployed in the immediate vicinity of the border were pulled back to avoid the outbreak of border-related hostilities of the kind that had led to the killing of a Soviet soldier during the Hungarian crisis in 1956.

Austria's policies were politically, if not ideologically, consistent with its neutral status. The Czech and Slovak reformers enjoyed a tremendous reputation in Austria, which was at least partly the result of the reports on Austrian television.

In 1968, most Austrians viewed Czechoslovakia as a country that was being deprived of its legitimate freedom; they were severely criticized for this view by the Soviets. There were also allegations that Austria had veered from its course as a neutral country. These allegations were a cause for considerable concern, especially for people in the gas industry. Would the Soviets still consider themselves bound by their contract to supply Austria with natural gas? They would. On 1 September 1968, gas deliveries started via a pipeline that pierced the Iron Curtain. What had looked like a test of Austria's neutrality in the crucible of the Cold War left behind no more than a mild sense of irritation, which evaporated in no time.

NOTES

Translated from German into English by Otmar Binder, Vienna.

1. For further information on the Soviet occupation of Austria, see *Die Rote Armee in Österreich: Sowjetische Besatzung 1945–1955*, vol. 1, *Beiträge*, vol. 2, *Dokumente*, ed. Stefan Karner et al., Veröffentlichungen des Ludwig Boltzmann-Instituts für Kriegsfolgen-Forschung, Sonderband 4, 5 (Graz: Oldenbourg, 2005).

2. Text of a statement delivered by Federal Chancellor J. Klaus, on Austrian television (ORF), 21 August 1968 (7:00 a.m.), Ktn. 1347, 129.266-6 (Pol.) 68, Austrian State Archives, Ministry of Foreign Affairs, Vienna (hereafter abbreviated as ÖStA, BMfaA).

3. Podtserob was a long-serving Soviet diplomat. Active in the People's Commissariat for Foreign Affairs from 1937, he had worked for Molotov from 1943. In 1952, he was promoted to deputy foreign minister, became head of the 1st European Department and ambassador to Turkey and, in 1956, to Austria, where he remained until 1971. For more details, see G. P. Kynin and J. Laufer, *SSSR i germanskii vopros: 22 iyunya 1941g.–8 maya 1945, SSSR i germanskii vopros 1941–1949*, Tom I. (Moscow: Mezhdunarodnye otnosheniya, 1996), 750.

4. Cf. the instructions for the Soviet ambassadors in different countries prepared by the Politburo of the CC CPSU. Politburo resolution of the CC CPSU P 96 (V), "On the declarations of the government of the USSR addressed to foreign governments concerning the events in Czechoslovakia," 19 August 1968, F. 3, op. 72, d. 198, pp. 4, 20–30, Russian State Archives of Contemporary History, Moscow (hereafter abbreviated as RGANI), reprinted in Karner et al., *Dokumente*, #165.

5. At the beginning of August, a group of Czechoslovak Communists loyal to Moscow around Vasil Bil'ak handed a "request" written in Russian to Leonid Brezhnev in Bratislava asking the Soviet leadership for "assistance." For details, see the Prozumenshchikov chapter in this volume.

6. From the official log of the ambassador of the USSR in Austria, B. F. Podtserob, 21 August 1968, F. 66, op. 47, p. 100, d. 6, pp. 163–64, Archives of the Foreign Ministry of Affairs, Moscow (hereafter abbreviated as AVP RF). In his 1968 *Krisen an Österreichs Grenzen*, Reiner Eger concluded that on the basis of the sources available at the time it was impossible to say with certainty whether on 21 August the Soviet ambassador had already given Chancellor Klaus "an assurance . . . that no Soviet moves of any kind would be taken against Austria," but he inferred quite correctly that this must have been the case. See Reiner Eger, *Krisen an Österreichs Grenzen: Das Verhalten Österreichs während des Ungarnaufstandes 1956 und der tschechoslowakischen Krise 1968. Ein Vergleich* (Vienna: Herold Verlag, 1981), 90–91.

7. ÖStA, BMfaA, Ktn. 1350, 124.434-6 (Pol.) 68.

8. ÖStA, BMfaA, Ktn. 1350, 124.434-6 (Pol.) 68.

9. ÖStA, BMfaA, Ktn. 1350, 124.434-6 (Pol.) 68; From the official log of the ambassador of the USSR in Austria, B. F. Podtserob, 21 August 1968, AVP RF, F. 66, op. 47, p. 100, d. 6, pp. 163–64. The transcript was made on 25 August 1968 and dispatched to Moscow by the Soviet embassy on 31 August 1968.

10. From the official log of the ambassador of the USSR in Austria, B. F. Podtserob, 21 August 1968, AVP RF, F. 66, op. 47, p. 100, d. 6, pp. 163–64. In the afternoon of the previous day, the first demonstrations outside the Soviet embassy occurred, which had resulted in two Molotov cocktails being thrown against the door of the embassy. One man was arrested. *Arbeiter-Zeitung*, 22 August 1968, p. 1 and 4.

11. Minutes no. 91a of the extraordinary session of the Austrian Council of Ministers, 21 August 1968 (1:25 p.m.).ÖStA, BMfaA, Ktn. 1347, 129.266-6 (Pol.) 68.

12. ÖStA, BMfaA, Ktn. 1347, 129.266-6 (Pol.) 68, official communiqué on the session of the Council of Ministers, 21 August 1968. Owing to the visit of the Soviet

ambassador, the beginning of the session of the Council of Ministers was delayed until 1:30 p.m. *Arbeiter-Zeitung*, 22 August 1968, p. 1.

13. Andreas Steiger, "'zum Schutz der Grenze bestimmt'? Das Bundesheer und die CSSR/Krise 1968," *ÖMZ* 5 (1998): 540–41.

14. From the official log of the ambassador of the USSR in Austria, B. F. Podtserob, 21 August 1968, AVP RF, F. 66, op. 47, p. 100, d. 6, pp. 165–66. The transcript was made on 29 August 1968 and dispatched to Moscow by the Soviet embassy on 31 August 1968. Waldheim had not lodged a formal protest, as Eger claims. Cf. Eger, *Krisen an Österreichs Grenzen*, 91.

15. For details, see the article by Horst Pleiner and Hubert Speckner, "Das österreichische Bundesheer und die ČSSR-Krise," in Karner et al., *Beiträge*, 1007–23; the Federal Army was prepared for an emergency and ready for deployment at 8:00 a.m. The marching order was not given until 4:00 p.m. See Eger, *Krisen an Österreichs Grenzen*, 108–9.

16. From the official log of the ambassador of the USSR in Austria, B. F. Podtserob, 21 August 1968, AVP RF, F. 66, op. 47, p. 100, d. 6, pp. 165–66.

17. From the official log of the ambassador of the USSR in Austria, B. F. Podtserob, 21 August 1968, AVP RF, F. 66, op. 47, p. 100, d. 6, pp. 165–66.

18. Cable of the Czechoslovak ambassador in Austria, P. Novotný, on the reaction of the Austrian government to Czechoslovakia's invasion by Warsaw Pact troops, Tlg. došlé, 7764/1968, Archives of the Ministry of Foreign Affairs, Prague (hereafter abbreviated as A MZV), reprinted in Karner et al., *Dokumente*, #174.

19. Text of the statement made by Chancellor J. Klaus on Austrian television (ORF) on 21 August 1968 (evening news), ÖStA, BMfaA, Ktn. 1347, 129.266-6 (Pol.) 68.

20. See Eger, *Krisen an Österreichs Grenzen*, 194–96.

21. The words "serious setback" (*schweren Rückschlag*) were added by hand, with the word "serious" being crossed out again.

22. The word "fortunately" was added by hand.

23. File memo and circular note on Waldheim's communiqué to APA, ÖStA, BMfaA, Ktn. 1350, 124.435-6 (Pol.) 68; Text of the APA report, 22 August 1968, ÖStA, BMfaA, Ktn. 1347, 129.266-6 (Pol.) 68.

24. Ibid.

25. Stenographic transcript of a meeting of the Communist and Workers' Parties of Bulgaria, Hungary, the GDR, Poland, and the USSR in Moscow, 18 August 1968, reprinted in Karner et al., *Dokumente*, #87. For details, see Silke Stern, "Die tschechoslowakische Emigration: Österreich als Erstaufnahme- und Asylland," in Karner et al., *Beiträge*, 1025–42.

26. Stern, "Die tschechslowakische Emigration," in Karner et al., *Beiträge*, 1025–42.

27. For details, see the Jakovina chapter in this volume.

28. Report of the head of the Central British Fund for Jewish Relief and Rehabilitation, 10 September 1968, UNHCR Archives, Geneva, 1.AUS.CZE/4, reprinted in Karner et al., *Dokumente*, #184; Report of the regional office of the UN High Commissioner for Refugees to Geneva, 9 September 1968, UNHCR Archives, Geneva, 1.AUS.CZE/2, reprinted in Karner et al., *Dokumente*, #183.

29. From the official log of the ambassador of the USSR in Austria, B. F. Podtserob, 23 August 1968, AVP RF, F. 66, op. 47, p. 100, d. 6, pp. 167–68. The transcript was made on 30 August 1968 and dispatched to Moscow by the Soviet embassy on 31 August 1968.

30. From the official log of the ambassador of the USSR in Austria, B. F. Podtserob, 23 August 1968, AVP RF, F. 66, op. 47, p. 100, d. 6, pp. 167–68; ÖStA, BMfaA, Ktn. 1350, 124.545 (Pol. 6) 68.

31. From the official log of the ambassador of the USSR in Austria, B. F. Podtserob, 23 August 1968, AVP RF, F. 66, op. 47, p. 100, d. 6, pp. 167–68.

32. The following words presumably led to irritation on the Soviet side: "In view of its strictly observed policy of neutrality the Federal Government can only express its disappointment that the events of the last 48 hours should call such a policy in doubt." From the official log of the ambassador of the USSR in Austria, B. F. Podtserob, 23 August 1968, AVP RF, F. 66, op. 47, p. 100, d. 6, 167–68; Chancellor J. Klaus's statement in the ORF evening news, 22 August 1968, ÖStA, BMfaA,., Ktn. 1347, 129.266 (Pol. 6) 68.

33. From the official log of the ambassador of the USSR in Austria, B. F. Podtserob, 23 August 1968; AVP RF, F. 66, op. 47, p. 100, d. 6, pp. 167–68. Kirchschläger had been recalled to Vienna from Yugoslavia, where he was on holiday, and was subsequently dispatched to Prague. See Klaus Eisterer, "The Austrian Legation in Prague and the Czechoslovak Crisis of 1968," in *Neutrality in Austria*, vol. 9, *Contemporary Austrian Studies*, ed. Günter Bischof et al. (New Brunswick, NJ: Transaction, 2001), 225.

34. From the official log of the ambassador of the USSR in Austria, B. F. Podtserob, 23 August 1968. The transcript was made on 30 August 1968 and dispatched to Moscow by the Soviet embassy on 31 August 1968, AVP RF, F. 66, op. 47, p. 100, d. 6, p. 171.

35. ÖStA, BMfaA, Ktn. 1350, 124.545 (Pol. 6) 68.

36. Michael Gehler, *Österreichs Außenpolitik der Zweiten Republik: Von der alliierten Besatzung bis zum Europa des 21. Jahrhunderts* (Innsbruck: Böhlau, 2005), 342.

37. Waldheim's report to the Executive Committee of Austria's parliament, 29 August 1968, ÖStA, BMfaA, Ktn. 1347, 129.266-6 (Pol.) 68.

38. On this occasion, the Soviet embassy counselor pointed out that the Czechoslovak ambassador had been given the opportunity to appear on Austrian television while in 1967 the request of the Soviet ambassador to be allowed to speak on TV on the occasion of the fiftieth anniversary of the October Revolution had been denied. What prompted this meeting was the latest edition of the *Deutsche Nationalzeitung* destined for sale in Austria, which in the words of the Soviet diplomat, "was brimful of highly insulting statements about the Soviet Union." The Austrian Foreign Ministry followed up on the matter and came to the conclusion that the Austrian edition of the periodical was produced entirely in Munich. See the file memo about a call paid to the Foreign Ministry by the Soviet embassy counselor, Bushmanov, 29 August 1968, ÖStA, BMfaA, Ktn. 1349, 124.904 (Pol. 6) 68.

39. File memo, 29 August 1968, ÖStA, BMfaA, Ktn. 1349, 124.904 (Pol. 6) 68.

40. File memo, 29 August 1968, ÖStA, BMfaA, Ktn. 1349, 124.904 (Pol. 6) 68.

41. Washington lodged an official protest with the Soviet Union regarding the "absurd claim" that the United States was violating Austrian neutrality. For details,

see the article by Günter Bischof, "'No Action': Die USA und die Invasion in die Tschechoslowakei," in Karner et al., *Beiträge*, 340.

42. Folder "8/28/68," cable of the secretary of state, D. Rusk, to the U.S. embassies in Vienna, Moscow, Prague, all NATO capitals, CINCEUR and USEUCOM, 28 August 1968, RG 59, Central Foreign Policy Files 1967–1969, POL 27-1 COM BLOC-Czech, Box 1995, NARA, reprinted in Karner et al., *Dokumente*, #180; for details see Günter Bischof, "'No Action,'" in Karner et al., *Beiträge*, 319–54.

43. From the official log of the ambassador of the USSR in Austria, B. F. Podtserob, 29 August 1968, AVP RF, F. 66, op. 47, p. 100, d. 6, pp. 177–78. The transcript was made on 30 August 1968 and dispatched to Moscow by the Soviet embassy on 31 August 1968.

44. Kurt Waldheim, *Im Glaspalast der Weltpolitik* (Düsseldorf: Econ, 1985), 64; Waldheim told the story also in an interview. See Gehler, *Österreichs Außenpolitik der Zweiten Republik*, 342, 346; AVP RF, F. 66, op. 47, p. 100, d. 6, pp. 177–78 (cf note 43).

45. Minutes of a meeting of the leadership of the CC CPSU with the leaders of the Communist parties of Bulgaria, Hungary, the GDR, and Poland, 8 May 1968, KC PVAR, p. 193, t. 24, Archivum Akt Nowych, Warsaw (hereafter abbreviated as AAN), reprinted in Karner et al., *Dokumente*, #77.

46. For details, see also report on the visit paid by the Soviet ambassador in Austria, Podtserob, to Austrian federal chancellor Klaus, 31 August 1968, AVP RF, F. 66, op. 47, p. 100, d. 6, 179–83, reprinted in Karner et al., *Dokumente*, #182.

47. See the article by Dieter Bacher and Harald Knoll, "Österreich als Drehscheibe ausländischer Geheimdienste?" in Karner et al., *Beiträge*, 1063–74.

48. For details on Ladislav Bittman, see Pavel Žaček, "Vzestupy a pády Bohumíra Molnára. Kariéra generála Státní bezpečnosti," in *Oči a uši strany: Sedm pohled do života StB*, ed. Petr Blažek et al. (Šenov, Ostrava: Nakl. Tilia, 2005), 95–99; Wendell L. Minnick, *Spies and Provocateurs: A Worldwide Encyclopedia of Persons Conducting Espionage and Covert Action 1946–1991* (Jefferson, NC: McFarland, 1992), 17–18; Ladislav Bittman, *Zum Tode verurteilt: Memoiren eines Spions* (Munich: Roitman, 1984); Ladislav Bittman, *Geheimwaffe D* (Bern: SOI, 1973); on the basis of these two publications, Bittman's activities were analyzed in Harald Irnberger, *Nelkenstrauß ruft Praterstern, Am Beispiel Österreich: Funktion und Arbeitsweise geheimer Nachrichtendienste in einem neutralen Staat* (Vienna: Verlag Promedia, 1983), 112–14.

49. From the official log of the ambassador of the USSR in Austria, B. F. Podtserob, 31 August 1968, AVP RF, F. 66, op. 47, p. 100, d. 6, pp. 179–83. The transcript was made on 2 September 1968 and dispatched to Moscow on the same day by the Soviet embassy.

50. From the official log of the ambassador of the USSR in Austria, B. F. Podtserob, 31 August 1968, AVP RF, F. 66, op. 47, p. 100, d. 6, pp. 179–83. Decidedly more inclined to criticism than Chancellor Klaus was Secretary for Information Karl Pisa in an interview he gave to the Austrian Press Agency (APA) on 28 August 1968 on the topic of the events in Czechoslovakia. He noted that there was no need for him to "hold forth" on the "nature of communism" now as he had "criticized both the communist idea and the encroachments of the Soviet occupying forces repeatedly even during Austria's occupation." ÖStA, BMfaA, Ktn. 1347, 129.266-6 (Pol.) 68.

51. From the official log of the ambassador of the USSR in Austria, B. F. Podtserob, 31 August 1968, AVP RF, F. 66, op. 47, p. 100, d. 6, pp. 179–83.

52. Transcript of a conversation between the Soviet ambassador B. F. Podtserob and Chancellor Klaus, 31 August 1968, reprinted in Eger, *Krisen an Österreichs Grenzen*, 213.

53. RGANI, F. 3, op. 72, d. 201, pp. 22, 41–55.

54. Excerpt from a statement by Kurt Waldheim at the UN Conference of Nuclear-Free States in Geneva, 6 September 1968, ÖStA, 129.266-6 (Pol.) 68.

55. Jonas was in Yugoslavia from 30 September to 5 October 1968. For details, see Eger, *Krisen an Österreichs Grenzen*, 103, and Gehler, *Österreichs Außenpolitik der Zweiten Republik*, 341.

56. Tito had paid Austria a state visit from 13 to 17 February 1967.

57. From the official log of the ambassador of the USSR in Austria, B. F. Podtserob, 28 September 1968, AVP RF, F. 66, op. 47, p. 100, d. 6, pp. 195–98. The transcript was made on 30 September 1968 and dispatched to Moscow on the same day by the Soviet embassy. See also Tvrtko Jakovina, "Tito, the Bloc-Free Movement, and the Prague Spring" in this volume, and Bischof, "'No Action,'" in Karner et al., *Beiträge*, 319–54.

58. From the official log of the ambassador of the USSR in Austria, B. F. Podtserob, 28 September 1968 (cf. note 56). A discussion on Austrian television (ORF) on 12 September 1968 was even mentioned in a report to the CC CPSU. According to its report, the Soviet embassy was reasonably pleased with the program. See the report of the deputy chairman of APN, V. Larin, to the Propaganda Department of the CC CPSU, RGANI, F. 5, op. 60, d. 38, p. 107, reprinted in Karner et al., *Dokumente*, #187.

59. For details, see Eger, *Krisen an Österreichs Grenzen*, 101.

60. In the 1966 declaration of its program, Austria's new federal government gave top priority to speeding up its negotiations for the country's accession to the EC. By linking the South Tyrolean question to the EC negotiations, Rome compromised these negotiations. Paris subsequently adopted Moscow's proposal, which provided for Vienna to conclude a trade treaty with the EEC's member states. The USSR considered Austria's potential EC membership as incompatible with the State Treaty (on the basis of the interdiction of the Anschluß with Germany). Similar fears surfaced in Moscow before Austria's accession to the European Union. For details, see Gehler, *Österreichs Außenpolitik der Zweiten Republik*, 310–58, and Robert Kriechbaumer, "Die Ära Klaus: Aufgeklärter Konservatismus in den 'kurzen' sechziger Jahren in Austria," in Gehler and Kriechbaumer, eds., *Die Ära Josef Klaus: Austria in den 'kurzen sechziger Jahren*, vol. 1, *Document*, Schriftenreihe des Forschungsinstitutes für politisch-historische Studien der Dr.Wilfried-Haslauer-Bibliothek, vol. 7/1 (Vienna: Böhlau, 1998), 63.

61. From the official log of the ambassador of the USSR in Austria, B. F. Podtserob, 28 September 1968, AVP RF, F. 66, op. 47, p. 100, d. 6, pp. 195–98.

62. From the official log of the ambassador of the USSR in Austria, B. F. Podtserob, 28 September 1968, AVP RF, F. 66, op. 47, p. 100, d. 6, pp. 195–98.

63. Eger, *Krisen an Österreichs Grenzen*, 97.

64. A KGB report mentioned that "500 Austrian plain-clothes policemen [had infiltrated the ČSSR] and had smuggled weapons into the country." The only charge

ever mentioned by the Soviet ambassador in his meetings with Federal Chancellor Klaus concerned the smuggling of German-made mobile radio stations into the ČSSR via Austria. See the official call by the Soviet ambassador in Austria, B. F. Podtserob, on the Austrian federal chancellor, J. Klaus, 31 August 1968, AVP RF, F. 66, op. 47, p. 100, d. 6, pp. 179–83, reprinted in Karner et al., *Dokumente*, #182. In an even more bizarre claim, the KGB reported that Austria's military intelligence had activated its agents in the ČSSR, "especially among the officers of the Czechoslovak army." According to the head of the KGB, Yuri Andropov, "the agents were given the task to set up underground organizations and carry out acts of terrorism against those who impeded the process of liberalization." See the report of the head of the KGB, Y. Andropov, to the CC CPSU, 13 October 1968, RGANI, F. 89, op. 61, d. 5, pp. 1–60, reprinted in Karner et al., *Dokumente*, #121.

   65. Gehler, *Österreichs Außenpolitik der Zweiten Republik*, 342–51.
   66. Gehler, *Österreichs Außenpolitik der Zweiten Republik*, 345–51.
   67. Eger, *Krisen an Österreichs Grenzen*, 98.

Appendix 1

"Counterrevolution" in Prague

Report by the ambassador of the GDR in the ČSSR, P. Florin, on the situation in the country.[1]

10 March 1968
[Prague]

The activities of the oppositional forces have been stepped up over the last few days; they are displaying counter-revolutionary traits ever more openly. Systematic attacks are being launched against the organs of the power of the state, against their representatives, against the pillars of a socialist society and against basic socialist principles. [The] writer Kohout calls for the publication of the so-called "Writers' Manifesto," which famously contains the demand for a return to a bourgeois parliamentary republic. On the 118th anniversary of Masaryk's birthday articles were published containing such passages as: "Our socialist society and its political system are connected by an umbilical cord to this historical development [i.e. the era of Masaryk] and not to the Soviet system, which came into being in totally different circumstances . . . Masaryk is for us a living compass between the past and the present" (*Mladá fronta*). The Trade Union paper *Prace* quotes Masaryk's phrase of a "social socialism" and states that today is the time to realize this idea.

[. . .] The press in general or at least the key papers, TV, radio, CTK and a large number of periodicals are in the hands of the oppositional forces. They are doing everything they can to foment an atmosphere of opposition, they allow no space for counterarguments and are working systematically to organize the counterrevolution. They have managed to bring about the

441

abolition of censorship and a new media law, in whose drafting the journalists themselves are to be given a say. Both measures have been passed
by the presidium of the CC. The presidium of the CC CPCz has also passed
a resolution that allows the practically unchecked importation of foreign
literature and news media.

[. . .] It is quite obvious that the oppositional forces are centrally coordinated. Presumably they have both an open center and an illegal one. The
personages of the open center include today Smrkovský (member of the
CC CPCz and Minister for Forestry), Šik (member of the CC), Goldstücker
(professor at Charles University and president of the writers' union),
Pelikan (director of state TV), Kohout (writer) and several journalists and
students. As can be gathered from the Western press, the illegal center is in
touch with capitalist circles and their organs abroad. Some Czechoslovak
comrades in leading positions have been attempting to this day to interpret
the activities of the oppositional forces as isolated extremist phenomena.
However in reality we are confronted with the centrally coordinated and
systematically developed preparation of a counterrevolution.

To date the situation has developed in analogy to the one on the eve of
the counter-revolutionary putsch of 1956 in Hungary. [. . .] If the comrades
in the party leadership do not take a determined stand soon, the other side
will be able to realize their plans in regard to public violent provocations.

(Florin)[2]
Ambassador

NOTES

1. For the policies of the GDR in connection with the events in Czechoslovakia,
see Manfred Wilke's chapter in this volume.

2. Autograph signature.

SOURCE

SAPMO-BA, DY 30/3616, S. 52–57 (reprinted in Karner et al., *Dokumente*, #3).

Appendix 2

"We Are Ready at Any Time . . . to Assist the Czechoslovak People Together with the Armies . . . of the Warsaw Pact"

Speech of the Minister of Defense of the USSR, Marshal of the Soviet Union A. A. Grechko, at the plenum of the CC CPSU.

10 April 1968

[. . .] The policies of our Party are continuously and fervently echoed by the Army and the Navy and meet with the unanimous approval of the entire personnel of the Armed Forces. The soldiers of the Soviet Union share the thoughts and the feelings of the party and the people. They are perfectly aware that they must be ready for international deployments, which are a consequence of the tremendous significance that our military power has for international events. They identify with everything that the party decrees, also in regard to foreign politics. Many of our soldiers have to serve outside the country. At present tens of thousands of communist and non-party soldiers are serving abroad in thirty-six different countries, where, as I am proud to report to the plenum, they discharge their duty with dignity and as propagators of the Leninist policy of the party.

The present situation is characterized by a tremendous surge in the bellicosity of the imperialists in general and of the Americans in particular. They resort increasingly frequently to the use of force in their attempts to crush the forces of progress and social liberation and they stage dangerous provocative acts in various regions of the world. Instigated by their masters in Washington, West German militarists and *revanchistes* openly demand a revision of the results of WWII and are becoming more assertive by the day. [. . .]

A source of deep concern for us are the events in China and the betrayal of Marxism-Leninism, the principles of proletarian internationalism, the unity of the worldwide communist movement and of the security of the Socialist states in the east by the group around Mao Tse-tung, which is going to inflict great harm.

The leaders in Peking are to blame for the fact that the stretch of the Socialist countries' defensive line that the Chinese are in charge of has proved to be the weakest. It is no coincidence that it is here, in Southeast Asia, that the American imperialism is at its most active.

[. . .] We are ready at any time, pending a party resolution, to assist the Czechoslovak people together with the armies of the countries of the Warsaw Pact if the imperialists and counterrevolutionaries should attempt to wrest socialist Czechoslovakia from the socialist camp.

[. . .] Let me add a few words on the situation in Vietnam. We all know about the latest triumphs that the Vietnamese army has achieved in its struggle with American imperialism. The steadfastness and perseverance of the Vietnamese people and its fighters are a source of deep satisfaction for all of us. At the same time it must be said that the military gains of the Vietnamese patriots are inseparably linked to the efforts of our people and our country that are aimed at assisting this heroic nation. To put it bluntly: this war is waged not only by the Vietnamese but by the Soviet people as well. It is common knowledge that both in the North and in the South it is our weapons that are used to fight the American aggressors.

Let me give you some figures. Only recently did we deliver to the Democratic Republic of Vietnam hundreds of Flak rocket launching pads and thousands of rockets; 3,000 or so flak cannon, 2,500 field cannon and grenade launchers, approximately 250,000 machine guns and carbines, approximately 400 airplanes and choppers and a great deal of other weapons and military technology. All this was given free of charge, with only one aim in mind—to assist the Vietnamese people in their struggle against the American aggressors. Our assistance is set to continue and we despatch weapons and military technology to Vietnam on a daily basis.

In addition to this we train whole regiments of flak soldiers, pilots and other specialists who are sent to the front when they are needed. In Vietnam there are hundreds of our advisers who help the Vietnamese control the war and handle modern weapons. Often our officers, non-commissioned officers and soldiers take part in the fighting, and many of the airplanes destroyed in the war were brought down by our brave fighters.

It needs to be said however that our Soviet military personnel are not treated as comrades taking part in a joint struggle. Contacts between our people and the Vietnamese soldiers are discouraged, their contacts with Vietnamese troops are limited, and those Vietnamese with sympathies for the Soviet state are subject to persecution. The truth about the war is kept secret and access to destroyed American airplanes is made difficult under one pretext or another.

All this seems to happen at the instigation of the Chinese who are active in the Vietnamese army as advisers and observers of one kind or another. Such attitudes towards soldiers from the Soviet Union obviously sadden us but we carry out our work regardless because we have been mandated to do so by the party in the name of our internationalist duty to pay tribute to our friendship with the Vietnamese people and to fight our common enemy, imperialism, and we will continue to do so by assisting the Vietnamese people.

[. . .] On behalf of the Armed Forces allow me to signal my unqualified approval [. . .] of the realization of the plenum's resolutions; the Armed Forces are standing by to implement them. [Applause.]

SOURCE

RGANI, F. 2, op. 3, d. 94, S. 1–15. Unedited stenographic notes. Translated from the German translation of the original Russian document (original Russian and German translation in Karner et al., *Dokumente*, #33).

Appendix 3

"Secret" Memorandum: Eugene V. Rostow to Dean Rusk, 10 May 1968

Subject: Soviet Threat to Czechoslovakia[1]

I have thought further about our conversation yesterday.

I conclude that it would be a serious mistake not to give the Soviets a private signal of concern about troop movements near Czechoslovakia.

1. In retrospect, our failure to deter the Communist takeover in Czechoslovakia in 1948 was one of the most serious mistakes of our foreign policy since the war. Firm diplomatic action then—a period of our nuclear monopoly—could well have prevented the Cold War. Similarly, our public statement in 1956 that we would not intervene gave the Soviets a full license. Obviously, the situation has profoundly changed.

2. What is at stake now is the process of movement towards détente— the policy of the President's speech of October 7, 1966; the NATO Resolution of last September accepting the Harmel Exercise Report; the German Eastern policy, and the possibility of real improvement in the political climate in Europe, leading to mutual balanced force reductions. Progress in this direction would be set back if the Soviets intervened in Czechoslovakia. I simply do not agree that Soviet efforts in Eastern Europe would fail to stamp out liberal trends. They have long since proved their capacity to keep the animals tame by police methods, and their willingness to do so.

3. The Russians must be hesitating. The moment to give them a deterrent signal is therefore now. It will be too late once they cross the border.

NOTE

1. On top of this memorandum is the handwritten note "No action DR" (Dean Rusk).

SOURCE

Folder "6/1/68," Box 1558, POL Czech—USSR DEF 4 NATO, Central Foreign Policy Files 1968–1969, RG 59, NARA.

Appendix 4

On the Results of the Warsaw Meeting of the Delegations of Communist Parties and Workers' Parties from Socialist Countries

Plenary Session of the CC CPSU
Speech by the General Secretary of the CC CPSU, L. I. Brezhnev
17 July 1968

Comrades!

The Poliburo of the CC CPSU has considered it imperative to convene this meeting, where our purpose is to report on the results of a meeting that took place in Warsaw on 14/15 July of the party and government leaders of Bulgaria, Hungary, the GDR, Poland and the Soviet Union.

The most important issue discussed at this meeting, indeed the issue around which the whole meeting revolved, was the dangerous sequence of events in Czechoslovakia. Before I proceed to present to this meeting the relevant documents let me remind you that after the April plenum of the CC the prevalent notion in the Politburo of the CC CPSU with regard to the events in Czechoslovakia had been the one expressed at that plenum; it held that assistance should be given to the healthy forces and above all to the communist party of Czechoslovakia in their efforts to fend off the loss of socialist achievements in Czechoslovakia as well as the country's alienation from the socialist camp. [. . .]

As they encountered no courageous and determined resistance, the rightist forces threw all moderation over board, with the result that four leading Czechoslovak papers simultaneously published an openly counter-revolutionary manifesto—the so-called "2,000 Words." It bore the signatures of a number of people, some of them well-known, others unknown. A detail that should be mentioned is the fact that some of the signatures are those of nonexistent people who have obviously been invented for the purpose.

This document is a direct attack on the KSČ, it is no less than a call to take up arms against the constitutional government. As we speak, it is being used to unite the antisocialist forces and to serve as a platform for their activities.

Immediately after the emergence of this hostile platform I spoke on the phone to Comrade Dubček and told him on behalf of the Poliburo of the CC that no time must be lost in engaging the antisocialist counter-revolutionary forces. We pointed out to him that the "2,000 Words" called for concerted actions against these forces, involving the support of the healthy forces in the party, in the working class and in the armed units of the People's Militia. Comrade Dubček told me that a meeting of the presidium of the CC KSČ was in progress at the time and that he was going to pass on our recommendations to the meeting; he assured us that a radical condemnation was forthcoming and that highly effective countermeasures were about to be taken. Unfortunately none of these things came to pass.

[. . .] What is happening in Czechoslovakia in our view is this: a carefully disguised, fully up-to-date counter-revolutionary process is taking place that is aiming to fundamentally alter the social structure, possibly without changing its outward attributes and without causing any changes up to now in the society's political and state leadership. The particular danger of this development consists in the initial confusion of the Czechoslovak working population and indeed even of the working class, who were completely in the dark as to where this development would eventually lead. It is also likely to cause confusion in communist circles outside the Soviet Union, as we can see from symptoms displayed by the Communist Parties of France, Italy and England.

[. . .] This manifest counterrevolution may yet cost the communists in Czechoslovakia dearly. The experience of events in Hungary teaches us that those who surrender to the reaction or strike a compromise with it expose the party to the onslaught of the counterrevolution.

[. . .] And the attempt to stem this process cannot be interpreted as an interference in the country's internal affairs. It is no more than the expression of our internationalist duty towards the communist movement, towards the working population of Czechoslovakia. [Applause.] Face to face with the danger that one of the member states of the socialist community might deviate from the path of Socialism, we have no right to lock ourselves up in our national houses. This would mean a betrayal of the interests of Communism.

Communism unfolds as an international movement and this in fact describes its very existence. This is the key to its victories and its achievements. Whoever deviates from internationalism has lost the right to call himself a communist. Our countries are tied to the ČSSR through treaties and agreements. These are no mere agreements between individuals but commitments entered into by peoples and states. They are based on the general striving to preserve Socialism in our countries and to protect it against fluke events.

No one has the right to shirk their internationalist duties, the duties that are part of our contractual obligations, and the demagoguery that one occasionally encounters in this context is, to be quite frank, totally misplaced.

We respect the rights that each party has, the rights of each people. We acknowledge the special characteristics that the construction of Socialism may assume in different countries. Yet we are equally convinced of the bond that unites our historical destinies. Protecting Socialism—that is the task to which all of us must be prepared to contribute. Our parties all agreed on this point when we met in Moscow in early May. We are convinced that the same consensus is going to prevail at our meeting this time.

It is simply without precedent for capitalism to reassert itself where victory has once fallen to Socialism and where Socialism has established itself. This has never been the case and we feel sure it never will. [Applause.] The guarantee for this is our joint readiness to do anything that is necessary to help a fraternal party and its people to scupper the plans of the counter-revolution and to foil the imperialists' designs on Czechoslovakia.

[. . .] As you can see, the imperialists' tactics are marked by cunning and subterfuge; we must be prepared to counter their machinations and to unmask them in a timely and irrefutable manner. We must not close our eyes to the direct link that unites the tactics of the imperialist reaction and the activities of the antisocialist and counter-revolutionary forces in Czechoslovakia.

[. . .] Before we resort to the most extreme measures at our disposal we will concentrate on political means in collaboration with the healthiest forces in the communist party of Czechoslovakia to decisively repulse the antisocialist and counter-revolutionary elements and to maintain the KSČ in its role of the leading force of Czechoslovak socialism. We count on your unqualified support, comrades, and are looking forward to your speeches. [Applause.]

SOURCE

RGANI, F. 2, op. 3, d. 114, pp. 27–54. Unedited stenographic notes. Translated from the German translation of the original Russian document (original Russian and German translation in Karner et al., *Dokumente*, #38).

Appendix 5

CC Urging the United States to Halt "Hostile U.S. Media Campaign" against the Soviet Union

Politburo resolution of the CC CPSU.
P 92/82
26 July 1968

82. *On the verbal message to the US Ambassador in Moscow concerning events in Czechoslovakia.*[1]

The draft of the verbal message of the Ministry of Foreign Affairs of the USSR to the U.S. Ambassador in Moscow on the issue in question is to be countersigned (Attachment).

[Attachment]

On Item 82 of Prot. no. 92

Text of the verbal message of the Ministry of Foreign Affairs of the USSR to the U.S. Ambassador in Moscow

Information has been received in Moscow about the verbal message Secretary of State Rusk delivered to the ambassador of the USSR in Washington, A. F. Dobrynin, on 22 July of this year in connection with the events in Czechoslovakia. Referring to comments in the Soviet press, notably to a *Pravda* article of 19 June, the Secretary of State expressed his concern about allegedly unfounded charges leveled at the Pentagon and the Central Intelligence Agency [CIA] regarding their interference in Czechoslovak affairs.

In this context it is necessary to make it quite clear at the outset that there is no reason why the American side should express their concern to the Soviet side. The Pravda article of 19 July that was cited by the Secretary of State is based on well documented evidence and the American authorities are obviously aware of the authenticity and credibility of the facts in question.

Generally speaking, we would have much more reason to direct the attention of the U.S. administration to the hostile campaign that is at present being waged in the United States against the USSR in connection with the events in Czechoslovakia. On a daily basis the American press, radio and TV spread all kinds of exaggerated reports, with the aim of giving comfort to the anti-Socialist counterrevolutionary forces in Czechoslovakia on one hand and, on the other, of causing bad feelings towards the Soviet Union and the other Socialist countries and use these to stoke tensions in Czechoslovakia.

Many statements of various U.S. officeholders, including members of the U.S. Congress, have been made with the same objectives in mind.

In the above mentioned conversation with the ambassador of the USSR, Secretary of State Rusk declared that events in Czechoslovakia were a matter that concerned solely the Czechs and the other countries of the Warsaw Pact; the U.S. administration did not want to get in any way involved.

If the U.S. administration does not want the situation concerning the events in Czechoslovakia to deteriorate drastically, the US administration should in our view do everything in its power to halt the campaign that is being waged against the Soviet Union in the United States. It goes without saying that this campaign has a very negative influence on public opinion in our country and on Soviet-American relations in general. The Soviet government believes it is essential to avoid anything that might lead to a deterioration in the relationship between our countries and to continue to seek ways and means to improve them. This is also the declared aim of President Johnson.

NOTE

1. The resolution was put to the vote and passed. Those who voted in favor were L. I. Brezhnev, G. I. Voronov, A. P. Kirilenko, A. N. Kosygin, K. T. Mazurov, A. J. Pel'she, N. V. Podgornyi, D. S. Polyanskii, M. A. Suslov, A. N. Shelepin, and P. E. Shelest.

SOURCE

RGANI, F. 3, op 72, d. 191, pp. 84–85. Translated from the German translation of the original Russian document (original Russian and German translation in Karner et al., *Dokumente*, #191).

Appendix 6

"Secret" Memorandum
by Nathaniel Davis,
"Czechoslovak Contingencies"

[No date, but from file location end of July/beginning of August 1968]

Tension continues to build, partly because tomorrow is the day the Czechs say the Soviets will start moving out. These are added disquieting signs: (1) [one line redacted] (2) Reportedly, an agreed paragraph in the Warsaw Pact announcement, saying Soviet troops would be leaving, was deleted when the announcement was made; and (3) An unspecified People's Militia "operation" is due to start at 9:00 tonight.

Possibilities include:

- The beginning of at least token withdrawals, followed by Czech-Soviet bilateral talks early next week and some sort of inconclusive accommodation.
- Soviet unwillingness to remove any troops, continued pressure and continued maneuver.
- Soviet provocation of an incident, perhaps in connection with an ostensible movement to withdraw, followed by a Warsaw Pact call for re-enforcements to protect existing forces.
- Public disorder and violence, in Prague or elsewhere, which would trigger an unraveling of the Czech party and government.
- Militia arrests of liberals, with or without Dubcek acquiescence, or moves toward a coup of some kind.

Alternatives for the United States:

We are obviously not prepared to intervene militarily. Recourse to the UN is probably an "after-the-fact" alternative—certainly not an immediate option. In the very short term, the following seem to be areas where we have alternatives:

1. World public attention. We could find ways to intensify world-wide press, public and government attention and concern. This might have some inhibiting effect on the Soviets. The disadvantage is that it could further destabilize the situation in Czechoslovakia—including the discipline and calm of the Czech public.
2. As a further step, we could make various kinds of official U.S. government statements. We could also stimulate European governments to parallel action. However, we must be careful we do not repeat the mistake of 1956, in creating expectations we are not prepared to follow through on.
3. [A word redacted] may have some capability of stimulating Western European or other Communist Parties and press to call on the Soviets to stop interfering in the internal affairs of a brother Communist Party and nation.

   Anything we could do to mobilize independent-minded Communist opinion, *before* rather than after the fact, would seem worth doing.
4. We might consider what kind of approach to the Romanians and/or Yugoslavs might be useful. Perhaps some discreet comparing of notes would be helpful.
5. We might consider what kind of diplomatic approach to the Russians could be helpful. The difficulty is that we are dealing with a vital interest of the USSR, and it is doubtful they would be responsive to any pressures we could apply or would be willing to bring to bear. Nevertheless, there might be some possibilities.

   We have a whole range of things we could do in our Soviet relationship—including cancelling the PanAm inaugural, suspending exchange negotiations, bringing Ambassador Thompson home on consultations, deferring our strategic-arms talks proposals, etc. However, our relationship with the Soviets has historically always been paramount, and our Eastern European interest secondary. This is, no doubt, still true.
6. Conceivably we might have some way through a third party, etc; to signal to the Czech leadership to "cool it," pull in their horns on reform, curb their press, etc.—if we think this is the best and only way to avert a debacle. There are certainly observers who think we should have done this sort of thing at an earlier stage in Hungary. On the other hand, we are not close enough to Czech developments or their leadership to have much realistic chance of trying to steer them.

Nathaniel Davis

SOURCE

Folder 5 "Memos Czechoslovakia, 1/68–8/68," Box 179, Country File Europe, USSR, Czechoslovakia, National Security File, LBJ Library.

Appendix 7

Memorandum from Ambassador McGhee to the Secretary of State, 21 August 1968

Subject: U.S. Reaction to Soviet Move Against Czechoslovakia

INFORMATION MEMORANDUM

1. We should, I believe, denounce in the clearest possible terms the action of the Soviets and certain of their Warsaw Pact allies against Czechoslovakia as being an unprovoked and unjustified act of aggression—both publicly at the highest level, in the Security Council and in the NATO, because:

   a. We must make it clear that we do not accept the Soviet interpretation of the move as being a purely internal Communist affair. Otherwise, both the Soviets and the peoples of Eastern Europe will assume that we have given the Soviets a free hand within the Communist sphere.

   b. We must disprove that we, as is often alleged in Europe, accept the status quo in Europe because of a desire to achieve a détente with the Soviets or a settlement in Vietnam.

   c. Since the UN was formed largely to prevent aggression, we have no choice but to raise a case of aggression against one of its members, even in the face of a certain veto in the Security Council.

   d. NATO, having been founded to defend against Communist encroachment against the Atlantic Nations, cannot ignore the drastic change in the European power balance caused by the Soviet move.

2. We should, at the same time, not give any impression that we intend to take unilateral action. It is not necessary to enunciate or explain

this since the world fully understands it. We should not, on the other hand, give as explanation the fact that the Czech leaders did not ask for assistance. Everyone understands that this was not practical in the circumstances.

3. The Soviet move demonstrates once more, as clearly as in Hungary in 1956 and in East Germany in 1953, their continuing intent to use whatever means are required to keep control over the Communist nations, even in the face of overwhelming world—and even other Communist opinion. This sets severe practical limits on our détente effort, which must be taken into account in our future negotiations with the Soviet Union. This is particularly true in the case of the FRG, whose goals in this regard have become increasingly unrealistic.

4. Although we should not, I believe backtrack on any bilateral agreements already negotiated, i.e. Civil Air and Consular, we should not in deference to reality and world opinion proceed with discussion of any new détente efforts for the time being. Our engagement in disarmament discussions would appear to many as being as cynical on our part—as on the part of the Soviets. The NPT, which is a largely fait accompli and stands on its own merits, should not be affected.

5. The Soviet action opens up excellent possibilities for exploitation to our and the free world advantage.

   a. Without any effort on our part, the implications of the present move are such that the world should now fully understand the nature of the Soviet regime and the lengths to which it will go to maintain its control over other countries. Although we should not stand back, we should let others carry the burden of explaining this wherever possible. In showing their hand so clearly, the Soviets move should have a particular effect on the attitude of the world youth. It should, if the young people involved are sincere in the goals they profess, bring the Soviets into their direct line of criticism and attack. Efforts should be made discreetly to encourage this.

   b. A new opportunity should be provided to obtain many of our objectives within NATO which we have not been able to accomplish on account of a general apathy on the part of other states. We should be able at least to stabilize present force goals.

   c. There is possibility that the Soviet action might precipitate a fundamental review of French policy, possibly leading to the French being willing to establish closer relations with the NATO organization and closer cooperation with U.S. and other NATO countries in their relations with the Soviet Union.

   d. The Soviet move will, it is believed, take the steam out of the efforts of those in Congress who have sought a drastic unilateral reduction in U.S. forces in Europe. The opportunity should be taken to try to get public statements recognizing the changed situation by some of the Congressional leaders involved, particularly Senators Russell, Mansfield and Symington.

6. The move against Czechoslovakia clearly demonstrates the renewed strong influence of Ulbricht on the Soviets (after what appeared to be a temporary eclipse), even though this influence largely stems from his personal weakness and that of his regime. Since this may presage Ulbricht's desire for renewed attacks against the FRG and threats to Berlin access, it might be advisable to warn the Soviets in advance of the serious consequences of such action.

SOURCE

Folder 1, Box 1, Czech Crisis Files, Lot 70 D 19, Office of the Executive Secretariat, RG 59, NARA.

Appendix 8

Svoboda about Dubček: "If He Were to Resign from His Post, It Would Be Better for All of Us"

Stenographic notes of the conversation between the Soviet leadership and the president of the ČSSR, L. Svoboda, and M. Klusák

23 August 1968[1]
[7:00 p.m.]
Top Secret[2]

Svoboda: In Prague parliament held a session and so did the government; there has also been a CC meeting. I was asked yesterday to form a new government but I think this would be unconstitutional.

Brezhnev: Sorry, I don't quite understand.

Svoboda: The situation has now changed for the better . . . In the Czechoslovak army 265 have been wounded and twenty-three killed, who are being buried now.

Podgornyi: And how many casualties among the Soviet comrades?

Svoboda: I can't say for sure but there are some. We have taken all measures so that there are as few casualties as possible.

(Comrade Svoboda proposes that Comrade Dubček go to Prague, openly confess his guilt and resign his powers. If some other course was adopted instead, it was likely to result in popular discontent.)

Brezhnev: Ludvík Ivanović [Svoboda], if Comrade Dubček resigns his powers, who would then become First Secretary?

Svoboda: It is obvious you have not understood me quite correctly. Where is Dubček now?

461

Brezhnev: He is alright.

Svoboda: If he were to resign from his post, it would be better for all of us. If he remains where he is, that is alright as well. In any case it is necessary for Comrade Dubček to step forward.

Brezhnev: Where, here?

Svoboda: No, in Prague. All the members of the government have said that they will keep their posts only if Černík becomes the head of the government. People say about Bil'ak that he is a traitor. Bil'ak cannot be the head of the government, he has no authority with most members of our party.

Brezhnev: That's all very well, Ludvík Ivanovič [Svoboda], but right now we should not be looking back, we should be looking ahead how we are going to avoid great bloodshed. Let's be frank: the whole country is in a psychosis. Even before the trip to Čierná nad Tisou an atmosphere of utmost nationalist tension was created. No other slogans were shouted there apart from Dubček, Dubček, save Dubček. A great tension was in evidence even then. I do believe there must be reason why this situation was brought about. Moreover it now transpires that various underground radio transmitters and arms caches have been discovered. Today for instance submachine guns and other arms were found in a cellar of the Ministry of Agriculture. The whole thing looks as if there was some group, let's cautiously call them rightists, counterrevolutionaries, that had been expecting things to take this turn. That they conducted the party conference in the way they did is further proof.

It is necessary for Comrades Dubček, Smrkovský and Černík as well as for your whole delegation to declare in advance that the present party conference has been convened illegally and has no function. This declaration has to be made first of all. Then the presidium becomes active in the old form which is considered legitimate. If you're going to consider the party conference as legally convened and neither Bil'ak nor Indra nor Švestka nor Kolder are there, if there are, to put it quite frankly, no healthy forces present, who is then supposed to be elected? This is a course we simply cannot give our consent to because it is for this very reason that we have sent our troops into Czechoslovakia: to prevent the country from going down the wrong road. [. . .]

We will evacuate our troops only when we have a binding commitment from you. We are under obligation to our allies, the other Socialist countries, and are unable to evacuate troops on our own.

Klusák: Were there German soldiers on Czechoslovak territory?

Podgornyi: No, not a single German set foot on Czechoslovak territory.

Klusák: Is it maybe necessary to put this point to the Minister of Defense?

Brezhnev: It is absolutely certain that there were no German soldiers on Czechoslovak territory. We kept them back.

Klusák: In Prague people are absolutely convinced that they're there even now.

Brezhnev: This is an act of provocation. Between you and me: the German comrades were offended because they felt that they were not being trusted somehow.

Podgornyi: We did this at your request. We took the whole situation into account even though they were to have marched with the others initially.[3]

NOTES

1. Added by hand in the original.
2. "Strictly classified" added by hand.
3. This is the final proof that the decision to refrain from deploying the NVA was made in Moscow at the request of the Czechoslovaks. See Rüdiger Wenzke, "Die Nationale Volksarmee der DDR: Kein Einsatz in Prag," in Karner et al., *Beiträge*, 673–86.

SOURCE

RGANI, F. 89, op. 38, d. 57, pp. 1–19. Translated from the German translation of the original Russian document (original Russian and German translation in Karner et al., *Dokumente*, #107).

Appendix 9

"Secret" and "Top Secret" Secretary of Defense Staff Meetings, 1968

"Secret" Secretary of Defense Staff Meeting, 1 July 1968
Mr. Clifford, Mr. Nitze, Mr. Resor, General Johnson, Mr. Ignatius, Admiral Moorer, Dr. Brown, General McConnell, General Wheeler, General Chapman, Dr. Enthoven, Mr. Warnke, et al.

1. *Personnel Matters*
Mr. Clifford began the meeting at 0937.
[. . .]
7. *Troop Reductions in Europe*
Mr. Clifford said that we are having an exceedingly difficult problem regarding our troops in Europe. He has talked with Senator Russell on this matter. Senator Symington has offered an amendment to the Appropriations Bill, which might pass in the current Congressional climate. He proposes to cut U.S. troops in Europe to 50,000. Senator Russell has indicated that he is prepared to vote for the proposal. Senator Mansfield has stated that he has sought Department of Defense cooperation to cut our troops in Europe. Unless Defense comes up with an alternative proposal, the Senate plans to go ahead with the Symington amendment. Mr. Clifford said he believed that the House was with us. Senator Russell feels we have to have a substitute plan because we can't beat something with nothing. We will want to give our preferred attention to this matter. We need to have a plan in addition to the 34,000 that are now scheduled to be out by 30 August 1968. When these troops return,

our European forces will total around 300,000. This latter figure is the one being used on the Hill and which they is excessive and should be brought down. We need to come up with a plan and take it up with our NATO allies. We may be able to work out something reasonable and intelligent.

Mr. Nitze stated that there would be the problem of coordinating any proposed reductions with State. Mr. Clifford said that the State Department feels that any reductions is all wrong. They have said that they can't agree with any kind of reduction. They want to stand firm. We feel we must "bend" with the wind. He will discuss the matter with Secretary Rusk.

[. . .]

The meeting adjourned at 1023

R. Eugene Livesay, Staff Secretary

"Top Secret" Secretary of Defense Staff Meeting, 15 July 1968

Mr. Nitze, Mr. Resor, General Westmoreland, General Walt (for General Chapman, Dr. Brown, General McConnell, Admiral Johnson (for General Wheeler), Mr. Earle (for Mr. Warnke), Mr. McGiffert, Mr. Stempler et al. Staff meeting convened at 0937 under Mr. Nitze's chairmanship.

Symington Amendment

Mr. Nitze summarized Mr. Clifford's and his meeting of last Thursday (11 July) with Senators Russell, Stennis, and Jackson. He reported that Mr. Clifford emphasized to the Senators:

(1) The importance of NATO to our strategic defense;
(2) The relationship and sensitivity of our European force deployments to:
   a. the political situation in France,
   b. the current commercial and travel problems involving Berlin,
   c. the Soviet deployments to the Mediterranean, and
   d. the political and economic changes in eastern Europe;
(3) The relationships of U.S. force reductions to the general proposition of NATO and Warsaw pact force reductions and to the forthcoming discussions with the Soviet union on arms limitations; and
(4) The troops withdrawals which have already been made (e.g., RE-FORGER).

Senator Russell replied that while he recognized the eloquence of Mr. Clifford's arguments, he had heard eloquent pleas before. The Senator remarked that the only new developments were the recent political changes in Czechoslovakia. Senator Russell said that while we had been maintaining sizable forces in Europe for twenty-three years, he wondered how much longer the U.S. planned to keep them there. He felt that our allies were not contributing their proportional share and that Mr. McNamara has not made the reductions in U.S. European force levels the Congress thought he was going to make. Senator Russell also said while he had not realized previously that the Symington proposal would reduce U.S. forces to 50,000, he thought [the] Symington Amendment would carry—in some form or another—unless an adequate substitute amendment could be presented. The Senator mentioned the possibility of developing a five-year reduction-in-strength program, or, alternatively, the withdrawal of some 50,000 men over an eighteen-month period.

Senator Stennis generally supported current U.S./NATO policies but was disturbed by the lack of adequate force contributions to the common NATO defense by our European allies. He noted that serious balance of payments problems still persist and that the various bilateral offset agreements hadn't been very satisfactory. Senator Stennis also said that a substitute amendment was desirable.

Senator Jackson was generally more sympathetic to the views expressed by Messrs. Clifford and Nitze and concurred in the view that the most practical alternative to the Symington Amendment was an acceptable substitute amendment.

Mr. Nitze expressed the view that the Executive branch should not be asked to develop "for-the-record" a substitute amendment because of the subsequent problems it would create with our NATO allies. The Senators accepted Mr. Nitze's suggestion but asked if State and Defense could work informally with them in developing an acceptable substitute.

At a White House meeting last Friday evening, (which General Wheeler and Mr. Clifford attended) Mr. Nitze had been told that while the President was pleased that Messrs. Clifford and Nitze had met with the Senators, he didn't want anyone in the Executive Branch taking positions which would endorse a withdrawal of U.S. forces from Europe. The net result of the President's instruction is that work should continue on the REDCOSTE proposals but that we should characterize this effort as an "investigation of possibilities and not as a "decision document."

Mr. Nitze said that notwithstanding the President's instructions of Friday evening, serious balance of payments problems persist. Dr. Brown remarked that the RECOSTE effort had been characterized as a series of proposals to reduce "people," not "forces." Mr. McGiffert asked if we were still obliged to work privately with Senators Jackson and Stennis. Mr. Stempler noted that the ground rule affecting our informal work on an acceptable substitute amendment with the Senators apparently had been changed. Mr.

Nitze said that since the Senatorial debate over the Symington Amendment would not take place for about two weeks, there would be an opportunity to review again the Executive Branch's position with the President. Mr. Nitze then suggested that if anyone had a good idea on how Senatorial support could be mobilized for current NATO deployments he should contact Jack Stempler.

[. . .]

Staff meeting adjourned at 1035.

Abbott C. Greenleaf, Colonel, USAF, Military Assistant

———

"Top Secret" Secretary of Defense Staff Meeting, 22 July 1968

Mr. Clifford, Nr. Nitze, Mr. Resor, General Westmoreland, Mr. Baird (for Mr. Ignatius), Admiral Claret (for Admiral Moorer), Dr. Brown, General Wheeler, Dr Enthoven, Mr. Warnke et al.

1. *Mr. Clifford's trip to Southeast Asia*

Mr. Clifford began the meeting at 0940.

[. . .]

5. *U.S. Forces in Europe*

Mr. Nitze said that with regard to the Symington Amendment to reduce U.S. military forces in Europe we have had two good editorials recently in the *New York [T]imes* and the *Washington Post*. We have the problem of how to handle Senator Jackson and work with him on alternative proposals. The President does not want to suggest moving any troops out of Europe. We have talked with Dorothy Fordick of Senator Jackson's staff. We are suggesting language in the report of the Senate committee covering several kinds of amendments that could be made rather than suggesting an amendment to the bill. Mr. Clifford emphasized that the President feels strongly on this matter and doesn't want to cut our forces in Europe at all at this time.

[. . .]

The meeting adjourned at 1042.

R. Eugene Livesay, Staff Secretary

———

"Secret" Secretary of Defense Staff Meeting, 29 July 1968

Mr. Clifford, Mr. Nitze, Mr. McGiffert (for Mr. Resor), General Palmer (for General Westmoreland), Mr. Ignatius, Admiral Moorer, Mr. Hoopes (for Dr. Brown), Lt. General McKee (for General McConnell), General Wheeler, Dr. Enthoven, Mr. Warnke et al.

1. *Negotiations in Paris*
Mr. Clifford began the meeting 0938.
[. . . .]
3. *Negotiations with the Soviets on Strategic Weapons*
Mr. Clifford said there is widespread public interest in the strategic talks with the Soviet Union. There is some indication that these could start within a month or two. He would caution that the press will be wanting to pick up pieces of information from Defense and State. All should be careful in this regard. No information of any kind whatsoever is to be given out. We can remain hopeful on the results of these talks. The talks will have a better chance of success if the lid is kept on comments.
4. *USSR/Czechoslovakia Confrontation*
Mr. Clifford said we are staying out of this one. We believe the best policy is to permit the Soviets and the Czechs to adjust their differences. We have a number of items going with the Soviet Union and it would be exceedingly unfortunate time to get involved. Here again he cautioned against comments on the situation by Defense personnel.
[. . .]
The meeting adjourned at 1038
R. Eugene Livesay, Staff Secretary

———

"Top Secret" Secretary of Defense Staff Meeting, 5 August 1968
Mr. Clifford, Mr. Nitze, Mr. McGiffert (for Mr. Resor), General Westmoreland, Mr. Ignatius, Admiral Moorer, Dr. Brown, General McConnell, General Wheeler, Dr. Enthoven, Mr. Warnke et al.

1. *Negotiations in Paris*
Mr. Clifford began the meeting at 0940.
[. . .]
2. *USSR/Czechoslovakia*
Mr. Clifford said although we do not have the whole story on the discussion by the Czechs, the Soviets and others, the results appear to be a signal accomplishment for Dubcek and the Czechs. The effects will run through the rest of Eastern Europe. The Soviets had a sticky problem. The 1968 Czechoslovakian crisis is a far cry from the 1956 Hungarian crisis. He feels that the Soviets wanted to do everything except march into Czechoslovakia. The manner in which the Soviets and other communist nations deployed troops around Czechoslovakia was interesting. General Wheeler said the Communists had elements of between eleven and eighteen divisions deployed in the southern portion of East Germany. Three Polish

divisions plus Soviets were deployed in Poland at the border. Other Soviet divisions were in the Carpathian District of the Soviet Union. In addition, there were two Soviet Divisions inside Czechoslovakia. Our intelligence people are looking into why we were unable to identify earlier some of the divisions deployed. One moved in radio silence and was not known to be in Czechoslovakia until our military attaché saw it while on a trip through the countryside. He noted around 3,000 vehicles. This casts some doubt on assumptions that we have made in the past that if the Communists plan a possible attack against NATO we would receive strategic warning. The Soviets imposed press censorship, security measures, radio silence and concentrated sizeable numbers of troops without our getting early notice. There is no question that they could have overrun Czechoslovakia in a matter of about two days. It would have been an easier task than in Hungary.

[. . .]

The meeting adjourned at 1048

R. Eugene Livesay, Staff Secretry

———

"Secret" Secretary of Defense Staff Meeting, 12 August 1968

Mr. Clifford, Mr. Nitze, Mr. Resor, General Westmoreland, Mr. Ignatius, Admiral Clarey (for Admiral Moorer), Mr. Hoopes (for Dr. Brown), General McConnell, Lt. General McPherson (for General Wheeler), Dr. Enthoven, Mr. Warnke et al.

1. *Negotiations in Paris*

Mr. Clifford began meeting 0936.

[. . .]

2. *MIRVs*

Mr. Clifford made reference to the decision to test MINUTEMAN III and POSEIDON. He again cautioned and asked all not to get into any discussions involving the U.S./USSR strategic missiles talks or these tests. We expect that the talks will be coming up within the next month or so. It will be a long, arduous, and sometimes frustrating negotiation. It will add to the burden of the negotiators if unauthorized statements are made. Over the weekend there was an article in the *Washington Post* by George Wilson entitled "Russians Slow Work on Anti-Ballistic Missile Defense Etc." The information in the article indicates that he got some of it from somebody either in the Pentagon or in the State Department. With problems on the Hill, being in the midst of a political campaign, it will prevent a lot of alarms and excursions if we do not talk about the talks and MIRVs.

[No separate item on "USSR/Czechoslovakia in the minutes of this meeting!]

[. . .]
The meeting adjourned at 1048
R. Eugene Livesay, Staff Secretary

"Top Secret" Secretary of Defense Staff Meeting, 26 August 1968
Mr. Clifford, Mr. McGiffert (for Mr. Resor), General Westmoreland, Mr. Ignatius, Admiral Moorer, Dr. Brown, General McConnell, General Chapman, Dr. Foster, Mr. Warnke et al.

1. *Review of Past Week*
Mr. Clifford began meeting 0937
[. . .]
    a. *Southeast Asia*
    [. . .]
    b. *Czechoslovakia*
Mr. Clifford said on Tuesday came the invasion of Czechoslovakia by the Soviets and other Warsaw Pact military forces. The first he heard of this action was in a phone call a little after 9:00 p.m. that evening to advise him to come to the White House for an NSC meeting. Soviet Ambassador Dobroynin [*sic*] had called on the President shortly after 8:00 p.m. to advise him as to why the Soviets were taking this step because of the presence of internal and external aggression against Czechoslovakia. Dobroynin [*sic*] stated that the Soviets had been petitioned to interfere by the government of Czechoslovakia. These statements created great skepticism that night. There is still no indication of who the individuals are that allegedly called on the Soviets to interfere.

Mr. Clifford said it is difficult to understand the manner of the Soviet action. From a military standpoint it was a sophisticated operation but politically it was a bust. He would have expected a prearranged plan for a new government in Czechoslovakia. He would have expected a group to step forward and say they are the individuals who asked the Soviets to interfere, and who were willing to have a new form of government. He personally thinks there was a debate within the Soviet politburo. He knows that they were having extensive meetings. The decision appears to have been made hurriedly. They were ready to move because of the training exercises and practice for invasion which have been conducted over a long period of time. The buttons were pushed and once they moved into Czechoslovakia the whole thing collapsed. Some of the Soviet troops shot at the Czechs and some didn't. The Russians could have made a contrived case of the external aggression accusing West Germany of infiltrating. The Soviet's [*sic*] haven't made a case in any sense of the word. World opinion thinks it is a shocking and appalling case of naked aggression.

Mr. Clifford said at the NSC meeting there was a discussion in great detail as to what we could do about the Soviet moves. From a military standpoint there was no doubt from the beginning that there was nothing we could do about it. Although we deplored the action no one suggested military action on our part. It was decided to proceed in the United Nations, first in the Security Council and then to the General Assembly. Instructions were issued for Ambassador Ball's presentation. They also discussed the possibility of issuing a presidential statement on the crisis. General Wheeler thought that the president should issue a statement that evening while Mr. Clifford said he voted for a delay until we could see out events were shaping up [*sic*]. In retrospect he believes that General Wheeler was right, although he doubts a twelve hour delay hurt much. When issued, the President's statement was a good one and forthright.

c. *Briefing of Governor Maddox*

Mr. Clifford said on Wednesday he participated in an incident which was a signal privilege. Mr. Rusk, Mr. Helms and he briefed Governor Maddox Twice the governor asked questions, but they not sure whether he was referring to Vietnam or Czechoslovakia so they covered both situations. Mr. Clifford said that he read in the paper yesterday that some arsonists had tried to burn down the Governor's library. It was reported that both books were destroyed, even one which he had not yet had a chance to color. Mr. Clifford said it was less than an inspiring experience.

d. *Deployment of Troops to Chicago*

On Thursday Mr. Clifford said he began conversations about possible trouble in Chicago [at the National Convention of the Democratic Party]. He and Mr. McGiffert attended a meeting in the White House, first with Mr. Califano and then with the President. As a result, the President decided to preposition troops. If the police first, and then the National Guard can't handle the situation, we would already have Army troops available on the scene. The president is concerned that if real trouble started it might turn out to be so big that the arrival of troops some 8 hours or so later would be able to do the job. The time to have the troops on hand is right after trouble starts. We have not given out the number of troops moved. The President hopes that their presence in Chicago will act as a deterrent.

e. *Congressional Briefing*

[. . .]

2. *Military Situation in Southeast Asia*

[. . .]

3. *Czechoslovakia*

Mr. Clifford asked General Wheeler to take a few minutes and give his observation and reactions on the Soviet invasion of Czechoslovakia and its effect on the European situation. General Wheeler said that over the weekend the Soviets had increased the number of their forces in Prague from about 30,000 to 50,000. The Soviets are starting now to rotate some Soviet units which came from East Germany. The French in a NATO Council meeting called attention to the fact that East German troops deployed into the area of the Sudentenland,[1] which the Germans have historically claimed; the Polish forces deployed into the areas claimed historically by Poland; and the Hungarian troops into the areas historically claimed by Hungary. The French raised the question as to whether this presages the partition of Czechoslovakia. Dr. Brown said this deployment could be explained geographically since these areas are adjacent to these countries.

General Wheeler said that there has been more trouble between the population and the occupation troops. There have been several incidents where the Soviets opened fire against demonstrators. Our embassy in Prague reports their people have suffered a series of incidents: their vehicles have been searched; the Soviets fired guns over a military attaché's car as he drove through Prague. Soviet soldiers broke into the apartment of an American and took a shot gun; and the Soviets intruded on the embassy grounds. Mr. Clifford said he read a cable in which the embassy reported it was surrounded. General Wheeler said yes, this was at the same time two or three Soviet soldiers broke into the grounds.

General Wheeler said that there is no confirmation that the Soviets plan to move into Rumania although they have the capability to do so. The Yugoslavs are getting somewhat upset. A meeting of the Yugoslav Communist party called for an end to the confrontation. They issued a warning that they would maintain Yugoslav sovereignty. They have cancelled military leaves and kept on duty those individuals who were scheduled to return to civilian life shortly.

Mr. Clifford asked how many foreign troops are in Czechoslovakia. General Wheeler said around 200,000. These consist of twelve to fifteen Soviet divisions, elements of four East German and four Polish divisions, and small detachments of Hungarian and Bulgarian forces. The Hungarians are stationed on the outskirts of Czechoslovakia. Tactical aircraft have been deployed to twelve Czechoslovakian airfields from the Western Soviet Union. The invasion forces have grown from 150,000 to 200,000 or more. Mr. Clifford asked how many of the 200,000 there are non-Soviet forces. General Wheeler said he would guess around 30 percent. Mr. Clifford said that this was higher than he would have thought.

Mr. Clifford asked Mr. Warnke for his comments. Mr. Warnke said it is difficult to sort out the various impacts. He would hope that the worst impact would be on the Soviet Union. Militarily it was a fine operation but politically a debacle that has stirred up adverse opinion around the world. In spite of our efforts at a détente the Soviets have made this move.

The impact in Europe appears extreme. There will be a loss of influence of various communist parties. He feels that the French and Italian communist parties will be negligible factors. As a result, the Rumanians and Yugoslavs are restless. The Soviet efforts have increased their diplomatic deficit. Both the Yugoslavs, the arch-heretics, and Communist China, the true believers, have criticized the Soviets.

Mr. Warnke said these events show the need for a significant American presence in Europe. The Soviets have not been transformed. It shows that we still cannot forecast whether the Soviets might take action against NATO. The invasion should put an end to the Symington amendment. We should maintain a strong defensive posture rather than credit the Soviets with becoming magnanimous.

Mr. Clifford said he feels these events point up the basic soundness of the DoD position taken on the Hill. It is better to negotiate with the Soviets from a position of strength. The Soviet actions have added to the efficacy of this argument. He recalled the effort required to sustain our position on the Hill on the SENTINEL ABM program. Opponents argued that the Soviets and communism had changed. We successfully debated this move. The opposition group should have substantially less support in the future. As General Wheeler said the whole area of support for NATO had a serious problem on hand. In Senator Mansfield's report to the President upon his recent return from Europe he was sanguine and optimistic about US/USSR relations. The ink had hardly dried on this report when the Soviets invaded. Unfortunately, however, the Soviet invasion will have an adverse effect on various important efforts we were making. The non-proliferation treaty is still hanging in the balance. The West Germans have not yet signed, the Israelis have not yet chosen to sign it, and many other nations haven't signed. The Soviet actions may have an adverse effect. Further, steps were fast approaching a climax to start the talks with the Soviets on the limitation of strategic weapons. He hoped as time moves on that we can select the right time and get started on these talks. In some respects the climate might even be better for these talks as a result of their moves. There will be more realistic feeling about the Soviet Union's attitudes.

4. *Civil Disturbances*

[. . .]

5. *French Hydrogen Bomb*

[. . .]

6. *Project 693 and FY 1970 Budget*

[. . .]

7. *Legislative Matters*

[. . .]

8. *F-111*

[. . .]

9. *South Vietnamese Navy*

[. . .]

10. *Czechoslovakia Postscript*

General Chapman said that the Soviet's [*sic*] invaded Czechoslovakia because Mother Russia was directly threatened. We would expect the Soviets to take additional preemptive actions under similar circumstances.

The meeting adjourned at 1053

R. Eugene Livesay, Staff Secretary

———

"Top Secret" Secretary of Defense Staff Meeting, 3 September 1968
Mr. Clifford, Mr. Nitze, Mr. Resor, General Palmer (for Westmoreland), Mr. Ignatius, Admiral Clarey (for Admiral Moorer), Dr. Brown, General McConnell, General Wheeler et al.

1. *Secretary Clifford's First Six Months*

Mr. Clifford began meeting 0935 stating that it was thoroughly fitting and proper to state that on 1 September he marked his first six months of service as the present Secretary of Defense.

[. . . .]

3. *Eastern Europe*

At one stage during the past week there were a number of reports that Soviet military forces were engaged in large scale maneuvers. Troops and arms appeared to be moving toward Rumania. There were also activities in Bulgaria and Hungary. Only Yugoslavia was not involved. These reports came in with such consistency as to create the greatest concern here. Mr. Clifford noted that the President's statements of the threat to world peace if the Soviets moved into Rumania. The Soviets have assured the President that they have no intentions toward Rumania and no desire to create trouble. They state that the Czechoslovakia situation is a family problem which is no concern to or of interest to the United States or otherwise. We should leave their personal problems to them and they will leave ours to us. All this is said in an amicable and conciliatory manner. They have stated that they hoped that the events of the last few weeks will not effect U.S./USSR talks on strategic weapons. Mr. Clifford said our posture should be one of careful, guarded, watchful waiting. He asked General Wheeler to report on the military situation in Eastern Europe.

General Wheeler said there are from fourteen to seventeen Soviet divisions, four Polish divisions, and elements of East German, Bulgarian and Hungarian forces of less than division size in Czechoslovakia. The Soviets have moved some aircraft back to their home stations. These moves appear to be consolidating their hold on Czechoslovakia and do so with lower visibility.

Western military attaches have seen no evidence of troop activity in Hungary. There have been field training exercises in Bulgaria. To date there have been primarily communications exercises, with no movement of ground troops. Yugoslavia is in a high state of alert. Rumania is on alert but has been dampening their polemics. We should keep an attitude of watchful waiting. General Wheeler is not convinced at all that we have seen the end of this.

Mr. Clifford said NATO is faced with a situation of considerable concern. NATO has noted with alarm the considerable number of Soviet troops in Czechoslovakia which has a common border with West Germany. NATO has demonstrated deep concern at the movement of Warsaw Pact forces which are in position to effect the interest of one of the NATO countries, Germany. There will be more discussion this week and he will report on these at next Monday's staff meeting.

[. . .]

The meeting adjourned at 1052

R. Eugene Livesay, Staff Secretary

—

"Top Secret" Secretary of Defense Staff Meeting, 9 September 1968
Mr. Clifford, Mr. Nitze, Mr. Resor, General Palmer (for General Westmoreland), Mr. Ignatius, Admiral Moorer, Dr. Brown, Dr. Enthoven, Mr. Warnke et al.

1. *Eastern Europe and NATO*

Mr. Clifford began meeting at 0935. [. . .]

Mr. Clifford said that each Monday he says this has been quite a week. The fact is that each week has been quite a week. There were a number of meetings at the White House. The Tuesday luncheon meeting was held on Wednesday with a long list of agenda items. The NSC meeting on Wednesday was devoted to Czechoslovakia and problems in Central Europe. The Cabinet meeting Thursday was devoted to Vietnam and reports on Czechoslovakia and Central Europe. A great deal of effort last week was devoted to these problems.

At this point the existing situation in Czechoslovakia is fluid. It is difficult to say which way it will turn. The Czechs are taking it as you would suppose they would. This has been an extraordinarily bitter pill for them to swallow. It will take a long time to get over the Soviet invasion. A disturbing factor in the whole situation is the erratic manner in which the Soviets went about their move. Militarily it went well, politically very bad. He would have expected the Soviets to have a good plan for the takeover. He would have expected that they would have had a group set up to invite them in, however, they couldn't find anyone who would step forward and say it was they who invited the Soviets in. This made the Soviets look foolish. Further they produced no evidence of either internal or external aggression. Mr. Clifford takes some comfort from the fact they did it so badly. However, if they can make mistakes in Czechoslovakia they could make them elsewhere. Apparently it is a dichotomy in the Kremlin. Apparently the hardliners have prevailed over the softliners. Since the hardliners took over they moved immediately without laying the diplomatic and political basis for their moves. We have to watch the Soviets with the greatest care.

Where Yugoslavia is now is also a matter of great concern. The Soviets have long deplored what went on there. If there is continued trouble in Czechoslovakia and the Rumanian comments are disturbing to the Soviets, the hardliners in the Kremlin might decide the time has come to clean up the whole situation. As far as Austria is concerned, if they should move against the Austrians we have a strong involvement there.

What NATO should do has been the subject of discussions and different approaches. Mr. Clifford said that he and General Wheeler had recommended that this is a good time for a NATO meeting. There are substantial Warsaw Pact forces across from a NATO ally, West Germany. Also, should NATO give attention to the Yugoslavia and Eastern Europe situation. Sometimes aggressors are held back by warnings.

Mr. Clifford said that he, Mr. Nitze and Mr. Warnke met with Ambassador Cleveland. He reported that our NATO allies are concerned that our reaction to the Soviet/Czechoslovakian venture continues mild and restrained. Some Europeans have the impression that our desire to have negotiations with the Soviets on Strategic Missiles is so great that there is an implied understanding that the Soviets will look after their sphere and we ours and that we will move towards agreement. An interesting sideline of this is that during the initial days of the Soviet invasion there was an alert in Cuba. The Cubans were concerned that the United States would move in and take them over because they were in our sphere. Mr. Clifford said we could put a stop to this type of talk by having a NATO meeting. It would show that we are deeply concerned over these events.

2. *National Press Club Speech*

Mr. Clifford said his speech came at a most propitious time. It was a sound and firm speech. The questions that he received after the speech were directed at current problems. He stressed that in order to negotiate in today's imperfect world one had to negotiate from strength. [. . .] It would be calamitous if the Soviets reached the conclusion that the world is not concerned about their adventures. Once this kind of adventurism begins experience in the past indicates that part of the world can become inflamed. [. . .]

[. . .]

The meeting adjourned at 1048

R. Eugene Livesay, Staff Secretary

———

"Top Secret" Secretary of Defense Staff Meeting, 16 September 1968
Mr. Clifford, Mr. Nitze, Mr. Resor, General Westmoreland, Mr. Ignatius,
Admiral Moorer, Dr. Brown, General McConnell, General Wheeler, Dr.
Enthoven, Mr. Warnke et al.

1. *Return of Marine Corps 27th Regimental Landing Team*
Mr. Clifford began meeting 0935.
[. . .]
2. *Central and East European Developments*
Mr. Clifford said that we and others are engaged in a study to determine why
the Soviets moved and when and how. We are seeking information concerning the size, deployment and equipment, and giving attention to possible next
Soviet moves. He noticed an article in the morning paper that the Yugoslavs
are deeply concerned. We feel that the Czech invasion is not the end of the
story. These developments have led to a great deal of thinking by the NATO
countries. There have been discussions of the holding of special meetings and
the development of special reactions. He asked Mr. Warnke to report.
Mr. Warnke said the State Department has proposed a series of NATO
meetings to make sure that when there is a full NATO ministerial meeting
that specific results can be achieved. One alternative is to have sessions of the
NATO foreign ministers at the United Nations, followed by a full ministerial
meeting in November, advancing the regularly scheduled one in December
by thirty days. Replies from NATO countries to these proposed meetings have
been mixed. The Germans feel that the Soviets would be tempted to construe
a unilateral declaration by the Germans as typical of German aggressiveness.
One opposition raised to the meetings included the fact that the first meeting
is proposed in connection with the United Nations. West Germany is not a
member of the UNO. Also in such circumstances should Mr. Brosio, the Secretary General, be present? Nevertheless it looks like there will be a prelimi-
nary meeting later this month involving the permanent representatives plus
a few deputy foreign ministers. There will be bilateral talks at the UN and the
ministerial meeting will be moved up to November. He doubts that there will
be concrete proposals for strengthening NATO until after theses meetings.
Mr. Clifford said that the Nuclear Planning Group meeting is scheduled for
10–11 October. So far there is no change in the schedule. This meeting could
be significant. General Wheeler said he will attend. The Germans are vitally
interested in these developments as they feel the impact of events the most.
They have a common border with Czechoslovakia. Dr. Birrenbach, Chancellor Kiesinger's personal representative, and Herr Schmidt, a party leader in
the *Bundestag*, have been among the German visitors to Washington. He
asked Mr. Nitze to comment on his meetings with them.

Mr. Nitze said that Dr. Birrenbach arrived with a paper provided by Chancellor Kiesinger. This paper discussed the origin of the Czechoslovakia crisis. It suggested that the real interest of the USSR is West Germany and the Czechoslovakian crisis was only a phase. The Soviets had previously sent notes to West Germany citing Article 47 and 103 of the UN Charter. These articles give UN Security Council members authority to take certain actions against former enemies without Security Council veto. Mr. Nitze said we in the U.S. feel that the Czechoslovakian crisis originated in developments in Czechoslovakia. The Germans also discussed the Nuclear Non-Proliferation Treaty. Mr. Nitze said he pointed out to both Dr. Birrenbach and Herr Schmidt that prior to the Czech crisis that we were encountering serious questions of maintaining forces in Europe without offset help. The twenty-three years that we have maintained forces in Europe has caused us a balance of payments problem. The key indication we needed on their part was that they are prepared to do something about it. They indicated they would do so but they could not be out in front. It was suggested we organize secret negotiations with the West Germans to get them to increase their Defense budget. If we can get others to bear part of the cost we might do, say, a tenth as much. Mr. Warnke said he had discussed this with State and JCS. Dr. Brown asked how would they offset our costs, by U.S. purchases? Mr. Warnke said yes and in addition take over some of the U.S. functions. Also we would like for them to fill out their own forces. It is important to get going on this.

General Wheeler said there is some consensus developing. Minister Harlan of Belgium feels they need the support of actions by other NATO nations to help them reverse the present Belgium course. We need concerted NATO effort. General Wheeler feels the Soviets seized the Czechoslovakian opportunity to put additional pressures on West Germany although the genesis of the Czech crisis was the situation developing in Czechoslovakia.

Mr. Clifford said he told Dr. Birrenbach that prior to the Czech crisis we had expected restrictions on what we could do. The crisis has been postponed because of the situation. He feels this may be NATO's last chance to take a new approach. We need to reconstruct, refurbish and reaffirm the Principles with which it was set up.

[. . .]

The meeting adjourned at 1055

R. Eugene Livesay, Staff Secretary

NOTE

1. Contrary to the widely held view of American intelligence and contemporary observers, no East German forces were deployed in the Warsaw Pact invasion of Czechoslovakia. See Brezhnev's statement, "It is absolutely certain that there were

no German soldiers on Czechoslovak territory. We kept them back [. . .] the German comrades were offended because they felt that they were not being trusted somehow," in appendix 8.

SOURCE

Folder "Minutes, Secretary of Defense, Staff Meeting, March–September 1968," Box 18, Papers of Clark Clifford, LBJ Library.

Appendix 10
"U.S. Propaganda Strengthening NATO"

Political report of the Soviet ambassador to the United States, A. Dobrynin.

3 October 1968
Washington
Classified
Copy Nr. 3

American anti-Soviet and anticommunist propaganda on the occasion of the invasion of Czechoslovakia by alliance troops was directed from the start towards achieving a number of clearly defined goals in the ideological and political struggle with the Soviet Union and other socialist countries. It was moreover a means used by reactionary forces to influence the US domestic situation and the mood prevailing in American society.

The question of the USA providing direct military "assistance" to Czechoslovakia arose neither on the spur of the moment nor later on. Even though for the purposes of propaganda the US administration does not support the "recognition of the attribution of spheres of influence" to the USA and the USSR respectively, both the United States' first reaction and its subsequent behavior in regard to Czechoslovakia are based on the factual acknowledgement that the country belongs to the socialist camp, to the USSR's sphere of interest and to the Warsaw Pact countries.

Against the backdrop of the weakening of U.S. positions abroad both in terms of ideology and foreign politics, which is mainly due to the Vietnam War and to the aggravation of racial and social conflicts in America, the US administration, its foreign policy and propaganda apparatus and diverse reactionary circles have attempted to initiate and to exploit a comprehensive campaign of anti-Soviet and anticommunist propaganda. [. . .]

At present attempts are made in the US to present the events in Czechoslovakia and the circumstances surrounding them as "proof of the Soviet Union's bellicosity"[1] and of the doctrine that the US must build its relationship with the Soviet Union *from a "position of strength,"* while making sure at the same time that it does not fail to engage in a dialogue on important international problems that are of general interest. (The latter argument is proof that the irrelevance of former Cold War slogans has been generally recognized in the US and that the events in Czechoslovakia have not led to a backsliding into the pro-war sentiments of the past.)

Propaganda efforts in this direction are very much in evidence in the U.S.— people are toying in this context with the idea of making American policy "tougher" and of boosting the arms race. American propaganda has been making much of the effectiveness and the precision with which the troop invasion was carried out in Czechoslovakia and has emphasized that the U.S. had *"underrated Russian military might.* At the same time *the idea is mooted* that Soviet troops *could invade Romania, Yugoslavia or the FRG at equally short notice.* Diverse rumors are being propagated about the "amassing" of Soviet troops on the borders of this or that country adjacent to the USSR etc.

Measures that are being recommended *in this context are the strengthening of NATO,* the "implementation of defensive measures" in the Mediterranean, etc. [. . .]

The Ambassador of the USSR in the USA

A. Dobrynin

NOTE

1. The text italicized here is underlined in the original document.

SOURCE

RGANI, F. 5, op. 60, d. 469, S. 57–69. Translated from the German translation of the original Russian document (original Russian and German translation in Karner et al., *Dokumente*, #217).

Index

About the Contributors

Csaba Békés is founding director of the Cold War History Research Center (www.coldwar.hu) and senior research fellow at the 1956 Institute, both in Budapest. His main fields of research are Cold War history, the history of East-West relations, Hungary's international relations after World War II, and the role of the East Central European states in the Cold War. He is the author or editor of eleven books, including *The 1956 Hungarian Revolution: A History in Documents* (with Malcolm Byrne and János M. Rainer), and more than sixty major articles and chapters, and he has participated at some seventy international conferences. Békés was a visiting professor at New York University and at Columbia University. He is also a contributor of the forthcoming three-volume *Cambridge History of the Cold War* and a member of the editorial boards of the *Journal of Cold War Studies* and *Cold War History*.

Günter Bischof is the Marshall Plan Professor of History and director of CenterAustria (www.centeraustria.org) at the University of New Orleans. He is the author of *Austria in the First Cold War 1945–55* (1999). He is the editor (with Saki Ruth Dockrill) of *Cold War Respite: The Geneva Summit of 1955* (2000) and many other books and coeditor of *Contemporary Austrian Studies* (seventeen volumes). Bischof was a guest professor at the Universities of Munich, Salzburg, Innsbruck, Vienna, the Vienna University of Economics and Business Administration, and Louisiana State University and serves on many boards.

Alessandro Brogi is associate professor at the University of Arkansas. His principal area of research is U.S. strategic and cultural relations with Western Europe during the Cold War. He is the author of three books: *L'Italia e l'egemonia*

505

americana nel Mediterraneo (Acqui Storia prize runner up); *A Question of Self-Esteem: The United States and the Cold War Choices in France and Italy, 1944–1958*; and *Confronting Anti-Americanism: America's Cold War against the French and Italian Communists* (forthcoming). Brogi was also at Yale University as lecturer and John Olin Fellow in International Security Studies (1999–2002), visiting professor at Johns Hopkins University's School of Advanced International Studies, Bologna Center, Italy (2004), and research fellow at the Peace Nobel Institute of Oslo, Norway (2007).

Mark Carson received his Ph.D. in history from the Louisiana State University. His master's thesis, "F. Edward Hebert and the Congressional Investigation of the Vietnam War" was published in *Louisiana History*. Carson was a guest lecturer at Loyola University and recently a visiting assistant professor at Tulane University. He is presently revising his dissertation, "Beyond the Solid South: Southern Members of Congress and the Vietnam War" and serves as an adjunct instructor at the University of New Orleans.

Saki Ruth Dockrill† was a professor and chair of contemporary history and international security at King's College, London. She was the author of many books and articles, including *Eisenhower's New Look National Security Policy, 1951–1961; Cold War Respite: The Geneva Summit of 1955* (with Günter Bischof); and *The End of the Cold War Era*.

Aleksei Filitov is a historian at the Russian Academy of Sciences and the author of many articles concerning Soviet foreign policy, especially toward Germany.

Tvrtko Jakovina is associate professor at the Department of History, Faculty of Humanities and Social Sciences, University of Zagreb. He is the author of *Socijalizam na američkoj pšenici* [Socialism on the American Grain] (2002) and *Američki komunistički saveznik: Hrvati, Titova Jugoslavija i Sjedinjene Američke Države 1945–1955* [The American Communist Ally: Croats, Tito's Yugoslavia and the United States, 1945–1955] (2003) and has written many articles dealing with the foreign policy of Tito's Yugoslavia and Croatian history in twentieth century. Jakovina is vice president of the Croatian Fulbright Alumni Association, lecturer at the Diplomatic Academy in Zagreb, and guest-lecturer at Instituti per l'Europa centro-orientale e balcanica, University of Bologna-Forli. He served as a visiting fellow at the London School of Economics.

Stefan Karner is the director of the Ludwig Boltzmann Institute for Research on War-Consequences, Graz-Vienna-Klagenfurt (see http://www.bik.ac.at) and a professor and the deputy director of the Department of

Economic, Social and Business History at the University of Graz. He is the chairman of the Austrian Part of the Austrian-Russian Commission of Historians, a member of the Czech-Austrian Commission of Historians, and a member of the editorial board of the *Jahrbuch für Historische Kommunismusforschung*, Berlin. In 1995 he received the prestigious Austrian Scientist of the Year award. Karner is the author of more than twenty books, including *Im Archipel GUPVI. Kriegsgefangenschaft und Internierung in der Sowjetunion 1941–1956* [In the GUPVI Archipelago: Prisoners of War and Internees in the Soviet Union 1941–1956], coeditor of *Die Rote Armee in Österreich. Sowjetische Besatzung 1945–1955* (2 volumes) [The Red Army in Austria: The Soviet Occupation 1945–1955], and the editor of several book series.

Harald Knoll is a senior fellow at the Ludwig Boltzmann Institute for Research on War-Consequences, Graz. He has published on prisoners of war in the USSR during and after World War II, especially on Stalin's legal persecution of POWs, on the Austrian resistance against the Nazi regime, and on espionage in the Soviet occupation zone in Austria (1945–1955).

Petr Kolář serves as the ambassador of the Czech Republic to the United States. He was educated at Charles University in Prague and majored in information technology and library science and ethnography. He held fellowships at the Woodrow Wilson International Center in Washington, DC, the University of London's Institute of Historical Research, and the Norwegian Nobel Institute in Oslo. He worked as a specialist at the Institute for Ethnography and Folklore Studies and the Research Center for Peace and Disarmament Issues, as well as a researcher at the Institute for Contemporary History, all of the Czechoslovak Academy of Science; he also worked as a chief researcher at the Institute for Strategic Studies of the Ministry of Defense and at the Institute for International Relations, both in Prague. Kolář joined the Czech Ministry of Foreign Affairs in the mid-1990s and served as director of the Department for Czechs Living Abroad and Nongovernmental Relations; director of the Eastern & Southern Europe Territorial Department, as well as foreign policy adviser to the foreign minister. He also served as an adviser for European Integration and the Balkans to Vaclav Havel, president of the Czech Republic 1999–2003, and as Czech ambassador to the Kingdom of Sweden and the Republic of Ireland, as well as a deputy minister of foreign affairs for bilateral relations.

Mark Kramer studied at Stanford and was a Rhodes scholar at Oxford University. He has been a driving force in making new documents from former communist countries available through the Cold War International History Project of the Woodrow Wilson Center in Washington, DC. He is the director of the Davis Center for Cold War Studies, Harvard University (see http://www.fas.harvard.edu/~hpcws/) and editor of the *Journal of Cold War Studies* (MIT Press). He is the author of numerous articles and signal analyses on the Soviet Union and Eastern Europe in the Cold War.

Nikita Petrov is leader of the research program on Soviet security studies at Memorial Moscow (see http://www.memo.ru/eng/memhrc/index .shtml). He is author of various books on the NKVD/KGB, including *Stalin's Loyal Executioner: People's Commissar Nikolai Ezhov, 1895–1940* (with Marc Jansen), *Kto rukovodil NKVD 1934–1941* [The Leaders of the NKVD 1934–1941] (with K. Skorkin), and *Pervyi predsedatel' KGB. Ivan Serov* [Ivan Servov: The First Chairman of the KGB].

Mikhail Prozumenshchikov is the deputy director of the Russian State Archives of Contemporary History (RGANI), Moscow (former Archives of the Central Committee of the CPSU). He is author of *Bol'shoy sport i bol'shaya politika* [Big Sport and Big Policy] and many books and articles on the history of international relations during the second half of the twentieth century, the history of the CPSU and its role on the formation of Soviet foreign and home affairs, and Soviet-Chinese relations. He is editor and the compiler of collections of documents concerning the XX Congress of CPSU in 1956, records of meetings of Presidium CC CPSU in the Khrushchev era, and the publication series "Culture and Power from Stalin to Gorbachev."

Peter Ruggenthaler is a fellow at the Ludwig Boltzmann Institute for Research on War-Consequences, Graz; he is also a member of the Austrian-Russian Commission of Historians and an expert and researcher for the International Commission for the Evaluation of the Crimes of the Nazi and Soviet Occupation Regimes in Lithuania (since 2004) and the Austrian Historians' Commission (2000–2002). He was coordinator of the international research project on the "Prague Spring 1968." He is the author of *Stalins großer Bluff. Die Geschichte der Stalin-Note in Dokumenten der sowjetischen Führung* [Stalin's Big Bluff: The History of the Stalin-Note in the Records of the Soviet Leadership] and coauthor of *Zwangsarbeit in der Land- und Forstwirtschaft auf dem Gebiet Österreichs 1939 bis 1945* [Forced Labor in Agriculture and Forestry on Austrian Territory 1939–1945].

Georges-Henri Soutou is professor emeritus at Paris-Sorbonne (Paris IV) University. He belongs to the Diplomatic Archives Commission of the French Foreign Ministry and also serves as a member of the editorial board of several scholarly journals, including *Relations Internationales, Revue Historique des Armées,* and *Contemporary European History;* he is coeditor of the *Revue d'histoire diplomatique.* He specializes in twentieth-century international history, particularly World War I, the Franco-German relationship, and East-West relations after 1945. In addition to numerous articles, Soutou has published *L'Or et le Sang. Les buts de guerre économiques de la Première guerre mondiale; L'Alliance incertaine. Les rapports politico-stratégiques franco-allemand 1943–1990s; La Guerre de Cinquante Ans. Les relations Est-Ouest 1943–1990;* and *L'Europe de 1815 à nos jours.*

Donald P. Steury is a historian working in the Central Intelligence Agency's Declassification Center. He previously served as a Soviet military analyst (1981–1992) and worked on the CIA History Staff from 1992 to 2007. He has written widely on the intelligence history in World War II and the Cold War and his publications include two documentary histories, *On the Front Lines of the Cold War: The Intelligence War in Berlin, 1946–1961* and *Intentions and Capabilities: Estimates on Soviet Strategic Forces, 1950–1983.* He has taught at the University of Southern California and the George Washington University and presently teaches at the University of Maryland University College. He also serves on the Academic Advisory Board of the Allied Museum in Berlin. He has a doctorate in modern European history from the University of California, Irvine.

Oldřich Tůma is the director of the Institute for Contemporary History of the Czech Academy of Sciences in Prague, Czech Republic (see http://www.cas.cz/en/institute_det.php?ID=61). He has held many fellowships and is the author of many articles on Czechoslovakia in the Cold War.

Manfred Wilke is a retired professor for sociology of the Professional School for Economics in Berlin (FHW). From 1992 to 2006 he was one of the two leaders of the research group on the SED state (*Forschungsverbund SED-Staat*) at the Free University of Berlin. He was a member of two Enquete-Commissions by the German *Bundestag* on the history of the SED dictatorship. He is the author of *Der SED-Staat; Prager Frühling. Das internationale Krisenjahr 1968* (2 vols.), 2008. He is currently the project manger at the Institute for Contemporary History (*Institut für Zeitgeschichte*) Munich-Berlin and the leader of the project The Berlin Wall: From SED Domestic Instrumentalization to Premier International Memory Site.

Vladislav Zubok is an associate professor in the Department of History at Temple University in Philadelphia. He is the author of numerous articles and several books, including the prize-winning *Inside the Kremlin's Cold War: From Stalin to Khrushchev* with C. Pleshakov (1996) and *A Failed Empire: The Soviet Union in the Cold War from Stalin to Gorbachev* (2007). Zubok's latest book, *Zhivago's Children: The Last Russian Intelligentsia,* was published in 2009. He is the director of the Carnegie Corporation's funded international educational project "Russia and the World in the 20th century" for junior faculty in humanities and social sciences from Russian regional universities and a former fellow of the National Security Archive, Woodrow Wilson International Center for Scholars, and current consultant of The Likhachev Foundation in St. Petersburg.